THE PROCESS
OF LEGAL RESEARCH

ASPEN PUBLISHERS

THE PROCESS OF LEGAL RESEARCH

Seventh Edition

Christina L. Kunz
Professor of Law
William Mitchell College of Law

Deborah A. Schmedemann
Professor of Law
William Mitchell College of Law

Ann L. Bateson
Director of the Schoenecker Law Library
Associate Dean and Professor of Law
University of St. Thomas School of Law

Matthew P. Downs
Director of the Law Library and Professor of Law
Florida International University College of Law

Mehmet Konar-Steenberg
Associate Professor of Law
William Mitchell College of Law

Wolters Kluwer
Law & Business

AUSTIN   BOSTON   CHICAGO   NEW YORK   THE NETHERLANDS

To contact Customer Care, e-mail customer.care@aspenpublishers.com, call 1-800-234-1660, fax 1-800-901-9075, or mail correspondence to:

Aspen Publishers
Attn: Order Department
PO Box 990
Frederick, MD 21705

Printed in the United States of America.

1 2 3 4 5 6 7 8 9 0

ISBN 978-0-7355-6977-5

Library of Congress Cataloging-in-Publication Data

The process of legal research / Christina L. Kunz . . . [et al.]. — 7th ed.
    p. cm.
  Includes bibliographical references and index.
  ISBN 978-0-7355-6977-5
  1. Legal research — United States. 2. Information storage and retrieval systems — Law — United States.
I. Kunz, Christina L.

KF240.P76 2008
340.072′073 — dc22

2008018822

About Wolters Kluwer Law & Business

Wolters Kluwer Law & Business is a leading provider of research information and workflow solutions in key specialty areas. The strengths of the individual brands of Aspen Publishers, CCH, Kluwer Law International and Loislaw are aligned within Wolters Kluwer Law & Business to provide comprehensive, in-depth solutions and expert-authored content for the legal, professional and education markets.

CCH was founded in 1913 and has served more than four generations of business professionals and their clients. The CCH products in the Wolters Kluwer Law & Business group are highly regarded electronic and print resources for legal, securities, antitrust and trade regulation, government contracting, banking, pension, payroll, employment and labor, and healthcare reimbursement and compliance professionals.

Aspen Publishers is a leading information provider for attorneys, business professionals and law students. Written by preeminent authorities, Aspen products offer analytical and practical information in a range of specialty practice areas from securities law and intellectual property to mergers and acquisitions and pension/benefits. Aspen's trusted legal education resources provide professors and students with high-quality, up-to-date and effective resources for successful instruction and study in all areas of the law.

Kluwer Law International supplies the global business community with comprehensive English-language international legal information. Legal practitioners, corporate counsel and business executives around the world rely on the Kluwer Law International journals, looseleafs, books and electronic products for authoritative information in many areas of international legal practice.

Loislaw is a premier provider of digitized legal content to small law firm practitioners of various specializations. Loislaw provides attorneys with the ability to quickly and efficiently find the necessary legal information they need, when and where they need it, by facilitating access to primary law as well as state-specific law, records, forms and treatises.

Wolters Kluwer Law & Business, a unit of Wolters Kluwer, is headquartered in New York and Riverwoods, Illinois. Wolters Kluwer is a leading multinational publisher and information services company.

*This book is dedicated to the thousands of students of
William Mitchell College of Law who have worked with and
helped us improve these materials during the past twenty-plus years*

and

*to the faculty, administrators, and staff of William Mitchell
College of Law, whose unwavering support for skills
instruction has made this book possible.*

Summary of Contents

CONTENTS

UNIT III   CASE LAW   147

EXHIBITS

Unit II Commentary

UNIT III   CASE LAW

Unit IV   Enacted Law

UNIT V   ADMINISTRATIVE MATERIALS

UNIT VI   RULES OF PROCEDURE AND LEGAL ETHICS

CHAPTER 16   RULES OF PROCEDURE

UNIT VII CONCLUSION

CHAPTER 18 DEVELOPING AN INTEGRATED RESEARCH STRATEGY

PREFACE

The first edition of this book was published in 1986, over two decades ago.

What has changed little since then is legal authority. Now, as then, the purpose of legal research is to locate pertinent cases, statutes, and rules — the law — governing the client's situation. Now, as then, commentators' discussion of the law is used to lead one to the law and to help one fully understand the law. Now, as then, new researchers must learn how the law is made, how different lawmaking bodies interact, how to discern which law is applicable when, how to read the law carefully, how to integrate the insights of commentators, and — most important — how to connect the law to the client's situation. As with earlier editions, this book emphasizes these matters. Today, as always, you must master these fundamentals to research competently.

What has changed greatly since 1986 is the technology of legal research. Legal materials have long been published, of course, in books and microforms (such as microfilm and microfiche). With the development of computers and related technology, legal research has become a multimedia endeavor. The researcher now has a sometimes bewilderingly wide range of options for locating a governing statute, for example: books, online subscription services offered by private publishers, Internet websites maintained by the government, and so forth. Indeed, some sources and tools are available only in computer-based media.

Technological change has brought other changes as well. The rate of product development has increased rapidly. Sources published in books tend to change infrequently; computer-based sources are reprogrammed far more easily and hence, far more often. Furthermore, the corporate structure of legal publishing is in flux, with large, well-established companies merging and small, new companies emerging.

So, it is an interesting time to teach and learn legal research. For us, it has been a challenge to write about a moving target. And we suspect you will find it challenging to adjust your research techniques on a nearly continual basis as publishers change their products.

In writing this book, we chose to take the following approach: We have set forth what you need to know about a type of legal authority. Then we have described what we consider the best practices currently employed by lawyers as they research that type of authority. Some practices have been in use for many years and likely will continue to be best practices. Others are newer and may well evolve as technology and research sources evolve. We have sought to cover the basics of the various practices; we hope that you will learn and appreciate the analytical processes lawyers employ in legal research. We have not discussed the mechanics and details of the best practices at length; these matters change, and you will be able to learn them easily enough once you master the basics.

Excellent researchers are curious, persistent, flexible people. We hope you approach this book with curiosity, persistence, and flexibility. If you do, we believe you will learn a great deal about an important and interesting process.

A Note to Professors: If you have used previous editions of this book, you will notice a number of changes in this edition:

☐ We have developed a template for each authority. The template specifies the major steps to take, such as finding pertinent material and updating it, along with the date of the research and citation information. The links between sources appear in the templates, e.g., the template might include a lead from a commentary source as a means of finding a statute and end with a reference to a case to read next.

☐ Each template also connects research to analysis: It begins with the issue, calls for the implications of the source for the client's situation, and ends with questions to consider and leads to follow.

☐ We have reduced some of the technical details to make the text less daunting and retention of key material more likely.

☐ We have incorporated more free online sources, especially government websites.

☐ We have included non-legal Internet research, such as Google, to help readers see how legal research is similar to yet also very different from these resources.

☐ We have moved the discussion of the sample case from the text to filled-in templates within the chapter and to interludes. The interludes generally appear at the end of a unit and describe in a more conversational tone how we researched the Canoga case. The interludes cover both good and not-so-good research, to show that research often requires persistence and re-thinking.

☐ We have updated where updating was needed, e.g., deletion of A.L.R. from LexisNexis and more coverage of HeinOnline.

We hope these changes work well for you and your students.

Last but not least, we welcome a new author — Professor Mehmet Konar-Steenberg, who brought fresh eyes and the perspective of a new generation to this project.

Deborah Schmedemann
Ann Bateson
Matthew Downs
Mehmet Konar-Steenberg

May 2008

Acknowledgments

First and foremost, the authors of this edition — Deborah Schmedemann, Ann Bateson, Matt Downs, and Mehmet Konar-Steenberg — would like to recognize the enduring contributions of authors who worked on earlier editions. Professor Christina Kunz began this book over twenty years ago, wrote major portions of the text, devised problem sets, collected illustrations, and managed its production. This edition, like its predecessors, is Chris's brainchild. Professor Peter Erlinder and Professor Clifford Greene, now in practice in Minneapolis, were our co-authors on portions of earlier editions. Former Professor Kevin Millard wrote the final draft of a chapter for the first edition of this book. Susan Catterall, a law firm librarian, assisted with the sixth edition.

Our colleague Professor Ken Kirwin has coordinated our legal research course ably, energetically, and enthusiastically for many years. He has been an uncommonly faithful and perceptive reader; we thank him for his many insights and suggestions.

We also would like to recognize the work of our research assistants: Karen Hazel, Jesse Klick, Adine Momoh, Marcus Ploeger, and Ryan Radtke. They worked hard, long, and diligently on various parts of this book, including Chapter 18 and the practice sets. We would also like to salute the work of our many research assistants on the previous editions. The perspectives and contributions of our research assistants have been invaluable in making this book more useful to our readers.

More so than other publications by law school faculty, this book draws on the talents and hard work of our law schools' librarians: Mary Ann Archer, Neal Axton, Janelle Beitz, Sean Felhofer, Jane Hopeman, Bill Jack, Anne Poulter, and Don Zhou at William Mitchell; Valerie Bowen, Deborah Hackerson, Rinal Ray, and Mary Wells at St. Thomas. They tracked down the sources, answered our questions, and offered top-notch suggestions.

We are grateful for the expertise of Cal Bonde and Linda Thorstad, who made sense of contorted and detailed revisions and constructed sophisticated exhibits from our mere sketches. Jane Andrews, Darlene Finch, and Nancy Urbina provided stellar administrative support.

Over the years, William Mitchell's faculty and administration have shown considerable interest and support for the project.

This book has been blessed with talented professionals on the publisher's end of the phone and computer. We want to recognize the work of Elizabeth Kenny, Christine Hannan, Christie Rears, and Jan Cocker for their patience and excellent work on the seventh edition. We are grateful for the efforts of the following people who nurtured this book and its

predecessors for the past twenty-plus years: Nick Niemeyer and Richard
Heuser (formerly at Little, Brown and Company), Carol McGeehan,
Elizabeth Kenny, and Melody Davies.

On a larger scale, we would like to thank the community of legal
writing and research teachers who have encouraged us and enriched us over
the years with their ideas about the pedagogy of legal skills education. The
same measure of gratitude and recognition goes to our students, who
remain our best source of insights about the process of learning legal
research.

We especially thank our spouses, companions, families, and friends for
their support and their interest in this project. Every three or four years,
they, like us, have been called upon to endure long hours and high stress. We
thank them from the bottom of our hearts.

We would also like to acknowledge those publishers who permitted us
to reprint copyrighted material in this book:

CHAPTER 1: THE LAY OF THE LAND: THE IMPORTANCE OF LEGAL RESEARCH, LEGAL AUTHORITIES, AND RESEARCH MEDIA

Exhibit 1.2: Judicial Case, from Loislaw (online source). Reprinted with permission
of Aspen Publishers, Inc. & Conway Greene Co.

Exhibit 1.3: Statute, from West's *New Mexico Statutes Annotated* (paper source).
Chapters 50-52, Employment Law, pp. 99-101 (2003). © Thomson West;
reprinted with permission.

Exhibit 1.4: Encyclopedia, from *American Jurisprudence, 2d* (paper source). Vol. 82,
Wrongful Discharge, pp. 637-38, 2003. © Thomson West; reprinted with
permission.

Exhibit 1.5: Legal Periodical Article, from *Albany Law Review* through LexisNexis
(online source). Vol. 70, pp. 117-19 (2006). Reprinted with permission of
LexisNexis; reprinted with permission of the publisher, Albany Law Review,
copyright 2006.

CHAPTER 2: FROM CURIOSITY TO CLOSURE: EIGHT COGNITIVE TASKS

Exhibit 2.6: Index, from *American Jurisprudence, 2d* (paper source). General Index
S-Z, p. 603 (2008). © Thomson West; reprinted with permission.

Exhibit 2.7: Table of Abbreviations, from *American Jurisprudence, 2d* (paper
source). General Index S-Z, p. xv (2008). © Thomson West; reprinted with
permission.

Exhibit 2.8: Table of Contents, from *American Jurisprudence, 2d* (paper source).
Vol. 82, Wrongful Discharge, pp. 582 & 586 (2003). © Thomson West;
reprinted with permission.

Exhibit 2.9: Table of Authorities, from *American Jurisprudence, 2d* (paper source).
General Index S-Z, p. 631 (2008). © Thomson West; reprinted with
permission.

Exhibit 2.12: Citation List, from Search in LexisNexis Periodicals Database (online
source). Reprinted with permission of LexisNexis.

CHAPTER 3: ENCYCLOPEDIAS

Exhibit 3.1: Encyclopedia Excerpt, from *American Jurisprudence, 2d* (paper source). Vol. 82, Wrongful Discharge, pp. 637-38 (2003). © Thomson West; reprinted with permission.

Exhibit 3.3: Encyclopedia Pocket Part, from *American Jurisprudence, 2d* (paper source). Vol. 82, Wrongful Discharge, p. 44 (2007 pocket part). © Thomson West; reprinted with permission.

CHAPTER 4: TREATISES

Exhibit 4.1: Treatise Text, from *Employment Discrimination 2d Ed.* (paper source). Vol. 9, pp. 155-45 & 155-46 (2007). Reprinted with permission of Matthew Bender & Company, Inc., a member of the LexisNexis Group.

CHAPTER 5: LEGAL PERIODICALS

Exhibit 5.2: Law Review Article, from *Albany Law Review* (paper source). Vol. 70, p. 128 (2006). Reprinted with permission of the publisher, Albany Law Review, © 2006.

Exhibit 5.5: Citation List, from Search in *Index to Legal Periodicals and Books* through WilsonWeb (online source). Reprinted with permission of H.W. Wilson Company.

Exhibit 5.6: Shepard's Report for Periodical Article, from LexisNexis (online source). Reprinted with permission of LexisNexis.

CHAPTER 6: A.L.R. ANNOTATIONS

Exhibit 6.2: A.L.R. Annotation Case Synopses (paper source). *American Law Reports Annotations 4th*, vol. 33, pp. 32-33, 1992. © Thomson West; reprinted with permission.

Exhibit 6.4: A.L.R. Annotation Opening Material (paper source). *American Law Reports Annotations 4th*, vol. 33, pp. 120-23 (1995). © Thomson West; reprinted with permission.

CHAPTER 7: RESTATEMENTS

Exhibit 7.2: Restatement Rule, Comments, Illustrations, and Reporter's Note, from *Restatement (Second) of Contracts* (paper source). Vol. 1, pp. 8-12 (1981). Copyright 1981 by the American Law Institute; reprinted with permission. All rights reserved.

Exhibit 7.5: Table of Contents, from *Restatement (Second) of Contracts* (paper source). Vol. 1, p. ix, 1981. Copyright 1981 by the American Law Institute; reprinted with permission. All rights reserved.

Exhibit 7.6: Case Annotations from Search in Westlaw Restatement Database (online source). © Thomson West; reprinted with permission.

Chapter 9: Case Reporters, Digests, and Their Alternatives

Exhibit 9.2: Judicial Case, from *Pacific Reporter 2d*, (paper source). Vol. 748, pp. 507-10, (1988). © Thomson West; reprinted with permission.

Exhibit 9.7: Digest Entries, from *New Mexico Digest* (paper source). Vol. 4B, p. 155 (2004). © Thomson West; reprinted with permission.

Exhibit 9.8: Topic Lists from *Minnesota Digest 2d* (paper source). Vol. 37, Descriptive-Word Index Dr-G. First page of exhibit shows Digest Topics from 2002 Main Volume; second page of exhibit shows Digest Topics and Abbreviations from 2007 pocket part. © Thomson West; reprinted with permission.

Exhibit 9.9: Descriptive Word Index, from *Minnesota Digest* (paper source). Vol. 37, Descriptive-Word Index Dr-G, p. 40, from 2007 pocket part. © Thomson West; reprinted with permission.

Exhibit 9.10: Outline of Digest Topic, from *New Mexico Digest* (paper source). Vol. 4B, p. 20 (2004). © Thomson West; reprinted with permission.

Exhibit 9.13: Terms-and-Connectors Citation List, from Search in Westlaw Cases Database (online source). © Thomson West; reprinted with permission.

Exhibit 9.14: Judicial Case, from LexisNexis Cases Database (online source). Copyright by LexisNexis, a division of Reed Elsevier, Inc. All rights reserved. No copyright is claimed as to any part of the original work prepared by government officer or employee as part of that person's official duties. Reprinted with permission of LexisNexis.

Exhibit 9.15: Citation List Showing Core Terms, from LexisNexis Cases Database (online source). Copyright by LexisNexis, a division of Reed Elsevier, Inc. All rights reserved. No copyright is claimed as to any part of the original work prepared by government officer or employee as part of that person's official duties. Reprinted with permission of LexisNexis.

Exhibit 9.17: Judicial Case, from New Mexico Court of Appeals Website (online source). (Use regulated by 14-3-15.5 NMSA 1978.)

Chapter 10: Case Citators

Exhibit 10.1: Shepard's Report for a Case, from LexisNexis (online source). Reprinted with permission of LexisNexis.

Exhibit 10.2: KeyCite Report for a Case, from Westlaw (online source). © Thomson West; reprinted with permission.

Exhibit 10.3: Citator Report for a Case, from Loislaw's GlobalCite Database (online source). Reprinted with permission of Aspen Publishers, Inc.

Chapter 11: Constitutions and Statutes

Exhibit 11.1: State Constitution, from *New Mexico Statutes Annotated* (paper source). Article 3, p. 50, 2003. Reprinted with the permission of Matthew Bender & Company, Inc., a member of the LexisNexis Group, and the New Mexico Compilation Commission.

Exhibit 11.2: State Statute, from New Mexico/LexisNexis Website (online source). Sections 50-11-1 to 50-11-6, 2007. Reprinted with permission of Matthew Bender & Company, Inc., a member of the LexisNexis Group, and New Mexico Compilation Commission.

Exhibit 11.10: Annotated Federal Statute, from *United States Code Service* (paper source). Annotations for Title 42, § 12102 (2007). Reprinted with permission of LexisNexis.

Exhibit 11.11: Update of Annotated Code, from *United States Code Service* (paper source). Annotations for Title 42, § 12102, from 2008 Cumulative Later Case and Statutory Service. Reprinted with permission of LexisNexis.

Exhibit 11.12: Advance Legislative Service Sections Affected Table, from *United States Code Service* (paper source). Index, p. 1852 (2007). Reprinted with permission of LexisNexis.

Exhibit 11.13: Advance Legislative Service Index, from *United States Code Service* (paper source). Reprinted with permission of LexisNexis.

Exhibit 11.15: Annotated Code, Art. 42, sec. 12201, from LexisNexis (online source). Reprinted with permission of LexisNexis.

Exhibit 11.17: Shepard's Report for a Statute, Art. 42, sec. 12201, from LexisNexis (online source). Reprinted with permission of LexisNexis.

Exhibit 11.18: KeyCite Report for Federal Statute, Art. 21, § 12201, from Westlaw (online source). © Thomson West; reprinted with permission.

Exhibit 11.19: Federal Session Law, from *United States Code Congressional and Administrative News* (paper source), Public Law 101-336 (July 26, 1990), vol. 104, p. 369, 1991. © Thomson West; reprinted with permission.

Exhibit 11.20: Local Ordinance Online, Municipal Ordinance, Sec. 3.60.020 for Taos, New Mexico, from Sterling Codifiers Website (online source). http:// www.sterlingcodifiers.com/ NM/Taos/05015000000002000.htm.

CHAPTER 12: LEGISLATIVE PROCESS MATERIALS

Exhibit 12.1: How a Bill Becomes Law (LexisNexis Congressional). Reprinted with permission of LexisNexis.

Exhibit 12.2: Senate Bill Online, Report for S. 933, 101st Congress, 1st Session, as introduced, from Westlaw Congressional Database (online source). © Thomson West; reprinted with permission.

Exhibit 12.4: Hearing Testimony, from CIS/Microfiche Library (microfiche source). CIS/Microfiche CIS 90: H341-4. 1990. Reprinted with permission of LexisNexis.

Exhibit 12.5: House Committee Report, from *United States Code Congressional and Administrative News* (paper source). Vol. 4, pp. 267-68 (1991). © Thomson West; reprinted with permission.

Exhibit 12.6: Floor Debate, from *Congressional Record* through LexisNexis Congressional Database (online source). 136 Congressional Record, S9684 - S9685, 1990. Reprinted with permission of LexisNexis.

Exhibit 12.7: Presidential Signing Statement, from *United States Code Congressional and Administrative News* (paper source). Vol. 4, p. 601 (1991). © Thomson West; reprinted with permission.

Exhibit 12.9: Legislative History Information in Annotated Code, from *United States Code Annotated* (paper source). Title 42, § 12102, p. 39 (2005). © Thomson West; reprinted with permission.

Exhibit 12.11: Legislative History Statement, from CIS-Legislative History through LexisNexis Congressional (online source). 101 CIS Legis. Hist, P.L. 336. Reprinted with permission of LexisNexis.

Exhibit 12.12: Graphical Display of Statute from Westlaw United States Code Annotated Database (online source). © Thomson West; reprinted with permission.

Exhibit 12.14: Bill Tracking Report, from Westlaw Bill Tracking Database (online source). Bill Tracking Report for Senate Bill 1881, 110th Congress, 1st Session. Reprinted with permission of LexisNexis.

CHAPTER 13: REGULATIONS

Exhibit 13.4: Annotated Federal Statute, from *United States Code Service* (paper source). Annotations for Title 29, § 164 (2007). Reprinted with permission of LexisNexis.

Exhibit 13.12: KeyCite Report for Agency Regulation, from Westlaw (online source). © Thomson West; reprinted with permission.

CHAPTER 14: AGENCY DECISIONS

Exhibit 14.4: Agency Decision Annotation in the Annotated Code, from *United States Code Service* (paper source). Title 29 Labor § 157, note 46, p. 580 (2007). Reprinted with permission of LexisNexis.

Exhibit 14.8: Shepard's Report for Agency Decision, from LexisNexis (online source). Reprinted with permission of LexisNexis.

CHAPTER 15: LOOSELEAF SERVICES

Exhibit 15.1: Looseleaf Service Updating Material, from BNA's *Labor Relations Reporter* Master Index I (paper source). Reproduced with permission from Labor Relations Reporter-Fair Employment Practices Manual, No. 1028 (Sept. 17, 2007). Copyright 2007 by The Bureau of National Affairs, Inc. (800-372-1033) http://www.bna.com.

Exhibit 15.2: Looseleaf Service General Index, from BNA's *Labor Relations Reporter* (paper source). Reproduced with permission from Labor Relations Reporter-Master Index, p. A 835 (Nov. 6, 2006). Copyright 2006 by The Bureau of National Affairs, Inc. (800-372-1033) http://www.bna.com.

Exhibit 15.3: Looseleaf Service Commentary, from BNA's *Labor Relations Reporter* (paper source). Reproduced with permission from Labor Relations Reporter-Labor Relations Expediter, pp. LRX 510.204: 860 (Mar. 28, 2005). Copyright 2005 by the Bureau of National Affairs, Inc. (800-372-1033) http://www.bna.com.

Exhibit 15.4: Online Service Overview, from BNA's Labor Relations Reporter (online source). Reproduced with permission from BNA's Labor & Employment Law Library, Introductory Page, http:// laborandemploymentlaw. bna.com. Copyright 2008 by The Bureau of National Affairs, Inc. (800-372-1033) http://www.bna.com.

CHAPTER 16: RULES OF PROCEDURE

Exhibit 16.2: Federal Rule of Civil Procedure, from *Federal Civil Judicial Procedure and Rules* Deskbook (paper source). Pp. 93, 94, 97 (2007). © Thomson West; reprinted with permission.

Exhibit 16.4: State Rule of Civil Procedure, from *New Mexico Rules Annotated* (paper source). © Thomson West; reprinted with permission. Vol. 1, pp. 82-83 (2007).

Exhibit 16.7: Treatise Discussion of a Rule of Procedure, from *Federal Practice and Procedure* (paper source). Pp. 520-521 (2007). © Thomson West; reprinted with permission.

Exhibit 16.8: Federal Form, from *Federal Civil Judicial Procedure and Rules* Deskbook (paper source). P. 378 (2007). © Thomson West; reprinted with permission.

CHAPTER 17: RULES OF PROFESSIONAL RESPONSIBILITY

Exhibit 17.2: Professional Responsibility Rule, from *New Mexico States Court Rules Annotated* (paper source). Vol. 1, pp. 42-44 (2007). © Thomson West; reprinted with permission.

Exhibit 17.5: Treatise Discussion, from *ABA/BNA Lawyer's Manual on Professional Conduct* (paper source). Reproduced with permission from ABA/BNA Lawyer's Manual on Professional Conduct, p. 31:309-31:310 (June 19, 2002). Copyright 2002 by the American Bar Association/The Bureau of National Affairs, Inc. (800-372-1033) http://www.bna.com.

Exhibit 17.6: State Bar Association Ethics Opinion, from Westlaw State Ethics Opinion Database (online source). © Thomson West; reprinted with permission.

PRACTICE SETS

Chapter 10 Problem Set—Case Citators: Reported Judicial Case, first page of Northwest Reporter 2d, (paper source). Vol. 338, p. 422 (1983). © Thomson West; reprinted with permission.

OVERVIEW

UNIT

I

THE LAY OF THE LAND: THE IMPORTANCE OF LEGAL RESEARCH, LEGAL AUTHORITIES, AND RESEARCH MEDIA

A. The Canoga Case
B. The Importance of Legal Research
C. Legal Authorities
D. Research Media
E. The Approach of This Book

Exhibit 1.1 Major Legal Research Materials by Category
Exhibit 1.2 Judicial Decision, from Loislaw (online source)
Exhibit 1.3 Statute, from West's New Mexico Statutes Annotated (paper source)
Exhibit 1.4 Encyclopedia, from American Jurisprudence 2d (paper source)
Exhibit 1.5 Legal Periodical Article, from LexisNexis (online source)
Exhibit 1.6 Lawyers' Media Choices

A. THE CANOGA CASE

Imagine yourself a lawyer or legal assistant* in a small firm in Taos, New Mexico. Consider the following fictional client problem:

> Your client, Emilia Canoga, began her career as a flutist for a small symphony orchestra in Taos, New Mexico, when she graduated from the Juilliard School five years ago. She has enjoyed her job and performed well. However, she has disagreed from time to time with the orchestra's general manager, especially over personnel issues. One such disagreement led to her termination on September 7, 2007.

---

*This text has several primary audiences: students in law schools, lawyers, students in legal assistant programs, and legal assistants. For ease of discussion, we generally refer to law students or lawyers; we trust that readers who plan to be or are legal assistants will read "legal assistant" where appropriate.

Throughout the preceding year, the general manager had been pressuring all smoking members of the orchestra to quit smoking. He argued that smoking is a health risk and that smoking by employees increases the orchestra's health care costs substantially. More specifically, he argued that smoking impairs the wind capacity, and hence performance, of brass and woodwind players. In January of 2007, he banned smoking at work. In early August, he issued a memo asking brass and woodwind players to sign either a statement indicating that they did not smoke off-duty or a pledge to embark on a no-smoking program. This memo was met with varying reactions and provoked significant discussion among the orchestra's members.

In particular, Ms. Canoga, a smoker who had tried to quit several times, was perturbed by the manager's early efforts and incensed by the August memo. She returned it with a signed note indicating that she intended to sign neither the statement nor the pledge.

The general manager called Ms. Canoga to his office shortly after receiving the note. A heated discussion ensued. Ms. Canoga accused the general manager of overstepping his bounds as an employer and intruding into her personal life. He told her she was fired for insubordination. Ms. Canoga angrily left his office.

Two days later, Ms. Canoga received her paycheck with a note stating that her services were no longer needed by the orchestra. Ms. Canoga sought advice from a senior colleague about how to get her job back. He suggested that she exercise her right to plead her case before the board of directors, as stated in the orchestra's employee handbook. Ms. Canoga received a copy of the handbook when she was hired, and the letter offering her the job refers to it. The handbook reads:

> It is the Orchestra's intent to resolve all employment disagreements amicably. If at any time, during your employment or thereafter, you are unable to resolve a disagreement by discussing the issue with management, you may bring the matter to the board. The board will make every effort to listen to both sides and facilitate a just solution.

Ms. Canoga wrote a letter to the board president requesting board consideration of her termination according to the handbook. About a week later, she received a letter stating that the board was aware of her situation, believed management had handled it appropriately, did not intend to revisit the topic, appreciated her contributions to the orchestra, and wished her well in her future endeavors. Hoping to get her job back or at least some type of compensation and a good reference, Ms. Canoga has sought your assistance.

In asking a lawyer for assistance, Ms. Canoga is seeking not just sympathy, but also a resolution of her problem according to the law and within the legal system. A lawyer would employ various skills to help her solve her problem: listening to Ms. Canoga to learn the facts of her situation and her concerns; investigating the facts through other sources; researching the law; analyzing her situation in light of applicable legal rules; identifying and assessing various means of obtaining a resolution, such as negotiating with the orchestra's lawyer, mediating the case, working through a government agency, or pursuing civil litigation; advocating for Ms. Canoga in those processes, in writing and orally; and, at all steps along the way, helping Ms. Canoga determine which actions should be taken on her behalf.

B.   THE IMPORTANCE OF LEGAL RESEARCH

Rule 1.1 of the Model Rules of Professional Conduct, a widely adopted ethics code for lawyers developed by the American Bar Association, states: "A lawyer shall provide competent representation to a client. Competent representation requires the legal knowledge, skill, thoroughness and preparation reasonably necessary for the representation."

This text teaches you how lawyers acquire this knowledge through legal research. As Ms. Canoga's advocate, you could not assess the strengths and weaknesses of her case against the orchestra if you did not know the pertinent law; nor could you negotiate effectively with the orchestra's lawyer or argue her case convincingly before a tribunal without a firm understanding of the law. Similarly, if the orchestra were your client and sought your advice before adopting its no-smoking policy, you could be of service only if you knew the legal constraints on employers in such situations. If you served as an advocate for an employer association or a public health organization before a legislature or agency considering laws on smoking by employees, you would need to be well informed about the current state of the law.

Furthermore, legal research is central to the ethical obligation that accompanies client representation: service to the legal system.[1] In representing Ms. Canoga ethically and effectively, you would promote the legal system as a peaceful means of resolving disputes; if her case led to adjudication, you would facilitate the development of the law. As the lawyer advising the orchestra, you would seek to secure the orchestra's compliance with the law. In either setting, you could not fulfill these roles without a firm understanding of the pertinent law.

Thus it is fitting, and not surprising, that poor legal research can have serious consequences not only for the client but also for the lawyer. In *Smith v. Lewis*,[2] a legal malpractice case, the court approved an award of $100,000 to the client and against a lawyer who had failed to apply principles of law commonly known to well informed attorneys and to discover principles readily accessible through standard research techniques. Poor research may lead to an

---

1. The Preamble to the Model Rules states: "A lawyer, as a member of the legal profession, is a representative of clients, an officer of the legal system and a public citizen having special responsibility for the quality of justice."

2. 530 P.2d 589 (Cal. 1975), *overruled on other grounds, In re Marriage of Brown*, 544 P.2d 561 (Cal. 1976).

award of attorney fees to the opposing party;[3] sanctions[4] against or a stern rebuke[5] of the lawyer; or professional discipline, such as suspension[6] or disbarment. Furthermore, no attorney can afford to tarnish his or her professional reputation by becoming known for poor research. It is primarily in law school that lawyers acquire their legal research skills.[7]

As you will soon see, legal research materials are voluminous, complex, and diffuse. Thus, good legal research is neither fast nor easy. It takes careful planning and persistence in execution, an appreciation of the big picture and an eye for detail, and a clear focus and openness to inspiration. Regardless of the topic or situation, good legal research is:

- □ *correct:* leading to the law governing your client's situation;
- □ *comprehensive:* addressing the various issues raised by the client's situation and incorporating an appropriate range of pertinent authorities;
- □ *credible:* focusing on authorities that carry weight because of their nature and quality; and
- □ *cost-effective:* obtaining results that justify the efforts devoted to research, in light of the client's interests and available research options.

These criteria are further developed throughout this text.

As you conduct legal research, you will encounter a wide range of legal materials. Materials used in legal research are not all created equal; rather, the law is a strongly hierarchical field, as discussed in Part C of this chapter. Part D provides an overview of the media in which these materials are published, mainly paper and online resources.

C.   LEGAL AUTHORITIES

Legal research materials are divided into three categories: the law, commentary, and finding tools. See Exhibit 1.1 (at page 7). This text uses the term "authority" to refer to the content of law and commentary, while "source" refers to the publications in which authorities appear.

3. *See, e.g., Lieber v. ITT Hartford Ins. Center, Inc.,* 15 P.3d 1030 (Utah 2000).
4. *See, e.g., Rodgers v. Lincoln Towing Serv., Inc.,* 771 F.2d 194 (7th Cir. 1985), *overruled on other grounds, Parmelee v. True,* No. 93 C 7362, 1995 U.S. Dist. LEXIS 17314 (N.D. Ill. Nov. 16, 1995).
5. *Massey v. Prince George's County,* 918 F. Supp. 905 (D. Md. 1996).
6. *See, e.g., Attorney Grievance Comm'n v. Zdravkovich,* 762 A.2d 950 (Md. Ct. App. 2000) (suspension for, inter alia, filing improper petition without consulting statute).
7. In a wide-ranging survey of practicing lawyers, over eighty percent indicated that the general law school curriculum was one of the three most important sources for developing library and computer legal research skills. (This was also true of legal analysis and reasoning.) *See* Bryant G. Garth & Joanne Martin, *Law Schools and the Construction of Competence* Table 8 (1992).

Exhibit 1.1	Major Legal Research Materials by Category

Authority
Law
  judicial case law
  enacted legislation
  administrative decisions and
    regulations
  rules of procedure and ethics

Major Forms of Commentary
  encyclopedias
  treatises
  periodicals
  A.L.R. Annotations
  Restatements

Finding Tools
  Library catalogs
  Internet search engines and directories
  Periodical indexes
  Case digests
  Statutory annotations

1.   The Law

Law is created by a branch of the government acting in its lawmaking capacity. In basic terms, United States law emanates from three types of government bodies: judicial, legislative, and administrative.

First, the federal and state judiciaries decide cases based on specific disputes that have arisen between two litigants (whether individuals or entities). In doing so, a court not only resolves the dispute for the litigants but also creates precedent. The result, rules, and reasoning in a decided case generally are to be followed in the resolution of future similar disputes within the court's jurisdiction. See Exhibit 1.2 (at pages 9–13), a case with significant implications for Ms. Canoga's situation.

Second, legislative bodies at the federal and state levels create constitutions and statutes; legislative bodies at the local level create charters and ordinances. Constitutions and charters create the government and define the rights of citizens vis-à-vis the government. Statutes and ordinances regulate a wide range of behavior by individuals, private entities, and the government. Legislation typically is written in broad, general terms. It is interpreted according to the legislature's intent; thus the materials created during the legislative process are of some importance. See Exhibit 1.3 (at pages 14–16), a statute pertaining to Ms. Canoga's situation.

Third, administrative agencies generate law through two chief mechanisms. Agencies issue decisions, which resemble judicial cases in that they simultaneously resolve specific disputes and can operate as precedent for future disputes. Agencies also promulgate regulations, which resemble statutes in that they address a range of behavior and are stated in general terms.

Often a client's situation is governed by some combination of legislative, judicial, and administrative agency law. Many client situations are governed by a statute interpreted in cases. For others, a statute creates an agency, that agency promulgates a regulation and applies it in a series of decisions, and the courts review the agency's actions.

In addition, all three branches create rules governing the functioning of the legal system. Rules governing the operation of a court system are created by the legislature, the courts, or both. Procedural rules promulgated by an agency govern litigation before that agency.

For any particular client's situation, some law is weightier than the rest. The weightier law is "mandatory" or "binding"; it emanates from the legislature, courts, or agency with jurisdiction over, or the power to regulate, the client's situation. Other law is "persuasive"; it emanates from a lawmaker without jurisdiction over the client's situation.

As you will see, Ms. Canoga's situation is governed by the following forms of law: statutes, judicial cases, regulations, and agency decisions at the federal level; New Mexico cases and a New Mexico statute; and rules governing litigation within the federal or New Mexico state courts (depending on where a suit may be brought). All of these laws are mandatory because they emanate from the federal or New Mexico governments, which have jurisdiction over the Canoga situation.

2.   Commentary

Commentary is not law. Rather, commentary is created by individuals, nongovernmental bodies, or government bodies not acting in a lawmaking capacity. All commentary describes what the law says, much also explains how the law came to be, some analyzes and critiques the law. Some commentary represents the author's view of what the law should be; on occasion, commentary does indeed influence lawmakers.

You will find that some forms of commentary resemble sources you have seen before in other fields, such as encyclopedias, treatises, and periodical articles. Exhibit 1.4 (at pages 17–18) is an excerpt from *American Jurisprudence 2d*, a legal encyclopedia; Exhibit 1.5 (at pages 19–20) is from a legal periodical article. Other forms of commentary, such as American Law Reports and the Restatements, are unique to the law. As you will see, every form of commentary has a particular place in legal research.

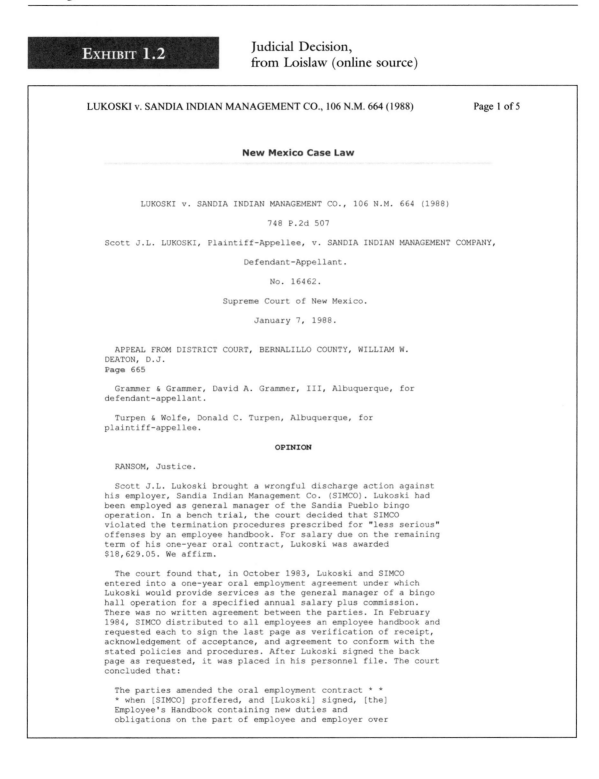

Exhibit 1.2

Judicial Decision,
from Loislaw (online source)

LUKOSKI v. SANDIA INDIAN MANAGEMENT CO., 106 N.M. 664 (1988)   Page 1 of 5

New Mexico Case Law

LUKOSKI v. SANDIA INDIAN MANAGEMENT CO., 106 N.M. 664 (1988)

748 P.2d 507

Scott J.L. LUKOSKI, Plaintiff-Appellee, v. SANDIA INDIAN MANAGEMENT COMPANY,

Defendant-Appellant.

No. 16462.

Supreme Court of New Mexico.

January 7, 1988.

APPEAL FROM DISTRICT COURT, BERNALILLO COUNTY, WILLIAM W.
DEATON, D.J.
Page 665

   Grammer & Grammer, David A. Grammer, III, Albuquerque, for
defendant-appellant.

   Turpen & Wolfe, Donald C. Turpen, Albuquerque, for
plaintiff-appellee.

                              OPINION

   RANSOM, Justice.

   Scott J.L. Lukoski brought a wrongful discharge action against
his employer, Sandia Indian Management Co. (SIMCO). Lukoski had
been employed as general manager of the Sandia Pueblo bingo
operation. In a bench trial, the court decided that SIMCO
violated the termination procedures prescribed for "less serious"
offenses by an employee handbook. For salary due on the remaining
term of his one-year oral contract, Lukoski was awarded
$18,629.05. We affirm.

   The court found that, in October 1983, Lukoski and SIMCO
entered into a one-year oral employment agreement under which
Lukoski would provide services as the general manager of a bingo
hall operation for a specified annual salary plus commission.
There was no written agreement between the parties. In February
1984, SIMCO distributed to all employees an employee handbook and
requested each to sign the last page as verification of receipt,
acknowledgement of acceptance, and agreement to conform with the
stated policies and procedures. After Lukoski signed the back
page as requested, it was placed in his personnel file. The court
concluded that:

   The parties amended the oral employment contract * *
   * when [SIMCO] proffered, and [Lukoski] signed, [the]
   Employee's Handbook containing new duties and
   obligations on the part of employee and employer over

EXHIBIT 1.2   *(continued)*

LUKOSKI v. SANDIA INDIAN MANAGEMENT CO., 106 N.M. 664 (1988)   Page 2 of 5

and above said oral contract, including Rules to be
obeyed by [Lukoski] and a termination procedure to be
followed by [SIMCO].

Although we determine the above-quoted language is a finding of
ultimate fact, rather than a conclusion of law, that is of no
consequence. *See Hoskins v. Albuquerque Bus Co.*, **72 N.M. 217**,
382 P.2d 700 (1963); *Wiggs v. City of Albuquerque*, **57 N.M. 770**,
263 P.2d 963 (1953). SIMCO challenges this finding and for the first
time on appeal raises two other issues. First, it claims that
Lukoski, as general manager, was not the type of employee
intended to be covered by the handbook. Distribution to all
employees with request for signatures constituted evidence to the
contrary, and resolution of any ambiguity regarding management
personnel would have been a specific question of fact. *See
Shaeffer v. Kelton*, **95 N.M. 182**, **619 P.2d 1226** (1980). Second,
SIMCO claims that any breach was not material because it neither
went to the substance of the contract nor defeated the object of
the parties. Materiality is likewise a specific question of fact.
See Bisio v. Madenwald (In re Estate of Bisio), **33 Or. App. 325**,
576 P.2d 801 (1978). As the contract stood after amendment, it
was not materiality, as argued by SIMCO, but rather severity of
offense that was at issue under the termination procedures. In
any event, by failing to tender requested findings, SIMCO waived
specific
Page 666
findings on these fact issues. SCRA 1986, 1-052(B)(1)(f).

There is substantial evidence supporting the court's findings
of ultimate fact that the termination procedures became an
amendment to Lukoski's contract, and that personality — not the
severe offenses of insubordination or disobedience — was the
cause for termination. He was terminated without warning or
suspension for a cause not so severe as to constitute cause for
immediate termination. His personality and interpersonal dealings
were found by the court to create an atmosphere of fear and
anxiety and bad morale among employees and managers.

Relying only on *Ellis v. El Paso Natural Gas Co.*, **754 F.2d 884**
(10th Cir. 1985), the thrust of SIMCO's appeal is that the
language of the employee handbook is "too indefinite to
constitute a contract" and lacks "contractual terms which might
evidence the intent to form a contract." It maintains that the
parties did not conduct themselves as if the employee handbook
was to govern Lukoski or as if they expected it to form the basis
of a contractual relationship. In support of its position, SIMCO
refers to the disciplinary action, suspension, and warning
provisions,**[fn1]** and argues that the language of the termination
policy is ambiguous and contains no required policy for
termination.

SIMCO's argument, however, overlooks the handbook's
characterization of the disciplinary policy regarding warnings,
suspensions and terminations as "an *established procedure*
regarding suspension of problem employees and termination for
those who cannot conform to Company Policy." (Emphasis added.)
Moreover, the language of the handbook does nothing to alert an
employee against placing reliance on any statement contained
therein or against viewing such discipline and termination policy

EXHIBIT 1.2   *(continued)*

LUKOSKI v. SANDIA INDIAN MANAGEMENT CO., 106 N.M. 664 (1988)   Page 3 of 5

as only a unilateral expression of SIMCO's intention that is
subject to revocation or change at any time, in any manner, at
the pleasure of SIMCO. To the contrary, from the language of the
handbook and the conduct of SIMCO in adopting the policy, it
could properly be found that the policy was part of the
employment agreement.

Whether an employee handbook has modified the employment
relationship is a question of fact "to be discerned from the
totality of the parties' statements and actions regarding the
employment relationship." *Wagenseller v. Scottsdale Memorial
Hosp.*, **147 Ariz. 370**, **383**, **710 P.2d 1025**, **1038** (1985) (en banc).

Evidence relevant to this factual decision includes
the language used in the personnel manual as well as
the employer's course of conduct and oral
representations regarding it. We do not mean to imply
that all personnel manual will become part of
employment contracts. Employers are certainly free to
issue no personnel manual at all or to issue a
personnel manual that clearly and conspicuously tells
their employees that the manual is not part of the
employment contract and that their jobs are
terminable
Page 667
at the will of the employer with or without reason.
Such actions * * * instill no reasonable expectations
of job security and do not give employees any reason
to rely on representations in the manual. However, if
an employer does choose to issue a policy statement,
in a manual or otherwise, and, by its language or by
the employer's actions, encourages reliance thereon,
the employer cannot be free to only selectively abide
by it. Having announced a policy, the employer may
not treat it as illusory.

Leikvold v. Valley View Community Hosp., **141 Ariz. 544**, **548**,
688 P.2d 170, **174** (1984). Here, substantial evidence supports the
finding of the trial court that the employee handbook modified
the employment relationship and created warning and suspension
procedures which were not followed in this case.

Accordingly, based upon the foregoing, the judgment of the
trial court is affirmed.

IT IS SO ORDERED.

SCARBOROUGH, C.J., SOSA, Senior Justice, and WALTERS, J.,
concur.

STOWERS, J., dissents.

[fn1] The referenced handbook provisions state:

OTHER DISCIPLINARY ACTION:

In order to protect the good employees [sic] jobs and Sandia
Indian Bingo, there is an established procedure regarding
suspension of problem employees and termination for those who
can not conform to Company Policy. Suspensions without pay

EXHIBIT 1.2   *(continued)*

LUKOSKI v. SANDIA INDIAN MANAGEMENT CO., 106 N.M. 664 (1988)   Page 4 of 5

may be given to employees who violate company policies. There
are violations which are so severe [including insubordination
and disobedience] that immediate termination may be
necessary. . . .

SUSPENSIONS:

Suspension without pay may be given when the incident is not
sufficiently serious to warrant discharge and/or the
particular employee's overall value to the Company [is
considered], if [in] the opinion of the Department Manager
[the employee] warrants another chance. Minimum suspensions
are (3) three days, maximum suspensions are (5) five days. No
employee may be suspended more than once in a year;
thereafter, if the incident would normally warrant suspension
he/she must be discharged.

DISCIPLINARY WARNING:

Disciplinary warning slips will be issued where the offense
is less serious and where corrective action may salvage an
employee. More than one (1) disciplinary warning, whether for
the same offense or not, may subject an employee to
suspension or termination. Warning slips become a permanent
part of an employee's personnel record.

STOWERS, Justice, dissenting.

I respectfully dissent from the majority's holding that SIMCO
did not abide with the termination procedures.

Substantial evidence does support the findings of the trial
court that the employee handbook modified the employment
relationship and that Lukoski was terminated for just cause. The
trial court erred, however, in concluding that SIMCO did not
follow the proper termination procedures. To the contrary, SIMCO
did not breach any of the provisions in the employee handbook
when it discharged Lukoski without a warning and suspension. The
handbook explicitly states that, "there are violations which are
so severe that *immediate termination may be necessary.*" (Emphasis
added).

Overwhelming evidence was presented at trial to show that
Lukowski's violations of company policies were of the type to
fall within the category of "so severe" that a warning and any
suspension procedures were not required. *See State ex rel.
Goodmans Office Furnishings, Inc. v. Page & Wirtz Constr. Co.,*
102 N.M. 22, 24, 690 P.2d 1016, 1018 (1984). Generally, this
evidence indicated that Lukowski had an overall attitude problem
towards his employees, other managers and representatives of the
Sandia Pueblo to the extent that SIMCO was in jeopardy of losing
its bingo contract with the Pueblo; moreover, he was abusive
towards the accountants, argued or fought publicly with
customers, the assistant bingo manager, the construction
supervisor and an admittance clerk; Lukoski also failed to
install proper security measures and verification methods, and
hired unqualified personnel. Further, testimony indicated that on
several occasions, Walker, Lukoski's supervisor, spoke to Lukoski
about this attitude problem, and, in fact, interceded on

EXHIBIT **1.2**   *(continued)*

LUKOSKI v. SANDIA INDIAN MANAGEMENT CO., 106 N.M. 664 (1988)   Page 5 of 5

Lukoski's behalf when the Sandia Pueblo desired to discharge
Lukoski.

As enumerated in the handbook, Lukoski's violations included,
"fighting on company property, refusal to obey reasonable orders
of a supervisor, discourtesy to customers, and disobeying or
ignoring established written or oral work rules or policies."
These are, and I again quote from the handbook, "violations which
are so severe that *immediate termination* may be necessary."
(Emphasis added.) Therefore, the trial court was in error when it
decided that SIMCO violated the termination procedures prescribed
for "less serious" offenses in the handbook. Lukoski was not
entitled to those termination procedures since his offenses were
not of the "less serious" type. Under the circumstances in this
case, the only process due Lukoski for the seriousness of his
violations was immediate termination. Thus, there was no breach
by SIMCO when it discharged him for just cause.

The judgment of the district court should be reversed and this
case remanded for dismissal.
Page 668

| EXHIBIT 1.3 | Statute, from West's New Mexico Statutes Annotated (paper source) |

ARTICLE 11
EMPLOYEE PRIVACY

Section
50–11–1. Short title.
50–11–2. Definitions.
50–11–3. Employers; unlawful practices.
50–11–4. Remedies.
50–11–5. Court fees and costs.
50–11–6. Mitigation of damages.

§ 50–11–1. Short title

This act may be cited as the "Employee Privacy Act".

L. 1991, Ch. 244, § 1.

Research References

Treatises and Practice Aids
Employee Privacy Law § 13:28.
Employment Coordinator P EP-18,346.
Employment Discrimination Coordinator P 97,605.

Guide to Employee Handbooks § 9:94.
Investigating Employee Conduct APP D.
Legal Guide to Human Resources APP. 32.

§ 50–11–2. Definitions

As used in the Employee Privacy Act:

A. "employee" means a person that performs a service for wages or other remuneration under a contract of hire, written or oral, express or implied, and includes a person employed by the state or a political subdivision of the state;

B. "employer" means a person that has one or more employees and includes an agent of an employer and the state or a political subdivision of the state; and

C. "person" means an individual, sole proprietorship, partnership, corporation, association or any other legal entity.

L. 1991, Ch. 244, § 2.

Research References

Treatises and Practice Aids
Employee Privacy Law § 13:28.
Employment Discrimination Coordinator P 97,630, P 97,631, P 97,632, P 97,641.5.

HRS Fair Employment Practices 324,500.

§ 50–11–3. Employers; unlawful practices

A. It is unlawful for an employer to:

(1) refuse to hire or to discharge any individual, or otherwise disadvantage any individual, with respect to compensation, terms, conditions or privileges of employment because the individual is a smoker or nonsmoker, provided that the individual complies with applicable laws or policies regulating smoking on the premises of the employer during working hours; or

99

EXHIBIT 1.3   *(continued)*

---

§ 50–11–3   **EMPLOYMENT LAW**

(2) require as a condition of employment that any employee or applicant for employment abstain from smoking or using tobacco products during nonworking hours, provided the individual complies with applicable laws or policies regulating smoking on the premises of the employer during working hours.

B. The provisions of Subsection A of this section shall not be deemed to protect any activity that:

(1) materially threatens an employer's legitimate conflict of interest policy reasonably designed to protect the employer's trade secrets, proprietary information or other proprietary interests; or

(2) relates to a bona fide occupational requirement and is reasonably and rationally related to the employment activities and responsibilities of a particular employee or a particular group of employees, rather than to all employees of the employer.

L. 1991, Ch. 244, § 3.

Library References

Civil Rights ⇒1231...
Westlaw Key Number Search: 78k1231.
C.J.S. Civil Rights §§ 64 to 65.

Research References

Treatises and Practice Aids
Avoiding and Discharging Wrongful Discharge Claims § 4:01.
Employee Privacy Law § 13:28.
Employment Discrimination Coordinator P 97,625, P 97,646, P 97,655, P 97,656, P 97,670, P 97,613.5, P 97,641.5.

Employment Law § 1.24.
HRS Fair Employment Practices 324,500.
Litigating Wrongful Discharge Claims §§ 2:100.
Termination of Employment § 34:19.

§ 50–11–4.   Remedies

Any employee claiming to be aggrieved by any unlawful action of an employer pursuant to Section 3 of the Employee Privacy Act may bring a civil suit for damages in any district court of competent jurisdiction. The employee may be awarded all wages and benefits due up to and including the date of the judgment.

L. 1991, Ch. 244, § 4.

Library References

Civil Rights ⇒1720.
Westlaw Key Number Search: 78k1720.
C.J.S. Civil Rights §§ 201 to 212, 214 to 217.

Research References

Treatises and Practice Aids
Employment Discrimination Coordinator P 97,682, P 97,715.

HRS Fair Employment Practices 324,500.
Termination of Employment § 34:19.

100

EXHIBIT 1.3   *(continued)*

EMPLOYEE PRIVACY   § 50–11–6

§ 50–11–5. Court fees and costs

In any civil suit arising from the Employee Privacy Act, the court shall award the prevailing party court costs and reasonable attorneys' fees.

L. 1991, Ch. 244, § 5.

Library References

Civil Rights ☞1773.
Westlaw Key Number Search: 78k1773.
C.J.S. Civil Rights § 222.

Research References

Treatises and Practice Aids
    Employment Discrimination Coordinator P
    97,683.

§ 50–11–6. Mitigation of damages

Nothing in the Employee Privacy Act shall be construed to relieve a person from the obligation to mitigate damages.

L. 1991, Ch. 244, § 6.

Library References

Civil Rights ☞1765.
Westlaw Key Number Search: 78k1765.
C.J.S. Civil Rights § 222.

Research References

Treatises and Practice Aids
    Employee Privacy Law § 13:28.
    Employment Discrimination Coordinator P
    97,682.
    Employment Law § 1.7.
    HRS Fair Employment Practices 324,500.
    Investigating Employee Conduct APP D.
    Legal Guide to Human Resources APP. 32.
    SE70 American Law Institute-American Bar
    Association 727.

SD52 American Law Institute-American Bar
    Association 697.
663 Practising Law Institute Litigation and
    Administrative Practice: Litigation 9.
637 Practising Law Institute Litigation and
    Administrative Practice: Litigation 1071.
614 Practising Law Institute Litigation and
    Administrative Practice: Litigation 843.
592 Practising Law Institute Litigation and
    Administrative Practice: Litigation 1191.
571 Practising Law Institute Litigation and
    Administrative Practice: Litigation 871.

| EXHIBIT 1.4 | Encyclopedia, from American Jurisprudence 2d (paper source) |

WRONGFUL DISCHARGE   § 44

response to different degrees of misconduct,[1] ranging from reprimand to discharge.[2] Generally, if a termination violates the progressive discipline procedure set forth in the employer's handbook, the employer has breached its promise of procedural fairness, and the employee may recover for wrongful discharge.[3] However, a memorandum warning an employee that she will be terminated within a certain time period if her behavior does not improve cannot modify a worker's employment at-will contract and the employer does not breach that contract when it terminates the worker's employment without cause; it is wholly irrational to assume that the memorandum will somehow ripen into an assured contract of progressive discipline over that time period.[4] Additionally, the provisions of an employee manual stating that termination can be expected upon receipt of a third disciplinary action do not expressly provide that an employee can be terminated only for cause so as to overcome the employment at-will doctrine.[5]

◆ **Caution:** Some cases suggest that once a company promulgates procedures for termination, they must be strictly followed.[6] Substantial compliance, or an attempt to adhere to the spirit of the procedure, may not always suffice.[7]

§ 44 Grievance and appeal procedures

Research References
West's Key Number Digest, Civil Rights ☞144; Master and Servant ☞30(1.5)

Some employee manuals contain provisions which give aggrieved employees the opportunity to appeal adverse employment decisions. Courts have held that an employer's failure to abide by its rules concerning posttermination appeals is a breach of contract.[1]

[Section 43]

[1]Long v. Tazewell/Pekin Consol. Communication Center, 215 Ill. App. 3d 134, 158 Ill. Dec. 798, 574 N.E.2d 1191 (3d Dist. 1991); Enyeart v. Shelter Mut. Ins. Co., 693 S.W.2d 120 (Mo. Ct. App. W.D. 1985); Sherman v. Rutland Hosp., Inc., 146 Vt. 204, 500 A.2d 230 (1985); Mobil Coal Producing, Inc. v. Parks, 704 P.2d 702 (Wyo. 1985).

[2]Pine River State Bank v. Mettille, 333 N.W.2d 622 (Minn. 1983).

[3]Shah v. General Elec. Co., 816 F.2d 264 (6th Cir. 1987); Thompson v. American Motor Inns Inc., 623 F. Supp. 409 (W.D. Va. 1985); ARCO Alaska, Inc. v. Akers, 753 P.2d 1150 (Alaska 1988); Foley v. Interactive Data Corp., 47 Cal. 3d 654, 254 Cal. Rptr. 211, 765 P.2d 373 (1988); Long v. Tazewell/Pekin Consol. Communication Center, 215 Ill. App. 3d 134, 158 Ill. Dec. 798, 574 N.E.2d 1191 (3d Dist. 1991); Cannon v. National By-Products, Inc., 422 N.W.2d 638 (Iowa 1988); Staggs v. Blue Cross of Maryland, Inc., 61 Md. App. 381, 486 A.2d 798 (1985); Damrow v. Thumb Co-op. Terminal, Inc., 126 Mich. App. 354, 337 N.W.2d 338 (1983); Pine River State Bank v. Mettille, 333 N.W.2d 622 (Minn. 1983); Small v. Springs Industries, Inc., 292 S.C. 481, 357 S.E.2d 452 (1987); Berube v. Fashion Centre, Ltd., 771 P.2d 1033 (Utah 1989).

[4]Mudlitz v. Mutual Service Ins. Companies, 75 F.3d 391 (8th Cir. 1996) (applying Minnesota law).

[5]Robinson v. Langdon, 333 Ark. 662, 970 S.W.2d 292 (1998).

[6]Damrow v. Thumb Co-op. Terminal, Inc., 126 Mich. App. 354, 337 N.W.2d 338 (1983); Pine River State Bank v. Mettille, 333 N.W.2d 622 (Minn. 1983).

[7]Damrow v. Thumb Co-op. Terminal, Inc., 126 Mich. App. 354, 337 N.W.2d 338 (1983).

[Section 44]

[1]Wagenseller v. Scottsdale Memorial

EXHIBIT 1.4   *(continued)*

§ 44   82 AM JUR 2d

◆ **Observation:** The existence of an internal appeal procedure permits an inference of a fair treatment and a just cause requirement. The cases which hold that violation of a grievance procedure is a material breach of contract are few. Still, at least one court has held that postdischarge remedies must be made available to a terminated employee even if he or she was not aware of the rules.[2] On the other hand, where a handbook that required an exit interview before termination also reserved the right to discharge at any time, the presumption of employment at-will was not rebutted and the handbook did not operate to limit the circumstances of arbitrary dismissal.[3]

In the absence of clear, promissory language, the language of a summary of policies and benefits which sets forth the employer's employment policies, including a grievance policy for the resolution of work-related problems, does not create enforceable employment contract rights sufficient to overcome the presumption of an employment relationship terminable at will.[4]

§ 45 Specification of grounds for discipline or discharge

Research References

West's Key Number Digest, Civil Rights ☞144; Master and Servant ☞30(1.5)

Where specific grounds for discharge and discipline are set forth in an employers' handbook or other employment guidelines, discharged employees have sometimes been successful in arguing that such specified grounds are exclusive and that, consequently, the discharge of an employee on other grounds is wrongful.[1]

However, just as nonexclusive discharge procedures impose no obligation

---

Hosp., 147 Ariz. 370, 710 P.2d 1025 (1985); Pavadore v. School Committee of Canton, 19 Mass. App. Ct. 943, 473 N.E.2d 205, 22 Ed. Law Rep. 882 (1985); Jeffers v. Bishop Clarkson Memorial Hosp., 222 Neb. 829, 387 N.W.2d 692 (1986); Mobil Coal Producing, Inc. v. Parks, 704 P.2d 702 (Wyo. 1985).

[2]Pavadore v. School Committee of Canton, 19 Mass. App. Ct. 943, 473 N.E.2d 205, 22 Ed. Law Rep. 882 (1985).

[3]Ford v. Blue Cross & Blue Shield of Michigan, 150 Mich. App. 462, 389 N.W.2d 114 (1986).

[4]Bjorn v. Associated Regional and University Pathologists, Inc., 208 Ill. App. 3d 505, 153 Ill. Dec. 459, 567 N.E.2d 417 (1st Dist. 1990).

An at-will employee of a university could be terminated involuntarily where a grievance procedure was not an employment contract itself; the university never represented to the employee that the grievance procedure was part of his employment agreement; the employee did not negotiate or bargain for the terms of the grievance procedure either individually or as part of a group of employees. Mix v. University of New Orleans, 609 So. 2d 958, 79 Ed. Law Rep. 1146 (La. Ct. App. 4th Cir. 1992), writ denied, 612 So. 2d 83 (La. 1993).

[Section 45]
[1]Mycak v. Honeywell, Inc., 953 F.2d 798 (2d Cir. 1992) (applying New York law); Conley v. Board of Trustees of Grenada County Hosp., 707 F.2d 175 (5th Cir. 1983); Towns v. Emery Air Freight, Inc., 3 I.E.R. Cas. (BNA) 911, 1988 WL 156258 (S.D. Ohio 1988) (applying Ohio law); Damrow v. Thumb Co-op. Terminal, Inc., 126 Mich. App. 354, 337 N.W.2d 338 (1983); Frazier v. Minnesota Min. and Mfg. Co., 82 Or. App. 328, 728 P.2d 87 (1986); Berube v. Fashion Centre, Ltd., 771 P.2d 1033 (Utah 1989); Cook v. Heck's Inc., 176 W. Va. 368, 342 S.E.2d 453 (1986); Mobil Coal Producing, Inc. v. Parks, 704 P.2d 702 (Wyo. 1985).

EXHIBIT 1.5   Legal Periodical Article,
               from LexisNexis (online source)

6 of 84 DOCUMENTS

Copyright (c) 2006 Albany Law Review
Albany Law Review

2006

70 Alb. L. Rev. 117

LENGTH: 12682 words

ARTICLE: IS LEISURE-TIME SMOKING A VALID EMPLOYMENT CONSIDERATION?

NAME: Karen L. Chadwick*

BIO: * Associate Professor of Law, Thomas M. Cooley Law School; J.D., University of Michigan (1981). I wish to thank Andrew Lane for his helpful research and thoughtful suggestions.

TEXT:
[*117]

I. Introduction

It has been over forty years since the Surgeon General first released a report stating that cigarette smoking is a health hazard and a primary contributor to lung disease. n1 Since that report, substantial research has established that smoking dramatically increases the risk of death from a plethora of conditions. n2 Despite widespread awareness and acceptance of the risks of smoking, n3 an estimated 44.5 million adults, or 20.9% of the United States population, continue to smoke. n4 It has been estimated that cigarette smoking is now responsible for 440,000 deaths annually in the United States. n5 Another estimated 8.6 million persons in the United States suffer from serious illnesses attributable to smoking. n6

In the years since the Surgeon General's initial report, the evidence has mounted that the costs attributable to smoking are reflected not only in smokers' decreased longevity and increased [*118] risk of disease, but also in the workplace. n7 The highest prevalence of smoking in the United States occurs during peak employment years in the twenty-five to forty-four-year-old age groups. n8 Health care costs for smokers are estimated to be as much as forty percent higher than those for nonsmokers. n9 Employers of smokers suffer a substantial loss of productivity attributable to smoking. n10 In the United States, productivity costs attributable to smoking total an estimated $ 92 billion annually. n11 Many of the employment costs attributable to employee smokers, including increased health insurance costs and productivity losses due to absenteeism, are ultimately shared by nonsmoking employees. n12

Currently, twenty-seven states and the District of Columbia have adopted statutes which prohibit enforcement of employment policies that penalize employees and potential employees for engaging in legal activities such as smoking during non-employment periods. n13 Notwithstanding the substantial support for legislation prohibiting [*119] lifestyle discrimination, a significant number of states continue to permit discrimination based on off-duty activities. n14 In those states, an increasing number of employers have opted to enact policies precluding the employment of smokers. n15 Currently, approximately six percent of companies refuse to hire smokers. n16 In contrast to the draconian no-smoking-ever approach taken by some employers in states that tolerate lifestyle discrimination, other employers in those states have adopted a middle-of-the-road approach to leisure-time smoking by employees. Those employers, rather than proscribing employment of smokers, have attempted to pass on at least some of the additional costs attributable to smoking to employees that smoke. n17

This Article examines the current approaches to employment discrimination based on off-duty smoking. Part I examines the constitutional, statutory, and common law background giving rise to the differing views regarding employer consideration of off-duty behavior in making employment decisions. Both federal and state constitutional attacks on employment discrimination against smokers have failed. n18 Similarly, no federal statute prohibits employers from re-

EXHIBIT 1.5   *(continued)*

70 Alb. L. Rev. 117, *   Page 10

tion between smokers and nonsmokers as to employer provided health benefits, the benefits provided to smokers are subsidized by nonsmoking employees. Id.

n13. Ariz. Rev. Stat. Ann. §36-601.02 (West 2006); Colo. Rev. Stat. Ann. §24-34-402.5 (West 2006); CONN. GEN. STAT. ANN. <SECT>31-40s (West 2006); D.C. CODE <SECT>7-1703.03 (2006); 820 ILL. COMP. STAT. ANN. 55/5 (West 2006); IND. CODE ANN. <SECT>22-5-4-1 (West 2006); KY. REV. STAT. ANN. <SECT>344.040 (West 2005); LA. REV. STAT. ANN. <SECT>23:966 (2006); ME. REV. STAT. ANN. tit. 26, <SECT>597 (2006); MINN. STAT. ANN. <SECT>181.938 (West 2006); MO. ANN. STAT. <SECT>290.145 (West 2006); MONT. CODE ANN. <SECT>39-2-313 (2005); NEV. REV. STAT. ANN. <SECT>613.333 (West 2005); N.H. REV. STAT. ANN. <SECT>275:37-a (2006); N.J. STAT. ANN. <SECT>34:6B-1 (West 2006); N.M. STAT. ANN. <SECT>50-11-13 (West 2006); N.Y. LAB. LAW <SECT>201-d (McKinney 2006); N.C. GEN. STAT. ANN. <SECT>95-28.2 (West 2006); N.D. CENT. CODE <SECT>14-02.4-03 (2005); OKLA. STAT. ANN. tit. 40, <SECT>500 (West 2006); OR. REV. STAT. ANN. <SECT>659A.315 (West 2005); R.I. GEN. LAWS. <SECT>23-20.7.1-1 (West 2004) (repealed 2005); S.C. CODE ANN. <SECT>41-1-85 (2005); S.D. CODIFIED LAWS <SECT>60-4-11 (2006); VA. CODE ANN. <SECT>2.2-2902 (West 2006); W. VA. CODE ANN. <SECT>21-3-19 (West 2006); WIS. STAT. ANN. <SECT>111.31 (West 2005); WYO. STAT. ANN. <SECT>27-9-105 (2005).

n14. The states that have not enacted employee-privacy statutes include: Alabama, Alaska, Arkansas, California, Delaware, Florida, Georgia, Hawaii, Idaho, Kansas, Maryland, Massachusetts, Mississippi, Nebraska, Ohio, Pennsylvania, Texas, Utah, Vermont, and Washington. Although Michigan has not enacted an employee-privacy statute, a bill has been introduced in the Michigan Senate which, if passed, would prohibit employer discrimination based on leisure-time activities. See S.B. 381 (Mich. 2005).

n15. See Nat'l Workrights Inst., Lifestyle Discrimination: Employer Control of Legal off Duty Employee Activities, http://www.workrights.org [hereinafter Nat'l Workrights Inst.] (noting that Kalamazoo Valley Community College in Michigan; Alaska Airlines; Schwitzer Engineering Laboratories in Pullman, Washington; Investors Property Management in Seattle, Washington; and Union Pacific and Montgomery Counties in Pennsylvania refuse to hire workers who smoke).

n16. Michele L. Tyler, Blowing Smoke: Do Smokers Have a Right? Limiting the Privacy Rights of Cigarette Smokers, 86 Geo. L.J. 783, 790 (1998).

n17. See, e.g., Julie Forster, NWA Smokers to Pay More for Insurance, Detroit Free Press, Oct. 18, 2005 ("Northwest Airlines plans to begin charging some of its workers who smoke an additional fee for health insurance."); Marguerite Higgins, Gannett Smokers to Pay, Wash. Times, Oct. 19, 2005 (reporting that Gannett Company employees who admit to smoking will be given the choice of enrolling in a company-funded cessation program or paying a fifty dollar per month fee for health insurance).

n18. See discussion infra Part II.A.

n19. See discussion infra Part II.B.

n20. See discussion infra Part II.C.

n21. See, e.g., Grusendorf v. City of Okla. City, 816 F.2d 539, 540 (10th Cir. 1987); City of N. Miami v. Kurtz, 653 So. 2d 1025, 1026 (Fla. 1995).

n22. See, e.g., Marsh v. Delta Air Lines, Inc., 952 F. Supp. 1458, 1462 (D. Colo. 1997). An airline employee discharged for writing a letter to a newspaper that was critical of his employer filed suit under a Colorado

3. Finding Tools

As you may have guessed, you will need assistance locating pertinent authorities. Finding tools help you do this. They are not authority, however, because they do not assert legal propositions or do so only incidentally.

Some finding tools cover a wide range or set of sources. For example, a library catalog covers many of the sources owned by or accessible in a particular library. Internet search engines and directories cover World Wide websites. Other finding tools are narrower, covering a particular type of authority. For example, periodical indexes are used to identify periodical articles, and digests are used to identify cases.

Many sources operate as finding tools for other authorities. For example, a court may cite to a statute; a treatise author may list cases from which he or she has drawn the legal rule under discussion; an online search for a case may yield references to commentary, along with the case.

Finally, keep in mind that people, including colleagues, professors, and reference librarians, can sometimes be very helpful "finding tools."

D. RESEARCH MEDIA

Until quite recently, legal materials were all published in books, and legal research took place in a library. Researchers worked with books and occasionally microforms.[8] Computer-assisted legal research debuted approximately three decades ago and has evolved through several phases since then. Initially, two commercial online services — now known as LexisNexis and Westlaw — dominated; they remain the dominant commercial online services for legal research today.[9] During the 1990s, CD-ROM products became fairly popular, especially for certain sources, such as a specific state's statutes.[10] In recent years, as CD-ROMs have faded in importance, the Internet has come to play a central role in legal research. Joining LexisNexis and Westlaw are more modest commercial services and public websites, such as a court's website where recent decisions are posted.

The Internet is a vast, unregulated, international network that connects thousands of computer networks; this is both the Internet's strength and weakness. You may locate a pertinent website on the Internet by four different methods:

☐ You may go directly to a known website by typing in its URL (uniform resource locator), that is, its Internet address.

---

8. Microform reels or fiche cards contain tiny photographs of printed pages, read through a microform reader.

9. Online services store information on a server at a remote location; the user gains access to the information through a computer and a network connection.

10. A CD-ROM (compact disc — read-only memory) contains information stored in "pits" and read via a computer.

☐ You may go to a website that serves as a portal to other websites, that is, it collects and organizes URLs for websites, especially government websites, and provides links to those sites. An early service in law and still a very well regarded academic website is that of the Legal Information Institute, provided by Cornell University's law school and located at www.law.cornell.edu.

☐ You may use an online subject directory, such as Findlaw, or a paper directory such as *The Legal List*.

☐ You may use a search engine by typing in words pertinent to websites you hope to locate. Many legal researchers use general-purpose search engines such as Google, Yahoo!, or Live Search for certain purposes. LawCrawler and Westlaw WebPlus are search engines focusing on legal materials.

Through the Internet, you will gain access to many websites containing legal materials, so you will need to exercise considerable judgment in selecting which to use. The online legal research industry is changing rapidly. Your prime objective is to locate a credible site; other important factors are coverage and cost. As of the writing of this text in mid-2007, most of the online services fit into one of the following categories:

☐ Government sites: Increasingly, federal and state governments are providing their legal materials to the public through free websites, such as www.access.gpo.gov, the federal government printing office website.

☐ Commercial sites: Various commercial publishers make legal materials available through the Internet for a fee, either by subscription or on a per-use basis. The two most prominent are, as mentioned previously, LexisNexis and Westlaw. Both companies also publish paper legal materials. Several less extensive sites also provide a fairly wide range of authorities; an example is Loislaw.

☐ Legal organizations: Recently, bar associations (professional organizations of lawyers) have begun to offer legal materials through the Internet. For example, you can locate materials regarding legal ethics at www.abanet.org, the free website of the American Bar Association. Some state bar associations offer access to online research services offering fairly recent cases and statutes as a benefit of membership.

☐ Academic sites: Although academic websites primarily serve as portals to other websites, some also provide selected documents as well. For example, the University of Pennsylvania's Biddle Law Library provides the archives of the Restatements, which are very influential commentary.

☐ Other organizations: Professional, trade, and public interest organizations provide some legal materials in their areas of interest on their websites. Some of these materials may be available to subscribers only. These websites generally are not as authoritative as those listed above because they may not be as accurate or updated and generally have an advocacy orientation.

EXHIBIT 1.6	Lawyers' Media Choices

According to the American Bar Association Legal Technology Resource Center's 2007 Survey Report, *Online Research Trends Report*, 52% of lawyers regularly use paper resources, 58% regularly use fee-based online resources, and 48% regularly use free online resources. Fee-based online resources receive higher satisfaction ratings than free resources:

	fee-based services	*free service*
ability to assess author's credentials	94%	76%
depth of coverage	97%	77%
search options	94%	70%
user-friendliness	86%	73%

A 2007 survey of Illinois attorneys* revealed that 80% researched every day or often. To some extent, media choices reflected years of practice; below are the answers to the question "What do you do most of your research in?"

	all	*0–5 years*	*16+ years*
paper	7.7%	1.4%	17.4%
LexisNexis or Westlaw	70%	87.1%	47.8%
other fee-based online	7.7%	5.7%	11.6%
free online	10.8%	2.9%	17.4%
other	3.6%	2.9%	5.8%

*Sanford Greenberg & Tom Gaylord, *Online Research Trend Report: Practitioner Surveys and Focus Groups on the Research Realities*, Back to the Future of Legal Research (Chicago, IL, May 18, 2007).

The exhibits in this chapter come from both paper and online sources: the *Lukoski* case from Loislaw online; the employee privacy statute from a paper code published by Michie, now owned by LexisNexis; the encyclopedia excerpt from a paper encyclopedia published by Thomson West; and the law review article from the LexisNexis U.S. and Canadian Law Reviews Combined database.

As you develop your legal research skills, you should aim to be ambidextrous — equally adept at paper and online research — for three reasons. First, some legal research materials are available in only one medium. Some materials are not yet available online, and some of those never will be. A fairly recent development in legal publishing is that some very new materials are available only online. Second, sometimes the medium you would prefer to use will be unavailable — books can be off the shelf, online networks can be down — or cost more than your client is willing to pay. Third, as you will see throughout this text, paper sources work better for some purposes, and online resources work better for other purposes. See Exhibit 1.6 (at page 23).

E.   THE APPROACH OF THIS BOOK

To maneuver successfully through the many sources involved in legal research, you must not only know the lay of the land, described above. You also must understand the distinct tasks involved in legal research, such as how to develop research terms and how to update your initial research results. These are the topics of Chapter 2.

With that groundwork set, the text explores the five major categories of research materials, each in its own unit:

- ☐ commentary in Unit II,
- ☐ case law in Unit III,
- ☐ enacted law in Unit IV,
- ☐ administrative law in Unit V, and
- ☐ rules of procedure and legal ethics in Unit VI.

You may wonder why commentary is discussed before the various forms of law. As you will see, although the law is well more important than commentary, often you will start your research in commentary and then proceed to one or more types of law.

Most chapters cover a set of closely related research materials and follow a standard format. They address the following questions:

- ☐ What is the authority?
- ☐ Why would you research in it?
- ☐ How do you research in it?
- ☐ How do you cite it?
- ☐ What else should you know?

These chapters come at their topics three ways: A general description and illustrative materials pertinent to the Canoga case appear in each chapter. Each chapter also contains a template, which is presented twice, blank and then filled in to reflect our research into the Canoga case. In addition, interludes at the end of each unit describe how we found the illustrative material and what we would draw from it.

Two of the questions listed previously merit a paragraph of explanation here. First, as to the *how do you research in it* discussion: Many types of legal authority can be researched multiple ways, in multiple sources. For example, you can research case law through a set of books, online commercial computer services, or in free websites. If we were to describe all of the ways to conduct legal research, this book would be enormous, and your capacity to fully learn any particular technique would be limited. Thus each chapter presents no more than a handful of research practices that we see as best practices because they likely will lead to correct, comprehensive, credible, and cost-effective research in most situations. As you become more expert, and technology and publication patterns evolve, you may develop new best practices, but they probably will build on the practices discussed here. We have synopsized the practices in shaded boxes, each of which presents either steps (signified by arrow bullets ▶) or options (signified by round bullets •).

Second, as to the *how do you cite it* discussion: Citation is the practice of providing the reader with a very brief description of an authority and a precise reference to its location. As you will see, legal citation is complicated and technical, but also manageable if you work through it in a systematic way. This text provides you with starting information on citation and refers you to the two leading manuals on legal citation. *The Bluebook: A Uniform System of Citation*, compiled by upper-level students at four prestigious law schools, was in its eighteenth edition at the time this book was written. *ALWD Citation Manual: A Professional System of Citation*, in its third edition at the time this book was written, is a product of the Association of Legal Writing Directors. Furthermore, some courts have their own citation protocols, which you should, of course, follow in appropriate cases.

Finally, Unit VII, a single chapter, presents research journals written by upper-level law students as they researched a typical client situation. These journals demonstrate various ways in which the sources and processes described in this text fit together.

From Curiosity to Closure: Eight Cognitive Tasks

Research is formalized curiosity. It is poking and prying with a purpose.
— Zora Neale Hurston, *Dust Tracks on a Road* (1942)

A. INTRODUCTION

Good legal research takes a lot of time, hard thinking, and discipline. To do it well, you will pass through the four phases — curiosity, content and context, consultation, and closure — and work through the eight steps listed in the chapter outline. Throughout the process, you will acquire information and make judgments based on what you have learned so far — this is the process of cognition. The more you are aware of the process, the better — the less likely you will lose track of your topic, pursue off-point materials, or spend too much time on a resource.

The eight tasks generally occur in the sequence set forth here. That is, you will:

☐ start by considering your client's situation (tasks 1 and 2);
☐ proceed to determining which authorities and resources to use (tasks 3 and 4);
☐ spend much of your time carefully working with those resources (tasks 5, 6, and 7); and
☐ stop researching (task 8).

As you will soon see, legal research is not a totally linear process. For example, if at task 5 you find little pertinent information in the sources you have selected, you may need to return to task 2 to generate additional research terms and issues, or to task 4 to identify additional sources to explore. In addition, your specific research plan will vary somewhat from project to project, reflecting the difficulty of the topic, your initial knowledge of the pertinent law, the time available, cost considerations, and other factors.

If you accomplish all eight tasks well, your research should meet the criteria stated in Chapter 1; it should be

☐ *correct:* leading to the law governing your client's situation;
☐ *comprehensive:* addressing the various issues raised by the client's situation and incorporating an appropriate range of pertinent authorities;
☐ *credible:* focusing on authorities that carry weight because of their nature and quality; and
☐ *cost-effective:* obtaining results that justify the effort, in light of the client's situation and available research options.

As you read through this chapter, you will not only read about a task but also see a simple drawing symbolizing the task. This chapter refers, a number of times, to the Canoga situation presented in Chapter 1 (at pages 3–4) and to the authorities presented in Chapter 1 (at pages 9–20). We encourage you to read or review those materials before proceeding.

B. CURIOSITY

Lawyers research the law because clients have problems to be solved, whether disputes to resolve or transactions to plan. Thus good research begins with careful consideration of the client's situation leading, ideally, to sufficient curiosity to sustain what may be a lengthy research process.

1. Learn and React to Your Client's Situation

On occasion, you will receive a tidy oral or written statement of a client's situation. This is far more common in law school than in real life. Most of the time in practice, you will learn about the client's situation through various sources of information: a conversation with the client, correspondence, documents, a visit to the site, etc.

From these various sources, you must construct a narrative of the client's situation. To develop a strong narrative, consider using one or more of the following activities:

☐ Write out a cast of characters, and identify the role each played.
☐ Create a timeline of key events.
☐ Discern what each of the main characters would say about the situation.
☐ Develop a short statement of what your client hopes will happen as a result of your representation.

Note that your client's situation involves not only facts but also the client's concerns and goals.

As you develop the narrative, you likely will realize that you do not know everything you would like to know. You may be able to get the missing information by contacting your client or by some other appropriate means. Fairly often, however, you will not know everything you want to know because the participants do not remember what you would like to know, because you are not yet in a position to contact the participant who might know, or because you are helping to structure a transaction that will take place in the future. Similarly, you may have conflicting information on some aspect of the situation and no means of resolving the conflict. Be sure to note any unknown or uncertain facts, and proceed in your research on the basis of one or more reasonable assumptions.

Once you have developed the narrative, reflect a bit on your client's situation. Ask yourself questions like these:

☐ What are the appealing aspects of my client's position?
☐ What are the appealing aspects of the position of my client's opponent or the other participants in the situation?
☐ What would be a fair and just outcome?
☐ If I were the lawmaker, not my client's lawyer, what would I think about this situation? What rule would I devise?

This process is often described as "weighing the equities" of a situation; hence, our symbol for this task is a scale.

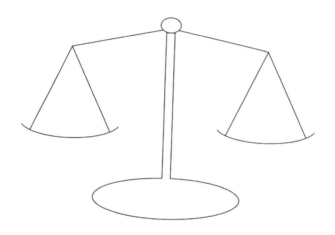

Finally, think about possible solutions that would meet your client's goals, address your client's concerns, and probably be accepted by your client's opponent or other participants in the situation. Once you begin your legal research, you will inevitably focus on the options available through the legal system. Keep in mind, however, that many situations involving legal questions are handled not through formal legal processes but rather through negotiation facilitated or conducted by lawyers.

The narrative of Ms. Canoga's situation appears in Chapter 1 at pages 3–4. The appealing aspects of Ms. Canoga's position include her interests in making her own decisions regarding her personal habits, being able to raise an issue of serious concern with management without losing her job, and having the board follow the procedures promised in the handbook. The appealing aspects of the orchestra's position include its interests in securing excellent performance by wind players, controlling health care costs, and preserving managerial prerogative.

2.   Develop Research Terms and Research Issues

a.   Understanding Legal Language

The law and commentary (and finding tools, too) consist of words used in particular ways. Of primary concern is the legal rule. A legal rule links factual conditions with legal consequences. For example, consider this excerpt from the New Mexico statute presented in Chapter 1 (at pages 14–16):

> It is unlawful for an employer to . . . require as a condition of employ-ment that any employee . . . abstain from smoking or using tobacco products during nonworking hours. . . . Any employee claiming to be aggrieved by [such an] unlawful action . . . may bring a civil suit for damages. . . . The employee may be awarded all wages and benefits due up to and including the date of the judgment.

This rule refers to the following factual condition: an employer prohibits an employee from smoking during non-working hours. That factual condition leads to the following legal consequence: the employee may sue the employer for lost wages and benefits.

Most of the words in this rule are familiar words. Indeed, some words are used just as you would use them in everyday speech, e.g., *smoking* and *tobacco products*. Others are primarily legal terms, e.g., *aggrieved*, *civil suit*, and *judgment*.

In some legal rules, one or more words are defined; that definition may or may not accord with its common meaning. For example, the New Mexico legislature defined *employer* to include various legal entities, including the state and its political subdivisions, that have one or more employees. In another statute, *employer* might include only private employers or entities with a specified minimum number of employees.

Most words in a legal rule are quite general, because rules describe classes of situations, not specific situations. For example, the New Mexico statute does not describe a specific employer or employee, particular tobacco pro-ducts, or a specific means of prohibiting smoking.

As is true outside the law, many legal concepts can be expressed various ways, as exemplified in the New Mexico statute:

- ☐ Some concepts are expressed not in one word, but in a phrase. Sometimes the words may be inverted with no loss of meaning; sometimes the words appear in a fixed order. For example: *during nonworking hours; conditions of employment* or *employment conditions*.
- ☐ Some concepts can be stated in one of several words or phrases with virtually the same meaning, i.e., synonyms. For example: *claim* and *civil suit*.
- ☐ Similarly, some words and phrases used in legal rules have antonyms. For example, the New Mexico statute excerpted above also has a rule governing *during working hours*.

☐ Some concepts can be expressed in broad or narrow terms. For example: *unlawful* and *civil suit for damages; damages* and *lost wages.*

☐ Finally, some concepts are subsets of larger legal concepts; that is, legal rules have elements. For example, the New Mexico statute has these elements: employer, employee, requirement of abstention from smoking, during nonworking hours.

Many legal authorities do more than state legal rules; they also use non-rule language. In describing the facts of a case, a court uses specific factual terms, such as the name of a specific person or company. For example, the *Lukoski* case, Exhibit 1.2 (at pages 9–13), refers to Mr. Lukoski, his employer SIMCO, and specific provisions of the SIMCO employee handbook. In critiquing or explaining a rule, a commentary writer may refer to abstract legal concepts and non-legal ideas. For example, the periodical article excerpted in Exhibit 1.5 (at pages 19–20) refers to *leisure-time smoking* and *lifestyle discrimination.*

b. Generating Research Terms

To research effectively in legal sources, you must excel in developing both research terms and research issues. A *research term* is an expression of a concept you plan to research; a *research issue* is a combination of terms in question form. Developing both requires wide-ranging and methodical analysis, broken down here into three steps.

Step 1: Think carefully about the following factual dimensions of the client's situation:

☐ *Who* is involved? The answer may be people or entities, such as a corporation or government body. Focus not on the exact identities of those involved, but on their roles.

☐ *What* is involved? The answer may be physical items, activities, or intangibles.

☐ *When* did (or will) the important events occur? Think not only about the precise date and time, but also about the sequence of events.

☐ *Where* did (or will) the important events occur? Think not only about the precise location, but also about the significance of the location.

☐ *Why* did (or will) the participants act in this way? Analyze their motives or states of mind.

Many of the factual concepts you identify will appear in some form in the factual conditions of the legal rule or rules governing your client's situation. Of course, not every factual concept will prove to be a useful research term, but to avoid overlooking something critical, you should include, rather than exclude, too much.

Your answers to two of these questions — *where* and *when* — will contribute to the correctness of your research. Your answer to the *where* question will help you identify the jurisdiction whose law you should research. Your answer to the *when* question will help you identify law that is current as of the time of your client's situation.

Step 2: Consider your problem's legal dimensions as well. Analyzing a situation from a legal standpoint entails fitting the client's situation into one or more legal framework(s) and connecting the client's facts to legal rules. The frameworks may be broad or narrow, created by courts or legislatures or agencies or a combination of these. For example, the statute in Chapter 1 (at pages 14–16) creates a fairly narrow framework that provides a set of rules governing employer efforts to regulate off-duty smoking by employees. The *Lukoski* case in Chapter 1 (at pages 9–13) creates a much broader framework that renders an employer's failure to follow its handbook a breach of contract.

Even before you begin your research, you may have some sense of what legal topics it might entail. Many legal rules are based on common notions of what is just and fair, and many legal rules are within common parlance. Hence you should think about the following legal dimensions:

☐ What is the *legal theory* applicable to this situation? Think about the possible legal basis for penalizing the wrongdoer, benefiting the wronged party, or excusing the wrong.
☐ What *relief* does the wronged party seek through the legal system?
☐ What is the *procedural posture* of the case? That is, if the client's situation involves litigation, identify the present stage of the litigation.

Although these questions, especially the last, assume that there is litigation, your client's situation may not actually involve litigation, now or ever. Nonetheless, as lawyers research, as a general rule, they imagine what the courts would do with a case involving the client's situation; hence you should look at your problem in this light. Ideally, many of the legal concepts you identify will appear in the legal consequences of applicable rules.

As phrased here, the eight questions—five factual, three legal—probably seem fairly distinct; in practice, you may find them to be less than distinct. Fortunately, it is not important that you properly categorize a particular concept. However, you should think through all eight questions so that your research is comprehensive. Each question is important; each is a piece of the whole research pie.

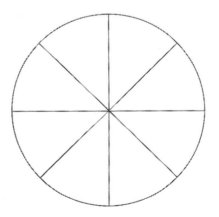

Step 3: To develop a full set of words conveying your research terms, work through the following three tasks: spinning off additional words, analyzing the roots of your words, and analyzing phrases.

First, for each important concept, think of words that are synonyms, antonyms, or broader or narrower terms. Two useful devices for doing so are a hub-and-spokes diagram and a ladder diagram. In the former, the original word appears at the center, with additional words circling it. In the latter, a broad term appears at the top rung and consecutively narrower terms appear below it. Examples appear in Exhibit 2.1 (below).

Second, consider whether a word has a root that is shared with other potentially pertinent words. For example, the root *employ* appears in various words: *employment, employee, employer, employing*, etc.; you probably would want to encompass all of these concepts. Also consider whether a word or its root has a non-pertinent meaning. For example, *employ* is used in many contexts unrelated to working for another for pay, as in employing a type of analysis to solve a problem.

| EXHIBIT 2.1 | Hub and Spokes and Ladder Diagrams |

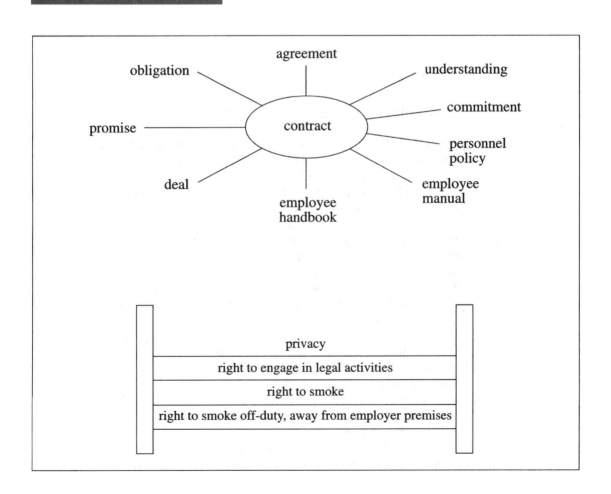

Third, consider any phrases you have generated, specifically whether the words always appear in a fixed order.

At the end of this process, you should have a well developed set of research items. See Exhibit 2.2 (below) for a set of terms for the Canoga case.

c.   Using Dictionaries and Thesauri

As you develop research terms, you may want to consult a dictionary or thesaurus for two reasons. First, you should look up your most important research terms in a legal dictionary, to be sure that your understanding is correct and comports with legal usage. Second, dictionaries and thesauri can help you identify additional research terms.

EXHIBIT 2.2	Research Terms for the Canoga Case

Factual and Legal Concepts

(1) *who:*   musician, flutist, smoker (tried to quit; failed), employee, employer, orchestra, general manager, board of directors

(2) *what:*   employment, termination, smoking, insubordination, denial of board review, employee manual, no-smoking policy, protest against smoking rules

(3) *when:*   September 7, 2007; five years after hire; smoking during non-working hours

(4) *where:*   Taos, New Mexico; smoking away from the orchestra's premises

(5) *why:*   protest against policy for privacy reasons, termination for insubordination or refusal to cease smoking

(6) *legal theory:*   breach of contract, discrimination against smokers, violation of privacy rights, protest against an illegal employer policy

(7) *relief sought:*   money (damages), return to work (reinstatement), cleared work record

(8) *procedure:*   nothing yet

Employee	*Discharge*
employ . . .	discharg(e) . . . of / from employment
employer	dismiss "
employee	separat(e) "
employment	terminat(e) "
work, worker	fir(e) . . .
labor, laborer	involuntar(y)
job	
orchestra / musician / flutist	

The parentheses indicate that various endings may follow a root word.

You will find quite an array of legal dictionaries and thesauri, each with strengths and weaknesses. The more comprehensive dictionaries, such as *Black's Law Dictionary*, cover a very wide range of terms and phrases, including some foreign-language phrases; include pronunciations and word derivations; and provide illustrative references to legal authorities. The more compact dictionaries, such as *Oran's Dictionary of the Law*, contain only the definitions of essential or basic legal terms. Thesauri primarily provide synonyms, antonyms, and associated concepts; some include basic definitions. See Exhibit 2.3 (at pages 36–38).

Dictionaries and thesauri are available in paper and online. *Black's* is available through Westlaw; *Ballentine's*, another major dictionary, is available through LexisNexis. Google has a dictionary that includes some legal definitions. In the early stage of research, a paper dictionary may be more useful than an online dictionary because you can browse more easily in a book.

Whichever dictionary you use, as you discover new terms within the definitions, be sure to look them up as well. Also, keep track of where you locate key definitions. While it is better to rely on the law for the definition of a legal term, you may rely on a dictionary for a definition of a term that is generic or undefined in your jurisdiction's law. For proper citation form for dictionaries, see *Bluebook* Rule 15.8 and *ALWD* Rule 25.

Exhibit 2.3 (at pages 36–38) presents pertinent definitions and synonyms for the Canoga case. The *contract* definitions focus on an obligation derived from a promise; the thesaurus provides numerous synonyms, such as *agreement* and *covenant*. The law formerly used *master* and *servant* to refer to employers and employees. A potentially important term is *employment at will*, which means employment that may be terminated at any time, with or without cause. Yet there also are *retaliatory* and *wrongful discharges* that violate the law or public policy.

d.   Formulating Legal Issues

As you analyze your client's situation and generate research terms, you probably will note that some concepts seem closely connected; certain factual concepts will seem to connect to certain legal concepts. From these connections, you may be able to formulate tentative research issues, that is, questions for which you are seeking legal answers.

Formulating legal issues is a critical step in legal research; it is what differentiates legal research from other types of research. Your task is not to discern whether the action in your client's situation is a good or bad idea, likely to lead to the intended result, well grounded in the best social or hard science research findings, or approved of (or not) by the general public (although the law may reflect these matters to some extent). Rather, your task is to find law that applies to that action to determine the legal significance of your client's situation. In the Canoga case, for example, you could undoubtedly find considerable material on whether an employer ban on off-duty smoking is wise or over-reaching; however, your legal research task is to ascertain the legal status and consequences of the ban. See Exhibit 2.4 (at page 38) for several issues for the Canoga case.

| EXHIBIT 2.3 | Excerpts from Dictionaries and Thesauri |

NOTE: The citations below comport with Rule 15 of *The Bluebook*. Rule 25 of *ALWD Citation Manual* also includes the publisher.

Google's *de · fine*, quoting from *The Collaborative International Dictionary of English v.0.44 [gcide]*.

Contract \Con″tract\ (k[o^]n″tr[a^]kt), *noun* [L. contractus, fr. contrahere: cf. F. contrat, formerly also **contract**.]

1.   (Law) The agreement of two or more persons, upon a sufficient consideration or cause, to do, or to abstain from doing, some act; an agreement in which a party undertakes to do, or not to do, a particular thing; a formal bargain; a compact; an interchange of legal rights. —Wharton.

2.   A formal writing which contains the agreement of parties, with the terms and conditions, and which serves as a proof of the obligation.

. . .

Syn. Covenant; agreement; compact, stipulation; bargain; arrangement; obligation. See {Covenant}.

Daniel Oran, *Oran's Dictionary of the Law* 100 (3d ed. 2000).

Contract. An agreement that affects or creates legal relationships between two or more persons. To be a *contract*, an agreement must involve: at least one promise, **consideration** (something of value promised or given), persons legally capable of making binding agreements, and a reasonable certainty about the meaning of the terms. A contract is called **bilateral** if both sides make promises (such as the promise to deliver a book on one side and a promise to pay for it on the other) or **unilateral** if the promises are on one side only. According to the **Uniform Commercial Code**, a contract is the "total legal obligation which results from the parties' agreement," and according to the Restatement of the Law of Contracts, it is "a promise or set of promises for the breach of which the law in some way recognizes a duty." For the many different types of contracts, such as **output**, **requirements**, etc., see those words.

William C. Burton, *Legal Thesaurus* 122 (4th ed. 2007).

CONTRACT, *noun*, accord, accordance, agreement, arrangement, articles of agreement, assurance, avouchment, avowal, bargain, binding agreement, bond, charter, collective agreement, commitment, compact, compromise, concordat, *condicio*, *conductio*, confirmation, *conventio*, covenant, deal, embodied terms, engagement, *entente*, guarantee, instrument

EXHIBIT 2.3   *(continued)*

evidencing an agreement, ironclad agreement, legal document, mutual agreement, mutual pledge, mutual promise, mutual undertaking, negotiated agreement, obligation, pact, paction, *pactum*, pledge, pledged word, private understanding, promise, ratified agreement, set terms, settlement, stated terms, stipulation, terms for agreement, understanding, undertaking, warranty, written terms

Jonathan S. Lynton, *Ballentine's Legal Dictionary and Thesaurus* 211 (1995).

employer [em · *ploy* · er] *n*. A person who hires another to work for her for pay in a relationship that allows her to control the work and direct the manner in which it is done. The earlier legal term for employer was **master**.

▶ master, contractor, director, boss, chief. *Ant*. employee, servant, agent.

Black's Law Dictionary 566 (8th ed. 2004).

employment. 1. The relationship between master and servant. See MASTER AND SERVANT. **2.** The act of employing. **3.** The state of being employed. **4.** Work for which one has been hired and is being paid by an employer.

. . .

employment at will. Employment that is usu. undertaken without a contract and that may be terminated at any time, by either the employer or the employee, without cause. — Also termed *at-will employment; hiring at will*. [Cases: Master and Servant key 20. C.J.S. *Apprentices* § 10; *Employer-Employee Relationship* §§ 40, 42-43.]

. . .

"The doctrine of employment at will prescribed that an employee without a contract for a fixed term could be hired or fired for any reason or no reason at all. . . . [The] rule provided that employees categorized as 'at will' had no legal interest in continuing job security. Whereas early American masters had some responsibility to the public as well as to their servants when they turned dependent servants out on the world, under [this] formulation, masters could simply fire employees who had no contracts." Mark A. Rothstein et al., *Employment Law* § 1.4, at 9-10 (1994).

Findlaw's Legal Dictionary quoting from *Merriam-Webster's Dictionary of Law* (1996).
discharge ['dis-'chärj]

1 a: the act of relieving of something that burdens or oppresses: "release"
  b: something that discharges or releases esp: a certification of or a document providing release or payment
2: the state of being discharged or released . . .
3: release from confinement . . .

Exhibit 2.3   *(continued)*

4: the act of removing an obligation or liability (as by payment of a debt or performance of a duty)

5 a: a dismissal from employment or office

  b: a release from service or duty

constructive discharge

: discharge of an employee effected by making the employee's working conditions so intolerable that he or she feels reasonably compelled to resign

retaliatory discharge

: a wrongful discharge that is done in retaliation for an employee's conduct (as reporting an employer's criminal activity) and that clearly violates public policy

wrongful discharge

: discharge of an employee for illegal reasons or for reasons that are contrary to public policy (as in retaliation for the employee's refusal to engage in unlawful activity)

Note: Findlaw had no entry for *fire* and a short one for *terminate*—"to discontinue the employment of."

Exhibit 2.4   Research Issues for the Canoga Case

☐ Was there a *breach of contract* when the board denied review to a terminated employee although board review was promised in the employee handbook?

☐ Was there a *violation of privacy rights* when an orchestra's policy prohibited smoking off-duty, a flutist resisted, and she was discharged as a result?

☐ Was there unlawful *discrimination against a smoker* when a flutist-smoker who could not quit smoking was fired by an orchestra for refusing to agree not to smoke off-duty and off-premises?

The legal theories are italicized above.

C. CONTENT AND CONTEXT

After you have developed your research terms and issues, and before you open a book or turn on your computer (dictionaries and thesauri aside), you should think carefully about which authorities in which media are most likely to be useful, that is, the content and publication context of the authorities you hope to locate.

3. List and Rank Potential Authorities

By learning and reacting to your client's situation, you should know two important facts: the location of the events and their timing.

From the location of the events, you can deduce potential jurisdictions whose law you should research. Until you learn otherwise, you should assume that both federal and state law might be involved. You also should assume that statutes, case law, and agency law are involved; if the problem involves litigation, rules of procedure also will be involved.

As to case law, as explained more thoroughly in Chapter 9, most court systems involve trial courts, each with a specific geographic territory; one or more intermediate appeals courts, each with a specific geographic territory; and a high court, typically called the "supreme court." Thus, you should discern which judicial districts encompass the location of your client's situation.

Timing is as important as location. In most situations, you will research the state of the law as of today. However, if your client's situation involves a statute, and the statute has changed over time, you will focus on the statutory language in effect as of the date of the events, as explained more thoroughly in Chapter 11.

Although your research and analysis should focus on the law of your jurisdiction, which is the bull's-eye in your research target, you very likely will research in other authorities as well. Law, especially cases, from outside your jurisdiction can be used as persuasive authority; this occupies the middle ring in your research target.

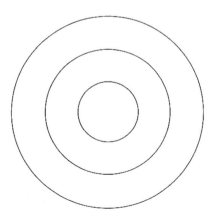

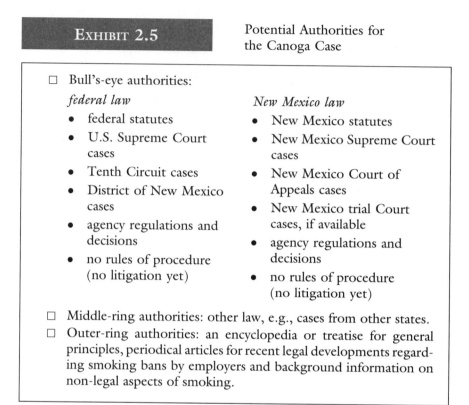

EXHIBIT 2.5   Potential Authorities for
                              the Canoga Case

☐ Bull's-eye authorities:

federal law

- federal statutes
- U.S. Supreme Court cases
- Tenth Circuit cases
- District of New Mexico cases
- agency regulations and decisions
- no rules of procedure (no litigation yet)

New Mexico law

- New Mexico statutes
- New Mexico Supreme Court cases
- New Mexico Court of Appeals cases
- New Mexico trial Court cases, if available
- agency regulations and decisions
- no rules of procedure (no litigation yet)

☐ Middle-ring authorities: other law, e.g., cases from other states.
☐ Outer-ring authorities: an encyclopedia or treatise for general principles, periodical articles for recent legal developments regarding smoking bans by employers and background information on non-legal aspects of smoking.

Unless you know a fair amount about the subject already, you most likely will start your research in commentary, which occupies the outer ring in your research target. Through commentary, you should learn whether federal or state law governs, whether a statute or agency is involved, etc. You also should acquire an overview of the subject and some references to pertinent law. As you will see in Unit II, there are many types of commentary, each with distinctive strengths and weaknesses, so you should think about which type is most likely to be helpful. See Exhibit 2.5 (above) for our list of potential authorities for the Canoga case.

4.   Assess Available Sources

An authority may well be available in multiple sources, and you may have print as well as online sources to choose from. As you make your choice, consider the following factors:

Scope of coverage: Does the source have as full a range of the authority as you need? For example, as to New Mexico case law, you would hope to find not only New Mexico Supreme Court cases but also important cases from the court of appeals.

Time period — retrospective and recent: Does the source go back far enough to encompass what you need? And does it have very recent material?

For example, a source containing cases from 1995 forward very likely is not sufficiently retrospective, and a case law source published in 2000 and not updated thereafter is not by itself recent enough.

Credibility: Is the source sufficiently credible that you could cite it to a court, should the situation develop into litigation? As you will learn in later chapters, for every type of authority, there are well regarded sources that you can use with confidence, because they have a strong track record and are published by well regarded companies or organizations. For example, as you will see in Chapter 9, an official court website, West paper case reporters, LexisNexis, and Westlaw are credible sources of state cases.

Ease and efficacy of access: Given limited time and energy, can you reasonably quickly identify both the source and pertinent passages within the source, without needing to work through extraneous passages? For example, a website that posts cases as they are published but does not provide an index or permit searching for key words is not very accessible. By contrast, the West reporter system — a set of books containing cases accompanied by a sophisticated digest (a well organized compilation of short descriptions of many cases) — is quite accessible.

Ease and efficacy of reading and retention: Given limited time and energy, can you reasonably quickly read what you need to read, scan what you need to scan, and obtain a copy of the important passages? In broad terms, paper and online sources have different strengths and weaknesses here. Many people find paper sources easier to look at for long periods of time, it is easier to look at an array of paper sources, and it is easier to scan nearby passages in the same paper source. However, it is easier to move from one authority to another in online sources that employ links, and many online sources cumulate older and more recent information into one document, whereas you may need to look at several volumes of a paper source. You will need to photocopy important passages in a paper source, whereas generally you can download, e-mail, and print pertinent passages from an online source.

Ease of updating: After you complete your research, you will need to stay current on developments that may alter the law. Online sources can be updated easily, and some online resources send you updating alerts by e-mail. Paper sources typically include periodic pamphlets containing new material, which take more time to publish and distribute.

Cost: Given your client's financial resources, how can you accomplish what you need to accomplish at a reasonably low price? Obviously, your bill will depend in large part on how much time you spend researching, which is a function of the source's ease and efficacy of access, reading, and retention. You also should be aware of the cost of the source itself. Once a book is bought, it does not cost money to use. Beyond the cost of an Internet service provider, the costs of online sources vary considerably:

- ☐ An online source can be free, most typically if it is a government website.
- ☐ An online source may be bought by subscription, e.g., a law firm pays a monthly or annual fee for access to HeinOnline, a major source of periodicals, among other things.

□   An online source may be purchased on a per-use basis, e.g., a lawyer runs a search in a specialized LexisNexis or Westlaw database not covered by the firm's monthly subscription.

Understanding cost structures of the options you have as well as the value of your time is key to performing cost-effective research.

If you have two or more available sources for the same authority, you may find it helpful to synopsize your assessment in a matrix. If there is no perfect source for commentary, this may not be a significant concern. However, if there is no perfect source for the law, you will need to use two or more sources, each with different strengths. For example, often you will research case law in paper reporters and then use an online service to bring your research up to date.

	Source A	Source B	Source C
coverage			
time			
credibility			
access			
reading & retention			
updating			
cost			

D.   CONSULTATION

Once you have thoroughly analyzed both your client's situation and legal authorities and sources to use in your research, you are ready to work with the sources. This entails locating pertinent materials within a source, carefully reading that material, and following up on the information you have acquired.

Sometimes you will find law that clearly and precisely addresses your client's situation and provides an indisputable answer. When this happens, lawyers say that the authority is "on all fours."[1] Much more often, you will find law that quite clearly but less precisely addresses your client's situation and thus provides guidance, but not an indisputable answer. When this happens, lawyers say that the authority is "on point." Most often, legal research is similar to consultation with an expert: The expert provides useful information, but you still must do a lot of thinking on your own. On occasion, you will find little law on point, and you will have to extrapolate from what you do

---

1. We are not sure of the origins of this phrase. The allusion may be to the four legs of a horse or other animal or to the four sides of a brick.

find. Should the situation lead to litigation, lawyers say it is a "case of first impression." Then creativity is a very important aspect of legal research.

5.   Use Your Terms and Issues to Locate Pertinent Passages

Introduction. Every source you use, whether a single issue of a legal periodical or a very large database, has means of access, that is, ways to use your terms and issues to locate pertinent passages within the source. The first time you work with a source, you should familiarize yourself with its means of access; there are likely to be several. The following discussion describes the most common means of access employed in legal research; you will find details and variations, source by source, throughout Units II through VI.

Success in the task of locating pertinent documents is measured by two criteria:

- □ *recall* — identification of all pertinent passages within a source, and
- □ *precision* — avoidance of nonpertinent passages.

Hence the image for this task is a double-square diagram: the large square represents all of the passages in the source that might be identified, and the small square surrounds the passages actually identified. P stands for pertinent passages, X for nonpertinent passages. The research depicted captures nearly all of the Ps; that is, it satisfies the recall criterion fairly well. However, the research also captures quite a few Xs, so it is not as successful from a precision standpoint.

The means of access you may use for a given source depend in part on its publication pattern. Consider first an encyclopedia: it is published as a set and there is an overarching organizational scheme, so its internal findings tools — the index and table of contents — provide ready access to the pertinent passages. Consider next a journal: it is published periodically, e.g., monthly or quarterly; the contents of the issues are not related to each other; thus you need an external finding tool to locate a pertinent article.

In addition, as you consider the means of access available to you, keep in mind how much you already know about the law governing your client's situation. Some means of access work well when you know fairly little; others should be used only when you already know a fair amount about the topic you are researching. Some means are primarily associated with paper sources, others with online sources.

Paper options. Consider the following: You are beginning to research the Canoga situation and have chosen to start in a legal encyclopedia, a set of books. To find pertinent material, two good options to start with are an index and a list of topics.

Many legal sources have an **index**, an alphabetical list of covered subjects with references to where each subject is discussed. Highly organized sources, such as encyclopedias, have their own indexes.[2] Legal indexes typically are long and complex, with multiple minor subjects and cross-references to other subjects. See Exhibit 2.6 (at page 45). Your task is to look for major and minor subjects that correspond to or are similar to your research terms; you can then move to the specified part of the source.

Many sources have an overall organizational scheme reflected in the **list of topics** as they appear in the source. See Exhibit 2.7 (at page 46). The organizing principle may be alphabetical or topical. You should skim the list of topics, looking for entries that correspond to or are similar to your research terms.

Once you have located a pertinent topic, explore the **table(s) of contents** listing sections within a topic; often you will find both general and detailed tables of content. See Exhibit 2.8 (at pages 47–48).

These means of access have advantages and disadvantages. Once you discern the authors' terms, you can easily locate and understand pertinent passages. On the other hand, your research will succeed only if you can tap into the authors' vocabulary; their vocabulary can be idiosyncratic or become stale if it does not evolve as concepts and usage evolve. For example, the terms *master* and *servant* have long been used for *employer* and *employee*; if a source continues to use this terminology and you do not think of it, you may not locate pertinent passages.

More important, these tools, especially tables of contents, provide legal frameworks into which you can place your client's situation. Often — very often when you are researching a topic that is new to you — you may use this framework to identify the important aspects of your client's situation and begin organizing your analysis accordingly. By fitting your legal issue into such a framework, you will be well oriented as you begin to read the materials you have identified.

If you know of a pertinent case or statute, you may take advantage of a paper source's **tables of authorities**. See Exhibit 2.9 (at page 49). Once

---

2. Some finding tools operate as an index for a set of periodically published sources, such as an index for legal periodicals.

EXHIBIT 2.6   Index,
                     from American Jurisprudence 2d (paper source)

AMERICAN JURISPRUDENCE 2d

WRONGFUL DISCHARGE—Cont'd
Compensation—Cont'd
  good faith and fair dealing, violations of
    covenants of, **WrongDisc** § 73-75
  legal rights, discharge for exercising,
    WrongDisc § 97-99
  lost earnings, *below*
  periodic compensation terms,
    WrongDisc § 31
  raises, **WrongDisc** § 34
Competition
  antitrust violations, discharge for refusal
    to commit, **WrongDisc** § 110, 111
  marriage to employee of competitor,
    WrongDisc § 141
Compromise and settlement, **WrongDisc**
  § 227, 228
Conflict of laws, **WrongDisc** § 209, 210
Consent. Mutual assent, *below*
Consideration
  generally, **WrongDisc** § 10, 11
  additional consideration, **WrongDisc**
    § 10
  evidence of consideration, **WrongDisc**
    § 11
  modification of implied contracts, --
    WrongDisc § 19
Conspiracy, **WrongDisc** § 88
Constitutional law
  generally, **WrongDisc** § 78-81
  freedom of speech, **WrongDisc** § 79, 80
Consumer protection, **WrongDisc** § 129, 130
Continuing employee benefits, **WrongDisc**
  § 36
Contract actions
  availability of contract remedies,
    WrongDisc § 226
  good faith and fair dealing, covenants of,
    WrongDisc § 67
  public policy exception to at-will
    employment, **WrongDisc** § 59
  punitive damages, **WrongDisc** § 245
Contracts
  actions and remedies. Contract actions,
    above
  employment contracts, *below*
  interference with contractual relations,
    below
Covenants. Good faith and fair dealing, covenants of, *below*
Criminal proceedings, participation in
  generally, **WrongDisc** § 103-105
  jury duty, **WrongDisc** § 104
  subpoenas, **WrongDisc** § 105
  witnesses, **WrongDisc** § 105
Customs and usages, **WrongDisc** § 40
Damages
  generally, **WrongDisc** § 233-247
  back pay, **WrongDisc** § 234
  emotional distress, **WrongDisc** § 239
  employee benefits, **WrongDisc** § 236
  expenses resulting from discharge,
    WrongDisc § 238

WRONGFUL DISCHARGE—Cont'd
Damages—Cont'd
  future earnings, **WrongDisc** § 235
  lost earnings, *below*
  mitigation of damages, **WrongDisc**
    § 243
  new employment, expenses of seeking,
    WrongDisc § 238
  pension rights, **WrongDisc** § 236
  punitive damages, *below*
  reduction of damages for lost earnings,
    WrongDisc § 241
  reputation, injury to, **WrongDisc** § 237
  sale of home, **WrongDisc** § 238
Defenses
  generally, **WrongDisc** § 177-208
  bad faith, defense of, **WrongDisc** § 184
  business, **WrongDisc** § 181
  collateral estoppel, *above*
  disloyalty, defense of, **WrongDisc** § 184
  exhaustion of remedies, **WrongDisc**
    § 178
  factual defenses, **WrongDisc** § 179-185
  financial condition, **WrongDisc** § 181
  good cause, **WrongDisc** § 179, 180
  government employees, **WrongDisc**
    § 178
  incompetence, defense of, **WrongDisc**
    § 182
  limitation of actions, defense of,
    WrongDisc § 186, 187
  misconduct of employee, **WrongDisc**
    § 183
  neglect of work, defense of, **WrongDisc**
    § 182
  perform, inability to, **WrongDisc** § 182
  preemption by federal law, *below*
  preemption by state statutory remedies,
    below
  procedural defenses, **WrongDisc** § 186-
    189
  public officers and employees,
    WrongDisc § 178
  res judicata, *below*
  statute of frauds, defense of, **WrongDisc**
    § 188
  voluntary resignation, defense of,
    WrongDisc § 185
  Workers' Compensation Act, defense of
    exclusivity of, **WrongDisc** § 189
Directed verdicts, motions for, **WrongDisc**
  § 222
Disability insurance, conflict of laws,
  ConflictLw § 173
Discipline and discharge procedures
  generally, **WrongDisc** § 41-47
  appeal and review, **WrongDisc** § 44
  cause, discharge only for, **WrongDisc**
    § 46, 47
  grievances, **WrongDisc** § 44
  grounds for discipline and discharge,
    WrongDisc § 45
  implied contracts, **WrongDisc** § 42

WRONGFUL DISCHARGE—Cont'd
Discipline and discharge procedures—Cont'd
  mutual assent, **WrongDisc** § 47
  progressive discipline, **WrongDisc** § 43
  reliance, **WrongDisc** § 47
Disclaimers by employers
  generally, **WrongDisc** § 25-27
  communication of disclaimer to
    employee, **WrongDisc** § 27
  conspicuousness of disclaimer,
    WrongDisc § 26
  express language, **WrongDisc** § 25
Discovery, punitive damages, **WrongDisc**
  § 247
Discrimination
  emotional distress, discharge as
    intentional infliction of, **WrongDisc**
    § 154-156
  jurisdiction, **WrongDisc** § 214
  opposition to discriminatory practices,
    discharge for, **WrongDisc** § 134
  preemption by federal law, **WrongDisc**
    § 200
Disloyalty, defense of, **WrongDisc** § 184
Dismissal, motions for, **WrongDisc** § 221
Diversity jurisdiction
  generally, **WrongDisc** § 210
  federal courts, **WrongDisc** § 212
Drug tests
  privacy, invasion of, **WrongDisc** § 169
  refusal of drug tests, discharge for,
    WrongDisc § 101
Drug use, discharge for, **WrongDisc** § 139
Educational pursuits, discharge for,
  WrongDisc § 142
Emotional distress, intentional infliction of
  generally, **WrongDisc** § 146-160
  accusations of theft, **WrongDisc** § 157
  age discrimination, **WrongDisc** § 156
  damages, **WrongDisc** § 239
  discrimination, **WrongDisc** § 154-156
  elements of action, **WrongDisc** § 146
  fiduciary relationship, **WrongDisc** § 149
  outrageousness of conduct, **WrongDisc**
    § 148-151
  quasi fiduciary relationship, **WrongDisc**
    § 149
  reasonableness, **WrongDisc** § 148-151
  religious harassment or discrimination,
    WrongDisc § 154
  retaliation, **WrongDisc** § 151
  severity of distress, **WrongDisc** § 152,
    153
  sexual harassment or discrimination,
    WrongDisc § 155
  susceptibility of plaintiff, **WrongDisc**
    § 150
  theft, accusations of, **WrongDisc** § 157
Emotional distress, negligent infliction of
  generally, **WrongDisc** § 158, 160
  damages, **WrongDisc** § 239
  workers' compensation, **WrongDisc**
    § 160

For assistance using this Index, call 1-800-328-4880

| EXHIBIT 2.7 | Topic List — Table of Abbreviations, from American Jurisprudence 2d (paper source) |

TABLE OF ABBREVIATIONS

Torts	Torts
Trademark	Trademarks and Trade names
Treaties	Treaties
Trespass	Trespass
Trial	Trial
Trusts	Trusts
Unemploy	Unemployment Compensation
UnitedSts	United States
Vagrancy	Vagrancy
Vendor	Vendor and Purchaser
Venue	Venue
Veterans	Veterans and Veterans Laws
Veterinar	Veterinarians
War	War
Warehouse	Warehouses
Waste	Waste
WaterCo	Waterworks and Water Companies
Waters	Waters
Weapons	Weapons and Firearms
Weights	Weights and Measures
Welfare	Welfare Laws
Wharves	Wharves
Wills	Wills
Witn	Witnesses
Workers	Workers' Compensation
WrongDisc	Wrongful Discharge
Zoning	Zoning and Planning

EXHIBIT 2.8   Tables of Contents,
                     from American Jurisprudence 2d (paper source)

EXHIBIT 2.8   *(continued)*

82 AM JUR 2d

b. Representations as to Particular Matters

(1) In General

(2) Regarding Discharge and Discipline

(3) Detrimental Reliance by Employee

C. PUBLIC POLICY EXCEPTION TO AT-WILL RULE; RETALIATORY DISCHARGE, IN GENERAL

EXHIBIT 2.9　Table of Authorities,
from American Jurisprudence 2d (paper source)

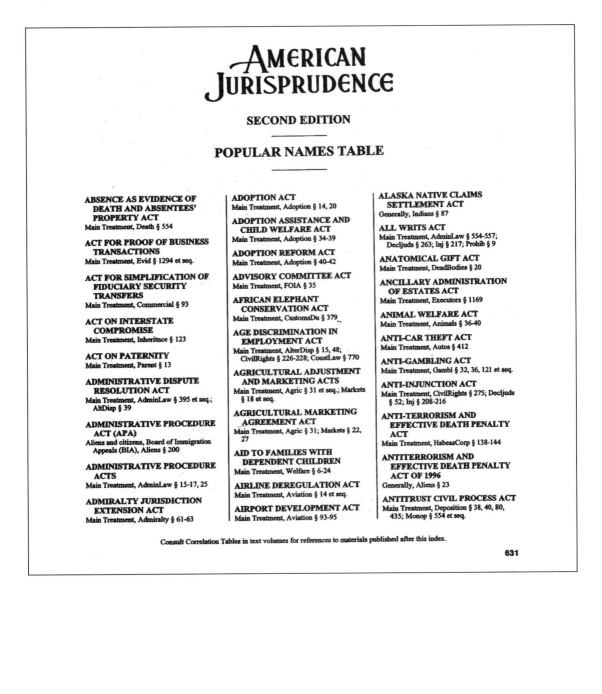

AMERICAN JURISPRUDENCE

SECOND EDITION

POPULAR NAMES TABLE

ABSENCE AS EVIDENCE OF DEATH AND ABSENTEES' PROPERTY ACT
Main Treatment, Death § 554

ACT FOR PROOF OF BUSINESS TRANSACTIONS
Main Treatment, Evid § 1294 et seq.

ACT FOR SIMPLIFICATION OF FIDUCIARY SECURITY TRANSFERS
Main Treatment, Commercial § 93

ACT ON INTERSTATE COMPROMISE
Main Treatment, Inheritnce § 123

ACT ON PATERNITY
Main Treatment, Parent § 13

ADMINISTRATIVE DISPUTE RESOLUTION ACT
Main Treatment, AdminLaw § 395 et seq.; AltDisp § 39

ADMINISTRATIVE PROCEDURE ACT (APA)
Aliens and citizens, Board of Immigration Appeals (BIA), Aliens § 200

ADMINISTRATIVE PROCEDURE ACTS
Main Treatment, AdminLaw § 15-17, 25

ADMIRALTY JURISDICTION EXTENSION ACT
Main Treatment, Admiralty § 61-63

ADOPTION ACT
Main Treatment, Adoption § 14, 20

ADOPTION ASSISTANCE AND CHILD WELFARE ACT
Main Treatment, Adoption § 34-39

ADOPTION REFORM ACT
Main Treatment, Adoption § 40-42

ADVISORY COMMITTEE ACT
Main Treatment, FOIA § 35

AFRICAN ELEPHANT CONSERVATION ACT
Main Treatment, CustomsDu § 379

AGE DISCRIMINATION IN EMPLOYMENT ACT
Main Treatment, AlterDisp § 15, 48; CivilRights § 226-228; ConstLaw § 770

AGRICULTURAL ADJUSTMENT AND MARKETING ACTS
Main Treatment, Agric § 31 et seq.; Markets § 18 et seq.

AGRICULTURAL MARKETING AGREEMENT ACT
Main Treatment, Agric § 31; Markets § 22, 27

AID TO FAMILIES WITH DEPENDENT CHILDREN
Main Treatment, Welfare § 6-24

AIRLINE DEREGULATION ACT
Main Treatment, Aviation § 14 et seq.

AIRPORT DEVELOPMENT ACT
Main Treatment, Aviation § 93-95

ALASKA NATIVE CLAIMS SETTLEMENT ACT
Generally, Indians § 87

ALL WRITS ACT
Main Treatment, AdminLaw § 554-557; Decljuds § 263; Inj § 217; Prohib § 9

ANATOMICAL GIFT ACT
Main Treatment, DeadBodies § 20

ANCILLARY ADMINISTRATION OF ESTATES ACT
Main Treatment, Executors § 1169

ANIMAL WELFARE ACT
Main Treatment, Animals § 36-40

ANTI-CAR THEFT ACT
Main Treatment, Autos § 412

ANTI-GAMBLING ACT
Main Treatment, Gambl § 32, 36, 121 et seq.

ANTI-INJUNCTION ACT
Main Treatment, CivilRights § 275; Decljuds § 52; Inj § 208-216

ANTI-TERRORISM AND EFFECTIVE DEATH PENALTY ACT
Main Treatment, HabeasCorp § 138-144

ANTITERRORISM AND EFFECTIVE DEATH PENALTY ACT OF 1996
Generally, Aliens § 23

ANTITRUST CIVIL PROCESS ACT
Main Treatment, Deposition § 38, 40, 80, 435; Monop § 554 et seq.

Consult Correlation Tables in text volumes for references to materials published after this index.

631

you find the authority in the table, you will learn where the source discusses that authority.

The three options discussed previously can be used in some online sources as well. For example, you can scan the table of contents of an online encyclopedia. By contrast, the options discussed in the following paragraphs are not available in paper sources because the options depend on the technology afforded by computers.

Online options. Consider the following: You are researching the Canoga situation, looking for an article on employee smoking in an online database of legal periodicals fairly early in your research process. One advantage of researching online is that you can formulate your own search for pertinent passages — a key-word search. This involves keying in sentences, words, or characters; the computer scans the selected database and retrieves documents meeting the requirements of your search.

This process has advantages and disadvantages. On one hand, you can customize a search, using words tailored to your research problem; if those words are distinctive enough, you should obtain excellent results. Because computers process searches quickly, computer research can be fast. On the other hand, if the words in your search are very common, the computer may retrieve too many documents to review. Even in a more manageable set of retrieved documents, you may well find nonpertinent documents. Conversely, you may fail to retrieve articles that are pertinent, because they do not use the words you have identified.

Equally important, key-word searching does little to provide a legal framework into which to place your client's situation. Because major legal principles are so common, they are problematic search terms; your search will likely focus on factual features of your client's situation. The documents the computer retrieves will be linguistically similar but may not be logically related to your client's legal situation.

To maximize the advantages and minimize the disadvantages of key-word searching, you will need to skillfully employ various search-drafting options. The options are fairly standard across most online services, although the expression varies from service to service. For simplicity, the examples in this section reflect the protocols of LexisNexis and Westlaw.

When your knowledge of the law is fairly limited or general, you may want to start with a **natural-language search**, which entails typing in a question that resembles ordinary English. The service may provide a thesaurus to help you identify alternatives for the major words in your question. In response to a natural-language search, a computer typically retrieves a prespecified number of documents, identified through application of a semantic-statistical algorithm that, among other steps, ranks your words for distinctiveness and assesses the prevalence and location of your search words in the many documents in the database you selected. For example, a natural-language search for the smoking issue in the Canoga situation is:

```
Can an employer prohibit an employee from smoking
during non-working hours?
```

| EXHIBIT 2.10 | Boolean Search Tasks and Protocols |

Task	*LexisNexis protocol*	*Westlaw protocol*
single term	! and * root expanders	! and * root expanders
several-word phrase	space between words	" " around words
multiple terms for the same concept	OR	space (or OR)
exclusion of non-pertinent usage	AND NOT NOT W/# NOT W/s NOT W/p	%
multiple-concept search	W/# or /# or PRE/# W/s or /s W/p or /p AND or &	/# and +/# /s and +/s /p and +p &

Some services permit you to refine a natural-language search by adding in your own alternative terms, designating a phrase (the program may do this for your common phrases), requiring a specific word, or excluding a specific word. To the extent you use these options, your natural-language search will come to resemble a Boolean search.

Once you have a fairly sound idea of the words used to discuss the topic you are researching, you may use a **Boolean search**,[3] also described as a terms-and-connectors search. Boolean searches can be simple or rather intricate. Exhibit 2.10 (above) lists the five major steps in constructing a Boolean search along with LexisNexis and Westlaw protocols for each step.

(1) One simple option is to enter one single-word term such as *smoking*; you thereby ask the computer to retrieve any document containing that term. The word you select may itself be or contain a root word. For example, *smoking* contains the root *smok*, used not only in *smoking*, but also in *smoke*, *smoker* (and its plural and possessives), *smokes*, etc. Some services automatically retrieve standard variations of search words, such as plurals and possessives. To search for variations that the service does not automatically retrieve, you may use root expanders. For example, on both LexisNexis and Westlaw:

smok!	→	will retrieve any word starting with *smok*.
smok***	→	will retrieve any word starting with *smok* and continuing for up to three letters.
mari*uana	→	will retrieve *marijuana* and *marihuana*.

(2) Some concepts are stated not with single words, but with several-word phrases. You should be very careful in searching for phrases. Some

---

3. The name refers to a nineteenth-century mathematician.

phrases can be inverted or phrased in slightly different terms. Furthermore, some phrases might be written with or without hyphens. For example, on Westlaw:

`"non-working hours"`	→	will retrieve *non-working hours* or *non working hours* or *nonworking hours*.

LexisNexis requires two forms—non-working and nonworking—and does not require the quotation marks.

(3) Often, you will want to search for multiple terms for the same concept by use of synonyms, antonyms, or broader or narrower terms. You will enter the terms, joined by the symbol for the connector *or*. For example:

`cigarette or tobacco`	→	will retrieve documents containing *cigarette* or *tobacco* or both.

See Exhibit 2.11 (below), in which the shaded area represents the retrieved documents.

(4) On occasion, you may want to exclude documents in which a non-pertinent usage appears by asking the computer to reject documents with some other word associated with the nonpertinent usage. You should use

EXHIBIT 2.11	Diagrams of Boolean Connectors

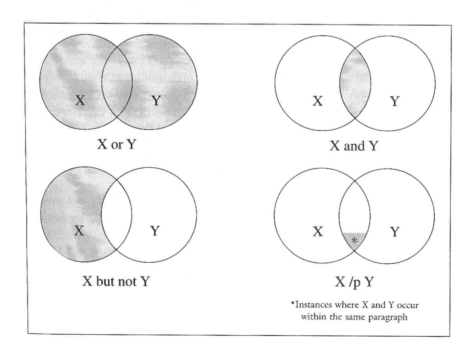

such a search only when you are quite certain that documents with the excluded term really are not pertinent. For example:

smok! and not marijuana	→	will retrieve documents that both do contain variants of *smoke* and do not contain *marijuana*.

Again, see Exhibit 2.11.

(5) If several concepts are likely to appear together, you should consider a multiple-concept search. Such a search is more focused than a single-concept search and hence more efficient. However, combining too many concepts may make your search too narrow and inadvertently exclude pertinent documents. Multiple-concept searches entail the use of a connector. The broadest connector signifies *and*, which requires that the joined terms appear in the same document. Tighter connectors link concepts in the same sentence, paragraph, or fixed number of words. In the rare instances in which you are sure that one concept will precede another, you can use a sequencing connector. As examples, consider the following searches:[4]

smok! & workplace	→	Both must appear anywhere in the document.
smok! /p workplace	→	Both must appear in the same paragraph.
smok! /s workplace	→	Both must appear in the same sentence.
smok! /20 workplace	→	Both must appear within twenty words of each other.
smok! +20 workplace smok! pre/20 workplace	→	Both must appear within twenty words of each other, *smok!* first.

Again, see Exhibit 2.11. Be sure you understand exactly how each connector works; for example, you should know whether the service counts insignificant words, such as articles or prepositions, when processing a numerical search.

You also should know the service's standard order of operations — the order in which the computer will process multiple connectors. LexisNexis[5] and Westlaw prioritize the commonly used connectors similarly:

☐ starting with phrases and *or*;
☐ moving through numerical (lower numbers first), sentence, paragraph, and *and* connectors;
☐ concluding with the *not* connector.

---

4. LexisNexis offers the following variations on the not connector: *not w/#*, *not w/sent*, and *not w/para*.

5. LexisNexis processes *not w/#* along with *w/#*, *not w/s* along with *w/s*, and *not w/p* along with *w/p*.

Some services permit you to create your own order of operations, typically by placing search words and a connector within parentheses. For example:

```
discharg!        →    The computer will search first for variants
(terminat!            of terminat within three words of variants
/3 employ!)           of employ, then search for documents
                      containing variants of discharg.
```

Without the parentheses, the computer would search for variants of *discharg* or *terminat* within three words of a variant of *employ*.

Here is an example of a search involving multiple concepts and connectors that we ran, while researching the Canoga case, in a LexisNexis database of periodical articles:

```
employ! /s       →    The computer will look for documents
smok! /s              containing some form of employ in the
privacy               same sentence as some form of smok in the
                      same sentence as privacy.
```

Exhibit 2.12 (at pages 56–57) is an excerpt from the results, with the search terms in context.

Quite often you will need to edit your initial search. If your search does not yield the number of pertinent documents you expect, first review the protocols for the service you are using and correct any drafting errors. Then consider the following remedies for common defects:

☐ Too many documents retrieved: Use tighter connectors, e.g., switch from & to /p. Add a concept. Use less common words for a concept. Limit your search to a component of a document (which, in effect, shrinks the database to a more manageable size). Restrict your search by dates.

☐ Too few documents retrieved: Use looser connectors, e.g., switch from /p to &. Delete a concept. Use alternative words for a concept; check the thesaurus for ideas.

☐ Too many inapt documents retrieved: Consider excluding a term associated with the inapt documents. Limit your search to a component of the documents that summarizes their content.

Note that a natural-language search generally will not retrieve the same documents as a Boolean search. In response to a natural-language search, the computer will retrieve the specified number of cases, whether they fit the search very well or only minimally. In response to a Boolean search, the computer will retrieve all cases meeting the requirements, however few or many that will be. Hence, it often is wise to run both kinds of searches.

Once you have a list of documents in response to your search, you will want to **sort the documents** as efficiently as possible. A mere citation list generally is not particularly revealing. Rather, view the passages in which the search terms are located. Another option is to view the document page by page with the search terms highlighted; often the first few paragraphs of a document summarize its content.

Sometimes, you will have sufficient knowledge to run a very **targeted search**. By adding a date restriction, you may limit the search to documents from a specified time period. In addition, you may confine your search to a particular component of a document; this is useful when your search terms very likely would appear in a specific place. For example, if, when we were researching the Canoga situation, a colleague had referred us to a periodical article written during the past few years on "leisure-time smoking," we would run a search in the title field with a date restrictor. In an even more focused search, if you already know the citation of a pertinent authority, you may **retrieve a known document**. For example, if you wanted a copy of the article starting at page 117 of volume 7 of the *Albany Law Review*, you would enter 70 Alb 1 rev 117 in Westlaw's Find or LexisNexis' LEXSEE program.

Hybrid means of access. As online tools have become more sophisticated, they have come to offer searches that combine options. For example, LexisNexis' Search by Topic or Headnote entails making a series of selections from broad to narrow subjects—which resembles scanning successively narrower tables of contents—and then adding search terms (i.e., key-word searching). The computer runs the key-word search in the documents categorized as fitting within the narrow topic selected in the first phase of the search.

All too often, law students become hooked on expensive online services, such as LexisNexis and Westlaw, during law school when there is no direct out-of-pocket cost to the student. It is quite wonderful to build expertise on these services during law school without having to pay for them, but you should be very mindful of the costs for the service once you are in practice. Excessive and expensive over-reliance on LexisNexis and Westlaw by law clerks and new lawyers is a very common complaint; the ability to research cost-effectively in paper and free or less costly online services, along with judicious use of LexisNexis and Westlaw, is highly valued.

6. Study Pertinent Passages

As you identify an authority that may be pertinent, scan it carefully enough to answer these questions:

- ☐ How weighty is it? You should, of course, focus more energy on law than commentary.
- ☐ How pertinent is it?
- ☐ How much assistance does it provide in and of itself?
- ☐ How much assistance does it provide through references to other potentially important authorities?

If the authority appears weighty, pertinent, and helpful, make a copy—by photocopying a paper source or by printing, downloading, or e-mailing an online source.

EXHIBIT 2.12	Boolean Search Results, from LexisNexis Periodicals Database (online source)

Page 1

1. Copyright (c) 2006 Albany Law Review Albany Law Review, 2006, 70 Alb. L. Rev. 117, 12682 words, ARTICLE: IS LEISURE-TIME SMOKING A VALID EMPLOYMENT CONSIDERATION?, Karen L. Chadwick*

... report stating that cigarette **smoking** is a health hazard and ...

... examines the current approaches to **employment** discrimination based on off-duty **smoking**. ... This approach rejects the current all-or- ...

... time discrimination against **employee smoking** and attempts to pass on at least some of the costs attributable to **employee smoking to those employees who smoke**. ... The Background and Basis for the Differing Views on **Employment** Discrimination Based on Leisure-Time **Smoking** ... " Similarly, the American Civil Liberties Union has denounced **employment** discrimination based on off-duty **smoking** on the basis that such discrimination infringes on ...

... liberties or inherent right to **privacy**. ... The belief that **employee privacy** is infringed by consideration of off-duty **smoking** has, no doubt, been the prime ...

... for legislation prohibiting **employment** discrimination based on off-duty **smoking**. ... " In the context of **employment** discrimination on the basis of **smoking**, this argument is generally stated: "If **employees** are not free to **smoke** outside the workplace, are we next ...

... middle approach of passing on the **employment** costs attributable to **smoking to the smoker** has two benefits. ...

... legitimate employment consideration. An **employee's** right to engage in leisure-time **smoking** without **employment** consequences is defended on both the basis of **privacy** and the connected notion that condoning discrimination against **smokers** constitutes a slippery- ...

... time scrutiny by **employers**. Part IV of this Article ...

... Constitutional Claims Based on **Privacy** Interests   In the public sector, it has been argued that **employer** discrimination against leisure-time **smoking** amounts to an impermissible constitutional violation of the state **employee** or applicant's constitutional right to **privacy** and due process. n25 However, ...

... leisure-time smoking. **Employer** discrimination based on off-duty **smoking** would only be prohibited under ...

... interests such as disability or race. However, because **smoking** rarely implicates a ...

... a common law **privacy** interest, **employers** are free to exercise their at-will ...

... arbitrarily or otherwise exclude **employees** who **smoke** from the workforce. n82 C. The ...

... Law Tort of Invasion of **Privacy** as the Basis for Claims ...

... Sector   The pervasive argument - that an **employer's** consideration of leisure-time **smoking** violates a legally protected common law **privacy** interest - is without legal ...

... least facially, because individual **privacy** is implicated by **employer** consideration of leisure-time **smoking**, the tort of invasion of **privacy** would be the most likely source of ...

... law protection for **employees**. n85 Recognition of an individual's ...

... others." n89 The right of **privacy** arguably implicated by a private **employer's** consideration of leisure-time **smoking** is an unreasonable intrusion upon the seclusion of another. n90 However, the **privacy** tort of unreasonable intrusion ...

... little protection for an **employee whose employer** discriminates against leisure-time **smokers**. The right to be free from intrusion ...

... fired. n100 Even if an **employee** or prospective **employee** could establish that she had a reasonable expectation of **privacy** in connection with her **smoking** habit, she would likely fail to surmount the obstacle of establishing that the **employer's** scrutiny into the **employee's smoking** was unreasonable. n101 A ...

... Liberties Union has denounced **employment** discrimination based on off-duty **smoking** on the basis that such discrimination infringes on ...

... liberties or inherent right to **privacy**. n121 The belief that **employee privacy** is infringed by consideration of off-duty **smoking** has, no doubt, been the prime ...

... for legislation prohibiting **employment** discrimination based on off-duty **smoking**. Advocates of such legislation continue to ...

... viewed by proponents of **smoker privacy** as further evidence of unwelcome economic control by **employers** and/or unwarranted paternalism. n162 ...

... Nonetheless, legislation which protects **smoker privacy** at the expense of **employers** and nonsmoking **employees** does not seem fair. n170 The clamor for **privacy** protection rings somewhat ...

... continue to be the tobacco industry and the **smokers** themselves. n171 The privacy ...

... attempted to balance individual **employee privacy** concerns with the cost burdens imposed on **employers** who are forced to hire **smokers**. n183 Under a ...

... Ann H. Zgrodnik, **Smoking** Discrimination: Invading an Individual's Right to **Privacy** in the Home and Outside the ...

EXHIBIT 2.12   *(continued)*

... states have laws regulating **smoking** in private places of **employment** and several other states regulate **smoking** by public **employees**).   n76. See, e.g., Smoke- ...
... See Victor Schachter, **Privacy** in the Workplace, in 6th Annual Institute on **Privacy** Law: Data Protection - The Convergence of **Privacy** and Security 153, 231 (...
... forbidding off-duty **smoking**] strikes [sic] at the heart of traditional notions of liberty, and **employer's** [sic] face an uphill ...
... against off-duty **smoking** or other legal activities ...
... a common law **privacy** action.").   n84. See ...

... non-national security **privacy** issues to center stage, including the question of what privacy rights, if any, employees should have with respect to their use of computers at ...
... lifestyle discrimination in **employment** could become a hot ...
... discrimination was centrally focused on **smokers'** rights laws. The prospects of this ...

15. Copyright (c) 2007 DePaul University DePaul Journal of Health Care Law, Spring, 2007, 10 DePaul J. Health Care L. 457, 15279 words, ARTICLE: IF YOU'RE SMOKING YOU'RE FIRED: HOW TOBACCO COULD BE DANGEROUS TO MORE THAN JUST YOUR HEALTH, Christopher Valleau*
... disagreed stating that cigarette **smoking** could be distinguished from the activities involving liberty or **privacy** that the Supreme Court had thus far recognized as fundamental rights. ... Because **smoking** cessation devices do exist, such as ...
... disability. ... Some of these statutes refer to **smoking** specifically and also include tobacco ...
... unfair and dangerous to allow **employers** to discriminate against certain **employees** because their private lifestyle choices are ...
... ADA, the only protection from **employment** discrimination that **smokers** can rely on exists ...
... state statutes prohibiting **employment** discrimination based on tobacco ...
... applicants seeking government **employment** a right of **privacy as to their smoking** habits. n59 The court ...

24. Copyright (c) 2006 The George Washington Law Review The George Washington Law Review, April, 2006, 74 Geo. Wash. L. Rev. 553, 9673 words, Note: You're Not the Boss of Me: A Call for Federal Lifestyle Discrimination Legislation, Ann L. Rives*
... in the form of general **employee privacy** rights as well as more ...
... off-duty activities, such as **smoking**. A company with locations ...
... healthcare costs. Although an **employee's** right to **privacy** must be respected, an **employer's** right to make a ...
... only increases for **employees** who have high risk factors, such as a history of **smoking** or obesity. n104 Although an ...

25. Copyright (c) 1998 Georgetown Law Journal Georgetown Law Journal, January, 1998, 86 Geo. L.J. 783, 16769 words, NOTE: Blowing Smoke: Do Smokers Have a Right? Limiting the Privacy Rights of Cigarette Smokers, MICHELE L. TYLER *
... in the workplace, informational **privacy** rights have been implicated when some government **employers** refused to hire **smokers**, insisting that new **employees** refrain from **smoking**, even while off duty.   n39 Potential **employees who smoke** claim that this policy invades their **privacy** because they must disclose their practice of a legal activity to their **employer.** Second, physical privacy ...
... condition to combat their on-the-job **smoke** exposure, the court held that the ...
... a firefighter's informational **privacy** interests are compromised by ...
... behavior that he would otherwise keep from his **employer,** it is not surprising that in the ...
... federal and state constitutional **privacy** right to **smoke** outside the course of **employment** and seeking to enjoin enforcement of the ...

Reading legal authority should be a slow and deliberate process, because nearly every word is significant. To read a legal authority as deeply as it deserves, consider following the SQ3R reading process:

- ☐ *Survey* the source to discern its components and organization.
- ☐ Pose *questions* that you think the source may answer.
- ☐ *Read* the source to find the answers.
- ☐ *Record* what you have learned.
- ☐ *Review* by looking over your notes.

The classic formulation of SQ3R uses *reciting* rather that *reviewing*; for difficult and important sources, reading pertinent material aloud may indeed be helpful. Because this task involves such painstaking work, its symbol is a magnifying glass.

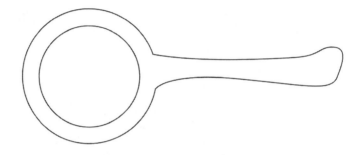

Avoid tempting shortcuts. Some sources include not only the authority itself but also summaries written by the publisher's staff. Focus your attention on the authority itself; use the editor's summary to confirm your understanding. Also, read the entire authority, especially cases, statutes, and other forms of law.

Read with your client's situation in mind. Be especially attentive to points that pertain to your client's situation, and sift out those that do not. Focusing too much on truly extraneous points will undermine the cost-effectiveness of your research.

As noted previously, some legal authority will be on all fours with your client's situation. Most legal authorities will be merely on point—both similar to and different from your client's situation. Be sure to note ways in which an on-point authority both converges on and diverges from your client's situation.

As you read, be sure to take careful notes about what you have learned. The content of your notes will vary from authority to authority. For example, a set of notes on commentary will include what the law is stated to be and perhaps policies underlying the law or critique of the law. Your notes on a case, statute, or other law should be more detailed. For example, you should brief a case by recording types of information, e.g., the facts, procedure, issue, holding (outcome), rule of law, and reasoning in a case, as discussed in Chapter 9. As best you can, resist the temptation to merely download important content. To properly analyze your client's position, you must actively process the text of the pertinent authorities; downloading by itself circumvents this process.

In addition to the content of the source, take notes on your research process and your ongoing analysis of your client's legal position. Although the details will vary somewhat from authority to authority, recording the following information is always a good idea:

- ☐ the issue being researched;
- ☐ the date of your research;
- ☐ the information needed to cite the authority;
- ☐ your research process — how you searched for and found pertinent material, e.g., how you used an index or a natural-language search;
- ☐ the information you obtained and its implications for your client's position; and
- ☐ next steps, including questions to consider and leads to pursue.

Note how extensively your client's situation pervades this list. Research is not an end in itself; rather, research serves your legal analysis, and your legal analysis serves your client.

One way to structure your note-taking and the notes themselves is to use a template with spaces for critical material. A general template is presented in Exhibit 2.13 (at page 60), with the italicized material connecting this chapter's eight cognitive tasks to the various spaces. Templates tailored to particular authorities appear throughout this book. Completing these templates will keep you focused — a critical condition of cost-effective legal research.

As counterintuitive as it may seem, jot down as well what did not work, e.g., a failed search, an unhelpful treatise. With these notes, you will avoid backtracking to determine whether you did try that search or looked at that treatise.

7.   Research Backward and Forward from Major Authorities

Nearly every legal authority you read will connect to other authorities. For your research to be comprehensive as well as correct, you will need to pursue some of the authorities connected to your major authorities. The more important an authority is, the more necessary it is to research connected authorities. It is useful to think of a timeline, with the date of the authority or source you are reading as the key date.

Lawyers tend to use the following terms in discussing this aspect of legal research:

- ☐ The *citing authority* is the authority you are currently reading. Within that authority are references to older authorities.
- ☐ The *cited authority* is the one cited in the authority you are currently reading.

EXHIBIT 2.13	General Research Template

Issue:	**Citation Information:**
1. Learn and react to your client's situation. *2. Develop research terms and research issues.*	*3. Rank potential authorities—citation reveals authoritativeness.*
Date of events:	
Date of research:	
Search and Find:	
Cells for particular types of sources reflect: *3. List and rank potential authorities.* *4. Assess available resources.*	
located pertinent topic and sections by . . . *5. Use your terms and issues to locate pertinent passages.*	updated by . . .
Information and Implications:	
6. Study pertinent passages.	
Next Steps:	
questions to consider:	leads to pursue: *7. Research backward and forward from major authorities.* *8. Stop researching—when nothing new appears here.*

For example, if you were reading an encyclopedia, the encyclopedia is the *citing* authority; the cases listed in the encyclopedia's footnotes are the *cited* authorities.

In many situations, you should research backward in time. For example,

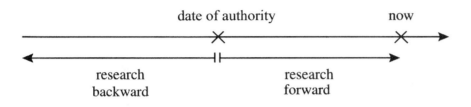

if a case cites a statute in a pertinent passage, you must read that statute. If an encyclopedia cites ten cases in support of a pertinent proposition, you should read any from your jurisdiction, but you probably can forgo reading the cases from other jurisdictions.

In addition, for your research to be current, you must research forward in time to be sure that a law is indeed current before you rely on it. For example, if you were reading *Lukoski*, a 1988 case from the New Mexico Supreme Court, in 2007, you would need to check that it has not been overruled by a more recent case. If you were reading the Employee Privacy Act in a source published in 2003, you would need to check that the New Mexico legislature has not amended that statute since then. Note that the validity of one type of law can be affected by law of a different sort; for example, a statute may supplant a case, and a case may render a statute unconstitutional. These topics are discussed in detail in Chapters 9 and 10 (case law) and Chapter 11 (statutes).

Similarly, you may want to check the influence of a commentary that is important to your analysis. For example, if you find a particularly useful point in a periodical article, you may want to determine whether that article has been cited in any cases since its publication; those citations add to the article's credibility.

Because of the importance of currency in legal research, there are many tools that update sources, including pocket parts, supplementary pamphlets, replacement pages, advance sheets, legislative services, citators, and alert messages provided by some online resources. You will learn about these throughout this text.

On occasion, a legal authority loses authoritativeness not because of subsequent legal developments but because of new nonlegal knowledge or changes in public policy. For example, advances in medical research regarding the effects of secondhand smoke may undermine an authority that predates those advances and rests on a view that secondhand smoke is innocuous.

E.   CLOSURE

8.   Stop Researching

There is, unfortunately, no magic test for when you should stop researching. Different research projects will require different amounts of time, based on your prior knowledge of the subject, the difficulty of the topic, the occasion for the research (you should spend less time for quick advice before a client takes a minor action than for an appeal before the highest court), and the client's resources. Nonetheless, you may find the following four-step process useful:

(1) Consider quitting when you are seeing the same authorities and the same legal rules over and over again. Legal research, like many activities, follows the principle of diminishing returns: after a certain point, each additional hour of effort brings fewer and fewer rewards. Hence the symbol for this task is a diminishing-returns graph.

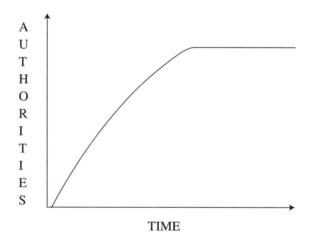

(2) At the point of diminishing returns, check through your research notes. Make sure that you have properly accomplished each of the seven tasks, and look for loose ends. For example, check that you have considered the various types of law (task 3), explored all research issues (task 5), ascertained that cases are still good law (task 7), etc. Review the leads-to-pursue entries in your templates.

(3) Read a commentary source that you have not yet read, or re-read one of the better ones you read earlier on. You should be able to say "I've looked into that" as you read through the discussion.

(4) Start to write out your analysis of the client's situation, or check in with your supervisor or another lawyer in your office. If you get stuck or you find it difficult to answer questions your colleague asks, you will know that your research is still not complete and which topics to work on some more.

Finally, keep in mind that your research may become stale as time passes. For example, a court may decide an important case, or a legislature may amend a statute after you complete your research. Most lawyers keep their research up to date by reviewing current-awareness publications, such as a weekly newspaper with new cases; by using an e-mail alert service, which sends an e-mail when a specified development occurs; and by repeating the research-forward task (task 7) from time to time or before major events, such as settlement discussions or oral argument.

F.   SUMMARY

As we worked on this book, we asked experts in teaching legal research — legal writing professors and reference librarians — to identify the most common missteps of novice legal researchers. Here are some of their answers, listed under the pertinent cognitive task outlined in this chapter:

1. **Learn and React to Your Client's Situation.**
   Failing to obtain all of the relevant facts.
   Getting *too* creative — pursuing issues that are not relevant.
   Researching too broadly, that is, including a related but not pertinent topic.

2. **Develop Research Terms and Research Issues.**
   Focusing on irrelevant facts.
   Failing to generate alternative broader and narrower terms.
   Failing to look up key words.
   Formulating a too-narrow research issue.
   Using the wrong key words or phrases and getting side-tracked.

3. **List and Rank Potential Authorities.**
   Not having an understanding of how all the sources fit together.
   Not using a broad source early on and then focusing on the precise issue.
   Under-relying on commentary early in the research process.
   Jumping too quickly to cases, especially in online form.
   Over-relying on persuasive cases and commentary.
   Failing to appreciate the importance of jurisdiction.
   Searching unnecessarily for commentary on matters covered by law.

4. **Assess Available Sources.**
   Not having enough patience to use different sources.
   Over-relying on online research, more specifically:
   ☐ Turning on the computer too soon.
   ☐ Trying to correct a problem by checking via a computer.

☐   Trying to research on LexisNexis or Westlaw before learning a fair amount about the topic.

☐   Over-relying on online resources in lieu of paper case law tools.

☐   Over-relying on online resources in lieu of paper statutory codes.

5.   **Use Your Terms and Issues to Locate Pertinent Passages.**
Not having enough patience to try different search terms.
Using only one word for an idea rather than searching under multiple words.
Not fully understanding the case digest system (a major and somewhat intricate source of locating pertinent cases).
Failing to fully utilize finding tools such as the case synopses in annotated statutes.
Failing to write searches well and thinking you can find what you need in ten or even thirty minutes on LexisNexis or Westlaw.

6.   **Study Pertinent Passages.**
Not stopping to read cases along the way.
Failing to recognize a case that is very useful.
Failing to fully understand a case, which includes failing to look up key concepts.
Failing to grasp the structure of statutory or procedural rules.
Not using the current statute.

7.   **Research Backward and Forward from Major Authorities.**
Relying on encyclopedias and other commentary rather than using these as a means to locate law and not reading the law.
Not finding and reading enough cases.
Not following through — copying something that seems to be on point without digging more deeply.
Relying on what a case says about a cited authority without reading that cited authority.
Failing to update.
Not citing cases along the way and failing to properly understand case citators (a process described in detail in Chapter 10).

8.   **Stop Researching.**
Deciding you are done when you find anything that appears to be on point, rather than looking at the issue from various angles before stopping.
Over-researching and leaving too little time for analysis and writing.
Never quitting because you are seeking a definitive case.

Easily the most commonly mentioned misstep is looking too soon, indeed immediately, for pertinent cases by running searches in LexisNexis or Westlaw. One legal writing teacher depicted this approach as looking for a needle in a haystack without knowing what a needle is. You can avoid such an exercise in futility by carefully undertaking all of the cognitive tasks described in this chapter in the various sources covered in this text.

INTERLUDE NO. 1: BROWSING THE INTERNET

Exhibit No. 1   National Institute on Drug Abuse Research Report, from Wikipedia Link (online source)

Exhibit No. 2   Google Results List (online source)

Exhibit No. 3   State Legislative Information, from American Lung Association (online source)

Many people regularly engage in some type of research through the Internet. By making information readily available and relatively easy to locate, the Internet has had a powerful impact on how people research a very wide variety of subjects. This interlude describes research conducted through four Internet tools: Wikipedia, Google,* Findlaw, and the Legal Information Institute of the Cornell University Law School.

Among the Internet's compilations of highly accessible information is Wikipedia, which contained 7 million articles in 200 hundred languages as of fall 2007. Articles are submitted and edited by people who know something they would like to share; this is what makes Wikipedia intriguing and also less than authoritative. Seeking to learn about nicotine addiction through Wikipedia, we found a piece on nicotine addiction, but an editor flagged it as possibly unbalanced and not meeting quality standards. We then found an extensive piece on addiction, including text analyzing nicotine addiction as a form of physical dependency. Relying on the Wikipedia piece itself would be unwise, but following some links brought us to a very authoritative research report of the National Institute on Drug Abuse, a branch of the National Institutes of Health, available for free printing and downloading. Among other points, the report states that most smokers understand the risks of smoking and yet use tobacco because they are addicted; only six percent who quit are successful for more than a month. See Exhibit No. 1 (at page 68).

Many people "Google" on a regular basis. According to Google's company overview, Google is the world's largest search engine, and users describe it as "the closest thing the Web has to an ultimate answer machine." So how well did Google work for the issues raised by Ms. Canoga's situation? The answer is a lawyer's favorite answer to many questions: it depends.

We researched employer smoking bans through Google Scholar. Google Scholar taps into journals in a wide range of nonlegal disciplines, including health sciences, business administration, and social sciences. In .15 seconds, Google identified 22,600 articles. See Exhibit No. 2 (at page 69). Working through the beginning of the list, we identified useful and credible articles,

* A study reported in the November 26, 2007, issue of *Time* magazine found that 71% of U.S. Internet users visited Google; 30% visited Wikipedia.

but the most interesting were not available without a fee or membership in the professional organization publishing the journal, such as the American Public Health Association.

We also used Google to look for material addressing the rights of smoking employees in New Mexico — "New Mexico" smoking employee. In .16 seconds, Google came up with 783,000 hits — very fast and very overwhelming.

The list began with a sponsored link (parallel to paid advertising) to an international law firm that represents employees in various types of litigation against their employers. There we found a brief article describing litigation on behalf of employees who lose jobs or pay more for benefits due to smoking. That article provided a link to a February 2005 article in the *New York Times* about a case the firm was litigating.

A link from the firm's website led to the American Lung Association's State Legislated Actions on Tobacco Issues website. There we found a description of New Mexico's laws on various tobacco topics, including the statute prohibiting employers from regulating off-duty smoking. The statute was paraphrased, but the description was so complete that one could assume that the statute was quoted verbatim. The statute's citation was also provided. See Exhibit No. 3 (at page 70).

The first ten nonsponsored links consisted of several articles in business magazines; several policies at New Mexico universities; the American Lung Association website; the website of an organization providing information about New Mexico's new clean indoor air act; and the website of a grass-roots group seeking to end smoking, which included links to research reports and provided information on statutes and ordinances.

Compare these results to Findlaw — a commercial but free portal for a wide range of free websites with legal information, some aimed at nonlawyers, others at legal professionals. Findlaw provided a link to the official version of the New Mexico statutes; we could find the pertinent statute by scanning the list of chapters or running a key-word search. Similarly, Findlaw also linked to federal statutes. Even more helpful were the links to federal agency sites, including that of the Equal Employment Opportunity Commission (EEOC), which administers federal antidiscrimination statutes and provides guidance to employers in various publications.

In Findlaw's Labor and Employment Law Library, we found brief pieces from lawyers on a wide range of topics, including at-will employment, discharge, discrimination, employee privacy, handbooks, and retaliation. Although the pieces would not carry much weight compared to the types of commentary discussed in Unit II, they did provide insight into very new developments and strategies for handling certain types of legal matters, e.g., the development of an employee handbook.

Finally, we visited LII — the Legal Information Institute, maintained by the Cornell University Law School, which is widely regarded as an excellent free portal for free websites containing legal information. LII provided overviews of various employment law topics. The most fruitful covered the law of employment discrimination, including federal statutes and the EEOC. Through a link or two, we found the pertinent federal statute. That statute dated to 2005 during our visit to LII in the fall of 2007; fortunately LII suggested various means of updating our research.

We then looked up New Mexico in LII's collection of state resources. There we found links to sources of New Mexico pending legislation, recent supreme court and court of appeals decisions, court rules, and administrative materials, as well as a link to the website of the New Mexico state bar association. Most of these links were to the New Mexico Compilation Commission, a government agency responsible for publication of New Mexico law. The statutes were very up to date — through the first special legislative session ending in 2007. A brief look at the cases database revealed that it was up to date but not sufficiently retrospective — it began in 1998.

There are several lessons to be learned through this tour of the Internet:

- ☐ Effective research entails not casual and random use of online tools but rather deliberate and targeted research, in which the resource to be used is carefully matched to the specific topic to be researched.
- ☐ Many legal problems have nonlegal dimensions. General-purpose resources, such as Wikipedia and Google, can lead to pertinent nonlegal information. The credibility and accuracy of information obtained this way should be critically evaluated.
- ☐ Legal research involves types of materials that are generally found more easily through law-specific online services than general-purpose online services. Here, even more than in nonlegal research, you must carefully evaluate what you are finding: who generated the content, whether what you have found is the law's language or a summary, how far back the database or document extends, how up to date the information is, and so on.

As a newcomer to legal research, you may find learning legal research a daunting prospect. It is true that there is much to learn; it also true that you can learn how to conduct legal research very well. This book seeks to make that process as efficient and interesting as possible.

EXHIBIT NO. 1

National Institute on Drug Abuse Research Report,
from Wikipedia Link (online source)

NIDA RESEARCH REPORT SERIES 3

Is nicotine addictive?

Yes. Most smokers use tobacco regularly because they are addicted to nicotine. Addiction is characterized by compulsive drug seeking and use, even in the face of negative health consequences. It is well documented that most smokers identify tobacco use as harmful and express a desire to reduce or stop using it, and nearly 35 million of them want to quit each year. Unfortunately, only about 6 percent of people who try to quit are successful for more than a month.

Research has shown how nicotine acts on the brain to produce a number of effects. Of primary importance to its addictive nature are findings that nicotine activates reward pathways—the brain circuitry that regulates feelings of pleasure. A key brain chemical involved in mediating the desire to consume drugs is the neurotransmitter dopamine, and research has shown that nicotine increases levels of dopamine in the reward circuits. This reaction is similar to that seen with other drugs of abuse, and is thought to underlie the pleasurable sensations experienced by many smokers. Nicotine's pharmacokinetic properties also enhance its abuse potential. Cigarette smoking produces a rapid distribution of nicotine to the brain, with drug levels peaking within 10 seconds of inhalation. However, the acute effects of nicotine dissipate in a few minutes, as do the associated feelings of reward, which causes the smoker to continue dosing to maintain the drug's pleasurable effects and prevent withdrawal.

Nicotine withdrawal symptoms include irritability, craving, cognitive and attentional deficits, sleep disturbances, and increased appetite. These symptoms may begin within a few hours after the last cigarette, quickly driving people back to tobacco use. Symptoms peak within the first few days of smoking cessation and may subside within a few weeks. For some people, however, symptoms may persist for months.

While withdrawal is related to the pharmacological effects of nicotine, many behavioral factors can also affect the severity of withdrawal symptoms. For some people, the feel, smell, and sight of a cigarette and the ritual of obtaining, handling, lighting, and smoking the cigarette are all associated with the pleasurable effects of smoking and can make withdrawal or craving worse. While nicotine gum and patches may alleviate the pharmacological aspects of withdrawal, cravings often persist. Other forms of nicotine replacement, such as inhalers, attempt to address some of these other issues, while behavioral therapies can help smokers identify environmental triggers of withdrawal and craving so they can employ strategies to prevent or circumvent these symptoms and urges.

Are there other chemicals that may contribute to tobacco addiction?

Yes, research is showing that nicotine may not be the only psychoactive ingredient in tobacco. Using advanced neuroimaging technology, scientists can see the dramatic effect of cigarette smoking on the brain and are finding a marked decrease in the levels of monoamine oxidase (MAO), an important enzyme that is responsible for the breakdown of dopamine. This change is likely caused by some tobacco smoke ingredient other than nicotine, since we know that nicotine itself does not dramatically alter MAO levels. The decrease in two forms of MAO (A and B) results in higher dopamine levels and may be another reason that smokers continue to smoke—to sustain the high dopamine levels that lead to the desire for repeated drug use.

Recently, NIDA-funded researchers have shown in animals that acetaldehyde, another chemical constituent of tobacco smoke, dramatically increases the reinforcing properties of nicotine and may also contribute to tobacco addiction. The investigators further report that this effect is age-related, with adolescent animals displaying far more sensitivity to this reinforcing effect, suggesting that the brains of adolescents may be more vulnerable to tobacco addiction.

What are the medical consequences of tobacco use?

Cigarette smoking kills an estimated 440,000 U.S. citizens each year—more than alcohol, cocaine, heroin, homicide, suicide, car accidents, fire, and AIDS combined. Since 1964, more than 12 million Americans have died prematurely from smoking, and another 25 million U.S. smokers alive today will most likely die of a smoking-related illness.

EXHIBIT NO. 2   Google Results List (online source)

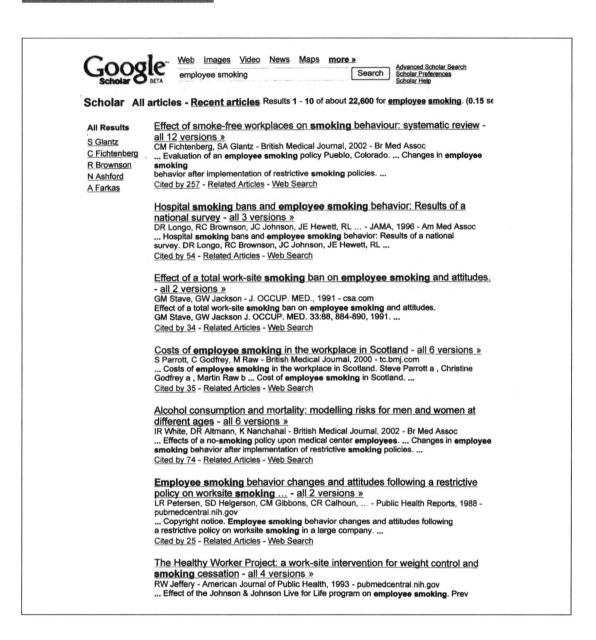

EXHIBIT NO. 3   State Legislative Information,
from American Lung Association Website (online source)

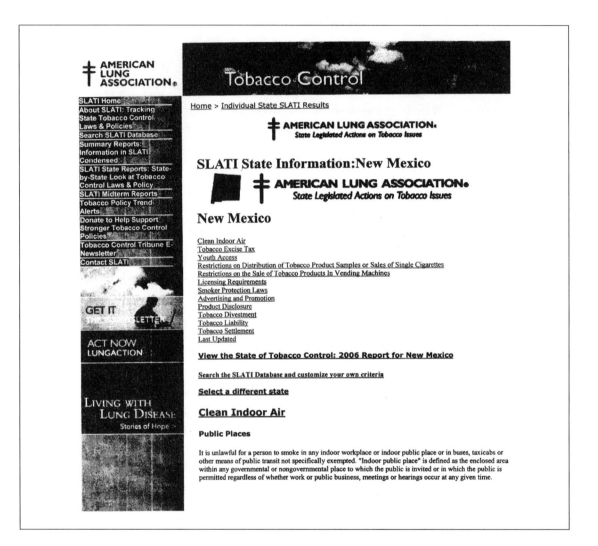

EXHIBIT NO. 3 *(continued)*

Warning signs shall be prominently displayed where a tobacco product vending machine is located. The sign shall read as follows: "A PERSON LESS THAN 18 YEARS OF AGE WHO PURCHASES A TOBACCO PRODUCT IS SUBJECT TO A FINE OF UP TO $1,000. A PERSON WHO SELLS A TOBACCO PRODUCT TO A PERSON LESS THAN 18 YEARS OF AGE IS SUBJECT TO A FINE OF UP TO $1,000." Violation is a misdemeanor subject to imprisonment for less than a year and/or not more than a $1,000 fine. When a municipality or county adopts an ordinance pertaining to the sales of tobacco products, the ordinance or regulation shall be consistent with state law.

N.M. STAT. ANN. §§ 30-49-9; 30-49-11; & 30-49-12 (1993).

Return to top

Licensing Requirements

Requirements

A person shall not engage in the manufacture or distribution of cigarettes in New Mexico without a license issued by the state Department of Taxation and Revenue. A license shall be issued for a term not to exceed one year. Violators are subject to a civil penalty of up to $1,000 for a first offense, $1,500 to $2,500 for a second offense and not less than $5,000 for a third or subsequent offense.

N.M. STAT. ANN. §§ 7-12-9.1 & 7-12-13.1 (2006).

Fee

Up to $100 each year for both distributors and manufacturers.

N.M. STAT. ANN. § 7-12-9.1 (2006).

License Suspension for Sales to Minors

None.

Return to top

Smoker Protection Laws

It is unlawful for an employer to refuse to hire or discharge any individual, or otherwise disadvantage any individual, with respect to compensation, terms, conditions or privileges of employment because the individual is a smoker or non-smoker, provided that the individual complies with applicable laws or policies regulating smoking on the premises of the employer during working hours. It is also unlawful for an employer to require as a condition of employment that any employee or applicant for employment abstain from using tobacco products during non-working hours. This does not apply to any activity that materially threatens an employer's legitimate conflict of interest policy reasonably designed to protect the employer's trade secrets, proprietary information or other proprietary interests; or relates to a bona fide occupational requirement and is reasonably and rationally related to the employment activities and responsibilities of a particular employee or a particular group of employees, rather than to all employees of the employer. Any employee claiming to be aggrieved by any unlawful action of any employer may bring a civil suit for damages.

N.M. STAT. ANN. §§ 50-11-1 et seq. (1991).

Return to top

Advertising and Promotion

None.

COMMENTARY

UNIT

II

INTRODUCTION

As you learned in Unit I, your ultimate goal is to discern the rule of law governing your client's situation. That rule derives from cases, statutes, administrative agency materials, or court rules. Yet this text suggests that you start your research in commentary.

There are several reasons for this seemingly circuitous approach. First, commentary sources describe, explain, analyze, and, in some cases, critique and suggest changes in the law. You often will find it easier to grasp the law when you begin with commentary than when you begin with the law itself. Second, commentary sources provide references to the law. Third, compared to sources containing the law itself, commentary sources are fairly accessible. As you will soon see, it is easier to locate a pertinent portion of a treatise, for example, than it is to locate a pertinent case, espe-cially if you are starting with little back-ground knowledge.

As you will see in this unit, each type of commentary has strengths and weaknesses. As you research in commentary sources, evaluate your research by the four criteria for competent research introduced in Chapter 1: correct, comprehensive, credible, and cost-effective. For some research projects, you will want to combine commentary sources to fully achieve these goals.

Chapters 3 through 7 each cover one of the major types of commentary. The sequence starts with sources that are analogous to nonlegal sources (such as encyclopedias and treatises) and then moves on to sources that are unique to the law (such as Restatements of the Law). Chapter 8 covers, in briefer form, several minor types of commentary and then discusses strategies for research in commentary that are correct, comprehensive, credible, and cost-effective.

ENCYCLOPEDIAS

A. What Is an Encyclopedia, and Why Are They Useful?

B. How Do You Research in and Cite Encyclopedias?

C. What Else?

Exhibit 3.1   Encyclopedia Excerpt, from American Jurisprudence
2d (paper source)

Exhibit 3.2   Encyclopedia Template

Exhibit 3.3   Encyclopedia Pocket Part, from American Jurisprudence
2d (paper source)

Exhibit 3.4   Encyclopedia Template for Canoga Case

A.   WHAT IS AN ENCYCLOPEDIA, AND WHY ARE THEY USEFUL?

Like nonlegal encyclopedias, legal encyclopedias cover a wide range of topics, present fairly general information, and order the topics alphabetically. Some topics are quite narrow, others very broad. Within each topic, the discussion is organized into parts and sections; each section consists of text along with footnotes citing to supporting authorities. Encyclopedias are written by authors on the publisher's editorial staff; they generally are not well known experts.

Two encyclopedias seek to provide broad coverage of American law, including state and federal law: *American Jurisprudence* second edition (Am. Jur. 2d) and *Corpus Juris Secundum* (C.J.S.). Both are successors to older encyclopedias and are now published by Thomson West. Both cover 400 or more topics and consist of approximately 150 books in paper form. In many states, a state encyclopedia covers all or many legal topics under that state's law.

For the typical research project, encyclopedias are most useful at the very beginning of the research process. You very likely will find a broad overview of your topic, which can be read fairly easily, and you can easily browse within an encyclopedia. Encyclopedias also operate as finding tools for the law. In addition, most encyclopedias are updated annually.

Encyclopedia research does have limitations. If you use Am. Jur. 2d or C.J.S., the text is likely to present general principles but not precisely state the law of your jurisdiction. Similarly, neither Am. Jur. 2d nor C.J.S. cites all pertinent cases, so there may not be a citation to your jurisdiction's law. Because these encyclopedias are not written by well recognized experts, they are not as authoritative as other forms of commentary. Thus they are cited most often for broad, well established points.

A state or specialized encyclopedia can be more useful than Am. Jur. 2d or C.J.S. The text generally is more detailed, there are more extensive citations to the law of your state, and a well researched and written state encyclopedia may be viewed with respect within the state.

For an example pertinent to the Canoga case, examine Exhibit 3.1 (at pages 77–78) from Am. Jur. 2d's discussion of Wrongful Discharge.

B.   HOW DO YOU RESEARCH IN AND CITE ENCYCLOPEDIAS?

Researching Encyclopedias: As shown in Exhibit 3.2 (at page 79), our encyclopedia template, researching in encyclopedias entails formulating, as best you can, a research issue; selecting an encyclopedia; locating and reading pertinent passages; deriving useful information and considering its implications for your clients' situation; and planning your next steps.

You can research encyclopedias online; for example, Am. Jur. 2d is available on Westlaw and LexisNexis; C.J.S. is available on Westlaw. However, paper research is often a better choice because encyclopedias are well organized with strong internal finding tools. Furthermore, browsing is a good strategy. Thus this text focuses on researching in Am. Jur. 2d and C.J.S. in books.

Encyclopedias in paper

► Use the index or topic list to identify a topic.
► Look over the topic's introductory materials.
► Read the topic's outline.
► Read the text.
► Look for and read updates in the pocket part or supplementary pamphlet.

There are two primary means of locating pertinent topics in an encyclopedia: the index and the topic list. Both Am. Jur. 2d and C.J.S. have multivolume indexes, issued annually and typically shelved at the end of the set; you may also find a supplement to the annual index. Review Exhibit 2.6

EXHIBIT 3.1	Encyclopedia Excerpt, from American Jurisprudence 2d (paper source)

WRONGFUL DISCHARGE   § 44

response to different degrees of misconduct,[1] ranging from reprimand to discharge.[2] Generally, if a termination violates the progressive discipline procedure set forth in the employer's handbook, the employer has breached its promise of procedural fairness, and the employee may recover for wrongful discharge.[3] However, a memorandum warning an employee that she will be terminated within a certain time period if her behavior does not improve cannot modify a worker's employment at-will contract and the employer does not breach that contract when it terminates the worker's employment without cause; it is wholly irrational to assume that the memorandum will somehow ripen into an assured contract of progressive discipline over that time period.[4] Additionally, the provisions of an employee manual stating that termination can be expected upon receipt of a third disciplinary action do not expressly provide that an employee can be terminated only for cause so as to overcome the employment at-will doctrine.[5]

◆ **Caution:** Some cases suggest that once a company promulgates procedures for termination, they must be strictly followed.[6] Substantial compliance, or an attempt to adhere to the spirit of the procedure, may not always suffice.[7]

§ 44 Grievance and appeal procedures

Research References

West's Key Number Digest, Civil Rights ⬤➛144; Master and Servant ⬤➛30(1.5)

Some employee manuals contain provisions which give aggrieved employees the opportunity to appeal adverse employment decisions. Courts have held that an employer's failure to abide by its rules concerning posttermination appeals is a breach of contract.[1]

[Section 43]
[1]Long v. Tazewell/Pekin Consol. Communication Center, 215 Ill. App. 3d 134, 158 Ill. Dec. 798, 574 N.E.2d 1191 (3d Dist. 1991); Enyeart v. Shelter Mut. Ins. Co., 693 S.W.2d 120 (Mo. Ct. App. W.D. 1985); Sherman v. Rutland Hosp., Inc., 146 Vt. 204, 500 A.2d 230 (1985); Mobil Coal Producing, Inc. v. Parks, 704 P.2d 702 (Wyo. 1985).

[2]Pine River State Bank v. Mettille, 333 N.W.2d 622 (Minn. 1983).

[3]Shah v. General Elec. Co., 816 F.2d 264 (6th Cir. 1987); Thompson v. American Motor Inns Inc., 623 F. Supp. 409 (W.D. Va. 1985); ARCO Alaska, Inc. v. Akers, 753 P.2d 1150 (Alaska 1988); Foley v. Interactive Data Corp., 47 Cal. 3d 654, 254 Cal. Rptr. 211, 765 P.2d 373 (1988); Long v. Tazewell/Pekin Consol. Communication Center, 215 Ill. App. 3d 134, 158 Ill. Dec. 798, 574 N.E.2d 1191 (3d Dist. 1991); Cannon v. National By-Products, Inc., 422 N.W.2d 638 (Iowa 1988); Staggs v. Blue

Cross of Maryland, Inc., 61 Md. App. 381, 486 A.2d 798 (1985); Damrow v. Thumb Co-op. Terminal, Inc., 126 Mich. App. 354, 337 N.W.2d 338 (1983); Pine River State Bank v. Mettille, 333 N.W.2d 622 (Minn. 1983); Small v. Springs Industries, Inc., 292 S.C. 481, 357 S.E.2d 452 (1987); Berube v. Fashion Centre, Ltd., 771 P.2d 1033 (Utah 1989).

[4]Mudlitz v. Mutual Service Ins. Companies, 75 F.3d 391 (8th Cir. 1996) (applying Minnesota law).

[5]Robinson v. Langdon, 333 Ark. 662, 970 S.W.2d 292 (1998).

[6]Damrow v. Thumb Co-op. Terminal, Inc., 126 Mich. App. 354, 337 N.W.2d 338 (1983); Pine River State Bank v. Mettille, 333 N.W.2d 622 (Minn. 1983).

[7]Damrow v. Thumb Co-op. Terminal, Inc., 126 Mich. App. 354, 337 N.W.2d 338 (1983).

[Section 44]
[1]Wagenseller v. Scottsdale Memorial

637

EXHIBIT 3.1   *(continued)*

---

§ 44   82 AM JUR 2d

◆ **Observation:** The existence of an internal appeal procedure permits an inference of a fair treatment and a just cause requirement. The cases which hold that violation of a grievance procedure is a material breach of contract are few. Still, at least one court has held that postdischarge remedies must be made available to a terminated employee even if he or she was not aware of the rules.[2] On the other hand, where a handbook that required an exit interview before termination also reserved the right to discharge at any time, the presumption of employment at-will was not rebutted and the handbook did not operate to limit the circumstances of arbitrary dismissal.[3]

In the absence of clear, promissory language, the language of a summary of policies and benefits which sets forth the employer's employment policies, including a grievance policy for the resolution of work-related problems, does not create enforceable employment contract rights sufficient to overcome the presumption of an employment relationship terminable at will.[4]

§ 45   Specification of grounds for discipline or discharge

Research References

West's Key Number Digest, Civil Rights ⊕144; Master and Servant ⊕30(1.5)

Where specific grounds for discharge and discipline are set forth in an employers' handbook or other employment guidelines, discharged employees have sometimes been successful in arguing that such specified grounds are exclusive and that, consequently, the discharge of an employee on other grounds is wrongful.[1]

However, just as nonexclusive discharge procedures impose no obligation

---

Hosp., 147 Ariz. 370, 710 P.2d 1025 (1985); Pavadore v. School Committee of Canton, 19 Mass. App. Ct. 943, 473 N.E.2d 205, 22 Ed. Law Rep. 882 (1985); Jeffers v. Bishop Clarkson Memorial Hosp., 222 Neb. 829, 387 N.W.2d 692 (1986); Mobil Coal Producing, Inc. v. Parks, 704 P.2d 702 (Wyo. 1985).

[2]Pavadore v. School Committee of Canton, 19 Mass. App. Ct. 943, 473 N.E.2d 205, 22 Ed. Law Rep. 882 (1985).

[3]Ford v. Blue Cross & Blue Shield of Michigan, 150 Mich. App. 462, 389 N.W.2d 114 (1986).

[4]Bjorn v. Associated Regional and University Pathologists, Inc., 208 Ill. App. 3d 505, 153 Ill. Dec. 459, 567 N.E.2d 417 (1st Dist. 1990).

An at-will employee of a university could be terminated involuntarily where a grievance procedure was not an employment contract itself; the university never represented to the employee that the grievance procedure was part of his employment agreement; the em-

ployee did not negotiate or bargain for the terms of the grievance procedure either individually or as part of a group of employees. Mix v. University of New Orleans, 609 So. 2d 958, 79 Ed. Law Rep. 1146 (La. Ct. App. 4th Cir. 1992), writ denied, 612 So. 2d 83 (La. 1993).

[Section 45]

[1]Mycak v. Honeywell, Inc., 953 F.2d 798 (2d Cir. 1992) (applying New York law); Conley v. Board of Trustees of Grenada County Hosp., 707 F.2d 175 (5th Cir. 1983); Towns v. Emery Air Freight, Inc., 3 I.E.R. Cas. (BNA) 911, 1988 WL 156258 (S.D. Ohio 1988) (applying Ohio law); Damrow v. Thumb Co-op, Terminal, Inc., 126 Mich. App. 354, 337 N.W.2d 338 (1983); Frazier v. Minnesota Min. and Mfg. Co., 82 Or. App. 328, 728 P.2d 87 (1986); Berube v. Fashion Centre, Ltd., 771 P.2d 1033 (Utah 1989); Cook v. Heck's Inc., 176 W. Va. 368, 342 S.E.2d 453 (1986); Mobil Coal Producing, Inc. v. Parks, 704 P.2d 702 (Wyo. 1985).

EXHIBIT 3.2	Encyclopedia Template

Issue:	Citation Information:
	• volume number
	• encyclopedia
Date of events:	• topic title and section
	• date(s)

Date of research:

Searching and Finding:

located pertinent topic and sections by . . .	updated by . . .

Information and Implications:

- look for rules
- note exact location — which section, in main volume or pocket part
- connect information to client's situation

Next Steps:

questions to consider:	leads to pursue:

(at page 45). Encyclopedia indexes are extensive, complex, and detailed,[1] so you should spend some time looking up alternative terms, pursuing cross-references, and reading through the entries and subentries. Through the index, you should be able to identify one or more pertinent topics and may also identify one or more pertinent sections within a topic.

The second primary means of locating pertinent topics (but not sections within a topic) is through the topic list. See Exhibit 2.7 (at page 46). Am. Jur. 2d and C.J.S. both provide alphabetical topic lists in their index volumes.

Once you have located a potentially useful topic, you should look over the introductory material to the topic. You may find a synopsis of the topic, cross-references to other topics, and references to other commentary. You also will find one or more topic outlines. Review Exhibit 2.8 (at pages 47–48) for a general outline and a detailed outline. Scanning the topic outline(s) is an excellent way to get a big-picture overview of the topic and identify the most pertinent sections to read.

As you read the most pertinent sections, seek first to learn the pertinent legal rules. Note the implications of the rules for your client's situation and the numbers of the pertinent sections. Second, look for references to potentially pertinent authorities. Reading all of the sections within a part of your topic is often a good strategy.

Finally, be sure that you have the most current information in the encyclopedia. Most of the time you will read the material in the main volume and then update that material by checking the pocket part. See Exhibit 3.3 (at page 81). A pocket part is a set of pages inserted into a pocket in the back of a bound volume; it provides additional citations and brings the bound volume up to date (or typically within no more than one year of the present). The pocket part may provide additional text with supporting authorities or simply additional references. Some volumes have no pocket parts because the main volume was published recently; others have so much updating material that they have a separate supplementary pamphlet instead of a pocket part.

To research as efficiently as possible when a main volume has been updated, skim the main volume to learn which sections are pertinent and what the law has been and may still be. Then check the updating material. Synthesize the main volume and updating material as you take your notes; be sure to note whether a point comes from the main volume or the pocket part.

Exhibit 3.4 (at page 82) presents our template for researching in encyclopedias, filled in to reflect our research on the issue of breach of contract in Am. Jur. 2d.

Citing Encyclopedias: A proper cite to an encyclopedia includes its volume number, abbreviated title, topic name, section number, and year. Here are two examples:

☐ *Bluebook* Rule 15.8(a): 82 Am. Jur. 2d *Wrongful Discharge* § 44 (2003).

☐ *ALWD* Rule 26: 82 Am. Jur. 2d *Wrongful Discharge* § 44 (2003).

---

1. According to Thomson West, the 2008 index to Am. Jur. 2d contains over one million entries.

EXHIBIT 3.3	Encyclopedia Pocket Part, from American Jurisprudence 2d (paper source)

§ 40

Termination or Demotion of a Public Employee in Retaliation for Speaking Out as a Violation of Right of Free Speech, 22 Am. Jur. Proof of Facts 3d 203

Wrongful discharge—Bad Faith Dismissal of At to Will Employee, 48 Am. Jur. Proof of Facts 2d 183

Implied Promise Not to Terminate At to Will Employment Without Cause, 34 Am. Jur. Proof of Facts 2d 259

Reduction or Mitigation of Damages—Employment Contract, 11 Am. Jur. Proof of Facts 2d 679

Retaliatory Termination of Private Employment, 7 Am. Jur. Proof of Facts 2d 1

Defending Wrongful Discharge Cases, 36 Am. Jur. Trials 419

Wrongful Discharge of At to Will Employee, 31 Am. Jur. Trials 317

Am. Jur. Legal Forms 2d, Employment Contracts §§ 99:152 to 99:153.1, 99:152 to 99:153.1

Am. Jur. Pleading and Practice Forms, Master and Servant §§ 35, 49, 50, 54, 67 to 78, 35, 49, 50, 54, 67 to 78

Andrews & Maroko, Employment to At to Will in New York Remains Essentially Unchanged After a Century of Refinements, 71 N.Y. St. B.J. 8 (1999)

Callahan & Dworkin, The State of State Whistleblower Protection, 38 Am. Bus. L.J. 99 (2000)

Dominick, What's the Definition of "Public Policy" Wrongful Discharge? Time for Idaho Courts to Provide Guidance, Without Judicial Legislation, of Public Policy by Interpreting the Wrongful Discharge Cause of Action, 35 Idaho L. Rev. 285 (1999)

Estlund, Wrongful Discharge Protections in an At to Will World, 74 Tex. L. Rev. 1655 (1996)

Galberry, Employers Beware: South Carolina's Exception to the At to Will Employment Doctrine Is Likely to Keep Expanding, 51 S.C. L. Rev. 406 (2000)

Hoffman, Whistleblower Protection: Is Retaliatory Discharge Allowed Under the Employment to At to Will Doctrine in Admiralty? 21 Tul. Mar. L.J. 171 (1996)

Knittig, Everything You Wanted to Know About Missouri's Public Policy Exception but Didn't Know You Should Ask, 61 Mo. L. Rev. 949 (1996)

Meadows, Dancing Around Employment At to Will: Can Fraud Provide Plaintiffs a Way to Hold Employers Liable? 65 Mo. L. Rev. 1003 (2000)

Moberly, Cranking the Wrongful Discharge Ratchet: Judicial Abrogation of Legislative Exceptions to the Public Policy Exception, 24 Seton Hall Legis. J. 43 (1999)

Moberly & Doran, The Nose of the Camel: Extending the Public Policy Exception Beyond the Wrongful Discharge Context, 13 Lab. Law. 371 (1997)

Vanse, Wrongful Discharge Law Turns Toward the Plaintiff, 27 Pepp. L. Rev. 281 (2000)

Wagoner, The Public Policy Exception to the Employment At Will Doctrine in Ohio: A Need

AMERICAN JURISPRUDENCE 2D

for a Legislative Approach, 57 Ohio St. L.J. 1799 (1996)

Walsh & Schwarz, State Common Law Wrongful Discharge Doctrines: Up to Date, Refinement, and Rationales, 33 Am. Bus. L.J. 645 (1996)

Chagnon, Termination of Employment

Holloway & Leech, Employment Termination: Rights and Remedies

Perritt, Employee Dismissal Law and Practice §§ 1.13 to 1.63 (3rd ed. 1992, Supp. 1995)

Practicing Law Institute, Wrongful Termination Claims: What Plaintiffs and Defendants Have to Know

Sessions, Wrongful Termination Law; Cases and Materials

(2) Regarding Discharge and Discipline

§ 41 Discipline and discharge procedures, generally

Cases

Employee of the District of Columbia's Alcoholic Beverage Regulation Administration (ABRA) was an at-will employee with no property interest in continued employment protected by the Fourteenth Amendment, despite claim that he had a legitimate expectation of continued employment arising from personnel regulations; those regulations did not establish any extra procedural protections for District employees, but only set forth additional categories of conduct for which employees could face disciplinary action. Evans v. District of Columbia, 391 F. Supp. 2d 160 (D.D.C. 2005).

§ 44 Grievance and appeal procedures

Research References

West's Key Number Digest, Civil Rights ⚓144, 157, 449; Contracts ⚓108(1); Counties ⚓67; Estoppel ⚓85; Federal Civil Procedure ⚓2497.1; Judgment ⚓181(21); Labor Relations ⚓773.1, 776; Master and Servant ⚓4, 6.10, 6.15, 6.30), 8(1), 18.5, 30(1 to 1.15, 54; Officers and Public Employees ⚓66; Principal and Agent ⚓33; States ⚓18.49

A.L.R. Digest, Master and Servant §§ 51 to 55

A.L.R. Index, Discharge from Employment or Office; Ethics and Ethical Matters; Labor and Employment; Professional Persons; Public Policy; Retaliation and Revenge

C.J.S., Employer to Employee Relationships §§ 68, 73, 77, 80 to 105

Termination or Demotion of a Public Employee in Retaliation for Speaking Out as a Violation of Right of Free Speech, 22 Am. Jur. Proof of Facts 3d 203

Wrongful Discharge—Bad Faith Dismissal of At to Will Employee, 48 Am. Jur. Proof of Facts 2d 183

Implied Promise Not to Terminate At to Will Employment Without Cause, 34 Am. Jur. Proof of Facts 2d 259

44

EXHIBIT 3.4	Encyclopedia Template for Canoga Case

Issue:	Citation Information:
Did the employer breach a contract by failing to follow the procedures in the handbook?	• *Vol. 82* • *Am. Jur. 2d* • *Wrongful Discharge § 44* • *2003 main volume; 2007 supplement*
Date of events: *Sept. 7, 2007*	

Date of Research: *Nov. 10, 2007*

Search and Find:

located pertinent topic and sections by . . . *2008 index: Employment Contracts →* *Wrongful Discharge → Discipline and* *Discharge Procedures → Grievances.*	updated by . . . *2007 pocket part.*

Information and Implications:

- *Some courts have held that an employer breaches a contract when it fails to abide by its rules regarding post-termination appeals. § 44 main volume*
- *The summary of policies must be in "clear, promissory language" to create an enforceable contract. Id.*
- *An appeal procedure permits inference of just cause. Id.*

- *The board in our case did not follow its handbook's procedures.*

Next Steps:

questions to consider: *Is the language clear and promissory enough?*	leads to pursue: • *No New Mexico case.* • *Wagenseller v. Scottsdale Memorial Hospital from Arizona — 710 P.2d 1025.* • *Lots of commentary and key number references in pocket part, including Labor Relations 773 & 776, Master & Servant 4, etc.*

C. WHAT ELSE?

Tables of Cited Laws and Cases: If you begin your research in Am. Jur. 2d or C.J.S. with a citation to a pertinent federal statute, regulation, court rule, or a uniform act, you can consult either encyclopedia's table of cited laws. Review Exhibit 2.9 (at page 49). Am. Jur. 2d also has a table listing statutes by their names, the Popular Names Table. C.J.S. has a table of cases, permitting you to locate a discussion of a known case.

New Topics Service: In addition to pocket parts, Am. Jur. 2d provides the New Topic Service, a looseleaf binder containing topics too new to be located in the appropriate bound volume; it merits a brief check as you complete your research in Am. Jur. 2d.

Correlation Tables: On occasion, a topic is reorganized to better reflect current law. If you know about a pertinent section from the older version of an encyclopedia and want to locate the corresponding material in a newer version, you should consult a correlation table.

Specialized Encyclopedias: Specialized encyclopedias cover some major areas of law, such as constitutional law and international law. Some are very authoritative within their fields.

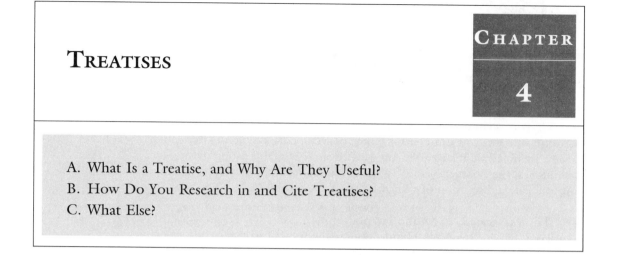

TREATISES

A.   WHAT IS A TREATISE, AND WHY ARE THEY USEFUL?

Put simply, a treatise is a form of commentary that systematically and extensively explores a legal subject. The subject may be quite broad (such as contracts or employment law), or it may be quite narrow (such as a single statute protecting disabled workers). Law professors and lawyers write treatises, as do the staffs of the major legal publishing companies.

A good treatise presents a thorough scholarly discussion of its subject. A treatise typically contains at least three parts: (1) the text itself, with footnotes or endnotes containing supporting citations and tangential remarks; (2) internal finding tools, such as an index, one or more tables of contents, and lists of authorities; and (3) supporting materials, such as an appendix of pertinent statutes. The text explains the law, setting out rules, policies, and examples. A few also critique the law and propose legal reforms. A treatise's text typically is organized by chapters and then by sections or paragraphs (rather than pages).

A treatise is often a good choice when you know what subject your client's situation involves but still need to learn about the legal framework and major rules. Furthermore, although treatises are commentary, not the law, a well written treatise by a highly respected author is highly credible.

In addition, a good treatise provides abundant references to the law and other commentary sources.

Treatises can have drawbacks. Some treatises are updated, but many are not. Some treatises are more credible, better researched, more clearly organized, and more comprehensive than others. Finally, although treatises abound, there may still be a few subjects, whether new or obscure, on which no one has yet written a good treatise.

Most treatises are published initially in books. A paper treatise may consist of a single volume or multiple volumes in hardbound, softbound, or looseleaf form. A looseleaf treatise consists of separate pages held together by some type of binder, which facilitates updating. In recent years, more and more treatises have become available online, typically through the commercial service of the treatise's publisher, e.g., a treatise published by Thomson West would be available through Westlaw.

As a novice legal researcher, you may find it difficult to determine what is and what is not a treatise. The word *treatise* may be, but generally is not, in the title. The following categories of books are not research treatises, although they are useful for other purposes:

- ☐ Textbooks: The titles of textbooks tend to include terms such as *cases and materials* or *readings in*. Textbooks typically present excerpts from the law rather than summarize and comment on the law.
- ☐ Study aids: Most study aids present the law in fairly simplified form and lack footnotes with supporting citations. This category includes series such as Thomson West's *Nutshells*, Aspen's *Examples and Explanations*, and LexisNexis' *Understanding* [a subject] series.
- ☐ Manuals for continuing legal education (CLE) courses: CLE manuals generally have terms such as *institute* or *seminar* in their titles. CLE manuals are covered in Chapter 8.

On the other hand, one type of book you may use for study purposes can serve you well early in your research: the hornbook.[1] A student hornbook is a single-volume treatise that explains the basic principles of law in a particular field, provides supporting citations, is written by a well regarded scholar in the field, and is designed for law students.

A treatise that is pertinent to the Canoga case is Lex K. Larson's *Employment Discrimination*. Two pages from that treatise appear as Exhibit 4.1 (at pages 86–87).

---

1. The term is derived from the name of a child's first book, covered with horn to protect it from soiling.

| Exhibit 4.1 | Treatise Text, from Employment Discrimination (paper source) |

on a benefit plan that provided twenty-four months of disability benefits for individuals suffering from a mental or psychological disability but provided a longer period of benefits for individuals suffering from physical benefits, the question was whether the different treatment of mental and physical disabilities was used as a subterfuge to evade the purposes of the ADA. The court rejected the plaintiffs' argument that the distinction had to rely on "sound actuarial principles" since the benefit plan was adopted prior to the enactment of the ADA. The court relied on earlier cases interpreting the subterfuge provision in the Age Discrimination in Employment Act and explained that the Supreme Court had recognized "that the ordinary meaning of subterfuge includes a specific intent to circumvent or evade a statutory purpose" and held that "there could be no such intent if the challenged provision had been adopted prior to the statute's enactment."[30]

§ 155.06   Restrictions on Smoking

The ADA provides that nothing in the Act prevents a covered entity from

---

Fitts v. Fannie Mae, 344 U.S. App. D.C. 310, 236 F.3d 1, 11 AD Cases 612 (2001). Following the rationale in EEOC v. Aramark Corp., 341 U.S. App. D.C. 38, 208 F.3d 266, 10 AD Cases 798 (2000), the court held that the difference in benefits for those suffering from mental disabilities and those suffering from physical disabilities did not violate the ADA because this difference was instituted prior to the enactment of the ADA. The court also rejected the plaintiff's argument that the retention of the policy after the ADA was enacted violated the ADA.

Leonard F. v. Israel Discount Bank, 199 F.3d 99, 10 AD Cases 13 (2d Cir. 1999). The district court dismissed the plaintiff's mental disability claim, holding that the long-term disability policy limiting the benefit period for mental disabilities but not for physical disabilities was protected under the safe harbor provisions of the ADA. The court held that the insurance policy's restrictions complied with state law and was not a subterfuge to evade the purposes of the ADA because it was adopted before the ADA's enactment. The Second Circuit, though agreeing with the district court's reasoning, held that it had erred by dismissing the complaint under Fed. R. Civ. P. 12(b)(6) based upon the finding that the policy predated the ADA when there was no information as to the date of its adoption in the pleadings.

Saks v. Franklin Covey Co., 117 F. Supp. 2d 318, 84 FEP 33, 11 AD Cases 11 (S.D.N.Y. 2000), aff'd on other grounds, 316 F.3d 337, 90 FEP 1266 (2d Cir. 2003), district court decision overruled in part on other grounds as stated in Kammeuller v. Loomis, Fargo & Co., 285 F. Supp. 2d 1200 (D. Minn. 2003), rev'd 383 F.3d 779, 15 AD Cases 1601 (8th Cir. 2004). The ADA became law in 1991 but this employer's insurance plan had excluded surgical impregnation procedures from coverage since 1989. The plan, therefore, could not have been adopted as a subterfuge to avoid the statute.

[29] 341 U.S. App. D.C. 38, 208 F.3d 266, 10 AD Cases 798 (2000).

[30] 208 F.3d at 269, 10 AD Cases at 801.

EXHIBIT 4.1   *(continued)*

---

§ 155D.01   EMPLOYMENT DISCRIMINATION   155-46

prohibiting or imposing restrictions on smoking in places of employment.[1] This clause curiously appears under the heading "Relationship to Other Laws." The legislative history does not provide any clues about how this came to be or what it means: does it imply that only government-imposed restrictions such as anti-smoking ordinances are referred to? The breadth of the language and the purposes of the ADA militate against any such narrow construction, so that purely employer-imposed workplace smoking rules are no doubt legitimized as well.

§ 155D.01   Digest of Additional Cases for § 155.01

Note 8— Discharge for misconduct, poor performance and the like can also be legitimate despite the fact that the misconduct or poor performance is related to or arises out of the worker's disability.

Seventh Circuit:

D. Illinois: Vieira v. Bombardier Motor Corp. of Am., 11 AD Cases 1663 (S.D. Ill. 2000). The plaintiff, who suffered from diabetes, was terminated after he violated the employer's attendance policy. The defendant successfully argued that the plaintiff was not terminated because of his diabetic condition, but rather because the plaintiff failed to follow medical advice, which led to an exacerbation of the condition and his absences. Contrary to his physician's orders, the plaintiff drank to the point of intoxication, sometimes on nights before he was to report to work at 7 a.m., and did not eat breakfast or take insulin in the morning before work. The court granted summary judgment for the defendant.

Eighth Circuit: See also:

Spades v. City of Walnut Ridge, 186 F.3d 897, 9 AD Cases 1015 (8th Cir. 1999). The plaintiff had previously shot himself in the head in a suicide attempt, but his depression was under control and no longer disabling. Nevertheless, defendant's concern about potential liability for negligent hiring of a police officer with a known history of violence constituted a legitimate nondiscriminatory reason for not rehiring him.

Harris v. Polk County, 103 F.3d 696, 6 AD Cases 545 (8th Cir. 1996). A legal stenographer, discharged after pleading guilty to a shoplifting charge, reapplied for employment with the county attorney years later. The county attorney refused to consider her application based on her criminal record. She sued for disability discrimination, alleging that the shoplifting was the result of a mental illness, which was now resolved, and that the county attorney discriminated against her

---

[1] 42 U.S.C. § 12201(b).

(Rel. 73-6/2006   Pub.626)

B. HOW DO YOU RESEARCH IN AND CITE TREATISES?

1. Researching in Treatises

Exhibit 4.2, our template for treatises, presents the elements of researching in treatises. In brief, treatise research entails formulating your research issue, locating and selecting a good treatise, locating and reading pertinent material, deriving useful information and considering its implications for your clients' situation, and planning your next steps. We recommend two approaches — paper treatises and online treatises — in that order.

Treatises in paper

▶ Locate treatises through a library catalog, shelf-browsing, a recommendation, or a reference in another source.

▶ Assess the value of various treatises.

▶ Use the index or tables of contents to locate pertinent material.

▶ Read the text.

▶ Check for updates.

Because you are likely to use a treatise when your knowledge is fairly limited, paper research, which permits easy browsing across parts of the book and reading at length, is generally a good choice. Furthermore, many treatises are not available online. When you search in a commercial publisher's databases, you may find only that publisher's treatises.

Locate and select a treatise: To find treatises on your research topic, think first about which legal subject encompasses the problem you are researching. You then may use any of these techniques:

☐ Look in your library's catalog.

☐ Find out the call number range of the subject. Then browse the shelves with those call numbers, or ask at the library reserve desk for treatises with those call numbers. Exhibit 4.3 (at page 90) lists the standard scheme of call numbers for legal subjects, developed by the Library of Congress.

☐ Ask a professor, librarian, lawyer, or colleague who is knowledgeable about the subject for a recommendation.

☐ Look in a textbook for a citation in the footnotes, endnotes, or bibliography.

EXHIBIT 4.2	Treatise Template

Issue:	Citation Information:
	• author • title • volume, page, section • date • possibly edition • *ALWD Manual:* publisher
Date of events:	
Date of research:	
Search and Find:	
located treatise by . . .	credibility factors: author's credentials, multiple editions, etc.
located pertinent passages by . . .	updated by . . .

Information and Implications:

- look for rules, policies, examples
- note exact location — which section, in main volume or update
- connect information to client's situation

Next Steps:

questions to consider:	leads to pursue:

EXHIBIT 4.3	Library of Congress Call Numbers

Administrative Law KF 5401-5425

Antitrust KF 1631-1657

Banking KF 966-1032

Bankruptcy KF 1501-1548

Business Associations, generally KF 1355-1480

Civil and Political Rights KF 4741-4786

Civil Procedure KF 8810-9075

Commercial Transactions KF 871-962

Conflict of Laws KF 410-418

Constitutional Law KF 4501-5130

Contracts, quasi-contracts KF 801-1244

Copyright KF 2986-3080

Corporations KF 1384-1480

Criminal Law KF 9201-9763

Criminal Procedure KF 9601-9763

Education Policy and Law KF 4101-4257

Employment Discrimination KF 3464-3470.5

Environmental Law KF 3775-3816

Equity KF 398-400

Evidence

   In civil cases KF 8931-8969

   In criminal cases KF 9660-9678

Family Law 501-553

Federal Courts KF 8700-8807

Immigration Law KF 4801-4836

Insurance Law KF 1146-1238

International Law JX or JZ or KZ

Jurisprudence KF 379-382

Juvenile Criminal Law and Procedure KF 9771-9827

Labor Law KF 3301-3580

Land-Use Planning KF 5691-5710

Legal History KF 350-374

The Legal Profession KF 297-334

Legal Research and Writing KF 240-251

Legislative Process KF 4945-4952

Local Government/Municipal Law KF 5300-5332

Medical Legislation KF 3821-3832

Mental Health Law KF 480, 3828-3828.5

Oil and Gas KF 1841-1870

Patents and Trademarks KF 3091-3194

Public Safety KF 3941-3977

Real Property KF 560-698

Regulation of Industry, Trade, and Commerce KF 1600-2940

Secured Transactions KF 1046-1062

Securities Regulations KF 1066-1084, KF 1428-1457

Social Legislation KF 3300-3771

Taxation KF 6271-6795

Torts KF 1246-1327

Trial Practice (Civil) KF 8911-8925

Uniform State Laws KF 165

Water Resources KF 5551-5590

Wills and Trusts KF 726-780

Whatever the medium of your library's catalog—most are computer databases—you most likely will be able to search for treatises in various ways. A subject search is the broadest search, so it usually will retrieve the largest number of treatises. Of course, you must work within the subject headings used by the cataloger, which usually are based on the Library of Congress system. Be sure to try various subjects if your initial choices do not work, and take advantage of the cross-references. Another alternative in an electronic catalog is to employ a key-word search, which permits you to locate all catalog entries containing the words you enter; especially if your topic has distinctive terms, key-word searching may be a useful place to start, with a subject search as a follow-up if you want more choices.

You may find more than one treatise on your subject. Treatises vary in quality and in usefulness for a particular project. To select an appropriate treatise for your needs, consider the following factors:

Coverage: Pick a treatise with the scope and level of detail you need. You might first read about your topic in a single-volume treatise with a broad scope, such as a hornbook, and then read a more detailed discussion in a multivolume treatise.

Currency: In general you will want to select a treatise that has been published or updated recently. Check the copyright dates of the main volume as well as any updating materials, described later. Because there always is a delay between the completion of the text and its publication, look too for any statements about the dates of coverage of the text. In general, looseleaf treatises are updated more frequently than others.

Credibility: Some treatises are known as the classics in their fields; these treatises are especially credible. Select a treatise that has been cited in a textbook or course syllabus, pick a treatise that is kept on reserve, or find a treatise that has been published in multiple editions. To determine whether the author is a true expert, check the author's credentials as noted in the treatise, check periodical indexes or library catalogs to see if the author has written extensively on the subject, or use a treatise written by the author of a textbook on your topic. Furthermore, select a book from a well regarded publisher. Aspen, BNA, LexisNexis and Matthew Bender, RIA, and Thomson West are highly reputable publishers.

Organization: Treatises are organized in a variety of ways, including topically, such as by statute or claims and defenses, or chronologically, such as by phases of a transaction or stages of litigation. They also vary in the number and quality of the tables of contents, indexes, and tables of authorities. Select a treatise that permits you to locate pertinent passages relatively easily.

Locate and read pertinent passages: Once you have selected a treatise, you most likely will use either the treatise's index or tables of contents to locate pertinent material within the treatise. If you use the index approach, be sure to consult all indexes; a treatise may have both a main index and one or more updates. Similarly, many treatises include both a summary table of contents and a detailed table of contents; start with the summary table of contents, then move to the detailed table of contents. If you already know the name of a pertinent case or the name or citation of a statute or rule on point, you could consult a table of cases, statutes, or rules, to learn where the case or statute is cited in the treatise.

As you read pertinent material, look for an explanation of the law— including rules, policies, and examples—as well as a critique of the law (if presented). In addition, note references to potentially pertinent law and commentary. Take time to browse sections adjacent to the one you start with; reading a part of or, indeed, an entire chapter is a very good idea. Finally, pursue cross-references.

Check for updates as well. Most multivolume treatises have updates, as do some single-volume treatises. Updates are organized by page, paragraph, or section to parallel the material in the main volume and come in several forms:

☐ Pocket parts: These updates are pamphlets that slip into a pocket on an inside cover of a volume. Pocket parts usually are replaced annually. If a pocket part becomes too large, it may be replaced by a softcover supplement.

☐ Supplemental volumes: Some treatises have separate hardbound or softcover updating volumes, which are usually shelved next to the volumes they update.

☐ Looseleaf supplements: Treatises published in looseleaf binders may be updated with looseleaf supplements that are inserted periodically into the looseleaf volumes behind a tab for supplemental pages.

☐ Looseleaf page replacements: Replacement pages are issued and inserted at regular intervals or on an as-needed basis. A replacement page typically indicates its date of issuance.

Updates usually contain supplementary indexes and tables, which you should be sure to consult. If the treatise you are using was not published in the last few years and has not been updated, check for a newer edition or online version, which may be more current.

Exhibit 4.4 (at page 93) is our treatises template filled in to reflect our research in a paper treatise discussing employment termination.

Treatises online

▶ Tap into the service's collection of sources on the subject area of your research.

▶ Assess the value of the treatise.

▶ Locate pertinent material by working through the tables of contents or run a key-word search in the index or the full text.

▶ Read the text.

Researching online treatises, if indeed there is one covering your topics, entails the same basic steps as researching in paper treatises. You may find it more difficult to read a treatise online than in paper. On the other hand, an online treatise offers several advantages over paper in locating pertinent information, connecting to sources cited in the treatise, and updating.

The main way to identify and locate a pertinent online treatise is to tap into the service's collection of sources pertinent to a practice area. Another option is to check for a known treatise in the service's directory. As you consider using a specific treatise, read its database description to learn about its authors, currency, and appendices.

EXHIBIT 4.4	Treatise Template for Canoga Case — Paper

Topic:	Citation Information:
Might nicotine addiction be a protected disability?	• *Lex K. Larson* • *Employment Discrimination* • *Vol. 9, § 155.06* • *2d ed.* • *Page is current to 6/2006; other pages to 2007* • *Matthew Bender*
Date of events: *Sept. 7, 2007*	

Date of Research: *Nov. 11, 2007*

Search and Find:

located treatise by . . .	credibility factors:
Subject search in library's catalog: Discrimination in Employment — Law and Legislation — U.S.	• *2d ed. plus update* • *1st ed. by Duke U. prof. & Sec'y of Labor* • *2d ed. by Duke lecturer* • *Matthew Bender/ LexisNexis*
located pertinent passages by . . .	updated by . . .
Summary table of contents → vol. 9 re ADA. *Vol. 9 table of contents → ch. 155.* *Scan of ch. 155 → § 155.06.*	• *Page is current to 6/2006.* • *New cases for part are described in digest section at end of part; none for § 155.06.*

Information and Implications:
• *42 U.S.C. § 12201(b) says that the Americans with Disabilities Act does not prevent an entity from prohibiting or imposing restrictions on smoking in the workplace. § 155.06.* • *The purpose of this is not clear; it should apply to employer workplace rules. Id.* • *This seems to permit the orchestra rule as to the workplace.* • *If smoking can be prohibited, nicotine addition is unlikely to be a protected disability.*

Next Steps:

questions to consider:	leads to pursue:
If this covers workplace rules, what is the rule for prohibitions of smoking outside the workplace?	*Federal ADA — 42 U.S.C. § 12201(b).*

Once you have selected a promising treatise, to locate pertinent material within its text, one good strategy is to scan the major topics in the table of contents and then drill down one or more levels to zero in on the most promising sections. Another good option is to search within the treatise's index or within the full text for key words that should appear in pertinent material; in this respect, online treatises offer more options than paper treatises.

Reading the pertinent information in an online treatise is both similar to and different from reading a paper treatise. The text may be identical in paper and online, although the online treatise may be updated more seamlessly. Browsing in a paper treatise is easier, although online treatises may permit moving to the previous section and the next one. The references to potentially pertinent law and commentary may be very similar; some online treatises have more references than their paper counterparts.

A major advantage of the online format is that it permits linking directly to the cited materials. This advantage can prove to be a disadvantage, however, if you pursue the links without keeping track of where you are and slowing down enough to read each source to ascertain its pertinence to your client's situation. Note that our template for each type of research includes a space for how you found the source and a space for leads to pursue.

Exhibit 4.5 (at page 95) is our treatise template, filled in to reflect our research in an online treatise covering discrimination on the basis of disability.

2.   Citing Treatises

A citation to a treatise includes the full name(s) of the author(s); the volume number (if the treatise has more than one volume); the main title of the treatise as it appears on the title page (not the cover); the page, section, or paragraph number; the edition (if other than the first); and the year of publication of the main volume or supplement you are using. The *ALWD Manual* also includes the publisher. Here are two examples:

☐ *Bluebook* Rule 15: 9 Lex K. Larson, *Employment Discrimination* § 155.06 (2d ed. Supp. 2007).
☐ *ALWD* Rule 22: Lex K. Larson, *Employment Discrimination* vol. 9, § 155.06 (2d ed., Matthew Bender Supp. 2007).

C.   WHAT ELSE?

Additional Techniques for Finding Treatises: The *Index to Legal Periodicals and Books* (covered in more detail in Chapter 5) indexes some treatises. On occasion, periodicals publish bibliographies on certain subjects, including treatises along with other sources. A fairly new tool is IndexMaster, a

EXHIBIT 4.5	Treatise Template for Canoga Case — Online

Topic:	**Citation Information:**
Might nicotine addiction be a protected disability?	• *Lex K. Larson* • *Employment Discrimination* • *Part LIV Americans with Disabilities Act of 1990* • *9-151 Summary and History § 151.05* • *LexisNexis/Mathew Bender*
Date of events: *Sept. 7, 2007*	

Date of research: *Nov. 10, 2007*

Search and Find:

located treatise by . . .	credibility factors:
LexisNexis: Legal → Area of Law — By Topic → Labor & Employment → Search Analysis, Law Reviews & Journals.	• *By president of Employment Law Research* • *Current to August 2007* • *LexisNexis/Mathew Bender.*
located pertinent passages by . . .	updated by . . .
Full-text terms-and-connectors search: *smok! w/p disab!*	• *Current to August 2007* • *Follow-up sections with digests of new cases (not so for our section).*

Information and Implications:

• *The ADA is clear that it does not affect the right to ban smoking in workplaces. § 151.05*

• *This seems to permit the orchestra rule as to the workplace.*
• *If smoking can be prohibited, nicotine addition is unlikely to be a protected disability.*

Next Steps:

questions to consider:	leads to pursue:
If this covers workplace rules, what is the rule for prohibition of smoking outside the workplace?	*§ 155.06 of treatise.*

subscription service that currently contains the tables of contents and indexes of over 8,000 legal treatises, searchable by key words, authors, or titles. WorldCat is a comprehensive database of materials in over 9,000 libraries, both legal and nonlegal, with over 85 million bibliographic records as of mid-2007. Keep in mind that your library will not own all of the treatises in these very extensive lists.

Keeping Up to Date: If you find a particularly pertinent section of an online treatise and will be working on the project for some time, you may want to sign up to receive alerts when new material on your topic is added, if possible.

Historical Legal Treatises: For history buffs or research projects on the origins or development of a modern law, several significant collections of historical treatises, such as *The Making of Modern Law*, are now online.

LEGAL PERIODICALS

A. WHAT IS A LEGAL PERIODICAL, AND WHY ARE THEY USEFUL?

A legal periodical, a form of commentary, contains articles on a range of legal topics and is published on a periodic basis, such as quarterly, monthly, or weekly. Most legal periodicals fall into one of four broad categories: law reviews, bar journals, commercial legal newspapers, and newsletters.

First, the most prominent type of legal periodical is the law review. Law review articles not only describe the current state of the law but also explore underlying policies, critique current legal rules, and advocate law reform. The articles are written by professors; lawyers; lawmakers, most often judges; and law students. Unlike most academic journals, most law reviews are staffed by upper-class students, who select and edit the work; relatively few are peer-reviewed. Not surprisingly, most law reviews carry the names of their host schools, e.g., the *Albany Law Review*. Most law reviews publish articles on a wide variety of topics, although some focus on a specific area, e.g., the *Berkeley Journal of Employment and Labor Law*, and a few are interdisciplinary, e.g., the *Law & Psychology Review*. There are about 150 general-scope and

250 special-focus law reviews in the United States. Most publish one volume per year in two to eight issues, each containing various types of papers, listed in Exhibit 5.1. For efficiency, this chapter uses *article* to refer to any type of paper.

Second, many legal organizations, known as "bar associations," publish journals. For example the American Bar Association, by far the largest national association of lawyers, publishes the *ABA Journal*. The articles in bar journals tend to be more practical than theoretical. Bar journals also report on important legal developments, such as changes in court rules, and cover nonlegal topics of interest to lawyers, such as law firm management. Some ABA sections publish journals that fairly closely resemble academic law reviews and focus on that section's area of law, such as *The Labor Lawyer*, published by the Section of Labor and Employment Law.

Third, for many areas of practice, commercial legal publishers publish journals with articles on emerging legal issues, oriented toward practicing lawyers. In addition, commercial legal newsletters alert readers to new cases, statutes, or rules and also cover recent conferences, studies, and other topics of interest to lawyers in the particular practice area; an example is *Employment Law Weekly*. Most newsletters are quite short and appear frequently, e.g., monthly, weekly, or even daily.

Fourth, commercial legal newspapers typically report on new court decisions and other changes in the law, carry legal notices, and present stories about interesting people or significant events in the legal profession. Some

EXHIBIT 5.1	Types of Periodical Articles
article	a long piece with extensive citations typically written by a professor, lawyer, or lawmaker (typically a judge)
essay	a shorter piece with fewer citations written by a professor, lawyer, or lawmaker
commentary	a short piece responding to a significant lead article by a prominent author
comment or note	a long piece written by a student
case comment or case note	a shorter piece written by a student that focuses on a specific case
recent developments or survey	a set of pieces all on one subject, generally written by a group of faculty and students
symposium	an issue consisting of articles and student-written pieces on one subject
book review	a critique of a recently published book

legal newspapers are national in scope, e.g., the *National Law Journal*; others cover one city or state, e.g., the *Los Angeles Daily Journal*.

A good periodical article can be very useful. Most articles cover their subjects in depth; indeed, you may find a lengthy article on a very narrow subject. You are likely to find a wealth of references to the law, such as cases and statutes; other commentary, such as treatises and other articles; and some nonlegal sources. Many articles also provide valuable background, such as historical information or statistical data. You may find a critique of present law and proposals for law reform; although law review articles are merely commentary, a few have indeed prompted changes in the law. Finally, compared to other commentary, law review articles can be written and published fairly quickly, so they are a good source for discussion of new legal topics.

Periodical articles have disadvantages as well. An article loses currency quickly because the information is current only to the date the article was completed, which may be some time ago, and there is no updating process, as with other types of commentary. In addition, some analysis is idiosyncratic; you need to consider whether it is too unusual to be accepted before you rely on it heavily. Finally, even though periodicals abound, it is possible there will be no article on your topic.

Most well established legal periodicals are published in paper. Because the Internet offers a means of quickly and widely distributing material, not surprisingly, online periodical collections have come to dominate the field. Lexis and Westlaw have large periodicals databases. HeinOnline, a subscription service, encompasses articles from 1,000 legal and law-related periodicals. At the time this was written, fairly few well regarded periodicals were published only online.

For an excerpt of an article pertinent to the Canoga case, examine Exhibit 5.2 (at page 100), copied from a paper volume. An excerpt from the online version of this article appears as Exhibit 1.5 (at pages 19–20).

B.   HOW DO YOU RESEARCH IN AND CITE LEGAL PERIODICALS?

1.   Researching in Periodicals

As shown in Exhibit 5.3 (at page 101), our legal periodicals template, researching in periodicals entails formulating a specific research issue, using an index of periodical articles or a key-word search in a periodicals database to identify pertinent article(s), reading the article(s) to derive useful information and considering its implications for your client's situation, and planning your next steps.

Two standard approaches to periodicals research start differently — in an index or with a key-word full-text search; both are described below. The major resources you are likely to use when researching periodicals are summarized in Exhibit 5.4 (at page 102). An optional follow-up step is to cite a helpful article to identify newer articles on the same topic and cases citing the article.

| EXHIBIT 5.2 | Law Review Article, from Albany Law Review (paper source) |

128   Albany Law Review   [Vol. 70

recognized it as a legitimate basis for legal redress.[87] The right to privacy is protected by four separate torts,[88] each of which protects individuals from interference with their interest in leading a "private life, free from the prying eyes, ears and publications of others."[89] The right of privacy arguably implicated by a private employer's consideration of leisure-time smoking is an unreasonable intrusion upon the seclusion of another.[90]

However, the privacy tort of unreasonable intrusion upon the seclusion of another affords little protection for an employee whose employer discriminates against leisure-time smokers. The right to be free from intrusion upon seclusion requires any actionable intrusion to be not only unreasonable, but also intrusive upon the private affairs of the plaintiff.[91] The mere fact that smoking may take place in the privacy of the home is insufficient to render it a private activity subject to tort protection.[92] In the case of off-duty smoking, those courts which have considered whether leisure-time smoking is a private affair implicating a legitimate privacy interest have concluded that it is not.[93] Smokers must disclose their status as smokers when being seated in restaurants, renting hotel and motel rooms, and renting cars.[94] Today, smokers must reveal that they smoke in almost every aspect of life.[95] Thus, a claim for intrusion upon seclusion cannot be maintained where the activity, like smoking, is one which is habitually disclosed or undertaken in public.[96]

In addition, most employers who police off-duty smoking require

---

[87] *See* RESTATEMENT (SECOND) OF TORTS § 652A cmt. a (noting that the first judicial recognition of the right to privacy was in 1905).

[88] The four tort actions under the rubric of invasion of privacy are: (1) "unreasonable intrusion upon the seclusion of another," (2) "appropriation of the other's name or likeness," (3) "unreasonable publicity given to the other's private life," and (4) "publicity that unreasonably places the other in a false light before the public." *Id.* § 652A(2).

[89] *Id.* § 652A cmt. b.

[90] *See id.* § 652B. The Restatement provides: "One who intentionally intrudes, physically or otherwise, upon the solitude or seclusion of another or his private affairs or concerns, is subject to liability to the other for invasion of his privacy, if the intrusion would be highly offensive to a reasonable person." *Id.*

[91] *Id.*

[92] *See, e.g.*, Swerdlick v. Koch, 721 A.2d 849, 858 (R.I. 1998) ("Activities occurring in plain view of the public are not entitled to the protection of [a] privacy statute merely because they occur on private property in the vicinity of the actor's home.").

[93] *See, e.g.*, City of N. Miami v. Kurtz, 653 So. 2d 1025, 1029 (Fla. 1995).

[94] *Id.* at 1028.

[95] *Id.*

[96] *See, e.g.*, Gill v. Hearst Publ'g Co., 253 P.2d 441, 445 (Cal. 1953) (finding that plaintiffs had waived their right to privacy when they were photographed in an affectionate pose in a public place).

EXHIBIT 5.3	Legal Periodicals Template

Issue:	Citation Information:
	• author
	• title
	• volume
	• journal
Date of events:	• page number
	• date

Date of Research:

Search and Find:

located article by . . .	selection factors: currency, scope, reputation of journal or author, etc.

Information and Implications:

- look for description of law
- look for critique
- look for pertinent nonlegal information
- note exact location of pertinent information
- connect information to client's situation

Next Steps:

questions to consider:	leads to pursue:

EXHIBIT 5.4	Major Online Periodicals Resources

Periodical Indexes	*Periodical Compilations*
Index to Legal Periodicals and Books • Westlaw • WilsonWeb	Hein Online • retrieve known article • full-text key-word search
LegalTrac/Legal Resource Index • Westlaw • Gale Group LexisNexis	LexisNexis' U.S. & Canadian Law Reviews, Combined • retrieve known article • full-text key-word searches
Periodical Citators LexisNexis' Shepard's Westlaw's KeyCite	Westlaw's JLR (Journals & Law Reviews) • retrieve known article • full-text key-word searching

Periodicals through indexes

▶ Select a periodicals index.
▶ Conduct a subject search and possibly also a key-word search in the index.
▶ Assess the identified articles.
▶ Scan and read the article(s) you have chosen.

Although paper indexes exist,[1] online indexes are preferable because they are very current; cumulate information over time (paper research involves multiple books and pamphlets); provide not only citations but also abstracts (short descriptions) of articles and, in some cases, the full text of the article; and afford key-word searching as well as searching by subject, author, and title. You can limit your search online, e.g., by dates, and some alert you to new articles fitting your search. You are most likely to use one of two indexes:

☐ *Index to Legal Periodicals and Books* is available through WilsonWeb and Westlaw (starting in 1981). *ILPB* covers almost 900 law reviews and journals, yearbooks, institutes, bar association publications, university publications, and government publications, as well as 1,400 monographs per year.

☐ *LegalTrac*, a division of *InfoTrac*, covers about 875 law reviews, legal newspapers, law specialty publications, bar association journals, and

---

1. The major paper indexes are *Index to Legal Periodicals* and *Current Law Index*.

international legal journals as well as law-related articles from 1,000 additional business and general-interest sources. It is also available as *Legal Resource Index* on Westlaw.

The main advantage of using a periodicals index is the framework of subject headings and subheadings into which articles are categorized. Thus, your goal is to identify a pertinent subject heading and obtain a list of articles on that subject. A good first step is a subject search, in which you enter a term you believe will be a subject heading. If the term you enter in a subject search is not itself a subject heading and does not lead to one, consider running a key-word search; once you find a pertinent article, you can discern under which subject heading(s) it is listed. See Exhibit 5.5 (at page 104). If the list of articles under the pertinent subject heading is lengthy, consider running a key-word search within that list to zero in on the most probably pertinent articles.

At a minimum, the article's entry will provide the article's author, title, and citation. You may also find an abstract, i.e. a brief summary of its content. Periodical article titles can be less than revealing; an abstract and the first paragraph or so of text should help you ascertain how pertinent the article is.

Depending on your circumstances, you may have several options for locating and reading articles identified through your index research. You may find a paper copy in a library; many researchers prefer to read articles on paper, in part because it is easy to flip from page to page and the text and corresponding footnotes appear on the same page. Online options include the index (if full text is available); the journal's website; or a commercial resource such as Westlaw, LexisNexis, or HeinOnline. You may be able to link to the materials cited in the article in an online version. Exhibit 1.5 (at pages 19–20) is the article featured in this chapter as obtained through LexisNexis; Exhibit 5.2 (at page 100) is from the paper version.

If you identify more than one pertinent article, you may well want to read several but not all of them. Keep the following factors in mind as you select articles to read:

- ☐ Coverage: Does the article focus on your topic and cover it thoroughly? Be sure that the article covers your jurisdiction; some articles focus on one state's law.
- ☐ Currency: Is the article fairly recent, so that the research and analysis are still current?
- ☐ Credibility: Is the author reputable, and is the periodical well respected? As you would surmise, student work is viewed as less credible than an article by a professor, for example, and law reviews from well known and highly ranked law schools tend to be viewed most highly.
- ☐ Quality of research and analysis: Do the footnotes cite sufficient authority to support the propositions, and does the analysis make sense?
- ☐ Persuasiveness: If the article argues for a change in the law, is the argument logical and convincing?

EXHIBIT 5.5   Periodicals Index Entries,
from Index to Legal Periodicals and Books
(online source)

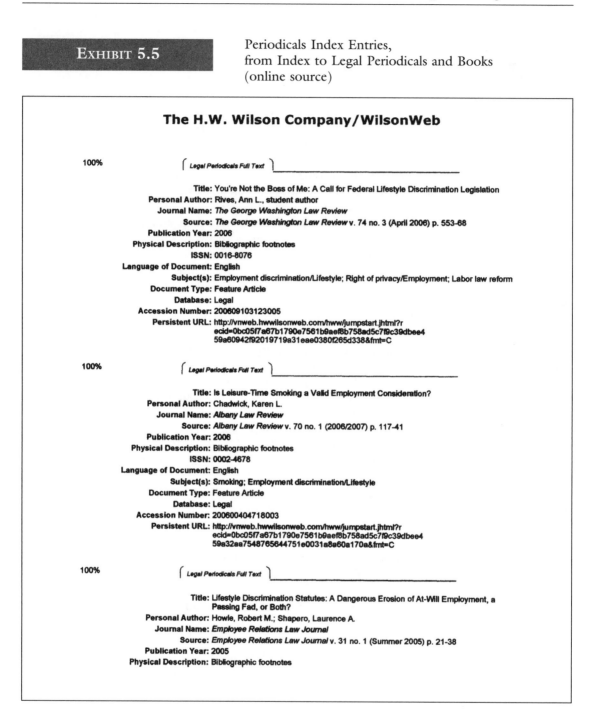

The H.W. Wilson Company/WilsonWeb

100%   ⌐ *Legal Periodicals Full Text* ⌐

Title: You're Not the Boss of Me: A Call for Federal Lifestyle Discrimination Legislation
Personal Author: Rives, Ann L., student author
Journal Name: *The George Washington Law Review*
Source: *The George Washington Law Review* v. 74 no. 3 (April 2006) p. 553-68
Publication Year: 2006
Physical Description: Bibliographic footnotes
ISSN: 0016-8076
Language of Document: English
Subject(s): Employment discrimination/Lifestyle; Right of privacy/Employment; Labor law reform
Document Type: Feature Article
Database: Legal
Accession Number: 200609103123005
Persistent URL: http://vnweb.hwwilsonweb.com/hww/jumpstart.jhtml?r
ecid=0bc05f7a67b1790e7561b9aef8b758ad5c7f9c39dbee4
59a60942f92019719a31eae0380f265d338&fmt=C

100%   ⌐ *Legal Periodicals Full Text* ⌐

Title: Is Leisure-Time Smoking a Valid Employment Consideration?
Personal Author: Chadwick, Karen L.
Journal Name: *Albany Law Review*
Source: *Albany Law Review* v. 70 no. 1 (2006/2007) p. 117-41
Publication Year: 2006
Physical Description: Bibliographic footnotes
ISSN: 0002-4678
Language of Document: English
Subject(s): Smoking; Employment discrimination/Lifestyle
Document Type: Feature Article
Database: Legal
Accession Number: 200600404718003
Persistent URL: http://vnweb.hwwilsonweb.com/hww/jumpstart.jhtml?r
ecid=0bc05f7a67b1790e7561b9aef8b758ad5c7f9c39dbee4
59a32aa7548765644751e0031a8a60a170a&fmt=C

100%   ⌐ *Legal Periodicals Full Text* ⌐

Title: Lifestyle Discrimination Statutes: A Dangerous Erosion of At-Will Employment, a
Passing Fad, or Both?
Personal Author: Howie, Robert M.; Shapero, Laurence A.
Journal Name: *Employee Relations Law Journal*
Source: *Employee Relations Law Journal* v. 31 no. 1 (Summer 2005) p. 21-38
Publication Year: 2005
Physical Description: Bibliographic footnotes

As you read an article, be sure to orient yourself first: read the synopsis on the first page, if there is one; look over the table of contents or, if there is no table of contents, the headings and subheadings within the article; and carefully read the introduction and conclusion. More likely than not, some parts will be more pertinent to your client's situation than others; read those parts carefully and skim the rest. Take care to differentiate the author's description of existing law, critique of the law, and proposed reforms.

Pay close attention as well to the footnotes. You will, of course, want to find any references to law from your jurisdiction. In addition, identify the legal basis for the article's pertinent points. You should read what the author relied on to make sure the analysis in the article is sound and to support your analysis of your client's situation. For example, if an article cites a statute, your analysis should be based on your reading of the statute, not the article's statement.

Periodicals in full-text key-word searching

▶   Select a service and database.

▶   Run a key-word search.

▶   Assess the retrieved articles.

▶   Scan and read the article(s) you have chosen.

As noted in Chapter 2, key-word searching is a good strategy when on online source follows a periodic (rather than highly organized) publication pattern. Both Westlaw and LexisNexis have very substantial legal periodicals databases. Westlaw's Journals & Law Reviews database contains selected articles from approximately 850 legal periodicals and similar publications. LexisNexis' U.S. and Canadian Law Reviews, Combined covers almost 700.

A newer resource, HeinOnline, offers more than 1,000 legal and law-related periodicals, all with coverage from the first issue, making it a good choice especially for researching in and finding older issues of periodicals that may not be available on Westlaw and LexisNexis. On the other hand, HeinOnline is generally current to the volume preceding the current volume; in some cases, current issues are available.

Because these databases are so large, you should think about ways to narrow your search. Options include confining your search to a subset of the periodicals database, searching the titles only, imposing a date restriction, and adding a term after you have obtained a large number of hits through your preliminary search. Viewing the results with the key words highlighted can help you discern which ones are pertinent. Review Exhibit 2.12 (at page 56).

Once you have located articles through full-text, key-word searching, sort and then read the articles as described previously.

> **Citing periodical articles**
>
> ► Select a periodicals citator.
> ► Cite the article.
> ► Follow up on the citing sources, as appropriate.

As in many other disciplines, if you find a particularly helpful article, you may want to learn whether its ideas have been received favorably by other scholars or the courts. The article you have read is the *cited* article, and the more recent authorities, such as other articles or cases, are the *citing* authorities.

Until quite recently, this process was done through a paper source, *Shepard's Law Review Citations.* Thus, one name for this is "Shepardizing." LexisNexis now offers Shepard's in electronic form. Westlaw has a comparable product in KeyCite; hence the second name for this process — "KeyCiting." We use the term "citing" to cover both.

Exhibit 5.6 (at page 107) is a Shepard's printout, but not for the 2006 article in the *Albany Law Review* featured in this chapter. When we wrote this text, the featured article was so new that there were no citations to it. Rather, the printout is for an earlier — 1998 — article on the same topic, which has been cited in twelve more recent articles, including the article featured in this chapter.

Exhibit 5.7 (at page 108) presents our periodicals template, filled in to reflect our research on the privacy issue in the Canoga case.

2.   Citing Periodical Articles

A proper cite to an article in a legal periodical includes the author's full name and, as needed, an indication that the author is a student; the title of the article; the volume; the periodical's abbreviation; the first page number; and the date. Here are two examples:

☐ *Bluebook* Rule 16: Karen L. Chadwick, *Is Leisure-Time Smoking a Valid Employment Consideration?*, 70 Alb. L. Rev. 117 (2006).

☐ *ALWD* Rule 23: Karen L. Chadwick, *Is Leisure-Time Smoking a Valid Employment Consideration?*, 70 Alb. L. Rev. 117 (2006).

C.   WHAT ELSE?

Current Index to Legal Periodicals (CILP). CILP is a weekly current awareness publication that gives researchers citations to new articles four to

EXHIBIT 5.6   Shepard's Periodical Article Entry, from LexisNexis (online source)

Copyright 2007 SHEPARD'S(R) - 12 Citing references

NOTE: Blowing Smoke: Do Smokers Have a Right? Limiting the Privacy Rights of Cigarette Smokers, 86 Geo. L.J. 783 (1998)

(TM):
Restrictions: *Unrestricted*
FOCUS(TM) Terms: *No FOCUS terms*
Print Format: *FULL*
Citing Ref. Signal Legend:
    ⬤{Warning} -- negative treatment indicated
    ◼{Questioned} -- validity questioned by citing refs.
    ▲{Caution} -- possible negative treatment
    ◆{Positive} -- positive treatment indicated
    Ⓐ{Analysis} -- cited and neutral analysis indicated
    Ⓘ{Cited} -- citation information available

PRIOR HISTORY (0 citing references)

    (CITATION YOU ENTERED):
    NOTE: Blowing Smoke: Do Smokers Have a Right? Limiting the Privacy Rights of Cigarette Smokers, 86
    Geo. L.J. 783 (1998)

LAW REVIEWS AND PERIODICALS (12 Citing References)

    1.   *ARTICLE: IS LEISURE-TIME SMOKING A VALID EMPLOYMENT CONSIDERATION?, 70 Alb. L. Rev.*
       117 (2006)
          70 Alb. L. Rev. 117 *p.117*

    2.   *ARTICLE: THE QUEST FOR PRIVACY: STATE COURTS AND AN ELUSIVE RIGHT, 65 Alb. L. Rev. 945*
       (2002)
          65 Alb. L. Rev. 945 *p.945*

    3.   *ARTICLE: Ameliorating Medication and ADA Protection: Use it and Lose it or Refuse it and Lose it?, 38*
       Am. Bus. L.J. 785 (2001)

    4.   *ARTICLE: "Lifestyle" Discrimination in Employment, 24 Berkeley J. Emp. & Lab. L. 377 (2003)*

    5.   *STUDENT NOTE: When Parents are on a Level Playing Field, Courts Cry Foul at Smoking: Smoking as a*
       Determining Factor in Child Custody Cases, 40 Fam. Ct. Rev. 238 (2002)

    6.   *NOTE: Seeing Through the Smoke: The Need for National Legislation Banning Smoking in Bars and*
       Restaurants, 75 Geo. Wash. L. Rev. 662 (2007)
          75 Geo. Wash. L. Rev. 662 *p.662*

    7.   *BOOK REVIEW LEARNING FROM HISTORY IN THE CIGARETTE DEBATE:, 10 Health Matrix 205*
       (2000)

    8.   *ARTICLE: American Workers Increase Efforts to Establish a Legal Right to Privacy as Civility Declines in*

EXHIBIT 5.7	Periodicals Template for Canoga Case

Issue: *Does an employer's rule prohibiting smoking off-duty violate the employee's privacy?*	**Citation Information:** • *Karen L. Chadwick* • *Is Leisure-Time Smoking a Valid Employment Consideration?* • *Vol. 70* • *Albany Law Review* • *Page 117*
Date of events: *Sept. 7, 2007*	• *2006*

Date of research: *Nov. 15, 2007*

Search and Find:

located article by . . .	selection factors: currency, scope, journal
In ILPB online: employee employer smoking → 14 hits, several pertinent → Employment Discrimination/Lifestyle subject. *In LexisNexis U.S. & Canadian Law Reviews: employ! /s smok! /s privacy.*	• *Very current* • *Professor* • *Extensive footnotes* • *Balanced recommendation*

Information and Implications:

As to tort of invasion of privacy: There are four different torts. The most pertinent is "unreasonable intrusion upon the seclusion of another." (1) Smoking is not private—smoking is habitually disclosed or undertaken in public. (2) The employer has permission to intrude; the employee is on notice. (3) A policy is not unreasonable if the employer has legitimate business reason i.e. health care costs. pp. 127-30.

The privacy tort probably won't succeed: smoking occurs in public; the orchestra has business interests, including the impact of smoking on performance.

Many states have statutes prohibiting employer bans on off-duty smoking. p. 118.

Next Steps:

questions to consider:	leads to pursue:
Maybe check what other orchestras do; could suggest this is unreasonable; but tort seems unlikely anyway. *Focus on the New Mexico statute.*	*N.M. Stat. Ann. §50-11-13.* *Restatement (Second) of Torts §§ 652A, 652B.*

six weeks before these articles are indexed in the major legal periodical indexes. CILP covers over 570 legal publications and organizes the contents of those publications within 100 subject headings.

Legal Scholarship Network (LSN). A leading example of Internet periodicals publication is the LSN, which is a division of the Social Science Research Network (SSRN). Subscribers may search the abstracts by author, title, or key words and download many articles from the SSRN collection. SSRN is particularly useful as a means of locating works-in-progress and social science scholarship. In addition, subscribers receive, by e-mail, abstracts on new articles as well as working papers, most of which will eventually appear in law reviews or other academic journals.

Specialized Indexes. As extensive as the indexes described in this chapter are, for some advanced research tasks, you may want to consult an index with a more specialized focus, e.g., *Index to Federal Tax Articles, Index to Periodical Articles Related to Law, Index to Foreign Legal Periodicals.*

Older Articles. To find pre-1981 articles, use the paper *Index to Legal Periodicals*, a paper index, or Legal Periodicals Retro on WilsonWeb.

A.L.R. ANNOTATIONS

A.   WHAT ARE *AMERICAN LAW REPORTS* ANNOTATIONS (A.L.R.), AND WHY ARE THEY USEFUL?

American Law Reports annotations (A.L.R.) are unique to legal research. Each annotation synopsizes the various cases on a fairly narrow legal topic. Most annotations focus on issues of some controversy, in which courts in different jurisdictions follow different rules, or issues that are factually sensitive so that differing facts result in different holdings. A typical A.L.R. annotation discusses the law in many jurisdictions within the United States, citing relevant authority in each of those jurisdictions. A.L.R. is published by Thomson West, and the annotations are written by its staff attorneys or attorneys hired to write particular annotations.

Accompanying the annotation (at the beginning of the annotation or back of the volume) is a leading or typical case on the topic — hence the word "reports" in the title, "reports" being a common term for a compilation of cases. Because other sources of case law are preferred (as discussed in Chapter 9), your primary focus in A.L.R. research will be the annotations.

A.L.R. is a large multivolume set, first published in 1919. Put together they cover more than 27,000 legal issues as of fall 2007. A.L.R. has been published in eight series, as listed in Exhibit 6.1. Publication in series is

| EXHIBIT 6.1 | A.L.R. Series |

Series	Dates	Topics
A.L.R.1st	1919-1948	state and federal
A.L.R.2d	1949-1965	state and federal
A.L.R.3d	1965-1969	state and federal
A.L.R.3d	1969-1980	state
A.L.R.4th	1980-1992	state
A.L.R.5th	1992-2004	state
A.L.R.6th	2005 to date	state
A.L.R. Fed.	1969-2005	federal
A.L.R. Fed.2d	2005 to date	federal

common in the law. After a good number of volumes, the publisher starts a new series and begins the numbering of volumes over with 1. In general, a new series does not replace an old series. In the case of A.L.R., although most recent annotations cover new topics, some do cover topics covered in, and thus supersede, earlier annotations.

Six to ten A.L.R. volumes are issued each year for each current series, and each volume contains approximately ten annotations. Each A.L.R. volume typically covers a wide range of subjects, such as contracts, torts, criminal law, and employment law. A.L.R. is also available in Westlaw.

An annotation is very useful for several reasons. It provides a general overview of its topic and synopses of the cases on the topic. Because the case descriptions are organized by rule or key facts or outcome, you can easily see the different approaches to the issue. Thus A.L.R. is often cited[1] to document the pattern of cases across the country on an issue. In addition, an annotation provides references to other commentary, such as encyclopedias. Finally, A.L.R. is timely: an annotation may be the first commentary published on a new topic, and A.L.R. is kept up to date in various ways.

However, A.L.R. has limitations. There may be no annotation on your research topic. Because the topics are quite narrow, you should turn to A.L.R. only after you have a good sense of the subject encompassing your research topic. Moreover, although the discussion is quite comprehensive, it is more descriptive than analytical or critical.

For an excerpt from an A.L.R. pertinent to the Canoga Case, see Exhibit 6.2 (at pages 112–13).

---

1. According to Thomson West, A.L.R. is the most often cited type of commentary.

EXHIBIT 6.2

Case Synopses,
from A.L.R. Annotation (paper source)

manager's testimony would allow jury to reasonably conclude that entire dismissal procedure was referring to "for cause" employees, one of whom was office manager. Beales v Hillhaven, Inc. (1992, Nev) 825 P2d 212, 7 BNA IER Cas 260.

Under state law, company's employment manual may contractually bind company. Key consideration in determining whether employment manual gives rise to contractual obligations is reasonable expectation of employees. Lawrence v National Westminster Bank (1996, CA3 NJ) 98 F3d 61, 18 ADD 693, 5 AD Cas 1796, 72 BNA FEP Cas 234 (applying NJ law).

When employer of substantial number of employees circulates manual that, when fairly read, provides that certain benefits are incident to employment (including, especially, job security provisions), judiciary, instead of "grudgingly" conceding enforceability of those provisions, should construe them in accordance with reasonable expectations of employees. There is no categorical test to determine whether an employment manual could give rise to reasonable expectations of employees that it confers enforceable obligations under state law; however, among important factors that court should consider are definiteness and comprehensiveness of policy and context of manual's preparation and distribution. Marzano v. Computer Science Corp. Inc., 91 F.3d 497, 71 Fair Empl. Prac. Cas. (BNA) 1120, 68 Empl. Prac. Dec. (CCH) ¶ 44256 (3d Cir. 1996) (applying NJ law).

Under New Jersey law, absent written contract of employment, there are only two exceptions to employment at-will doctrine: where employee is terminated in violation of clear expression of public policy, or where employee handbook creates implied contract of employment. Barone v Gardner Asphalt Corp. (1997, DC NJ) 955 F Supp 337.

New Jersey law recognizes claim for breach of employer's stated termination policies. Boginis v Marriott Ownership Resorts (1994, ED Va) 855 F Supp 862, 9 BNA IER Cas 1024, 129 CCH LC ¶ 57784 (applying NJ law).

Entire manual gave rise to implied contract of employment, even though employee received only excerpt on disciplinary procedures, due to terms of manual—including most importantly those relating to employment security—and its wide distribution. That contract included rights and obligations in section that plaintiff employee in wrongful-discharge action actually received. Nicosia v Wakefern Food Corp. (1994) 136 NJ 401, 643 A2d 554, 9 BNA IER Cas 1338.

If plaintiff can prove that employment manual containing job security and termination

procedures could reasonably be understood by an employee to create binding duties and obligations between employer and its employees, manual will constitute, in effect, unilateral offer to contract that an employee may accept through continued employment. Only in those circumstances will employment manual overcome presumption that employment is at-will. Witkowski v Thomas J. Lipton, Inc. (1994) 136 NJ 385, 643 A2d 546, 9 BNA IER Cas 1332.

Employment manual promising that discharge would occur only upon just cause constituted more than mere expression of employer's philosophy; thus, trial court erred in granting summary judgment to employer, where engineer contended that he had been dismissed without just cause after having refused to resign. Woolley v Hoffmann-La Roche, Inc. (1985) 99 NJ 284, 491 A2d 1257, 1 BNA IER Cas 995, 119 BNA LRRM 2380, 102 CCH LC ¶ 55496, mod on other gnds 101 NJ 10, 1985 NJ 10, 499 A2d 515, 4 BNA IER Cas 403.

Although neither employee handbook nor policies and procedures manual expressly declared that employees would be fired only for just cause, such contractual agreement was created in view of widespread distribution of respective policy manuals and their application to employer's workforce at large; required reading and signing of employee handbooks; provision of progressive scheme of discipline for enumerated types of prohibited conduct; testimony of employer's human resources director that it was employer's general policy to terminate employees only for cause, and, most important, various representations of maximum job security. Having offered representations as attractive alternative to collective bargaining, employer could not avoid its obligations on basis of semantic differences. Preston v Claridge Hotel & Casino, Ltd. (1989) 231 NJ Super 81, 555 A2d 12, 4 BNA IER Cas 493.

Personnel manual gives rise to implied contract, for purposes of implied contract exception to employment at will doctrine, if it controls employer-employee relationship and employee can reasonably expect employer to conform to procedures it outlines. Garcia v Middle Rio Grande Conservancy Dist. (1996, NM) 918 P2d 7, 11 BNA IER Cas 1328.

In wrongful discharge action against employer, substantial evidence supported finding that employee handbook modified employment relationship and created warning and suspension procedures which were not followed; termination procedures became amendment to employee's contract and personality, not se-

32

EXHIBIT 6.2   *(continued)*

vere offenses of insubordination or disobedience, caused employee's termination. Handbook characterized disciplinary policy regarding warnings, suspensions, and terminations as established procedure and language of handbook did nothing to alert employee that it was subject to revocation at any time or that employee should not rely on it. Lukoski v Sandia Indiana Management Co. (1988, NM) 748 P2d 507, 2 BNA IER Cas 1650. LC ¶ 55496, mod on other gnds 101 NJ 10, 1985 NJ 10, 499 A2d 515.

Evidence was sufficient to overcome presumption that employment contract was terminable at will and to support finding that implied employment provision for discharge only for good reason was in effect between employer and employee, where during initial employment negotiations, employee's immediate supervisor made clear that employment would be long term and permanent as long as employee did job, other supervisory employees stated employer released permanent employees for good reason, just cause, and where neither insurance benefits manual nor severance pay plan and policy manual addressed effect of without cause termination of employment. Kestenbaum v Pennzoil Co. (1988) 108 NM 20, 766 P2d 280, 4 BNA IER Cas 67, cert den (US) 104 L Ed 2d 1026, 4 BNA IER Cas 672.

Presumption that, absent agreement establishing fixed duration, employment relationship is at will does not apply when employer had promulgated policies in personnel manual specifying procedures or grounds for termination; these procedures become part of employment contract and must be followed. Thus, job security policy stated in handbook contractually bound employer and did not amount to nonbinding general statements of policy and supervisory guidelines, where policy set forth very specific and detailed procedure for work force reduction in mandatory and unqualified terms. Further, severance pay provision was explicitly invoked and followed in case of discharged employee asserting cause of action for breach of contract in connection with reduction in force. Handbook's general language of qualification that stated "in the final analysis, specific judgment and discretion will govern," did not negate binding force of handbook's more specific provisions under state law. Mycak v. Honeywell, Inc., 953 F.2d 798, 7 I.E.R. Cas. (BNA) 117, 120 Lab. Cas. (CCH) ¶ 56780 (2d Cir. 1992) (applying New York law).

Under New York law, at-will employee can have cause of action of breach of implied contract against employer where he or she is discharged in absence of circumstances or procedures specified in employer's handbook.

Thus, terminated at-will executive of registered securities broker-dealer satisfied all elements of state cause of action for wrongful discharge alleging that employer's manual created implied contract of employment because it assured continued employment as long as employee did not transgress manual's provisions; that employer breached implied contract where it did not fire him for any stated ground contained in manual, but rather for no apparent or stated reason or cause, evidence indicated that no misconduct occurred before firing. Reeves v. Continental Equities Corp. of America, 767 F. Supp. 469 (S.D. N.Y. 1991) (applying New York law).

Employer may be bound by express statements in its policy manual limiting its otherwise unfettered right to discharge its employees. Disciplined or terminated employee may seek Article 78 review to determine whether employer contravened any of its own rules or regulations in taking that disciplinary action. Hanchard v Facilities Dev. Corp. (1995) 85 NY2d 638, 628 NYS2d 4, 651 NE2d 872, 10 BNA IER Cas 1004, 130 CCH LC ¶ 57921.

Discharged employee may recover damages by establishing that employer made employee aware of its express written policy limiting its right of discharge and that employee detrimentally relied on that policy in accepting employment. Mika v. New York State Ass'n for Retarded Children, Inc., 230 A.D.2d 744, 646 N.Y.S.2d 168 (2d Dep't 1996).

At-will auditor for brokerage house who alleged he was discharged for reporting illegal money-laundering scheme possessed cause of action for breach of contract, where employment manual contained requirement that employees report misconduct and also contained reciprocal promise to protect reporters from retaliation. Mulder v Donaldson, Lufkin & Jenrette (1995, 1st Dept) 208 App Div 2d 301, 623 NYS2d 560, 10 BNA IER Cas 631.

To sustain cause of action for breach of employment contract, employee must demonstrate that employment manual contained clear and express limitation that employee would not be terminated or disciplined except for cause, and that employee specifically relied on this language. Charyn v National Westminster Bank, U.S.A. (1994, 2d Dept) 204 App Div 2d 676, 612 NYS2d 432.

Employee can rebut presumption of employment at will by establishing that employee was made aware of written policy of limitation on employer's right to discharge at time employment commenced, and in accepting employment, employee relied on termination only for cause limitation. For manual or other written policy to limit employer's right to terminate, it

33

B.   How Do You Research in and Cite A.L.R.s?

1.   Researching in A.L.R.

Exhibit 6.3 (at page 115), our A.L.R. template, presents the elements of researching in A.L.R. In brief, A.L.R. research entails formulating a specific research issue, using a paper index or online search tools to locate a pertinent annotation, using the annotation's finding tools to identify pertinent material, reading that material to derive useful information and considering its implications for your client's situation, and planning your next steps.

There is no single dominant approach for A.L.R. research. Researching in paper and online both work well.

A.L.R. in paper

▶ Consult the *ALR Index* or tables of cases or laws to identify pertinent annotations.
▶ Read the opening material.
▶ Use the various finding tools to identify pertinent passages.
▶ Read the text of the annotation.
▶ Consult the references section.
▶ Update your research.

An efficient means of locating a pertinent A.L.R. annotation in paper is to use the *ALR Index*, a multivolume set encompassing the second through sixth and both federal series of A.L.R. The *ALR Index* is updated, so you should check the pocket part as well as the main volume. As an alternative, if you already know of a pertinent case, statute, rule, or regulation, you can locate an annotation discussing that authority by consulting the appropriate table of authorities.

Once you have located a potentially pertinent annotation, read the opening material to learn the scope of the annotation and to obtain an overview of the topic. To locate pertinent material within the annotation, consult the outline of the annotation, its index, and the list of jurisdictions represented. See Exhibit 6.4 (at pages 117–20).

Exhibit 6.3	A.L.R. Annotations Template

Issue:	Citation Information:
	• author
	• title
	• volume and series
Date of events:	• date(s)
	• begining page number

Date of research:

Search and Find:

located ALR by . . .	checked for my state's cases . . .
located pertinent material by . . .	updated by . . .

Information and Implications:
• look for rules and factors determining outcomes
• look for descriptions of factually similar cases
• note exact location
• connect information to client's situation

Next Steps:

questions to consider:	leads to pursue:

As you read the text of the annotation, focus on cases in your jurisdiction, seek to discern patterns in the case law from other jurisdictions, and look for cases with factual parallels to your client's situation. You should read the case reported along with the annotation if it is from your jurisdiction; if it is from a different jurisdiction, you may want to scan it because the author considered it an illustrative case on the topic.

Next, consult the references section in the opening pages for citations to other commentary sources. New A.L.R.s include references to Westlaw topical databases, suggested searches, and references to pertinent government and private websites.

Recent annotations are updated several ways; you should explore all three for comprehensive research:

- ☐ First, check the pocket part for additional case synopses.
- ☐ Second, check for a more recent annotation. The pocket part or the Annotation History Table in the tables volume, may indicate that the annotation has been superseded.
- ☐ Third, you may bring your research up-to-the-minute by e-mailing or calling the Latest Case Service hotline for cases decided since the last supplement.

If the annotation you are reading was published some time ago, you may want to check the pocket part earlier in your research process, perhaps even before you read the text of the annotation. This way, you may learn of a superseding annotation before you invest too much time reading the older one. In addition, you may learn of more recent cases; in general, recent cases are more significant than older ones (as discussed in Chapter 9).

A.L.R. in Westlaw

▶   Select the A.L.R. database.
▶   Run a key-word search (with a segment restriction).
▶   Read the annotation (which is updated automatically).
▶   Pull in cases via links.

Most A.L.R. volumes are available online as well; Westlaw offers all but the first series. The approach stated previously works with some modifications online. For example, on Westlaw, a `ci(index)` command permits you to search the index to locate a pertinent annotation.

Because A.L.R. is periodically published and has no overall topical organization, searching for key words is a sensible approach. You can use natural-language or Boolean searches. Because the entire A.L.R. database is very large, unless you can craft a very specific search, you may want to use segment restrictions. For example, A.L.R. titles generally are comprehensive

EXHIBIT 6.4	Opening Material, from A.L.R. Annotation (paper source)

ANNOTATION

RIGHT TO DISCHARGE ALLEGEDLY "AT-WILL" EMPLOYEE AS AFFECTED BY EMPLOYER'S PROMULGATION OF EMPLOYMENT POLICIES AS TO DISCHARGE

by

Theresa Ludwig Kruk, J.D.

TOTAL CLIENT-SERVICE LIBRARY® REFERENCES

53 Am Jur 2d, Master and Servant §§ 34, 43–70

Annotations: See the related matters listed in the annotation, infra.

7 Am Jur Legal Forms 2d, Employment Contracts §§ 99:111, 99:121, 99:146–99:147

7 Am Jur Proof of Facts 2d 1, Retaliatory Termination of Private Employment; 11 Am Jur Proof of Facts 2d 679, Reduction or Mitigation of Damages—Employment Contract; 29 Am Jur Proof of Facts 2d 335, Wrongful Discharge of At-Will Employee

US L Ed Digest, Master and Servant § 21

ALR Digests, Master and Servant § 51

L Ed Index to Annos, Contracts; Labor and Employment; Waiver or Estoppel

ALR Quick Index, Contracts; Discharge from Employment; Estoppel and Waiver; Manuals; Master and Servant; Restitution and Implied Contracts

Federal Quick Index, Contracts; Discharge from Employment; Labor and Employment; Manuals and Handbooks; Restitution and Implied Contracts; Waiver and Estoppel

Auto-Cite®: Any case citation herein can be checked for form, parallel references, later history, and annotation references through the Auto-Cite computer research system.

Consult POCKET PART in this volume for later cases

120

EXHIBIT 6.4   *(continued)*

33 ALR4th   EMPLOYMENT AT WILL—RESTRAINTS ON DISCHARGE
33 ALR4th 120

**Right to discharge allegedly "at-will" employee as affected by
employer's promulgation of employment policies as to discharge**

§ 1. Introduction:
[a] Scope
[b] Related matters

§ 2. Background, summary, and comment:
[a] Generally
[b] Practice pointers

§ 3. View that right to discharge at-will employee not affected by employer's
promulgation of policies as to discharge

§ 4. Particular theories restricting right of discharge—contract:
[a] Right of discharge held restricted
[b] Right of discharge held not restricted

§ 5. —Equitable estoppel

INDEX

Advisory committee, summons before, § 3
Amendments to handbook, § 3
Application for employment, § 4[a]
Background, § 2
Board of directors' adoption of policies, § 4[a]
Campus security guard, § 4[b]
Comment, § 2
Consideration, mutuality of, § 3
Contract theory restricting right of discharge, § 4
Conversations with management personnel, § 3
Directors' adoption of policies, § 4[a] ✓
Disloyalty as basis for discharge, § 4[a]
Equitable estoppel theory restricting right of discharge, § 5 ✓
Executive director preparing manual, § 4[a]
Forward to personnel manual, § 4[a]
Grievance hearing, § 4[a]
Grounds for discharge listed in handbook, § 3
Handbook or manual, §§ 3-5
Hearing, § 4[a]
Implied contracts, §§ 3-5 ✓
Inquiry by employee regarding job security, § 4[a]
"Just cause" dismissal, § 3 ✓
Labor union activities, § 5
Layoff, § 4[a]
Length of service, §§ 4[a], 5

Loyalty to company, § 4[a]
Manual or handbook, §§ 3-5
Mission society, § 4[a]
Mutuality of consideration, § 3
Notice of resignation, § 4[a]
Oral contract, §§ 3, 4[a]
Personnel manual, §§ 3-5
Police on campus, § 4[b]
Policy manual, §§ 3-5
Practice pointers, § 2[b]
Pre-employment negotiations as necessary, § 4[a]
Probationary period, discharge during, § 4[a]
Publications of employer, §§ 3-5
Question by employee regarding job security, § 4[a]
Reduction in work force, § 4[a]
Rehabilitation set out in handbook, § 4[a]
Related matters, § 1[b]
Reprimands, § 4[a]
Review of behavior by executive officer, § 4[a]
Scope of annotation, § 1[a]
Security guard, § 4[b]
Seniority considerations, §§ 4[a], 5
Summary, § 2
Summons before advisory committee, § 3
Suspension, § 4[a]
Tripartite disciplinary procedure, § 4[a]
"Unilateral contract modification" theory, § 4[a]

121

EXHIBIT 6.4   *(continued)*

§ 1[a]   EMPLOYMENT AT WILL—RESTRAINTS ON DISCHARGE   33 ALR4th
33 ALR4th 120

Union activities, § 5	Withdrawal of handbook by employer, § 3
Vacation pay loss, § 4[a]	Work force reduction, § 4[a]
Warning slip, § 3	"Writing up" of employee, § 4[b]

TABLE OF JURISDICTIONS REPRESENTED
Consult POCKET PART in this volume for later cases

US: §§ 3, 4[a]	Mich: § 4[a]
Ala: § 3	Minn: § 4[a] ✓
Cal: § 5	Mont: § 4[b]
Del: § 3	Neb: § 3
DC: §§ 3, 4[a]	NY: §§ 4[a], 5
Fla: § 3	NC: § 3
Ill: §§ 4[a], 4[b]	Or: §§ 4[a], 4[b]
Ind: §§ 3, 4[a]	Pa: § 4[a]
Kan: §§ 3, 4[a]	SD: § 4[a]
Ky: § 4[a]	Tex: § 3
La: § 3	Va: § 3
Me: § 3	Wis: § 4[b]

§ 1. Introduction

[a] Scope

This annotation[1] collects the state and federal cases that consider whether an employer's promulgation of employment policies regarding the procedures and reasons for termination or discharge of employees[2] affects an employer's right to discharge an at-will employee at any time and for any or no reason.

This annotation includes only those cases in which an at-will employee relies upon the policy statements of his or her employer regarding termination or discharge and contends that his or her discharge was effectuated in a manner or for reasons contrary to the express general policy of the employer,[3] as opposed to personal assurances or representations by the employer, regardless of whether such policy was written or unwritten, and the employer defends against such a charge by asserting the at-will status of the employee.

[b] Related matters

Recovery for discharge from employment in retaliation for filing workers' compensation claim. 32 ALR4th 1221.

Modern status of rule that employer may discharge at-will employee for any reason. 12 ALR4th 544.

---

1. This annotation supersedes § 7 of 12 ALR4th 544.

2. For treatment of cases dealing with an at-will employee's right to severance pay as provided by an employer's general policy on severance, see 53 Am Jur 2d, Master and Servant § 81.

3. For a discussion of cases involving

at-will employees who claim to have been hired as "permanent" employees or "for life," see generally 53 Am Jur 2d, Master and Servant §§ 20, 32–34. See also the annotation in 24 ALR3d 1412 entitled "Employer's misrepresentation as to prospect, or duration of, employment as actionable fraud."

122

EXHIBIT 6.4   *(continued)*

33 ALR4th   EMPLOYMENT AT WILL—RESTRAINTS ON DISCHARGE   **§ 2[a]**
33 ALR4th 120

Liability for discharging at-will employee for refusing to participate in, or for disclosing, unlawful or unethical acts of employer or coemployees. 9 ALR4th 329.

Right of corporation to discharge employee who asserts right as stockholder. 84 ALR3d 1107.

Reduction in rank or authority or change of duties as breach of employment contract. 63 ALR3d 539.

Employee's arbitrary dismissal as breach of employment contract terminable at will. 62 ALR3d 271.

Employer's termination of professional athlete's services as constituting breach of employment contract. 57 ALR3d 257.

Nature of alternative employment which employee must accept to minimize damages for wrongful discharge. 44 ALR3d 629.

Employer's misrepresentation as to prospect, or duration of, employment as actionable fraud. 24 ALR3d 1412.

Elements and measure of damages in action by schoolteacher for wrongful discharge. 22 ALR3d 1047.

Liability of federal government officer or employee for causing discharge or separation of subordinate. 5 ALR Fed 961.

§ 2. Background, summary, and comment

[a] Generally

The common-law rule regarding the termination of an at-will employ-

ment contract is that if the employment is not for a definite term, and if there is no contractual or statutory restriction on the right of discharge, an employer may lawfully discharge an employee whenever and for whatever cause, without incurring liability for wrongful discharge.[4] Few legal principles have been better settled than the at-will concept, whose roots date back to the 19th century laissez-faire policy of protecting freedom to contract. In recent years, however, there has been a growing trend toward a restricted application of this rule in order to comport with express and implied public policy, as well as statutory concerns. Some jurisdictions have been willing to depart from the traditional contract rule of terminability at will and to impose an implied contractual duty not to discharge an employee for reasons regarded as violative of public policy or to recognize the tortious nature of a discharge violative of public policy, whether such policy is expressly codified or implied.[5]

In keeping with this modern trend of judicial re-evaluation and legislative modification, a number of jurisdictions have held or recognized that under particular circumstances, the right of an employer to freely discharge at-will employees may be contractually restricted as a result of the promulgation of corporate employment policies specifying the proce-

---

4. Although the at-will rule is generally regarded as vesting in the employer absolute discretion to terminate employment, this "right" is actually a rule of contract construction rather than a right grounded in substantive law. Absent an express contractual provision specifying the term of employment, the duration depends upon the intention of the parties as determined from the circumstances of each case. It is

still the general rule that an indefinite hiring, under circumstances that do not permit the implication of any fixed period of duration, is presumed to be terminable at the will of either party, with the burden on the party asserting a fixed period. 53 Am Jur 2d, Master and Servant §§ 27, 43.

5. See generally, the annotation in 12 ALR4th 544, for a discussion of the modern status of the at-will rule.

123

and precise; hence, a title search may succeed well, and so might a date-restricted search.

Once you locate a pertinent annotation, you should work through it much as you would in paper, although the online version is presented somewhat differently. For example, once you identify a pertinent section in the outline or index, you can link to that section. You can also link from a section to a cumulative update. New case synopses are added weekly. Furthermore, you will receive a notice if the annotation has been superseded and can easily link to the new annotation. You can quickly move to a pertinent case through the link in the annotation. However, note that the accompanying case from the book version is not part of the online version.

Exhibit 6.5 (at page 122) presents our A.L.R. template, filled in to reflect our research, both in paper and online, into the issue of a breach of contract.

2. Citing A.L.R.s

A cite to an A.L.R. annotation includes the author's full name (if available), the title of the annotation, the volume and series, beginning page number, and date. Here are two examples:

☐ *Bluebook* Rule 16.6.6: Theresa L. Kruk, Annotation, *Right to Discharge Allegedly "At-Will" Employee as Affected by Employer's Promulgation of Employment Policies as to Discharge*, 33 A.L.R.4th 120 (1984 & Supp. 2007).

☐ *ALWD* Rule 24: Theresa L. Kruk, *Right to Discharge Allegedly "At-Will" Employee as Affected by Employer's Promulgation of Employment Policies as to Discharge*, 33 A.L.R.4th 120 (1984 & Supp. 2007).

C. WHAT ELSE?

Lawyers' Edition Annotations: In addition to A.L.R. annotations, annotations discussing United States Supreme Court cases on certain major topics appear in a publication called *United States Supreme Court Reports Lawyers' Edition.*

Quick Indexes: These two single-volume indexes cover the third through sixth series and the federal series.

West's ALR Digest: This new finding tool uses the framework West has created for categorizing cases by topic. Once you have identified a pertinent topic and key number within that topic (a system described in detail in Chapter 9), you can look up that topic and key number and learn whether there is a pertinent A.L.R.

EXHIBIT 6.5	A.L.R. Annotations Template for Canoga Case

Issue:	Citation Information:
Did the orchestra breach a contract by not following its handbook language providing for a hearing by the board of directors?	• *Theresa Ludwig Kruk* • *Right to Discharge Allegedly "At-Will" Employee as Affected by Employer's Promulgation of Employment Policies as to Discharge* • *Vol. 33 of A.L.R. 4th, page 120* • *Main volume 1984; pocket part 2007*
Date of events: *Sept. 7, 2007*	

Date of research: *Nov. 17, 2007*

Search and Find:

located ALR by . . .	checked for my state's cases . . .
• *Paper index: Discharge from Employment or Office → At-Will Employee → this A.L.R.* • *Westlaw: ti(discharg! terminat! & employe! & policy handbook manual).*	*Table of jurisdictions.*
located pertinent material by . . .	updated by . . .
Annotation index and outline.	*Paper: 2007 pocket part to main volume. Online: extensive listing of cases decided after the original annotation.*

Information and Implications:
• *Employment at will permits discharging an employee for any reason. § 2* • *Some courts have held that this right can be restricted by an employer policy re discharge. Id.* • *New Mexico cases are cited in the 2007 pocket part.* • *This rule benefits Canoga if the circumstances are right; there is policy re discharge.*

Next Steps:

questions to consider:	leads to pursue:
The handbook does not state that the orchestra must have a good reason. Rather, the policy addresses post-discharge procedures — are they also within this rule?	*Lukoski v. Sandia Indian Management Co. — New Mexico 1988 — 748 P.2d 507.*

Citing A.L.R. Annotations: It is possible to citate, i.e., find authorities citing to, A.L.R. annotations in both LexisNexis' Shepard's and Westlaw's KeyCite services. The most likely reason for doing this is to find additional cases and commentary.

Some Features of the Older Series: A.L.R.1st has its own index; the same is true of A.L.R.2d. The annotations in the first series are supplemented by the *A.L.R. Blue Book of Supplemental Decisions;* A.L.R.2d annotations are updated by *A.L.R.2d Later Case Service.*

RESTATEMENTS

A. What Are the Restatements, and Why Are They Useful?
B. How Do You Research in and Cite Restatements?
C. What Else?

A. WHAT ARE THE RESTATEMENTS, AND WHY ARE THEY USEFUL?

The Restatements are a distinctly legal form of commentary; they are the most law-like of the various types of commentary. To use the Restatements effectively, you need to understand why they came to be, how they are created, how they are formatted, and how courts view them.

During the early twentieth century, two schools of legal scholarship battled. The rationalists believed that the common law — that is, the body of law comprised of decisions of the courts — consisted of immutable principles that could be expressed in an organized manner. The realists believed that the common law reflected the needs of the litigants, the biases of judges, and prevailing social norms. In 1923, the rationalists mobilized to organize the American Law Institute (ALI). The ALI's goal was to promulgate one highly authoritative, rule-like source stating the common law. Because the purpose of the source was not to create law, but rather to state what already existed, the source was named the Restatements. The first Restatement, covering the law of contracts, was promulgated in 1932.

EXHIBIT 7.1	Restatement Subjects, Series, and Adoption Dates

Subject	Series and Date(s) of Adoption
Agency	first 1933, second 1957, third 2005
Conflict of Laws	first 1934, second 1969, 1988
Contracts	first 1932, second 1979
Foreign Relations	second 1962, 1964, 1965, third 1986
Judgments	first 1942, second 1980
Law Governing Lawyers	third 1998
Property	first 1936, 1940, 1944
Landlord and Tenant	second 1976
Donative Transfers	second 1981, 1984, 1987, 1990
Mortgages	third 1996
Servitudes	third 1998
Wills & Other Donative Transfers	third 1998
Restitution	first 1936
Security	first 1941
Suretyship & Guaranty	third 1995
Torts	first 1934, 1938, 1939, second 1963, 1964, 1976, 1977
Apportionment of Liability	third 1999
Products Liability	third 1997
Trusts	first 1935, second 1957, third 2001, 2003, 2007
Prudent Investor Rule	third 1990
Unfair Competition	third 1993

In development (as of fall 2007):
Restitution and Unjust Enrichment;
Torts — Liability for Physical Harm and Liability for Economic Loss; and
Employment Law.

The ALI has continued to promulgate Restatements over the past seventy-five years. See Exhibit 7.1 (at page 125). Note that the Restatements do not cover every legal subject. Note as well that each Restatement carries not only the name of the subject but also a series designation reflecting the date of adoption: the first series Restatements were adopted in 1932–1942, the second series in 1957–1981, and the third in 1986 to the present.

As the Restatements have matured, there has been a shift in policy. Early on, the Restatements were to state the rule followed by the majority of courts around the country, even if the minority rule were wiser. This policy could slow the development of the law, however. Recent Restatements state the minority rule when it is deemed wiser than the majority rule.

Each Restatement is the product of a lengthy and wide-ranging deliberative process, which generally involves the following steps: preparation of a draft by the reporter, an eminent scholar in the particular field; review of that draft by a panel of experts; consideration by the ALI Council — a group of approximately sixty judges, attorneys, and professors; consideration by the entire ALI membership (including up to 3,000 elected members); submission to the public and the legal profession for comment; and approval by the ALI Council and membership. This process is, obviously, far more extensive than the process used to create any other type of commentary.

Given the purpose of the Restatements and the ALI process, it is not surprising that the Restatements consist not only of expository prose but also rather finely honed sentences, each stating a distinct rule, which appears in boldface[1] in the official books. Each rule, or section, is followed by explanatory material:

- ☐ comments, which discuss the rule's scope, meaning, and rationale;
- ☐ illustrations, which are short stories that illustrate the application of the rule and typically reflect influential cases from which the rule was derived; and
- ☐ for more recent Restatements, reporter's notes, which typically explain the history of the rule and refer to leading cases and commentary.

The rules and supporting materials on a particular subject are compiled into chapters organized to reflect the logical structure of the subject.

Given the Restatements' purpose, means of creation, and format, it is not surprising that the Restatements are widely viewed as the most authoritative commentary and that courts around the country routinely cite and indeed even adopt Restatement rules. A court is not obligated to follow the Restatement: a court may reject a Restatement rule, adopt only part of a rule, incorporate one illustration but not another, etc. According to the *ALI Annual Report* for 2002, as of April 1, 2002, the Restatements had been cited by the courts almost 155,000 times.

For the most part, the Restatements are not where you will begin your research. There may not be a Restatement on your research topic, and even if

---

1. You may hear the term "black-letter law," which means a legal rule that is fundamental and well settled. Although many Restatement rules amount to black-letter law, the term refers not to the boldface print of the Restatement, but rather to books printed in Gothic type, which is very bold.

there is one, the Restatements are not as easy to read as other types of commentary. Rather, you are likely to use a Restatement once you already know something about your research topic, in particular for the following purposes:

- ☐ to obtain a succinct and very credible statement of the law on a settled topic;
- ☐ to discern some of the nuances in and policies underlying a rule, through the comments and illustrations; and
- ☐ to obtain a highly credible statement of a rule, when the case law in your jurisdiction has no rule on your topic or an outmoded rule that differs from the Restatement rule.

As you work with the Restatements, keep in mind that they do have limitations. The Restatements are not revised on a regular basis, as you can see from Exhibit 7.1, and the law may develop differently from the Restatement rule. There is no attempt to capture or explain the variations in approach from courts around the country. A few rules are thought not to restate the law or the desirable rule, but rather the views of the primary authors or an awkward compromise of the various views proposed during the deliberations.

To counter some of these limitations, before you rely to a significant extent on a Restatement rule, you should research how it has been received by courts. Most important is whether it has been adopted, noted, rejected, or not discussed in the case law of your jurisdiction. If you find no indication of your jurisdiction's view of the rule, you should examine how it has been received by other courts.

Researching the employee handbook issue in the Canoga case in the Restatement of Contracts (Second), we found section 2, which defines "promise," a key element of an enforceable contract. See Exhibit 7.2 (at pages 128–32).

B. HOW DO YOU RESEARCH IN AND CITE RESTATEMENTS?

As shown in Exhibit 7.3 (at page 133), our Restatements template, researching in the Restatements entails formulating a legal issue involving general principles, selecting the pertinent Restatement, identifying the pertinent section, reading the rule and supporting materials, considering the implications for your client's situation, and looking for key cases citing the Restatements.

You can research the Restatements in paper or online through Lexis-Nexis and Westlaw. In some ways, a Restatement resembles a treatise because it has a strong internal organization; this suggests researching in paper. On the other hand, a Restatement resembles an A.L.R. annotation because thorough Restatement research entails looking for key cases citing a Restatement section in what can be a large set of case summaries; this suggests online research. Thus the approach presented here is a hybrid. See Exhibit 7.4 (at page 134) for an overview of the major resources for Restatements research.

EXHIBIT 7.2	Restatement Rule and Explanatory Material, from Restatement (Second) of Contracts (paper source)*

§ 1   CONTRACTS, SECOND   Ch. 1

Wis. L. Rev. 303; Macauley, Contract Law and Contract Research, 20 J. Legal Ed. 452 (1968); Farnsworth, The Past of Promise: An Historical Introduction to Contract, 69 Colum. L. Rev. 576 (1969); Macneil, The Many Futures of Contract, 47 So. Cal. L. Rev. 691 (1974); Macneil, Restatement, Second, of Contracts and Presentation, 60 Va. L. Rev. 589 (1974); Atiyah, Contracts, Promises and the Law of Obligations, 94 L. Q. Rev. 193 (1978); see also Leff, Contract as Thing, 19 Amer. U. L. Rev. 131 (1970).

Comments a and b. For a concise discussion of what constitutes a contract, how it can be created and its relation to tort actions for fraud, see Steinberg v. Chicago Medical School, 69 Ill.2d 320, 371 N.E.2d 634 (1977).

Comment e. Illustration 1 is new.

Comment f. Section 12 of the original Restatement defined unilateral and bilateral contracts. It has not been carried forward because of doubt as to the utility of the distinction, often treated as fundamental, between the two types. As defined in the original Restatement, "unilateral contract" included three quite different types of transaction: (1) the promise which does not contemplate a bargain, such as the promise under seal to make a gift, (2) certain option contracts, such as the option under seal (see §§ 25, 45), and (3) the bargain completed on one side, such as the loan which is to be repaid. This grouping of unlike transactions was productive of confusion.

Moreover, as to bargains, the distinction tends to suggest, erroneously, that the obligation to repay a loan is somehow different if the actual delivery of the money was preceded by an advance commitment from the obligation resulting from a simultaneous loan and commitment. It also causes confusion in cases where performance is complete on one side except for an incidental or collateral promise, as where an offer to buy goods is accepted by shipment and a warranty is implied. Finally, the effect of the distinction has been to exaggerate the importance of the type of bargain in which one party begins performance without making any commitment, as in the classic classroom case of the promise to pay a reward for climbing a flagpole.

The principal value of the distinction has been the emphasis it has given to the fact that a promise is often binding on the promisor even though the promisee is not bound by any promise. This value is retained in § 25 on option contracts. But the terms unilateral and bilateral are generally avoided in this Restatement.

§ 2.   Promise; Promisor; Promisee; Beneficiary

(1) A promise is a manifestation of intention to act or refrain from acting in a specified way, so made as to justify a promisee in understanding that a commitment has been made.

(2) The person manifesting the intention is the promisor.

See Appendix for Court Citations and Cross References

EXHIBIT 7.2   *(continued)*

Ch. 1   **MEANING OF TERMS**   **§ 2**

(3) The person to whom the manifestation is addressed is the promisee.

(4) Where performance will benefit a person other than the promisee, that person is a beneficiary.

Comment:

a.   Acts and resulting relations.   "Promise" as used in the Restatement of this Subject denotes the act of the promisor. If by virtue of other operative facts there is a legal duty to perform, the promise is a contract; but the word "promise" is not limited to acts having legal effect. Like "contract," however, the word "promise" is commonly and quite properly also used to refer to the complex of human relations which results from the promisor's words or acts of assurance, including the justified expectations of the promisee and any moral or legal duty which arises to make good the assurance by performance. The performance may be specified either in terms describing the action of the promisor or in terms of the result which that action or inaction is to bring about.

b.   Manifestation of intention.   Many contract disputes arise because different people attach different meanings to the same words and conduct. The phrase "manifestation of intention" adopts an external or objective standard for interpreting conduct; it means the external expression of intention as distinguished from undisclosed intention. A promisor manifests an intention if he believes or has reason to believe that the promisee will infer that intention from his words or conduct. Rules governing cases where the promisee could reasonably draw more than one inference as to the promisor's intention are stated in connection with the acceptance of offers (see §§ 19 and 20), and the scope of contractual obligations (see §§ 201, 219).

c.   Promise of action by third person; guaranty.   Words are often used which in terms promise action or inaction by a third person, or which promise a result obtainable only by such action. Such words are commonly understood as a promise of conduct by the promisor which will be sufficient to bring about the action or inaction or result, or to answer for harm caused by failure. An example is a guaranty that a third person will perform his promise. Such words constitute a promise as here defined only if they justify a promisee in an expectation of some action or inaction on the part of the promisor.

d.   Promise of event beyond human control; warranty.   Words which in terms promise that an event not within human control will occur may be interpreted to include a promise to answer for harm caused by the failure of the event to occur. An example is a warranty

---

See Appendix for Court Citations and Cross References

1 A.L.I.Contracts 2nd—2

EXHIBIT 7.2   *(continued)*

---

§ 2   **CONTRACTS, SECOND**   **Ch. 1**

of an existing or past fact, such as a warranty that a horse is sound, or that a ship arrived in a foreign port some days previously. Such promises are often made when the parties are ignorant of the actual facts regarding which they bargain, and may be dealt with as if the warrantor could cause the fact to be as he asserted. It is then immaterial that the actual condition of affairs may be irrevocably fixed before the promise is made.

Words of warranty, like other conduct, must be interpreted in the light of the circumstances and the reasonable expectations of the parties. In an insurance contract, a "warranty" by the insured is usually not a promise at all; it may be merely a representation of fact, or, more commonly, the fact warranted is a condition of the insurer's duty to pay (see § 225(3)). In the sale of goods, on the other hand, a similar warranty normally also includes a promise to answer for damages (see Uniform Commercial Code § 2–715).

Illustrations:

1. A, the builder of a house, or the inventor of the material used in part of its construction, says to B, the owner of the house, "I warrant that this house will never burn down." This includes a promise to pay for harm if the house should burn down.

2. A, by a charter-party, undertakes that the "good ship Dove," having sailed from Marseilles a week ago for New York, shall take on a cargo for B on her arrival in New York. The statement of the quality of the ship and the statement of her time of sailing from Marseilles include promises to pay for harm if the statement is untrue.

e. Illusory promises; mere statements of intention. Words of promise which by their terms make performance entirely optional with the "promisor" whatever may happen, or whatever course of conduct in other respects he may pursue, do not constitute a promise. Although such words are often referred to as forming an illusory promise, they do not fall within the present definition of promise. They may not even manifest any intention on the part of the promisor. Even if a present intention is manifested, the reservation of an option to change that intention means that there can be no promisee who is justified in an expectation of performance.

On the other hand, a promise may be made even though no duty of performance can arise unless some event occurs (see §§ 224, 225(1)). Such a conditional promise is no less a promise because there is small likelihood that any duty of performance will arise, as in the case of a promise to insure against fire a thoroughly fireproof building. There

---

See Appendix for Court Citations and Cross References

EXHIBIT 7.2   *(continued)*

Ch. 1   **MEANING OF TERMS**   **§ 2**

may be a promise in such a case even though the duty to perform depends on a state of mind of the promisor other than his own unfettered wish (see § 228), or on an event within the promisor's control.

Illustration:

> 3. A says to B, "I will employ you for a year at a salary of $5,000 if I go into business." This is a promise, even though it is wholly optional with A to go into business or not.

f. Opinions and predictions. A promise must be distinguished from a statement of opinion or a mere prediction of future events. The distinction is not usually difficult in the case of an informal gratuitous opinion, since there is often no manifestation of intention to act or refrain from acting or to bring about a result, no expectation of performance and no consideration. The problem is frequently presented, however, whether words of a seller of goods amount to a warranty. Under Uniform Commercial Code § 2–313(2) a statement purporting to be merely the seller's opinion does not create a warranty, but the buyer's reliance on the seller's skill and judgment may create an implied warranty that the goods are fit for a particular purpose under Uniform Commercial Code § 2–315. In any case where an expert opinion is paid for, there is likely to be an implied promise that the expert will act with reasonable care and skill.

A promise often refers to future events which are predicted or assumed rather than promised. Thus a promise to render personal service at a particular future time commonly rests on an assumption that the promisor will be alive and well at that time; a promise to paint a building may similarly rest on an assumption that the building will be in existence. Such cases are the subject of Chapter 11. The promisor may of course promise to answer for harm caused by the failure of the future event to occur; if he does not, such a failure may discharge any duty of performance.

Illustration:

> 4. A, on seeing a house of thoroughly fireproof construction, says to B, the owner, "This house will never burn down." This is not a promise but merely an opinion or prediction. If A had been paid for his opinion as an expert, there might be an implied promise that he would employ reasonable care and skill in forming and giving his opinion.

g. Promisee and beneficiary. The word promisee is used repeatedly in discussion of the law of contracts, and it cannot be avoided here. In common usage the promisee is the person to whom the prom-

See Appendix for Court Citations and Cross References

EXHIBIT 7.2   *(continued)*

§ 2   CONTRACTS, SECOND   Ch. 1

ise is made; as promise is defined here, the promisee might be the person to whom the manifestation of the promisor's intention is communicated. In many situations, however, a promise is complete and binding before the communication is received (see, for example, §§ 63 and 104(1)). To cover such cases, the promisee is defined here as the addressee. As to agents or purported agents of the addressee, see § 52 Comment *c*.

In the usual situation the promisee also bears other relations to the promisor, and the word promisee is sometimes used to refer to one or more of those relations. Thus, in the simple case of a loan of money, the lender is not only the addressee of the promise but also the person to whom performance is to be rendered, the person who will receive economic benefit, the person who furnished the consideration, and the person to whom the legal duty of the promisor runs. As the word promisee is here defined, none of these relations is essential.

Contractual rights of persons not parties to the contract are the subject of Chapter 14. The promisor and promisee are the "parties" to a promise; a third person who will benefit from performance is a "beneficiary." A beneficiary may or may not have a legal right to performance; like "promisee", the term is neutral with respect to rights and duties. A person who is entitled under the terms of a letter of credit to draw or demand payment is commonly called a beneficiary, but such a person is ordinarily a promisee under the present definition. See Uniform Commercial Code § 5–103.

REPORTER'S NOTE

This Section substitutes the concept of a "manifestation of intention to act . . . " for the phrase used in former § 2(1): "an undertaking . . . that something shall happen. . . . " The older definition did not identify the essential characteristics of an undertaking. See Gardner, An Inquiry Into the Principles of Contracts, 46 Harv. L. Rev. 1, 5 (1932). The present definition of promise is based on 1 Corbin, Contracts § 13 (1963 & Supp. 1980). See also 1 id. § 15; 1 Williston, Contracts § 1A (3d ed. 1957). The definitions of "promisor," "promise" and "beneficiary" are new. Compare Gardner, Massachusetts Annota-

tions, Restatement of Contracts, Chapter 6, at 64 (1935).

Comment a. See Coffman Industries, Inc. v. Gorman-Taber Co., 521 S.W.2d 763 (Mo. Ct. App. 1975); Farnsworth, The Past of Promise: An Historical Introduction to Contract, 69 Colum. L. Rev. 576 (1969).

Comment d. This Comment is based on former § 2(2). Illustrations 1 and 2 are based on Illustrations 2 and 3 to former § 2.

Comment e. See Pappas v. Bever, 219 N.W.2d 720 (Iowa 1974). Illustration 3 is based on Illustration 4 to former § 2.

See Appendix for Court Citations and Cross References

EXHIBIT 7.3	Restatements Template

Issue:	Citation Information: • Restatement • series • section(s), explanatory material • date of publication
Date of events:	

Date of research:

Search and Find:

located pertinent section by . . .	located pertinent cases by . . .

Information and implications:

- look for rule
- look for pertinent comments and illustrations
- look for references in reporter's note
- note exact location, e.g., rule number, illustration letter
- connect information to client's situation

Next Steps:

questions to consider:	leads to pursue:

	EXHIBIT 7.4	Major Restatements Resources

Paper	*LexisNexis*	*Westlaw*
Rule Volumes • browse table of contents • look up terms in index	Restatement Database without Case Summaries • browse or search table of contents • full-text key-word search	Restatement Datebase with Case Summaries • browse or search table of contents • full-text key-word searching — including case summaries
Case Summaries • main volume • pocket part • appendix • appendix pocket part • pamphlets • *Interim Case Citations*	Database of Case Summaries • full-text key-word search	Restatement Database with Case Summaries • full-text key-word searching

---

Restatements in paper and online

▶ Select the applicable Restatement and series.

▶ Use the table of contents or index to identify one or more pertinent sections.

▶ Read the rules, comments, illustrations, and reporter's note.

▶ Locate and review important cases citing the rule and pertinent explanatory material.

Researching the Restatements: To locate a pertinent Restatement rule, you must first determine which Restatement, e.g., the Restatement of Contracts or the Restatement of Torts, covers your research topic. If you have already done some research in commentary, this should not be difficult. If your topic is covered by more than one series, you generally should start with the more recent.

To locate pertinent sections in paper, look up your research terms in the index, or read over the table of contents for the Restatement you chose. See Exhibit 7.5 (at page 136). As in paper, the best online option is browsing the table of contents; another option is key-word searching if your topic has one or more distinctive legal terms or a common factual setting. Look not just for one pertinent section; for many research topics, you will want to read a number of related sections, typically all sections in a chapter, as well as any pertinent definitions or overarching principles covered in the first chapter.

As you read the pertinent section(s), first study the rule, then read the supporting material. Take care to glean as much as possible, including:

- ☐ the exact language of the rule;
- ☐ comments on the rule that pertain to your client's situation;
- ☐ illustrations that factually parallel your client's situation;
- ☐ any discussion of the rule's derivation, e.g., whether it is a majority or minority rule, how it relates to an earlier Restatement;
- ☐ references to other related Restatement sections; and
- ☐ references to leading cases (especially any from your jurisdiction) and commentary.

As noted previously, if you plan to rely to a significant degree on a Restatement rule, you should learn how it has been received in your jurisdiction and perhaps in other jurisdictions as well. Happily, the ALI editors prepare summaries of cases citing Restatement sections. Each summary contains a brief statement of the facts and outcome, as well as a citation to the case. See Exhibit 7.6 (at page 137). The case summaries appear in various print publications, each covering a certain time span: the main volume, its pocket part, separate appendix volumes, their pocket parts, supplementary pamphlets, *Interim Case Citations to the Restatements of the Law*, and in the Table of Citations in *Interim Case Citations*. Because the summaries appear in alphabetical order by state, you can fairly easily locate the summaries from your jurisdiction.

Identifying key cases citing a pertinent section is easier to do online than in paper because the online database is more comprehensive than the various paper volumes and can be searched for key words. To find cases in your jurisdiction, search for the various abbreviations of your jurisdiction's courts. To find factually similar cases, search for distinctive factual terms.

If the Restatement you are using is not the first on the subject and has few citing cases, especially if you have not found a case summary from your jurisdiction, you may want to engage in retrospective research. Although the newer version is meant by the ALI to supercede the previous version, some courts may not support the newer version, so you should look for citations to the earlier version. You would most likely do this retrospective research if reliance on a Restatement section is critical to your analysis.

Exhibit 7.7 (at page 138) presents our Restatement template filled in to reflect our research for the Canoga case in the Restatement (Second) of Contracts.

Citing Restatements: A cite to Restatement material includes the name (including the series) of the Restatement, the section number, and the date of publication. Here are two examples:

- ☐ *Bluebook* Rule 12.8.5: Restatement (Second) of Contracts § 2 (1981).
- ☐ *ALWD* Rule 27.1: *Restatement (Second) of Contracts* § 2 (1981).

EXHIBIT 7.5   Restatement Table of Contents (paper source)*

TABLE OF CONTENTS

Volume 1

Foreword by Herbert Wechsler
Introduction

Chapter 1

MEANING OF TERMS

Section

Chapter 2

FORMATION OF CONTRACTS—PARTIES AND CAPACITY

Chapter 3

FORMATION OF CONTRACTS—MUTUAL ASSENT

TOPIC 1.   IN GENERAL

TOPIC 2. MANIFESTATION OF ASSENT IN GENERAL

1 A.L.I. Contracts 2nd   IX

| EXHIBIT 7.6 | Restatement Case Summaries, from Westlaw (online source) |

REST 2d CONTR § 2   FOR EDUCATIONAL USE ONLY   Page 17

Restatement (Second) of Contracts § 2 (1981)

statements that the bank would continue to support them, the farmers elected to stay in the dairy business and did not participate in a government dairy buyout program. State Bank of Standish v. Curry, 442 Mich. 76, 85, 500 N.W.2d 104, 108.

Neb.1991. Subsec. (1) quot. in disc. and quot. in case cit. in disc. A purchaser of cable television systems sued the sellers for failing to deliver the promised amount of subscribers specified in the contract. The sellers claimed that the purchaser forfeited any right to damages because it did not comply with the contract notice provisions. The trial court granted the purchaser partial summary judgment on the issue of the sellers' liability for the subscriber shortfall and damages were awarded. Affirming in part, vacating in part, and remanding, this court held, inter alia, that the notice provisions in the contract were promissory rather than conditional and, therefore, the purchaser's noncompliance did not discharge the sellers' liability. The court stated that the absence of any language indicative of a condition precluded a conclusion that the parties clearly intended the notice requirements to constitute a condition to the creation of a contract. Harmon Cable Com. v. Scope Cable Tele., 237 Neb. 871, 468 N.W.2d 350, 359.

N.M.App.1993. Subsec. (1) quot. in diss. op. Terminated employee sued employer for wrongful discharge, alleging that he was fired in retaliation for requesting that occupational health and safety bureau investigate chemical usage and employee health problems at defendant's workplace. The parties entered into settlement agreement approved by the bureau. The trial court entered partial summary judgment for defendant, holding that the agreement settled plaintiff's claim for wrongful discharge and gave rise to an accord and satisfaction of that claim. This court reversed and remanded for trial including factual issue whether parties intended a universal accord and satisfaction. A dissent would affirm, contending that plaintiff failed to rebut the presumption of a complete accord and satisfaction. It argued that private thoughts of parties to contract were of no consequence in interpreting contract terms, and argued that test of contract's meaning was objective, based on what parties said and did and surrounding circumstances. Gutierrez v. Sundancer Indian Jewelry, 117 N.M. 41, 868 P.2d 1266, 1277.

N.D.App.1992. Cit. in disc. The clerk of the state district court fired the deputy clerk. The deputy clerk then appealed her termination to the county board of commissioners, which reinstated her to her former position. Former deputy clerk rejected her reinstatement and later sued the county and the clerk for damages for wrongful termination, asserting, inter alia, that her contractual employment rights under the county personnel manual were breached. Trial court granted summary judgment to defendants, holding that former deputy clerk was an at-will employee without contractual employment rights. Reversing and remanding, this court held that deputy clerk had raised genuine issues of material fact about whether she had contractual employment rights under the personnel manual. The personnel manual had to be examined to determine whether it disclosed an intent to overcome the presumption of at-will employment. Schmidt v. Ramsey County, 488 N.W.2d 411, 413.

Ohio App.1991. Subsec. (1) quot. in disc. Employees sued employer for wrongful termination under contract and promissory estoppel theories. The trial court granted employer summary judgment. Affirming on the contract theory, this court held that employer laid employees off for legitimate economic reasons and that no provision in employment contracts insulated employees from such layoffs. Reversing on the promissory estoppel theory and remanding for further proceedings, this court held that, while neither the personnel manual nor pension plan conveyed any promise preventing employer from laying off employees, supervisor's statements regarding length of future employment presented a genuine issue of material fact on the issue of promissory estoppel. Stull v. Combustion Engineering, Inc., 72 Ohio App.3d 553, 595 N.E.2d 504, 507.

Pa.Super.1994. Cit. in headnote, com. (e) quot. in ftn. Sellers contracted to sell land upon which they operated recreation vehicle firm to purchaser that intended to construct warehouse. Buyer's agent requested sellers to immediately vacate premises by evicting tenants and making inventory storage available for buyer. Sellers complied with request, after informing agent that request would require sellers to drastically reduce their own inventory and lose discounts and inventory for future sale. When buyer failed to perform, sellers sued for losses sustained as result of making property immediately available. Trial court granted buyer summary judgment,

EXHIBIT 7.7	Restatements Template for Canoga Case

Issue:	Citation Information:
Does it matter whether the orchestra did not mean the handbook to be viewed as a contract?	• *Restatement of Contracts* • *Second* • *§ 2* • *1981*
Date of events: *Sept. 7, 2007*	

Date of research: *Nov. 9, 2007*

Search and Find:

located pertinent rule by . . .	located pertinent cases by . . .
Reading paper list of chapters and chapter outlines.	*Westlaw: retrieved § 2; ran search for (1) abbreviations of New Mexico courts and (2) employee /s handbook manual.*

Information and Implications:

A promise is a "manifestation of intention to act . . . , so made as to justify a promisee, in understanding that a commitment has been made." § 2

The focus is the external expression — not undisclosed intention. Comment (b).

Words of promise that make performance "entirely optional with the 'promisor' whatever may happen" are not a promise. Comment e.

We need not be concerned with what the board thought but rather with the handbook and Canoga's justifiable understanding.

Next Steps:

questions to consider:	leads to pursue:
How does the entire handbook read? How did she come to receive it?	*Gutierrez v. Sundancer Indian Jewelry, 868 P.2d 1266 — N.M. App. 1993 case re meaning of settlement; § 2 cited in dissenting opinion.* *Continental Airlines, Inc. v. Keenan, 731 P.2d 708 — Colorado case with similar facts.*

If you are citing to a comment or illustration, you would so indicate, as follows (using the *Bluebook* typeface):

- ☐   Restatement (Second) of Contracts § 2 cmt. a (1981).
- ☐   Restatement (Second) of Contracts § 2 illus. 1 (1981).

C.   WHAT ELSE?

Work in Progress. You can follow the development of a pending Restatement through three ALI publications: *Annual Reports, Proceedings,* and *The ALI Reporter,* which are available in paper and online. More specifically, the drafts of a Restatement in progress are available through the ALI website, LexisNexis, and Westlaw.

   Historical Materials. To research the evolution of an existing or past Restatement section, you could visit the University of Pennsylvania's Biddle Law Library, use HeinOnline, or search in Westlaw's Restatements archives database.

   Citing the Restatements. You can cite the Restatements through LexisNexis' Shepard's and Westlaw's KeyCite services. These services will be more up-to-date than the case summaries, and you will find references not only to citing cases but also to selected commentary, such as law reviews. However, you will not find summaries of the cases—just their citations.

ADDITIONAL TYPES OF COMMENTARY AND STRATEGY

A. Additional Types of Commentary
B. Strategies for Commentary Research

Exhibit 8.1   Commentary Research Factors

A.   ADDITIONAL TYPES OF COMMENTARY

In addition to the types of commentary described in the other chapters in this unit, several other types merit mention.

Jury Instructions.   At the end of a jury trial, the jury is instructed on the law applicable to the case. Often the instructions are drawn from a set of jury instructions or a jury instruction guide (JIG). JIGs typically are written by private authors (professors or lawyers), a group of judges, a bar association committee, or a combination of these, and they state the law of a specific jurisdiction. Each instruction states the rule in a form similar to a Restatement section and typically is supplemented by notes stating the source of the instruction and discussing the pertinent cases and statutes. Thus JIGs can be useful not only when you are seeking sample instructions in a trial setting but also in nonlitigation settings. Of the authorities discussed in this chapter, JIGs are the most citable; in particular you would cite to a JIG in a trial memorandum or in an appellate brief discussing how the jury was instructed.

Practice Materials.   After researching and analyzing a client's problem, a lawyer often moves on to various activities designed to solve that problem, such as drafting documents or filing a lawsuit. Some commentary sources provide practical advice and model forms for such activities; some also provide an overview of the law behind the advice or form. Examples of practice materials with broad coverage are *American Jurisprudence Trials, American Jurisprudence Proof of Facts, Causes of Action, American Jurisprudence Legal Forms, American Jurisprudence Pleading and Practice Forms*, and *West's Legal Forms*; some are now in their second or third series. There are numerous subject-specific sources of this type as well, such as form books focused on corporate or tax law. These practice materials are rarely used as authority for the legal propositions they state, but they can provide a helpful bridge between legal analysis and actions to be taken on the client's behalf.

CLE Materials.   Many states require lawyers to take courses to continuously improve their skills. Presenters at continuing legal education (CLE) programs prepare written materials containing outlines, checklists, sample documents, and important cases and statutes. CLE materials can be useful because they address practical aspects of a topic, typically provide significant detail about a specific jurisdiction's law, and may provide the first discussion of new developments. However, they are rarely cited.

B.   STRATEGIES FOR COMMENTARY RESEARCH

1.   Choosing Among Commentary Sources

All of the sources covered in this unit serve dual functions as commentary and finding tools for other sources, including the law. You do not need to use every source on every research project. How do you know when to use which source, so as to produce comprehensive, correct, and credible research and yet avoid costly excessive effort?

Exhibit 8.1 (at page 142) presents factors to consider as you choose among commentary sources. Although the characteristics are grouped under the four research goals (cost-effectiveness, comprehensiveness, etc.), many of the characteristics relate to more than one research goal. For instance, accuracy and lack of bias relate to both correctness and credibility. As you fill in the chart, you may notice some patterns.

A wide scope of coverage usually comes at the expense of detailed coverage. For example, encyclopedias cover a very full range of legal subjects in general terms, while A.L.R. annotations and legal periodical articles provide detailed coverage of specific subjects. The generality of an encyclopedia can be helpful at the outset of a research project when you need big-picture information. A narrow yet pertinent A.L.R. annotation or legal periodical article may be more helpful when you have come to focus on a well defined research topic.

Some sources excel at providing a coherent and comprehensive overview of a subject that is fairly static; others excel at providing a shorter analysis of targeted hot topics. For example, periodicals and A.L.R. annotations are published periodically, so they are better able to respond quickly to changes in the law than are encyclopedias and Restatements.

Authorities written by staff members of publishers tend to differ in nature from those produced other ways. The former tend to be descriptive, the latter analytical and critical. Not coincidentally, the citability of sources varies accordingly. Treatises and periodicals, especially those written by recognized

EXHIBIT 8.1	Commentary Research Factors

	Correctness		Comprehensiveness			
	Accuracy, Lack of Bias	Updating Means & Frequency	Breadth of Topics Covered	Depth of Coverage of Each Topic	Attention to Rules, Facts, & Principles	Description Only, or Critique Too
Encyclopedia						
Treatises						
Periodical Articles						
A.L.R. Annotations						
Restatements						

	Credibility			Cost-Effectiveness			
	Reputation of Author(s), Publisher, or Book	Strength of Supporting Citations	Clarity, Persua- siveness	Clarity of Organization	Means of Access (index, Boolean search, etc.)	Ease of Reading and Retention	Total Cost (fees & time)
Encyclopedia							
Treatises							
Periodical Articles							
A.L.R. Annotations							
Restatements							

experts, are quite citable, and Restatements, promulgated by a group of experts through a long deliberative process, are highly citable.

Furthermore, you may have several periodical articles, for example, from which to choose. If you plow through your list in no particular order, you may find yourself reading more material than you need to; this is not cost-effective research. Instead, you first should rank the authorities by how much promise they show. Give high priority to the authorities with your research terms in their titles and subject descriptions. If you come across more than one citation to a source, pursue that source before others.

2. Deciding Whether to Cite Commentary

As you research, keep in mind which sources you eventually will be able to cite in the final written product embodying your research. You should cite to the law — cases, statutes, administrative materials, rules of procedure — whenever possible, of course. Commentary sources are most often cited for several purposes:

- ☐ A general proposition, such as the number of jurisdictions adopting a rule or a very widely agreed-upon principle, may not need a citation to the law.
- ☐ A commentary source may be cited when your jurisdiction has not considered your research topic.
- ☐ A commentary source may be cited for its criticism or policy analysis of an established rule of law.
- ☐ Commentary sources supporting a proposition that diverges from current law can be cited in an argument that the law should change.

You should not rely on a commentary source without reading the sources on which it relies. Only by reading the law itself will you get the full flavor of the law and detect ambiguities, misinterpretations, and perhaps even mistakes made by the commentary author.

INTERLUDE NO. 2: RESEARCH IN COMMENTARY

Not surprisingly, we found useful information in all five types of commentary reasonably smoothly.

We started out researching the breach-of-contract issue in Am. Jur. 2d in paper. We meandered in the index a bit — master and servant? employer and employee? employment contract? — before settling on the Wrongful Discharge topic. Once there, we quickly zeroed in on section 44, discussing grievance and appeal procedures. The text seems to suggest that sometimes the employer's manual does create a contract, sometimes not. Key to the outcome is how clear and promissory the language is. We found cites to several cases from other states, but no cites to New Mexico cases.

It seems likely that the orchestra board and management saw the manual as not promissory. But does it matter what management and the board thought? Does that govern the issue of "promissory"? To get at the meaning of "promise," we turned to the Restatement (Second) of Contracts. Browsing the table of contents quickly led us to section 2, which defines "promise."[1] The comment indicates that the focus is on a party's external manifestation, not its undisclosed intention. We found a New Mexico case citing this section — the first case on our list. On one hand, the facts look similar to Canoga's situation: a potentially wrongful termination of an employee. But the type of contract — a settlement agreement — is very different from an employee handbook, and the citation to section 2 is in the dissent. With luck, we will find cases that fit our topic more closely.

Feeling fairly comfortable with the general landscape of the contract issue, we sought to get into the case-by-case nature of this topic, as suggested in Am. Jur., by looking for an A.L.R. annotation on our topic. We ran a title search — discharg! terminat! & employee & policy handbook manual — in Westlaw and discovered a 1984 annotation precisely on point, with reams of cases in the updating material. By looking in the table of jurisdictions, we easily identified and then read the synopses of six New Mexico cases, including *Lukoski*, the case featured in Unit III on case law.

We had two other potential issues to look into before leaving commentary research. First, does the no-smoking requirement violate Canoga's privacy? This is a hot issue, so we looked for a pertinent periodical article. Our first strategy was to search in the WilsonWeb version of ILPB. A rough-cut search — employee employer smoking — yielded fourteen hits, with the pertinent ones categorized under Employment Discrimination/Lifestyle, a concept we had not yet come across. Once we looked under that subject heading, we found several more pertinent articles. Our second strategy was to run a key-word search in the LexisNexis periodicals database; the search was employ! /s smok! /s privacy, which yielded a rather large number of

---

1. More likely than not, you would know this from your Contracts course.

hits. Seeing the terms in context permitted us to quickly sort through the newer ones.

Both searches led us to a very recent article in the *Albany Law Review* that is squarely on point. We learned that many states — including New Mexico — have statutes prohibiting employers from banning off-duty smoking. We got the statute's citation — a definite lead to pursue. We also learned that the common law tort of invasion of privacy is not a good fit for employer bans on off-duty smoking.

Second, we had wondered about discrimination early on, on the theory that nicotine addiction might somehow be a form of disability. As described in the interlude to Unit I, after a bit of research into the nonlegal topic of nicotine addiction, we learned that nicotine addiction is a physical dependency and that few people quit for more than a month. Our theory has some factual support.

To examine the legal treatment of nicotine addiction, we turned to a treatise on employment discrimination. We found the multivolume treatise through our library's catalog and worked our way to the volume on disability discrimination and from there to a discussion of smoking. We discovered that the federal statute, the Americans with Disabilities Act, has a section indicating that an "entity" may prohibit or impose restrictions on smoking in the workplace. This raised several questions. The author discussed one question: Should this provision apply to employers? But he didn't address the other two: Can an employer prohibit or impose restrictions on off-duty smoking? And could nicotine addiction be a protected disability?

In summary, we decided that the breach-of-contract and statutory privacy claims merited further research. We were less convinced and clear about the pertinence of the federal statute on disability discrimination.

CASE LAW

UNIT
—
III

INTRODUCTION

In the U.S. legal system, there are many sources of law: cases decided by courts; constitutions and statutes passed by legislatures; regulations and decisions issued by agencies; rules of procedure and practice created by courts and legislatures. Furthermore, law is made at the federal, state, and local levels. This unit is the first of four discussing research in the law itself, a category some call "primary authority."

This unit focuses on the cases decided by courts and has two chapters:

☐ Chapter 9 explains what cases are and why they are so important in legal research; it then covers various ways of identifying and obtaining pertinent cases.

☐ Chapter 10 covers a critical next step in case law research: citing a case to determine the case's status and to expand your research.

This unit continues to illustrate the research on the Canoga case stated at pages 3–4. One of the issues in that case (suggested by our research in commentary presented in Unit II) is whether the orchestra breached its contract with Ms. Canoga when it terminated her employment without following the procedures stated in the handbook. This unit focuses on that issue, and the interlude at the end of the unit describes our research into that issue.

Finally, note that the term "case" has several meanings for lawyers: a matter handled on behalf of a client, a dispute that is litigated in the courts, and the decision of a court. This book uses the term in all three senses.

CASE REPORTERS, DIGESTS, AND THEIR ALTERNATIVES

A. What Is a Case?
B. Why Would You Research Which Cases?
C. How Do You Research Cases?
D. How Do You Cite Cases?
E. What Else?

A.   WHAT IS A CASE?

Courts decide cases for two essential purposes. First, the decision provides a peaceful and principled resolution to a dispute the parties were unable to resolve otherwise. Second, the decision serves as a guideline for participants in future similar situations as they resolve their own disputes or engage in business or other activities. Both purposes are served by the court's written explanation of the case's facts, the outcome, and the reasoning behind the outcome.

1.   How Does a Case Come to Be Decided?

Courts are reactive institutions. They resolve disputes brought to them by litigants; they do not render legal opinions on issues unconnected to actual disputes. The lawyers for the litigants bring the facts to the court's attention, frame the issues, and develop the arguments on both sides.

A dispute enters litigation when one party, the plaintiff, sues the other, the defendant. (Complex cases may involve more than two parties.) The case is handled initially by a trial court, typically called a "district court." This court provides the forum for presentation of the facts to a jury or judge, determination of the facts in dispute, and application of the law to the facts to yield an initial resolution of the dispute. Many cases are, of course, resolved by the parties themselves. Many more are decided by a judge through motion practice, in which one side or the other moves for, i.e., requests, a favorable ruling. For example, the judge may dismiss the case early in the proceedings, with little development of the facts, if the plaintiff has sued on a theory without adequate legal support. A case that has not settled or been decided through motion practice may be resolved through a trial, at which witnesses testify orally, documents and items are reviewed, and the jury renders a verdict or the court renders judgment.

A party that loses in whole or in part in the trial court may appeal. The party bringing the appeal is the appellant or petitioner, whereas the party defending against the appeal is the appellee or respondent. Appellate proceedings differ from trial court proceedings. The appellate court relies on the record of the trial court proceedings along with the written and oral arguments of the lawyers. Cases are decided by panels of three or more judges; the panel may be drawn from the court's membership, or the case may be heard by the entire court en banc.

Court systems have one or two tiers of appellate courts. In the typical two-tier appellate structure, the judges of the intermediate court, typically called the "court of appeals," review the trial court's handling of the case for reversible errors. The justices of the highest court, typically titled the "supreme court," conduct a second review for errors but focus primarily on the development of legal doctrine. Typically, appeal to the intermediate court is as of right, whereas the supreme court affords discretionary review.

In a simpler one-tier structure, the sole appellate court handles both appellate functions and reviews all appeals.

2. How Are Court Systems Structured?

The federal court system is a complex court system with three tiers. The federal trial courts are called "United States District Courts"; each state has one to four district courts, with each court covering part or all of the state. The intermediate appellate courts are called "United States Courts of Appeals"; there are eleven numbered circuits, each covering several states, and the District of Columbia Circuit. See Exhibit 9.1 at (below). The United States Supreme Court hears cases on discretionary review from the courts of appeals. Furthermore, specialized trial and appeals courts exist in areas such as bankruptcy and international trade.

| EXHIBIT 9.1 | Federal Courts Map, from www.uscourts.gov |

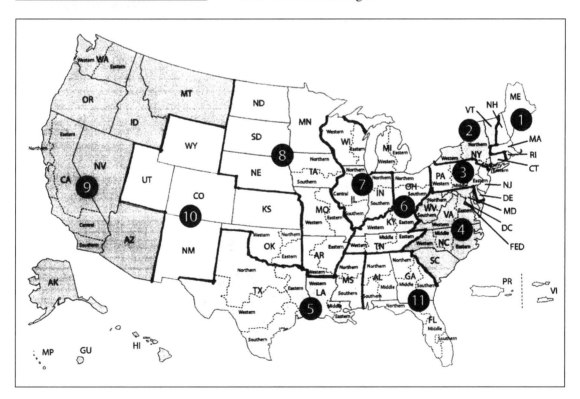

New Mexico's system is typical for state courts; it is somewhat simpler than the federal system. The trial courts are called "district courts." The New Mexico Court of Appeals handles appeals from all district courts. The highest court is the New Mexico Supreme Court.

Table T.1 of *The Bluebook* and *ALWD Citation Manual* Appendix 1 list the courts for U.S. jurisdictions.

3.   What Does a Published Case Look Like?

Many cases are published one way or another so lawyers may research them. For more than a century, West Publishing Company, now Thomson West, has been the dominant publisher of federal and state cases. Most cases published by West follow a fairly standard framework, labeled in the margins of Exhibit 9.2 (at pages 153–56), which shows the case of *Lukoski v. Sandia Indian Management Co.*, a key New Mexico case pertinent to the breach-of-contract issue in the Canoga matter.

The opening block includes the names of the parties and their positions in the litigation (item 2), the court deciding the case (item 4), the docket number assigned to the case by the court for administrative purposes (item 3), and the date of decision (item 5). The opening block also may contain a parallel citation (item 1); parallel citations are discussed in Parts C and D of this chapter.

Following the opening block are several brief paragraphs describing the main points in the case. There may be the following elements in this section:

☐   a syllabus, written by the court itself or by the court's staff;

☐   a synopsis, a one-paragraph overview of the facts and outcome written by the publisher's staff (item 6); and

☐   headnote paragraphs, each describing a discrete legal point made in the case, written by West editors (item 7).

You should not view these materials as legal authority; the opinion itself is the legal authority. The lawyers handling the case appear next (item 8).

Of course, most of the published case is the court's opinion. Each opinion begins with the name of the judge or justice who wrote the opinion (item 9). Note that "judge" refers to a jurist of a trial court or intermediate appellate court; high court jurists are "justices." The text of the opinion (item 10) typically includes a summary of the facts of the case, the course of the litigation, the court's holding, and its reasoning. The holding is the legal outcome of the case; it may be understood in procedural terms (e.g., the lower court's grant of a motion is affirmed) and in substantive terms (e.g., the defendant is liable for breach of contract and must pay damages). The reasoning typically includes a statement of the legal rule, references to and discussion of pertinent legal authorities, analysis of how the law applies to the facts of the case, and perhaps discussion of public policies. The court also may opine about a matter not necessary to its decision; this material is called "obiter dicta" (or "dictum" in the singular) and is not as authoritative as the rest of the opinion.

| EXHIBIT 9.2 | Judicial Case, from Pacific Reporter 2d (paper source) |

LUKOSKI v. SANDIA INDIAN MANAGEMENT CO.   N.M.   507
Cite as 748 P.2d 507 (N.M. 1988)

court's finding of damages, it is our opinion that an "as is" clause provides absolute protection to a seller such as Horizon only when the buyer and seller possess equal knowledge of the property. Here, while Lambert's knowledge of the property was equal to that of Horizon's insofar as most essentials of the contract were concerned, Lambert relied on Horizon for its knowledge of the total acreage in the property, and for such information as would have informed him about the realignment of Golf Course Road. Hence the trial court did not err in finding damages as to the realignment of Golf Course Road despite the "as is" clause. *See Archuleta v. Kopp,* 90 N.M. 273, 562 P.2d 834 (Ct.App.), *cert. dismissed,* 90 N.M. 636, 567 P.2d 485 (1977).

THE ISSUE OF THE ARROYO

[5]   If as to the issue of the realignment of Golf Course Road and the total number of acres conveyed the parties were not in possession of equal knowledge, when the issue of the arroyo is raised, it is clear that Lambert did have knowledge of the property equal to that of Horizon. Indeed, it appears from the testimony of past officers of Horizon that Lambert's knowledge as to the arroyo may in some respects have been superior to that of Horizon. Lambert's principal argument against the terms of paragraph 6 of the contract insofar as it applies to the arroyo is that he talked to Horizon's legal counsel before signing the contract and was told that "natural drainageway" did not refer to the arroyo, but referred to a swale running north and south across the property.

Yet, the court found in its findings of fact that Lambert (1) "read and agreed to all the terms and conditions of the Contract," (2) "had personal knowledge of, and had inspected and investigated" the property before entering into the contract, (3) that George Lambert "is a knowledgeable and sophisticated real estate broker with 20 years of experience" and that he had available to him certain engineering drainage studies dealing with the problems of the arroyo, and (4) "[a]n Arroyo is a natural drainageway." We have no reason to dis-

pute any of these findings since they are all supported by substantial evidence. "[T]he circumstances surrounding the Agreement, the import of that Agreement as a whole, and the undisputed parol evidence of the parties show that [Lambert's] right to acquire [Horizon's] interests was not conditioned upon ..." [an interpretation of "natural drainageway" as a "swale".] *Schaefer v. Hinkle,* 93 N.M. 129, 131, 597 P.2d 314, 316 (1979); *see also Smith v. Price's Creameries,* 98 N.M. 541, 544, 650 P.2d 825, 828 (1982), which likewise involved the issue of a conflict between contractual language and alleged oral assurances modifying the contractual language.

The judgment of the trial court is affirmed.

IT IS SO ORDERED.

WALTERS and RANSOM, JJ., concur.

KEY NUMBER SYSTEM

106 N.M. 664 ————————— ❶

Scott J.L. LUKOSKI, Plaintiff-Appellee,

v.

SANDIA INDIAN MANAGEMENT   ❷
COMPANY, Defendant-Appellant.

No. 16462. ———————————————— ❸

Supreme Court of New Mexico. ——— ❹

Jan. 7, 1988. ———————————————— ❺

Former general manager brought action against former employer for wrongful discharge. The District Court, Bernalillo County, William W. Deaton, D.J., entered judgment in favor of manager. Employer appealed. The Supreme Court, Ransom, J., held that evidence established that employee handbook amended employment contract and that employer breached contract by failing to comply with warning and suspension procedures.   ❻

Notes:	1. parallel citation	4. court
	2. parties	5. date of decision
	3. docket number	6. publisher's synopsis

EXHIBIT 9.2   *(continued)*

---

508 N.M.   748 PACIFIC REPORTER, 2d SERIES

(7a) Affirmed.

Stowers, J., dissented and filed opinion.

1. Trial ⟵392(1)

Defendant waived specific findings of fact on issues on which it failed to tender requested findings. SCRA 1986, Rule 1-052, subd. B(1)(f).

2. Master and Servant ⟵40(3)

(7) Evidence supported trial court's conclusions that termination procedures in employee handbook amended general manager's employment contract, that handbook created warning and suspension procedures which were not followed, and that personality, rather than insubordination, caused employment termination; handbook characterized disciplinary policy regarding warnings, suspensions, and terminations as established procedure; and handbook did not indicate that it was subject to revocation at any time or that employees should not rely on it.

---

(8) Grammer & Grammer, David A. Grammer, III, Albuquerque, for defendant-appellant.

Turpen & Wolfe, Donald C. Turpen, Albuquerque, for plaintiff-appellee.

OPINION

(9) RANSOM, Justice.

(10) Scott J.L. Lukoski brought a wrongful discharge action against his employer, Sandia Indian Management Co. (SIMCO). Lukoski had been employed as general manager of the Sandia Pueblo bingo operation. In a bench trial, the court decided that SIMCO violated the termination procedures prescribed for "less serious" offenses by an employee handbook. For salary due on the remaining term of his one-year oral contract, Lukoski was awarded $18,629.05. We affirm.

The court found that, in October 1983, Lukoski and SIMCO entered into a one-year oral employment agreement under which Lukoski would provide services as the general manager of a bingo hall opera-

tion for a specified annual salary plus commission. There was no written agreement between the parties. In February 1984, SIMCO distributed to all employees an employee handbook and requested each to sign the last page as verification of receipt, acknowledgement of acceptance, and agreement to conform with the stated policies and procedures. After Lukoski signed the back page as requested, it was placed in his personnel file. The court concluded that:

> The parties amended the oral employment contract * * * when [SIMCO] proffered, and [Lukoski] signed, [the] Employee's Handbook containing new duties and obligations on the part of employee and employer over and above said oral contract, including Rules to be obeyed by [Lukoski] and a termination procedure to be followed by [SIMCO].   **(11)**

(11) Although we determine the above-quoted language is a finding of ultimate fact, rather than a conclusion of law, that is of no consequence. *See Hoskins v. Albuquerque Bus Co.*, 72 N.M. 217, 382 P.2d 700 (1963); *Wiggs v. City of Albuquerque*, 57 N.M. 770, 263 P.2d 963 (1953). SIMCO challenges this finding and for the first time on appeal raises two other issues. First, it claims that Lukoski, as general manager, was not the type of employee intended to be covered by the handbook. Distribution to all employees with request for signatures constituted evidence to the contrary, and resolution of any ambiguity regarding management personnel would have been a specific question of fact. *See Shaeffer v. Kelton*, 95 N.M. 182, 619 P.2d 1226 (1980). Second, SIMCO claims that any breach was not material because it neither went to the substance of the contract nor defeated the object of the parties. Materiality is likewise a specific question of fact. *See Bisio v. Madenwald (In re Estate of Bisio)*, 33 Or.App. 325, 576 P.2d 801 (1978). As the contract stood after amendment, it was not materiality, as argued by SIMCO, but rather severity of offense that was at issue under the termination procedures. In any event, by failing to tender requested findings, SIMCO waived specific

---

Notes:	7. headnotes	10. majority opinion
	7a. topic and key number	11. bracketed headnote reference
	8. counsels' names	
	9. justice who wrote majority opinion	

EXHIBIT **9.2**   *(continued)*

LUKOSKI v. SANDIA INDIAN MANAGEMENT CO.   N.M. **509**
Cite as 748 P.2d 507 (N.M. 1988)

findings on these fact issues. SCRA 1986, 1–052(B)(1)(f).

[2] There is substantial evidence supporting the court's findings of ultimate fact that the termination procedures became an amendment to Lukoski's contract, and that personality—not the severe offenses of insubordination or disobedience—was the cause for termination. He was terminated without warning or suspension for a cause not so severe as to constitute cause for immediate termination. His personality and interpersonal dealings were found by the court to create an atmosphere of fear and anxiety and bad morale among employees and managers.

Relying only on *Ellis v. El Paso Natural Gas Co.,* 754 F.2d 884 (10th Cir.1985), the thrust of SIMCO's appeal is that the language of the employee handbook is "too indefinite to constitute a contract" and lacks "contractual terms which might evidence the intent to form a contract." It maintains that the parties did not conduct themselves as if the employee handbook was to govern Lukoski or as if they expected it to form the basis of a contractual relationship. In support of its position, SIMCO refers to the disciplinary action, suspension, and warning provisions,[1] and argues that the language of the termination policy is ambiguous and contains no required policy for termination.

SIMCO's argument, however, overlooks the handbook's characterization of the disciplinary policy regarding warnings, suspensions and terminations as "an *estab-*

lished procedure regarding suspension of problem employees and termination for those who cannot conform to Company Policy." (Emphasis added.) Moreover, the language of the handbook does nothing to alert an employee against placing reliance on any statement contained therein or against viewing such discipline and termination policy as only a unilateral expression of SIMCO's intention that is subject to revocation or change at any time, in any manner, at the pleasure of SIMCO. To the contrary, from the language of the handbook and the conduct of SIMCO in adopting the policy, it could properly be found that the policy was part of the employment agreement.

Whether an employee handbook has modified the employment relationship is a question of fact "to be discerned from the totality of the parties' statements and actions regarding the employment relationship." *Wagenseller v. Scottsdale Memorial Hosp.,* 147 Ariz. 370, 383, 710 P.2d 1025, 1038 (1985) (en banc).

Evidence relevant to this factual decision includes the language used in the personnel manual as well as the employer's course of conduct and oral representations regarding it. We do not mean to imply that all personnel manual will become part of employment contracts. Employers are certainly free to issue no personnel manual at all or to issue a personnel manual that clearly and conspicuously tells their employees that the manual is not part of the employment contract and that their jobs are termina-

---

1. The referenced handbook provisions state:
OTHER DISCIPLINARY ACTION:
In order to protect the good employees [sic] jobs and Sandia Indian Bingo, there is an established procedure regarding suspension of problem employees and termination for those who can not conform to Company Policy. Suspensions without pay may be given to employees who violate company policies. There are violations which are so severe [including insubordination and disobedience] that immediate termination may be necessary....
SUSPENSIONS:
Suspension without pay may be given when the incident is not sufficiently serious to warrant discharge and/or the particular employee's overall value to the Company [is con-

sidered], if [in] the opinion of the Department Manager [the employee] warrants another chance. Minimum suspensions are (3) three days, maximum suspensions are (5) five days. No employee may be suspended more than once in a year; thereafter, if the incident would normally warrant suspension he/she must be discharged.
DISCIPLINARY WARNING:
Disciplinary warning slips will be issued where the offense is less serious and where corrective action may salvage an employee. More than one (1) disciplinary warning, whether for the same offense or not, may subject an employee to suspension or termination. Warning slips become a permanent part of an employee's personnel record.

EXHIBIT 9.2   *(continued)*

---

510 N.M.   **748 PACIFIC REPORTER, 2d SERIES**

ble at the will of the employer with or without reason. Such actions * * * instill no reasonable expectations of job security and do not give employees any reason to rely on representations in the manual. However, if an employer does choose to issue a policy statement, in a manual or otherwise, and, by its language or by the employer's actions, encourages reliance thereon, the employer cannot be free to only selectively abide by it. Having announced a policy, the employer may not treat it as illusory. *Leikvold v. Valley View Community Hosp.*, 141 Ariz. 544, 548, 688 P.2d 170, 174 (1984). Here, substantial evidence supports the finding of the trial court that the employee handbook modified the employment relationship and created warning and suspension procedures which were not followed in this case.

Accordingly, based upon the foregoing, the judgment of the trial court is affirmed.

IT IS SO ORDERED.

SCARBOROUGH, C.J., SOSA, Senior Justice, and WALTERS, J., concur.

STOWERS, J., dissents.

STOWERS, Justice, dissenting.

I respectfully dissent from the majority's holding that SIMCO did not abide with the termination procedures.

Substantial evidence does support the findings of the trial court that the employee handbook modified the employment relationship and that Lukoski was terminated for just cause. The trial court erred, however, in concluding that SIMCO did not follow the proper termination procedures. To the contrary, SIMCO did not breach any of the provisions in the employee handbook when it discharged Lukoski without a warning and suspension. The handbook explicitly states that, "there are violations which are so severe that *immediate termination may be necessary*." (Emphasis added).

Overwhelming evidence was presented at trial to show that Lukoski's violations of company policies were of the type to fall within the category of "so severe" that a

warning and any suspension procedures were not required. *See State ex rel. Goodmans Office Furnishings, Inc. v. Page & Wirtz Constr. Co.*, 102 N.M. 22, 24, 690 P.2d 1016, 1018 (1984). Generally, this evidence indicated that Lukoski had an overall attitude problem towards his employees, other managers and representatives of the Sandia Pueblo to the extent that SIMCO was in jeopardy of losing its bingo contract with the Pueblo; moreover, he was abusive towards the accountants, argued or fought publicly with customers, the assistant bingo manager, the construction supervisor and an admittance clerk; Lukoski also failed to install proper security measures and verification methods, and hired unqualified personnel. Further, testimony indicated that on several occasions, Walker, Lukoski's supervisor, spoke to Lukoski about this attitude problem, and, in fact, interceded on Lukoski's behalf when the Sandia Pueblo desired to discharge Lukoski.

As enumerated in the handbook, Lukoski's violations included, "fighting on company property, refusal to obey reasonable orders of a supervisor, discourtesy to customers, and disobeying or ignoring established written or oral work rules or policies." These are, and I again quote from the handbook, "violations which are so severe that *immediate termination* may be necessary." (Emphasis added.) Therefore, the trial court was in error when it decided that SIMCO violated the termination procedures prescribed for "less serious" offenses in the handbook. Lukoski was not entitled to those termination procedures since his offenses were not of the "less serious" type. Under the circumstances in this case, the only process due Lukoski for the seriousness of his violations was immediate termination. Thus, there was no breach by SIMCO when it discharged him for just cause.

The judgment of the district court should be reversed and this case remanded for dismissal.

Note: 12. dissenting opinion

If the court consists of more than one judge, there is, of course, the potential for disagreement and multiple opinions. In these situations, each opinion is one of the following:

☐ The majority opinion garners more than half of the votes and resolves the case.

☐ A dissent expresses the view of judges who would have reached a different result in the case.

☐ A concurrence expresses the view of judges who favor the majority's result, but for different reasons.

☐ A plurality opinion arises when no opinion garners over half of the votes. As the opinion garnering the largest number of votes, the plurality opinion generally is the most influential and resolves the dispute between the parties.

There was a dissent in the *Lukoski* case (item 12).

B. WHY WOULD YOU RESEARCH WHICH CASES?

1. The Common Law, Stare Decisis, and Precedent

In a common law system, as in the United States, case law forms part of the law of the land. The operative principle in a common law system is *stare decisis et non quieta movere*, which means "to adhere to precedent and not to unsettle things which are settled." According to stare decisis, a court should follow previously decided cases, or precedents, on the same topic. Hence, as you research the law applicable to a client's situation, even if you hope and reasonably anticipate that the situation will never come before a court, you should try to deduce how the court would handle the situation based on pertinent precedents.

Stare decisis has several chief advantages. Situations involving similar facts are treated consistently. Outcomes are based on legal principles, rather than the unconstrained biases of judges and juries. Because it generally is possible to predict the outcome of a case by looking to precedents, many cases can be settled. Furthermore, people can conform their conduct to the law by looking to precedents.

Yet overly strict adherence to precedent would produce a static legal rule. Although some areas of law benefit from stability, others do not. When social values change, information improves, or new situations develop, the law should evolve.

Fortunately, the U.S. legal system provides for change. A court may distinguish an earlier case by finding factual differences between it and the pending case; then the court may apply a different rule to the case before it. A court may modify the common law by revising the rule in a new case. Indeed, a court may overrule precedent in response to a significant need for change.

Finally, the legislature may enact a statute modifying the common law to a greater or lesser degree (as explained in Chapter 11).

Through your research, you may find many cases pertaining to your research topic. Not all cases are of equal importance. To focus on the most important cases, you should consider the following factors:

☐ You should focus first on whether the case is mandatory or persuasive precedent, given the jurisdiction of your client's situation.

☐ Then you must ascertain that the case is what lawyers call "good law" — a case that, indeed, currently states the law of the jurisdiction. In deciding whether a case is good law, you will consider its history and treatment as well as its publication status.

☐ Finally, if you have more cases than you can handle well, you should assess several additional factors, such as factual similarity to your client's situation and the quality of the reasoning.

2.   Mandatory versus Persuasive Precedent: Federalism, Jurisdiction, and Level of Court

As to a particular situation, some cases are binding or mandatory, whereas others are merely persuasive. The distinction between mandatory and persuasive precedent is critical: Stare decisis applies only to mandatory precedents. Persuasive precedents may influence a court, but they do not bind it. The distinction between mandatory and persuasive precedent is based on two main factors: jurisdiction and court level.

The U.S. legal system is a federal system, that is, a collection of legal systems. A particular legal topic, or issue, may be governed by federal law, state law, or both. A few issues are governed by local (e.g., municipal or county) law.

If the legal issue is governed by federal law, then mandatory precedents emanate from the federal courts. If the legal issue is governed by state law, then mandatory precedents emanate from the courts of the pertinent state. Decisions from other courts, which lawyers call "sister courts" or "sister jurisdictions," are only persuasive.

The term "jurisdiction" has several common meanings in the law. Often it is used to refer to a legal system of a particular geographic region. In a more technical sense, jurisdiction is the power of a specific court to render and enforce a decision in a particular case. That is, a state court has the power to render and enforce decisions in cases arising under the law of that state, and a federal court has the power to render and enforce decisions in cases arising under federal law and within its geographic region.

In several situations, a court may apply law that is not its own. For example, in diversity jurisdiction, a federal court has the power to decide cases arising under state law if the case involves citizens of different states and the amount in controversy is high enough. Similarly, under supplemental jurisdiction, a federal court has the power to decide a case arising in part under state law if the case also involves a federal claim. Moreover, Congress has given state and federal courts concurrent jurisdiction over certain claims stated in federal law. Finally, the courts of one state may apply the law of a different state if a multistate contract identifies the second state's law as governing.

In these situations, the mandatory precedents are those decisions from the courts whose law governs. For example, when operating in diversity or supplemental jurisdiction, a federal court will follow the law of the state that governs the claim and will seek to emulate the approach of that state's highest court; the decisions of other federal courts are not as weighty.

Unfortunately, there are few broadly applicable principles to explain the distribution of legal topics among the three levels of government, and jurisdiction can be complex. As you begin to research, you should assume that federal, state, and local law are all potentially applicable, and you should be alert to jurisdictional possibilities. Your research in commentary will provide preliminary guidance, which you should verify in researching the law itself.

An additional determinant of mandatory versus persuasive precedent is the level of the court issuing the decision. Stare decisis operates hierarchically. Any particular court is bound by decisions of higher courts within the same court system and must take its own decisions into account. It is not, however, bound by decisions issued by other courts at the same level or by lower courts. Hence, you would rely on a supreme court decision over that of an intermediate appeals court; similarly, you would rely on an intermediate appeals court decision over that of a trial court.

3. Good Law: History, Treatment, and Publication Status

Before you rely on a case, you first must determine that it is what lawyers call "good law." A case's status is a function primarily of its subsequent history and treatment:

☐ Subsequent history consists of later rulings in the same litigation.
☐ Treatment consists of decisions rendered in later litigation involving different parties.

Subsequent history nearly always affects whether a case is good law; a case's treatment may or may not do so. See Exhibit 9.3 (at page 160). Whether the court issuing the decision designates it as published or unpublished may also affect its status, although less significantly.

a. Subsequent History

Before you rely on a decision from a court other than the highest court, you must know whether one or both of the parties brought an appeal; whether the

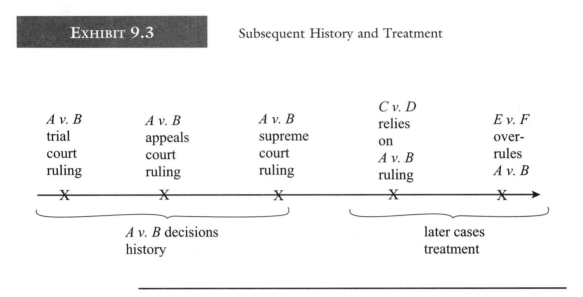

EXHIBIT 9.3   Subsequent History and Treatment

decision has indeed been reviewed by a higher court; and, if so, what the outcome was. The higher court may affirm the lower court's decision, reverse the lower court's decision, or take intermediate action, e.g., modifying or remanding to the lower court. These later decisions in the same litigation involving the same parties constitute the original decision's subsequent history. In Exhibit 9.3, the history of the case is comprised of the three *A v. B* decisions.

Obviously, your research is not complete until you have identified the subsequent history of any decision you intend to rely on. Then you must carefully read any subsequent decision you find to discern its impact on your client's situation. The impact will generally be one of the following:

☐ If the subsequent decision adversely affects the outcome and reasoning you plan to rely on, it is incorrect to rely on the original decision.

☐ If the subsequent decision affirms the material you plan to rely on, the original decision has greater credibility. Ordinarily you will rely on the higher court's decision.

☐ When the higher court does not expressly rule on a point that is stated by the lower court and important to your case, and the point is consistent with the higher court's ruling, you may rely on the lower court decision.

Furthermore, if you intend to rely on a decision that is very recent and not from the highest court, you should check whether an appeal is pending before a higher court and be prepared to adjust your analysis when the higher court rules.

b.   Treatment

As noted previously, judges often refer to decisions rendered in earlier similar cases. The court may follow an earlier decision, distinguish it, criticize it, modify it, or even overrule it. For any decided case, there may be several, a dozen, or many more references in later cases. Your research is not complete until you have discerned how later cases have treated the case you intend to rely on. You should focus on courts in the same court system because those courts have the greatest power to undermine the case's validity or enhance its credibility. In Exhibit 9.3, the decisions in *C v. D* and *E v. F* constitute the treatment of *A v. B.*

You should attend first to adverse treatment. See *E v. F* in Exhibit 9.3. You should be especially concerned with indications that the case has been overruled; it is then no longer good law. You also should be wary of relying on a case that has been modified, criticized significantly, or distinguished frequently by courts in your jurisdiction. When you discover such adverse treatment, you must read the new case(s) carefully. If the original case makes more than one point, you should figure out whether the overruling, modification, or criticism in the new case affects the point on which are you relying. It may be that the original case remains good law as to the point you plan to rely on; nonetheless, you should use the case with caution.

Adverse treatment from sister jurisdictions is, of course, not nearly as significant. A sister court cannot overrule a case in your jurisdiction. Nor does criticism by one or more sister courts render a case less precedential in its own jurisdiction, although you may want to consider seriously what the basis of the criticism is.

Favorable treatment of a case, by courts in your jurisdiction or sister jurisdictions or both, enhances the case's credibility. See *C v. D* in Exhibit 9.3. If you find many instances of favorable treatment, the case may be what lawyers call a "leading" or "seminal" case, that is, the case that first or most persuasively established a particular legal rule.

c.   Publication Status

Courts in the United States issue decisions at an astounding rate. According to the *2006 Judicial Business of the United States Courts* report, the regional appellate courts disposed of approximately 67,000 cases that year, the district courts approximately 340,000 cases. Although every decision matters a great deal to the litigants, some decisions are, of course, more significant than others to the development of the law.

Courts seek to reflect the relative importance of a decision by deciding whether to publish the decision. The highest courts in each court system designate nearly every decision as published, intermediate appellate courts a smaller percentage, and trial courts even fewer. A court is likely to designate a decision for publication if it establishes a new legal rule, develops or significantly explains an existing rule, criticizes or questions existing law, involves an issue as to whether there is a conflict in the case law, discusses a little-discussed rule, applies an existing rule to a new factual situation, or discusses an issue of significant public interest. Approximately eighty percent of federal appellate decisions are designated as unpublished.[1]

As contradictory as it may seem, unpublished decisions are, as a matter of fact, published. This phenomenon has varied over time. Until a few decades ago, a court would provide an unpublished decision only to the parties, not to publishers of cases. Although you could generally obtain a copy of a decision from the clerk of court if you knew about the case, as a practical matter, these unpublished decisions were minimally published and not easily researched. For several decades, Westlaw and LexisNexis have provided unpublished decisions in their case law databases, discussed in Part C. More recently, West has begun to provide some unpublished decisions in paper case reporters, also discussed in Part C. Many courts now post their decisions — published and unpublished — on their websites. These developments have made unpublished decisions very researchable.

There remains the question of whether unpublished decisions are precedential. Different courts have their own rules on whether unpublished decisions may be cited. Federal Rule of Appellate Procedure 32.1 forbids federal courts from prohibiting the citation of unpublished decisions issued on or after January 1, 2007. Some state courts prohibit citing an unpublished decision except in the same litigation; others permit citation to an unpublished case as persuasive, but not binding, precedent. Some rules require the party citing an unpublished case to provide a copy to the court and opposing counsel.

Thus, as you research in case law, you should learn your jurisdiction's position on this issue and view any unpublished decisions you discover accordingly. Although court rules on this issue directly address only the use of unpublished cases in documents filed in court, you should take guidance from these rules as you analyze your client's situation and provide advice in other contexts, such as settling a dispute or structuring a business transaction.

4.   Additional Factors

Your research may well yield multiple mandatory published precedents that are good law — more than you can reasonably focus on. Consider the following factors as you select cases to emphasize:

☐ Similarity: The higher the degree of similarity between the facts and legal issues of your client's situation and those of the case you have located, the better. Your goal is to obtain both factual and legal parallelism, to the extent possible.

---

1. Dione Christopher Greene, *The Federal Courts of Appeals, Unpublished Decisions, and the "No-Citation" Rule*, 81 Ind. L.J. 1503 (2006).

- ☐ Clarity: The clearer and more convincing the reasoning of the case you have located, the better. A clear, well reasoned case is inherently more credible than one with flawed reasoning.
- ☐ Recency: The more recent the case you have located, the better, all else being equal. Age by itself does not make an old case bad law. However, an old case may be less credible than a new case, because a new case may more closely reflect current values and perspectives.

On some occasions, you may need to rely on persuasive precedent: when there is a dearth of mandatory precedent, the mandatory precedent is outdated, or the mandatory precedent is adverse to your client's interest and you want to seek a change in the law. In selecting from possible persuasive precedents, you should consider the following factors, in addition to those stated previously: which courts or cases are viewed as leaders in the subject matter, how closely the law of the sister jurisdiction tracks the law of your jurisdiction on related legal topics, how closely the policies underlying the precedent mesh with your jurisdiction's policies, and how geographically close the sister jurisdiction is to yours. Your research in commentary will help you assess some of these factors.

C.   HOW DO YOU RESEARCH CASES?

1.   Introduction

As synopsized in Exhibit 9.4 (at page 164), our case law template, case law research entails developing a well-honed issue, identifying one or more pertinent cases, reading and briefing each case you have selected, verifying that it is good law, connecting the law from the case to your client's situation, and planning your next steps.

Given the importance of case law in the U.S. legal system, it is not surprising that published cases are available in multiple media from various publishers, as follows:

- ☐ Slip opinion: This is the decision as the court issues it, traditionally in paper; sends it to the parties; and maintains it in the files of the clerk of court.
- ☐ Official publications: In most jurisdictions, the court will post the decision electronically on a public Internet website. In addition, there may be an official reporter, that is, a set of books containing the court's decisions published by or under the auspices of the government.

| EXHIBIT 9.4 | Case Law Template |

Issue:	**Citation Information:** • case name • reporter or database • volume and page number • court • date • GOOD LAW?
Date of events:	
Date of research:	
Search and Find:	

located case by . . .

Information and Implications:
- facts
- procedure
- outcome and holding
- rule
- reasoning
- dissent/concurrence
- note exact location
- connection to client's situation: application of rule and case comparison

Next Steps:

questions to consider:	leads to follow:

☐ Unofficial publications: Various commercial publishers publish new cases very quickly, for example, in a legal newspaper. Not long thereafter, commercial publishers add editorial enhancements designed to assist the researcher and publish the case in paper unofficial reporters, in online databases, or both. In some jurisdictions, a commercially published reporter is considered the official reporter.

As noted in Part B of this chapter, some unpublished cases are available online in court websites and commercial databases; a few also are available in paper.

As depicted in Exhibit 9.5 (below), many avenues lead to pertinent cases. If you have researched in commentary well, you should have one or more cases to consider when you turn to case law research. Only rarely should you stop there, however, because the commentary author was not researching your client's specific situation. Rather you should develop and implement a plan for your specific research topic. This chapter covers the sources of cases (the rectangle) and their finding tools (the lines below the rectangle). Chapter 10 covers case citators, which you will use to determine whether a case is good law and find additional cases. Chapter 11 covers annotated statutes; Chapters 16 and 17 cover annotated rules.

Given the number of resources, the number of options each provides, and the speed at which existing resources evolve and new resources appear,

EXHIBIT 9.5   Avenues to Cases

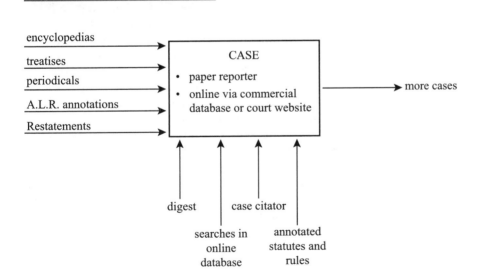

you should view the following discussion as illustrative, not exhaustive. You should stay current with developments in case law research, so that your research is as effective and efficient as current sources permit. We have organized our discussion by resource:

☐ West's paper reporters and digest system;
☐ Westlaw and LexisNexis, the two major commercial online resources, which offer extensive case law databases and a wide range of search options;
☐ several less extensive and elaborate commercial online resources; and
☐ free court websites.

As appropriate, we have featured the following search strategies within the resource discussions:

☐ looking for cases fitting within the resource's topical framework;
☐ Boolean, i.e., terms-and-connectors, full-text searching;
☐ natural-language full-text searching; and
☐ retrieving a known case.

One way to think of these resources (as of fall 2007) is an analogy to modes of transportation. West's paper reporters and digests are similar to public transportation: The routes are mapped for you, you need to navigate systematically within that framework, it takes time to get where you want to go, you will know when you have arrived, and the cost is low. Westlaw and LexisNexis are the fully loaded sports-utility vehicles of legal research: You plan the route, with some assistance; you get somewhere very quickly, although you may not know fully where you are; there are features you may never use; the look and sometimes the functioning of the systems are evolving; the cost is high. Other commercial online resources are the compact cars of legal research: less power, fewer features, and less costly than Westlaw and LexisNexis. Finally, free websites are the bicycles of legal research: Only a few bike paths and destinations currently exist, but they cost nothing and are worth using in the right situations. Depending completely on someone else's research, such as a treatise or periodical, is hitchhiking: the destination is imprecise, and the driver may or may not drive well, so it generally is not a good idea.

An important note: The discussion in this part covers the bulk of case law research — identifying, locating, and reading pertinent cases. The critical step of discerning the subsequent history and treatment of a case is covered in Chapter 10 on case citators.

2. Paper Research

Cases through West digests and reporters

▶ Select an appropriate digest.
▶ Identify a topic and key numbers via the topic list or Descriptive Word Index.
▶ Assemble the digest volumes and supplements you need.
▶ Skim the outline of the topic in the digest.
▶ Peruse the digest paragraphs under pertinent key numbers.
▶ Use the references in the digest to locate cases in reporters.
▶ Read each case for its facts, procedure, outcome and holding, rule, reasoning, and references.
▶ Cite each case (see Chapter 10).

Paper research in case law involves two interlocking sources: digests and reporters, used in that order. A digest is a finding tool that leads you to cases published in a reporter. To use digests well, you need to understand reporters and the role played by digests.

Understanding reporters and digests. A case reporter is a book containing the decisions issued during a particular time period by a single court or a set of courts. As already noted, reporters are official or unofficial. Official reporters do not contain the editorial enhancements of unofficial reporters and are not as useful for the researcher.

The National Reporter System, published by Thomson West beginning in the late 1800s, is the most prominent set of reporters. Indeed in some states, the West reporter serves as the official reporter. The West system is synopsized in Exhibit 9.6 (at page 168).

West currently publishes reporters containing decisions of the federal courts as follows:

☐ *Supreme Court Reporter* for decisions of the U.S. Supreme Court;
☐ *Federal Reporter,* now in its third series, for decisions of the various courts of appeals; and
☐ *Federal Supplement,* now in its second series, for decisions of the various district courts.

Although all decisions of the Supreme Court are published, only those decisions of the lower federal courts designated for publication appear in the *Federal Reporter* and the *Federal Supplement.* In 2001, West began to publish the *Federal Appendix,* containing decisions from the courts of appeals not designated for publication. In addition to the West reporters, there is an official reporter for the Supreme Court, *United States Reports,* but not for the lower federal courts.

As for case law from state courts, West has divided the country into seven regions, drawn from the perspective of a Minnesota publisher in the nineteenth century. Each region contains four to fifteen states, and each is served by one of the regional reporters. Again, see Exhibit 9.6. The regional reporters contain the decisions designated for publication by the various state appellate courts; decisions of lower state courts typically are not published. West's regions are not synonymous with jurisdiction; a case from a sister state within the same West region as your state is no more binding than a case from a sister state outside your state's West region. West also publishes two

| EXHIBIT 9.6 | West Reporters and Digests |

Cases from these courts	*appear in these West reporters*	*and are digested in these West digests*
Federal Courts		
Supreme Court	*Supreme Court Reporter*	*United States Supreme Court Digest* *Federal Practice Digest* (currently in fourth series) older cases covered by *Modern Federal Practice Digest* and *Federal Digest*
courts of appeals for various circuits	*Federal Reporter* (currently in third series) *Federal Appendix* (unpublished decisions)	*Federal Practice Digest* (currently in fourth series) older cases covered by *Modern Federal Practice Digest* and *Federal Digest* (also separate digests for Fifth and Eleventh Circuits)
district courts	*Federal Supplement* (currently in second series) older cases in *Federal Reporter*	*Federal Practice Digest* (currently in fourth series) older cases covered by *Modern Federal Practice Digest* and *Federal Digest*
State Courts*		
Connecticut Delaware District of Columbia Maine Maryland New Hampshire New Jersey Pennsylvania Rhode Island Vermont	*Atlantic Reporter* (currently in second series)	*Atlantic Digest* state digests (except Delaware) including federal cases from state

*Appendix 1 of *ALWD Citation Manual* indicates, for each state, whether the West reporter is the official reporter.

	EXHIBIT 9.6	(continued)

Cases from these courts	appear in these West reporters	and are digested in these West digests
Illinois Indiana Massachusetts New York Ohio	*North Eastern Reporter* (currently in second series) also *New York Supplement* (currently in second series)	state digests, including federal cases from state
Iowa Michigan Minnesota Nebraska North Dakota South Dakota Wisconsin	*North Western Reporter* (currently in second series)	*North Western Digest* state digests (North and South Dakota are merged), including federal cases from state
Alaska Arizona California Colorado Hawaii Idaho Kansas Montana Nevada New Mexico Oklahoma Oregon Utah Washington Wyoming	*Pacific Reporter* (currently in third series) also *California Reporter* (currently in third series)	*Pacific Digest* state digests (except Nevada and Utah), including federal cases from state
Georgia North Carolina South Carolina Virginia West Virginia	*South Eastern Reporter* (currently in second series)	*South Eastern Digest* state digests (Virginia and West Virginia are merged), including federal cases from state
Arkansas Kentucky Missouri Tennessee Texas	*South Western Reporter* (currently in third series)	state digests, including federal cases from state
Alabama Florida Louisiana Mississippi	*Southern Reporter* (currently in second series)	state digests, including federal cases from state

single-state reporters, for California and New York; these contain some cases not published in the regional reporters. Some states publish official reporters; others in effect rely on the West reporters.

For many reporters, West has published more than one series, e.g., F., F.2d, F.3d for the *Federal Reporter*. The first series of a reporter contains the oldest cases, while the second or third series contains the newest. Numbering of the volumes starts over with a new series.

Most volumes of a reporter are hardbound books. However, the most recent decisions appear in advance sheets, which are softcover pamphlets that can be published quickly. Once the hardbound book is prepared, it replaces the advance sheets.

Cases are published in case reporters as they arrive at the publisher and clear the editorial process. Case reporters are organized chronologically, not topically. To locate cases on your research topic, you need a digest, that is, a tool for locating pertinent cases within the many volumes of a reporter. A digest presents brief statements of the legal points made in the covered cases, written by the publisher's editorial staff and then fit into a framework of major legal topics and subtopics. See Exhibit 9.7 (at page 171). West's digests are the most highly developed and widely used legal digests.

Select an appropriate digest. Your first step in researching in digests and reporters is to select an appropriate digest. There is a rough correlation between West's reporters and its digests, as indicated in Exhibit 9.6. For example, the main federal digest is the *Federal Practice Digest*, which covers the *Supreme Court Reporter*, the *Federal Reporter*, the *Federal Supplement*, and the *Federal Appendix*. West publishes digests for the Atlantic, North Western, Pacific, and South Eastern regional reporters. It also publishes digests for most states; these digests cover state court decisions published in the regional reporters as well as federal cases arising in or appealed from the state.

Identify a topic and key numbers. Your next step is to identify a pertinent topic and key number. West has divided the law into approximately 450 main topics. Each topic is divided into subtopics and indeed into sub-subtopics. The subtopics and sub-subtopics are assigned numbers, called "key numbers." The configuration of topics and key numbers is the same across the West system.

One way to find a pertinent topic, but not key numbers, is by scanning the topic list in the digest volume. See Exhibit 9.8 (at pages 172–73). (Note that the first page is from a 2002 main volume; the second page is from a 2007 pocket part.) To find not only a pertinent topic but also pertinent key numbers, you would consult the Descriptive Word Index, which appears in its own volumes and typically is updated by pocket parts or pamphlets. See Exhibit 9.9 (at page 174). To obtain a thorough list of potentially pertinent topics and key numbers, look up various research terms, read the entries carefully, and check out cross-references.

Assemble a full set of digests. The next step is to assemble the necessary digest volumes and supplements covering your topics and key numbers for the time period you are researching. Many digests consist of more than one bound series. Later series typically contain more recent information than

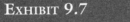

| EXHIBIT 9.7 | Digest Entries, from New Mexico Digest (paper source) |

4B N M D—155   **LABOR & EMPLOYMENT**   ☞57

For references to other topics, see Descriptive-Word Index

evidentiary function in implied employment contracts, indicating that parties intended to place limitation on employer's right to discharge, but evidentiary function is something distinct from showing of consideration as essential element of contract.

> Hartbarger v. Frank Paxton Co., 857 P.2d 776, 115 N.M. 665, certiorari denied 114 S.Ct. 1068, 510 U.S. 1118, 127 L.Ed.2d 387.

☞55. —— Presumptions and burden of proof.

Presumption of at-will employment, see ☞40.

☞56. —— Admissibility.

For other cases see the Decennial Digests and WESTLAW.

☞57. —— Weight and sufficiency.

C.A.10 (N.M.) 1994. Under New Mexico law, evidence did not support finding that ranch manager and ranch hand (manager's daughter and her husband) had implied contracts of employment and, thus, they were employees at-will and were properly terminated; only statements ranch owner made were ambiguous, promising manager place to live as long as owner retained ranch, owner made no statements to ranch hands at all, and length of their employment and their responsibilities, such as manager's power of attorney and authority to take out loans in his own name for business, did not support finding of implied contract of employment.

> Watson v. Blankinship, 20 F.3d 383.

C.A.10 (N.M.) 1987. Finding that employment contract between newspaper organization and publisher and plan of reorganization by which publisher sold newspaper to organization were inseparable, and that publisher could thus sue organization for breach of employment contract even though it was not signatory to contract, was supported by record.

> McKinney v. Gannett Co., Inc., 817 F.2d 659.

N.M. 1993. Explicit promise would support jury's finding of mutual assent in context of implied employment contract.

> Hartbarger v. Frank Paxton Co., 857 P.2d 776, 115 N.M. 665, certiorari denied 114 S.Ct. 1068, 510 U.S. 1118, 127 L.Ed.2d 387.

Where there was sufficient evidence to support finding that employee received earlier edition of employee handbook, but did not receive later edition, Supreme Court would accept find-

ing that employment relationship was affected only by earlier edition.

> Hartbarger v. Frank Paxton Co., 857 P.2d 776, 115 N.M. 665, certiorari denied 114 S.Ct. 1068, 510 U.S. 1118, 127 L.Ed.2d 387.

Totality of evidence was insufficient to support finding of promise by employer that employee would be terminated only for just cause; evidence did not show sufficiently explicit offer or promise to terminate only for just cause in employee handbook, employer's custom of only terminating employees for good reason, oral statements by employer, written statements by employer, or employer's retirement plan.

> Hartbarger v. Frank Paxton Co., 857 P.2d 776, 115 N.M. 665, certiorari denied 114 S.Ct. 1068, 510 U.S. 1118, 127 L.Ed.2d 387.

N.M. 1988. Evidence supported trial court's conclusions that termination procedures in employee handbook amended general manager's employment contract, that handbook created warning and suspension procedures which were not followed, and that personality, rather than insubordination, caused employment termination; handbook characterized disciplinary policy regarding warnings, suspensions, and terminations as established procedure; and handbook did not indicate that it was subject to revocation at any time or that employees should not rely on it.

> Lukoski v. Sandia Indian Management Co., 748 P.2d 507, 106 N.M. 664.

N.M. 1967. Finding, in action to recover compensation allegedly due for plugging an oil well, that relationship between plaintiff and defendant corporation president was that of master-servant or employer-employee was supported by substantial evidence, including evidence that defendant had stated that a certain person would supervise the entire operation and that that person had met plaintiff's crew at job site and had told them what to do and how to go about it every day.

> Platco Corp. v. Shaw, 428 P.2d 10, 78 N.M. 36.

N.M.Terr. 1857. In action by master against servant, evidence was insufficient to show any contract of service or any indebtedness on part of servant to master.

> Jaremillo v. Romero, 1 N.M. 190, 1 Gild. 190.

N.M.App. 2000. Evidence was sufficient to find implied contract for severance pay on behalf of terminated employee, as basis of damages against former employer for breach of contract, where employer led employee to believe that he was entitled to severance pay, and

† This Case was not selected for publication in the National Reporter System

EXHIBIT 9.8	Topic Lists, from Minnesota Digest (paper source)*

DIGEST TOPICS

114	Customs Duties	165	Extortion and	212	Injunction
115	Damages		Threats	213	Innkeepers
116	Dead Bodies	166	Extradition and	216	Inspection
117	Death		Detainers	217	Insurance
117G	Debt, Action of	167	Factors	218	Insurrection and
117T	Debtor and Creditor	168	False Imprisonment		Sedition
118A	Declaratory	169	False Personation	219	Interest
	Judgment	170	False Pretenses	220	Internal Revenue
119	Dedication	170A	Federal Civil	221	International Law
120	Deeds		Procedure	222	Interpleader
122A	Deposits and	170B	Federal Courts	223	Intoxicating Liquors
	Escrows	171	Fences	224	Joint Adventures
123	Deposits in Court	172	Ferries	225	Joint-Stock
124	Descent and	174	Fines		Companies and
	Distribution	175	Fires		Business Trusts
125	Detectives	176	Fish	226	Joint Tenancy
126	Detinue	177	Fixtures	227	Judges
129	Disorderly Conduct	178	Food	228	Judgment
130	Disorderly House	179	Forcible Entry and	229	Judicial Sales
131	District and		Detainer	230	Jury
	Prosecuting	180	Forfeitures	231	Justices of the Peace
	Attorneys	181	Forgery	232	Kidnapping
132	District of Columbia	183	Franchises	232A	Labor Relations
133	Disturbance of	184	Fraud	233	Landlord and
	Public	185	Frauds, Statute of		Tenant
	Assemblage	186	Fraudulent	234	Larceny
134	Divorce		Conveyances	235	Levees and Flood
135	Domicile	187	Game		Control
135H	Double Jeopardy	188	Gaming	236	Lewdness
136	Dower and Curtesy	189	Garnishment	237	Libel and Slander
137	Drains	190	Gas	238	Licenses
138	Drugs and Narcotics	191	Gifts	239	Liens
141	Easements	192	Good Will	240	Life Estates
142	Ejectment	193	Grand Jury	241	Limitation of Actions
143	Election of	195	Guaranty	242	Lis Pendens
	Remedies	196	Guardian and Ward	245	Logs and Logging
144	Elections	197	Habeas Corpus	246	Lost Instruments
145	Electricity	198	Hawkers and	247	Lotteries
146	Embezzlement		Peddlers	248	Malicious Mischief
148	Eminent Domain	199	Health and	249	Malicious
148A	Employers' Liability		Environment		Prosecution
149	Entry, Writ of	200	Highways	250	Mandamus
150	Equity	201	Holidays	251	Manufactures
151	Escape	202	Homestead	252	Maritime Liens
152	Escheat	203	Homicide	253	Marriage
154	Estates in Property	204	Hospitals	255	Master and Servant
156	Estoppel	205	Husband and Wife	256	Mayhem
157	Evidence	205H	Implied and	257	Mechanics' Liens
158	Exceptions, Bill of		Constructive	257A	Mental Health
159	Exchange of		Contracts	258A	Military Justice
	Property	206	Improvements	259	Militia
160	Exchanges	207	Incest	260	Mines and Minerals
161	Execution	208	Indemnity	265	Monopolies
162	Executors and	209	Indians	266	Mortgages
	Administrators	210	Indictment and	267	Motions
163	Exemptions		Information	268	Municipal
164	Explosives	211	Infants		Corporations

* We used the Minnesota version because our library carries it and does not carry the New Mexico version. This is because the topics and key numbers are identical across the system.

EXHIBIT 9.8   *(continued)*

DIGEST TOPICS AND ABBREVIATIONS

152	Escheat	Escheat		200	Highways	High
154	Estates in Property	Estates		201	Holidays	Holidays
156	Estoppel	Estop		202	Homestead	Home
157	Evidence	Evid		203	Homicide	Homic
158	Exceptions, Bill of	Exceptions Bill of		205	Husband and Wife	Hus & W
				205H	Implied and Constructive Contracts	Impl & C C
159	Exchange of Property	Exch of Prop				
160	Exchanges	Exchanges		206	Improvements	Improv
161	Execution	Execution		207	Incest	Incest
162	Executors and Administrators	Ex & Ad		208	Indemnity	Indem
				209	Indians	Indians
163	Exemptions	Exemp		210	Indictment and Information	Ind & Inf
164	Explosives	Explos				
165	Extortion and Threats	Extort		211	Infants	Infants
166	Extradition and Detainers	Extrad		212	Injunction	Inj
				213	Innkeepers	Inn
167	Factors	Fact		216	Inspection	Inspect
168	False Imprisonment	False Imp		217	Insurance	Insurance
169	False Personation	False Pers		218	Insurrection and Sedition	Insurrect
170	False Pretenses	False Pret				
170A	Federal Civil Procedure	Fed Civ Proc		219	Interest	Interest
				220	Internal Revenue	Int Rev
170B	Federal Courts	Fed Cts		221	International Law	Intern Law
171	Fences	Fences		222	Interpleader	Interpl
172	Ferries	Ferries		223	Intoxicating Liquors	Int Liq
174	Fines	Fines		224	Joint Adventures	Joint Adv
175	Fires	Fires		225	Joint-Stock Companies and Business Trusts	Joint-St Co
176	Fish	Fish				
177	Fixtures	Fixt		226	Joint Tenancy	Joint Ten
178	Food	Food		227	Judges	Judges
179	Forcible Entry and Detainer	Forci E & D		228	Judgment	Judgm
				229	Judicial Sales	Jud S
180	Forfeitures	Forfeit		230	Jury	Jury
181	Forgery	Forg		231	Justices of the Peace	J P
183	Franchises	Franch		231E	Kidnapping	Kidnap
184	Fraud	Fraud		231H	Labor and Employment	Labor & Emp
185	Frauds, Statute of	Frds St of				
186	Fraudulent Conveyances	Fraud Conv		233	Landlord and Tenant	Land & Ten
				234	Larceny	Larc
187	Game	Game		235	Levees and Flood Control	Levees
188	Gaming	Gaming				
189	Garnishment	Garn		236	Lewdness	Lewd
190	Gas	Gas		237	Libel and Slander	Libel
191	Gifts	Gifts		238	Licenses	Licens
192	Good Will	Good Will		239	Liens	Liens
193	Grand Jury	Gr Jury		240	Life Estates	Life Est
195	Guaranty	Guar		241	Limitation of Actions	Lim of Act
196	Guardian and Ward	Guard & W		241E	Limited Liability Companies	Ltd Liab Cos
197	Habeas Corpus	Hab Corp				
198	Hawkers and Peddlers	Hawk & P		242	Lis Pendens	Lis Pen
198H	Health	Health		245	Logs and Logging	Logs

Exhibit 9.9	Descriptive Word Index, from Minnesota Digest (paper source)*

EMPLOYMENT

37 Minn D 2d–40

References are to Digest Topics and Key Numbers

EMPLOYMENT LAW—Cont'd
ADVERSE employment decisions, actions regarding,—Cont'd

Supervisor liability, Labor & Emp ⟸ 857
Time to sue, Labor & Emp ⟸ 856
Variation between proof and pleading, Labor & Emp ⟸ 858

ALIENS. See heading ALIENS, EMPLOYMENT

ARBITRATION and award. See heading ARBITRATION AND AWARD, EMPLOYMENT law.

ASYLUMS, employees and officers. See heading ASYLUMS, EMPLOYEES.

AT-WILL employment,
Generally, Labor & Emp ⟸ 40
Implied contracts, Labor & Emp ⟸ 36
Termination of employment, Labor & Emp ⟸ 40(2)

BORROWED servant,
Workers' compensation, Work Comp ⟸ 203-210

CONTRACTS,
Generally, Labor & Emp ⟸ 32

DISCHARGE,
Generally, Labor & Emp ⟸ 825
Bad faith, Labor & Emp ⟸ 843
Bankruptcy, Labor & Emp ⟸ 768
Breach of contract, Labor & Emp ⟸ 835
Cause, necessity of, Labor & Emp ⟸ 40(2)
Compensation,
Deductions and forfeitures, Labor & Emp ⟸ 210
Condonation, Labor & Emp ⟸ 829
Conflict of laws, Labor & Emp ⟸ 756
Constitutional rights, exercise of, Labor & Emp ⟸ 812
Constructive discharge, Labor & Emp ⟸ 826
Contract, breach of, Labor & Emp ⟸ 835
Criminal conviction, Labor & Emp ⟸ 763
Criticism, Labor & Emp ⟸ 776
Disability, Labor & Emp ⟸ 764
Discrimination. See heading EMPLOYMENT DISCRIMINATION, DISCHARGE.
Disobedience, Labor & Emp ⟸ 766
Effect of discharge, Labor & Emp ⟸ 835
ERISA violation, Labor & Emp ⟸ 793
Fair dealing requirement, Labor & Emp ⟸ 843
Garnishment, Labor & Emp ⟸ 768
Good faith requirement, Labor & Emp ⟸ 843
Grounds in general, Labor & Emp ⟸ 760
Health and safety regulations, exercise of rights under, Labor & Emp ⟸ 800
Incompetence, Labor & Emp ⟸ 765
Insubordination, Labor & Emp ⟸ 766
Intoxication, Labor & Emp ⟸ 767
Malicious procurement of discharge, liability of third party, Labor & Emp ⟸ 914
Misconduct, Labor & Emp ⟸ 763
Motive, Labor & Emp ⟸ 843
Neglect of duty, Labor & Emp ⟸ 765
Operation of discharge, Labor & Emp ⟸ 835

EMPLOYMENT LAW—Cont'd
DISCHARGE—Cont'd

Performance, unsatisfactory, Labor & Emp ⟸ 765
Political rights, exercise of, Labor & Emp ⟸ 812
Procedural requirements, Labor & Emp ⟸ 828
Public policy considerations, Labor & Emp ⟸ 759
Reason, necessity for, Labor & Emp ⟸ 40(2)
Reemployment after discharge, Labor & Emp ⟸ 877
Refusal to perform wrongful act, Labor & Emp ⟸ 781
Reports of wrongdoing to employer or outside entities, Labor & Emp ⟸ 775
Third party's liability for malicious procurement of discharge, Labor & Emp ⟸ 914
Unsatisfactory performance, Labor & Emp ⟸ 765
Waiver, Labor & Emp ⟸ 852
Whistle blowing, Labor & Emp ⟸ 775
Wrongful act, refusal to perform, Labor & Emp ⟸ 781

DISCRIMINATION. See heading EMPLOYMENT DISCRIMINATION, generally.

HANDBOOKS, Labor & Emp ⟸ 49

IMMIGRANTS. See heading ALIENS, EMPLOYMENT

INDEMNITY,
Operation of law, indemnification by, Indem ⟸ 71

RETALIATORY discharge or discipline,
Generally, Labor & Emp ⟸ 770
Civil rights laws, filing of claims under,
Armed services, civilian employees, Armed S ⟸ 27(4, 5), 102
Hospital employees, Health ⟸ 266

EMPLOYMENT TAXES

Generally, Tax ⟸ 3260

ACTIONS and proceedings,
Assessment, Tax ⟸ 3291(9)

AGRICULTURAL employment excepted, Tax ⟸ 3288

APPROVAL of state laws by federal authorities, Tax ⟸ 3265

ASSESSMENT,
Generally, Tax ⟸ 3291(1)
Actions and proceedings, Tax ⟸ 3291(9)
Burden of proof, Tax ⟸ 3291(7)
Evidence. See subheading EVIDENCE, generally, under this heading.
Matters considered, Tax ⟸ 3291(3)
Notice, Tax ⟸ 3291(1)
Presumptions, Tax ⟸ 3291(7)
Time, Tax ⟸ 3291(4)

BURDEN of proof, Tax ⟸ 3291(7)

BUSINESSES controlled by same interests, Tax ⟸ 3275

---

* We used the Minnesota version because our library carries it and does not carry the New Mexico version. This is because the topics and key numbers are identical across the system.

earlier series; some later series incorporate the information from the previous series. Typically, the most recent bound digest is updated by a pocket part inserted into the back of the bound volume; some pocket parts become so big that they are reissued as pamphlets or bound volumes. Even more recent information appears in pamphlets that cover multiple bound volumes and generally are shelved at the end of a digest set. The most recent information appears in digest pages found within the most recent reporter hardbound volumes and advance sheets, discussed later. Because recent cases generally are more useful than older cases, and because the newer publications contain fairly few entries, experienced researchers typically follow this sequence:

- ☐ the bound volume from the current series,
- ☐ its pocket part or pamphlets,
- ☐ the supplementary pamphlet for the digest,
- ☐ the most recent digest material in recent reporter hardbound volumes and advance sheets, and
- ☐ the older series bound volume (if the newer series does not incorporate its material).

Read the topic outline and headnotes. As you turn to the digest material covering your topic, skim the general and detailed outlines at the outset of your topic. See Exhibit 9.10 (at page 176), a detailed outline. There may be additional pertinent key numbers you have not yet identified; rarely is there only one pertinent key number for a legal issue. Furthermore, you may find the organization of the topic to be informative.

Then peruse the entries under the pertinent key numbers. The entries are called "digest paragraphs," and they are identical to the headnote paragraphs appearing with the case in the West reporter. Compare Exhibit 9.2 (at page 153) and 9.7 (at page 171). At the end of each digest paragraph is a citation to the case from which it is drawn.

The digest paragraphs are ordered by one or more of the following principles:

- ☐ hierarchical: federal before state, higher courts before lower courts;
- ☐ reverse chronological: newer before older;
- ☐ alphabetical: for example, Iowa before Michigan; and
- ☐ numerical: for example, First Circuit before Second Circuit.

The court and date appear in bold letters at the beginning of the digest paragraph, so you can quickly prioritize which to read first.

On occasion, you may know the name of one or both parties in a pertinent case, but not the citation of the case. Hence, you need assistance locating the case in the reporter. Digests contain tables permitting you to look up the plaintiff or defendant by name and providing the case's citation.

Locate and read the cases in reporters. When you finish with the digest, you will have a list of pertinent cases along with their locations in the case reporters and a basic idea of what each case stands for. It is essential, of course, to take the next step — to read the case in full.

EXHIBIT 9.10	Outline of Digest Topic, from New Mexico Digest (paper source)

LABOR & EMPLOYMENT

4B N M D—20

I. IN GENERAL.—Continued.

    34. —— Formation; requisites and validity.
        (1). In general.
        (2). Particular cases.
    35. —— Construction and operation in general.
    36. —— Implied contracts.
    37. Term, duration, and termination.
    38. —— In general.
    39. —— Commencement of relation.
    40. —— Definite or indefinite term; employment at-will.
        (1). In general.
        (2). Termination; cause or reason in general.
        (3). Particular cases.
    41. —— Hiring for a period of time.
        (1). In general.
        (2). By the year.
        (3). By the month.
        (4). Other particular time periods.
    42. —— Lifetime or permanent employment.
    43. —— Other particular terms.
    44. —— Termination by mutual agreement.
    45. —— Termination by employee.
        (1). In general.
        (2). Abandonment; constructive resignation.
    46. —— Changed circumstances.
    47. Modification or rescission of contract.
    48. Renewal or continuation.
    49. Manuals, handbooks, and policy statements.
    50. —— In general.
    51. —— Particular cases.
    52. Actions or proceedings in general.
    53. Evidence of employment.
    54. —— In general.
    55. —— Presumptions and burden of proof.
    56. —— Admissibility.
    57. —— Weight and sufficiency.
    58. Questions of law and fact as to employment status.

II. GOVERNMENT REGULATION IN GENERAL.

    ☞60. In general.
    61. Constitutional and statutory provisions.
    62. Administrative boards and officers and agents in general.
    63. Regulations in general.
    64. Enforcement procedures.
    65. Evidence.
    66. Review.
    67. Searches and inspections.

III. RIGHTS AND DUTIES OF EMPLOYERS AND EMPLOYEES IN GENERAL.

    ☞70. In general.

As you read the case, take care to use the headnotes properly. Relying only on the headnote is unwise because it will not tell you everything you need to know about the case, it may not reflect an important nuance of the case, and (rarely) it may be erroneous. You can use the headnotes to help you pinpoint the most pertinent portions of the case; the number preceding each headnote in the case reporter is keyed to a small bracketed number West editors insert within the opinion itself. See item 11 in Exhibit 9.2 (at page 153). Nonetheless, you should at least skim the apparently less pertinent passages, to be sure you fully understand the legal and factual context of the pertinent passages.

Read the case carefully so that you correctly derive the legal rule for which it stands. Because a case supplies not only a legal rule but also an example of the rule's application, you should also brief the case. A case brief should include the facts, procedure, outcome and holding, rule, and reasoning. With this information recorded, you will be well situated not only to use the legal rule in your analysis of your client's situation but also to compare the case and your client's situation; reasoning by analogy is a powerful tool in legal analysis.

Finally, take advantage of the case as a finding tool for additional authorities. A case may refer to authorities you have not yet identified. Furthermore, there may be a headnote assigned to a topic and key number you have not yet identified; pursue that topic and key number in the digest, as described previously.

The process described thus far is not complete. You still must employ a citator to verify that your case is good law, that is, to ascertain its subsequent history and treatment. Citators are discussed in Chapter 10.

Exhibit 9.11 (at page 178) presents the cases template filled in to reflect our research for the Canoga case, performed in the West digests and reporters.

3. Online Resources

As noted previously, various online resources offer case law databases. Each has its strengths and weaknesses. To become a skilled researcher, you must not only be proficient in paper research but also in the use of online resources. Exhibit 9.12 (at page 179) summarizes some key factors to consider.

Cases in Westlaw

► Select an appropriate database.
► Draft and run one or more searches — natural language, terms and connectors, key number, KeySearch — with restrictions, as appropriate.
► Sift the results to identify pertinent cases.
► Read each pertinent case.
► Cite each case (see Chapter 10).

| EXHIBIT 9.11 | Case Law Template for Canoga Case |

Issue:	Citation Information:
Did the orchestra breach a contract with Canoga by failing to follow the procedures set out in the employee handbook?	• *Lukoski v. Sandia Indian Management Co.* • *Pacific Reporter 2d* • *Vol. 748, p. 507* • *N.M. Sup. Ct.* • *1988* • *Citing as per Chapter 10: KeyCite: green C. Shepard's: yellow caution — need to check distinguishing case.*
Date of events: *Sept. 7, 2007*	
Date of research: *Nov. 30, 2007*	

Search and Find:

located case by . . .

> *New Mexico Digest: Old topic list → Master & Servant; new topic list → Labor & Employment.*
> *Descriptive Word Index → Handbooks under Labor & Emp. 49.*
> *Topic outline → Evidence of Employment 53–58.*

Information and Implications:

- *Lukoski was general manager of bingo operation. No written contract to start. Feb. 1984: all employees got handbook; signed form acknowledgment. See fn. 1 re procedures. Lukoski was fired without warning or suspension for personality issues, not severe offense or insubordination or disobedience. Severe offense could lead to immediate termination.*
- *Bench trial: judgment for Lukoski.*
- *Judgment affirmed: Sandia breached contract with Lukoski; Lukoski awarded $18,000+ for salary due on rest of one-year oral contract.*
- *Whether employee handbook has modified employment relationship is question of fact to be discerned from totality of parties' statements and actions. p. 509*
- *Handbook referred to warnings and suspensions as established procedures. Nothing in handbook alerted employees not to rely on it or see it as unilateral expression of intention Sandia could revoke at any time.*
- *Dissent: Lukoski's conduct was severe enough to justify immediate termination.*

- *Handbook can be contract depending on circumstances. Process rights can be enforced. Lukoski handbook's language is stronger than orchestra's, however.*

Next Steps:

questions to consider:	leads to follow:
• *How did Canoga get handbook? Any acknowledgment form?* • *Look into rest of handbook language to check for disclaimers of binding contract.*	• *Maybe Wagenseller — AZ decision.* • *Citate Lukoski for more recent N.M. cases.*

| EXHIBIT 9.12 | Major Case Law Resources and Strategies |

	West's Paper Reporters and Digests	LexisNexis Westlaw	Other Online Commercial Services	Court Websites
Scope of compilation— retrospective	+	+	limited	very limited
Scope of compilation— current	typically within three to four months	+	varies	+
Examining cases in publisher's topical framework	✓	✓		
Boolean or natural-language full-text searching		✓	✓	varies— generally no
Retrieve a known case	✓	✓	✓	✓

In addition to the National Reporter System, Thomson West not surprisingly provides a significant online resource for case law research: Westlaw. Westlaw provides a very wide range of cases and many means of access to those cases.

In some respects, research through Westlaw has advantages over paper research:

☐ Westlaw provides more recent cases than paper sources.

☐ Westlaw provides unpublished cases, which may not be available in paper.

☐ You may use specific factual concepts in constructing a Westlaw search that would not be used in the means of access provided in a paper source.

☐ Westlaw's case law databases are automatically cumulated, whereas paper research generally entails working through multiple publications, e.g., a main volume, pocket part, and supplement pamphlet.

On the other hand, Westlaw research does not always work well. In particular, if your research terms are very common words, it will be difficult to draft an effective search. If you do not write your search well, you may believe that you have located all pertinent cases when in fact you have not. For example, if your search focuses on a distinctive fact, you will not retrieve pertinent cases that state the applicable law but do not include the distinctive fact. Furthermore, Westlaw can be expensive. Pricing structures vary, so you should always be aware of the fees associated with the research you conduct in

Westlaw. The key to appropriate use of Westlaw is being strategic in selecting database(s), constructing searches, and sifting the results.

Select an appropriate database. Westlaw offers many case law databases, most drawn along jurisdictional lines, others along subject-matter lines. As a general principle, you should start in the narrowest database containing the mandatory precedent for your jurisdiction, then switch to wider or different databases as needed, e.g., if you want to find factually parallel cases in other states because you have found no factually similar cases in your jurisdiction. As you begin your research, always be sure to check the scope of the database you have chosen.

Draft and run one or more searches. Westlaw offers four main search options for case law research; you may well want to combine two or three to assure comprehensive results. Two options rest in part on the work of West editors. The other two rest entirely on your search drafting. Search drafting is discussed in detail in Chapter 2.

First, key-number searching entails entering West's code for a pertinent topic and key number as your search term. You may find pertinent topics and key numbers in commentary, through your research in digests, through a pertinent case you already have located, or by browsing or searching the online key-number service. See Exhibit 9.2 item 7a (at page 154). A variation on key-number searching is KeyCite Notes, in which you click on that icon adjacent to a pertinent headnote in a case you are reading online. Either way, the computer will retrieve cases with headnotes under that key number.

Second, KeySearch entails taking advantage of searches already written by West's staff. You select a topic and subtopic, in effect adopting West's search for that subtopic. You will be told what the search is, and you may add your own search terms as well.

Third, natural-language searching entails stating an issue, possibly using the thesaurus to expand your terms, and obtaining a specified number of documents that best fit the search as determined by a semantic-statistical algorithm. The cases are presented from best fit to least fit.

Fourth, terms-and-connectors searching is Westlaw's version of Boolean searching. This entails keying in words, with or without root expanders, along with connectors, such as &, /s, and /#, and a space for or. All cases meeting the requirements of the search will be retrieved and presented from newest to oldest.

Note that the results will differ from search to search. For example, a key-number search will retrieve only published cases that have key numbers; for the most part, West has not assigned key numbers to unpublished cases. Natural-language and terms-and-connectors searches are processed differently.

For various reasons, you may want to restrict your search. For example, you would add a date restrictor if you are seeking only recent cases, because you are updating your research in paper sources or updating research done some time ago. Or you may want to restrict your search to a specific "field" (Westlaw's term for components of a document). As an example, if your research terms are quite common and you want to, in effect, shrink the database to a manageable size, you could confine your search to the synopsis field or the digest field (which contains both the key-number classifications and the headnotes).

Sift the results, and read the pertinent cases. However you construct your search, your next step is to sift through the results to identify pertinent cases. To identify cases that probably will be pertinent, read the synopsis and headnotes, read the passages of the case in which your search terms appear, or both. For an example of a printout from a terms-and-connectors search in the synopsis and digest fields, see Exhibit 9.13 (at page 182). As you sift your results, if your research yields unpublished cases, consider carefully how precedential they are. Most, if not all, of the cases you select should be published cases.

You may want to use Westlaw, versus more modest online resources, because of Westlaw's added features. For example, once you find a pertinent case, the ResultsPlus feature provides links to various West commentary sources, such as A.L.R.s and encyclopedias, discussing the topic of the case.

On occasion, you will use Westlaw to obtain a known case or locate and obtain a nearly known case. If you know the citation of a case, you can obtain the case through the Find function. If you know some information about a case, such as the name of one of the parties or the judge or one of the lawyers, you can run a search in the appropriate database with that information in the appropriate field.

As you read a pertinent case located and obtained through Westlaw, you should look for the same information detailed previously for paper research. And, as with paper research in cases, you must use a citator to verify that your case is still good law. As discussed in Chapter 10, citating through Westlaw is one good option.

Cases in LexisNexis

▶ Select an appropriate database.
▶ Draft and run searches.
▶ Sift the results to identify pertinent cases.
▶ Read each pertinent case.
▶ Citate each case (see Chapter 10).

As with Westlaw, LexisNexis provides a wealth of cases along with many means of access to those cases. It offers several advantages over paper research: very recent cases, unpublished cases, use of research terms drawn from the specific facts of your client's situation, and automatic cumulation of new material into existing databases. On the other hand, it is difficult to draft a good search for some research topics, you cannot tell what you have missed, and LexisNexis use can be expensive.

For many years, LexisNexis relied on the editorial material developed by West, chiefly the key number system. More recently, LexisNexis has developed its own editorial material. This includes the following:

☐ the prior and subsequent history of the case;
☐ a description of its procedural posture;
☐ an overview of the events;

Exhibit 9.13	Results of Westlaw Terms-and-Connectors Search, Run in New Mexico State Cases Database (online source)

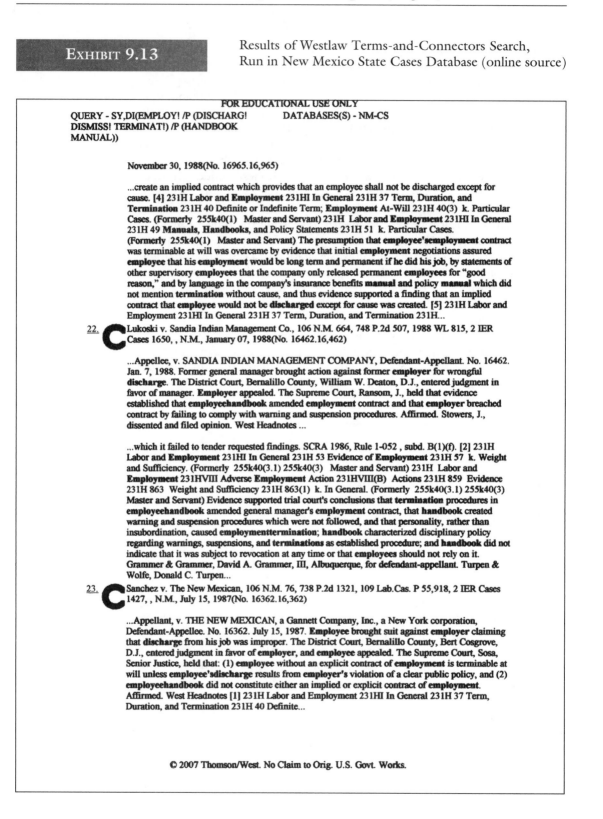

FOR EDUCATIONAL USE ONLY

QUERY - SY,DI(EMPLOY! /P (DISCHARG!   DATABASES(S) - NM-CS
DISMISS! TERMINAT!) /P (HANDBOOK
MANUAL))

November 30, 1988(No. 16965.16,965)

...create an implied contract which provides that an employee shall not be discharged except for cause. [4] 231H Labor and **Employment** 231HI In General 231H 37 Term, Duration, and **Termination** 231H 40 Definite or Indefinite Term; **Employment** At-Will 231H 40(3) k. Particular Cases. (Formerly 255k40(1) Master and Servant) 231H Labor and **Employment** 231HI In General 231H 49 **Manuals, Handbooks,** and Policy Statements 231H 51 k. Particular Cases. (Formerly 255k40(1)   Master and Servant) The presumption that **employee'semployment** contract was terminable at will was overcome by evidence that initial **employment** negotiations assured **employee** that his **employment** would be long term and permanent if he did his job, by statements of other supervisory **employees** that the company only released permanent **employees** for "good reason," and by language in the company's insurance benefits **manual** and policy **manual** which did not mention **termination** without cause, and thus evidence supported a finding that an implied contract that **employee** would not be **discharged** except for cause was created. [5] 231H Labor and Employment 231HI In General 231H 37 Term, Duration, and Termination 231H...

22.   **C** Lukoski v. Sandia Indian Management Co., 106 N.M. 664, 748 P.2d 507, 1988 WL 815, 2 IER Cases 1650, , N.M., January 07, 1988(No. 16462.16,462)

...Appellee, v. SANDIA INDIAN MANAGEMENT COMPANY, Defendant-Appellant. No. 16462. Jan. 7, 1988. Former general manager brought action against former **employer** for wrongful **discharge**. The District Court, Bernalillo County, William W. Deaton, D.J., entered judgment in favor of manager. **Employer** appealed. The Supreme Court, Ransom, J., held that evidence established that **employeehandbook** amended **employment** contract and that **employer** breached contract by failing to comply with warning and suspension procedures. Affirmed. Stowers, J., dissented and filed opinion. West Headnotes ...

...which it failed to tender requested findings. SCRA 1986, Rule 1-052 , subd. B(1)(f). [2] 231H Labor and **Employment** 231HI In General 231H 53 Evidence of **Employment** 231H 57 k. Weight and Sufficiency. (Formerly 255k40(3.1) 255k40(3) Master and Servant) 231H Labor and **Employment** 231HVIII Adverse **Employment** Action 231HVIII(B) Actions 231H 859 Evidence 231H 863 Weight and Sufficiency 231H 863(1) k. In General. (Formerly 255k40(3.1) 255k40(3) Master and Servant) Evidence supported trial court's conclusions that **termination** procedures in **employeehandbook** amended general manager's **employment** contract, that **handbook** created warning and suspension procedures which were not followed, and that personality, rather than insubordination, caused **employmenttermination; handbook** characterized disciplinary policy regarding warnings, suspensions, and **terminations** as established procedure; and **handbook** did not indicate that it was subject to revocation at any time or that **employees** should not rely on it. Grammer & Grammer, David A. Grammer, III, Albuquerque, for defendant-appellant. Turpen & Wolfe, Donald C. Turpen...

23.   **C** Sanchez v. The New Mexican, 106 N.M. 76, 738 P.2d 1321, 109 Lab.Cas. P 55,918, 2 IER Cases 1427, , N.M., July 15, 1987(No. 16362.16,362)

...Appellant, v. THE NEW MEXICAN, a Gannett Company, Inc., a New York corporation, Defendant-Appellee. No. 16362. July 15, 1987. **Employee** brought suit against **employer** claiming that **discharge** from his job was improper. The District Court, Bernalillo County, Bert Cosgrove, D.J., entered judgment in favor of **employer**, and **employee** appealed. The Supreme Court, Sosa, Senior Justice, held that: (1) **employee** without an explicit contract of **employment** is terminable at will unless **employee'sdischarge** results from **employer's** violation of a clear public policy, and (2) **employeehandbook** did not constitute either an implied or explicit contract of **employment**. Affirmed. West Headnotes [1] 231H Labor and Employment 231HI In General 231H 37 Term, Duration, and Termination 231H 40 Definite...

☐   the outcome;
☐   and headnotes, which consist of concept chains beginning with the broadest and ending with the narrowest, along with a pertinent quotation from the case.

See Exhibit 9.14 (at page 184). At the same time, LexisNexis recognizes the preeminence of the West reporters by providing the citation of the case in the West system and star pagination — numbers scattered throughout the case that reflect the pagination of the case in the West reporters. LexisNexis does this as well for any official reporter of a case. LexisNexis also provides, of course, its own citation and page numbers.

Select an appropriate database; draft and run appropriate searches. LexisNexis offers many cases databases. It also offers various search options. An early decision to be made in LexisNexis is whether to construct your own search or work within the topical framework LexisNexis has developed.

If you opt to construct your own search, the first step would be to select a database. Start with the narrowest database containing mandatory precedents; switch to wider or different databases as needed. Be sure to check the scope of each database you use.

LexisNexis offers both of the standard search options. Natural-language entails stating an issue, adding suggested words as you desire, and obtaining a pre-determined number of cases, presented from most likely pertinent to least pertinent. Terms-and-connectors (Boolean) searching entails keying in words, with or without root expanders, and connectors; the computer retrieves all cases meeting the requirements of the search and presents them within jurisdiction and level of court from newest to oldest. You may use tools such as date restrictions and running your search in specified segments to sharpen your search. The results of natural language and terms-and-connectors searches may well vary. Search drafting is covered in detail in Chapter 2.

If you opt to work within the LexisNexis framework, you would use the Source by Topic or Headnote program. You would first pick a main topic and then continue to choose subtopics; in a way, this parallels using a table of contents. Once you have chosen the smallest subtopic, you would select the appropriate database from a list of sources including commentary as well as sources of law. You may then run the search you have created as you chose the topic and subtopics. To refine the search, you may search the LexisNexis headnotes, add in a natural-language or terms-and-connectors search, impose a date restriction, or focus your search on specific segments of a case.

Sift the results, and read the pertinent cases. Whatever your search may be, your next step is to sift through the results. You may peruse a citation list containing a case overview and list of core terms prepared by the Lexis-Nexis staff, as well as see your research terms in context. See Exhibit 9.15 (at page 185). To further identify cases that probably will be pertinent, peruse the editorial material at the beginning of the decision or read the passages in which your search terms appear. In addition, attend carefully to whether or not the case is published.

You may want to use LexisNexis, versus more modest online resources, because of its additional features. For example, once you find a pertinent case,

| EXHIBIT 9.14 | First Page of Case, from LexisNexis's New Mexico State Courts Database (online source) |

LEXSEE 748 P2D 507

Caution
As of: Nov 20, 2007

Scott J.L. LUKOSKI, Plaintiff-Appellee, v. SANDIA INDIAN MANAGEMENT
COMPANY, Defendant-Appellant

No. 16462

SUPREME COURT OF NEW MEXICO

106 N.M. 664; 748 P.2d 507; 1988 N.M. LEXIS 17; 2 I.E.R. Cas. (BNA) 1650

January 7, 1988

SUBSEQUENT HISTORY: January 7, 1988, Filed

PRIOR HISTORY: [***1] Appeal from the District Court of Bernalillo County, William W. Deaton, District Judge.

CASE SUMMARY:

PROCEDURAL POSTURE: Defendant employer sought review of the decision from the District Court of Bernalillo County (New Mexico) which ruled in favor of plaintiff employee in a wrongful discharge action.

OVERVIEW: The employee brought a wrongful discharge action against the employer. The trial court found that the employer had violated the termination procedures prescribed for "less serious" offenses by an employee handbook. The employee was awarded the salary due on the remaining term of his one-year oral contract. On appeal, the employer claimed the employee, as general manager, was not the type of employee intended to be covered by the handbook. The court affirmed. It found that distribution of the handbook to all employees with request for signatures refuted the employer's claims. There was substantial evidence supporting the trial court's findings of ultimate fact that the termination procedures became an amendment to the employee's contract. The employee was terminated without warning or suspension for a cause not so severe as to have constituted cause for immediate termination. Substantial evidence supported the finding of the trial court that the employee handbook modified the employment relation-

ship and created warning and suspension procedures which were not followed.

OUTCOME: The judgment of the trial court was affirmed.

LexisNexis(R) Headnotes

Civil Procedure > Trials > Jury Trials > Province of Court & Jury
Contracts Law > Breach > Causes of Action > General Overview
Contracts Law > Breach > Material Breach
[HN1] Materiality is a specific question of fact.

Civil Procedure > Trials > Jury Trials > Province of Court & Jury
Labor & Employment Law > Wrongful Termination > Breach of Contract > General Overview
[HN2] Whether an employee handbook modifies the employment relationship is a question of fact to be discerned from the totality of the parties' statements and actions regarding the employment relationship.

Labor & Employment Law > Employment Relationships > At-Will Employment > General Overview
Labor & Employment Law > Wrongful Termination > Breach of Contract > General Overview
[HN3] If an employer does choose to issue a policy statement, in a manual or otherwise, and, by its language

EXHIBIT 9.15	Results of LexisNexis Terms-and-Connectors Search, Run in New Mexico State Courts Database (online source)

OVERVIEW: Where an employee was not deprived of any "property right," had no civil rights claim, and no termination procedures were applicable, summary judgment was properly granted to the university in the employee's wrongful termination action.

CORE TERMS: summary judgment, entitlement, handbook, employment contract, genuine issue, material fact, faculty

... legitimate entitlement to employment at the University.   ...
... in a faculty handbook constituted an entitlement   ...
... the plaintiff, no termination procedures are applicable   ...
... renewal of his employment contract. He does not   ...
... to review his discharge. See Roth, 408 U.S. at 578, 92 S.Ct. at 2710 ...

19. Lukoski v. Sandia Indian Management Co., No. 16462, SUPREME COURT OF NEW MEXICO, 106 N.M. 664;
748 P.2d 507; 1988 N.M. LEXIS 17; 2 I.E.R. Cas. (BNA) 1650, January 7, 1988 , January 7, 1988, Filed ▲
Caution, As of: Nov 20, 2007

OVERVIEW: Where the employee handbook modified the employment relationship and created warning and suspension procedures which were not followed, the employer was liable to the employee for wrongful termination of employment.

CORE TERMS: termination, suspension, warning, employee handbook, handbook, severe, bingo, employment relationship, personnel manual, disciplinary ...

... brought a wrongful discharge action against his employer, Sandia Indian Management   ...
... Lukoski had been employed as general manager   ...
... SIMCO violated the termination procedures prescribed for "   ...
... offenses by an employee handbook. For salary due   ...
... one-year oral contract, Lukoski was awarded   ...
... one-year oral employment agreement under which   ...
... distributed to all employees an employee handbook and requested each   ...
... amended the oral employment contract * * * when [SIMCO] proffered,   ...
... Lukoski] signed, [the] Employee's Handbook containing new duties   ...
... the part of employee and employer over and above said oral contract, including Rules to   ...
... Lukoski] and a termination procedure to be   ...
... the type of employee intended to be covered by the handbook. Distribution to all employees with request for   ...
... substance of the contract nor defeated the   ...
... Bisio v. Madenwald (In re Estate of Bisio), 33 Or.App. 325, 576 P.2d 801 (1978). As the contract stood after amendment,   ...
... issue under the termination procedures. In any   ...
... language of the employee handbook is "too indefinite to constitute a contract" and lacks "contractual   ...
... to form a contract." It maintains that   ...
... as if the employee handbook was to govern   ...
... language of the termination policy is ambiguous   ...
... required policy for termination ...

20. Boudar v. E.G. & G., Inc., No. 16167, SUPREME COURT OF NEW MEXICO, 106 N.M. 279; 742 P.2d 491; 1987
N.M. LEXIS 3717; 2 I.E.R. Cas. (BNA) 1420, August 27, 1987 , Rehearing Denied September 16, 1987. ●
Analysis, As of: Nov 20, 2007

OVERVIEW: On rehearing, the court agreed with employee that the expanded public policy exception to the terminable at-will rule applied to her cause, and also held that employee stated a breach of implied contract claim against employer.

you can leverage your successful research in the same or different databases, through the More-Like-This function.

LexisNexis can be used to obtain a known case, through its LEXSEE function.

As you read a pertinent case located and obtained through LexisNexis, look for the same information you would seek in a paper reporter. And be sure to cite the case; as discussed in Chapter 10, using the Shepard's tool on LexisNexis is one good option.

Other commercial case law resources

▶ Assess the utility of the source.
▶ Use various means to identify and retrieve pertinent cases.
▶ Read each case.
▶ Citate each case (see Chapter 10).

One of two significant developments in case law research over the last decade has been the rise of online commercial resources that are less extensive, less elaborate, and hence less expensive than Westlaw and LexisNexis. These services are aimed at smaller law offices.

For example, Casemaker operates through state bar associations; thirty bar associations were members when this text was written. For members, Casemaker offers both federal and state materials, including cases, statutes, rules, regulations, and some commentary. However, a limitation of Casemaker is that its case databases are less retrospective than the West reporter system, Westlaw, and LexisNexis. You can research via Boolean and natural-language searches, targeted searches run in fields such as the citation and syllabus, and retrieval of a known case. When you locate a case, you also obtain a list of cases citing the located case; you can then use the Casecheck feature to see the discussion of the cited case in the citing case. Citators are discussed in Chapter 10.

Similarly, Fastcase, with over 275,000 members as of 2007, provides federal and state cases as well as statutes, regulations, and rules. As is true of Casemaker, Fastcase's databases are less retrospective than the West reporter system, Westlaw, and LexisNexis. You can research via Boolean and natural-language searches, targeted field searches, and retrieval of a known case. You can sort the cases by date; relevance; and citation analysis, which displays the number of cases citing the cases the search retrieved. Authority Check lists the cases citing the case you have located, helping you determine whether a case is good law. Again, citators are discussed in Chapter 10.

Loislaw, the oldest of the three services discussed here, has much the same content as Casemaker and Fastcase, along with online treatises, reflecting its connection with Aspen Publishers. See Exhibit 1.2 (at pages 9–13), which is the *Lukoski* case as it appears on Loislaw. Loislaw's standard approach to key-word searching is to type the desired terms within the box for the

Exhibit 9.16	Search-and-Find Component of Case Law Template for Canoga Case — Online Searches Yielding Featured Case

WESTLAW

Key-Number search for *Lukoski*'s most pertinent headnote: only 5 cases.

KeySearch: Employment Law → Handbooks and Manuals, run in NM State Cases with West Headnotes: 34 cases; *Lukoski* was #27.

Natural language: Can an employer discharge an employee without following the procedures in the employee handbook?, run in NM-CS: *Lukoski* was #1.

Terms-and-connectors search: sy,di(employ! p (discharg! dismiss! terminat!) /p (handbook manual)), run in NM-CS: 28 cases; *Lukoski* was #22.

LEXISNEXIS

Source by Topic or Headnote: Labor & Employment Law → Wrongful Termination → Breach of Contract → Employer Handbooks, run in NM Labor & Employment Cases yielded too many cases to process; adding procedure OR process and after 1980 reduced the number to 60 cases.

Terms-and-connectors search: employ! /p (discharg! or dismiss! or terminat!) /p (handbook or manual) /p contract, run in New Mexico State Courts: 45 cases; *Lukoski* was #19; More-Like-This search based on *Lukoski* yielded 26 cases.

LOISLAW

Terms-and-connectors: (terminate or discharge) NEAR/30 employee NEAR/30 (handbook or manual), run in New Mexico Caselaw: 30 cases; *Lukoski* was #25.

selected field; one option is the entire document. You may also retrieve a known case. Loislaw's GlobalCite lists the documents citing the case you have located along with language from the citing case, so you can get some insight into whether the case is good law. One more time: citators are discussed in Chapter 10.

Exhibit 9.16 (above) lists searches run in Westlaw, LexisNexis, and Loislaw that yielded *Lukoski*.

> **Court websites**
>
> ▶ Retrieve recent decisions.
> ▶ In some sites, conduct a key-word search.

The second significant development in case law research over the last decade has been the court website. On the federal level, the Supreme Court posts its decisions and keeps them posted until they are published in *United States Reports* (its official paper publication). Each court of appeals also posts its decisions, and most district courts post at least selected decisions. Every state has a website for appellate decisions, with some including not only the highest court's decisions but also the intermediate appellate court's decisions. One good way to find a court website is through a portal such as Cornell University's Legal Information Institute.

Court websites typically are free resources. What you retrieve from a court website is almost the official decision; if the online version varies from the paper slip opinion, the latter governs.

However, most court websites reach back to the late 1990s, if that. Some courts remove opinions once they are published elsewhere. You will find only a chronological list of cases; but many court websites do not provide keyword searching or similar means of access. There will be no editorial enhancements and no citator. Thus, as of fall 2007, lawyers generally used a court website as a way to retrieve a recent known case, not as a major tool for researching case law.

See Exhibit 9.17 (at page 189) for the first page of a case as it appears on a court website.

4.   Summary

Because cases are primary authority, you must excel in researching cases. Seek cases that are mandatory precedent, good law, published decisions, strong parallels to your client's situation, and well reasoned discussions of your research topic. In addition to following up on leads from commentary, use one or more of the following strategies:

- ☐ Use case digests to find pertinent cases in paper reporters.
- ☐ Use the various Westlaw and LexisNexis tools — tapping into their topical frameworks and conducting key-word searching — to find pertinent cases.
- ☐ As available, perform less powerful and lower cost research in other commercial resources.
- ☐ When appropriate, visit court websites to obtain recent cases.

EXHIBIT 9.17	First Page of Case, from New Mexico Compilation Commission Website (online source)

Certiorari denied, No. 27,145, October 18, 2001

IN THE COURT OF APPEALS OF THE STATE OF NEW MEXICO

Opinion Number: 2001-NMCA-089

Filing Date: August 29, 2001

Docket No. 20,160

JANIE MEALAND,

    Plaintiff-Appellant,

v.

EASTERN NEW MEXICO MEDICAL CENTER,

    Defendant-Appellee.

APPEAL FROM THE DISTRICT COURT OF CHAVES COUNTY
William P. Lynch, District Judge

Chris Key
Albuquerque, NM

Keith Oas
Roswell, NM

    for Appellant

W.R. Logan
Lisa Entress Pullen
Civerolo, Gralow & Hill, P.A.
Albuquerque, NM

    for Appellee

OPINION

ALARID, Judge.

{1} The opinion heretofore filed in this case is withdrawn and the following substituted therefor. The motion for rehearing (reconsideration) is denied.

{2} This case arises out of a hospital's discharge of a registered nurse. The principal issue presented by this appeal is whether an employee handbook promulgated by the hospital gave rise to a reasonable expectation that Plaintiff would be discharged only after being afforded a fair opportunity to respond to charges of misconduct. We conclude that the evidence before the trial court established a genuine issue of fact as to whether the Eastern New Mexico Medical Center (ENMMC) employee handbook supported

For instance, you may use paper digests and reporters to start, then shift to Westlaw to update your research and find cases with similar facts to your client's situation. You may start your research in Loislaw, then shift to LexisNexis to run a More-Like-This search starting with a pertinent case you found via Loislaw.

However your research in case law begins, it is not complete until you cite your cases, as discussed in Chapter 10.

D.   HOW DO YOU CITE CASES?

Case law citation is in a state of flux. For a very long time, citation to cases has focused on paper resources. As online sources of cases have become more prevalent, it has seemed that citation should evolve accordingly. Furthermore, some courts have promulgated their own citation rules, in part in response to technological change and in part as a reflection of the preferences of the judges.

Under any citation rule you may be bound by, you will provide the name of the case; a means of locating it; the court and date of decision; and the case's subsequent history and adverse treatment, if any. As to each of these items, both *The Bluebook* and *ALWD Citation Manual*, for example, have rather particular rules about how to abbreviate party names, how to abbreviate court names,* how specifically to state the date of decision, how to order this information. See *Bluebook* Rule 10 and *ALWD* Rule 12.

The major open issue is how to provide information about the location of a case. For any particular case, one could provide citations to an official reporter, an unofficial reporter, various commercial databases, and one or more court websites. Some argue that the best solution is source-neutral citation; knowing a case name, decision number, court, and date should permit a reader to locate a case in various media. This approach is called "medium-neutral citation" or "public-domain citation."

Both citation manuals list when to use which source. In many situations, the *Lukoski* case would be cited to the Pacific Reporter 2d as follows:

☐ *Bluebook: Lukoski v. Sandia Indian Mgmt. Co.,* 748 P.2d 507 (N.M. 1988).
☐ *ALWD: Lukoski v. Sandia Indian Mgt. Co.,* 748 P.2d 507 (N.M. 1988).

If a parallel citation to the official state reporter were required, the cite (using the *Bluebook* abbreviation for the title of the case) would be:

☐ *Lukoski v. Sandia Indian Mgmt. Co.,* 106 N.M. 664, 748 P.2d 507 (1988).

---

* If the citation appears in a text sentence, the case name is abbreviated less than when the citation appears in its own sentence or clause. The examples here are citations in a citation, not text, sentence.

A New Mexico Rule of Appellate Procedure calls for inclusion of a public domain citation for cases decided in 1996 and later along with a citation to the regional reporter, the official reporter, or both. Were there a public domain citation for *Lukoski*, the citation (again using the *Bluebook* abbreviation for the title) would be:

> ☐ *Lukoski v. Sandia Indian Mgmt. Co.*, 1988-NMSC-123, 106 N.M. 664, 748 P.2d 507.

If *Lukoski* was not published and you found it through LexisNexis, the citation would be:

> ☐ *Bluebook: Lukoski v. Sandia Indian Mgmt. Co.*, No. 16462, 1998 N.M. Lexis 17 (Jan. 7, 1988) (unpublished decision).
> ☐ *ALWD: Lukoski v. Sandia Indian Mgt. Co.*, 1988 N.M. Lexis 17 (Jan. 7, 1988) (unpublished decision).

We favor a parenthetical noting the unpublished status of the case.

The standard citation to a federal case, illustrated with the *Ellis* case cited in *Lukoski*, is:

> ☐ *Bluebook: Ellis v. El Paso Natural Gas*, 754 F.2d 884 (10th Cir. 1985).
> ☐ *ALWD: Ellis v. El Paso Nat. Gas*, 754 F.2d 884 (10th Cir. 1985).

You may have obtained a case from a different source than you are required to cite. Much of the time, you will find the information you need to properly cite the case listed at the beginning of the case. See the information at the beginning of the LexisNexis version of *Lukoski*, Exhibit 9.14 (at page 184). Scattered throughout the case in brackets may be page numbers from other sources. Another way to find information about the various sources of a case is to use a case citator, as discussed in Chapter 10.

E. WHAT ELSE?

State Versions of Regional Reporters. You may have available to you a state-specific version of a regional reporter, that is, a volume containing only the cases from one of the states covered by a regional reporter, reprinted as they appear in the regional reporter. The advantage of such a reporter is its small size and cost.

Updating of Key Numbers. As the law or legal vocabulary evolves, West occasionally changes topics and key numbers. Generally, you will find a conversion table at the end of the outline of the revised topic.

Master Digests. West has combined the information in its various federal, regional, and state digests into master — and hence voluminous — digests:

Century Digests, *Decennial Digests*, and *General Digests*, covering multiple decades, multiyear periods, and years, respectively. You generally will use these master digests only when you already have explored a narrower digest for your jurisdiction and have decided to seek cases from outside your jurisdiction.

Specialized Reporters and Looseleaf Services.   Specialized reporters contain cases on a single area of law. For example, West publishes *Federal Rules Decisions*, a reporter with cases pertaining only to federal civil or criminal procedure rules. Furthermore, looseleaf services, discussed in Chapter 15, include cases and digests along with statutes, regulations, and commentary materials on a single area of law.

Lawyers' Edition.   Another unofficial case reporter is *United States Supreme Court Reports, Lawyers' Edition*, which encompasses Supreme Court cases. The set includes a digest, summaries of the briefs written by the lawyers, and references to commentary.

Paper Sources of Very New Cases.   At both the national and state levels, legal newspapers and newsletters provide copies of very recent cases, typically within a week of issuance by the court. For example, *The United States Law Week* publishes decisions of the U.S. Supreme Court, as well as information on cases pending before the Court and significant cases from other courts, on a weekly basis. Your state may have a similar source.

Updating an Online Search.   If you craft an effective search in Westlaw or LexisNexis, and you want to update that search, you may use the update feature (Westlaw's WestClip, LexisNexis' Save as Alert) so that you receive automatic updates, if there are new results.

CASE CITATORS

A. What Are Case Citators, and Why Would You Use Them?
B. How Do You Use Case Citators?
C. Why and How Should You Bolster Your Research in
   Case Citators?

Exhibit 10.1 Shepard's Report (online source)
Exhibit 10.2 KeyCite Report (online source)
Exhibit 10.3 GlobalCite Report (online source)
Exhibit 10.4 Ways of Undermining a Case

A. WHAT ARE CASE CITATORS, AND WHY WOULD YOU USE THEM?

A citator is a research tool that is not itself authority of any kind but, rather, points you to potentially significant authorities. More precisely, it lists authorities that cite an authority you already have found. Using citators is the most technical task — and one of the most important — in legal research. Lawyers use the following terms when using citators:

- ☐ The authority you are currently reading is the "cited authority." You will seek the report for this authority.
- ☐ The authorities that cite the cited authority are the "citing authorities." They are listed in the report for the cited authority.
- ☐ For many years, Shepard's Citators, a paper source, were by far the most prominent citators. Many lawyers still call research in citators "Shepardizing." Shepard's is now aviailable online in LexisNexis.
- ☐ Some lawyers call this research "KeyCiting," which is the name of Westlaw's citator.

For this chapter, for ease of understanding, we will call this process of using a citator "citing" and the case you already have read and on which you plan to rely the "case-in-hand."

As you will see, case citators are very sophisticated, reflecting the critical role they play in case law research and the intricacies of legal research. You will use a case citator for five reasons stated in the order the information appears in a case's report:

1. To learn of the case-in-hand's parallel citation(s).   Most likely, the case-in-hand is published in several or more sources. Citation rules may require you to provide a citation to a source other than the one you are using. If the source you are using does not provide the citation information for that other source, you can find it in the citator report.

2. To discern the history of the case-in-hand.   Recall from Chapter 9 that you should rely on a case only if it is good law. You cannot tell whether this is so from reading the case-in-hand itself, because, in general, a case is not removed from case law sources or altered when its validity is undermined by a later case. Hence you need a tool that alerts you to subsequent cases affecting the validity of the case-in-hand. These may be later decisions in the same litigation, that is, subsequent history. For example, if your case-in-hand is a decision of the intermediate appellate court, you should know whether the supreme court reviewed your case-in-hand. In addition, you may learn about an earlier decision in the litigation that gave rise to the case-in-hand, that is, its prior history. (For further discussion, see Part B, section 3, of Chapter 9.)

3. To learn of the case-in-hand's treatment in other cases from your jurisdiction.   Whether a case is good law depends not only on its subsequent history but also on its treatment, that is, decisions in later cases from your jurisdiction that involve different parties but the same legal topic. Most important are later cases that treat the case-in-hand adversely. Later cases that treat the case-in-hand favorably are also important because they strengthen the credibility of the case-in-hand and are more recent cases on the topic. (For further discussion, again see Part B, section 3, of Chapter 9.)

Good law can be a matter of nuance. Many cases involve more than one topic, so you should focus on the topic pertaining to your client's situation. An overruled case is, obviously, no longer good law as to the topic for which it has been overruled, but it may be good law on a different topic. Whether a case that has been distinguished often or criticized recently is still good law is a closer call. The major citators use color-coded symbols to signal the calls of their editors. The more a case matters to your analysis, the less you should rely on those symbols, and the more carefully you should read the significant citing cases yourself.

4. To expand and update your research by finding additional cases. Case citators list any case that cites the case-in-hand, including cases from other jurisdictions. Persuasive cases can be helpful, for example, when your state's courts have not considered a factually similar case and a sister state's court has done so.

5. To expand your research in commentary.   You may find some commentary, such as law review articles or A.L.R. annotations, that you have not yet found.

B.   HOW DO YOU USE CASE CITATORS?

1.   Introduction

Citing your cases should be an integral part of your research in cases. Once you decide that you may rely on a case-in-hand if it is good law, you should cite it. Be sure to check at the end of the research process that you have cited all of the cases you plan to rely on. When you come back to your research at a later time, you should update your research by again citing the major cases.

You are very likely to cite your cases online through Shepard's or Key-Cite; indeed, citing is the research function best suited to online research. On both LexisNexis and Westlaw, you can begin the citation function two ways: by typing in the case's citation in the Shepard's or KeyCite box or by clicking into Shepard's or KeyCite when you are reading the case-in-hand, or a reference to it, online.

The challenging aspect of citation is to decipher the report you thus obtain. Before you try to read the report, be sure you know the details of the service's current protocols; the reports in this chapter date to fall 2007.

2.   LexisNexis' Shepard's Citator

Exhibit 10.1 (at pages 197–202) is a Shepard's report for the *Lukoski* case featured in Chapter 9. Shepard's synopsizes the status of the case-in-hand as good law through six symbols, which appear not only in the Shepard's report but also elsewhere in LexisNexis, for example, beside the case as it appears on the screen. The symbols and their meanings are as follows:

- ☐ Red stop sign: The case has strong negative history or treatment, e.g., it has been reversed or overruled.
- ☐ Square with the letter Q: The citing authorities question the case's validity.
- ☐ Yellow triangle: The case has some negative history or treatment that may be significant, e.g., it has been limited or criticized.
- ☐ Green diamond: The case has positive history or treatment, e.g., it has been affirmed or followed.
- ☐ Blue circle with the letter A: There is treatment that is neither positive nor negative, e.g., the case has been explained. The A means that the citing case has been analyzed by the Shepard's staff.
- ☐ Blue circle with the letter I: There is information about citing sources but without analysis, e.g., the citing sources are law reviews.

Shepard's presents a summary of the citing references. Note that the summary alludes to the Shepard's case analysis codes. The most commonly used case analysis codes, from the most positive to the most negative, are affirmed, followed, explained, distinguished, questioned, criticized, limited, modified, overruled, and reversed.

Shepard's presents the citing cases by court, with the most weighty decisions listed first and reverse chronology within a court. Some of the listings include a case analysis code; some do not. Shepard's provides a full citation to the citing case as well as the exact pages on which each cite to the case-in-hand appears. For some cases, Shepard's also provides information about which headnote in the case-in-hand is discussed in the citing case.

Shepard's also directs you to commentary citing the case-in-hand. These references are not as important as references to cases, but you should check for any potentially pertinent authorities you have not yet seen.

Below is the explanation of the *Hartbarger* entry, the third case on page 198.

Shepard's *Hartbarger* Entry (No. 3)	
Hartbarger v. Frank Paxton Co.	case name
115 N.M. 665	official reporter citation
857 P.2d 776	Pacific Reporter 2d citation
1993 N.M. LEXIS 187	Lexis citation
32 N.M. B. Bull. 635 8 I.E.R. Cas. (BNA) 1114 127 Lab. Cas. (CCH) P57664 (1993)	other citations: New Mexico bar journal and two unofficial paper services with reporters focusing on employment law
yellow triangle	status of *Hartbarger* (not *Lukoski*)
LexisNexis Headnotes HN2	LexisNexis headnote for which *Hartbarger* cites *Lukoski*; see the end of the report (page 202) for that headnote

Distinguished by:
    115 N.M. 665 *p.673*
    857 P.2d 776 *p.784*
Cited by:
    115 N.M. 665 *p.669*
    857 P.2d 776 *p.780*
	two *Lukoski* citations in *Hartbarger*, including specific pages in the official and Pacific Reporter 2d reporters, in which *Hartbarger* distinguishes *Lukoski* and cites *Lukoski*

EXHIBIT 10.1	Shepard's Report (online source)

Shepard's Batch Delivery Request Report
Shepard's Citation: 1988 N.M. LEXIS 17 - FULL
References: 33
Restricted: No
FOCUS Terms: No
Deliver Shepard's Report: Yes - Completed
Available LexisNexis(R) HEADNOTES from Lukoski v. Sandia Indian Management Co.: Yes - Completed
Selected Citing Documents: None Selected
Date of Request: 11/20/2007

Citing Reference Number	Citations	Full Text Request

Key:
Completed - Full-text retrieved and delivered below.
Table Case - Multiple documents found for this citation; insufficient information to choose one.
Error - Full-text could not be retrieved and/or delivered.
LexisNexis is a trademark, and LEXSEE and LEXSTAT and Shepard's are registered trademarks of Reed Elsevier
Properties, Inc., used under license. ALR is a registered trademark of West Licensing Corp.
Copyright **** LexisNexis, a division of Reed Elsevier Inc. All Rights Reserved.

Copyright 2007 SHEPARD'S(R) - 33 Citing references

Lukoski v. Sandia Indian Management Co., 106 N.M. 664, 748 P.2d 507, 1988 N.M. LEXIS 17, 2 I.E.R. Cas. (BNA) 1650 (N.M. 1988)

SHEPARD'S Signal(TM): ⚠ *Caution: Possible negative treatment*
Restrictions: *Unrestricted*
FOCUS(TM) Terms: *No FOCUS terms*
Print Format: *FULL*
Citing Ref. Signal Legend:
  ⬤ {Warning} -- negative treatment indicated
  ▣ {Questioned} -- validity questioned by citing refs.
  ⚠ {Caution} -- possible negative treatment
  ◆ {Positive} -- positive treatment indicated
  Ⓐ {Analysis} -- cited and neutral analysis indicated
  ❶ {Cited} -- citation information available

SHEPARD'S SUMMARY

Unrestricted *Shepard's* Summary
No subsequent appellate history.
Citing References:
⚠ Cautionary   **Distinguished (1)**
Analyses:
  Positive Analyses: Followed (4)
  Neutral Analyses: Concurring Opinion (1), Dissenting Op. (1), Explained (1)
  Other Sources: Law Reviews (4), Treatises (6), Court Documents (2)

EXHIBIT **10.1**   *(continued)*

SHEPARD'S® - 106 N.M. 664 - 33 Citing References

LexisNexis Headnotes: HN1 (1), HN2 (8), HN3 (4)

PRIOR HISTORY   (0 citing references)

> ***(CITATION YOU ENTERED):***
> *Lukoski v. Sandia Indian Management Co.*, 106 N.M. 664, 748 P.2d 507, 1988 N.M. LEXIS 17, 2 I.E.R. Cas. (BNA) 1650 (N.M. 1988).▲

CITING DECISIONS   (21 citing decisions)

NEW MEXICO SUPREME COURT

1.   **Cited by:**
      Cockrell v. Bd. of Regents, 2002 NMSC 9, 132 N.M. 156, 45 P.3d 876, 2002 N.M. LEXIS 158, 41 N.M. B. Bull. No. 20 19, 41 N.M. B. Bull. 20, 146 Lab. Cas. (CCH) P34521, 7 Wage & Hour Cas. 2d (BNA) 1444 (2002)▲
            132 N.M. 156 *p.167*
            45 P.3d 876 *p.887*

2.   **Followed by:**
      Garcia v. Middle Rio Grande Conservancy Dist., 1996 NMSC 29, 121 N.M. 728, 918 P.2d 7, 1996 N.M. LEXIS 202, 11 I.E.R. Cas. (BNA) 1328 (N.M. 1996)▲ **LexisNexis Headnotes HN3**
            1996 NMSC 29
            121 N.M. 728 *p.732*
            918 P.2d 7 *p.11*

3.   **Distinguished by, Cited by:**
      Hartbarger v. Frank Paxton Co., 115 N.M. 665, 857 P.2d 776, 1993 N.M. LEXIS 187, 32 N.M. B. Bull. 635, 8 I.E.R. Cas. (BNA) 1114, 127 Lab. Cas. (CCH) P57664 (1993)▲ **LexisNexis Headnotes HN2**
            Distinguished by:
            115 N.M. 665 *p.673*
            857 P.2d 776 *p.784*

            Cited by:
            115 N.M. 665 *p.669*
            857 P.2d 776 *p.780*

4.   **Cited by:**
      Chavez v. Manville Prods. Corp., 108 N.M. 643, 777 P.2d 371, 1989 N.M. LEXIS 241, 4 I.E.R. Cas. (BNA) 833, 122 Lab. Cas. (CCH) P56927 (N.M. 1989)▲ **LexisNexis Headnotes HN2**
            108 N.M. 643 *p.646*
            777 P.2d 371 *p.374*

5.   **Cited by:**
      Paca v. K-Mart Corp., 108 N.M. 479, 775 P.2d 245, 1989 N.M. LEXIS 189, 4 I.E.R. Cas. (BNA) 727 (N.M. 1989)◆
            108 N.M. 479 *p.481*
            775 P.2d 245 *p.247*

EXHIBIT **10.1** *(continued)*

SHEPARD'S® - 106 N.M. 664 - 33 Citing References

6. **Followed by:**
    Newberry v. Allied Stores, 108 N.M. 424, 773 P.2d 1231, 1989 N.M. LEXIS 139, 4 I.E.R. Cas. (BNA) 562
    (N.M. 1989)△ **LexisNexis Headnotes HN2**
    >   108 N.M. 424 *p.426*
    >   773 P.2d 1231 *p.1233*

7. **Cited by:**
    Kestenbaum v. Pennzoil Co., 108 N.M. 20, 766 P.2d 280, 1988 N.M. LEXIS 326, 4 I.E.R. Cas. (BNA) 67
    (N.M. 1988)△ **LexisNexis Headnotes HN2**
    >   108 N.M. 20 *p.24*
    >   766 P.2d 280 *p.284*

NEW MEXICO COURT OF APPEALS

8. **Cited by:**
    Whittington v. State Dep't of Pub. Safety, 2004 NMCA 124, 136 N.M. 503, 100 P.3d 209, 2004 N.M. App.
    LEXIS 108, 21 I.E.R. Cas. (BNA) 1862 (N.M. Ct. App. 2004)Ⓐ **LexisNexis Headnotes HN3**
    >   2004 NMCA 124
    >   136 N.M. 503 *p.508*
    >   100 P.3d 209 *p.214*

9. **Cited by:**
    Heye v. Am. Golf Corp., 2003 NMCA 138, 134 N.M. 558, 80 P.3d 495, 2003 N.M. App. LEXIS 95, 20
    I.E.R. Cas. (BNA) 1268 (N.M. Ct. App. 2003)△
    >   134 N.M. 558 *p.562*
    >   80 P.3d 495 *p.499*

10. **Cited in Concurring Opinion at, Cited by:**
    Mealand v. Eastern. N.M. Med. Ctr., 2001 NMCA 89, 131 N.M. 65, 33 P.3d 285, 2001 N.M. App. LEXIS
    79, 40 N.M. B. Bull. No. 48 33, 40 N.M. B. Bull. 48 (2001)Ⓐ **LexisNexis Headnotes HN3**
    >   **Cited in Concurring Opinion at:**
    >   2001 NMCA 89
    >   131 N.M. 65 *p.76*
    >   33 P.3d 285 *p.296*
    >
    >   **Cited by:**
    >   131 N.M. 65 *p.69*
    >   33 P.3d 285 *p.289*

11. **Cited by:**
    Campos De Suenos, Ltd. v. County of Bernalillo, 2001 NMCA 43, 130 N.M. 563, 28 P.3d 1104, 2001 N.M.
    App. LEXIS 36, 40 N.M. B. Bull. 28, 40 N.M. B. Bull. No. 28 19 (2001)△
    >   2001 NMCA 43
    >   130 N.M. 563 *p.571*
    >   28 P.3d 1104 *p.1112*

12. **Cited by:**

EXHIBIT 10.1   *(continued)*

SHEPARD'S® - 106 N.M. 664 - 33 Citing References

Famiglietta v. Ivie-Miller Enters., Inc., 1998 NMCA 155, 126 N.M. 69, 966 P.2d 777, 1998 N.M. App.
LEXIS 126, 37 N.M. B. Bull. 45, 37 N.M. B. Bull. No. 45 16 (1998)🅰 **LexisNexis Headnotes HN1**
    1998 NMCA 155
    37 N.M. B. Bull. No. 45 16 *p.18*
    126 N.M. 69 *p.74*
    966 P.2d 777 *p.782*

13.   **Cited by:**
        Silva v. Town of Springer, 1996 NMCA 22, 121 N.M. 428, 912 P.2d 304, 1996 N.M. App. LEXIS 4, 33
        N.M. B. Bull. 11 (1996)△ **LexisNexis Headnotes HN2**
            1996 NMCA 22
            121 N.M. 428 *p.431*
            912 P.2d 304 *p.307*

14.   **Cited by:**
        Delisle v. Avallone, 117 N.M. 602, 874 P.2d 1266, 1994 N.M. App. LEXIS 44, 33 N.M. B. Bull. 843
        (1994)△
            117 N.M. 602 *p.609*
            874 P.2d 1266 *p.1273*, Headnote: N.M. - 1

NEW MEXICO

15.   **Followed by:**
        1996 N.M. LEXIS 261, 1996 NMSC 29, 1996 N.M. LEXIS 261◆
            1996 N.M. LEXIS 261

10TH CIRCUIT - COURT OF APPEALS

16.   **Followed by:**
        Sullivan v. Am. Online, Inc., 219 Fed. Appx. 720, 2007 U.S. App. LEXIS 3277 (10th Cir. N.M. 2007)🅰
        LexisNexis Headnotes HN2
            219 Fed. Appx. 720 *p.723*

17.   **Cited in Dissenting Opinion at, Cited by:**
        Zaccardi v. Zale Corp., 856 F.2d 1473, 1988 U.S. App. LEXIS 12339, 3 I.E.R. Cas. (BNA) 1249, 110 Lab.
        Cas. (CCH) P55976 (10th Cir. Utah 1988)△ **LexisNexis Headnotes HN2, HN3**
            Cited in Dissenting Opinion at:
            856 F.2d 1473 *p.1478*

            Cited by:
            856 F.2d 1473 *p.1476*

10TH CIRCUIT - U.S. DISTRICT COURTS

18.   **Cited by:**
        Parker v. Hammons Hotel, 914 F. Supp. 467, 1994 U.S. Dist. LEXIS 20891, 135 Lab. Cas. (CCH) P58313
        (D.N.M. 1994)🅘 **LexisNexis Headnotes HN2**
            914 F. Supp. 467 *p.470*

EXHIBIT **10.1**   *(continued)*

SHEPARD'S® - 106 N.M. 664 - 33 Citing References

CALIFORNIA COURTS OF APPEAL

19.   **Explained by:**
      Ladas v. California State Auto. Ass'n, 19 Cal. App. 4th 761, 23 Cal. Rptr. 2d 810, 1993 Cal. App. LEXIS
      1058, 93 Cal. Daily Op. Service 7886, 93 D.A.R. 13441, 8 I.E.R. Cas. (BNA) 1628 (Cal. App. 1st Dist.
      1993)▲
         19 Cal. App. 4th 761 *p.771*
         23 Cal. Rptr. 2d 810 *p.815*

WASHINGTON SUPREME COURT

20.   **Cited by:**
      Swanson v. Liquid Air Corp., 118 Wn.2d 512, 826 P.2d 664, 1992 Wash. LEXIS 71, 7 I.E.R. Cas. (BNA)
      366, 125 Lab. Cas. (CCH) P57376, 126 Lab. Cas. (CCH) P57556 (1992)▲
         118 Wn.2d 512 *p.524*
         826 P.2d 664 *p.671*

21.   **Cited by:**
      Swanson v. Liquid Air Corp., 126 Lab. Cas. (CCH) P57556 (Wash. Mar. 5, 1992)▲
         126 Lab. Cas. (CCH) P57556

LAW REVIEWS AND PERIODICALS (4 Citing References)

22.   *TRENDS IN NEW MEXICO LAW: 1995-96: CONTRACTS-Implied Employment Contracts Based on
      Written Policy Statements Are Not Subject to Governmental Immunity: Garcia v. Middle Rio Grande
      Conservancy District*, 27 N.M. L. Rev. 649 (1997)

23.   *ARTICLE: RECONSIDERING THE LOUISIANA DOCTRINE OF EMPLOYMENT AT WILL: ON THE
      MISINTER-PRETATION OF ARTICLE 2747 AND THE CIVILIAN CASE FOR REQUIRING "GOOD
      FAITH" IN TERMINATION OF EMPLOYMENT*, 69 Tul. L. Rev. 1513 (1995)

24.   *SYMPOSIUM: BEYOND COLLECTIVE BARGAINING AND EMPLOYMENT AT WILL: THE FUTURE OF
      WRONGFUL DISMISSAL CLAIMS: WHERE DOES EMPLOYER SELF INTEREST LIE?*, 58 U. Cin. L.
      Rev. 397 (1989)

25.   *COMMENT: COMBATTING SEXUAL HARASSMENT IN THE WORKPLACE WITHOUT RISKING A
      WRONGFUL DISCHARGE LAWSUIT: AN EMPLOYER'S DILEMMA? **, 42 U. Kan. L. Rev. 437 (1994)

TREATISE CITATIONS (6 Citing Sources)

26.   *E1-1 Business Law Monographs I1.01*

27.   *E2-16A Business Law Monographs Scope*

28.   *4-52A Doing Business in the United States @ 52A.04*

29.   *1-23 Employment Law Deskbook @ 23.32*

30.   *10-274 Labor and Employment Law @ 274.32*

EXHIBIT 10.1   *(continued)*

SHEPARD'S® - 106 N.M. 664 - 33 Citing References

31.   *1-8 Unjust Dismissal @ 8.04*

MOTIONS (2 Citing Motions)

32.   *MOGHBEL v. STATE GEN. SERVS. DEP'T*, 2007 U.S. Dist. Ct. Motions 898977, 2006 U.S. Dist. Ct. Motions LEXIS 53565 (D.N.M. Dec. 28, 2006)

33.   *TYREE v. DEPARTMENT OF TRANSPORATION*, 2005 U.S. Dist. Ct. Motions 5532, 2006 U.S. Dist. Ct. Motions LEXIS 51079 (D.N.M. Mar. 6, 2006)

Available LexisNexis (R) HEADNOTES from Lukoski v. Sandia Indian Management Co.

Civil Procedure > Trials > Jury Trials > Province of Court & Jury
Contracts Law > Breach > Causes of Action > General Overview
Contracts Law > Breach > Material Breach
[HN1] Materiality is a specific question of fact.

Civil Procedure > Trials > Jury Trials > Province of Court & Jury
Labor & Employment Law > Wrongful Termination > Breach of Contract > General Overview
[HN2] Whether an employee handbook modifies the employment relationship is a question of fact to be discerned from the totality of the parties' statements and actions regarding the employment relationship.

Labor & Employment Law > Employment Relationships > At-Will Employment > General Overview
Labor & Employment Law > Wrongful Termination > Breach of Contract > General Overview
[HN3] If an employer does choose to issue a policy statement, in a manual or otherwise, and, by its language or by the employer's actions, encourages reliance thereon, the employer cannot be free to only selectively abide by it. Having announced a policy, the employer may not treat it as illusory.

---

3.   Westlaw's KeyCite

Exhibit 10.2 (at pages 205–08) is a KeyCite report for the *Lukoski* case featured in Chapter 9. KeyCite presents three forms of history, as applicable for a specific case-in-hand: (1) direct history tracing the case-in-hand through its litigation, including prior and subsequent history; (2) negative indirect history in cases outside the litigation of the case-in-hand, that is, adverse treatment such as overruling in a later decision from the same court; and (3) related references, which are decisions arising from the litigation that gave rise to the case-in-hand but involve different topics or topics.

KeyCite synopsizes the status of the case-in-hand as good law through one of four symbols, which appear not only in the KeyCite report but also elsewhere in Westlaw, for example, the case as it appears on the screen. The symbols and their meaning are as follows:

- ☐ Red flag: The case is no longer good law for at least one of its points.
- ☐ Yellow flag: The case has some negative indirect history (adverse treatment) but has not been reversed or overruled.
- ☐ Blue H: The case has history that gives rise to neither a red nor a yellow flag.
- ☐ Green C: The case has citing references but no direct or indirect negative history.

The bulk of most KeyCite reports is the list of positive citing cases. The cases are arrayed from four stars to one star:

****   examined, i.e., an extended discussion of the case-in-hand that runs a page or more of text;

***   discussed, i.e., more than a paragraph but less than a page;

**   cited, i.e., a paragraph or less; and

*   mentioned, i.e., only a brief reference to the case-in-hand.

Each case listing includes several key pieces of information about the citing case, as applicable:

- ☐ the case's name and citation(s), including the page(s) on which the case-in-hand is discussed;
- ☐ quotation marks signifying that the case-in-hand is quoted in the citing case;
- ☐ references to the case-in-hand's West headnotes linked to the points for which the citing case cites the case-in-hand; and
- ☐ in the lefthand margin, the citing case's (not the case-in-hand's) KeyCite symbol.

KeyCite also lists commentary sources that cite your case-in-hand. Although these citing authorities are not as important as cases are, you should check for potentially pertinent authorities you have not yet seen. KeyCite also lists administrative materials, briefs, and other court documents.

On the next page is the explanation of the *Hartbarger* entry, the second case at page 205.

KeyCite's *Hartbarger* Entry (No. 2)	
*** Discussed	extent of discussion of *Lukoski* in *Hartbarger*
yellow flag in left margin	*Hartbarger*'s status (not *Lukoski*)
Hartbarger v. Frank Paxton Co.	case name
857 P.2d 776, 780+	*Hartbarger*'s Pacific Reporter 2d citation and page where *Lukoski* is cited
115 N.M. 665, 669+	official reporter citation and page where *Lukoski* is mentioned
127 Lab.Cas. P 57,664, 57664+ 8 IER Cases 1114, 1114+	two unofficial paper services with reporters focusing on employment law
N.M. Jun 14, 1993	court and date of decision
NO. 19,913	docket number
""	indication that *Hartbarger* quotes *Lukoski*
HN: 2(P2d)	West headnote in *Lukoski* for which *Hartbarger* cites *Lukoski*

| EXHIBIT 10.2 | KeyCite Report (online source) |

AUTHORIZED FOR EDUCATIONAL USE ONLY

Date of Printing: NOV 02,2007

KEYCITE

C Lukoski v. Sandia Indian Management Co., 106 N.M. 664, 748 P.2d 507, 2 IER Cases 1650 (N.M., Jan 07, 1988) (NO. 16,462)

Citing References
Positive Cases (U.S.A.)
★★★★ Examined

C   1 Zaccardi v. Zale Corp., 856 F.2d 1473, 1476+, 110 Lab.Cas. P 55,976, 55976+, 3 IER Cases 1249, 1249+ (10th Cir.(Utah) Sep 12, 1988) (NO. 86-1748) **HN: 1,2 (P.2d)**

★★★ Discussed

▷   2 Hartbarger v. Frank Paxton Co., 857 P.2d 776, 780+, 115 N.M. 665, 669+, 127 Lab.Cas. P 57,664, 57664+, 8 IER Cases 1114, 1114+ (N.M. Jun 14, 1993) (NO. 19,913) "" **HN: 2 (P.2d)**

▷   3 Newberry v. Allied Stores, Inc., 773 P.2d 1231, 1233+, 108 N.M. 424, 426+, 4 IER Cases 562, 562+ (N.M. May 01, 1989) (NO. 17,712) "" **HN: 2 (P.2d)**

▷   4 Ladas v. California State Auto. Assn., 23 Cal.Rptr.2d 810, 816+, 19 Cal.App.4th 761, 772+, 8 IER Cases 1628, 1628+ (Cal.App. 1 Dist. Oct 22, 1993) (NO. A057353) "" **HN: 2 (P.2d)**

★★ Cited

▷   5 Cockrell v. Board of Regents of New Mexico State University, 45 P.3d 876, 887+, 132 N.M. 156, 167+, 146 Lab.Cas. P 34,521, 34521+, 7 Wage & Hour Cas.2d (BNA) 1444, 1444+, 2002-NMSC-009, 009+ (N.M. Mar 27, 2002) (NO. 26,338) "" **HN: 2 (P.2d)**

▷   6 Garcia v. Middle Rio Grande Conservancy Dist., 918 P.2d 7, 11+, 121 N.M. 728, 732+, 11 IER Cases 1328, 1328+, 1996-NMSC-029, 029+ (N.M. May 21, 1996) (NO. 22,790) "" **HN: 2 (P.2d)**

▷   7 Chavez v. Manville Products Corp., 777 P.2d 371, 374+, 108 N.M. 643, 646+, 58 USLW 2084, 2084+, 122 Lab.Cas. P 56,927, 56927+, 4 IER Cases 833, 833+ (N.M. Jul 05, 1989) (NO. 17,596)

C   8 Paca v. K-Mart Corp., 775 P.2d 245, 247, 108 N.M. 479, 481, 4 IER Cases 727, 727 (N.M. May 31, 1989) (NO. 17,983)

H   9 Kestenbaum v. Pennzoil Co., 766 P.2d 280, 284, 108 N.M. 20, 24, 4 IER Cases 67, 67 (N.M. Nov 30, 1988) (NO. 16,965)

▷   10 Whittington v. State Dept. of Public Safety, 100 P.3d 209, 214, 136 N.M. 503, 508, 21 IER Cases 1862, 1862, 2004-NMCA-124, 124 (N.M.App. Aug 27, 2004) (NO. 24,376)

▷   11 Heye v. American Golf Corp., Inc., 80 P.3d 495, 499+, 134 N.M. 558, 562+, 20 IER Cases 1268, 1268+, 2003-NMCA-138, 138+ (N.M.App. Sep 30, 2003) (NO. 22,920) **HN: 2 (P.2d)**

H   12 Mealand v. Eastern New Mexico Medical Center, 33 P.3d 285, 289+, 131 N.M. 65, 69+, 2001-NMCA-089, 089+ (N.M.App. Aug 29, 2001) (NO. 20,160) "" **HN: 2 (P.2d)**

▷   13 Campos de Suenos, Ltd. v. County of Bernalillo, 28 P.3d 1104, 1112, 130 N.M. 563, 571, 2001-NMCA-043, 043 (N.M.App. Apr 18, 2001) (NO. 20,918) **HN: 2 (P.2d)**

H   14 Famiglietta v. Ivie-Miller Enterprises, Inc., 966 P.2d 777, 782, 126 N.M. 69, 74, 1998-NMCA-155, 155 (N.M.App. Aug 19, 1998) (NO. 17,922) **HN: 1 (P.2d)**

▷   15 Silva v. Town of Springer, 912 P.2d 304, 307, 121 N.M. 428, 431, 1996-NMCA-022, 022 (N.M.App. Jan 29, 1996) (NO. 16,015) **HN: 2 (P.2d)**

H   16 DeLisle v. Avallone, 874 P.2d 1266, 1273, 117 N.M. 602, 609 (N.M.App. Jan 27, 1994) (NO. 13,652) **HN: 1 (P.2d)**

AUTHORIZED FOR EDUCATIONAL USE ONLY

C   17 Sullivan v. America Online, Inc., 219 Fed.Appx. 720, 723 (10th Cir.(N.M.) Feb 12, 2007) (Table, text in WESTLAW, NO. 06-2129) HN: 2 (P.2d)

C   18 Bayliss v. Contel Federal Systems, Inc., 930 F.2d 32, 32+ (10th Cir.(N.M.) Mar 21, 1991) (Table, text in WESTLAW, NO. 89-2310) "" HN: 2 (P.2d)

C   19 Parker v. John Q. Hammons Hotels, Inc., 914 F.Supp. 467, 470 (D.N.M. Apr 26, 1994) (NO. CIV 93-0038MV/DJS) HN: 2 (P.2d)

★ Mentioned

▷   20 Swanson v. Liquid Air Corp., 826 P.2d 664, 671, 118 Wash.2d 512, 524, 125 Lab.Cas. P 57,376, 57556, 126 Lab.Cas. P 57,556, 7 IER Cases 366, 366 (Wash. Mar 05, 1992) (NO. 57358-1) HN: 2 (P.2d)

Secondary Sources (U.S.A.)

H   21 Right to discharge allegedly "at-will" employee as affected by employer's promulgation of employment policies as to discharge, 33 A.L.R.4th 120 (1984)

22 18 Causes of Action 229, Cause of Action for Wrongful Discharge from Employment in Breach of Contract (2007)

23 Emp. Discrim. Coord. Analysis of Related Issues s 35:12, s 35:12. References to discharge procedures (2007) HN: 2 (P.2d)

24 Emp. Discrim. Coord. Analysis of Related Issues s 35:8, s 35:8. Application of contract theory (2007) HN: 2 (P.2d)

25 Emp. Discrim. Coord. Analysis of Related Issues s 35:9, s 35:9. Evidence of intent (2007) HN: 2 (P.2d)

26 Guide to Employment Law and Regulation 2d s 1:41, s 1:41. Implied contract claims (2007) HN: 2 (P.2d)

27 Litigating Wrongful Discharge Claims APP A, APPENDIX A. STATE-BY-STATE COMPENDIUM OF LEADING AND REPRESENTATIVE DECISIONS RELATING TO IMPLIED CONTRACTS ARISING FROM HANDBOOKS AND OTHER REPRESENTATIONS (2007) HN: 2 (P.2d)

28 Litigating Wrongful Discharge Claims s 4:1, s 4:1. Introduction (2007)

29 Litigating Wrongful Discharge Claims s 4:17, s 4:17. Progressive discipline policy (2007)

30 Litigating Wrongful Discharge Claims s 4:2, s 4:2. In general (2007)

31 Termination of Employment s 34:27, s 34:27. Employment contracts (2007) HN: 2 (P.2d)

32 CJS Trial s 1083, s 1083. Waiver (2007) HN: 1 (P.2d)

33 CONTRACTS-IMPLIED EMPLOYMENT CONTRACTS BASED ON WRITTEN POLICY STATEMENTS ARE NOT SUBJECT TO GOVERNMENTAL IMMUNITY: GARCIA v. MIDDLE RIO GRANDE CONSERVANCY DISTRICT, 27 N.M. L. Rev. 649, 660+ (1997) HN: 2 (P.2d)

C   34 RECONSIDERING THE LOUISIANA DOCTRINE OF EMPLOYMENT AT WILL: ON THE MISINTERPRETATION OF ARTICLE 2747 AND THE CIVILIAN CASE FOR REQUIRING "GOOD FAITH" IN TERMINATION OF EMPLOYMENT, 69 Tul. L. Rev. 1513, 1599 (1995) HN: 2 (P.2d)

C   35 THE FUTURE OF WRONGFUL DISMISSAL CLAIMS: WHERE DOES EMPLOYER SELF INTEREST LIE?, 58 U. Cin. L. Rev. 397, 430 (1989) HN: 2 (P.2d)

C   36 COMBATTING SEXUAL HARASSMENT IN THE WORKPLACE WITHOUT RISKING A WRONGFUL DISCHARGE LAWSUIT: AN EMPLOYER'S DILEMMA?, 42 U. Kan. L. Rev. 437, 460 (1994) HN: 2 (P.2d)

C   37 AT-WILL EMPLOYMENT: GOING, GOING . . ., 24 U. Rich. L. Rev. 187, 209+ (1990) HN: 2 (P.2d)

38 TRENDS IN WRONGFUL TERMINATION LAW AND COMMON LAW TORT CLAIMS, 508 PLI/Lit 695, 735 (1994) HN: 2 (P.2d)

EXHIBIT **10.2**   *(continued)*

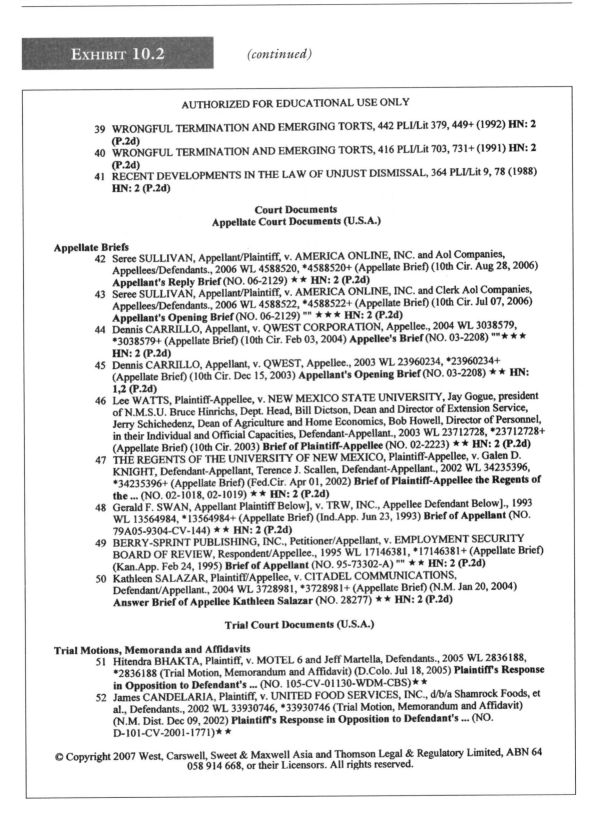

AUTHORIZED FOR EDUCATIONAL USE ONLY

39   WRONGFUL TERMINATION AND EMERGING TORTS, 442 PLI/Lit 379, 449+ (1992) **HN: 2 (P.2d)**

40   WRONGFUL TERMINATION AND EMERGING TORTS, 416 PLI/Lit 703, 731+ (1991) **HN: 2 (P.2d)**

41   RECENT DEVELOPMENTS IN THE LAW OF UNJUST DISMISSAL, 364 PLI/Lit 9, 78 (1988) **HN: 2 (P.2d)**

Court Documents
Appellate Court Documents (U.S.A.)

Appellate Briefs

42   Seree SULLIVAN, Appellant/Plaintiff, v. AMERICA ONLINE, INC. and Aol Companies, Appellees/Defendants., 2006 WL 4588520, *4588520+ (Appellate Brief) (10th Cir. Aug 28, 2006) **Appellant's Reply Brief** (NO. 06-2129) ★★ **HN: 2 (P.2d)**

43   Seree SULLIVAN, Appellant/Plaintiff, v. AMERICA ONLINE, INC. and Clerk Aol Companies, Appellees/Defendants., 2006 WL 4588522, *4588522+ (Appellate Brief) (10th Cir. Jul 07, 2006) **Appellant's Opening Brief** (NO. 06-2129) "" ★★★ **HN: 2 (P.2d)**

44   Dennis CARRILLO, Appellant, v. QWEST CORPORATION, Appellee., 2004 WL 3038579, *3038579+ (Appellate Brief) (10th Cir. Feb 03, 2004) **Appellee's Brief** (NO. 03-2208) "" ★★★ **HN: 2 (P.2d)**

45   Dennis CARRILLO, Appellant, v. QWEST, Appellee., 2003 WL 23960234, *23960234+ (Appellate Brief) (10th Cir. Dec 15, 2003) **Appellant's Opening Brief** (NO. 03-2208) ★★ **HN: 1,2 (P.2d)**

46   Lee WATTS, Plaintiff-Appellee, v. NEW MEXICO STATE UNIVERSITY, Jay Gogue, president of N.M.S.U. Bruce Hinrichs, Dept. Head, Bill Dictson, Dean and Director of Extension Service, Jerry Schichedenz, Dean of Agriculture and Home Economics, Bob Howell, Director of Personnel, in their Individual and Official Capacities, Defendant-Appellant., 2003 WL 23712728, *23712728+ (Appellate Brief) (10th Cir. 2003) **Brief of Plaintiff-Appellee** (NO. 02-2223) ★★ **HN: 2 (P.2d)**

47   THE REGENTS OF THE UNIVERSITY OF NEW MEXICO, Plaintiff-Appellee, v. Galen D. KNIGHT, Defendant-Appellant, Terence J. Scallen, Defendant-Appellant., 2002 WL 34235396, *34235396+ (Appellate Brief) (Fed.Cir. Apr 01, 2002) **Brief of Plaintiff-Appellee the Regents of the ...** (NO. 02-1018, 02-1019) ★★ **HN: 2 (P.2d)**

48   Gerald F. SWAN, Appellant Plaintiff Below], v. TRW, INC., Appellee Defendant Below]., 1993 WL 13564984, *13564984+ (Appellate Brief) (Ind.App. Jun 23, 1993) **Brief of Appellant** (NO. 79A05-9304-CV-144) ★★ **HN: 2 (P.2d)**

49   BERRY-SPRINT PUBLISHING, INC., Petitioner/Appellant, v. EMPLOYMENT SECURITY BOARD OF REVIEW, Respondent/Appellee., 1995 WL 17146381, *17146381+ (Appellate Brief) (Kan.App. Feb 24, 1995) **Brief of Appellant** (NO. 95-73302-A) "" ★★ **HN: 2 (P.2d)**

50   Kathleen SALAZAR, Plaintiff/Appellee, v. CITADEL COMMUNICATIONS, Defendant/Appellant., 2004 WL 3728981, *3728981+ (Appellate Brief) (N.M. Jan 20, 2004) **Answer Brief of Appellee Kathleen Salazar** (NO. 28277) ★★ **HN: 2 (P.2d)**

Trial Court Documents (U.S.A.)

Trial Motions, Memoranda and Affidavits

51   Hitendra BHAKTA, Plaintiff, v. MOTEL 6 and Jeff Martella, Defendants., 2005 WL 2836188, *2836188 (Trial Motion, Memorandum and Affidavit) (D.Colo. Jul 18, 2005) **Plaintiff's Response in Opposition to Defendant's ...** (NO. 105-CV-01130-WDM-CBS) ★★

52   James CANDELARIA, Plaintiff, v. UNITED FOOD SERVICES, INC., d/b/a Shamrock Foods, et al., Defendants., 2002 WL 33930746, *33930746 (Trial Motion, Memorandum and Affidavit) (N.M. Dist. Dec 09, 2002) **Plaintiff's Response in Opposition to Defendant's ...** (NO. D-101-CV-2001-1771) ★★

(continued)

AUTHORIZED FOR EDUCATIONAL USE ONLY

53 Remijio SAUCEDA, Plaintiff, v. NEW MEXICO STATE HIGHWAY and Transportation
Department, Defendant., 2001 WL 35808563, *35808563 (Trial Motion, Memorandum and
Affidavit) (N.M. Dist. Jul 16, 2001) **Plaintiff's Memorandum Response in Opposition to ...** (NO.
CV-99-08368)★★

54 Tommy HUDSON, Plaintiff, v. VILLAGE INN PANCAKE HOUSE OF ALBUQUERQUE, INC.,
Defendant., 1999 WL 34590294, *34590294+ (Trial Motion, Memorandum and Affidavit) (N.M.
Dist. May 03, 1999) **Plaintiff's Trial Brief** (NO. CV95-10632)★★

55 Frank TRUJILLO and Lorriane Trujillo, husband and wife, Plaintiffs, v. NORTHERN RIO
ARRIBA ELECTRIC COOPERATIVE, INC., Defendant., 1998 WL 35182554, *35182554 (Trial
Motion, Memorandum and Affidavit) (N.M. Dist. Sep 21, 1998) **Plaintiffs' Memorandum Brief in
Opposition to ...** (NO. RA97-375(C))★★

4. Citing Strategies

As you work through a citator report, you should engage in a sort of research triage. Keep in mind that some information must be checked out, for example, cases identified as undermining your case-in-hand; other information is optional, for example, cases from sister jurisdictions and commentary. Newer cases merit more attention than older cases; higher court decisions merit more attention than lower court decisions. Look more seriously at cases that the citator has designated as discussing your case-at-hand in some depth. Furthermore, if your case-at-hand has several headnotes, some pertinent and others not, focus on citing cases that are designated as citing the case on the topic of pertinent headnotes. Regardless of headnote, however, you should check out all cases that are designated as reversing or overruling your case-at-hand to be sure you do not miss something important. Focus on cases that themselves appear to be good law, based on the symbol assigned in the report.

Two strategies entail condensing the report. If there is a distinctive term that should appear in pertinent cases and not in nonpertinent cases, you may run a search for that term in the various citing cases. If the report is so lengthy that it is not practical to consider all of it, especially if the case is not significant to your analysis, you can restrict the report by some or all of the following: type of document (case versus commentary), jurisdiction, date, headnote, and type or depth of treatment.

It is common for Shepard's and KeyCite reports for the same case-in-hand to be similar but not identical. Differences in citing commentary are to be expected and matter little. Different lists of citing cases and case status designations are more significant. Most of the time, both citators will have the same published cases but differ as to unpublished cases. The difference in case status will generally be a matter of judgment, for example, whether a case's distinguishing of the case-in-hand merits a cautionary designation or not. In some situations, it may make sense to both Shepardize and KeyCite an especially important case.

This chapter has focused on Shepard's and KeyCite because they are by far the best established and most sophisticated case citators. As alluded to in Chapter 10, less extensive commercial online resources also provide a citator function. If you have located your case-in-hand through one of those resources, it makes sense to employ its citator function. See Exhibit 10.3 (at page 210) for a page from Loislaw's GlobalCite. The citing cases may be the same, but the information provided in each entry typically is less complete than the information provided by Shepard's and KeyCite.

| EXHIBIT 10.3 | GlobalCite Report (online source) |

 # 21
California Courts of Appeal Reports
LADAS v. CALIFORNIA STATE AUTO. ASSN., 19 Cal.App.4th 761 (1993)
Docket No. A057353.
October 22, 1993. **[Opinion certified for partial publication.[fn*]]**
... [fn3] Appellants' claim that Ellis has been **"overruled"** by the New Mexico Supreme Court in Lukoski v. Sandia I
Management Co. (1988) 186 N.M. 664 [748 P.2d 507] (Lukoski), is meritless. Lukoski involved an oral contract of e
which the employer promulgated an employee handbook containing specific procedures regarding discipline, susp
termination of company employees. The handbook was signed by the employee and kept in his personnel file. ...

 # 22
New Mexico Case Law
HARTBARGER v. FRANK PAXTON CO., 115 N.M. 665 (1993)
No. 19913.
June 14, 1993. Rehearing Denied July 21, 1993.
... N.M. 20, 24-26, 766 P.2d 280, 284-86 (1988) **(affirming** finding of implied contract based on words and conduc
cert. denied, 490 U.S. 1109, 109 S.Ct. 3163, 104 L.Ed.2d 1026 (1989); Lukoski v. Sandia Indian Management Co.
667, 748 P.2d 507-510 (1988) **(upholding** finding of oral contract amended by employee handbook); Forrester v. I
781, 782, 606 P.2d 191, 192 (1980) (holding that, when terminating non-probationary employee, employer is boun

 # 23
Washington Supreme Court Reports
SWANSON v. LIQUID AIR CORPORATION, 118 Wn.2d 512 (1992)
No. 57358-1.
March 5, 1992.
... Globe, 150 Ariz. 82, 86, 722 P.2d 250, 254 (1986); Tuttle v. ANR Freight Sys., Inc., 797 P.2d 825, 827 (Colo.Ct.
Haselrig v. Public Storage, Inc., 86 Md. App. 116, 585 A.2d 294 (1991); Lukoski v. Sandia Indian Mgt. Co., 106 N.I
P.2d 507, Page 525 509 (1988); Small v. Springs Indus., Inc., 292 S.C. 481, 486, 357 S.E.2d 452, 454 (1987); Coi
176 W. Va. 368, 342 S.E.2d 453 (1986); Thompson v. Kings Entertainment Co., 674 F. Supp. 1194 (E.D. Va. 1987

 # 24
New Mexico Case Law
CHAVEZ v. MANVILLE PRODUCTS CORP., 108 N.M. 643 (1989)
No. 17596.
July 5, 1989. Rehearing Denied August 8, 1989.
... F.2d 1225 (6th Cir. 1988); Reid v. Sears, Roebuck & Co., 790 F.2d 453 (6th Cir. 1986); Eliel v. Sears, Roebuck
Mich. App. 137, 387 N.W.2d 842 (1985). Similarly, this Court, in Lukoski v. Sandia Indian Management Co., 106 N
P.2d 507 (1988), recognized that various means exist whereby employers may limit their employees' reasonable e
concerning the employment relationship. ...

 # 25
New Mexico Case Law
PACA v. K-MART CORP., 108 N.M. 479 (1989)
No. 17983.
May 31, 1989.
... Also, the handbook clearly stated that K-Mart employees were terminable "at will." Personnel manuals containin
statement do not create an implied contract altering the parties' "at will" relationship. Lukoski v. Sandia Indian Man
106 N.M. 664, 666-67, 748 P.2d 507, 509-10 (1988). Thus, we conclude that the trial court correctly found no genu
breach of contract. ...

C. WHY AND HOW SHOULD YOU BOLSTER YOUR RESEARCH IN CASE CITATORS?

As good as case citators are, they do not directly cover all of the ways a case may lose its status as good law. Exhibit 10.4 (at page 212) summarizes the possibilities. In addition to adverse subsequent history and adverse treatment, numbers 1 and 2 in Exhibit 10.4, a case can become bad law through indirect adverse treatment. This occurs when a recent case overrules or otherwise undermines an older case without actually citing the older case. For example, the court may identify one or two of the older cases and generally refer to the rest, for example, "We thus overrule *Case X* and its progeny."

Indirect adverse treatment may appear in several forms. First, assume that your case-in-hand is *Alpha*. *Beta* relies on *Alpha*. A third case, *Chi*, overrules *Beta* without mentioning *Alpha*. Citing *Alpha* would not lead you to *Chi*. If you cite *Beta* before you rely on it, however, you should come across *Chi*. See Exhibit 10.4 number 3.

Second, assume that a new case, *Chi*, expressly overrules not your case-in-hand *Alpha* but rather *Omega*, a case predating *Alpha*. If *Alpha* refers to *Omega*, you can learn about *Chi* through the table-of-authorities feature of both Shepard's and KeyCite. This feature functions as a reverse citator: it extracts the cases referred to in your case-in-hand and cites them. In our example, it cites *Omega*, revealing *Chi*. See Exhibit 10.4 number 4.

Third, assume the same situation except that *Alpha* does not refer to *Omega*. Neither the case citator's main function nor the table-of-authorities function will alert you to *Chi* and its indirect adverse treatment of *Alpha*, unless this situation is revealed through citing a different case on the topic. See Exhibit 10.4 number 5.

A case can also be undermined, indeed overruled in effect, by legislation that takes a different approach to the issue than the case. In general, statutes trump cases, as discussed in Chapter 11. A case citator will not alert you to this situation unless a case interpreting the statute refers to your case-in-hand. See Exhibit 10.4 number 6.

Fortunately, your research in commentary, case law resources covered in Chapter 10, and sources discussed in later chapters, if done well, will generally provide insight into these intricate situations. While many legal subjects experience little change over time, others do change. It is the possibility of change that makes updating steps, such as citing and checking pocket parts, so critical.

Finally, the day after you cite a case, new developments may occur. One way to be sure you know of the most recent developments is, of course, to re-cite the case. Through LexisNexis' Shepard's Alert and Westlaw's KeyCite Alert, you may set up automatic updates for cases you have cited, and you may have these reports e-mailed to you on a schedule you specify.

EXHIBIT 10.4	Ways of Undermining a Case

The Situations	Citator Functions
1. A higher court reverses a lower court's decision.	Citing the lower court decision reveals this.
Below, the case-in-hand is _Alpha_. _Chi_ overrules the _Alpha_ rule.	
2. _Chi_ refers to and overrules _Alpha_.	Citing _Alpha_ reveals this.
3. _Beta_ relies on _Alpha_. _Chi_ refers to and overrules _Beta_ but does not mention _Alpha_.	Citing _Alpha_ does not reveal this. Citing _Beta_ does reveal this.
4. _Alpha_ relies on _Omega_. _Chi_ refers to and overrules _Omega_, but does not mention _Alpha_.	Citing _Alpha_ does not reveal this. The table-of-authorities function citates the cases _Alpha_ cites and thus would reveal _Chi_.
5. _Alpha_ relies on _Omega_. _Chi_ refers to and overrules neither _Alpha_ nor _Omega_, but rather other cases on the topic using the same rule as _Alpha_ and _Omega_.	Neither citing _Alpha_ nor a table-of-authorities check run on _Alpha_ reveals _Chi_.
6. Legislation overturns the decision by creating a different rule.	Case citators do not directly cover legislation; they do cover cases citing statutes.

INTERLUDE NO. 3 RESEARCH IN CASE LAW

Reading *Lukoski*. When we turned to researching the breach-of-contract issue in case law, we already had three cases from our A.L.R. research to check out. *Lukoski v. Sandia Indian Management Co.*, decided by the New Mexico Supreme Court in 1988, looked like a good case to read. The contract issue is a state law question (as is generally true of contract law). New Mexico is the jurisdiction of the client's situation, and New Mexico state court decisions, such as *Lukoski*, are mandatory precedent for a court in New Mexico deciding the Canoga case. The case was about twenty years old.

Because we had the cite to the West reporter, we read the case in volume 748 of the second series of the Pacific Reporter starting at page 507. See Exhibit 9.2 (at pages 153–56). (Yes, the Pacific Reporter covers New Mexico; indeed, it also covers Kansas.)

Reading the case, we learned that Scott Lukoski, the plaintiff-appellee, sued the Sandia Indian Management Company, the defendant-appellant. Mr. Lukoski, a manager, was terminated for poor interpersonal dealings, yet the employer did not follow the suspension procedures for less serious misconduct that were outlined in its handbook. The case was tried to the judge, who ruled in favor of Mr. Lukoski and awarded him money damages.

The case then proceeded to the New Mexico Supreme Court because contract cases did not go to the court of appeals at that time. The supreme court affirmed. Relying on various state and federal decisions, Justice Ransom, writing for the majority, reasoned that the handbook language about suspensions was enforceable as a contract, and Mr. Lukoski's difficulty in interpersonal dealings should have been handled through the suspension process. Justice Stowers dissented; he would have ruled that the interpersonal problems were so severe as to permit immediate termination under the disciplinary procedures provision of the handbook.

The facts of *Lukoski* and the Canoga situation are similar, and the issues are nearly identical. Although Mr. Lukoski alleged that his employer should have suspended him, whereas Ms. Canoga would argue that the employer must provide board review, this difference is not substantial.

Looking for leads to pursue, we noted that in *Lukoski* the court relied heavily on a persuasive precedent from Arizona, *Wagenseller v. Scottsdale Memorial Hospital*, 710 P.2d 1025 (Ariz. 1985). *Wagenseller* was a recent case from a nearby state, involving fairly similar facts and the same legal issues as *Lukoski*. The *Lukoski* court noted, but did not much rely on, a federal case too — *Ellis v. El Paso Natural Gas Co.*, 754 F.2d 884 (10th Cir. 1985). That case was decided by the Tenth Circuit, so it could involve New Mexico law. The Tenth Circuit encompasses New Mexico, Colorado, Utah, and Wyoming (a more sensible configuration than the West regions). But even if *Ellis* does apply New Mexico law, it is less weighty than decisions by New Mexico state courts.

Before relying on *Lukoski*, we needed to cite it, to be sure it is good law. What we learned through several citators is covered here in our discussion of Westlaw, LexisNexis, and Loislaw.

Paper Digests and Reporters. If we did not have citations to pertinent cases when we turned to researching case law, a good starting point would be the West paper digests and reporters. To find case law in New Mexico on an issue of state law, we used the *New Mexico Digest*. Another good option would be the *Pacific Digest*.

Finding the pertinent topics and key numbers took some meandering.[1] A scan of the topic list led to Master & Servant. See the first page of Exhibit 9.8 (at pages 172–73). On the other hand, when we looked up various terms in the Descriptive Word Index, we found references to various Labor & Emp subtopics. See Exhibit 9.9 (at page 174). We solved the mystery by looking at the topic list in the 2007 pocket part in the Descriptive Word Index; there we discovered that the Master & Servant material had moved to a new topic, Labor & Employment. See the second page of Exhibit 9.8 (at pages 172–73). In the Descriptive Word Index, we found over forty subtopics under Discharge, falling in the 700-800 range—this must be a very big topic. We also saw that Contract and Handbooks were covered earlier on, around key numbers 30-40. See Exhibit 9.9 (at page 174).

Given the imprecision of our research thus far, we decided to read through the table of contents of the new Labor & Employment topic before selecting subtopics to read. See Exhibit 9.10 (at page 176). When we conducted this research, the *New Mexico Digest* consisted of a 2004 main volume and pocket part for 2008. We started out focusing on the contract discussion, which had fewer subtopics and key numbers than the termination portion. The contract topic started at key number 31; the discussion of manuals, handbooks, and policy statements started at key number 49. Under key number 57—weight and sufficiency of evidence of employment—we found a paragraph describing *Lukoski*. Under the same and nearby subtopics, we found other cases, such as *Hartbarger v. Frank Paxton Co.*, 857 P.2d 776 (N.M. 1993). Not surprisingly, our research in paper digests and reporters worked well.

Because the Labor & Employment topic is so large, we had some concern that we might miss cases filed in places we did not expect. For this reason, to update our paper research, and to seek a factually similar persuasive case, we turned to online research. Please note: We have presented a number of searches for illustrative purposes; we would not use them all or even most of them.

Westlaw. Although our research in the West digests and reporters was very fruitful, we also ran various searches in Westlaw. For the most part, we ran our searches in the NM-CS database, which contains cases from the New Mexico Supreme Court and the New Mexico Court of Appeals as well as a limited number of trial court decisions; includes not only published cases but also recent cases not yet in the Pacific Reporter and cases that will not be

---

1. We did this phase of the research in the *Minnesota Digest*. All West digests use the same topics and key numbers, and our library did not carry the New Mexico set.

published; and reaches back to 1852. A somewhat broader database is NM-CS-ALL, which also contains federal court cases that are authoritative in New Mexico, e.g., Tenth Circuit cases.

We tried KeySearch first. We picked the Employment Law topic and the Handbooks and Manuals subtopic. The search written by the West staff to cover this subtopic was `he(employ! personnel /3 hand-book manual)`. Note that `he` signifies a search in headnotes. This search, run in NM State Cases with West Headnotes, yielded thirty-four cases.

Our natural-language search was: `Can an employer discharge an employee without following the procedures in the employee handbook?` *Lukoski* was the first case on the list of twenty (the default number).

Finally, our initial terms-and-connectors search was `employ! /p (discharg! dismiss! terminat!) /p (handbook manual)`. This search yielded sixty-three cases. To narrow the search, we searched in the synopsis and digest fields; the revised search yielded twenty-eight cases. When we sought `smoke!` as well, we learned of *Mealand v. Eastern New Mexico Medical Center*, 33 P.3d 285 (N.M. Ct. App. 2001).

The numbers of retrieved cases may sound daunting—the New Mexico courts were busy deciding cases like Canoga's over the past twenty years. To figure out which cases to focus on, we compared the results of the various searches. We thus identified another frequently noted case, *Newberry v. Allied Stores, Inc.*, 733 P.2d 1231 (N.M. 1989), and approximately ten cases appearing on two of the lists.

When we had *Lukoski* on the screen, we looked at the ResultsPlus list of commentary, which included references to the Am. Jur. 2d discussion and A.L.R. annotation we found in our commentary research, among others.

We learned through KeyCite that *Lukoski* was still good law—no overruling, criticism, or distinguished designations; it was labeled with a green C. According to KeyCite, *Lukoski* was positively examined, discussed, cited, or mentioned in fourteen New Mexico state court decisions, five federal cases, one California case, and one Washington case. If we were inclined to return to commentary research, KeyCite listed twenty-one commentary citations, including A.L.R., C.J.S., and law review articles.

Finally, before leaving Westlaw, we sought a factually similar case in a sister jurisdiction. We used the MLB-CS database, a multistate database containing cases from various jurisdictions in the area of labor and employment law. Our search was `(discharg! dismiss! terminat!) /p (smok! /s off-duty)`; it yielded fifteen cases. Fifth on that list was a South Dakota case, *Wood v. South Dakota Cement Plant*, 588 N.W.2d 227 (S.D. 1999), which involved an assistant kiln operator who was fired for off-duty, off-premises use of tobacco. We also found cases involving bans on off-duty smoking by firefighters and police officers. *E.g., Town of Plymouth v. Civil Service Comm'n*, 686 N.E.2d 188 (Mass. 1997).

Researching in LexisNexis. We searched for New Mexico cases on the breach-of-contract issue various ways in LexisNexis. We started the first search by selecting New Mexico State Courts as our database. Our search was `employ! /p (discharg! OR dismiss! OR terminat!) /p` (handbook OR manual) /p contract. This search yielded forty-five cases when run in the full-text of the cases. When we narrowed the search by running it in the points of law i.e., LexisNexis' headnotes, the list dropped to five. Forty-five is a lot to handle; five is perhaps too few. We ran a More-Like-This search based on *Lukoski*, which listed fifteen terms (we struck "bingo"); this search yielded twenty-six cases, most of them apparently pertinent, including *Mealand* and *Hartbarger*.

Following the Source by Topic or Headnote process entailed selecting the following chain of topics and subtopics: Labor & Employment Law → Wrongful Termination (from a choice of eighteen) → Breach of Contract → Employer Handbooks. Running that search in NM Labor & Employment Cases yielded about 100 cases; we obtained the same list searching by the headnote. A list of 100 cases is really a lot to manage. We tried paring the list by adding specific terms but made little progress.

Shepardizing *Lukoski*, we encountered a yellow caution sign, signifying possible negative treatment. More specifically, we saw that *Hartbarger* cited but also distinguished *Lukoski* as to LexisNexis headnote 2, which is the topic for which we would use *Lukoski*. *Hartbarger* went on our list of cases to read soon. *Lukoski*'s Shepard's report listed twenty-one citing decisions, including New Mexico state courts, the federal courts covering New Mexico, and California and Washington state courts.

Other commercial online resources. Westlaw and LexisNexis yielded two to three handfuls of pertinent cases. A fair question is whether the less extensive services would work as well.

We chose Loislaw, more specifically the New Mexico Caselaw database. It reached back to 1923 for the supreme court, 1966 for the court of appeals. After a bit of drafting and re-drafting searches, we found thirty cases in response to employee NEAR/30 (terminate OR discharge) NEAR/30 (handbook OR manual). Because we could quickly read a synopsis for each case, thirty was a manageable number. *Lukoski* was the twenty-fifth; the other cases cited in this interlude were also on the list.

GlobalCite is Loislaw's approximation of KeyCite and Shepard's. It listed twenty-eight cases citing *Lukoski* and provided text surrounding the citations but not a rating system of the sort provided by KeyCite and Shepard's. GlobalCite also listed two treatises.

Court websites. We would not use a court website for this project, but we gave it a shot for illustrative purposes. Seeking a court website for New Mexico state cases through a Google search, we came up with two interesting sites. One, nmcourts.com, had a case look-up function, but it appeared to be for the docket of the lower courts in New Mexico; we could have figured out that it was not an official court website from ".com." We also found the Judicial Education Center, an organization that provides education and training to judges and posts summaries of very recent civil and criminal decisions.

Working through LII (generally a better idea), we came to supreme-court.nm.gov, which is maintained by the New Mexico Compilation Commission. There we could retrieve decisions of the New Mexico Supreme Court and Court of Appeals from 1998 to date. We tested it by pulling up one of the cases we had identified various ways, *Mealand v. Eastern New Mexico Medical*

Center, decided by the court of appeals in 2001. The version we obtained from the website indicated that the supreme court denied certiorari (denied the request for review). The case seemed particularly promising because, as noted above, it contained some version of *smok*. The employer's handbook provided for discipline for unauthorized smoking, but the nurse was fired for reasons unrelated to smoking.

As could be expected, the federal Tenth Circuit site, at ca10.uscourts. gov, was expansive and sophisticated. The database extended back to 1995, and it was searchable. Our search for ``New Mexico'' ``employee handbook'' yielded twenty-six cases, arrayed by how well they fit the search. We obtained a pertinent case arising out of New Mexico and applying New Mexico law; unfortunately, it ran eighty pages. The lack of editorial material was a definite disadvantage of the court website in this situation.

Summary. As one would expect, all roads led to *Lukoski* and a handful or two of other cases. We could tell from our research that three — *Hartbarger*, *Mealand*, and *Newberry*—warranted particular attention as we shifted from locating to reading cases. Our next task was to read and citate them, then synthesize the cases.

Note: For illustrative purposes, we researched in cases more ways than you should do in practice.

ENACTED LAW

INTRODUCTION

Previous units have covered how to use commentary sources to locate and understand the law and how to research one form of law — case law. In this unit, you will learn to research an additional type of law — enacted law, primarily statutes and constitutions, along with related materials.

This unit has two chapters. Chapter 11 explains what statutes and constitutions are, how they relate to case law, and why they are so important in legal research. It then covers various ways of researching enacted laws and related case law. Chapter 12 covers methods of researching the legislative process; this research helps you discern what a legislature meant when it enacted a statute, as well as what a legislature is considering enacting for the future. As you will see, statutory research often has a broad scope. Complete statutory research is the sum of the following:

☐ commentary — which provides descriptions of and references to statutes;

☐ statutes — the law itself that is currently in effect;

☐ session laws, as needed — older or newer law than the statute;

☐ cases interpreting the statute, if any — which assess the constitutionality of the statute and apply it to specific situations; and

☐ legislative history materials, as needed and available — which are used to gain insight into the legislature's intent.

This unit continues to illustrate the research of the Canoga case stated in Chapter 1 (at pages 3–4). This unit addresses two of the issues in that case, suggested by the commentary research in Unit II:

(1) Does a prohibition of off-duty smoking impermissibly intrude on the employee's privacy?

(2) Does a prohibition of off-duty smoking impermissibly discriminate against employees who are disabled due to nicotine addiction?

Finally, a bit of vocabulary:

☐ A bill is potential legislation under consideration by a legislature.

☐ A law is a bill that has passed, thereby becoming law.

☐ A statute is the law on a particular topic that has been created by the legislature through one or more enacted laws and that is in effect on a specific date.

In addition, this unit uses "constitution" to refer to federal and state constitutions and local government charters. Similarly, "statutes" refers to federal and state statutes and local ordinances. "Enacted law" includes all of these.

CONSTITUTIONS AND STATUTES

CHAPTER

11

A. What Are Constitutions and Statutes, and Why Would You Research Them?

B. How Do You Research Constitutions and Statutes?

C. How Do You Cite Constitutions and Statutes?

D. What Else?

Exhibit 11.18   KeyCite Report for Federal Statute, from Westlaw (online source)

Exhibit 11.19   Federal Session Law, from United States Code Congressional and Administrative News (paper source)

Exhibit 11.20   Local Ordinance, from Sterling Codifiers (online source)

A.   WHAT ARE CONSTITUTIONS AND STATUTES, AND WHY WOULD YOU RESEARCH THEM?

United States law is dominated by enacted law, created at the federal, state, and local levels. Federal and state constitutions and local charters create government structures, defining the powers of the government and the rights of the governed. Federal and state statutes and local ordinances govern a wide range of activities by public and private entities and individuals. Constitutions and statutes have somewhat different roles in the United States legal system, yet they resemble each other and are researched in much the same way.

Succinctly stated, you research constitutions and statutes because they are the law. They are mandatory authority if validly enacted by the legislature in your jurisdiction and approved or ratified. Because courts interpret and apply enacted law, researching enacted law also entails researching case law.

1.   What Is a Constitution, and Why Would You Research It?

A constitution is the highest law in a constitutional democratic regime. A constitution sets the structure of the government, its inherent powers, and limits on the government's authority with regard to certain matters.

The United States Constitution dates to the late 1700s. In 1781, the Articles of Confederation created the United States of America. However, certain defects soon became apparent in the Articles of Confederation, and a constitutional convention was assembled in Philadelphia in 1787. The major political figures at that time submitted drafts that were debated and revised many times. The Constitution was finally ratified and became effective in 1789. The Bill of Rights, comprised of the first ten amendments to the Constitution, which spell out specific protections afforded the governed, soon followed.

To amend the Constitution, a proposed amendment must pass two-thirds of both houses of Congress, or the legislatures of two-thirds of the states must support it by constitutional convention. It then must be ratified by three-fourths of the states. In more than 200 years, only twenty-seven amendments (including the Bill of Rights) have been made to the Constitution.

The federal Constitution creates the three branches of the federal government. The Constitution creates the Congress, empowers it to enact legislation, and places limits on that power. For example, the First Amendment limits the power of Congress to pass statutes that infringe on the freedoms of speech, the press, and religion. The Constitution also creates the federal court system, describing the selection of Supreme Court justices, defining the jurisdiction of the federal courts, and granting Congress the right to establish lower federal courts. Constitutional provisions pertaining to the executive branch detail how presidents are elected, impeached, and succeeded. The Constitution also provides for presidential powers such as the right to veto legislation (subject to congressional override), to negotiate international treaties, and to serve as commander-in-chief of the military.

Under our federalist system, each state also has a separate constitution, which likewise details the structure of the state and local governments, grants them powers to act in certain areas, and protects the rights of persons within the state. Some states have had several constitutions, and state constitutions are amended more frequently than the federal Constitution. In the typical process, amendments are initiated by the state legislature or by public initiative and are then approved by public referendum. Typically, the rights protected by a state constitution mirror the rights protected by the federal constitution. However, a state constitution may grant additional rights to its people, so long as those rights do not conflict with the federal Constitution.

Because constitutions generally regulate only governmental action, they are primarily pertinent in two circumstances: (1) when a party attacks the validity of a law or (2) when a party seeks to challenge action taken by a government official, on constitutional grounds. On rare occasions, non-governmental entities may be governed by a constitution when their actions are quasi-governmental or tightly enmeshed in government functions. In addition, some state constitutional provisions are written broadly enough to apply to private actors as well.

A constitution states broad principles that are intended to stand the test of time, so most provisions have little detail or explanation. A constitution is organized by parts and subparts, such as articles and clauses. Generally, amendments are not integrated into the text of the original constitution, but rather appear as separate provisions in the order ratified.

Exhibit 11.1 (at page 224) is an excerpt from the New Mexico Constitution; it is a part of New Mexico's Bill of Rights.

2.   What Is a Statute, and Why Would You Research It?

Statutes are enacted by the federal Congress or a state legislature in a highly collaborative process involving legislators; the executive branch; and members of the public, who act both as lobbyists and as interested individuals. Legislatures are both reactive and proactive institutions. Interested individuals and groups bring concerns to the legislature, and legislators also seek to anticipate or respond to evolving problems and issues they identify. The legislative process is open to all constituencies, so it is inevitably political in the sense that a government body listens to the diverse interests of its constituents and decides how to honor those interests.

Nearly anyone may generate a bill — a new piece of proposed legislation, which must be introduced by a legislator. In a typical process, the bill then

| EXHIBIT 11.1 | Constitution, from West's New Mexico Statutes Annotated (paper source) |

Art. 2, § 1

CONSTITUTION OF NEW MEXICO

proceeds of contracts between federal government and private contractors performed on Indian reservations, see Arizona Dept. of Revenue v. Blaze Const. Co., U.S.Ariz.1999, 119 S.Ct. 957, 526 U.S. 32.

Utility regulation,

Utility regulation, Supremacy Clause, filed rate doctrine, interstate power rates binding on state utility commission determination of intrastate rates, see Entergy Louisiana, Inc. v. Louisiana Public Service Commission, La.2003, 123 S.Ct. 2050.

Notes of Decisions

Full faith and credit   1

_____

1. Full faith and credit
Fact that an adoption judgment entered by a Colorado court could not have been entered by

a New Mexico court, because it would have offended public policy of New Mexico, did not permit New Mexico courts to deny it full faith and credit. U.S.C.A.Const. art. 4, § 1. Delaney v. First Nat. Bank in Albuquerque, 1963, 73 N.M. 192, 386 P.2d 711. Adoption ⚭ 25

§ 2.   Government by the people

All political power is vested in and derived from the people: all government of right originates with the people, is founded upon their will and is instituted solely for their good.

Cross References

Comparable provision, see Kearny Bill of Rights (1846), ¶ 1.

Library References

Constitutional Law ⚭82(6.1).
Westlaw Key Number Search: 92k82(6.1).
C.J.S. Right to Die § 2.

§ 3.   Sovereign and independent state

The people of the state have the sole and exclusive right to govern themselves as a free, sovereign and independent state.

Library References

Constitutional Law ⚭82(6.1).
Westlaw Key Number Search: 92k82(6.1).
C.J.S. Right to Die § 2.

Notes of Decisions

In general   1

_____

1. In general
Section 301, providing for the appointment of the board of directors for the conservancy dis-

trict by district court, does not violate section 3 of article 2 of the Constitution of New Mexico. In re Proposed Middle Rio Grande Conservancy Dist., 1925, 31 N.M. 188, 242 P. 683. Levees And Flood Control ⚭ 2

§ 4.   Inalienable rights

All persons are born equally free, and have certain natural, inherent and inalienable rights, among which are the rights of enjoying and defending life and liberty, of acquiring, possessing and protecting property, and of seeking and obtaining safety and happiness.

passes through committee hearings, committee deliberations, full-chamber floor debates, and votes in both houses of the legislature before the bill is sent to the executive, i.e., governor or president, for approval or veto. Of course, the bill may be amended or perish at any of these steps.

A law once passed is not written in stone. Should circumstances or public sentiment change, a legislature may return to the statute, to amend it or even repeal it, through the process described previously. Some statutes have been amended many times.

Although the statutory law on a topic may consist of a single brief section, many statutes consist of multiple related sections. An elaborate statute has many of the following provisions:

- ☐ opening provisions: the statute's name, its definitions, and scope;
- ☐ operative provisions: the general rule, any exceptions to the rule, the consequences of violating the rule, and enforcement provisions;
- ☐ closing provisions, for example, whether the statute is severable (if part of it is invalid, the rest continues to operate), when the statute becomes effective.

In an elaborate statute, the sections and subsections are separately numbered (sometimes with gaps in the numbering sequence to accommodate later additions and to set off separate topics).

Not all statutes fit this description. Compact statutes do not contain all of these components. In other statutes, the components may be unlabeled or presented in a different order.

When a statute is amended, the old text must, of course, give way to new text. Obsolete language is deleted, and new language is inserted. Generally this revision is accomplished within the organizational framework set by the original statute.

Timing is very important in statutory research. For your research to be correct, you must find the language in effect at the time of your client's situation. Although there are some exceptions, enacted law is prospective, that is, a law governs conduct occurring on or after its effective date. The effective date of a law is the date stated in the law's effective-date provision or, if none, the default date for the jurisdiction. For federal legislation, the default effective date is the date of the president's approval. Once effective, a statute remains in effect unless it is repealed or replaced; is declared unconstitutional, as discussed in section 4; or expires by operation of a provision in the statute so stating, often called a "sunset provision."

Statutes have potentially broad application; they govern many facets of the economy and social relations. Many statutes apply to private actions, some to governmental actions, some to both. The statute itself indicates or implies how broadly it applies. For example, a statute may set standards for an industry, provide that someone injured by noncompliance may sue, or create an agency to monitor compliance. Because statutes are so prevalent, you should assume that your research topic is governed by a statute.

Exhibit 11.2 (at pages 226–27) is New Mexico's Employee Privacy Act, a compact statute addressesing the privacy aspect of the Canoga Case.

| EXHIBIT 11.2 | State Statute,
from New Mexico Government Website (online source) |

ARTICLE 11
Employee Privacy
Section

50-11-1. Short title.
This act [50-11-1 to 50-11-6 NMSA 1978] may be cited as the "Employee Privacy Act".

50-11-2. Definitions.
As used in the Employee Privacy Act [50-11-1 NMSA 1978]:
A.   "employee" means a person that performs a service for wages or other remuneration under a contract of hire, written or oral, express or implied, and includes a person employed by the state or a political subdivision of the state;
B.   "employer" means a person that has one or more employees and includes an agent of an employer and the state or a political subdivision of the state; and
C.   "person" means an individual, sole proprietorship, partnership, corporation, association or any other legal entity.

50-11-3. Employers; unlawful practices.
A.   It is unlawful for an employer to:
(1)   refuse to hire or to discharge any individual, or otherwise disadvantage any individual, with respect to compensation, terms, conditions or privileges of employment because the individual is a smoker or nonsmoker, provided that the individual complies with applicable laws or policies regulating smoking on the premises of the employer during working hours; or
(2)   require as a condition of employment that any employee or applicant for employment abstain from smoking or using tobacco products during nonworking hours, provided the individual complies with applicable laws or policies regulating smoking on the premises of the employer during working hours.
B.   The provisions of Subsection A of this section shall not be deemed to protect any activity that:
(1)   materially threatens an employer's legitimate conflict of interest policy reasonably designed to protect the employer's trade secrets, proprietary information or other proprietary interests; or
(2)   relates to a bona fide occupational requirement and is reasonably and rationally related to the employment activities and responsibilities of a particular employee or a particular group of employees, rather than to all employees of the employer.

EXHIBIT 11.2 *(continued)*

50-11-4. Remedies.
Any employee claiming to be aggrieved by any unlawful action of an employer pursuant to Section 3 [50-11-3 NMSA 1978] of the Employee Privacy Act may bring a civil suit for damages in any district court of competent jurisdiction. The employee may be awarded all wages and benefits due up to and including the date of the judgment.

50-11-5. Court fees and costs.
In any civil suit arising from the Employee Privacy Act [50-11-1 NMSA 1978], the court shall award the prevailing party court costs and reasonable attorneys' fees.

50-11-6. Mitigation of damages.
Nothing in the Employee Privacy Act [50-11-1 NMSA 1978] shall be construed to relieve a person from the obligation to mitigate damages.

Exhibit 11.3 (at pages 228–29) is just a list of the fifty sections of the much longer federal Americans with Disabilities Act (ADA). The ADA is a complex statute prohibiting discrimination based on disability not only in employment, but also in public services, transportation, and public accommodations (such as restaurants).

3. Whose Law Governs?

Under our federal system, federal and state governments have separate as well as overlapping rights to enact law within constitutionally prescribed limits. For example, the federal government has authority to govern in areas that preserve its national sovereignty or that have been expressly granted to it by the United States Constitution. State governments have authority to govern matters that are state concerns, have been delegated to them by Congress, or are not expressly assigned to the federal government.

The federal system is hierarchical in that federal law sometimes preempts state law on the same topic. In areas of potential federal authority, Congress can dictate whether its laws preempt state laws or coexist with them. If Congress is silent, then the courts must decide whether the federal law impliedly preempts the state law; courts consider the strength of the state interest and the potential for interference with the overall federal regulatory scheme.

Often you will learn whose law governs through your research in commentary. If you are uncertain, begin with research in federal law, then turn to state and then local law. If you find that your topic does involve overlapping federal and state statutes, first be sure that you fully understand their relationship. In employment law, for example, the federal statute may govern employers of a certain size, whereas the state statute contains no such limits.

EXHIBIT 11.3

Outline of Federal Statute,
from United States Code (paper source)

(D) include annual and five-year cost estimates for individual programs under this chapter; and

(E) identify program areas for which funding levels have been changed from the previous year's Plan.[2]

(6) Within one year after October 24, 1992, the Secretary shall submit a revised management plan under this section to Congress. Thereafter, the Secretary shall submit a management plan every three years at the time of submittal of the President's annual budget submission to the Congress.

(c) Report on options

As part of the first report submitted under subsection (a) of this section, the Secretary shall submit to Congress a report analyzing options available to the Secretary under existing law to assist the private sector with the timely commercialization of wind, photovoltaic, solar thermal, biofuels, hydrogen, solar buildings, ocean, geothermal, low-head hydro, and energy storage renewable energy technologies and energy efficiency technologies through emphasis on development and demonstration assistance to specific technologies in the research, development, and demonstration programs of the Department of Energy that are near commercial application.

(Pub. L. 101–218, § 9, Dec. 11, 1989, 103 Stat. 1868; Pub. L. 102–486, title XII, § 1202(c), (d)(5), title XXIII, § 2303(b), Oct. 24, 1992, 106 Stat. 2959, 2960, 3093.)

AMENDMENTS

1992—Subsec. (a). Pub. L. 102–486, § 1202(d)(5), substituted "and projects" for ", projects, and joint ventures".

Subsec. (b)(1). Pub. L. 102–486, § 1202(c)(1), inserted "three-year" before "management plan".

Subsec. (b)(4). Pub. L. 102–486, § 2303(b), inserted before period at end "and the plan developed under section 5905 of this title".

Subsec. (b)(5), (6). Pub. L. 102–486, § 1202(c)(2), added pars. (5) and (6) and struck out former par. (5) which read as follows: "The plan shall accompany the President's annual budget submission to the Congress."

TERMINATION OF REPORTING REQUIREMENTS

For termination, effective May 15, 2000, of provisions of law requiring submittal to Congress of any annual, semiannual, or other regular periodic report listed in House Document No. 103–7 (in which reports required under subsecs. (a) and (b) of this section are listed as the 20th item on page 84 and the 19th item on page 86), see section 3003 of Pub. L. 104–66, as amended, set out as a note under section 1113 of Title 31, Money and Finance.

SECTION REFERRED TO IN OTHER SECTIONS

This section is referred to in section 12003 of this title.

§ 12007. No antitrust immunity or defenses

Nothing in this chapter shall be deemed to convey to any person, partnership, corporation, or other entity immunity from civil or criminal liability under any antitrust law or to create any defenses to actions under any antitrust law. As used in this section, "antitrust laws" means those Acts set forth in section 12 of title 15.

(Pub. L. 101–218, § 10, Dec. 11, 1989, 103 Stat. 1869.)

[2] So in original. Probably should not be capitalized.

EXHIBIT 11.3   *(continued)*

Page 659   TITLE 42—THE PUBLIC HEALTH AND WELFARE   § 12101

CHAPTER REFERRED TO IN OTHER SECTIONS

This chapter is referred to in sections 290bb–34, 608, 1760, 1786, 3796gg–7, 15007, 15024 of this title; title 2 sections 1302, 1331, 1371, 1434; title 3 sections 402, 421; title 16 sections 410aaa–41, 410aaa–52; title 20 sections 1011, 1140c, 1415, 8507; title 23 section 133; title 25 section 2005; title 26 section 44; title 29 sections 720, 721, 762, 764, 781, 793, 795, 3011; title 49 sections 5302, 5307, 5314, 5323, 5335, 47102.

§ 12101. Findings and purpose

(a) Findings

The Congress finds that—

(1) some 43,000,000 Americans have one or more physical or mental disabilities, and this number is increasing as the population as a whole is growing older;

(2) historically, society has tended to isolate and segregate individuals with disabilities, and, despite some improvements, such forms of discrimination against individuals with disabilities continue to be a serious and pervasive social problem;

(3) discrimination against individuals with disabilities persists in such critical areas as employment, housing, public accommodations, education, transportation, communication, recreation, institutionalization, health services, voting, and access to public services;

(4) unlike individuals who have experienced discrimination on the basis of race, color, sex, national origin, religion, or age, individuals who have experienced discrimination on the basis of disability have often had no legal recourse to redress such discrimination;

(5) individuals with disabilities continually encounter various forms of discrimination, including outright intentional exclusion, the discriminatory effects of architectural, transportation, and communication barriers, overprotective rules and policies, failure to make modifications to existing facilities and practices, exclusionary qualification standards and criteria, segregation, and relegation to lesser services, programs, activities, benefits, jobs, or other opportunities;

(6) census data, national polls, and other studies have documented that people with disabilities, as a group, occupy an inferior status in our society, and are severely disadvantaged socially, vocationally, economically, and educationally;

(7) individuals with disabilities are a discrete and insular minority who have been

4. How Does Enacted Law Relate to Case Law?

Although cases and statutes are both law, they develop and are analyzed differently. As discussed in Chapter 9, case law develops case by case, each case focusing on the situation that prompted the litigation. Cases serve as binding or persuasive precedent for future disputes involving similar situations. In contrast, enacted laws are enacted by legislators who are seeking to describe and set rules for a broad class of situations that will arise in the future.

Constitutions are the supreme law in a jurisdiction, yet most provisions are framed in vague and general terms. Hence the courts play a very active role in the development of constitutional law. It is up to the courts to discern what spare constitutional language means in myriad particular circumstances. As you research a constitutional issue, you most likely will find yourself grappling with a substantial body of case law.

Statutes bear various relationships to common law. Some statutes codify, clarify, or supplement pre-existing common law. Some statutes overturn the common law. Still other statutes create whole new areas of law not covered in the common law. Because the Constitution grants the legislative branch broad powers, statutes usually take precedence over common law.

In turn, statutes are interpreted in case law as courts apply statutes to disputes in litigation. Courts have two primary tasks in such cases, one common, the other rare. First, courts interpret the legislature's language and use it to resolve the parties' dispute. Second, and less commonly, courts assess whether the statute is constitutional; if not, the statute is declared unconstitutional and has no further effect. Stare decisis applies in the statutory setting; a court asked to interpret a statute will follow the interpretation of courts that create the precedents it must follow.

The number of interpreting cases varies greatly from statute to statute, depending on the breadth of the statute's impact, the clarity of its language, and its age. Some statutes have no interpreting cases; some have thousands. Thus, as you research a statute, you will also research case law interpreting the statute. Otherwise, your research will be incomplete.

5. When Do Sister Jurisdictions' Statutory Cases Matter?

First, noted previously, in some areas, federal and state statutes overlap. A state court may seek to interpret its state statute the same as the federal statute, especially if the language is identical or very nearly so. Often you will find many cases interpreting the federal statute and only a few interpreting the state statute; you may then look to a federal case that has decided a question not yet addressed by your state's courts.

Second, courts look to the cases of a sister jurisdiction when their statutes derive from uniform or model acts. Uniform acts are proposals for statutes drafted by public or private organizations that seek to standardize the statutory law of the fifty states. Model acts address topics that may not be of critical concern to all jurisdictions or that likely will not be enacted by a substantial number of jurisdictions. The drafters of both uniform and model acts seek to persuade state legislatures to enact the proposed language. The Uniform Commercial Code is an example of a widely adopted uniform act.

Uniform and model acts come from a variety of sources: The National Conference of Commissioners on Uniform State Laws, consisting of attorneys, judges, legislators, and law professors appointed from each state, has approved over 100 model and uniform acts. The American Law Institute (which promulgates Restatements of the Law, discussed in Chapter 7) also drafts model codes. Section committees of the American Bar Association and the Council of State Governments promulgate model acts on occasion. Finally, private individuals, most notably law faculty, occasionally propose model legislation.

Complete uniformity is rarely achieved because few acts are enacted by every jurisdiction and because few uniform or model acts are enacted verbatim. Nonetheless, achieving some uniformity in state statutes through these efforts promotes and simplifies interstate activities.

If your state's statute closely or completely tracks the language of a uniform or model act, you may expand your research to include leading cases from other states. Furthermore, you may find helpful material in the notes or comments accompanying the uniform or model act, which function much like the Restatements' explanatory material.

Third, if your state's statute resembles that of another state, even though they do not derive from uniform or model acts, you may look to a case from that other state, especially if your state's courts have not interpreted your statute or that other state's court is seen as particularly expert in the subject.

B.   HOW DO YOU RESEARCH CONSTITUTIONS AND STATUTES?

1.   Introduction

As synopsized in Exhibit 11.4 (at page 232), our statutes template, statutory research entails developing a well-honed issue; locating the statute governing your client's situation, which is a function of its content and currency; carefully reading that statute; locating and reading cases interpreting the statute, where appropriate; connecting the law from the statute, with or without interpreting cases, to your client's situation; and planning your next steps.

Given the importance of statutory law in the U.S. legal system, it is not surprising that statutes are available in multiple media from various publishers, as follows:

☐   Slip law: This is the individual law as enacted. The slip law carries the public law number (for federal laws) or chapter number (typically

EXHIBIT 11.4	Statutes Template

Issue:	Citation Information:
	• code • necessary numbers, e.g., title, section • date of code
Date of events:	
Date of research:	

Search and Find:	
located statute by . . .	updated by . . .
	as needed, found former law by . . .

Information and Implications:

- purpose or other introductory section
- definition and scope
- general rule
- exceptions
- consequences
- enforcement
- connection to client's situation

Next Steps:

questions to consider:	leads to follow:

used for state laws), which reflects the legislative session when it passed and its place in that session's laws.
- ☐ Session laws: The slip laws for a session are collected and published in order of enactment in the session laws.
- ☐ Official code: This is a set of statutes currently in force, organized topically and published by the government or its designated publisher.[1] Thus if a new law amends an existing statute, the old language is displaced by the new language. If a new law instead covers new ground, it is inserted near other statutes on the same broad subject. Codes have fairly elaborate numerical schemes; for example, the federal code uses title, chapter, and section numbers. A law thus has two numbers: its session law number and its code number.
- ☐ Unofficial code: Published by a private company, the unofficial code uses the same numbering scheme and should contain the same statutory language (subject to differences in updating and minor editorial features) as the official code.[2] Unlike most official codes, most unofficial codes are annotated, that is, they provide background information and descriptions of cases interpreting the statute; references to related laws, such as administrative materials; and references to commentary discussing the topic of the statute. Unofficial codes are updated more frequently than official codes.

Some states have only one code, published by a private company with annotations on contract with the state. Table T.1 of *The Bluebook* and Appendix I of *ALWD Citation Manual* list the session laws and codes for U.S. jurisdictions.

Statutory materials have long been and continue to be published in paper. They also are now available online through commercial services and public websites. Thus for any particular statute, you will very likely have several research resources from which to choose. This part discusses options one could use in 2007. Others may well develop, so you should keep abreast of major developments. More likely than not, the changes will be variations on the practices discussed here.

As depicted in Exhibit 11.5 (at page 234), many avenues lead to pertinent statutes. Quite often, you will find a reference to a pertinent statute through your commentary research; indeed, this is very desirable. You may also become aware of a statute when you read a pertinent case that discusses it. However, you should not rely solely on such leads; you should also develop and implement your own search for pertinent statutes.

---

1. A jurisdiction's code typically contains only public permanent laws, not private laws (which relate to a particular person or specific situation) or temporary laws (such as appropriations for government agencies).

2. Although there rarely is conflict among session laws, official codes, and unofficial codes, there is a hierarchy among them. From time to time, Congress examines specific titles of the official code and re-enacts those titles as positive law; once re-enacted, those titles are the law. Titles that have not been re-enacted as positive law are only prima facie (presumptively correct) evidence of the law, and the session law governs in the event of a conflict. A similar process occurs at the state level.

| EXHIBIT 11.5 | Avenues to Statutes |

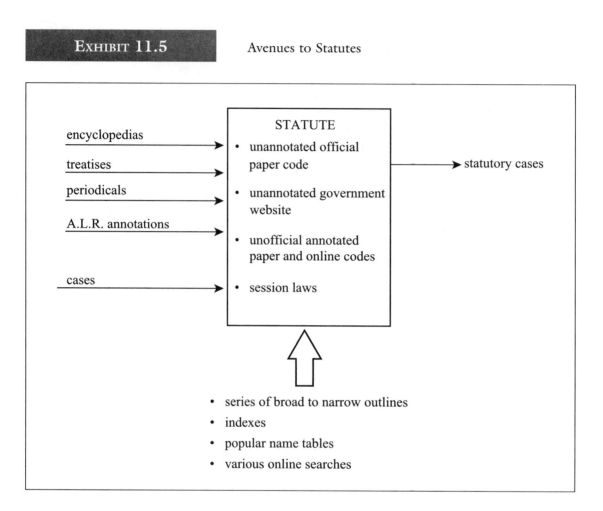

In the abstract, statutory research is straightforward: find the language pertaining to your client's situation. Sometimes statutory research is indeed straightforward when, for example, a short, fairly recently enacted statute applies in a clear way to your client's situation. In other situations, statutory research can be complicated: the statute is lengthy, has been amended, is ambiguous as applied to your client's situation, has been interpreted in a number of cases, or some combination of these. Generally state statutes are easier to research than federal statutes because there are fewer cases interpreting state statutes.

The following discussion starts with basic statutory sources and moves into more sophisticated sources. This progression is intended in part to assist your learning; it is easier to understand the sources discussed in this chapter by starting with the less elaborate ones. This progression is also a common way of coming at statutory research, especially when you are researching an area of law you have not worked with before, because it is the best way to keep your initial focus on the statute itself. Along the way, the discussion covers federal, state, and local sources; official and unofficial codes; paper sources, commercial online sources, and free websites.

In Chapter 9, we compared case law sources to modes of transportation; for example, we equated the paper reporter and digest system to public transportation and Westlaw and LexisNexis to fully loaded sport-utility vehicles. Devising a similar comparison for statutory research sources is more difficult because differentiating among them is more difficult. For example, although the scope of coverage varies across case law sources, all of the statutory sources discussed in this part have the same statutory content. Thus think of them all as recreational boats: state statute sources are small rowboats, federal statute sources are forty-foot sail boats. For each, you can operate without a motor, i.e., in paper, or with a motor, i.e., online. Some come with many amenities, i.e., annotations, while others do not.

As you consider the various options, which operate in much the same way for statutes and constitutions, keep several attributes of the sources in mind: how one finds the pertinent statute within the source; how up to date — or up-to-date-able — the source is; on rare occasions, how retrospective the source is; how much information the source provides beyond the statutory language; and how much cost, in addition to your time, there is to using the source.

After the discussion of researching in federal and state codes are discussions of researching statutory cases; research in session laws, which does not come up often but is important to know; and researching local ordinances.

This chapter does not discuss several tools that have important but less central roles in statutory research. Chapter 12 discusses legislative process materials, which are used to establish the legislature's intent in passing a statute or to track pending bills.

2.   Statutory Codes

> **Official codes in paper and codes on legislative websites**
>
> ▶ Identify the paper code; use the means of access it affords to find the pertinent statute.
> ▶ Or identify an appropriate website; use the means of access afforded by the website to find the pertinent statute.
> ▶ Update the results as permitted.
> ▶ Study the statute.

An official code generally is the sparest source of a jurisdiction's statutes. Thus it often is the most manageable source and a good place to start. If the code's organization is straightforward, the publisher has written a good index, or you already have the statute's citation, finding the pertinent statute in an official paper code is relatively easy.

An abundance of statutory material is available through public websites. In general, you should focus on websites maintained by the legislature itself or a similarly credible government agency. On these websites, you can expect to find the current statutes in force, basic search options, and not much information beyond the statute itself. An online code can be more useful than a paper code because it may be updated sooner and affords online search options. However, some legislatures' websites do not claim that the code presented there is the official code. The concern is that the posting process may lead to inadvertent changes.

Although the specific steps for researching on legislative websites vary from site to site, the outline is the same. First, identify an appropriate website; a good strategy is to use a site identified by a well regarded portal, such as LII (maintained by Cornell University). Second, figure out the website's scope of coverage, especially the most recent legislative session and law it covers. Third, discern how to search the site and do so. Ideally, the site will permit full-text searches and browsing of the chapters or titles and parts or articles.

Once you identify a pertinent statute, carefully study the complete statutory language. If you are working with a multi-section statute, first look over the statute to discern how it is organized. Then read through it as follows:

- ☐ statement of purpose or other introductory section,
- ☐ definitions and scope,
- ☐ the general rule,
- ☐ exceptions,
- ☐ consequences, and
- ☐ enforcement provisions.

If you are working with a shorter statute or one without these labels, seek to understand the statute in these terms, because they facilitate your analysis of the statute's application to your client's situation. See Exhibit 11.2 (at pages 222–23), the New Mexico statute on off-duty smoking which, although short, follows the classic form.

Many statutes are self-contained; others refer to and rely on provisions in other statutes. Every time you read a reference to another section of the same statute or a different statute, be sure to note and follow up on these references. Likewise, read provisions at the beginning of the chapter in which the statute is located; they may apply throughout the chapter. Finally, pay close attention to every word in a statute. Unlike cases, statutes do not contain dicta. You should assume that each word has a purpose and is potentially significant.

Depending on when you research relative to the legislature's session, the code may not be fully up to date. If so, look for a way to update your research by tapping into very new laws; this function may be provided elsewhere on the legislature's website.

As you work on understanding the statute, be sure to determine the version in effect as of the time of your client's situation. As sketched in Exhibit 11.6 (at page 238):

☐ If the client is seeking advice about its future plans, the current language is the correct language.
☐ If the client's events occurred since the most recent enactment's effective date, again, the current language will be the correct language.
☐ If the client's events occurred before the most recent enactment's effective date, however, old language is the correct language.

To sort this out, read whatever information the site provides about the statute's history. This varies from site to site; ideally you will find a list of laws with enactment dates. If your client's events occurred very close to the enactment of a pertinent law, you will need to pinpoint that law's effective date. If you need timing information beyond that provided by the website, you should consult sources described in the remainder of this section, especially session laws.

You may wonder why you should attend to the current language if an older version is the correct language for your client's situation. Often, new language helps you understand older language or infer what the legislature's concerns are and have been.

The official federal code in paper is the *United States Code* (U.S.C.), prepared by the Office of Law Revision Counsel of the U.S. House of Representatives. As you might expect, there is a sophisticated website for federal legislation, uscode.house.gov, also prepared by the Office of Law Revision Counsel. This website offers a wide variety of search strategies, including Boolean searching, searching by topic, and limiting searches to over ten fields. What you might not expect is that the website's currency varies from statute to statute. This is because the website is based on U.S.C., which is republished over six years on a rolling basis, several titles per year. When you locate a pertinent statute at uscode.house.gov, you will see how recent that statute is; as needed, you can then check for your statute in the classification table, which identifies the code sections affected by new laws.

The Legal Information Institute at Cornell University offers a federal statute database based on information provided by the House of Representatives. Among the options are retrieving a known statute, drilling through the titles and chapters, and Boolean searching; for efficiency, the site recommends running a search within a title. The site provides an easy means of updating through a message indicating the currency of the statute and a table alerting you to new laws affecting your statute, if any.

Exhibit 11.2 (at pages 226–27) is the New Mexico statute on employer smoking bans as found in the New Mexico website. Exhibit 11.6 (at page 238) is the statutes template filled in to reflect our research in the New Mexico Employee Privacy Act.

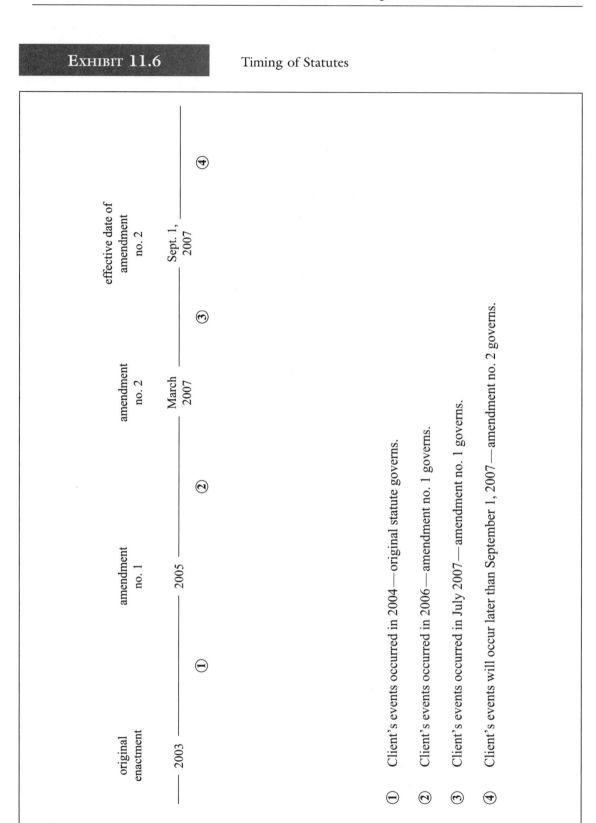

EXHIBIT 11.6   Timing of Statutes

① Client's events occurred in 2004—original statute governs.

② Client's events occurred in 2006—amendment no. 1 governs.

③ Client's events occurred in July 2007—amendment no. 1 governs.

④ Client's events will occur later than September 1, 2007—amendment no. 2 governs.

EXHIBIT 11.7	Statutes Template for Canoga Case — State Privacy Statute

Issue:	Citation Information:
Did the orchestra impermissibly violate Canoga's privacy by prohibiting off-duty smoking?	• *West's New Mexico Statutes Annotated* • *§§ 50-11-1 to 50-11-6* • *2003*
Date of events: *September 7, 2007*	
Date of research: *Dec. 10, 2007*	

Search and Find:

located statute by . . . *Employee Privacy Act in index.*	updated by . . . *2007 pocket part—nothing new. Nothing new in advance legislative service.*
	as needed, found former law by . . . *NA; statute dates to 1991.*

Information and Implications:

"Employee" is a person performing a service for wages — § 2A. True of Canoga.
"Employer" is a person that has one or more employees; a corporation can be a person — § 2B & C. Orchestra qualifies.
It is unlawful for an employer to require as a condition of employment that an employee abstain from smoking during nonworking hours, provided the individual complies with policies regulating smoking on the employer's premises during working hours. § 3A(1) Orchestra's ban does this.
There is an exception for bona fide occupational requirement that is reasonably and rationally related to the employment activities of a particular employee or group of employees — § 3B(2). Possibly true of ban.
An aggrieved employee can sue for damages (wages and benefits) — § 4.
A prevailing party receives costs and reasonable attorney fees — § 5.

Next Steps:

questions to consider:	leads to follow:
Is not smoking reasonably and rationally related to the performance of wind and brass players?	*No cases. Perhaps look for similar statutes with cases in other states?*

Statutes in annotated codes in paper

▶ Select an appropriate annotated code.

▶ Use the index, statutory outlines, or popular names table to identify the pertinent statute.

▶ Locate the statute's current language in the main volume, updating materials, or both.

▶ Read the correct and complete statutory language.

▶ Review the annotation: statutory history notes, case descriptions, and references to related law and commentary.

Paper unofficial annotated codes exist at both the federal and state levels. These codes are very useful because they provide annotations: the statute's background; descriptions of cases citing the statute; and references to other sources, such as administrative regulations, related statutes, and commentary. Furthermore, unofficial annotated codes are updated fairly quickly.

Although each annotated code is unique, they share various general characteristics. Exhibit 11.1 (at page 224) is an excerpt from the New Mexico Constitution from an annotated unofficial code. This part focuses on federal codes. Exhibit 11.10 (at pages 245–50) is the ADA provision defining "disability," found in one of the two main unofficial annotated federal codes.

Select an appropriate code. Your first step is to select an annotated code for your jurisdiction. Federal statutes appear in two unofficial codes: *United States Code Annotated* (U.S.C.A.), published by Thomson West, and *United States Code Service* (U.S.C.S.), published by LexisNexis. These two codes contain the same statutory sections and use the same organizational scheme as U.S.C., the official code. Exhibit 11.10 is from U.S.C.S.

Use an index, outlines, or table. To locate a pertinent statute within a code, you generally will choose from three research approaches.

The index approach is probably the most successful in most situations. U.S.C.A. and U.S.C.S. both have a multivolume general index that is issued annually, so it is fairly current. In addition, most of the fifty titles in U.S.C.A. and U.S.C.S. have an individual title index, which usually is located in the last hardbound volume of the title.

A second method for finding a pertinent statute within a code is to use the statute's outlines. For many codes (including the federal codes), you will start with a list of titles, then move to a list of chapters within a title, and then to a list of sections within a chapter. Exhibit 11.8 (at page 241) lists the titles of the federal code. In U.S.C.A. and U.S.C.S., the list of chapters for each title appears at the front of each volume for the title or at the beginning of a new title in midvolume; the list of sections within a chapter is found at the

EXHIBIT 11.8	Titles of United States Code

1. General Provisions
2. The Congress
3. The President
4. Flag and Seal, Seat of Government, and the States
5. Government Organization and Employees
6. Domestic Security
7. Agriculture
8. Aliens and Nationality
9. Arbitration
10. Armed Forces
11. Bankruptcy
12. Banks and Banking
13. Census
14. Coast Guard
15. Commerce and Trade
16. Conservation
17. Copyrights
18. Crimes and Criminal Procedure
19. Customs Duties
20. Education
21. Food and Drugs
22. Foreign Relations and Intercourse
23. Highways
24. Hospitals and Asylums
25. Indians

26. Internal Revenue Code
27. Intoxicating Liquors
28. Judiciary and Judicial Procedure
29. Labor
30. Mineral Lands and Mining
31. Money and Finance
32. National Guard
33. Navigation and Navigable Waters
*34. [Navy]
35. Patents
36. Patriotic and National Observances, Ceremonies and Organizations
37. Pay and Allowances of the Uniformed Services
38. Veterans' Benefits
39. Postal Service
40. Public Buildings, Property, and Works
41. Public Contracts
42. The Public Health and Welfare
43. Public Lands
44. Public Printing and Documents
45. Railroads
46. Shipping
47. Telegraphs, Telephones, and Radiotelegraphs
48. Territories and Insular Possessions
49. Transportation
50. War and National Defense

*This title has been eliminated by the enactment of Title 10.

beginning of each chapter. The outline approach can be more difficult than the index approach if the title topics are very general, as is often true.

If you already know the name of the statute you are seeking, a third approach is to use a popular names table. Some, but not all, statutes have official or popular names for easy identification. U.S.C.A. and U.S.C.S. both have a Popular Names Table volume.

Locate the current language. After you have identified a potentially pertinent statute, your next task is to locate its current language. Much of the time, the current language will be in the main volume. Sometimes, however, the current language will be newer than the main volume and thus will appear in updating materials.

Most codes are updated in stages:

☐ First, the initial update generally is an annual pocket part or supplement pamphlet, filed in the back of or after the main hardbound volume to which it pertains. The initial update for a looseleaf code generally consists of supplement pages filed under a supplement tab in the same binder.

☐ Second, even newer information appears in one or more supplements that update the entire code and accordingly are shelved at the end of the code; these pamphlets appear as needed and may or may not be cumulative.

☐ Third, the advance legislative service provides the language of newly enacted laws.

U.S.C.A. and U.S.C.S. both use these various supplements.

The first and second updating publications contain material that is similar in kind to that found in the main volume, and they typically are organized as the annotated code itself is, so it is easy to see whether there is any updating material for your statute. New statutory language is presented so that its relationship to the old language is clear. For example, there may be references to the main volume for sections or subsections that were not changed, whereas an amended section will be printed as amended. There generally is not new statutory language; more often, the new material is additional annotations. Exhibit 11.11 (at page 251) is from a U.S.C.S. cumulative supplementary pamphlet.

By contrast, advance legislative service pamphlets contain reprints of new laws; they do not contain annotation material. Because advance legislative service pamphlets typically are not organized so as to parallel the code, but rather chronologically, as laws are enacted, they typically have two means of access. First, the table of statutory sections affected by new legislation is useful when you have located a pertinent statute in the code and want to see whether it has changed. See Exhibit 11.12 (at page 252). Second, the subject index is most useful when there is no pertinent statute in the code. See Exhibit 11.13 (at page 253). Because these two means of access serve somewhat different functions, you should check both.

Recall that statutes generally operate prospectively, so you need to locate the language that was or will be in effect at the time of your client's events. Most of the time, that language will be in the main volume or update. However, if your client's facts occurred some time ago, check the notes at the end of each provision to learn about your statute's date(s) of enactment. If language other than what is presented in the main volume applies to your client's situation, you generally will need to use session laws, described later. See Exhibit 11.9 (at page 243).

Study the correct and complete language. The tasks of locating and reading the pertinent language tend to overlap. You probably will skim the language you find first, typically in the main volume or perhaps in a pocket part, to ascertain whether it is indeed pertinent. Next you will want to check for newer language and discern how new language fits with the older language. Then you will study the statute, as you have assembled it. The process of carefully reading a statute is described previously. Discern the various elements of the statute, check cross-references, and focus on every word of the pertinent provision(s).

EXHIBIT 11.9	Timing of Statutes and Paper Code Publications

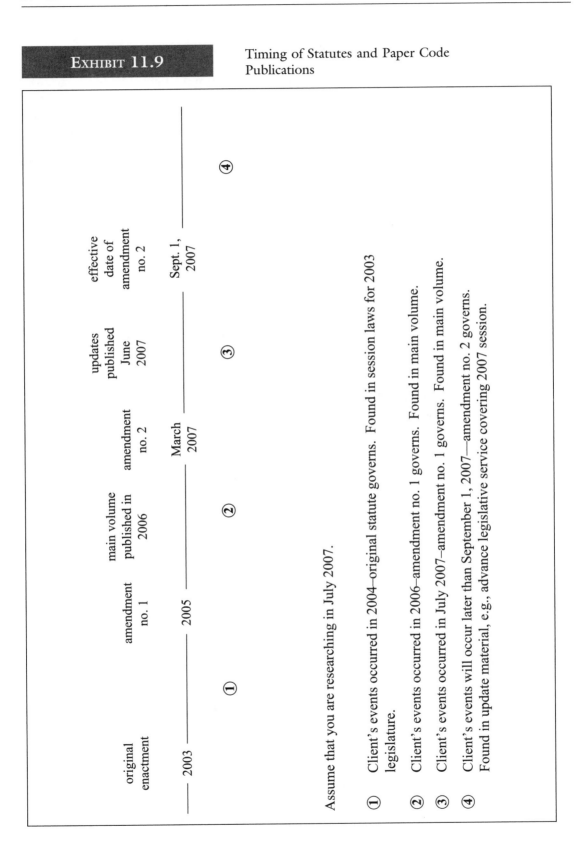

original enactment

amendment no. 1

main volume published in 2006

amendment no. 2

March 2007

updates published June 2007

effective date of amendment no. 2

Sept. 1, 2007

2003 — 2005 — ① ② ③ ④

Assume that you are researching in July 2007.

① Client's events occurred in 2004–original statute governs. Found in session laws for 2003 legislature.

② Client's events occurred in 2006–amendment no. 1 governs. Found in main volume.

③ Client's events occurred in July 2007–amendment no. 1 governs. Found in main volume.

④ Client's events will occur later than September 1, 2007—amendment no. 2 governs. Found in update material, e.g., advance legislative service covering 2007 session.

Review the annotation. Once you have studied the statute itself, you should review the annotation, in the main volume and updating volumes. Again, see Exhibit 11.10 (at pages 245–50) and Exhibit 11.11 (at page 251).

Of particular importance are the descriptions of cases interpreting the statute. There may be a few to literally hundreds of case descriptions, depending on how much litigation the statute has spawned. The editors likely created a topical framework for the case descriptions; if so, be sure to review that framework to discern where cases pertinent to your research problem should appear and focus on those portions of the annotation. See Exhibit 11.9 (at page 243). As you read the case descriptions, look for cases that will be particularly useful to you, based on your legal issue, factual similarity to your client's situation, court, and date of decision.

Next, review the rest of the annotation material. You may, for example, find references to administrative agency materials or potentially pertinent commentary.

U.S.C.A. and U.S.C.S. both provide abundant annotation material; however, there are some differences. For example, U.S.C.A. provides references to pertinent West key numbers; U.S.C.S. does not. Because the two competing annotated codes are not identical, you may research in both at times, particularly when the first one you consult has no pertinent case descriptions or does not present the case descriptions in a framework that fits your research needs.

Exhibit 11.14 (at page 254) is our statutes template filled in to reflect our research into the ADA definition of "disability."

EXHIBIT 11.10	Annotated Federal Statute, from United States Code Service (paper source)

OPPORTUNITIES FOR DISABLED

42 USCS § 12102

action under ADA (42 USCS §§ 12101 et seq.), even though he claims he is disabled within meaning of ADA, and food allowances were denied him, where problem with allowances was rectified to his satisfaction within matter of months, because there is no remaining claim that he was denied benefits because of disability. Hook v Mutha (2001, SD NY) 168 F Supp 2d 77.

13. Miscellaneous

Individual, who was dismissed, due to hypertension, from mechanic's job which required driving commercial motor vehicles, is not regarded as "having substantially limiting impairment" under Americans with Disabilities Act (42 USCS §§ 12101 et seq.). Murphy v UPS (1999) 527 US 516, 144 L Ed 2d 484, 119 S Ct 2133, 99 CDOS 4857, 99 Daily Journal DAR 6259, 9 AD Cas 691, 1999 Colo J C A R 3749, 12 FLW Fed S 435.

City and state officials shall install curb ramps or slopes on every city street, at any intersection having curbs or other barriers to access, where bids for resurfacing were let after January 26, 1992, where Justice Department regulations promulgated under 42 USCS § 12134 require installation of curb ramps or other sloped areas on "altered" streets, roads, and highways, and advocates for disabled claim this applies to resurfaced streets, because broad interpretation of regulation to include resurfaced streets is consistent with § 12101 statement of purpose specifically identifying "discriminatory effects of architectural barriers" as evil to be addressed. Kinney v Yerusalim (1993, ED Pa) 812 F Supp 547, 1 ADD 369, 2 AD Cas 444, affd (1993, CA3 Pa) 9 F3d 1067, 3 ADD 444, 2 AD Cas 1470, cert den (1994) 511 US 1033, 128 L Ed 2d 196, 114 S Ct 1545, 3 AD Cas 448.

Massachusetts statute, ALM GL c 123 § 18A, requiring patients in state mental health facilities to contribute to cost of representation, when representative is appointed by court, violates due process clause of Fourteenth Amendment and Americans with Disabilities Act, 42 USCS §§ 12101 et seq. T.P. v DuBois (1993, DC Mass) 843 F Supp 775, 5 ADD 764, 3 AD Cas 288.

In action alleging that provision of Georgia's Medicaid plan, by providing reimbursement for necessary liquid diet only to individuals in nursing homes, has tendency to isolate and segregate individuals with disabilities in contravention of intent of 42 USCS § 12101 to end such segregation, section

cited by plaintiff does not itself provide cause of action to him. Hodges v Smith (1995, ND Ga) 910 F Supp 646, 49 Soc Sec Rep Serv 866, 13 ADD 1100, 5 AD Cas 229.

Medical technologist's disclosure of his HIV status to supervisor was not result of job-related inquiry that was consistent with business necessity, as would require employer to keep confidential such disclosure under 42 USCS § 12101, where before disclosure employer made no inquiry into technologist's health, and information was obtained through private medical exam, which was non-work related. Ballard v Healthsouth Corp. (2001, ND Tex) 147 F Supp 2d 529, 11 AD Cas 1717.

In employee's suit for discrimination due to his disability under Americans with Disability Act (ADA), 42 USCS § 12101 et seq., where collective bargaining agreement covering employee prohibited discrimination against any employee, and employee alleged that he was fired, reinstated, and then fired again in retaliation for earlier discrimination claims, court found that (1) employee's hybrid claim under 29 USCS § 185 was barred by six month limitations period; (2) employee's claim filed with Maine Human Rights Commission (MHRC) gave adequate notice to union of employee's complaints, including his claim that union did not fairly represent him at second arbitration so as to constitute exhaustion of his administrative remedies; (3) employee's ADA claim adequately stated claims that union deliberately acquiesced in employer's discrimination and that union breached its duty of fair representation; and (4) his claim of retaliation was adequate where he alleged that union failed to assist him in grievance process. Greenier v Pace, Local No. 1188 (2002, DC Me) 201 F Supp 2d 172, 13 AD Cas 127.

Action brought by physician who claimed his license was revoked in violation of Americans with Disabilities Act, 42 USCS § 12101 et seq., was dismissed as barred by Rooker-Feldman doctrine. Harris v N.Y. State Dep't of Health (2002, SD NY) 202 F Supp 2d 143.

Where employee was assigned to smoke-free division to accommodate her asthma, under ADA, if she wished accommodation of being assigned to "totally" smoke-free building she had to make that request; employer, who would not be held liable for failing to provide accommodation that employee had not requested in first place, was granted summary judgment. Thorner-Green v N.Y. City Dep't of Corr. (2002, ED NY) 207 F Supp 2d 11.

§ 12102. Definitions

As used in this Act:

(1) Auxiliary aids and services. The term "auxiliary aids and services" includes—

EXHIBIT 11.10   *(continued)*

42 USCS § 12102   PUBLIC HEALTH AND WELFARE

(A) qualified interpreters or other effective methods of making aurally delivered materials available to individuals with hearing impairments;

(B) qualified readers, taped texts, or other effective methods of making visually delivered materials available to individuals with visual impairments;

(C) acquisition or modification of equipment or devices; and

(D) other similar services and actions.

(2) Disability. The term "disability" means, with respect to an individual—

(A) a physical or mental impairment that substantially limits one or more of the major life activities of such individual;

(B) a record of such an impairment; or

(C) being regarded as having such an impairment.

(3) State. The term "State" means each of the several States, the District of Columbia, the Commonwealth of Puerto Rico, Guam, American Samoa, the Virgin Islands, the Trust Territory of the Pacific Islands, and the Commonwealth of the Northern Mariana Islands.

(July 26, 1990, P. L. 101-336, § 3, 104 Stat. 329.)

HISTORY; ANCILLARY LAWS AND DIRECTIVES

References in text:

"This Act", referred to in this section, is Act July 26, 1990, P. L. 101-336, 104 Stat. 327, popularly referred to as the Americans with Disabilities Act of 1990, which appears generally as 42 USCS §§ 12101 et seq. For full classification, consult USCS Tables volumes.

Other provisions:

Termination of Trust Territory of the Pacific Islands. For termination of Trust Territory of the Pacific Islands, see note preceding 48 USCS § 1681.

CROSS REFERENCES

This section is referred to in 20 USCS §§ 1003, 1228c, 2302, 9202; 29 USCS § 2801; 40 USCS § 550; 47 USCS § 255; 42 USCS §§ 280B-1c, 3796gg-7, 3796hh, 12211, 12581, 12594.

RESEARCH GUIDE

Federal Procedure:

8 Moore's Federal Practice (Matthew Bender 3d ed.), Jury Trial of Right § 38.33.

10 Moore's Federal Practice (Matthew Bender 3d ed.), Judgments; Costs § 54.171.

19 Moore's Federal Practice (Matthew Bender 3d ed.), Reviewability of Issues § 205.07.

6 Fed Proc L Ed, Civil Rights §§ 344, 346.

Am Jur:

45A Am Jur 2d, Job Discrimination §§ 16–21, 27–104, 168–213.

45B Am Jur 2d, Job Discrimination § 821.

45C Am Jur 2d, Job Discrimination §§ 2539–2541, 2543, 2544, 2654, 2657, 2661, 2664, 2699, 2717, 2733, 2798.

EXHIBIT 11.10   *(continued)*

OPPORTUNITIES FOR DISABLED   **42 USCS § 12102**

79 Am Jur 2d, Welfare § 18.
82 Am Jur 2d, Workers' Compensation §§ 368, 606, 611.
Am Jur 2d, New Topic Service, Americans with Disabilities Act §§ 1–4, 7,
10, 18, 19, 29, 34, 259, 260, 311, 314, 321, 322, 332, 359, 489, 609, 615–
619, 624, 659, 670, 681, 693.

Am Jur Trials:
74 Am Jur Trials, Disability Discrimination Based on Dyslexia in Employment Actions Under the Americans with Disabilities Act, p. 255.

Forms:
5 Fed Procedural Forms L Ed, Civil Rights §§ 10:216, 217, 222, 229, 232–
234, 245, 246.
11B Am Jur Legal Forms 2d, Leases of Real Property §§ 161:971–981.

Annotations:
Who is qualified individual with disability, for purposes of Americans with
Disabilities Act of 1990, as amended (ADA) (42 USCS §§ 12101 et seq.)—
Supreme Court cases. 143 L Ed 2d 1133.
The Propriety, Under ERISA (29 USCS §§ 1001 et seq.) and the Americans
With Disabilities Act (42 USCS §§ 12101 et seq.) of Capping Health In-
surance Coverage for HIV–Related Claims. 131 ALR Fed 191.
What Constitutes Substantial Limitation on Major Life Activity of Work-
ing for Purposes of Americans with Disabilities Act (42 USCS §§ 12101–
12213). 141 ALR Fed 603.
When is Individual Regarded as Having, or Perceived to Have, Impairment
Within Meaning of Americans With Disabilities Act (42 U.S.C.A
§ 12102(2)(C) [42 USCS § 12102(2)(C)]). 148 ALR Fed 305.

Law Review Articles:
Teitelbaum. Accessibility of ATMs to handicapped persons. 45 Bus Law
1981.
Murphy. Disabilities discrimination under the Americans with Disabilities
Act. 36 Cath Law 13, 1995.
Hamilton. New protections for persons with mental illness in the workplace
under the Americans with Disabilities Act of 1990 40 Clev St L Rev 63,
1992.
DuYang. Women with disabilities in the work force: outlook for the 1990's.
13 Harv Women's L J 13.
Laarman. The effect of the Americans with Disabilities Act on health and
other employee benefit plans. 50 Inst on Fed Tax'n 1.1, 1992.
ADA study and commentary. 79 Iowa L Rev 853, May 1994.
Blanck. Employment integration, economic opportunity, and the Americans
with Disabilities Act: empirical study from 1990–1993. 79 Iowa L Rev 853,
May 1994.
Rischitelli. Avoiding discriminatory drug testing practices under the Ameri-
cans with Disabilities Act. 14 J Legal Med 597, December 1993.
DeSario; Slack. The Americans with Disabilities Act and refusals to provide
medical care to persons with HIV/AIDS. 27 J Marshall L Rev 347, Winter
1994.
Feldblum. The Americans With Disabilities Act definition of disability. 7
Lab Law 11, Winter 1991.

EXHIBIT 11.10	*(continued)*

42 USCS § 12102   PUBLIC HEALTH AND WELFARE

Krugel. AIDS and the ADA: maneuvering through a legal minefield. 44 Lab LJ 408, July 1993.

Calloway. Dealing with diversity: changing theories of discrimination. 10 St John's J Legal Comment 481, Summer 1995.

Stabile. AIDS, insurance and the ADA. 10 St John's J Legal Comment 533, Summer 1995.

Peplow. Uncharted ground: the extent of insurance coverage under the Americans with Disabilities Act. 10 St John's J Legal Comment 551, Summer 1995.

Silberman. The interaction of the Americans with Disabilities Act and alternative dispute resolution within the EEOC. 10 St John's J Legal Comment 573, Summer 1995.

Spencer. Clearing the docket: alternative dispute resolution under the Americans with Disabilities. 10 St John's J Legal Comment 589, Summer 1995.

Outten. Alternative dispute resolution and the Americans with Disabilities Act. 10 St John's J Legal Comment 597, Summer 1995.

Adler. Arbitration and the Americans with Disabilities Act. 37 St Louis U LJ 1005, Summer 1993.

Zaken. The confusion created by the Carparts [Carparts Distribution Center, Inc. v. Automotive Wholesaler's Association, 37 F.3d 12 (1st Cir. 1994)] decision. 10 St. John's J Legal Comment 543, Summer 1995.

Hanssens. Healthcare insurance, AIDS and the ADA. 10 St. John's J Legal Comment 567, Summer 1995.

Dryovage. Your office and the ADA. 30 Trial 36, January 1994.

Hodges. The Americans with Disabilities Act in the unionized workplace. 48 U Miami L Rev 567, January 1994.

SHEPARD'S® Citations Service. For further research of authorities referenced here, use SHEPARD'S to be sure your case or statute is still good law and to find additional authorities that support your position. SHEPARD'S is available exclusively from LexisNexis™.

INTERPRETIVE NOTES AND DECISIONS

I. WHAT CONSTITUTES DISABILITY, IN GENERAL

A. General Considerations
1. Generally
2. Relation to other laws
3. Consideration of mitigating or corrective measures
4. Temporary or permanent nature of condition

B. What Is "Major Life Activity"
5. Generally
6. Awareness of surroundings
7. Caring for others
8. Cleaning and housework
9. Concentration
10. Daycare attendance
11. Engaging in sexual relations
12. Interacting with others
13. Lifting, bending or reaching
14. Liver function
15. Reproduction or procreation
16. Sleeping
17. Speaking
18. Writing or keyboarding
19. Miscellaneous

C. Impairment that Substantially Limits Major Life Activity
20. Generally
21. What constitutes physical or mental impairment
22. Direct or indirect effect of impairment

EXHIBIT 11.10   *(continued)*

OPPORTUNITIES FOR DISABLED	42 USCS § 12102, n 1

OPPORTUNITIES FOR DISABLED

23. Duration, episodic nature or long-term impact of impairment
24. Severity or percentage of impairment
25. Range or breadth of limitation
26. Mitigating or corrective measures
27. Individualized or case-by-case assessment of effect of impairment
28. Eligibility for social security disability benefits
29. Particular impairments effecting job activity
30. —Inability to return to particular job or narrow class of jobs
31. —Particular restrictions on job- related activities
32. —Temporary, episodic or recurring impairment or limitation
33. Other particular impairments and activities
34. Miscellaneous

D. Record of Impairment

35. Generally
36. Particular circumstances

E. Being Regarded as Having Impairment

37. Generally
38. Awareness of impairment or symptoms
39. Falsity of perception of disability
40. Incapacity as to single job or narrow range of jobs
41. Restrictions on amount or type of work
42. Temporary incapacity or limitation
43. Employer's efforts at accommodation
44. Request for medical examination
45. Other particular circumstances

II. PARTICULAR CONDITIONS AS DISABILITIES

46. Allergies or chemical sensitivities
47. Aneurysm
48. Arthritis
49. Asthma
50. Back injuries
51. —Particular weight-lifting restrictions
52. Brain, head or neck injury or condition
53. Breast conditions
54. Cancer and tumors
55. Carpal tunnel syndrome
56. Cervical injury or condition
57. Chronic fatigue syndrome
58. Cirrhosis
59. Colitis
60. Cystic fibrosis
61. Diabetes
62. Drug or alcohol dependency
63. Epilepsy and seizures
64. Epstein-Barr syndrome
65. Eye conditions
66. Facial disfigurement
67. Flu
68. Hand, arm or shoulder injury or condition
69. Hearing impairment or condition
70. Hernia

42 USCS § 12102, n 1

71. Heart condition
72. Hepatitis
73. High blood pressure and circulatory conditions
74. HIV and AIDS
75. Infertility
76. Irritable bowel syndrome
77. Learning disability
78. Leg, foot, knee and hip injuries and conditions
79. —Use of brace
80. Lupus
81. Mental disorders
82. —Attention deficit hyperactivity disorder
83. —Bi-polar or manic depressive disorder
84. —Depression
85. ——Use of medication
86. —Mental retardation
87. —Obsessive compulsive disorder
88. —Phobias and panic disorders
89. —Schizophrenia
90. —Stress disorders; post-traumatic stress disorder
91. Migraine headaches
92. Miscarriage
93. Multiple sclerosis
94. Obesity
95. Pain
96. Pregnancy
97. Skin condition
98. Sleep disorder or deprivation
99. Tendinitis
100. Other repetitive stress injuries
101. Miscellaneous

I. WHAT CONSTITUTES DISABILITY, IN GENERAL

A. General Considerations

1. Generally

Americans with Disabilities Act, by defining disability "with respect to individual" (42 USCS § 12102(2)) and in terms of impact of impairment on "such individual" (42 USCS § 12102(2)(B)), expresses mandate to determine existence of disabilities on case-by-case basis. Albertson's, Inc. v Kirkingburg (1999) 527 US 555, 144 L Ed 2d 518, 119 S Ct 2162, 99 CDOS 4846, 99 Daily Journal DAR 6243, 9 AD Cas 694, 1999 Colo J C A R 3740, 12 FLW Fed S 443.

Former employee who was totally and permanently disabled and who conceded that she could not perform essential functions of her former job with or without accommodation was not qualified individual with disability within meaning of ADA (42 USCS §§ 12101 et seq.). EEOC v CNA Ins. Cos. (1996, ND Ill) 14 ADD 48, 5 AD Cas 1763, affd (1996, CA7 Ill) 96 F3d 1039, 18 ADD 759, 5 AD Cas 1769, 20 EBC 1949 (criticized in Ford v Schering-Plough Corp. (1998, CA3 NJ) 145 F3d 601, 8 AD Cas 190, 22 EBC 1866).

EXHIBIT 11.10   *(continued)*

---

42 USCS § 12102, n 61

PUBLIC HEALTH AND WELFARE

Rehabilitation Act (29 USCS §§ 701 et seq.), where his diabetes merely ''requires medication, fixed meal schedule, timely snack breaks, and opportunity to use bathroom very frequently during work day,'' because he fails to show that any major life activities are substantially limited by his diabetes. Sepulveda v Glickman. (2001, DC Puerto Rico) 167 F Supp 2d 186, 12 AD Cas 1255, 87 BNA FEP Cas 539.

62. Drug or alcohol dependency

Recovering drug or alcohol abuser who is not currently using drugs or alcohol is ''disabled'' under ADA (42 USCS §§ 12101 et seq.) by reason of having record of substance addiction; however, individual who merely has record of drug or alcohol use, but not addiction, is not disabled. Buckley v Consolidated Edison Co. (1997, CA2 NY) 127 F3d 270, 24 ADD 758, 7 AD Cas 794, vacated on other grounds (1998, CA2 NY) 155 F3d 150, 8 AD Cas 847.

Pharmacist who had sought treatment for his cocaine addiction was not disabled by reason of being perceived by his employer as drug addict, where pharmacist presented no evidence that employer regarded him as being substantially limited in major life activity of working. Zenor v El Paso Healthcare Sys., Ltd. (1999, CA5 Tex) 176 F3d 847, 9 AD Cas 609.

Alcoholism is impairment, and where alcoholics are unable to maintain abstinence and continued recovery in independent living situation, they are substantially limited in their ability to care for themselves, and thus such individuals are disabled under ADA (42 USCS § 12102). Reg'l Econ. Cmty. Action Program, Inc. v City of Middletown (2002, CA2 NY) 281 F3d 333, 12 AD Cas 1317, corrected (2002, CA2 NY) 294 F3d 35, cert den (2002, US) 154 L Ed 2d 16, 123 S Ct 74.

Drug addiction that substantially limits one or more major life activities is recognized disability under ADA (42 USCS § 12102). Thompson v Davis (2002, CA9 Cal) 282 F3d 780, 2002 CDOS 2307, 2002 Daily Journal DAR 2743, 12 AD Cas 1551, amd (2002, CA9 Cal) 13 AD Cas 500 and amd, reprinted as amd (2002, CA9 Cal) 295 F3d 890, 2002 CDOS 6038, 2002 CDOS 6040, 2002 Daily Journal DAR 7595.

Assistant to union executive failed to make showing that executive considered assistant to be disabled by being substantially limited in major life activity of working, owing to alcoholism problem, as required to maintain action under 42 USCS § 12102(2)(A). Wilson v International Bhd. of Teamsters (1999, DC Dist Col) 47 F Supp 2d 8.

Former employee's 2 hospitalizations for alcoholism within 10-year period were not ''record of such impairment'' such as would support claim that she had history of alcoholism that substantially limited major life activity under 42 USCS § 12102(2), where

employee never provided employer with any medical restrictions throughout her term of employment, and her personnel file was devoid of any indication that she suffered from alcoholism. Bilodeau v Mega Indus. (1999, DC Me) 50 F Supp 2d 27, 9 AD Cas 850.

Recovering alcoholic corrections officer cannot state prima facie case under Americans with Disabilities Act (ADA) (42 USCS §§ 12101 et seq.), even though he asserts he was denied promotions discriminatorily on account of his alcoholism, because alcoholism is not disability per se under ADA, and officer failed to demonstrate that his alcoholism substantially interfered with major life activity. Roberts v New York State Dep't of Correctional Servs. (1999, WD NY) 63 F Supp 2d 272.

Recovering heroin addicts, who were prospective clients for proposed methadone treatment clinic opposed by city residents, were ''persons with disabilities'' under 42 USCS § 12102(2), where addiction was long-term problem affecting major life activities of working and parenting, at minimum, and prospective clients had record of or were regarded as being disabled. MX Group, Inc. v City of Covington (2000, ED Ky) 106 F Supp 2d 914, 13 AD Cas 317, affd (2002, CA6 Ky) 293 F3d 326, 13 AD Cas 323, 2002 FED App 205P.

Former employee did not establish that he was disabled under 42 USCS § 12102(2)(C) because employer regarded him as impaired, based on one incident in which supervisor suggested that employee was forgetful because he had drinking problem. Pace v Paris Maint. Co. (2000, SD NY) 107 F Supp 2d 251, 11 AD Cas 990, 55 Fed Rules Evid Serv 558, affd (2001, CA2 NY) 7 Fed Appx 94.

Whether denominated as ''nicotine addiction'' or not, tobacco smoking is not ''disability'' within meaning of 42 USCS § 12102. Brashear v Simms (2001, DC Md) 138 F Supp 2d 693.   *

Terminated real estate marketer's disability discrimination claim against former employer is denied, even though he endured short stays in treatment programs and temporary hospitalization, where effects of his inebriation were no different than those experienced by overindulging social drinkers, because, while his alcoholism and depression may have caused him some difficulties and affected how he lived and worked, he has not shown that he had impairment that substantially limited major life activity. Lottinger v Shell Oil Co. (2001, SD Tex) 143 F Supp 2d 743, 6 BNA WH Cas 2d 1825.

Teacher was not impaired in major life activity of working as result of her alcoholism, and, thus, she was not disabled within meaning of 42 USCS § 12102(2), where teacher was terminated for poor performance allegedly related to her alcoholism, but she continued to work in teaching profession as substitute teacher, and she continued to interview for full-time positions. Nucifora v Bridgeport Bd. of Educ. (2001, DC Conn) 188 F Supp 2d 197, affd (2002, CA2 Conn) 36 Fed Appx 472.

EXHIBIT 11.11   Update of Annotated Code,
                     from United States Code Service (paper source)

---

42 USCS § 12101, n 12   PUBLIC HEALTH AND WELFARE

nated before employer knew extent of damage. Head v Glacier Northwest, Inc. (2006, DC Or) 17 AD Cas 1546.

Court did not have jurisdiction to hear disabled hotel patron's motion for attorney's fees following entry of consent decree because patron did not have standing under ADA, as there was no evidence that her injury was "actual or imminent"; patron could not establish standing by showing later actions or intent to return to hotel or geographic area formed after filing of suit. D'Lil v Best Western Encina Lodge & Suites (2006, CD Cal) 415 F Supp 2d 1048.

Store and its owners were not entitled to dismissal of action related to architectural barriers under Americans with Disabilities Act, 42 USCS § 12101 et seq., and Unruh Civil Rights Act, Cal. Civ. Code § 51 et seq., for failure to join operator of common area because operator was not necessary and indispensable party under Fed. R. Civ. P. 19; although store was in shopping center, majority of alleged violations were on property owned and operated by store owners and, therefore, meaningful relief could be granted to complainants in absence of common area operator. Hubbard v Rite Aid Corp. (2006, SD Cal) 433 F Supp 2d 1150.

Employee's Americans with Disabilities Act (ADA), 42 USCS § 12101 et seq., claim was barred because employee did not file timely charge with Equal Employment Opportunities Commission (EEOC) under 42 USCS § 2000e-5(e) because it was filed after expiration of 300 days from his termination; furthermore, equitable tolling did not apply because there was no trickery or other exceptional circumstances. Reid v Rexam Bev. Can Co. (2006, ND Ohio) 434 F Supp 2d 500.

Employer argued that firefighter's Age Discrimination in Employment Act of 1967 (ADEA), 29 USCS § 621 et seq., and Americans with Disabilities Act of 1990 (ADA), 42 USCS § 12101 et seq., claims were time-barred as firefighter failed to file his discrimina-

tion charge with Equal Employment Opportunity Commission within 300 days of alleged discriminatory act—failure to promote firefighter; firefighter did not dispute this argument and recognized that these causes of action were time-barred; in addition, firefighter's argument that he was subject to several continuing violations of ADA and ADEA, which would not be time-barred, failed; not only did firefighter fail to raise these issues in his Equal Employment Opportunity Commission charge, but he failed to raise them in his complaint. Morris v Mayor (2006, DC Md) 437 F Supp 2d 508.

13. Miscellaneous

28 CFR § 35.130(b)(7) makes clear that duty to accommodate is independent basis of liability under Americans with Disabilities Act, 42 USCS §§ 12101 et seq. Wis. Cmty. Servs. v City of Milwaukee (2006, CA7 Wis) 18 AD Cas 918.

Discrimination claims that pretrial detainee who suffered from acute psychosis, and died after he was returned to jail because there was no available hospital bed, failed to demonstrate Eighth and Fourteenth Amendments' deliberate indifference on part of county sheriffs, or violation of Title II of ADA; detainee had refused to take his medication and sheriffs had done everything possible to get him in hands of medical professionals. Winters v Ark. HHS (2006, ED Ark) 437 F Supp 2d 851.

Employee's disability discrimination claims under Americans with Disabilities Act (ADA), 42 USCS §§ 12101 et seq., and Pennsylvania Human Rights Act (PHRA), 42 Pa. Cons. Stat. § 931 et seq., survived employer's motion for summary judgment because material facts were in dispute with respect to whether job requirements identified by employer were essential functions of sales representative's job, whether reasonable accommodations were available, and who was responsible for alleged breakdown in interactive process. Johnson v McGraw-Hill Cos. (2006, WD Pa) 451 F Supp 2d 681, 98 BNA FEP Cas 1659.

§ 12102.   Definitions

RESEARCH GUIDE

Am Jur Proof of Facts:
93 Am Jur Proof of Facts 3d, Parents' or Student's Proof in Action for Educational Services or Tuition Reimbursement Under the Special Education Laws, p. 1.

Law Review Articles:
Stein; Waterstone. Disability, Disparate Impact, and Class Actions. 56 Duke LJ 861, December 2006.

INTERPRETIVE NOTES AND DECISIONS

I. WHAT CONSTITUTES DISABILITY, IN GENERAL

A. General Considerations

2. Relation to other laws

To extent that ADA and 12 USCS § 1831j irreconcilably conflict with 12 USCS § 341(Fifth), these statutes have impliedly amended § 341(Fifth) to grant Federal Reserve Bank limited power to dismiss any of its officers at pleasure by its board of directors, not extending to dismissal on grounds prohibited by ADA or 12 USCS § 1831j; corollary is that as impliedly amended by ADA and 12 USCS § 1831j, 12 USCS

§ 341(Fifth) bestows qualified immunity from liability arising from its exercise, allowing only specified relief, with limits and/or bars against compensatory and/or punitive damages. Fasano v FRB (2006, CA3 NJ) 457 F3d 274, 18 AD Cas 321.

Summary judgment was entered against employee on his suit under Rehabilitation Act of 1973, 29 USCS §§ 701-795, because employee did not offer cognizable evidence sufficient to justify reasonable factfinder in concluding that he suffered impairment satisfying definition of disability found in 42 USCS § 12102(2). Rolland v Potter (2006, DC Mass) 453 F Supp 2d 223.

2622

| EXHIBIT 11.12 | Advance Legislative Service Sections Affected Table, from United States Code Service (paper source) |

TABLE OF CODE SECTIONS ADDED, AMENDED, REPEALED, OR OTHERWISE AFFECTED
110TH CONGRESS FIRST SESSION
(110-1--110-84)

Section	Effect	Public Law No.	
		TITLE 42 (cont'd)	
prec. 7381a	Added	110-69	Sec. 5003(d)(1)
7381a	Amd.	110-69	Sec. 5003(a)
	Amd.	110-69	Sec. 5003(d)(1)
7381b	Amd.	110-69	Sec. 5003(d)(1)
7381c	Amd.	110-69	Sec. 5003(d)(1)
7381d	Amd.	110-69	Sec. 5003(c)
	Amd.	110-69	Sec. 5003(d)(1)
7381e	Amd.	110-69	Sec. 5003(d)(1)
	Amd.	110-69	Sec. 5003(d)(2)
prec. 7381g	Added	110-69	Sec. 5003(d)(3)
7381g	Added	110-69	Sec. 5003(d)(3)
7381g nt.	New	110-69	Sec. 5003(b)
7381h	Added	110-69	Sec. 5003(d)(3)
prec. 7381j	Added	110-69	Sec. 5003(d)(3)
7381j	Added	110-69	Sec. 5003(d)(3)
prec. 7381*l*	Added	110-69	Sec. 5003(d)(3)
7381*l*	Added	110-69	Sec. 5003(d)(3)
prec. 7381n	Added	110-69	Sec. 5003(d)(3)
7381n	Added	110-69	Sec. 5003(d)(3)
prec. 7381p	Added	110-69	Sec. 5003(d)(3)
7381p	Added	110-69	Sec. 5003(d)(3)
prec. 7381r	Added	110-69	Sec. 5003(d)(3)
7381r	Added	110-69	Sec. 5003(d)(3)
9858 nt.	New	110-28	Sec. 8303
10301 nt.	Amd.	110-5	Sec. 2
11319 nt.	New	110-5	Sec. 2
12651i	New	110-5	Sec. 2
12651i nt.	New	110-5	Sec. 2
15302	Amd.	110-28	Sec. 6301(a)
15302 nt.	New	110-28	Sec. 6301(b)
15801 nt.	New	110-69	Sec. 5001
16311	Amd.	110-69	Sec. 5007
16515	New	110-5	Sec. 2
16531	New	110-69	Sec. 5002

| EXHIBIT 11.13 | Advance Legislative Service Index, from United States Code Service (paper source) |

110TH CONGRESS 1ST SESSION

COURT OF APPEALS FOR THE ARMED FORCES.
Amendments to rules of practice and procedure, p. 659.

COURT OF APPEALS FOR THE 1ST CIRCUIT.
Amendments to court rules, p. 177.

COURT OF APPEALS FOR THE 10TH CIRCUIT.
General order no. 95-01, p. 1435.

COURT OF APPEALS FOR THE 11TH CIRCUIT.
Amendment of circuit rules, p. 65.
Amendments to rules and internal operating procedures, p. 187.
Amendments to rules and internal operating procedures and Addendum Five, p. 1443.
General order 33.
Pilot program for electronic records on appeal from the Southern District of AL, extension, p. 65.

COURT OF APPEALS FOR THE 2ND CIRCUIT.
Amendments to local rules, p. 673.

COURT OF APPEALS FOR THE 4TH CIRCUIT.
Amendments to CJA plan and docketing statement forms, p. 1667.
Amendments to local rules, p. 677.
Amendments to rules and internal operating procedures, p. 181.

COURT OF APPEALS FOR THE 8TH CIRCUIT.
Electronic filing, administrative order regarding, p. 457.

COURT OF APPEALS FOR THE 9TH CIRCUIT.
Amendments to rules, p. 813.

COURT OF APPEALS FOR VETERANS CLAIMS.
Amendments to rules, 669, pp. 545.

COURTS-MARTIAL.
Amendments to the manual for courts-martial, United States, Exec. Or. 13430, Exec. Or. 13447, p. 306, p. 1736.

COYLE, ROBERT E.
Fresno, CA.
Robert E. Coyle United States Courthouse designated, P.L. 110-46, p. 782.

CRIME VICTIMS' RIGHTS WEEK, 2007, Proc. 8130, p. 282.

CUBA.
Continuation of national emergency relating to Cuba, regulation of anchorage and movement of vessels, 2007, Pres. Not. February 26, p. 109.

D

D.A.R.E. DAY, 2007, Proc. 8123, p. 269.

DAVIS, CLIFFORD.
Memphis, TN.
Clifford Davis and Odell Horton federal building, designation, P.L. 110-20, p. 158.

DEFENSE DEPARTMENT.
John Warner national defense authorization act for FY2007.
Assignment of certain reporting functions, 2007, Pres. Mem. June 12, p. 703.

DISABLED PERSONS.
National disability employment awareness month, 2007, Proc. 8182, p. 1719.

DISASTERS.
National preparedness month, 2007, Proc. 8170, p. 1695.

DISTRICT OF COLUMBIA.
Lyndon Baines Johnson Department of Education building, designation, P.L. 110-15, p. 142.
Public education.
Home rule act, amendment to reflect charter revisions, P.L. 110-33, p. 649.

DOMESTIC VIOLENCE.
National domestic violence awareness month, 2007, Proc. 8183, p. 1721.

DOMINICAN REPUBLIC.
Dominican Republic-Central America-US free trade agreement, Proc. 8111, p. 83.

DONATE LIFE MONTH, 2007, Proc. 8118, p. 259.

DRUGS AND NARCOTICS.
Columbia.
Continuation of US drug interdiction assistance to government of Columbia, Pres. Det. 2007-28, p. 1467.
Foreign assistance act of 1961.
Largest exporting and importing countries of certain precursor chemicals, Pres. Det. 2007-14, p. 102.

| Exhibit 11.14 | Statutes Template for Canoga Case — Federal Disability Discrimination No. 1 |

Issue:	Citation Information:
Is Canoga protected against disability discrimination? Is nicotine addiction a disability? (If so, additional elements of claim and defense should be analyzed.)	• *United States Code Service* • *Title 42, § 12102* • *2003*
Date of events: *Sept. 7, 2007*	
Date of research: *Dec. 10, 2007*	

Search and Find:	
located statute by . . . *Larson treatise discussion of Americans with Disabilities Act.* *Index to U.S.C.S.: Civil Rights/Disabled Persons/Labor & Employment/Job Discrimination . . .* *Scan of outline — definitions are in second section.*	updated by . . . *Supplementary pamphlet dated October 2007 — nothing new.* *U.S.C.S.'s advance legislative service — nothing new.* *Search in federal courts database for 42 /5 12102 /p smok! nicotine.*
	as needed, found former law by . . . *NA; statute dates to 1990.*

Information and Implications:

" *'Disability' means, with respect to an individual — (A) a physical or mental impairment that substantially limits one or more of the major life activities of such individual; (B) a record of such an impairment; or (C) being regarded as having such an impairment." § 12102(2).*
Need to show impact on major life activities — need more information. As for playing music, Canoga says she can perform well enough; orchestra thinks not.

Next Steps:

questions to consider:	leads to follow:
If smoking does not adversely affect Canoga's performance, but the orchestra thinks it does, could she have a claim under C — being regarded as having an impairment?	*Brashear v. Simms, 138 F. Supp. 2d (D. Md. 2001): in prison context, nicotine addiction is not a disability.*

> **Statutes in commercial online services**
> ▶ Select an appropriate service and code database.
> ▶ Run one or more searches.
> ▶ Obtain and carefully study the correct language.
> ▶ Review the annotation for additional information.

Paper is a medium well suited to statutes. As discussed previously, a paper statutory code is a well organized source, accompanied by several helpful means of access—indexes, outlines, and popular name tables. In addition, you often will move back and forth through a statute, reading various sections. Thus, many lawyers research statutes primarily in paper.

On the other hand, commercial services, especially Westlaw and LexisNexis, provide substantial federal and state statute databases. These databases and the search methods they afford have several distinct advantages:

☐ The information is very current. Because electronic publication is a quick process, you may find very recent changes.

☐ The databases are cumulative; you need not work through several separate publications to be up to date.

☐ It is easier to use specific factual concepts as research terms. A factual term may not appear in a paper code's table of contents or index, but it may appear in a case description or elsewhere in an annotation.

☐ You may move quite easily from one section of the statute to other sections and from the statute to cases and other sources covered in the references.

It is important, of course, to consider the costs of using a commercial service as well. See Exhibit 11.15 (at pages 257–62), the LexisNexis version of the ADA provision permitting prohibition of workplace smoking.

In broad strokes, researching in a statutory database parallels researching in paper annotated codes. You will select an appropriate source; use some means of access to identify the pertinent statute and sections; obtain and carefully study the correct statute; and review the annotation for background information about the statute and references to other sources. The following discussion focuses on how online research differs from paper research. The discussion focuses on federal research; although the volume of materials for state statutes is likely to be much smaller, the research techniques are the same.

Select an appropriate code database. After selecting a service, the initial decision to make is whether to search in an unannotated or annotated code. An unannotated code is smaller, and generally it is wise to search in the smallest useful database. However, the information provided in an annotation generally proves very useful; for example, the terms in your Boolean search may very well appear not in the statute itself but in a case description. Thus, the better choice overall is an annotated code. Especially if you are researching federal statutes, which are voluminous, you may want to use a subject-specific database rather than the large database encompassing all federal statutes.

As with all online research, be sure you know the scope and currency of the database, including the most recent legislative session it covers.

Run one or more searches. To identify and obtain pertinent sections, you may use various means of access — some paralleling paper research, some available only online. The options are many; the following lists the most commonly used, beginning with options used when you know fairly little about your research topic and ending with options used when you already know about a statute.

☐ Browse or run a key-word search in the index only (which may be a separate database). Browsing parallels using a paper index.

☐ Run a key-word search in or browse the table of contents (which also may be a separate database). Browsing the table of contents parallels reading the outlines of a paper code.

☐ Run a natural-language search in the entire database.

☐ Run a Boolean search in the entire database.

☐ Run a Boolean search in certain documents in the database, for example, the pertinent title or even chapter identified through browsing the table of contents.

☐ Run a Boolean search in certain components of the documents in the database. For example, if the terms you are using are very common, you may want to confine your search to the material at the beginning of the document, e.g., the title, chapter, and section names.

☐ If you already know the name but not the citation of the statute, run a search in the popular names table or in the material at the beginning of the document. The former parallels use of a paper popular names table.

☐ If you already know the citation of the statute, use the document retrieval function to obtain the statute.

Obtain and study the correct language. Nearly always, the statutory language you obtain through an electronic service will be the language currently in effect. Indeed this is one of the advantages of online statutory research. If the service provides a means of checking for very recent legislative activity involving the statute, be sure to do so. To be sure you are using the correct language for your client's situation, read the information about the statute's effective date. If the current language was not in effect at the time of your client's situation, seek the correct language in session laws, discussed later.

As you read a statute online, take care to read the complete statute governing your client's situation. Often your search will lead you to a specific section, but you will need to read additional sections of the statute as well. Use the service's means of switching to adjacent documents, and use links to pursue cross-referenced sections.

Review the annotation. If you are researching in an annotated code, you will obtain not only the statutory language but also the annotation. Peruse this material as you would when researching in a paper annotated code, focusing on cases that will be particularly useful, based on jurisdiction, legal issue, and factual similarity to your client's situation.

Exhibit 11.16 (at page 263) is our statutes template filled in to reflect our research into the explicit treatment of smoking in the ADA.

EXHIBIT 11.15   Annotated Code Online,
from LexisNexis (online source)

---

41 of 41 DOCUMENTS

UNITED STATES CODE SERVICE
Copyright © 2007 Matthew Bender & Company, Inc.,
one of the LEXIS Publishing (TM) companies
All rights reserved

*** CURRENT THROUGH P.L. 110-133, APPROVED 12/6/2007 ***

TITLE 42. THE PUBLIC HEALTH AND WELFARE
CHAPTER 126. EQUAL OPPORTUNITY FOR INDIVIDUALS WITH DISABILITIES
MISCELLANEOUS PROVISIONS

Go to the United States Code Service Archive Directory

42 USCS § 12201

§ 12201. Construction

(a) In general. Except as otherwise provided in this Act, nothing in this Act shall be construed to apply a lesser standard than the standards applied under title V of the Rehabilitation Act of 1973 (29 U.S.C. 790 et seq.) or the regulations issued by Federal agencies pursuant to such title.

(b) Relationship to other laws. Nothing in this Act shall be construed to invalidate or limit the remedies, rights, and procedures of any Federal law or law of any State or political subdivision of any State or jurisdiction that provides greater or equal protection for the rights of individuals with **disabilities** than are afforded by this Act. Nothing in this Act shall be construed to preclude the prohibition of, or the imposition of restrictions on, **smoking** in places of employment covered by title I [42 USCS §§ 12111 et seq.], in transportation covered by title II or III [42 USCS §§ 12131 et seq. or 12181 et seq.], or in places of public accommodation covered by title III [42 USCS §§ 12181 et seq.].

(c) Insurance. Titles I through IV of this Act shall not be construed to prohibit or restrict--
     (1) an insurer, hospital or medical service company, health maintenance organization, or any agent, or entity that administers benefit plans, or similar organizations from underwriting risks, classifying risks, or administering such risks that are based on or not inconsistent with State law; or
     (2) a person or organization covered by this Act from establishing, sponsoring, observing or administering the terms of a bona fide benefit plan that are based on underwriting risks, classifying risks, or administering such risks that are based on or not inconsistent with State law; or
     (3) a person or organization covered by this Act from establishing, sponsoring, observing or administering the terms of a bona fide benefit plan that is not subject to State laws that regulate insurance.

Paragraphs (1), (2), and (3) shall not be used as a subterfuge to evade the purposes of title [titles] I and III [42 USCS §§ 12111 et seq., 12181 et seq.].

(d) Accommodations and services. Nothing in this Act shall be construed to require an individual with a **disability** to accept an accommodation, aid, service, opportunity, or benefit which such individual chooses not to accept.

HISTORY:
    (July 26, 1990, P.L. 101-336, Title V, § 501, 104 Stat. 369.)

HISTORY; ANCILLARY LAWS AND DIRECTIVES

EXHIBIT 11.15   *(continued)*

---

42 USCS § 12201

References in text:
"This Act", referred to in this section, is Act July 26, 1990, P.L. 101-336, 104 Stat. 327, popularly referred to as the Americans with Disabilities Act of 1990, which appears generally as 42 USCS §§ 12101 et seq. For full classification, consult USCS Tables volumes.
"Title I through IV of this Act", referred to in this section, refers to Titles I-IV of Act July 26, 1990, P.L. 101-326, 104 Stat. 330, which appear generally as 42 USCS §§ 12111 et seq. For full classification of such Titles, consult USCS Tables volumes.

Explanatory notes:
The bracketed word "titles" has been inserted in the concluding matter of subsec. (c) to indicate the word probably intended by Congress.

NOTES:

Code of Federal Regulations:
Office of Thrift Supervision, Department of the Treasury--Contracting outreach programs, 12 CFR Part 517.
Office of the Secretary of Transportation--Transportation services for individuals with disabilities (ADA), 49 CFR Part 37.
Office of the Secretary of Transportation--Americans with Disabilities Act (ADA) accessibility specifications for transportation vehicles, 49 CFR Part 38.

Related Statutes & Rules:
This section is referred to in 29 USCS §§ 791, 793, 794.

Research Guide:

Federal Procedure:
6 Fed Proc L Ed, Civil Rights §§ 11:445, 446.
21 Fed Proc L Ed, Job Discrimination § 50:209.

Am Jur:
43 Am Jur 2d, Insurance § 555.
45A Am Jur 2d, Job Discrimination §§ 16-21, 27-35, 40-104, 168-213, 398, 624-731.
45B Am Jur 2d, Job Discrimination §§ 782, 797, 803, 828, 862.
48 Am Jur 2d, Labor and Labor Relations §§ 29, 47.
Am Jur 2d, New Topic Service, Americans with Disabilities Act §§ 27, 29, 50, 74, 119, 124, 253, 257, 277, 314, 615-617, 659, 666.

Am Jur Trials:
74 Am Jur Trials, Disability Discrimination Based on Dyslexia in Employment Actions Under the Americans with Disabilities Act, p. 255.
79 Am Jur Trials, Obtaining Workers' Compensation for Back Injuries, p. 231.

EXHIBIT 11.15	*(continued)*

42 USCS § 12201

Am Jur Proof of Facts:
  33 Am Jur Proof of Facts 3d, Proof of "Disability" Under the Americans With Disabilities Act, p. 1.

Forms:
  5 Fed Procedural Forms L Ed, Civil Rights (2006) §§ 10:188, 190-192, 210, 213, 214, 216, 217, 219.
  12 Fed Procedural Forms L Ed, Job Discrimination §§ 45:296, 297, 320, 322.
  10A Fed Procedural Forms L Ed, Government Officers and Employees (2005) § 35:259.
  11B Am Jur Legal Forms 2d, Leases of Real Property §§ 161:971-981.

Labor and Employment:
  9 Larson on Employment Discrimination, ch 151, Summary and History § 151.05.
  9 Larson on Employment Discrimination, ch 152, Coverage § 152.09.
  9 Larson on Employment Discrimination, ch 154, Prohibited Practices § 154.03.
  9 Larson on Employment Discrimination, ch 155, Permitted Practices; Defenses §§ 155.05, 155.06.
  9 Larson on Employment Discrimination, ch 158, Remedies § 158.03.
  9 Larson on Employment Discrimination, ch 161, Definition of "Individual with a Disability" § 161.02.
  10 Larson on Employment Discrimination, ch 170, Employee Health--AIDS Discrimination § 170.03.
  5 Labor and Employment Law (Matthew Bender), ch 136, An Overview of the Americans with Disabilities Act §
136.09.
  5 Labor and Employment Law (Matthew Bender), ch 139, Prohibition of Discrimination Against a Qualified Individual with a Disability §§ 139.04, 139.08.
  5 Labor and Employment Law (Matthew Bender), ch 142, Enforcement of the ADA and Establishing Discrimination
Under the Act § 142.05.
  6 Labor and Employment Law (Matthew Bender), ch 156, Other Federal Laws Affecting Employee Welfare Benefit
Plans § 156.03.
  7 Labor and Employment Law (Matthew Bender), ch 173, Interaction with Other Laws § 173.02.

Annotations:
  Use of "Last Chance" or "Return to Work" Agreements Under Americans with Disabilities Act.   6 ALR Fed 2d 453.
  Construction and Application of Association Section of Americans with Disabilities Act of 1990, § 102(b)(4), 42
U.S.C.A. § 12112(b)(4) [42 USCS § 12112(b)(4)].   7 ALR Fed 2d 447.
  Parents' Mental Illness or Mental Deficiency As Ground for Termination of Parental Rights--Applicability of Amer-
icans With Disabilities Act.   119 ALR5th 351.

Law Review Articles:
  Davidson. The Civil Rights Act of 1991.   1992 Army Law 3, March 1992.
  Shaller. "Reasonable accommodation" under the Americans with Disabilities Act--what does it mean?   16 Empl Rel
L J 431, Spring 1991.
  Burgdorf. The Americans With Disabilities Act: analysis and implications of a second-generation civil rights statute.
26 Harv C R-C L L Rev 413, Summer 1991.
  Ryan. Americans with disabilities: the legal revolution.   60 J Kan B A 13, Nov 1991.
  Mahoney; Gibofsky. The Americans with Disabilities Act of 1990.   13 J Legal Med 51, March 1992.
  Clegg. Introduction: a brief legislative history of the Civil Rights Act of 1991.   54 La L Rev 1459, July 1994.
  Broas; Nager. Enforcement issues: a practical overview.   54 La L Rev 1473, July 1994.
  Gray. Disparate impact: history and consequences.   54 La L Rev 1487, July 1994.

EXHIBIT 11.15   *(continued)*

---

42 USCS § 12201

Thornburgh. The Americans with Disabilities Act: what it means to all Americans.   41 Lab L J 803, December 1990.

Hernicz. The Civil Rights Act of 1991: from conciliation to litigation--how Congress delegates lawmaking to the courts.   141 Mil L Rev 1, Summer 1993.

Greenberger. A productivity approach to disparate impact and the Civil Rights Act of 1991.   72 Or L Rev 253, Summer 1993.

Geslewitz. Understanding the 1991 Civil Rights Act.   38 Prac Law 57, March 1992.

Miller. How the Americans with Disabilities Act affects your clients.   8 Prac Real Est Law 13, March 1992.

Blumrosen. Society in transition IV: affirmation of affirmative action under the Civil Rights Act of 1991.   45 Rutgers L Rev 903, Summer 1993.

Jones; Leibold; Sola. Civil Rights Act of 1991: race to the finish--civil rights, quotas, and disparate impact in 1991.   45 Rutgers L Rev 1043, Summer 1993.

Thornburgh. The Americans With Disabilities Act: what it means to all Americans.   64 Temp L Rev 375, Summer 1991.

Mikochik. The Constitution and the Americans with Disabilities Act: some first impressions.   64 Temp L Rev 619, Summer 1991.

Harkin. Our newest civil rights law: the Americans with Disabilities Act.   26 Trial 56, December 1990.

Addiction as disability: the protection of alcoholics and drug addicts under the Americans with Disabilities Act of 1990.   44 Vand L Rev 713, April 1991.

Buchanan. A dramatic expansion of rights and remedies: the Americans With Disabilities Act.   64 Wis Law 16, Nov 1991.

Interpretive Notes and Decisions:
  1. Generally   2. Relation to other laws   3.--**Smoking** regulations   4.--Worker compensation laws   5. Insurance safe harbor provisions   6.--Distinction between mental and physical **disabilities**   7.--Use as subterfuge

1. Generally

Claim by city police officer against police pension fund trustees alleging violation of ADA (42 USCS §§ 12101 et seq.) is dismissed since pursuant to 42 USCS § 12201 board was exempt from requirements of ADA. Rodriguez v City of Aurora (1995, ND Ill) 887 F Supp 162, 8 ADD 107, 4 AD Cas 967.

ADA (42 USCS §§ 12101 et seq.) requires employer to offer qualified employee reasonable accommodation, but ADA does not require employer to force or coerce employee into accepting accommodation; in fact, such force or coercion would contravene ADA, which clearly states that employee need not accept proffered accommodation. Roberts v County of Fairfax (1996, ED Va) 937 F Supp 541, 18 ADD 1034, 8 AD Cas 919.

Individual cannot sue directly under Title V "Miscellaneous Provisions" of ADA (42 USCS §§ 12201 et seq.), since there is no indication that Congress intended to create private right of action. Doukas v Metropolitan Life Ins. Co. (1996, DC NH) 950 F Supp 422, 20 ADD 245, 6 AD Cas 262.

Motion to dismiss of Retirement Board of Fireman's Annuity and Benefit Fund was denied where Board was exempt pursuant to § 501(c) of Americans with Disabilities Act of 1990 (ADA), 42 USCS § 12101 et seq., because (1) former fire paramedic brought his claim against Board pursuant to Title II of ADA, conceding that Board was public entity; (2) all parties also agreed that Board administered bona fide benefit plans; (3) pursuant to § 501(c), administrators of bona fide benefit plans were exempt from provisions of ADA; (4) thus, paramedic's claim that Board violated ADA when it refused to reinstate paramedic's suspended duty disability benefits failed to state claim upon which relief can be granted; and (5) paramedic's subterfuge argument could not have saved his claim because subterfuge exception only applied to subchapters I and III of ADA and paramedic's claim was brought pursuant to subchapter II. King v City of Chicago (2003, ND Ill) 15 AD Cas 357, summary judgment gr, judgment entered (2004, ND Ill) 15 AD Cas 359.

Methadone clinic produced sufficient evidence to overcome county's motion for summary judgment on issue of whether its clients were disabled by producing evidence showing that, inter alia, its clients were substantially limited in their ability to care for themselves absent methadone and rehabilitative treatment and that even with treatment they suffered from chronic relapsing illness, their clients were required to demonstrate record of drug use for more than one

Exhibit 11.15   *(continued)*

42 USCS § 12201

year to be admitted into clinic's program, and clients were regarded as disabled by both county and its citizens, as evidenced by protests and news reports. A Helping Hand, L.L.C. v Baltimore County (2005, DC Md) 17 AD Cas 642.

2. Relation to other laws

Provision of Americans with Disabilities Act of 1990 (ADA) (42 USCS § 12201(a))--directing that except as otherwise provided, nothing in ADA shall be construed to apply lesser standard than standards applied under Title V of Rehabilitation Act of 1973 (29 USCS §§ 790 et seq.) or regulations issued by federal agencies pursuant to Title V--requires that ADA be construed to grant at least as much protection as provided by regulations implementing Rehabilitation Act. Bragdon v Abbott (1998) 524 US 624, 141 L Ed 2d 540, 118 S Ct 2196, 98 CDOS 5021, 98 Daily Journal DAR 6973, 8 AD Cas 239, 1998 Colo J C A R 3268, 11 FLW Fed S 726.

When interpreting ADA (42 USCS §§ 12101 et seq.), 42 USCS § 12201(a) does not require court to incorporate into ADA more restrictive language of Rehabilitation Act (29 USCS §§ 701 et seq.), but rather directs court not to do so. McNely v Ocala Star-Banner Corp. (1996, CA11 Fla) 99 F3d 1068, 18 ADD 614, 10 FLW C 542, 6 AD Cas 78, 10 FLW Fed C 542, cert den (1997) 520 US 1228, 137 L Ed 2d 1028, 117 S Ct 1819, 6 AD Cas 1314 and (criticized in Pernice v City of Chicago (2001, CA7 Ill) 237 F3d 783, 11 AD Cas 608) and (criticized in McLeod v Parsons Corp. (2003, CA6 Tenn) 73 Fed Appx 846).

Under 42 USCS § 1981, claimant is not prevented from recovering greater damages under state law claim that is virtually identical to capped federal claim. Gagliardo v Connaught Labs. (2002, CA3 Pa) 311 F3d 565, 13 AD Cas 1345.

Because directive of 42 USCS § 12201(a) required courts to construe Americans with Disabilities Act (ADA), 42 USCS § 12101 et seq., to grant at least as much protection as was provided by regulations implementing Rehabilitation Act of 1973, 29 USCS § 701 et seq., and ADA's legislative history expressly stated that ADA incorporated many of standards of discrimination that were set out in Rehabilitation Act's implementing regulations, including obligation to provide reasonable accommodations unless it would result in undue hardship on operation of employer's business, it was plain that ADA required employers to provide reasonable accommodations for employees that they regarded as disabled. D'Angelo v Conagra Foods (2005, CA11 Fla) 422 F3d 1220, 16 AD Cas 1825, 18 FLW Fed C 908.

Given express provision of 42 USCS § 12201(b), ADA (42 USCS §§ 12101 et seq.) does not completely supplant state laws concerning discrimination against individuals with disabilities so that any action under such law would necessarily state federal claim; thus, action brought in state court, alleging violations of state's Civil Rights Act for Handicapped Persons, is not properly removed by defendant corporation to federal district court on theory that action necessarily states claim under ADA, and plaintiff's motion to remand case to state court will be granted.   Beaumont v Exxon Corp. (1994, ED La) 4 ADD 684, 2 AD Cas 1865.

Plaintiff may properly pursue state law claim of fraud in conjunction with his claim under ADA (42 USCS §§ 12101 et seq.), since Act explicitly states that it is not intended to limit, preempt, or foreclose any state remedies which plaintiff might have which might potentially provide plaintiff with greater or different relief than he might be entitled to under ADA. Anderson v Martin Brower Co. (1994, DC Kan) 6 ADD 126, 3 AD Cas 829, 10 BNA IER Cas 1693.

In action alleging that nursing home violated ADA (42 USCS §§ 12101 et seq.) by denying plaintiff admission because of her size and medical condition, plaintiff is not required to exhaust her administrative remedies before bringing federal suit, particularly since exhaustion is not required under Rehabilitation Act (29 USCS §§ 701 et seq.) in such case, and ADA was meant to follow Rehabilitation Act and not to apply lesser standard. Grubbs v Medical Facilities of Am. (1994, WD Va) 7 ADD 570.

Action by police officers alleging that city and board of trustees of pension fund denied officers opportunity to participate in city's police pension fund because of their disabilities is not barred by § 501(b) of ADA (42 USCS § 12201(b)) for failure to initiate state administrative review proceedings to challenge decisions of board. Piquard v City of E. Peoria (1995, CD Ill) 887 F Supp 1106, 11 ADD 428, 4 AD Cas 1716 (criticized in King v City of Chicago (2003, ND Ill) 15 AD Cas 357).

Parties agreed that jury's award of $ 2.5 million in compensatory damages should be allocated entirely to employee's state law claim under N.Y. Exec. Law § 296 instead of under employee's claim under Americans with Disabilities Act of 1990 (ADA), 42 USCS § 12101 et seq., because ADA explicitly preserved employee's right to recover damages under state law not available under federal law, 42 USCS § 12201(b), and N.Y. Exec. Law § 296 placed no limit

EXHIBIT 11.15   *(continued)*

42 USCS § 12201

on amount of compensatory damages that employee could recover. Brady v Wal-Mart Stores, Inc. (2005, ED NY) 16 AD Cas 1672.

Under 42 USCS § 12201(b), 42 USCS § 1983 claim by disabled transit authority customers to redress Americans with Disabilities Act of 1990 (ADA) violations was available against transit authority manager; legislative history of ADA confirmed that 42 USCS § 12201(b) was intended in part to ensure that remedies under 42 USCS § 1983 were available to redress violations of ADA. Disability Rights Council of Greater Wash. v Wash. Metro. Area Transit Auth. (2006, DC Dist Col) 239 FRD 9.

3.–Smoking regulations

Congress did not intend to isolate effects of **smoking** from protections of ADA (42 USCS §§ 12101 et seq.) by leaving regulation of **smoking** to states and municipalities; rather, states and other political subdivisions remain free to offer greater protection for **disabled** individuals than ADA provides, but violations of ADA should not go unredressed merely because state has chosen to provide some degree of protection to those with **disabilities;** further, total ban on **smoking** is permissible if court finds it appropriate under ADA. Staron v McDonald's Corp. (1995, CA2 Conn) 51 F3d 353, 9 ADD 481, 4 AD Cas 353 (criticized in Neff v American Dairy Queen Corp. (1995, CA5 Tex) 58 F3d 1063, 11 ADD 92, 4 AD Cas 1170, 136 ALR Fed 671).

ADA (42 USCS §§ 12101 et seq.) does not, by itself, mandate blanket ban on smoking in fast food restaurants; allergies to tobacco smoke must be considered on case-by-case basis. Staron v McDonald's Corp. (1994, DC Conn) 7 ADD 336.

4.–Worker compensation laws

Relationship to other laws section of ADA (42 USCS § 12201) was not intended to require ADA (42 USCS §§ 12101 et seq.) to defer to certain state statutes; rather, provision of California's workers' compensation statute which established workers' compensation payments as exclusive remedy for certain injuries sustained on job is preempted by ADA with regard to claim by injured worker that her employer refused to return her to her former position. Wood v County of Alameda (1995, ND Cal) 875 F Supp 659, 60 Cal Comp Cas 71, 8 ADD 875, 4 AD Cas 43, summary judgment den, injunction gr (1995, ND Cal) 13 ADD 908, 5 AD Cas 173.

Laws such as Florida workers' compensation statute are expressly addressed and permitted under ADA (42 USCS §§ 12101 et seq.), since Florida statute provides protection at least equal to that of ADA with regard to individuals with disabilities and makes no distinction between individuals with disabilities and non-disabled individuals. Cramer v Florida (1995, MD Fla) 885 F Supp 1545, 9 ADD 846, 4 AD Cas 687, subsequent app (1997, CA11 Fla) 117 F3d 1258, 23 ADD 22, 7 AD Cas 115, 11 FLW Fed C 232.

ADA (42 USCS §§ 12101 et seq.) does not preempt Florida's workers' compensation laws since state and federal statutes do not conflict with one another, but rather complement each other, with state laws providing workers with benefits in addition to rights granted under ADA. Harding v Winn-Dixie Stores (1995, MD Fla) 907 F Supp 386, 13 ADD 833, 5 AD Cas 129, 9 FLW Fed D 466.

5. Insurance safe harbor provisions

Where evidence shows that particular medical treatment is non-experimental, and insurance plan provides such treatment for other conditions directly comparable to one at issue, denial of that treatment arguably violates ADA (42 USCS §§ 12101 et seq.), and plaintiff is entitled to injunction requiring insurer to guarantee payment for treatment. Henderson v Bodine Aluminum (1995, CA8 Mo) 70 F3d 958, 12 ADD 77, 4 AD Cas 1505, 19 EBC 2047, mod, on reconsideration, reh gr, motion gr, application den (1995, CA8 Mo) 1995 US App LEXIS 31036.

Safe-harbor provision does not serve to insulate insurance industry completely from other requirements of ADA (42 USCS §§ 12101 et seq.) with regard to provision of insurance coverage; rather, insurance practices are protected by safe-harbor provision only to extent that they are consistent with "sound actuarial principles," "actual reasonably-anticipated experience," and "bona fide risk classification." Parker v Metropolitan Life Ins. Co. (1996, CA6 Tenn) 99 F3d 181, 18 ADD 669, 5 AD Cas 1804, 20 EBC 2033, 1996 FED App 338P, vacated, reh, en banc, gr (1997, CA6) 107 F3d 359, 6 AD Cas 547 and different results reached on reh (1997, CA6 Tenn) 121 F3d 1006, 24 ADD 174, 6 AD Cas 1865, 21 EBC 1369, 1997 FED App 230P, cert den (1998) 522 US 1084, 139 L Ed 2d 768, 118 S Ct 871, 8 AD Cas 224 and (criticized in Boots v Northwestern Mut. Life Ins. Co. (1999, DC NH) 77 F Supp 2d 211) and (criticized in

EXHIBIT 11.16	Statutes Template for Canoga Case — Federal Disability Discrimination No. 2

Issue:	Citation Information:
Is Canoga, a smoker, protected against disability discrimination? Does the ADA address smoking?	• *United States Code Service online* • *Title 42, § 12201*
Date of events: *Sept. 7, 2007*	
Date of research: *Dec. 10, 2007*	

Search and Find:

located statute by . . .	updated by . . .
Larson treatise discussion of Americans with Disabilities Act, with specific reference to § 12201.	*Current to December 6, 2007.*
	as needed, found former law by . . .
	NA; statute dates to 1990.

Information and Implications:

Nothing in the ADA "shall be construed to preclude the prohibition of . . . smoking in places of employment . . . ." § 12201(b).
This permits the orchestra (if language encompasses an employer) to regulate workplace smoking. But the issue here is smoking outside the workplace.

Next Steps:

questions to consider:	leads to follow:
We could say statute permits only workplace prohibitions — not off-duty prohibitions. Or we could say the statute's permitting prohibition of smoking suggests that smoking is disfavored and nicotine addiction is not a disability. Which is better?	*Staron v. McDonald's Corp., 51 F.3d 353 (2d Cir. 1995); Neff v. American Dairy Queen Corp., 58 F.3d 1063 (5th Cir. 1995) — both re restaurant bans on smoking.*

3.   Statutory Cases and Updating

> **Options for researching statutory cases**
> - Commentary
> - Reporters and digests
> - Case law databases
> - Case citators
> - Statutory citators

Research in paper and online annotated codes should yield the major cases interpreting the statute. However, the codes may not cover all cases, or you may find it difficult to locate cases particularly pertinent to your client's situation in a lengthy annotation. Ways to deepen your research in cases interpreting a statute are the following:

☐ Read commentary, such as a law review article or A.L.R. annotation, that is very specific to your research issue. (See Unit II.)

☐ Use the West digest and reporter system; its classification may be more helpful than the statutory annotation. (See Chapter 9.)

☐ Run a search in an appropriate case law database using the statute's citation and other distinctive search terms. (See Chapter 9.)

☐ Identify and cite a strong case. (See Chapter 10.)

A final step is to cite the statute through Shepard's on LexisNexis or KeyCite on Westlaw. Statutory citators operate as case citators do; the cited authority is the statute. Using a statutory citator is not nearly as important as using a case citator, because the various resources described in this part will likely lead you to the most important information provided by the citator. On the other hand, a statutory citator may list more cases, including very recent cases. Exhibit 11.17 (at page 265) is the beginning of the Shepard's printout for § 12201(b); the symbols are listed there. Exhibit 11.18 (at page 266), is the beginning of the KeyCite report for § 12201(b). KeyCite's symbols are as follows:

☐ Green C: The statute has citing references.

☐ Yellow flag: A case has limited or questioned the validity of the statute, a prior version received negative judicial treatment, recent or pending legislation would affect the statute, or the statute has been renumbered and transferred recently.

☐ Red flag: The statute has been amended, repealed, superseded, or held invalid on constitutional or preemption grounds in whole or in part.

KeyCite also provides links to legislative history materials, discussed in Chapter 12.

| EXHIBIT 11.17 | Shepard's Report for Federal Statute, from LexisNexis (online source) |

Copyright 2007 SHEPARD'S(R) - 69 Citing references

42 U.S.C. sec. 12201 (b), 42 U.S.C. sec. 12201 (b)

(TM):
Restrictions: *Unrestricted*
FOCUS(TM) Terms: *No FOCUS terms*
Print Format: *FULL*
Citing Ref. Signal Legend:
⬤ {Warning} -- negative treatment indicated
🔲 {Questioned} -- validity questioned by citing refs.
△ {Caution} -- possible negative treatment
◆ {Positive} -- positive treatment indicated
Ⓐ {Analysis} -- cited and neutral analysis indicated
❶ {Cited} -- citation information available

CITING DECISIONS (63 citing decisions)

1ST CIRCUIT - COURT OF APPEALS

1. **Cited by:**
    Dichner v. Liberty Travel, 141 F.3d 24, 1998 U.S. App. LEXIS 7362, 5 Accom. Disabilities Dec. (CCH) P5-091, 8 Am. Disabilities Cas. (BNA) 111 (1st Cir. Mass. 1998)🔲
    141 F.3d 24 *p.32*

2. **Cited by:**
    Ellenwood v. Exxon Shipping Co., 984 F.2d 1270, 1993 U.S. App. LEXIS 362, 2 Am. Disabilities Cas. (BNA) 415, 1 Am. Disabilities Dec. 414, 60 Empl. Prac. Dec. (CCH) P41964, 8 I.E.R. Cas. (BNA) 364 (1st Cir. Me. 1993)△
    984 F.2d 1270 *p.1277*

1ST CIRCUIT - U.S. DISTRICT COURTS

3. **Cited by:**
    Schomburg v. Dell, Inc., 2006 U.S. Dist. LEXIS 72532 (D.N.H. Oct. 4, 2006)△
    2006 U.S. Dist. LEXIS 72532

4. **Cited by:**
    Schomburg v. Dell, Inc., 2006 U.S. Dist. LEXIS 59324 (D.N.H. Aug. 22, 2006)△
    2006 U.S. Dist. LEXIS 59324

5. **Cited by:**
    Iwata v. Intel Corp., 349 F. Supp. 2d 135, 2004 U.S. Dist. LEXIS 24973, 11 Accom. Disabilities Dec. (CCH) P11-213, 16 Am. Disabilities Cas. (BNA) 681, 34 Employee Benefits Cas. (BNA) 1633 (D. Mass. 2004)△

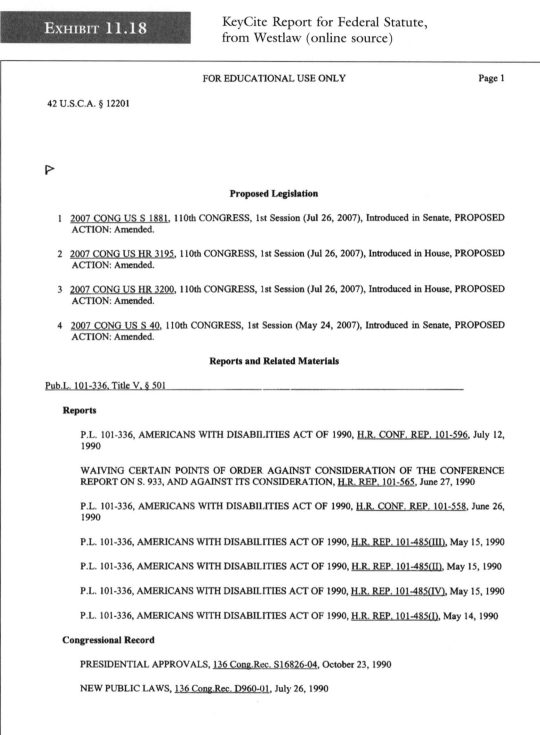

EXHIBIT 11.18   KeyCite Report for Federal Statute,
                 from Westlaw (online source)

FOR EDUCATIONAL USE ONLY   Page 1

42 U.S.C.A. § 12201

▷

Proposed Legislation

1   2007 CONG US S 1881, 110th CONGRESS, 1st Session (Jul 26, 2007), Introduced in Senate, PROPOSED
    ACTION: Amended.

2   2007 CONG US HR 3195, 110th CONGRESS, 1st Session (Jul 26, 2007), Introduced in House, PROPOSED
    ACTION: Amended.

3   2007 CONG US HR 3200, 110th CONGRESS, 1st Session (Jul 26, 2007), Introduced in House, PROPOSED
    ACTION: Amended.

4   2007 CONG US S 40, 110th CONGRESS, 1st Session (May 24, 2007), Introduced in Senate, PROPOSED
    ACTION: Amended.

Reports and Related Materials

Pub.L. 101-336, Title V, § 501 _____

Reports

P.L. 101-336, AMERICANS WITH DISABILITIES ACT OF 1990, H.R. CONF. REP. 101-596, July 12,
1990

WAIVING CERTAIN POINTS OF ORDER AGAINST CONSIDERATION OF THE CONFERENCE
REPORT ON S. 933, AND AGAINST ITS CONSIDERATION, H.R. REP. 101-565, June 27, 1990

P.L. 101-336, AMERICANS WITH DISABILITIES ACT OF 1990, H.R. CONF. REP. 101-558, June 26,
1990

P.L. 101-336, AMERICANS WITH DISABILITIES ACT OF 1990, H.R. REP. 101-485(III), May 15, 1990

P.L. 101-336, AMERICANS WITH DISABILITIES ACT OF 1990, H.R. REP. 101-485(II), May 15, 1990

P.L. 101-336, AMERICANS WITH DISABILITIES ACT OF 1990, H.R. REP. 101-485(IV), May 15, 1990

P.L. 101-336, AMERICANS WITH DISABILITIES ACT OF 1990, H.R. REP. 101-485(I), May 14, 1990

Congressional Record

PRESIDENTIAL APPROVALS, 136 Cong.Rec. S16826-04, October 23, 1990

NEW PUBLIC LAWS, 136 Cong.Rec. D960-01, July 26, 1990

4. Session Laws

> **Session laws**
>
> ▶ Locate the pertinent law via its public law number from the code or via the session laws' subject index.
> ▶ Study the language of the law.

As complete as codes, especially annotated codes, are, you may research in session laws from time to time as well, for several reasons:

☐ As already discussed, a very new law may be available in session law form before it is codified.

☐ Codes are designed to provide the law of the present, although they may provide some historical material as well. If your client's situation arose under a law preceding that now stated or explained in the code, you will research in session laws (or an old code, if still available).

☐ Session laws make it possible to track changes in a statute from year to year, which can assist you in discerning the legislature's thinking and hence the intended meaning of the statute.

☐ Session laws contain all the laws enacted during a particular legislative session, including private laws (which affect a particular person or specific situation) and temporary laws that are not codified.

This discussion focuses on the federal session laws; similar sources exist at the state level.

The official compilation of federal session laws is *United States Statutes at Large (Statutes at Large)*, organized primarily by public law numbers. *Statutes at Large* is also available in a Thomson West publication, *United States Code Congressional and Administrative News*. The federal Government Printing Office provides public and private laws on its website, gpoaccess.gov; coverage begins with laws passed in 1995, and the site is searchable by subject as well as public law and statute citations. HeinOnline also provides *Statutes at Large*. Exhibit 11.19 (at page 268) is an excerpt from *Statutes at Large*, showing a portion of the ADA as passed by Congress in 1990.

Your first task is to locate the pertinent law within the session law volumes. Annotated codes generally provide the public law designations for statutes currently in force immediately following the text of the statute; some also provide this information for obsolete language in historical notes. If you do not have a reference from a code or elsewhere, you may use the subject index to the sessions laws to locate acts on your topic or a key-word search online. Every *Statutes at Large* volume contains an index that pertains to the acts of that session.

EXHIBIT 11.19

Federal Session Law,
from United States Code Congressional
and Administrative News (paper source)

PUBLIC LAW 101-336—JULY 26, 1990   104 STAT. 369

"(i) within 180 days after the complaint is filed with such State; or
"(ii) within a shorter period as prescribed by the regulations of such State; or
"(B) the Commission determines that such State program is no longer qualified for certification under subsection (f).".
(b) CONFORMING AMENDMENTS.—The Communications Act of 1934 (47 U.S.C. 151 et seq.) is amended—
(1) in section 2(b) (47 U.S.C. 152(b)), by striking "section 224" and inserting "sections 224 and 225"; and
(2) in section 221(b) (47 U.S.C. 221(b)), by striking "section 301" and inserting "sections 225 and 301".

SEC. 402. CLOSED-CAPTIONING OF PUBLIC SERVICE ANNOUNCEMENTS.

Section 711 of the Communications Act of 1934 is amended to read as follows: 47 USC 611.

"SEC. 711. CLOSED-CAPTIONING OF PUBLIC SERVICE ANNOUNCEMENTS.

"Any television public service announcement that is produced or funded in whole or in part by any agency or instrumentality of Federal Government shall include closed captioning of the verbal content of such announcement. A television broadcast station licensee—
"(1) shall not be required to supply closed captioning for any such announcement that fails to include it; and
"(2) shall not be liable for broadcasting any such announcement without transmitting a closed caption unless the licensee intentionally fails to transmit the closed caption that was included with the announcement.".

TITLE V—MISCELLANEOUS PROVISIONS

SEC. 501. CONSTRUCTION.   42 USC 12201.

(a) IN GENERAL.—Except as otherwise provided in this Act, nothing in this Act shall be construed to apply a lesser standard than the standards applied under title V of the Rehabilitation Act of 1973 (29 U.S.C. 790 et seq.) or the regulations issued by Federal agencies pursuant to such title.
(b) RELATIONSHIP TO OTHER LAWS.—Nothing in this Act shall be construed to invalidate or limit the remedies, rights, and procedures of any Federal law or law of any State or political subdivision of any State or jurisdiction that provides greater or equal protection for the rights of individuals with disabilities than are afforded by this Act. Nothing in this Act shall be construed to preclude the prohibition of, or the imposition of restrictions on, smoking in places of employment covered by title I, in transportation covered by title II or III, or in places of public accommodation covered by title III.
(c) INSURANCE.—Titles I through IV of this Act shall not be construed to prohibit or restrict—
(1) an insurer, hospital or medical service company, health maintenance organization, or any agent, or entity that administers benefit plans, or similar organizations from underwriting risks, classifying risks, or administering such risks that are based on or not inconsistent with State law; or
(2) a person or organization covered by this Act from establishing, sponsoring, observing or administering the terms

Your second task is to study the law, as you would study a statute in a code. Be sure to examine any editorial enhancements, such as cross-references to related statutes and margin notes. Take particular note of the effective date provision, typically located at the end of the law.

5. Local Ordinances

Options for researching local ordinances

- The clerk's office or the government's website
- Websites specializing in ordinances
- Westlaw or LexisNexis databases

Most local ordinances cover matters that are very local, such as land use, streets, and public services. Some cover topics also covered by federal or state law; many of these ordinances implement the directives of the federal or state law. See Exhibit 11.20 (at page 270), a Taos ordinance implementing the ADA.

Until recently, the main source for researching the law made by cities or counties, i.e., ordinances, was the clerk's office. This continues to be a practical approach. In addition, if the local government has a website, its ordinances may appear there.

Several companies publish ordinances through publicly accessible websites. These include Municipal Code Corporation (with over 1,600 codes), Sterling Codifiers, and American Legal Publishing. Exhibit 11.20 is from the Sterling Codifiers website. The codes provided vary from service to service, so you may need to check several. Furthermore, LexisNexis' database of municipal codes is free.

6. Summary

Because enacted laws — constitutions and charters, statutes and ordinances — are the law, you must excel in researching them. Because courts interpret statutes, proficiency in statutory research includes strong case law research skills as well. Your research will be correct, comprehensive, credible, and cost-effective if you use the following tools strategically:

- ☐ official codes in paper and legislative websites,
- ☐ unofficial annotated codes in paper,
- ☐ unofficial annotated codes online,
- ☐ case law research tools,
- ☐ statutory citators,

Exhibit 11.20	Local Ordinance, from Sterling Codifiers (online source)

3.60.020: AMERICANS WITH DISABILITIES ACT (ADA) POLICY AND GRIEVANCE PROCEDURE:

A. Purpose: The purpose of this section is to provide a reasonable policy and procedure that will ensure: 1) equal opportunities for disabled persons to participate in and benefit from services, programs or activities sponsored by the town; 2) a bias free environment for disabled employees, or for disabled persons who seek employment with the town; and 3) prompt and equitable resolution of complaints alleging discrimination on the basis of a disability.

B. Statement Of Policy: The town does not discriminate on the basis of race, color, national origin, sex, religion, age, marital status. It is the intent of the town to guarantee disabled persons equal opportunity to participate in or enjoy the benefits of town services, programs or activities, and to allow disabled employees a bias free work environment. The town, upon request, will provide reasonable accommodation in compliance with the Americans with disabilities act (ADA).

The town is committed to creating an environment in which facilities for public meetings and general public use are accessible. Furthermore, the town will provide auxiliary aids and services if necessary if such reasonable accommodation can be provided without undue hardship to the town.

The town has a commitment to ensure equal opportunities for disabled town employees. Every reasonable effort will be made to provide an accessible work environment and additional accommodations. Employment practices (e.g., hiring, training, testing, transfer, promotion, compensation, benefits, termination, etc.) will be administered in such manner as to not promote discrimination of disabled employees.

Recruitment and selection processes will grant equal opportunity for employment to qualified applicants and will not discriminate on the basis of disability. Reasonable accommodation will be provided upon request during an application/interview process.

The town is also committed to ensure equal opportunity for disabled persons to participate on boards and commissions.

In the event citizens, employees, or other participants in the town's programs, services and activities feel the town has violated their rights under the ADA, this policy provides a grievance procedure for handling such complaints.

Town staff will be trained to ensure that disabled persons may participate in and benefit from town programs, services and activities.

C. Grievance Procedure: The town adopts the following internal grievance procedure providing for prompt and equitable resolution of complaints alleging any action prohibited by the equal employment opportunity commission (EEOC) regulations implementing title I of the ADA and the U.S. department of justice regulations implementing title II of the ADA. Title I of the ADA states that "no covered entity shall discriminate against a qualified individual with a disability because of the disability of such individual in regard to job application procedures, the hiring, advancement, or discharge of employees, employee compensation, job training, and other terms, conditions, and privileges of employment". Title II of the ADA

☐ session laws, and
☐ sources of local ordinances, as appropriate.

Often you will combine these resources, for example, beginning with a legislative website, working with an annotated code in paper, and concluding with a statutory citator. In some situations, chiefly a key statute with ambiguous language and no interpreting cases, you may supplement your statutory research by researching the statute's legislative history, covered in Chapter 12.

C. HOW DO YOU CITE CONSTITUTIONS AND STATUTES?

The form for citing a constitutional provision is quite spare. Here are two citations to the New Mexico constitutional provision in Exhibit 11.1 (at page 224):

- *Bluebook* Rule 11: N.M. Const. art. II, § 4.
- *ALWD* Rule 13: N.M. Const. art. II, § 4.

The citation forms for statutes and session laws are more elaborate. Any particular law may be located in several sources, and there is a hierarchy among them for citation purposes. *Bluebook* Rule 12's hierarchy is: the current official code, the current unofficial code, session laws, and other sources including electronic databases. *ALWD* Rule 14's hierarchy is: the official code, whether paper or electronic; the unofficial code, whether paper or electronic; the session laws; the slip law.

The citation forms for these sources include an abbreviation of the publication's name; the numbers needed to permit the reader to locate the exact section(s) of interest; for most forms, a date; and, where helpful, the statute's name. Note that the date is the year of the code, not the date of enactment, when you cite to a code. By contrast, when you cite to session laws, the date is the year of enactment or the date the statute became effective.

The federal Americans with Disability Act provision found in Exhibit 11.10 (at pages 245–50) would be cited nearly the same under the *Bluebook* and *ALWD* rules, as follows:

- *Bluebook* Rule 12: 42 U.S.C.S. § 12012 (LexisNexis 2003).
- *ALWD* Rule 12.4: 42 U.S.C.S. § 12102 (Lexis 2003).

However, the citation should be to the official U.S.C. if the language is available there:

- 42 U.S.C. § 12102 (2000).

Exhibit 11.19 (at page 268), the session law, would be cited as follows:

- *Bluebook* Rule 12.4: Americans with Disabilities Act of 1990, Pub. L. No. 101-336, § 501, 104 Stat. 327, 369 (to be codified at 42 U.S.C. § 12101).
- *ALWD* Rule 14.7: Americans with Disabilities Act of 1990, Pub. L. No. 101-336, § 501, 104 Stat. 327, 369 (1990) (to be codified at 42 U.S.C. § 12101).

Note that we have included the title in the session law citations; it could be included in the code citations too.

The Taos ordinance, Exhibit 11.20 (at page 270), would be cited somewhat differently under the two citation manuals, as follows:

- *Bluebook* Rule 12.8.2: Taos, N.M., Code § 3.60.020 (2005).
- *ALWD* Rule 18: Taos City Code (N.M.) § 3.60.020 (2005).

D.   WHAT ELSE?

More on the Constitution. The United States Constitution is among the most analyzed legal texts in the world. *The Constitution of the United States of America: Analysis and Interpretation* is prepared by the Library of Congress and provides case summaries, historical information, and extensive commentary. Scholarly commentary includes treatises (such as those by Professors Tribe, Nowak, Rotunda, and Chemerinsky) and periodicals specializing in constitutional law. Some state annotated codes include the United States Constitution.

Statutory construction tools. If you encounter vague, ambiguous, or conflicting language, you may want to locate rules of statutory construction. Some jurisdictions have statutory provisions that set forth rules for analyzing statutory language. Another option is to consult a treatise on the topic; an example is Norman J. Singer, *Statutes and Statutory Construction* (6th ed. 2000).

Conversion Tables. If you know a session law citation or public law number for a statute but not its code citation, or if you have an outdated section number for a statute that has been renumbered, you can consult conversion tables. For example, the federal annotated codes' *Statutes at Large* tables list statutes in chronological order, by public law number, along with corresponding code sections. The federal annotated codes' tables of revised titles show where renumbered sections now appear.

KeyCite and Shepard's Alerts. When you use these services, you receive updates to the search you have run.

Researching Uniform Laws: You are most likely to research uniform and model acts when your jurisdiction has adopted one and you are seeking information about how it has been interpreted in other jurisdictions. *Uniform*

Laws Annotated, published by West and available in paper and online, functions much like an annotated code. For each act, you can discern which states have adopted it and find the commissioners' commentary, West key numbers, references to cases from various jurisdictions, and references to selected secondary sources. The Council of State Governments annually publishes its model acts in a publication entitled *Suggested State Legislation*.

Compilations of State Laws. Should you seek information about the statutes of multiple states on a subject, you should check whether a compilation exists on that subject. The following list state statutes on various major subjects: *Subject Compilations of State Laws; National Survey of State Laws;* and *Statutes Compared: A U.S., Canadian, Multinational Research Guide to Statutes by Subject*.

Interstate Compacts. States may enter into agreements with each other, with the approval of Congress. These compacts appear in *Statutes at Large*, the session laws and codes of the involved states, and *Interstate Compacts & Agencies* (a publication of the Council of State Governments).

Treaties. Treaties (compacts with other countries that are ratified by Congress) are not codified into the federal code. They appear in official slip form in *Treaties and Other International Acts Series* and *United States Treaties and Other International Agreements*, the official source of treaties since 1950. Other options include *Treaties and International Agreements Online*, Westlaw and LexisNexis databases, HeinOnline's collection, and websites for particular treaties.

LEGISLATIVE PROCESS MATERIALS

A. Introduction: The Legislative Process
B. Legislative History
C. Pending Legislation
D. Concluding Points

A. INTRODUCTION: THE LEGISLATIVE PROCESS

1. Introduction

This chapter covers the legislative process and its relationship to the statutory sources described in Chapter 11. Part A describes the legislative process. The next two parts describe how to research legislative process materials in two rather different situations:

- ☐ Part B identifies the legislative history materials generated during a statute's enactment; it then explains how to locate those materials and evaluate their usefulness in discerning the legislative intent behind an enacted law that governs your client's situation.
- ☐ Part C covers how to track pending legislation to learn of its content or its progress. Lawyers track pending legislation so they can counsel clients about laws that may affect their future operations and assist clients who want to participate in the legislative process.

This chapter continues to illustrate the research of the Canoga case with a focus on Congress' enactment of the Americans with Disabilities Act (ADA), which is discussed in Chapter 11. If the ADA governs Ms. Canoga's situation and she can prove that her smoking is caused by an addiction to nicotine, her employer may be prohibited from discriminating against her due to that addiction. Thus a key issue is whether nicotine addiction is a "disability" under the ADA.

2. The Legislative Process

The process of enacting a statute is similar at the federal and state levels. The following discussion focuses on the federal Congress. See Exhibit 12.1 (at page 276) for a diagram of how a bill becomes law. The diagram shows a common path; not all bills follow the same path.

The legislative process typically begins with the introduction of a bill. Although anyone can draft a bill, only a member of Congress can introduce a bill. Some bills have multiple sponsors, to reflect broad political support. When a bill is introduced, it is given a number. A Senate bill number begins with "S." for Senate, a House bill number with "H.R." for House of Representatives. Because bill numbering starts over again in each Congress, a complete bill number also includes the number of the Congress in which a bill was introduced. The exact same bill may be introduced in both the House and Senate; the bill then has two bill numbers, and the two bills are companion bills. Different bills on the same subject also may be introduced in either or both chambers.

| EXHIBIT 12.1 | How a Bill Becomes Law,
from LexisNexis Congressional (online source) |

How a Bill Becomes Law.

<u>Step-by-step review</u> of the process by which a bill becomes a law, noting the pitfalls and politics involved. Includes tips relating to online research as well as research in printed or microfiche congressional information resources.

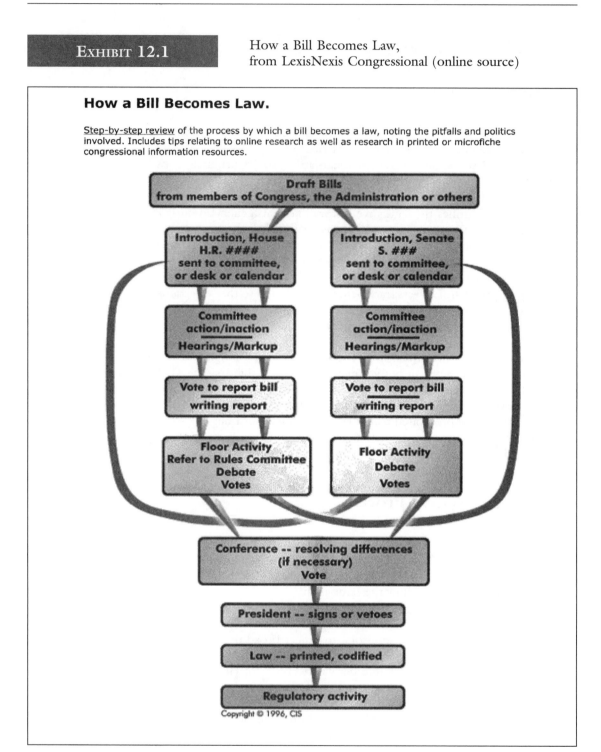

Copyright © 1996, CIS

After a bill is introduced, it may be referred to one or more committees, held at the desk of the chamber, or placed on a legislative calendar for floor action. A bill that is held at the desk may be placed on a calendar at any time.

If a bill is referred to a committee, the committee chair may refer the bill to one or more subcommittees, or the chair may handle the bill at the committee level. A subcommittee, the full committee, or (more rarely) both may hold a hearing on the bill. One or more of the bill's sponsors will appear. Witnesses may include representatives of the executive branch and of groups affected by the proposed legislation, representatives of public interest groups, and experts on the topic. Other interested parties can submit written comments for the hearing record.

After the hearing, or at any time if there is no hearing, the subcommittee or the full committee may meet to consider and mark up the bill. If a subcommittee approves a bill, with or without changes in the original language, it forwards the bill to the full committee. If the full committee approves the bill, with or without changes, it prepares a committee report, setting forth its analysis and recommendations, and reports the bill to its parent body.

Next, the bill goes to the floor of the House or the Senate for debate. Floor managers explain the bill and respond to questions about it. Other members may offer arguments for and against the bill, and amendments may be offered and either passed or defeated.

If the bill passes in one chamber, it becomes known as an "act," and it is sent to the other chamber. The second chamber may pass the bill without change, or it may amend the bill and return it to the first chamber. The first chamber may accept the amendment, or it may amend the amendment and return the bill to the other chamber, or it may insist on its version of the bill and request a conference committee to resolve the differences.

If the second chamber agrees to a conference committee, leaders of both chambers appoint conferees. If the conferees reach agreement, they prepare a conference committee report with the text of the compromise bill and an explanation. If both chambers vote to accept the compromise bill, it is sent to the President.

The President has ten days, excluding Sundays, in which to sign or veto a bill. If the President signs a bill, the bill becomes effective upon signing, unless a different date is specified in the bill. If the President vetoes a bill, the bill and the President's objections are returned to Congress, where the bill dies unless two-thirds of each chamber vote to override the veto. If the President does not act on a bill within ten days and Congress is still in session, the bill becomes law without the President's signature. If Congress has adjourned, however, the bill dies; this is called a "pocket veto."

Each Congress has two one-year sessions. If a bill does not pass by the end of the Congress in which it was introduced, the bill dies. However, it may be reintroduced with a new bill number in a subsequent Congress.

B. LEGISLATIVE HISTORY

1. What Are Legislative History Materials?

In the broadest sense, legislative history consists of all of the background and events giving rise to the enactment of a law. In a narrower sense, "legislative history" refers to the materials considered or created by the legislature at each stage of the legislative process. The legislative process just described generates seven categories of materials, although some legislation may lack some materials.

First, a **bill or act** is printed in various versions:

- □ an introduced bill;
- □ a reported bill — the bill as it is reported out of a committee to a particular chamber;
- □ an engrossed bill — an official copy of a bill as it passed a particular chamber;
- □ an act — the version as it passed one chamber and is printed for consideration in the other; and
- □ an enrolled act — the official version prepared for presentation to the President.

Because each version reflects a different stage in the legislative process, it is important to understand which version you are reading. In addition, sometimes you may need to examine amendments that were proposed but not adopted and that therefore never appeared in any version of the bill. Exhibit 12.2 (at page 280) is the first page of an introduced bill, and Exhibit 12.3 (at pages 281–82) is a proposed amendment.

Second, if a committee or subcommittee holds a hearing, it may publish a **record of a committee hearing**. The record may include the witnesses' oral and written statements, committee questions and answers, statements and exhibits submitted by interested parties, and supplemental material added to the hearing record by committee members and staff. See Exhibit 12.4 (at page 283) for an example of hearing testimony.

Third, a committee may rely on research reports prepared by committee staff, consultants, the Library of Congress, or others. These reports, published as **committee prints**, may contain statistics, scientific and social studies, historical data, bibliographies, compilations of statutes, bill comparisons, and other analyses.

Fourth, a communication from the president or an executive agency, such as a message proposing or vetoing legislation, may appear as a **House or Senate document**. Reports of committee activities, the texts of committee-sponsored studies, background information reports, and some other miscellaneous materials also may be issued as House and Senate documents.

Fifth, **committee reports** typically include a description and analysis of the bill, a discussion of its background, the committee's findings and recommendations, the text of the recommended bill, any minority views, and an estimate of the costs or revenues produced by the bill. See Exhibit 12.5 (at pages 284–85). Of particular importance are conference committee reports, which contain the text of the compromise bill and an analysis of how the compromise was reached.

Sixth, **floor debates and proceedings** include statements made and actions taken in a chamber of Congress. The *Congressional Record* contains more or less verbatim transcripts of floor debates and reports of proceedings, including remarks by members of Congress, their votes, proposed amendments, conference committee reports, messages from the President, and on occasion the text of the bills under consideration. The *Congressional Record* report is not a completely accurate account of what transpired because members of Congress may revise their remarks and may add extended remarks, that is, comments never made on the floor. See Exhibit 12.6 (at pages 286–87).

Seventh, **presidential messages** include signing statements and veto messages, as appropriate. See Exhibit 12.7 (at page 288).

2.   Why Would You Research Legislative History Materials?

Legislative history is a unique form of legal authority. The materials created during the legislative process are generated by a government body while creating primary authority — a statute — but they are subordinate to the statute itself. Thus you will research in legislative history materials when the meaning of a statute is difficult to discern and there is no authoritative case on point. The premise is that the statute should be interpreted so as to effectuate legislative intent, which may be revealed in legislative history materials.

Legislative history research is not without controversy. Some state courts and legislatures disfavor the use of legislative history as a source of the legislature's intent, so you should determine a jurisdiction's stance toward these materials before researching in them. In addition, although a state legislature may produce the materials described previously, those materials generally may not be readily available, especially for older statutes, e.g., you may have to listen to tapes at a state law library or historical society. Researching the legislative history of a state statute is an unusual step.

It is far more common to research the legislative history of a federal statute, at least when a significant issue arises as to its meaning and the client can afford the expense. Researching the legislative history of a federal statute is quite possible, although often time-consuming and sometimes tedious. In the right circumstances, the federal courts fairly readily accept legislative history as indicating Congress' intent. Thus, this part thus focuses on federal legislative history.

As you work with legislative history materials, keep in mind that the legislature may not have had any intent as to your client's situation. Legislators may not have thought of your client's situation, or circumstances may have changed since the statute's enactment. Even if you find a legislative statement on point, that statement may itself be ambiguous or inconclusive. You may even find conflicting statements.

EXHIBIT 12.2

Senate Bill,
from Westlaw (online source)

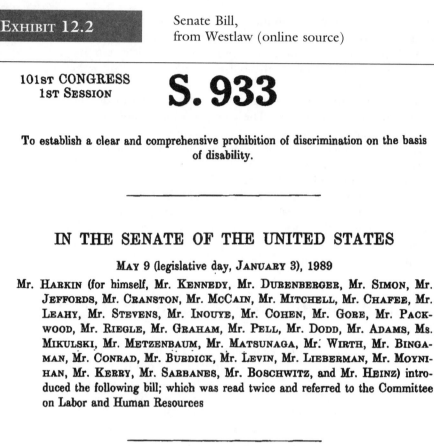

101ST CONGRESS
1ST SESSION

S. 933

To establish a clear and comprehensive prohibition of discrimination on the basis
of disability.

IN THE SENATE OF THE UNITED STATES

MAY 9 (legislative day, JANUARY 3), 1989

Mr. HARKIN (for himself, Mr. KENNEDY, Mr. DURENBERGER, Mr. SIMON, Mr. JEFFORDS, Mr. CRANSTON, Mr. McCAIN, Mr. MITCHELL, Mr. CHAFEE, Mr. LEAHY, Mr. STEVENS, Mr. INOUYE, Mr. COHEN, Mr. GORE, Mr. PACKWOOD, Mr. RIEGLE, Mr. GRAHAM, Mr. PELL, Mr. DODD, Mr. ADAMS, Ms. MIKULSKI, Mr. METZENBAUM, Mr. MATSUNAGA, Mr. WIRTH, Mr. BINGAMAN, Mr. CONRAD, Mr. BURDICK, Mr. LEVIN, Mr. LIEBERMAN, Mr. MOYNIHAN, Mr. KERRY, Mr. SARBANES, Mr. BOSCHWITZ, and Mr. HEINZ) introduced the following bill; which was read twice and referred to the Committee on Labor and Human Resources

---

A BILL

To establish a clear and comprehensive prohibition of
discrimination on the basis of disability.

1   *Be it enacted by the Senate and House of Representa-*

2   *tives of the United States of America in Congress assembled,*

3   SECTION 1. SHORT TITLE; TABLE OF CONTENTS.

4   (a) SHORT TITLE.—This Act may be cited as the

5   "Americans with Disabilities Act of 1989".

6   (b) TABLE OF CONTENTS.—The table of contents is as

7   follows:

Exhibit 12.3	Proposed Amendment and Vote, from THOMAS (online source)

THIS SEARCH	*THIS DOCUMENT*	*THIS CR ISSUE*	*GO TO*
Next Hit	Forward	Next Document	New CR Search
Prev Hit	Back	Prev Document	HomePage
Hit List	Best Sections	Daily Digest	Help
	Contents Display		

Congressional Record article 5 of 10	*Printer Friendly Display* - 812 bytes.[Help]

ARMSTRONG (AND HATCH) AMENDMENT NO. 722 (Senate - September 07, 1989)

[Page: S10833]

Mr. ARMSTRONG (for himself and Mr. **Hatch**) proposed an amendment to the bill S. 933, supra, as follows:

At the end of the bill, add the following:

Under this act the term `disability' does not include `homosexuality,' `bisexuality,' `transvestism,' `pedophilia,' `transsexualism,' `exhibitionism,' `voyeurism,' `compulsive gambling,' `kleptomania,' or `pyromania,' `gender identity disorders,' current `psychoactive substance use disorders,' current `'psychoactive substance-induced organic mental disorders,' as defined by DSM-III-R which are not the result of medical treatment, or other sexual behavior disorders.'

EXHIBIT 12.3   *(continued)*

The Library of Congress > THOMAS Home > Bills, Resolutions > Search Results

NEW SEARCH | HOME | HELP

S.AMDT.722
Amends: S.933
Sponsor: Sen Armstrong, William L. [CO] (submitted 9/7/1989) (proposed 9/7/1989)

AMENDMENT PURPOSE:
To more clearly define the term "disability".

TEXT OF AMENDMENT AS SUBMITTED: CR S10833

STATUS:

> **9/7/1989:**
> Proposed by Senator Armstrong.
> **9/7/1989:**
> Amendment SP 722 agreed to in Senate by Voice Vote.

COSPONSORS(1):

> Sen Hatch, Orrin G. [UT] - 9/7/1989

THOMAS Home | Contact | Accessibility | Legal | FirstGov

EXHIBIT 12.4   Hearing Testimony,
                             from CIS/Microfiche Library

TESTIMONY OF

EVAN J. KEMP, JR., COMMISSIONER

U. S. EQUAL EMPLOYMENT OPPORTUNITY COMMISSION

BEFORE THE HOUSE SUBCOMMITTEES ON SELECT

EDUCATION AND EMPLOYMENT OPPORTUNITIES

SEPTEMBER 13, 1989 AT 10:00 A.M.

I am here today not as a Commissioner of the U.S. Equal Employment
Opportunity Commission, but as a person with a disability. I am
100% for the Americans With Disabilities Act. But there are those
who ask "Does it make economic sense to integrate disabled people
into society?" Other people inquire "How many disabled people are
there really?" While others ask "Does it really matter? Isn't
medical science going to cure most disabling conditions?" Both
disabled people and nondisabled and politician and nonpoliticians
have all asked these questions many times.

To answer these questions and others, I have found it necessary
and helpful to have a philosophical framework to work from. I
would like to share it with you.

The disability rights movement addresses the problems of all our
citizens who are different in some respect from what society
considers to be an acceptable American: the 28 year old, 5'10",

EXHIBIT 12.5	Committee Report, from United States Code Congressional and Administrative News (paper source)

AMERICANS WITH DISABILITIES ACT OF 1990

P.L. 101–336, see page 104 Stat. 327

DATES OF CONSIDERATION AND PASSAGE

Senate: September 7, 1989; July 11, 13, 1990
House: May 22, July 12, 1990

Senate Report (Labor and Human Resources Committee)
No. 101–116, Aug. 30, 1989
[To accompany S. 933]

House Report (Public Works and Transportation Committee) No.
101–485(I), May 14, 1990
[To accompany H.R. 2273]

House Report (Education and Labor Committee) No. 101–485(II),
May 15, 1990
[To accompany H.R. 2273]

House Report (Judiciary Committee) No. 101–485(III), May 15,
1990
[To accompany H.R. 2273]

House Report (Energy and Commerce Committee) No. 101–
485(IV), May 15, 1990
[To accompany H.R. 2273]

House Conference Report No. 101–558, June 26, 1990
[To accompany S. 933]

House Conference Report No. 101–596, July 12, 1990
[To accompany S. 933]

Cong. Record Vol. 135 (1989)

Cong. Record Vol. 136 (1990)

The Senate bill was passed in lieu of the House bill after amending its language to contain much of the text of the House bill. The House Report (Parts I (this page), II (page 303), III (page 445), IV (page 512)) is set out below and the second House Conference Report (page 565) and the President's Signing Statement (page 601) follow.

HOUSE REPORT NO. 101–485(I)

[page 1]
The Committee on Public Works and Transportation, to whom was referred the bill (H.R. 2273) to establish a clear and comprehensive prohibition of discrimination on the basis of disability, having considered the same, report favorably thereon with an amendment and recommend that the bill as amended do pass.

*   *   *   *   *

267

EXHIBIT **12.5** *(continued)*

LEGISLATIVE HISTORY
HOUSE REPORT NO. 101–485(I)

[page 24]

*   *   *   *   *

INTRODUCTION

The Americans With Disabilities Act (ADA) will permit the United States to take a long-delayed but very necessary step to welcome individuals with disabilities fully into the mainstream of American society. The specific provisions of the bill which lie within the jurisdiction of the Committee on Public Works and Transportation are primarily within Titles II and III, dealing with publicly and privately provided transportation services.

With regard to publicly provided transportation services, the bill requires the purchase of new transit vehicles for use on fixed route systems which are readily accessible to, and usable by, individuals with disabilities, including individuals who use wheelchairs. The bill also requires the provision of paratransit services for those individuals whose disabilities preclude their use of the fixed route system.

Transit agencies across the United States have already made some progress in the provision of accessible transit services—35% of America's transit buses are currently accessible. As more and more transit authorities make the commitment to provide fully accessible bus service, the percentage of new bus purchases which are accessible has grown to more than 50% annually. By the mid-1990's many American cities will have completely accessible fixed route systems. Furthermore, many of the transit systems in America already provide some type of paratransit services to the disabled. So, the passage of the ADA will not break sharply with existing transit policy. It will simply extend past successes to even more cities, so that this country can continue to make progress in providing much needed transit services for individuals with disabilities.

With regard to privately provided transportation services, which do not receive the high levels of federal subsidies that publicly provided services do, the requirements of the bill vary according to the size and type of vehicle, as well as according to the type of system on which the vehicle operates.

Nonetheless, in all cases, the Americans with Disabilities Act provides strong guarantees that individuals with disabilities will be

[page 25]

treated with respect and dignity while using transporatation services. After all, the Americans With Disabilities Act is ultimately a civil rights bill. The history of the United States is rich with examples of diversity triumphing over discrimination, but not so rich that this country can ever afford to exclude, or segregate in any way, the significant number of its citizens who have disabilities.

SECTION 1. SHORT TITLE; TABLE OF CONTENTS

Subsection (a) of this section provides that the Act may be cited as the "Americans with Disabilities Act of 1990".

SECTION 2. FINDINGS AND PURPOSES

This section describes the findings and purposes of the Act.

EXHIBIT 12.6	Floor Debate, from Congressional Record through LexisNexis Congressional (online source)

LEXSEE 136 CONG REC S 9684

Congressional Record   -- Senate

Friday, July 13, 1990;
(Legislative day of Tuesday, July 10, 1990)

101st Cong. 2nd Sess.

136 Cong Rec S 9684

REFERENCE: Vol. 136 No. 89; Continuation of House Proceedings of July 12, 1990, Issue No. 88; and Proceedings of July 13, 1990, Issue No. 89.

TITLE: AMERICANS WITH DISABILITIES ACT -- CONFERENCE REPORT

SPEAKER: Mr. ARMSTRONG; Mr. CHAFEE; Mr. CRANSTON; Mr. DOLE; Mr. DURENBERGER; Mr. HARKIN; Mr. HATCH; Mr. INOUYE; Mr. JEFFORDS; Mr. KASTEN; Mr. KENNEDY; Mr. KOHL; Mr. McCAIN; Mr. MET-ZENBAUM; Mr. MITCHELL; Mr. REIGLE; Mr. SIMON; Mr. THURMOND

TEXT: [*S9684] The PRESIDENT pro tempore. The Senate will resume consideration of the conference report on S. 933, which the clerk will report.

The legislative clerk read as follows:

The committee of conference on the disagreeing votes of the two Houses on the amendment of the House to the bill (S. 933) to establish a clear and comprehensive prohibition of discrimination on the basis of disability having met, after full and free conference, have agreed to recommend and do recommend to their respective Houses this report, signed by a majority of the conferees.

The Senate resumed consideration of the conference report.

The PRESIDENT pro tempore. Under the order, the vote on adoption of the conference report on S. 933 will occur at the hour of 9:30 a.m. today. Meanwhile, the time until that hour will be equally divided between Mr. Harkin of Iowa and Mr. Hatch of Utah.

Who yields time?

Mr. HARKIN. Mr. President, I am glad to yield out of my time whatever time he needs to the Senator from Arizona.

Mr. HATCH. I am happy to yield 4 minutes to the distinguished Senator from Arizona.

The PRESIDENT pro tempore. The Senator from Arizona is recognized.

Mr. McCAIN. Mr. President, I am pleased to strongly support final passage of the Americans With Disabilities Act. This landmark legislation will mark a new era for the disabled in our Nation. For far too long, we have ignored the talents and gifts of certain Americans. Now, Mr. President, our Nation is proudly reasserting its claim as the world's torchbearer of freedom and opportunity.

On March 8, 1990, for the first time in the Senate's history, a deaf chaplain gave the invocation that sets the tone for the Senate's day. He very appropriately stated, " *** Especially, we ask Your blessing on people with disabling conditions. We pray that they receive not pity but respect; not shame but dignity; not neglect but inclusion."

Mr. President, it is time we took these words to heart. The ADA is a final proclamation that the disabled will never again be excluded, never again treated by law as second-class citizens. Each and every American has something unique and special to offer, and our Nation is a better place because of them.

EXHIBIT 12.6   *(continued)*

136 Cong Rec S 9684, *

I am particularly pleased to have played a part in the passage of this legislation. Over 2 years ago, I sought to ensure that our Nation's telecommunication's network was accessible to the 24 million hearing and speech impaired Americans. At that time, the Congress rightly moved to make the Federal Government's telecommunication's network fully accessible.

The telephone has become an essential part of our daily lives. For most people, it is impossible to imagine being without one. Yet for more than 100 years, deaf and hearing impaired individuals have been denied full access to the telephone. We are obligated to correct that situation. Title IV of the ADA will move us closer than ever toward granting the hearing and speech impaired the independence and greater opportunities sought in the other sections of the Americans With Disabilities Act. I am enormously gratified to see its final passage.

Mr. President, this bill is an important step in making the American dream available to all. But I urge the real champions of this legislation, the 43 million disabled Americans, to never allow their vigil to wane. The power of law is great, but it cannot change opinion or overcome prejudice. The freedom to be respected for your abilities is a tenuous concept, and the heroes of this legislation have proved that every person has value and deserve our respect and admiration.

The freedom to pursue the American dream is at the heart of what makes our Nation great. That freedom that encourages diversity makes us a stronger nation. We must never loose sight of it. I want to thank my colleagues, Senators Harkin, Hatch, Dole, and Kennedy for all they have done to make sure that those who are disabled are never again denied what is rightfully theirs, the opportunity to pursue their dreams. But most importantly, Mr. President, I thank the 43 million disabled individuals who never stopped believing in themselves, and never gave up the battle for their equal rights. Our Nation is better for their struggle.

Mr. President, I yield back the remainder of my time.

The PRESIDENT pro tempore. Who yields time?

Mr. HARKIN. Mr. President, I yield myself such time as I may consume.

The PRESIDENT pro tempore. The Senator from Iowa is recognized.

Mr. HARKIN. Mr. President, I am only going to take a minute now and reserve the balance of time toward the end of the period of time that we have before the vote.

I shall take a minute to say how proud I am of the actions the Senate and all of our friends who worked so hard on this legislation have taken. As I said, I will have more to say later, but as the chief sponsor of this bill I just could not be more proud of my fellow Senators, Members of the House, and especially people with disabilities, who have worked so hard for this day. It may be raining outside, but this is truly a day of sunshine for all Americans with disabilities.

Before I go any further, I wish to thank Senator McCain for his work on the section of the bill dealing with the relay system for deaf and hard of hearing people. That means a great   [*S9685]   deal to me personally and a great deal to my brother, who is deaf. I personally thank Senator McCain for all of his work, effort, and diligence.

Mr. President, I reserve about 5 or 6 minutes for myself later on, so I will yield the floor at this time.

The PRESIDENT pro tempore. The Senator from Utah [Mr. Hatch] is recognized.

Mr. HATCH. Mr. President, I am very proud to be here this morning. I believe this legislation is going to be good for America. For too long the valuable resources available to this Nation from individuals with disabilities have been wasted needlessly. Why? Because of senseless discrimination, intended or not, which subjected persons with disabilities to isolation and robbed America of the minds, the spirit, and the dedication we need to remain a competitive force in worldwide economy.

Today, we are going to unlock these resources through the Americans With Disabilities Act and bring individuals with disabilities into the mainstream of the economic structure of this country. In employment, in public accommodations, in transportation, in communications services, all of which many of us take for granted today, we area simply saying that no longer can we tolerate the exclusion of the disabled because of ignorance, fear, or intolerance.

I think America will be a better place, a far better place because of the actions we are about to take today. When we look at the demographic changes in America and the coming shortages of labor, particularly skilled labor, I think America's ability to compete on balance will be improved rather than injured by this bill.

| EXHIBIT 12.7 | Presidential Signing Statement, from United States Code Congressional and Administrative News (paper source) |

SIGNING STATEMENT
P.L. 101–336

STATEMENT BY PRESIDENT OF THE UNITED STATES

STATEMENT BY PRESIDENT GEORGE BUSH UPON SIGNING S. 933

26 Weekly Compilation of Presidential Documents 1165,
July 30, 1990

Today, I am signing S. 933, the "Americans with Disabilities Act of 1990." In this extraordinary year, we have seen our own Declaration of Independence inspire the march of freedom throughout Eastern Europe. It is altogether fitting that the American people have once again given clear expression to our most basic ideals of freedom and equality. The Americans with Disabilities Act represents the full flowering of our democratic principles, and it gives me great pleasure to sign it into law today.

In 1986, on behalf of President Reagan, I personally accepted a report from the National Council on Disability entitled "Toward Independence." In that report, the National Council recommended the enactment of comprehensive legislation to ban discrimination against persons with disabilities. The Americans with Disabilities Act (ADA) is such legislation. It promises to open up all aspects of American life to individuals with disabilities—employment opportunities, government services, public accommodations, transportation, and telecommunications.

This legislation is comprehensive because the barriers faced by individuals with disabilities are wide-ranging. Existing laws and regulations under the Rehabilitation Act of 1973 have been effective with respect to the Federal Government, its contractors, and the recipients of Federal funds. However, they have left broad areas of American life untouched or inadequately addressed. Many of our young people, who have benefited from the equal educational opportunity guaranteed under the Rehabilitation Act and the Education of the Handicapped Act, have found themselves on graduation day still shut out of the mainstream of American life. They have faced persistent discrimination in the workplace and barriers posed by inaccessible public transportation, public accommodations, and telecommunications.

Fears that the ADA is too vague or too costly and will lead to an explosion of litigation are misplaced. The Administration worked closely with the Congress to ensure that, wherever possible, existing language and standards from the Rehabilitation Act were incorporated into the ADA. The Rehabilitation Act standards are already familiar to large segments of the private sector that are either Federal contractors or recipients of Federal funds. Because the Rehabilitation Act was enacted 17 years ago, there is already an extensive body of law interpreting the requirements of that Act. Employers can turn to these interpretations for guidance on how to meet their obligations under the ADA.

The Administration and the Congress have carefully crafted the ADA to give the business community the flexibility to meet the requirements of the Act without incurring undue costs. Cost may be taken into account in determining how an employee is "reasonably accommodated," whether the removal of a barrier is "readily achievable," or whether the provision of a particular auxiliary aid would result in an "undue burden." The ADA's most rigorous access requirements are reserved for new construction where

601

Some legislative history materials are weightier than others; the key factors are who generated the materials, how the materials were generated, and how closely they relate to the law as enacted (rather than earlier versions). The hierarchy of legislative documents is as follows:

- ☐ The various versions of a bill as well as rejected and adopted amendments may be very persuasive evidence of legislative intent.
- ☐ Committee reports are usually considered key documents because they are formally prepared and adopted by the committee that has expertise on the topic and was charged with making a recommendation on the bill. Conference committee reports are especially important because they arise late in the legislative process and explain the resolution of differences between the House and Senate.
- ☐ Hearing records typically carry less weight. Although they may contain useful information, must of the testimony is not given by those who vote on the bill and may reflect the biased positions of those testifying.
- ☐ Floor debates are controversial because legislators sometimes seek to use them to establish a reading of the legislation that they were unable to incorporate into the statute itself. Nevertheless, courts do rely on such statements, particularly when they are made by the bill's sponsors.
- ☐ Committee prints are less commonly used but may contain factual background information from which you can infer the concerns of the legislature.
- ☐ Reports of executive branch agencies also are less commonly used but may discuss the problems that a law was designed to remedy.
- ☐ The executive's action in approving or vetoing a bill may provide indirect evidence of legislative intent, particularly for legislation passed after a veto.

To use legislative history materials properly, you must acquaint yourself thoroughly with a law's full legislative history. Otherwise, you will be at risk of relying on unrepresentative fragments.

3. How Do You Research Legislative History?

As you no doubt have surmised, the legislative process and the materials it produces can be lengthy and complicated. Thanks to online information technology, researching in these materials is less cumbersome than it used to be. Lawyers used to have to visit a federal depository library, use paper indexes, read documents on microfilm or microfiche, and obtain some documents from the Government Printing Office. Now legislative history research involves very current online reports, searches run in extensive and easily accessible databases, and links from source to source. This chapter focuses on these online options, available for fairly recent statutes, because lawyers generally research the legislative history of recent statutes.

Unfortunately, online sources do not extend backward in time more than several decades, so for older statutes, you still will engage in a much more cumbersome process. Should you find yourself in this situation, you would do well to consult with a reference librarian at a federal depository library.

Researching legislative history entails two closely linked tasks: (1) identifying the law's steps en route to enactment and (2) obtaining and reading the documents created at the various steps. Accomplishing the first task well is fundamental to success on the second. Furthermore, starting with basic sources may help you ground your research before you move on to more extensive sources. Thus this part proceeds as follows:

☐ Derive as much information as you can from the statutory code.

☐ Read the material selected by the editors of the *United States Code Congressional and Administrative News*, the most established and highly accessible source for federal legislative history.

☐ Check for a compiled legislative history for your law; compiled legislative histories are prepared for significant statutes.

☐ Explore the materials available through THOMAS, an online service of the Library of Congress.

☐ Explore the material available through a commercial online resource.

Within each of the major legislative history resources, you may search in various sequences. Thus, some of the descriptions below list options, not necessarily steps in a sequence.

Exhibit 12.8, (at page 291) our template for legislative history research, differs from the others. The left column lists legislative process documents from most to least weighty; this is a sensible order in which to read a set of documents. Once the list is prepared, you can take on the more substantial task — obtaining and reading the documents — in an organized way.

Legislative history in statutory codes

- Purpose statement
- Dates and numbers of bills

Before you set aside the code in which you have researched, look for a statement in the statute itself. A few statutes include a purpose provision, typically the first or second section of the statute. Because this provision is part of the statute, it is highly authoritative.

Next, examine the historical notes following the statute. The amount and type of information will vary depending on the code you are using. For example, the three federal codes all provide the following information: the public law number, date of approval, and *Statutes at Large* (session laws) citation for the original and amending legislation. *United States Code Annotated* (U.S.C.A.) also refers to one or more documents printed in *United States Code Congressional and Administrative News,* a basic legislative history source. See Exhibit 12.9 (at page 292), the ADA definition of "disability" from U.S.C.A.

| EXHIBIT 12.8 | Legislative History Template |

Document and Source:	Information and Implications:
purpose provision in statute:	
bills and amendments:	
hearing testimony:	
committee reports:	
floor statements:	
committee prints:	
executive agency reports:	
presidential statements:	

EXHIBIT 12.9	Legislative History Information in Annotated Code, from United States Code Annotated (paper source)

Ch. 126   AMERICANS WITH DISABILITIES   **42 § 12102**

(C) acquisition or modification of equipment or devices; and

(D) other similar services and actions.

(2) Disability

The term "disability" means, with respect to an individual—

(A) a physical or mental impairment that substantially limits one or more of the major life activities of such individual;

(B) a record of such an impairment; or

(C) being regarded as having such an impairment.

(3) State

The term "State" means each of the several States, the District of Columbia, the Commonwealth of Puerto Rico, Guam, American Samoa, the Virgin Islands, the Trust Territory of the Pacific Islands, and the Commonwealth of the Northern Mariana Islands.

(Pub.L. 101–336, § 3, July 26, 1990, 104 Stat. 329.)

HISTORICAL AND STATUTORY NOTES

Revision Notes and Legislative Reports
1990 Acts. House Report No. 101–485(Parts I–IV), House Conference Report No. 101–596, and Statement by President, see 1990 U.S. Code Cong. and Adm. News, p. 267.

CROSS REFERENCES

Auxiliary aids and services as defined in this section for purposes of national service trust fund program, see 42 USCA § 12581.
"Disability" defined as having same meaning as under this section for purposes of—
Access by persons with disability, see 47 USCA § 255.

LAW REVIEW AND JOURNAL COMMENTARIES

AIDS Discrimination in employee health benefits: Is there a federal remedy for modification of a plan once an employee develops AIDS? 18 Law & Psychol.Rev. 377 (1994).
AIDS in the food industry. Rebecca Winterscheidt, 28 Ariz.Att'y 13 (Mar. 1992).
AIDS-related benefits equation: Costs times needs divided by applicable law. Peter D. Blanck, Clifford H. Schoenberg and James P. Tenney, 211 N.Y.L.J. 1 (Feb. 28, 1994).
Americans With Disabilities Act: Obligations and employer knowledge. Alexandra Krueger Hedrick, 70 Fla.B.J. 73 (Oct. 1996).
Americans with Disabilities Act as it relates to AIDS in the workplace. Vimal K. Shah, 6 CBA Rec. 33 (Nov. 1992).
Americans with Disabilities Act "readily achievable" requirement for barrier removal: Proposal for the allocation of responsibility between landlord and tenant. 15 Cardozo L.Rev. 569 (1993).
An employer's guide to the Americans with Disabilities Act: From job qualifications to reasonable accommodations. Lawrence P. Postol and David D. Kadue, 24 J.Marshall L.Rev. 693 (1991).

39

> **Legislative history in *United States Code Congressional and Administrative News* (U.S.C.C.A.N.)**
>
> ▶ Locate pertinent materials through a U.S.C.A. reference, public law number, *Statutes at Large* citation, or the U.S.C.C.A.N. subject index.
> ▶ Read the opening material to obtain references to additional materials and proceedings.
> ▶ Read the materials reprinted in U.S.C.C.A.N.

U.S.C.C.A.N., published by Thomson West, is a convenient source of session laws and up to several legislative history documents for major laws. It does not, however, contain all or even most of the documents for a law. It is an accessible source often used at the outset of legislative history research (after the statutory code). Exhibits 12.5 and 12.7 (at pages 284–85 and 288) are from U.S.C.C.A.N.

Each set of bound volumes covers a particular session of Congress and contains two sections: reprints of the *Statutes at Large* session laws and the legislative history documents. The two sections typically appear in separate volumes, and both are organized by public law number.

You can locate the legislative history material for your law by using the reference in U.S.C.A., locating the materials by public law number, finding the reference in the *Statutes at Large* section of U.S.C.C.A.N., or looking up your research terms in the subject index. Once you locate the pertinent material, note the information on the opening page. See the first page of Exhibit 12.5 (at pages 284–85). The legislative history section of U.S.C.C.A.N. typically provides the following information for a public law:

- □ its public law number and its *Statutes at Large* citation,
- □ the dates of consideration and passage of the legislation by both chambers,
- □ the numbers of the House and Senate bills,
- □ the committees to which the bills were assigned,
- □ the numbers and dates of committee reports,
- □ the numbers and dates of conference committee reports, and
- □ the volumes and years of the *Congressional Record* in which the debates appear.

U.S.C.C.A.N. typically provides one or more committee reports and perhaps also a presidential signing statement. The committee reports are edited to remove duplicative or less helpful information; omissions are shown by asterisks, and the official page numbers are in brackets.

Westlaw's U.S.C.C.A.N. database contains portions of U.S.C.C.A.N. with coverage varying by type of document. U.S.C.C.A.N. on Westlaw affords Boolean and natural-language searching, which can be useful when your research topic is a narrow one captured in distinctive search terms.

The most common document provided in U.S.C.C.A.N. is a committee report. Most include the committee's recommendation on the bill; the text of the bill as recommended; section-by-section summaries of the bill; concurring and dissenting views of individual committee members; reports from the Congressional Budget Office, estimating the cost of the law; and analysis of changes that the bill as recommended would make in existing law. A conference committee report catalogs the differences between the House and Senate bills and notes which version prevailed.

When you read a legislative history document, proceed carefully:

☐ Read all or most of the document. At least scan parts that may seem off-point; you may find helpful information in a surprising location.

☐ Keep an open mind about what you will find: You may indeed find a statement directly and specifically addressing your topic. More often you will find only broad statements about the law's purpose, or you may need to extrapolate from the facts known to and emphasized by legislators.

☐ Also, look for both favorable and unfavorable statements, as you would in any other legal source.

☐ Guard against placing too much weight on a sentence or two; be sure to note the context of each pertinent statement.

☐ Be sure to examine how influential the pertinent statements were. For example, you should not rely on a statement by a proponent of an amendment that was soundly defeated.

Compiled legislative histories

• Consult a bibliography of compiled legislative histories, and procure and peruse the compilation.

• Or identify and search a LexisNexis, Westlaw, or HeinOnline database for your statute.

If your research project merits further consideration of the law's legislative history, a good next step is to determine whether there exists a compiled legislative history, that is, a collection of pertinent legislative materials or citations to those materials. As a general rule, compiled legislative histories exist for legislation of widespread importance.

To find out whether a paper compiled legislative history exists for your law, search an online catalog for the name of the law and "legislative history." Another option is to consult a source such as Nancy P. Johnson, *Sources of Compiled Legislative Histories: A Bibliography of Government Documents, Periodical Articles, and Books*, or Bernard D. Reams, *Federal Legislative Histories: An Annotated Bibliography and Index to Officially Published*

Sources. These directories identify legislative histories, by law, and state for each compilation its bibliographic information, some means by which to find it, and the citations and documents provided. Your next task is, of course, to obtain the compiled history and peruse its contents. Some may be voluminous, others smaller and less complete; some have an index, others only a table of contents.

For some major statutes, LexisNexis, Westlaw, and HeinOnline offer legislative history databases. The chief advantages of an electronic compilation are the availability of key-word and full-text searching and the ability to search all documents simultaneously.

Legislative history through THOMAS

- Bill Summary & Status
- All Congressional Actions
- Various versions of the legislation
- Amendments and outcomes
- *Congressional Record*
- Committee reports

In 1995, the Library of Congress introduced THOMAS,[1] a free Web-based legislative information service located at thomas.loc.gov. THOMAS tracks the history of bills, beginning with bills introduced in 1973. Its full-text coverage begins later, for example, the text of the *Congressional Record* from 1989 to date, committee reports from 1995 to date.

THOMAS provides several means of access. Most of the time, the best option is to search by bill number in the Bill Summary & Status service for the session that passed the law you are researching. At first, you will see a table of links to various categories of information. A good first step is to link to and peruse the law's All Congressional Actions report (with or without the amendments), which lists the events in the law's legislative process in great detail. See Exhibit 12.10 (at page 296). With that information serving as a framework, link to and read potentially pertinent information or documents from the following categories:

☐ titles;
☐ related bills, such as the House companion to a Senate bill that passed;
☐ text of legislation, which includes various versions, e.g., introduced, reported, engrossed, enrolled;
☐ cosponsors;
☐ amendments;

---

1. The Library of Congress was founded in 1800 by Congress. The original materials were destroyed by fire. Thomas Jefferson offered his personal collection as a replacement; Congress accepted the offer in 1815.

Exhibit 12.10	Beginning of All Congressional Acts Report, from THOMAS (online source)

NEW SEARCH | HOME | HELP | ABOUT STATUS

S.933
Title: A bill to establish a clear and comprehensive prohibition of discrimination on the basis of disability.
Sponsor: Sen Harkin, Tom [IA] (introduced 5/9/1989)   Cosponsors (63)
Related Bills: H.RES.427, H.R.2273
Latest Major Action: 7/26/1990 Became Public Law No: 101-336.

ALL ACTIONS: (Floor Actions/Congressional Record Page References)

5/9/1989:
>Read twice and referred to the Committee on Labor and Human Resources.
>**5/9/1989:**
>>Committee on Labor and Human Resources. Hearings held. Hearings printed: S.Hrg. 101-156.
>>**5/10/1989:**
>>>Subcommittee on Handicapped (Labor and Human Res.). Hearings held.
>>**5/16/1989:**
>>>Subcommittee on Handicapped (Labor and Human Res.). Hearings held.
>**6/22/1989:**
>>Committee on Labor and Human Resources. Hearings held.
>**8/2/1989:**
>>Committee on Labor and Human Resources. Ordered to be reported with an amendment in the nature of a substitute favorably.

8/30/1989:
>Committee on Labor and Human Resources. Reported to Senate by Senator Kennedy under the authority of the order of Aug 2, 89 with an amendment in the nature of a substitute. With written report No. 101-116. Additional views filed.

8/30/1989:
>Placed on Senate Legislative Calendar under General Orders. Calendar No. 216.

9/7/1989:
>Measure laid before Senate by unanimous consent.

9/7/1989:
>The committee substitute as amended agreed to by Voice Vote.

9/7/1989:
>Passed Senate with an amendment by Yea-Nay Vote. 76-8. Record Vote No: 173.

9/12/1989:
>Message on Senate action sent to the House.

9/12/1989 2:41pm:
>Received in the House.

9/12/1989 2:42pm:
>Held at the desk.

10/16/1989:
>Senate ordered measure printed as passed with amendments of the Senate numbered.

□ related committee prints; and

□ summary of the law.

A particular strength of THOMAS is its extensive coverage of amendments, both the text and the votes. See Exhibit 12.3 (at pages 281–82), an amendment and information about the voting on that amendment.

Another option is to conduct a key-word search in one of the document databases, such as committee reports or the *Congressional Record*. This approach entails selecting a session and then keying in your search terms for a full-text search. Yet another option is to browse an index.

Legislative history through LexisNexis Congressional and Congressional Information Service

- Legislative history
- Bill tracking report
- *Congressional Record*
- Abstracts of other documents (available from Congressional Information Service)

LexisNexis Congressional (LNC) is a commercial electronic service, provided by LexisNexis, that is based on an extensive paper and microfiche source, Congressional Information Service (CIS). For relatively recent legislation, from 1970 to date, LNC provides a statement of the main events in a statute's enactment process. In addition, LNC provides the text of some documents.

To research a specific law, you would search in the CIS Legislative Histories component by entering the public law number, bill number, or *Statutes at Large* citation. The statement thus obtained includes the following information:

□ the law's title and a summary of the law;

□ the bill numbers for the enacted and related bills;

□ descriptions of debates as reported in the *Congressional Record*;

□ the titles, dates, and numbers of committee reports;

□ the same information for committee hearings;

□ the same information for committee prints; and

□ a reference to presidential remarks.

See Exhibit 12.11 (at pages 298–303). Note that the legislative history statement covers not only the session in which the law was enacted but also previous sessions, if any, in which Congress considered related legislation.

| EXHIBIT 12.11 | Legislative History, from CIS-Legislative History through LexisNexis (online source) |

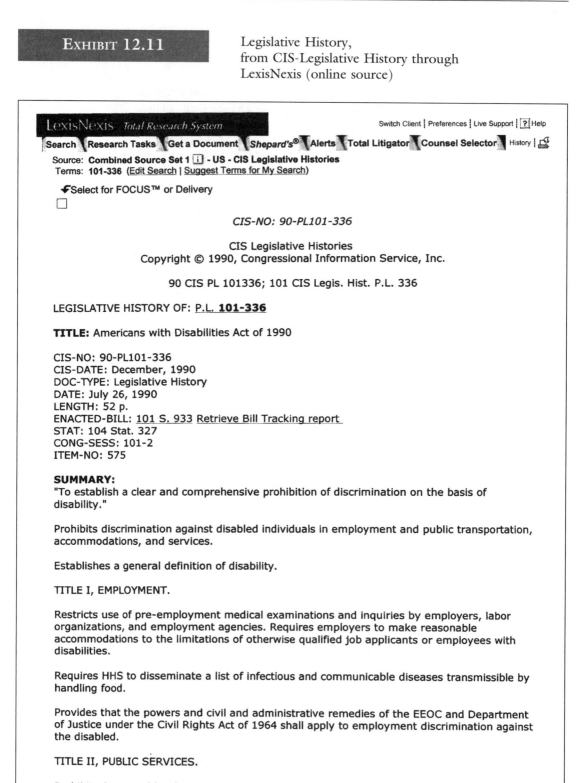

LexisNexis *Total Research System*   Switch Client ┊ Preferences ┊ Live Support ┊ [?] Help

Search ❭ Research Tasks ❭ Get a Document ❭ *Shepard's®* ❭ Alerts ❭ Total Litigator ❭ Counsel Selector ❭ History ┊

Source: **Combined Source Set 1** [i] **- US - CIS Legislative Histories**
Terms: **101-336** (Edit Search | Suggest Terms for My Search)

⨍Select for FOCUS™ or Delivery
☐

CIS-NO: 90-PL101-336

CIS Legislative Histories
Copyright © 1990, Congressional Information Service, Inc.

90 CIS PL 101336; 101 CIS Legis. Hist. P.L. 336

LEGISLATIVE HISTORY OF: P.L. **101-336**

TITLE: Americans with Disabilities Act of 1990

CIS-NO: 90-PL101-336
CIS-DATE: December, 1990
DOC-TYPE: Legislative History
DATE: July 26, 1990
LENGTH: 52 p.
ENACTED-BILL: 101 S. 933 Retrieve Bill Tracking report
STAT: 104 Stat. 327
CONG-SESS: 101-2
ITEM-NO: 575

SUMMARY:
"To establish a clear and comprehensive prohibition of discrimination on the basis of disability."

Prohibits discrimination against disabled individuals in employment and public transportation, accommodations, and services.

Establishes a general definition of disability.

TITLE I, EMPLOYMENT.

Restricts use of pre-employment medical examinations and inquiries by employers, labor organizations, and employment agencies. Requires employers to make reasonable accommodations to the limitations of otherwise qualified job applicants or employees with disabilities.

Requires HHS to disseminate a list of infectious and communicable diseases transmissible by handling food.

Provides that the powers and civil and administrative remedies of the EEOC and Department of Justice under the Civil Rights Act of 1964 shall apply to employment discrimination against the disabled.

TITLE II, PUBLIC SERVICES.

Prohibits State and local governments and Amtrak from excluding from programs or services

EXHIBIT 12.11   *(continued)*

disabled individuals who meet specified eligibility requirements if reasonable modifications of policies or removal of barriers would enable them to participate.

Provides that enforcement for discrimination against the disabled by public entities shall be the remedies in the Rehabilitation Act of 1973.

Requires new vehicles purchased by public entities operating fixed route transportation systems to be readily accessible to and usable by the disabled.

Requires public entities operating fixed route transportation systems to provide paratransit services for individuals whose disabilities preclude the use of the fixed route system.

Requires Amtrak and all commuter rail systems to have at least one car per train readily accessible to and usable by disabled individuals within five years.

Requires Amtrak and key commuter stations to be made readily accessible to disabled individuals within specified time frames.

TITLE III, PUBLIC ACCOMMODATIONS AND SERVICES OPERATED BY PRIVATE ENTITIES.

Prohibits discrimination on the basis of disability by private businesses and other providers of goods, services, or accommodations. Requires businesses to remove barriers and make reasonable modifications of policies in order to provide equal benefits to the disabled, unless such changes are not readily achievable or would result in undue hardship.

Requires OTA to conduct a study to determine transportation access needs of the disabled, and the most cost-effective method of providing disabled individuals with access to buses and bus services.

Requires the Department of Justice to issue regulations regarding prohibition of discrimination in privately owned accommodations and services and DOT to issue regulations on land-based public transportation services.

TITLE IV, TELECOMMUNICATIONS.

Amends the Communications Act of 1934 to require that all telephone common carriers provide relay services for the hearing-impaired and speech-impaired so that they can communicate with persons who are not impaired. Extends FCC regulatory authority to intrastate common carriers for purposes of implementing the relay services requirement.

Requires closed-captioning of all TV public service announcements produced using Federal funds.

TITLE V, MISCELLANEOUS PROVISIONS.

Includes a provision to require the Architectural and Transportation Barriers Compliance Board to issue guidelines for removal of barriers that make goods and services inaccessible to the disabled.

Provides that nothing in the Wilderness Act shall be construed as prohibiting use of wheelchairs in wilderness areas.

Prohibits discrimination on the basis of disability by members of Congress and legislative branch employees.

Amends the Rehabilitation Act of 1973 to revise definitions and make conforming amendments.

EXHIBIT 12.11　　　*(continued)*

CONTENT-NOTATION: Discrimination against the handicapped, prohibition

BILLS: 100 H.R. 192; 100 H.R. 1546; 100 H.R. 4498; 100 S. 2345; 101 H.R. 2273; 101 H.R. 3171; 101 H.R. 4807; 101 S. 1452

DESCRIPTORS:
　AMERICANS WITH DISABILITIES ACT; DISCRIMINATION AGAINST THE HANDICAPPED; DISCRIMINATION IN EMPLOYMENT; TRANSPORTATION OF THE HANDICAPPED; MEDICAL EXAMINATIONS AND TESTS; LABOR UNIONS; EMPLOYMENT SERVICES; DEPARTMENT OF HEALTH AND HUMAN SERVICES; GOVERNMENT INFORMATION AND INFORMATION SERVICES; COMMUNICABLE DISEASES; FOOD POISONING; EQUAL EMPLOYMENT OPPORTUNITY COMMISSION; DEPARTMENT OF JUSTICE; CIVIL RIGHTS ACT; ADMINISTRATIVE LAW AND PROCEDURE; CIVIL PROCEDURE; FEDERAL-STATE RELATIONS; FEDERAL-LOCAL RELATIONS; NATIONAL RAILROAD PASSENGER CORP.; ARCHITECTURAL BARRIERS; RAILROAD ROLLING STOCK; MOTOR BUS LINES; TRANSPORTATION REGULATION; GOVERNMENT AND BUSINESS; OFFICE OF TECHNOLOGY ASSESSMENT; DEPARTMENT OF TRANSPORTATION; TELECOMMUNICATION REGULATION; COMMUNICATIONS ACT; TELEPHONE AND TELEPHONE INDUSTRY; HEARING AND HEARING DISORDERS; SPEECH DISORDERS; TELEVISION; FEDERAL COMMUNICATIONS COMMISSION; REHABILITATION ACT; ARCHITECTURAL AND TRANSPORTATION BARRIERS COMPLIANCE BOARD; WILDERNESS ACT; WILDERNESS AREAS; CONGRESSIONAL EMPLOYEES

REFERENCES:

DEBATE:

135 Congressional Record, 101st Congress, 1st Session - 1989
　Sept. 7, Senate consideration and passage of S. 933, p. S10701.

136 Congressional Record, 101st Congress, 2nd Session - 1990
　May 17, House consideration of H.R. 2273, p. H2410.
　May 22, House consideration of H.R. 2273, consideration and passage of S. 933 with an amendment, and tabling of H.R. 2273, p. H2599.
　May 24, House insistence on its amendments to S. 933, request for a conference, and appointment of conferees, p. H3070.
　June 6, Senate disagreement to the House amendments to S. 933, agreement to a conference, and appointment of conferees, p. S7422.
　June 26, Submission in the House of the conference report on S. 933, p. H4169.
　July 11, Senate passage of motion to recommit the conference report on S. 933, p. S9527.
　July 12, Submission in the House of the second conference report on S. 933, and House agreement to the conference report, p. H4582.
　July 13, Senate agreement to the conference report on S. 933, p. S9684.

REPORTS:

101st Congress

S. Rpt. 101-116 on S. 933, "Americans with Disabilities Act of 1989," Aug. 30, 1989.
　CIS NO: 89-S543-11
　LENGTH: 107 p.
　SUDOC: Y1.1/5:101-116

EXHIBIT 12.11   *(continued)*

H. Rpt. 101-485, pt. 1 on H.R. 2273, "Americans with Disabilities Act of 1990," May 14, 1990.
  CIS NO: <u>90-H643-1</u>
  LENGTH: 65 p.
  SUDOC: Y1.1/8:101-485/pt.1

H. Rpt. 101-485, pt. 2 on H.R. 2273, "Americans with Disabilities Act of 1990," May 15, 1990.
  CIS NO: <u>90-H343-6</u>
  LENGTH: 167 p.
  SUDOC: Y1.1/8:101-485/pt.2

H. Rpt. 101-485, pt. 3 on H.R. 2273, "Americans with Disabilities Act of 1990," May 15, 1990.
  CIS NO: <u>90-H523-8</u>
  LENGTH: 94 p.
  SUDOC: Y1.1/8:101-485/pt.3

H. Rpt. 101-485, pt. 4 on H.R. 2273, "Americans with Disabilities Act of 1990," May 15, 1990.
  CIS NO: <u>90-H363-9</u>
  LENGTH: 83 p.
  SUDOC: Y1.1/8:101-485/pt.4

H. Rpt. 101-558, conference report on S. 933, "Americans with Disabilities Act of 1990," June 26, 1990.
  CIS NO: <u>90-H343-12</u>
  LENGTH: 87 p.
  SUDOC: Y1.1/8:101-558

H. Rpt. 101-596, conference report on S. 933, "Americans with Disabilities Act of 1990," July 12, 1990.
  CIS NO: <u>90-H343-20</u>
  LENGTH: 91 p.
  SUDOC: Y1.1/8:101-596

HEARINGS:

100th Congress

"Hearing on Discrimination Against Cancer Victims and the Handicapped," hearings before the Subcommittee on Employment Opportunities, Committee on Education and Labor. House, June 17, 1987.
  CIS NO: <u>88-H341-4</u>
  LENGTH: iii+115 p.
  SUDOC: Y4.Ed8/1:100-31

"Americans with Disabilities Act of 1988," hearings before the Subcommittee on the Handicapped, Senate Labor and Human Resources Committee, and the Subcommittee on Select Education, House Education and Labor Committee, Sept. 27, 1988.
  CIS NO: <u>89-S541-17</u>
  LENGTH: v+96 p.
  SUDOC: Y4.L11/4:S.hrg.100-926

EXHIBIT 12.11   *(continued)*

"Oversight Hearing on H.R. 4498, Americans with Disabilities Act of 1988," hearings before the Subcommittee on Select Education, Committee on Education and Labor. House, Oct. 24, 1988.
   CIS NO: 89-H341-36
   LENGTH: v+235 p.
   SUDOC: Y4.Ed8/1:100-109

101st Congress

"Americans with Disabilities Act of 1989," hearings before the Subcommittee on the Handicapped, Committee on Labor and Human Resources. Senate, May 9, 10, 16, June 22, 1989.
   CIS NO: 89-S541-37
   LENGTH: v+849 p.
   SUDOC: Y4.L11/4:S.hrg.101-156

"Joint Hearing on H.R. 2273, the Americans with Disabilities Act of 1989," hearings before the Subcommittee on Select Education and the Subcommittee on Employment Opportunities, Committee on Education and Labor. House, July 18, 1989.
   CIS NO: 89-H341-81
   LENGTH: iii+146 p.
   SUDOC: Y4.Ed8/1:101-37

"Americans with Disabilities Act of 1989," hearings before the Subcommittee on Civil and Constitutional Rights, Committee on the Judiciary. House, Aug. 3, Oct. 11, 12, 1989.
   CIS NO: 90-H521-37
   LENGTH: iv+446 p. il.
   SUDOC: Y4.J89/1:101/58

"Field Hearing on Americans with Disabilities Act," hearings before the Subcommittee on Select Education, Committee on Education and Labor. House, Aug. 28, 1989.
   CIS NO: 90-H341-2
   LENGTH: iii+112 p.
   SUDOC: Y4.Ed8/1:101-56

"Hearing on H.R. 2273, the Americans with Disabilities Act of 1989," hearings before the Subcommittee on Employment Opportunities and the Subcommittee on Select Education, Committee on Education and Labor. House, Sept. 13, 1989.
   CIS NO: 90-H341-4
   LENGTH: iii+168 p.
   SUDOC: Y4.Ed8/1:101-51

"Americans with Disabilities Act," hearings before the Subcommittee on Surface Transportation, Committee on Public Works and Transportation. House, Sept. 20, 26, 1989.
   CIS NO: 90-H641-25
   LENGTH: xlix+524 p.
   SUDOC: Y4.P96/11:101-32

"Americans with Disabilities: Telecommunications Relay Services," hearings before the Subcommittee on Telecommunications and Finance, Committee on Energy and Commerce. House, Sept. 27, 1989.
   CIS NO: 90-H361-20
   LENGTH: iii+62 p.
   SUDOC: Y4.En2/3:101-96

"Americans with Disabilities Act," hearings before the Subcommittee on Transportation and Hazardous Materials, Committee on Energy and Commerce. House, Sept. 28, 1989.

Exhibit 12.11   *(continued)*

CIS NO: 90-H361-19
LENGTH: iii+174 p.
SUDOC: Y4.En2/3:101-95

"Hearing on H.R. 2273, Americans with Disabilities Act of 1989," hearings before the Subcommittee on Select Education, Committee on Education and Labor. House, Oct. 6, 1989.
CIS NO: 90-H341-3
LENGTH: iv+115 p.
SUDOC: Y4.Ed8/1:101-57

"Americans with Disabilities Act," hearings before the Committee on Small Business. House, Feb. 22, 1990.
CIS NO: 90-H721-24
LENGTH: iii+213 p.
SUDOC: Y4.Sm1:101-45

COMMITTEE PRINTS:

101st Congress

"Legislative History of Public Law **101-336,** the Americans with Disabilities Act, Vol. 1," committee print issued by the House Education and Labor Committee, Dec. 1990. (Not available at time of publication.)

"Legislative History of Public Law **101-336,** the Americans with Disabilities Act, Vol. 2," committee print issued by the House Education and Labor Committee, Dec. 1990. (Not available at time of publication.)

"Legislative History of Public Law **101-336,** the Americans with Disabilities Act, Vol. 3," committee print issued by the House Education and Labor Committee, Dec. 1990. (Not available at time of publication.)

MISCELLANEOUS PUBLICATIONS:

Weekly Compilation of Presidential Documents, Vol. 26 (1990): July 26, Presidential remarks and statement.

Source: **Combined Source Set 1** ⓘ **- US - CIS Legislative Histories**
Terms: **101-336** (Edit Search | Suggest Terms for My Search)
View: Full
Date/Time: Wednesday, December 19, 2007 - 3:39 PM EST

Search | Research Tasks | Get a Document | *Shepard's*® | Alerts | Total Litigator | Counsel Selector
History | Delivery Manager | Switch Client | Preferences | Help

To learn about the law's enactment process, read its bill tracking report. This report provides the statute's legislative chronology, step by step, including referrals to committees, information about hearings, additions of sponsors, and proposals and actions on amendments.

Links in the legislative history statement and bill tracking report lead to various documents, some to the text of the document, others to a detailed abstract. See Exhibit 12.6 (at pages 286–87), a *Congressional Record* excerpt obtained through LexisNexis. Should you be interested in reading a document based on the information in an abstract, you may obtain it in microfiche from the CIS, which is organized by accession numbers provided in the abstract.

Legislative history in Westlaw

- Graphical Statutes
- Previous versions of the statute
- Searchable public laws, committee reports, presidential messages, *Congressional Record*
- Compiled legislative histories

Quite recently, Westlaw has created a service consolidating disparate information about a statute — Graphical Statutes — that is available for fairly recent federal statutes and some states' statutes. Once you find a pertinent section, you can click into its graphical presentation. Exhibit 12.12 (at page 305) is the entry point for § 12102 of the ADA.

The prior text column provides access to previous versions of the statute, in some cases by directing you to the credits material found immediately after the statutory language in U.S.C.A. A click or two away is a searchable U.S.C.A. database from the years that some version of the statute has been in effect.

The middle column provides links to the current statute and a wealth of legislative history documents: public laws, committee reports, presidential messages, and the *Congressional Record*. A significant benefit of researching these documents in Westlaw is the availability of a locate search within a document. For some statutes, Westlaw also links to a compiled legislative history.[2]

The Graphical Statutes display also alerts you to the validity of the current statute, including a KeyCite flag and references to cases negatively impacting the statute. The right column provides links to proposed legislation that would amend the statute.

Exhibit 12.13 (at page 306) is our legislative history template filled in to reflect some of our research for the Canoga case.

---

2. As of late fall 2007, Westlaw planned to add laws back to 1915 within four years.

EXHIBIT **12.12**   Graphical Statutes Display,
                          from United States Code Annotated
                          Online in Westlaw (online source)

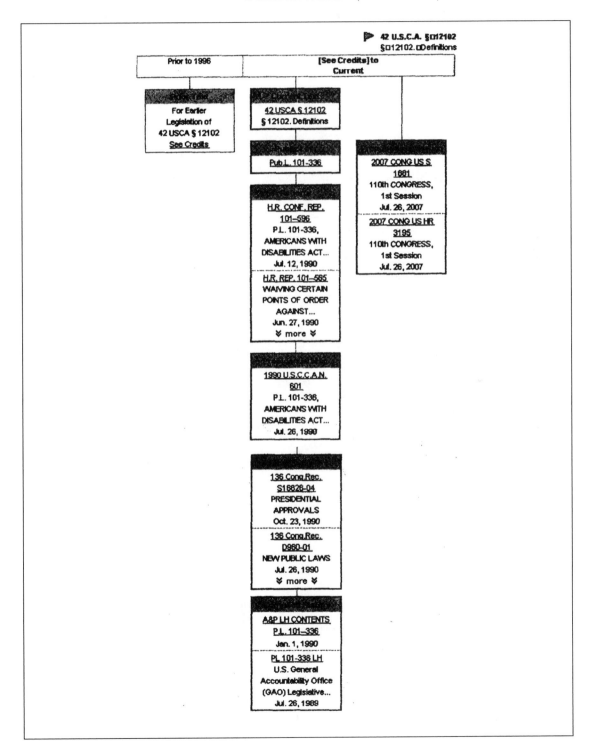

EXHIBIT 12.13	Legislative History Template for Canoga Case

Document and Source:	Information and Implications:
purpose provision in statute:	*"some 43,000,000 Americans have one or more physical or mental disabilities."*
bills: • *S. 933 101st Congress, 1st session (Westlaw).* • *H.R. 2273.* • *amendment no. 722, passed Sept. 7, 1989 (THOMAS).*	*Excludes certain types of drug addiction.*
committee reports: • *House Report No. 101-485(II), Education & Labor Comm., May 15, 1990.*	—
hearing testimony: • *Evan J. Kemp, Jr., EEOC Commissioner, House Subcomms on Select Educ. & Empl. Opportunities, Sept. 13, 1989.*	—
floor statements: • *John McCain, July 13, 1990, Cong. Rec. S9,684.*	*Real champions of legislation are 43 million disabled Americans.*
committee print:	
executive agency reports:	
presidential signing statement: • *Pres. George Bush, 26 Weekly Compilation of Presidential Documents 1165, July 30, 1990 (U.S.C.C.A.N.).*	—

4. How Do You Cite Legislative Materials?

Each type of legislative history document has its own citation requirements.

Enacted bills are cited as statutes unless they are used to document legislative history, in which case they are cited as unenacted bills. Unenacted bills are cited with the chamber's abbreviation, the bill number, the number of the Congress, the section number (if any), and the year or date. The name of the bill may be included; if the unenacted bill can be found in a published hearing record, that information may be added. Here are two examples:

- ☐ *Bluebook* Rule 13.2: S. 933, 101st Cong. § 1 (1989).
- ☐ *ALWD* Rule 15.1: Sen. 933, 101st Cong. § 1 (May 9, 1989).

The form for a hearing transcript includes the subject matter title, the bill number, the committee name(s), the number of the Congress, the page number, the date, and identifying information about the witness. Here are two examples:

- ☐ *Bluebook* Rule 13.3: *Americans with Disabilities Act of 1989: Hearing on H.R. 2273 Before the Subcomm. on Employment Opportunities and the Subcomm. on Select Education of the House Comm. on Education and Labor*, 101st Cong. 5 (1989) (statement of Evan J. Kemp, Commissioner, EEOC).
- ☐ *ALWD* Rule 15.7: H.R. Subcomm. on Empl. Opportunities & Subcomm. on Select Educ. of the Comm. on Educ. and Labor, *Americans with Disabilities Act of 1989: Hearing on H.R 2273*, 101st Cong. 5 (Sept. 13, 1989).

For committee reports, the form includes the name of the chamber, the numbers of the Congress and the report, page number (if you are citing a particular page), and year or date. If the report is published in U.S.C.C.A.N., a U.S.C.C.A.N. citation should be added. Here are two examples:

- ☐ *Bluebook* Rule 13.4: H.R. Rep. No. 101-485(II) (1990), as *reprinted in* 1990 U.S.C.C.A.N. 267.
- ☐ *ALWD* Rule 15.9: H.R. Rpt. 101-485(II) (May 14, 1990) (reprinted in 1990 U.S.C.C.A.N. 267).

Congressional debates are cited to the *Congressional Record*; the permanent version must be cited if available. The speaker should be identified. Here are two examples:

- ☐ *Bluebook* Rule 13.5: 136 Cong. Rec. S9,684 (daily ed. July 13, 1990) (statement of Sen. McCain).

☐ *ALWD* Rule 15.12: 136 Cong. Rec. S9684 (daily ed. July 13, 1990) (statement of Sen. John McCain).

5.   What Else?

Congressional Information Service. The Congressional Information Service in paper and microfiche covering statutes from 1970 to date has the following major components:

☐ *CIS Annual/Abstracts,* which provides descriptions of various legislative history documents and is organized by a system of accession numbers;

☐ *CIS Annual Index,* which contains detailed indexes, for example, by subject or bill number, listing the CIS accession numbers of pertinent documents;

☐ *Legislative Histories of U.S. Public Laws,* which is a collection of the Legislative History statements discussed above in regard to Lexis-Nexis Congressional; and

☐ microfiche collection, which encompasses bills, hearing records, committee reports and prints, and other documents.

The first two components are updated on a monthly basis.

CIS also provides paper and electronic indexes and microfiche sets of hearing records, committee prints, and executive documents and reports for pre-1970 legislation. Some are now available in the CIS digital collection.

The United States Congressional Serial Set. The Serial Set, one of the most important resources for U.S. history, has been published in one form or another, under one title or another, since 1789 by the Government Printing Office. It includes committee reports, House and Senate documents (including presidential statements), and some committee prints. Sources of the Serial Set include CIS and LexisNexis.

Congressional Record. The *Congressional Record,* the primary source for debates and votes, is issued on a daily basis and reissued in annual volumes. The daily version has four separately paginated parts: Senate; House; extensions of remarks; and the daily digest, which summarizes a day's proceedings. The annual *Congressional Record* includes a History of Bills and Resolutions, which provides a brief description of a bill and its key events.

Weekly Compilation of Presidential Documents. This publication is the primary source of presidential signing and veto statements. It is issued weekly and is accompanied by weekly, quarterly, and annual indexes.

GPO Access. The Government Printing Office has long provided copies of federal government documents. Recently, it has made many documents available through the website GPOAccess.gov. At present, the following documents are available from the year listed to date: history of bills from 1983, published bills from 1993, the *Congressional Record* from 1995, hearings from 1995, and committee prints from 1997. You may search the documents from the current session or search the archives.

LexisNexis and Westlaw Databases. In addition to the databases mentioned previously, LexisNexis and Westlaw both provide databases composed of categories of legislative history documents, e.g., bill texts from a recent session, the *Congressional Record*.

State Legislative History. Researching state legislative history generally is not easy. Before embarking on state legislative history research, look for a book on legal research in your state, consult your state legislative website; consult with your state's legislative reference librarian; or consult a text on state legislative history, such as *State Legislative Sourcebook: A Resource Guide to Legislative Information in the Fifty States.*

C. PENDING LEGISLATION

Legislative process sources can be used not only to research the legislative history of enacted laws but also to track the status of pending legislation. Although statutes generally operate prospectively, some clients wisely seek to know about probable new laws so they can plan ahead. Also, some clients seek to lobby the legislature to secure favorable new laws. Information technology has made this type of research very feasible.

On the federal side, THOMAS and both LexisNexis and LexisNexis Congressional offer much the same materials for bills as they do for laws. You can use bill numbers, if you have one, or key-word searching to find bills you may not know about. Thus, you can easily secure the text of the bill and the steps taken on the bill to date. See Exhibit 12.14 (at pages 310–11), which is the report for a bill before Congress in late 2007 that would amend the definition of "disability" in the ADA.

If you use the Graphical Statutes feature on Westlaw, you will be informed of pending legislation that would affect the statute. Westlaw provides the text of bills and a bill-tracking function, although the information is less extensive than that provided by THOMAS and LexisNexis.

LexisNexis and Westlaw provide bill tracking programs for state legislation as well. Another less expensive option is to visit the state legislature's website. At New Mexico's website, legis.state.nm.us, for example, is a "bill finder" searchable by bill number, sponsor, locator (status in the enactment process and present location), keyword, and subject. At the end of a session, the latter provides a topical list of the various bills and their progress. See Exhibit 12.15 (at page 312). The website also provides a "bill watcher" function, through which you would receive alerts of activity involving a specified bill.

| EXHIBIT 12.14 | Federal Bill Tracking Report,
from LexisNexis (online source) |

1 of 2 DOCUMENTS

Copyright 2007 Congressional Information Service, Inc
Bill Tracking Report

110th Congress
1st Session
U. S. Senate

S 1881

2007 Bill Tracking S. **1881**; 110 Bill Tracking S. **1881**

AMERICANS WITH DISABILITIES ACT RESTORATION ACT OF 2007

Retrieve full text version

SPONSOR: Senator Tom Harkin D-IA

DATE-INTRO: July 26, 2007

LAST-ACTION-DATE: November 15, 2007

STATUS: Introduced in the Senate, 07/26/07

TOTAL-COSPONSORS: 2 Cosponsors: 1 Democrats / 1 Republicans

SYNOPSIS: A bill to amend the **Americans with Disabilities Act** of 1990 to restore the intent and protections of that Act, and for other purposes

 Display Major Actions Only

Display All Legislative Actions (default)

ACTIONS: Committee Referrals:
 07/26/2007 Senate Committee on Health, Education, Labor, and Pensions

Legislative Chronology:

 1st Session Activity:

07/26/2007 153 Cong Rec S 10148
        Referred to the Senate Committee on Health, Education, Labor, and Pensions.

07/26/2007 153 Cong Rec S 10151
        Remarks by Sen. Harkin (D-IA)

11/15/2007 153 Cong Rec D 1537
        Hearing held by Senate Committee on Health, Education, Labor, and Pensions

BILL-DIGEST: (from the CONGRESSIONAL RESEARCH SERVICE)

EXHIBIT 12.14   *(continued)*

Bill Tracking Report S 1881

Digest :

Americans with Disabilities Act Restoration Act of 2007 - Amends the **Americans with Disabilities Act** of 1990 to define "disability" as a physical or mental impairment (under current law, a physical or mental impairment that substantially limits one or more of the major life activities of such individual), a record of a such impairment, or being regarded as having a such impairment.
Prohibits, in determining whether an individual has an impairment, considering whether the individual uses a mitigating measure, the impact of any mitigating measures, or whether any impairment manifestations are episodic, in remission, or latent. Defines the term "mitigating measure."
Defines "physical" and "mental" (used regarding impairment), "record of physical or mental impairment," and "regarded as having a physical or mental impairment."
Declares that an adverse action because of an individual's use of a mitigating measure constitutes discrimination under the Act.
Prohibits employment discrimination on the basis of disability (currently, against a qualified individual with a disability because of the disability).
Allows, as a defense to a charge of discrimination, that the individual alleging discrimination is not a qualified individual with a disability.
Requires that the Act's provisions be broadly construed. Entitles duly issued federal regulations and guidance to deference by administrative agencies or officers and courts.

CRS Index Terms:

Display Co-Sponsor List

Display Co-Sponsor List By Date

Display Co-Sponsor List By Political Party

Display Co-Sponsors (Default)

CO-SPONSORS:
 (Display Co-Sponsor List by Date -- ascending order)
Original Cosponsors:
    Specter R-PA
 Added 07/30/2007:
    Kennedy D-MA

SUBJECT: AMERICANS WITH DISABILITIES ACT (94%); LEGISLATION (90%); LABOR & EMPLOY-MENT LAW (90%); DISABLED PERSONS (90%); AGENCY RULEMAKING (78%); EMPLOYMENT (75%); EMPLOYMENT DISCRIMINATION (67%);

COUNTRY: UNITED STATES;

LOAD-DATE: 11/20/2007

| EXHIBIT 12.15 | Subject Index of State Legislation, from New Mexico Legislature's Website (online source) |

Legislative Council Service

48TH LEGISLATURE, FIRST SESSION, 2007

Subject Index

Legislation		Title	Sponsor	Location
ELECTIONS				
SB	52	ELIMINATE STRAIGHT PARTY BALLOT OPTION	Komadina	API
SB	179	VOTING SYSTEM AUDITS & ACCURACY	McSorley	API
SB	**342**	CANDIDATE WITHDRAWAL REQUIREMENTS	**Duran**	**Chapter 274**
SB	354	MAIL-IN CONSERVANCY DISTRICT ELECTION BALLOTS	Sanchez M	API
SB	360	MUNICIPAL ELECTIONS BY COUNTY CLERKS	Sanchez M	API
SB	**363**	ELECTRONIC CAMPAIGN REPORT FILING PROVISIONS	**Sanchez M**	**Veto**
SB	400	CONTRIBUTIONS TO STATE AGENTS & CANDIDATES	Ingle	API
SB	434	MAIL-IN IRRIGATION DISTRICT ELECTION BALLOTS	Harden	API
SB	**444**	CHANGE CANDIDATE REPORTING REQUIREMENTS	**Boitano**	**Chapter 202**
SB	449	AUTOMATIC RECOUNTS IN CERTAIN ELECTIONS	Feldman	API
SB	488	CONSERVANCY DISTRICT ELECTORS & VOTING	Harden	API
SB	**506**	INDEPENDENT CANDIDATE QUALIFICATIONS	**Duran**	**Chapter 25**
SB	508	EMERGENCY VOTING REQUIREMENTS	Duran	API
SB	510	REPLACEMENT OF CANDIDATES ON BALLOT	Duran	API
SB	571	USE OF ABSENTEE BALLOTS AS BACKUPS	Campos P	API
SB	603	ABSENTEE BALLOTS IN LIEU OF POLLING PLACES	Duran	API
SB	666	ELECTION OF PRESIDENT BY POPULAR VOTE	Altamirano	API
SB	**671**	CANDIDATE WITHDRAWAL REQUIREMENTS	**Lopez**	**Veto**
SB	737	CAMPAIGN DISCLOSURE LAWS & CERTAIN CONTRACTS	Robinson	API
SB	796	LEGISLATIVE CAMPAIGN FUNDS FOR OFFICE DUTIES	Garcia MJ	API
SB	799	PUBLIC FINANCING OF STATEWIDE CAMPAIGNS	Feldman	API
SB	800	CAMPAIGN REPORTING REQUIREMENTS	Feldman	API
SB	860	SAME-DAY VOTER REGISTRATION	McSorley	API
SB	928	ELECTION OF CERTAIN SCHOOL DISTRICT BOARDS	Ortiz y Pino	API
SB	948	ELECTION CODE TERMINOLOGY UPDATES	Lopez	API
SB	956	ELECTION CODE PROCEDURE REVISIONS	Lopez	API
SB	959	ALBUQUERQUE SCHOOL BOARD ELECTIONS	Ortiz y Pino	API
SB	962	WATER & SANITATION DISTRICT AUTHORITY	Cisneros	API
SB	980	VARIOUS ELECTION CODE CHANGES	Lopez	API
SB	**984**	COMMUNITY COLLEGE BOARD MEMBER ELECTIONS	**Jennings**	**Chapter 27**
SB	1027	SAN MIGUEL COUNTY BUREAU OF ELECTIONS STAFF	Campos P	API
SB	**1105**	ALTERNATE NATIVE AMERICAN VOTING LOCATIONS	**Lovejoy**	**Veto**
SJR	18	ALBUQUERQUE SCHOOL BOARD ELECTION, CA	Ortiz y Pino	API
EMPLOYER & EMPLOYEE (including workers' comp)				
HB	8	DEVELOPMENT TRAINING PROGRAMS	**Lujan B**	**Chapter 363**
HB	51	FILM INDUSTRY CHILD LABOR PROVISIONS	Swisstack	API
HB	80	FARM & RANCH WORKERS' COMP COVERAGE	Lujan A	API
HB	**88**	ATHLETIC TRAINER AS HEALTH CARE PROVIDER	**Taylor T**	**Chapter 327**
HB	110	WORKFORCE TRAINING PROGRAMS & SOFTWARE	Gutierrez	API
HB	193	LEAVE FOR CRIME VICTIMS AT LEGAL PROCEEDINGS	Chasey	API
HB	**247**	UNEMPLOYMENT PAYMENT RATE INCREASES	**Stewart**	**Chapter 137**
HB	335	FAIR SHARE FOR HEALTH CARE ACT	Garcia MP	API
HB	339	MENTORING SERVICES IN UNDERSERVED AREAS	Barela	API
HB	**342**	FEDERAL PUBLIC BENEFIT LAW COMPLIANCE	**Varela**	**Chapter 350**
HB	419	NORTHERN NM SUMMER YOUTH EMPLOYMENT	Vigil	API
HB	434	PERMANENT HIGH-WAGE JOBS TAX CREDIT	Heaton	API
HB	493	WORKERS' COMP BENEFITS FOR INCARCERATED	Maestas	API
HB	543	BERNALILLO WORKFORCE DEVELOPMENT PROGRAM	Anderson	API
HB	559	RIGHT TO WORK ACT	Ezzell	API
HB	**613**	BREAST PUMP USE IN WORKPLACES	**Picraux**	**Chapter 18**
HB	632	CHILD CARE PROVIDER COLLECTIVE BARGAINING	Garcia MP	API

D. CONCLUDING POINTS

Legislative process materials are researched for two purposes:

- ☐ legislative history: to gain insight into the legislature's intent in enacting a law, and
- ☐ bill tracking: to track progress on pending legislation.

Most legislative history research involves federal statutes. For any law there may be many documents, including various bills and amendments, hearing records, committee reports, floor debates, and presidential statements; some documents are more authoritative than others. Many legislative history sources exist, so there are, in turn, many approaches to researching in them. After gleaning basic information from the statutory code, you may do any of the following:

- ☐ Consult *United States Code Congressional and Administrative News*, which provides key documents in a highly accessible paper source as well as a Westlaw database.
- ☐ Peruse a compiled legislative history if your statute is of widespread significance.
- ☐ Work through THOMAS, a free web-based legislative information service of the Library of Congress.
- ☐ Explore the Congressional Information Service through LexisNexis, which provides not only information about a law's legislative process but also many of the documents generated in Congress.
- ☐ Work through the links provided through Westlaw's Graphical Statutes tool.

In legislative history research, more than in any other area of legal research, technology has made information and documents readily available and relatively easy to research.

To track the status of pending legislation, which is fairly easily accomplished at both the state and federal levels, you may use some of the sources listed previously, bill-tracking services on LexisNexis and Westlaw, and the legislature's own website.

INTERLUDE NO. 4 RESEARCH IN ENACTED LAW

1. New Mexico's Employee Privacy Act

Our commentary research, namely the periodical article discussed in Chapter 5, had directed us to a New Mexico statute squarely addressing employer regulation of off-duty smoking. Could we have found it another way? Yes — quite easily.

We found two direct routes to New Mexico statutes online: Googling our way to the New Mexico Legislature's website, legis.state.nm.us and using the LII (Cornell University) portal. We learned that a private company, ConwayGreene Co., collaborates with the New Mexico Compilation Commission to maintain a database of New Mexico statutes. The site was current through the 2007 special bill-tracking session, during our research in the fall of 2007. The site also provided a list of new laws organized by topic — a good list to monitor during the legislative session.

At the New Mexico legislature's website, we could browse the table of contents or run a terms-and-connectors search. Browsing went very smoothly: chapter 50 covers Employment Law; article 11 covers Employee Privacy; there we found the smoking statute. On the other hand, writing a successful terms-and-connectors search was difficult, until we read the protocols and adjusted our search accordingly, to smok* & employ* (* is the same thing as ! on other systems). That search yielded section 3 of the pertinent statute, the main section prohibiting employer bans on off-duty smoking. The website provided only the statutory language — not even the year or session law of enactment.

Because our library carries West's New Mexico Statutes Annotated, we looked there as well. Again, this went very easily. The table of contents led directly to the statute, and so did the index entry Employee Privacy Act. As shown in Exhibit 1.3 (at pages 14–16), this version provided information beyond the statutory language: the citation for the law creating the statute (L. 1991, Ch. 244); references to commentary, such as the encyclopedia C.J.S.; and key numbers for use in West's reporters and digests. Unfortunately there were no case descriptions. The main volume was published in 2003. We found nothing additional in the 2007 pocket part.

To double-check for very new legislation, we looked in West's New Mexico Session Law Service. According to the table of sections affected, there were no changes in chapter 50, article 11. However, under Labor and Employment in the index, we learned that the legislature adopted a new statute on breast-feeding (actually, pumping milk to feed the baby later on) in the workplace. The statute was slotted into the chapter on Human Rights, rather than the Employment Law chapter. This demonstrates what can challenge those who codify statutes and the people who research them — a new law may pertain to more than one existing chapter, yet it will appear in only one. As you research, you should always keep this possibility in mind.

The Employee Privacy Act squarely addresses Ms. Canoga's situation. On her side, the statute prohibits an employer from requiring as a condition of employment that an employee abstain from smoking during nonworking hours. On the other hand, there is an exception for a bona fide (good faith) occupational requirement that is rationally related to a particular group of employees, and the orchestra's ban covered only brass and woodwind players.

2. The Federal Statute: Americans with Disabilities Act (ADA)

Happily, our research in treatises, described in Chapter 4, directed us to the federal Americans with Disabilities Act (ADA), more specifically to § 12201 of title 42 of the United States Code. We could find that provision and another provision defining "disability" other ways — but only with considerable effort. For illustrative purposes, we have recounted here more steps than one would usually take.

Definition of Disability. Working with the online version at LII's website,[1] we found that locating the pertinent statute by working from broad to narrow outlines was difficult: the statute appears in title 42 covering the Public Health and Welfare; that title has over 170 chapters, some that seemed but were not pertinent, in a sequence that is far from obvious. It worked better to run a search within that title — disability smoking — which yielded three hits, including § 12201, which indicates that the ADA does not prohibit workplace smoking bans. Title 42 dated to January of 2005, so we needed to check the update, which showed no legislative activity since then.

When, for fun, we tried a search in the entire code at the House website, our first searches yielded as many as 12,000 hits (ouch). After reading through the very clear protocols and many more tries, we crafted a search — disability near/40 smoking or smoke near/40 employee — that yielded nine hits, including § 12201. That House version had more background information than the LII version.

Next, we sought the assistance provided in the commercial annotated codes in paper. The U.S.C.A. index worked well: Disabled Persons → Handicapped Persons → Equal Opportunity for Individuals with Disabilities → many references to the ADA including § 12102, the definition section. We ran around in circles a bit in the U.S.C.S. index — looking at Civil Rights, Disabled Persons, Labor & Employment, and Job Discrimination; indeed we initially identified a different statute governing federal agencies and organizations contracting with federal agencies. Eventually we located the entry for the ADA.

---

1. When we conducted our research in the fall of 2007, not only did we see federal statutes on the screen, but also an appeal for donations and a link saying "Study Law Abroad, Cornell Paris Institute" — the beginning, perhaps, of sponsorships of the well regarded service.

After a quick comparison of U.S.C.A. and U.S.C.S., we chose to work with the U.S.C.S. version of the definitions section, § 12102, because the framework for the case descriptions made more sense. We found a little statutory language — forty-two words defining "disability" — accompanied by a brief statement of the statute's history, a few cross-references to other statutes, a slew of references to commentary, and over 100 pages of case descriptions filed under 100 topics. One topic was Drugs or Alcohol Dependency; there we found a reference to a case deciding that a prisoner's nicotine addiction is not a "disability" under the ADA, *Brashear v. Simms*, 138 F. Supp. 2d 693 (D. Md. 2001) — definitely worth a read, unfortunately. We learned nothing new in the updating publications.

To pursue this issue another step, we ran a search in Westlaw in the federal courts databases using the search 42 /5 12102 /p smok! nicotine. This search yielded twenty cases, all but one involving the employee's reaction to others' smoke. One case did involve an employee with a nicotine addiction, but he had many other impairments as well. *Anderson v. Indep. School Dist. No. 281*, Civ. No. 01-560, 2002 WL 31242212 (D. Minn. Oct. 4, 2002).

Workplace Smoking Bans. For variety, we turned to LexisNexis. Pretending that we did not know about § 12201, we decided to see whether smoking was specifically discussed in a federal employment statute. We selected the Labor & Employment subject area — which confined the search to eight titles with some material on employment issues — and searched in the heading segment for smok! /p disability or disable!. At the end of the list of forty-one hits, which we easily browsed, was § 12201. The annotation was similar in content to that for § 12102 but considerably smaller — this section has received much less discussion. We found two cases involving smoking bans in fast-food restaurants: *Staron v. McDonald's Corp.*, 51 F.3d 353 (2d Cir. 1995), and *Neff v. American Dairy Queen Corp.*, 58 F.3d 1063 (5th Cir. 1995). Given how few cases we had found, they merited some attention.

We followed up our research into § 12201 by Shepardizing it (easily done while reading the statute on LexisNexis). We learned that subdivision (b) has been cited sixty-three times. Would it make sense to look at all of these? Probably not. The language we cared about is found in the second sentence; many of the cases could pertain to the broader first sentence. A good middle ground was to read only the cases in the Tenth (New Mexico's) Circuit; neither pertained to our issue.

Toward the end, being concerned about very recent legislation, we checked both the table of code sections affected during the 110th Congress, First Session and the index to recent laws in the U.S.C.S. advance legislative service. There was no change in the ADA, although Congress apparently proclaimed some month National Disability Employment Awareness Month — interesting, but not worth following up on.

We also KeyCited the statute. KeyCite gave it a yellow flag because bills in Congress, if passed, would amend it. References and links to these bills appear in West's Graphical Statutes display for § 12102.

Legislative History. Not surprisingly, when we turned to research Congressional intent, we found a great abundance of material generated during the ADA's enactment. The House and Senate considered separate bills, two committee reports (one involving four House committees) and two conference committee reports were written, debate spanned two years, the Senate bill eventually passed, and the President wrote a signing statement.

Also not surprisingly, our research did not yield a direct statement about nicotine addiction as a disability. We searched for mentions of nicotine addiction or smoking in various databases, for example, U.S.C.C.A.N., the legislative history compiled by a major Washington D.C. law firm (Arnold & Porter) available through Westlaw — no hits other than the provision permitting workplace smoking bans.

We did find bits and pieces of information that permitted some extrapolation about coverage of nicotine addiction. For example, in several places, such as the purpose statement in the ADA itself and Sen. John McCain's statement during the Senate debate, we saw a reference to 43 million Americans having one or more physical or mental disabilities. When the ADA was passed, the U.S. population was approximately 250 million, and 51 million American adults smoked (we learned from Census Bureau information obtained through Google). It seems unlikely that the 43 million figure was based on smoking statistics.

This analysis is found in the *Brashear* case. The court assumed that the ADA applied to a prison, then ruled that a prisoner's nicotine addiction was not a "disability." The court reasoned that Congress would not have intended to cover 25–30% of the American population within the ADA. Furthermore, nicotine addiction is remediable, and remediable conditions are not covered by the ADA under *Sutton v. United Airlines, Inc.*, 527 U.S. 471 (1999).

Incidentally the bill used as the example in our bill-tracking discussion seeks to broaden the definition of "disability," in part by overturning the rule that remediable conditions are not disabilities.

3.   The Taos City Code

Our research in the Taos City Code was very fast. We found it at sterlingcodifiers.com; ran a search for `discrimination`; and obtained section 3.60.020, which addresses discrimination by the city on the basis of disability and other traits. The ordinance did not apply to Ms. Canoga's situation because the city is not her employer. We browsed the titles; no other ordinance looked pertinent.

Again: We have shown you a wide range of research options in this interlude. In practice, we would use fewer.

ADMINISTRATIVE MATERIALS

In the United States, law is made not only by the judiciary and the legislature, but also by administrative agencies. Administrative agencies are involved in almost every aspect of American life. They regulate the environment, issue drivers' licenses, and inspect restaurants. Agencies operate at the federal, state, and local levels. For some matters, a single agency may operate alone; in other fields, there may be an overlap.

Many agencies regulate an industry, such as nuclear energy; others regulate certain practices, such as employment relations of various industries. Some gather data, such as the Census Bureau, and some provide scientific or other expertise in a specialized field. An agency may have the power to promulgate regulations, adjudicate cases, prosecute violations of the law, inspect operations, issue licenses, or conduct studies.

Agencies have two lawmaking functions: rulemaking and case adjudication. Rulemaking resembles legislative activity, and case adjudication resembles judicial activity. In this unit, we will use "regulation" to refer to the product of agency rulemaking and "agency decision" to refer to the product of case adjudication. As to both, the agency acts in concert with and under the supervision of the legislature, executive, and courts.

☐ The legislature by statute establishes the scope of the agency's authority, the goals the agency is to pursue, and its lawmaking functions. Subsequent statutes may direct the agency to adopt regulations in specific areas, investigate particular policy issues, or perform other tasks. Laws establishing agencies and endowing them with lawmaking power are often referred to as "organic" or "enabling" statutes. We will use the term "enabling statute" in our discussion. Legislatures also oversee and fund agencies.

☐ The links between agencies and the executive vary. Typically agency commissioners are appointed by the executive, and the agency may be highly influenced by the executive on matters of policy and budget.

☐ The courts review agency actions. If a court finds the agency's action to be unconstitutional, contrary to law, inadequately supported by the factual record, or insufficiently explained, it may invalidate the action.

Agency procedures for making regulations and adjudicating cases are usually governed by a separate administrative procedure statute. The federal version of this law is known as the Administrative Procedure Act, and there are similar state laws. Although these laws often govern, legislatures sometimes override these general procedures and establish more specific requirements for certain agencies or subject matters.

This unit has three chapters:

☐ Chapter 13 covers regulations, with a focus on official sources.
☐ Similarly, Chapter 14 covers agency decisions, with a focus on official sources.
☐ Chapter 15 covers commercial sources, usually referred to as "looseleaf services," which pull together a wide range of legal authorities in a specific practice area. Looseleaf services are especially useful in areas involving administrative agencies, so they are covered in this unit.

This unit explores a new issue in the Canoga case. Recall that Ms. Canoga's concern over the no-smoking policy was shared to some extent by her coworkers. See the Canoga case on pages 3–4. Hence, she might claim that the orchestra violated her right to act in concert with her workers. A federal statute, the National Labor Relations Act (NLRA), safeguards this right and enables the operations of a major federal agency, the National Labor Relations Board (Board). The Board protects employees who engage in concerted activity, whether through a union or without a union on the scene. The Board has the authority to promulgate regulations and prosecute and adjudicate cases involving violations of the NLRA, called "unfair labor practices."

This unit focuses throughout on federal law. There are analogous authorities, sources, and research methods at the state level.

REGULATIONS

A. What Are Regulations, and Why Would You Research Them?
B. How Do You Research and Cite Regulations?
C. What Else?

A.   WHAT ARE REGULATIONS, AND WHY WOULD YOU RESEARCH THEM?

Federal and state agencies promulgate various types of regulations:

☐ Legislative, or substantive, regulations are based on a specific statutory delegation of power from the legislature. Typically, the statute identifies in general terms the conduct to be regulated and the penalties that may be assessed; the statute then delegates to the agency the task of filling in the specifics of the regulatory scheme, consistent with the statute.

☐ Interpretative regulations are an agency's statement of its interpretation of its enabling statute; these regulations have substantially less force than legislative regulations.

☐ Procedural regulations address how the agency operates.

All regulations provide insight into what the law is. Indeed, a legislative regulation is law, so long as it meets constitutional and statutory requirements and was properly promulgated. Somewhat in contrast, an interpretative regulation is a significant statement of the agency's interpretation of the pertinent statute, but it is not itself law; it may be disregarded by a court that interprets the statute differently. Even so, courts often rely on or defer to such agency interpretations, in recognition of the agency's technical expertise and role in our government. Finally, procedural regulations are important for obvious reasons: they set out the steps, timelines, and details of how to handle a matter before the agency.

To create a legislative regulation, an agency may follow one of several processes, as specified in an administrative procedure act, enabling statute, or other statute. The dominant model is informal rulemaking, also known as notice-and-comment rulemaking. This process begins when the agency gives notice to the public of the topic it is about to consider. The public then has an opportunity to provide pertinent information to the agency through written submissions or, sometimes, through written or oral testimony at agency hearings. The agency considers these comments as it develops the final regulation and then promulgates the regulation with a statement of its basis and purpose. A less common approach is formal rulemaking, which entails a trial-type hearing in which participants may cross-examine witnesses and provide evidence. In formal rulemaking, the agency must issue findings and conclusions to support its regulation. In addition to these two general approaches, agencies are sometimes required by law to supplement these procedures with additional procedural steps or to consider additional substantive issues before promulgating a regulation. This is often referred to as hybrid rulemaking.

The process for adopting interpretative regulations is usually much less elaborate than for legislative regulations. Often, the agency may simply issue a final interpretative regulation based on its own internal deliberations, although it may provide for public participation. This relative lack of process is usually explained by the fact that interpretative regulations are not intended to have the same binding effect on regulated parties as do legislative regulations.

In form, an agency regulation resembles a statute. See Exhibit 13.1 (at page 324). A regulation consists of general rules applicable to a range of persons engaging in certain conduct. Regulations use fairly specific terms because they are intended to give precision to broad statutory language and are to be applied to specific situations. Many use numerical tests or technical concepts, based on the agency's particular area of expertise.

Finding out which agency regulates a particular topic is not always easy. Agencies exist at federal, state, and local levels. Typically, if a federal statute governs, there is a federal agency, and federal regulations will govern, too. Similarly, if a state statute governs, you will be concerned with a state agency and its regulations. In some areas, however, federal and state statutes may overlap — consumer protection is a good example. In other areas, such as regulation of the environment, federal law may create a cooperative arrangement between the federal and state agencies. In these situations, federal and state (and even local) regulations may apply.

Another factor in locating the correct law is timing: You must identify the regulation in effect as of the time of your client's fact situation. A regulation is presumed to be prospective, applying to events arising after its promulgation. Hence, as you research regulations, you must attend to their effective date and currency.

Exhibit 13.1 is one of the relatively few regulations promulgated by the National Labor Relations Board. It pertains to the Board's exercise of jurisdiction over orchestras.

B. HOW DO YOU RESEARCH AND CITE REGULATIONS?

1. Researching Regulations

Regulations research shares many similarities with research in statutes, as a comparison of our regulations template, Exhibit 13.2 (at page 325), with the statutes template, Exhibit 11.4 (at page 232), suggests. This makes sense when you consider that regulations, like statutes, are a form of codified law. Regulations currently in force appear in a code of regulations. Like a statutory code, a code of regulations is organized topically and has a structure that may include titles, chapters, parts, and sections. Indeed, the organization of the code of regulations may parallel the organization of the statutory code authorizing the regulations.

Regulations also appear in a publication reporting the activities of the jurisdiction's various agencies on a frequent basis, for example, daily or weekly; a common name for this publication is "register." In addition to newly promulgated regulations, registers contain explanations of new

| EXHIBIT 13.1 | Regulation, from Code of Federal Regulations (paper source) |

Las Vegas	8:30 a.m.–5 p.m.
29—Brooklyn	9 a.m.–5:30 p.m.
30—Milwaukee	8 a.m.–4:30 p.m.
31—Los Angeles	8:30 a.m.–5 p.m.
32—Oakland	8:30 a.m.–5 p.m.
33—Peoria	8:30 a.m.–5 p.m.
34—Hartford	8:30 a.m.–5 p.m.

[57 FR 4158, Feb. 4, 1992]

PART 103—OTHER RULES

Subpart A—Jurisdictional Standards

Sec.
103.1 Colleges and universities.
103.2 Symphony orchestras.
103.3 Horseracing and dogracing industries.

Subpart B—Election Procedures

103.20 Posting of election notices.

Subpart C—Appropriate Bargaining Units

103.30 Appropriate bargaining units in the health care industry.

Subpart E [Reserved]

Subpart F—Remedial Orders

103.100 Offers of reinstatement to employees in Armed Forces.

AUTHORITY: 29 U.S.C. 156, in accordance with the procedure set forth in 5 U.S.C. 553.

Subpart A—Jurisdictional Standards

§ 103.1 Colleges and universities.

The Board will assert its jurisdiction in any proceeding arising under sections 8, 9, and 10 of the Act involving any private nonprofit college or university which has a gross annual revenue from all sources (excluding only contributions which, because of limitation by the grantor, are not available for use for operating expenses) of not less than $1 million.

[35 FR 18370, Dec. 3, 1970]

§ 103.2 Symphony orchestras.

The Board will assert its jurisdiction in any proceeding arising under sections 8, 9, and 10 of the Act involving any symphony orchestra which has a gross annual revenue from all sources (excluding only contributions which are because of limitation by the grant-

or not available for use for operating expenses) of not less than $1 million.

[38 FR 6177, Mar. 7, 1973]

§ 103.3 Horseracing and dogracing industries.

The Board will not assert its jurisdiction in any proceeding under sections 8, 9, and 10 of the Act involving the horseracing and dogracing industries.

[38 FR 9507, Apr. 17, 1973]

Subpart B—Election Procedures

§ 103.20 Posting of election notices.

(a) Employers shall post copies of the Board's official Notice of Election in conspicuous places at least 3 full working days prior to 12:01 a.m. of the day of the election. In elections involving mail ballots, the election shall be deemed to have commenced the day the ballots are deposited by the Regional Office in the mail. In all cases, the notices shall remain posted until the end of the election.

(b) The term *working day* shall mean an entire 24-hour period excluding Saturdays, Sundays, and holidays.

(c) A party shall be estopped from objecting to nonposting of notices if it is responsible for the nonposting. An employer shall be conclusively deemed to have received copies of the election notice for posting unless it notifies the Regional Office at least 5 working days prior to the commencement of the election that it has not received copies of the election notice.

(d) Failure to post the election notices as required herein shall be grounds for setting aside the election whenever proper and timely objections are filed under the provisions of § 102.69(a).

[52 FR 25215, July 6, 1987]

Subpart C—Appropriate Bargaining Units

§ 103.30 Appropriate bargaining units in the health care industry.

(a) This portion of the rule shall be applicable to acute care hospitals, as defined in paragraph (f) of this section: Except in extraordinary circumstances and in circumstances in which there

EXHIBIT 13.2	Regulations Template

Issue:	Citation Information:
	• code, e.g., C.F.R., state or local code
Date of events:	• necessary numbers, e.g., title, part
Date of research:	• date of code

Search and Find:	
located regulation by . . .	enabling statute:
	updated by . . .

Information and Implications:
- definition and scope
- general rule
- exceptions
- consequences
- enforcement
- connection to client's situation

Next Steps:	
questions to consider:	leads to follow:

regulations, proposed regulations, and notices of various sorts. You will research in a register for four reasons: to update your code research, to learn about the agency's thinking in promulgating the regulation, to find a regulation that has been removed, and to track proposed regulations of interest to your client.

Codes and registers typically are available in paper and online, in official and commercial sources. This chapter focuses on official sources; Chapter 15 discusses commercial sources.

Only rarely will you research regulations alone. Most of the time, you also will research both the enabling statute that authorizes the agency to make regulations and agency decisions and judicial cases evaluating, interpreting, and applying those regulations. Thus this part starts with a few words about research in statutes and concludes with a few words about research in agency decisions and judicial case law. See Exhibit 13.3 (below) for an overview of regulations research. This part focuses on federal regulations; you will use similar sources and practices at the state level.

Regulations research in statutes

▶ Read the enabling statute for the legal standard and the agency's authority to promulgate regulations.

▶ Seek references to the regulatory code.

An important step in regulations research is locating and reading the enabling statute authorizing the agency to adopt regulations on the subject in question. Chapter 11 covers statutory research. As you read the statute, look for the legal standard that the legislature has set for the conduct you are concerned with as well as indications of the agency's authority to promulgate regulations regarding that conduct. Furthermore, you should look in the annotation for references to relevant regulations adopted under this statutory authority.

| EXHIBIT 13.3 | Overview of Regulations Research |

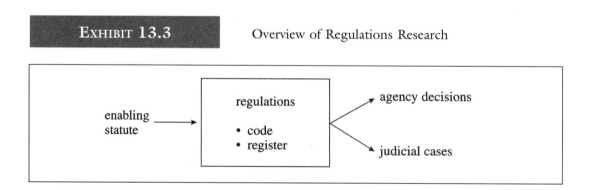

Exhibit 13.4 (at pages 328–30) is the statutory authority for the National Labor Relations Board to adopt regulations defining categories of employers over which it may decline to exercise jurisdiction; the included annotation refers to the pertinent regulation.

> **Regulations research in paper regulatory codes (*Code of Federal Regulations*)**
>
> ▶ Identify the pertinent regulation by a reference from a secondary source, enabling statute, or the code's finding aids.
> ▶ Read the pertinent regulation and related regulations.
> ▶ Note the administrative history information.
> ▶ Determine the currency of the code.

The *Code of Federal Regulations* (C.F.R.) is a codification of the regulations promulgated by the various federal agencies that are currently in force. C.F.R. is published by the United States Government Printing Office (GPO) and is thus the official compilation of federal regulations. C.F.R. is organized topically, and the organization roughly parallels the organization of the federal statutory code. For example, labor statutes appear in title 29 of U.S.C., and labor regulations appear in title 29 of C.F.R. C.F.R. is divided into titles, subtitles, chapters, subchapters, parts, and sections. C.F.R. is republished annually in four pieces: titles 1–16 as of January 1, titles 17–27 as of April 1, titles 28–41 as of July 1, and titles 42–50 as of October 1.

C.F.R. in paper is a large, multivolume set of softcover books. The color of the cover changes each year, so you can easily see the updating pattern. There are several ways to locate pertinent regulations in the paper C.F.R.:

☐ You may already have a reference from your research in commentary and statutes.

☐ If you do not already have a reference, you may look up your research terms in the subject index in *CFR Index and Finding Aids*, a separate volume accompanying C.F.R.

☐ In the same volume, you may skim the List of CFR Titles, Chapters, Subchapters, and Parts, which outlines C.F.R. With the organizational similarity between C.F.R. and the federal statutes, this process is quite easy if you have a statutory citation.

EXHIBIT 13.4   Annotated Federal Statute,
                                      from United States Code Service (paper source)

29 USCS § 163, n 16   LABOR

which protects against interferring with, impeding or diminishing in any way right to strike. Quaker State Oil Refining Corp. v NLRB (1959, CA3) 270 F2d 40, 44 BNA LRRM 2297, 37 CCH LC ¶ 65535, cert den (1959) 361 US 917, 4 L Ed 2d 185, 80 S Ct 261, 45 BNA LRRM 2249.

17. Miscellaneous

Strike, in which employees distribute handbills defaming quality of employer's product as concerted activity, is not protected by 29 USCS § 163. NLRB v International Brotherhood of Electrical Workers (1953) 346 US 464, 98 L Ed 195, 74 S Ct 172, 33 BNA LRRM 2183, 24 CCH LC ¶ 68000.

Union is clearly outside its legitimate function when it demands employer discharge foreman for reason that he or she is "crabby" or too-strict disciplinarian, so that strike called following employer's refusal to discharge foreman is illegal. NLRB v Aladdin Industries, Inc. (1942, CA7) 125

F2d 377, 9 BNA LRRM 548, 5 CCH LC ¶ 60879, cert den (1942) 316 US 706, 86 L Ed 1773, 62 S Ct 1310, 10 BNA LRRM 939.

Wildcat strike in which discharged employees were engaged and for which they were discharged is not such concerted action as falls within protection of 29 USCS § 157. NLRB v Draper Corp. (1944, CA4) 145 F2d 199, 15 BNA LRRM 580, 8 CCH LC ¶ 62368, 156 ALR 989.

Where employer is given notice by two unions that each of them represents his employees, and one union calls strike without offering proof of its majority representation or giving employer opportunity to request such proof or to talk to union's officials, strike is illegal; thus, company is within its rights in discharging strikers, and they are not entitled to reinstatement. Ohio Ferro-Alloys Corp. v NLRB (1954, CA6) 213 F2d 646, 34 BNA LRRM 2327, 26 CCH LC ¶ 68496.

§ 164.   Supervisory employees' rights to organize—Membership as condition of employment—Local law applicable—Declination of jurisdiction by board

(a) Supervisors as union members. Nothing herein shall prohibit any individual employed as a supervisor from becoming or remaining a member of a labor organization, but no employer subject to this Act [29 USCS §§ 151–158, 159–169] shall be compelled to deem individuals defined herein as supervisors as employees for the purpose of any law, either national or local, relating to collective bargaining.

(b) Agreements requiring union membership in violation of State law. Nothing in this Act [29 USCS §§ 151–158, 159–169] shall be construed as authorizing the execution or application of agreements requiring membership in a labor organization as a condition of employment in any State or Territory in which such execution or application is prohibited by State or Territorial law.

(c) Power of Board to decline jurisdiction of labor disputes; assertion of jurisdiction by State and Territorial courts. (1) The Board, in its discretion, may, by rule of decision or by published rules adopted pursuant to the Administrative Procedure Act, decline to assert jurisdiction over any labor dispute involving any class or category of employers, where, in the opinion of the Board, the effect of such labor dispute on commerce is not sufficiently substantial to warrant the exercise of its jurisdiction: Provided, That the Board shall not decline to assert jurisdiction over any labor dispute over which it would assert jurisdiction under the standards prevailing upon August 1, 1959.

(2) Nothing in this Act [29 USCS §§ 151–158, 159–169] shall be deemed to prevent or bar any agency or the courts of any State or Territory (including the Commonwealth of Puerto Rico, Guam, and the Virgin Islands), from assuming and asserting jurisdiction over labor disputes over

EXHIBIT 13.4   *(continued)*

LABOR-MANAGEMENT RELATIONS   **29 USCS § 164**

which the Board declines, pursuant to paragraph (1) of this subsection, to assert jurisdiction.
(July 5, 1935, ch 372, § 14, 49 Stat. 457; June 23, 1947, ch 120, Title I, § 101 in part, 61 Stat. 151; Sept. 14, 1959, P. L. 86-257, Title VII, § 701(a), 73 Stat. 541.)

HISTORY; ANCILLARY LAWS AND DIRECTIVES

References in text:

"The Administrative Procedure Act," referred to in subsec. (c)(1), is Act June 11, 1946, ch 324, 60 Stat. 237, which was repealed by Act Sept. 6, 1966, P. L. 89-554, § 8, 80 Stat. 653, which re-enacted similar provisions as 5 USCS §§ 551–559, 701–706, 1305, 3105, 3344, 5362, and 7521.

Amendments:

1947. Act June 23, 1947 (effective 60 days after enactment, as provided by § 104 of such Act, which appears as 29 USCS § 151 note), amended this section generally. The section formerly related to resolution of conflicts of this Act with other laws; see 29 USCS § 165.

1959. Act Sept. 14, 1959, added subsec. (c).

CODE OF FEDERAL REGULATIONS

National Labor Relations Board–Statements of procedures, 29 CFR Part 101.
National Labor Relations Board–Rules and regulations, Series 8, 29 CFR Part 102.

CROSS REFERENCES

This section is referred to in 18 USCS § 1951.

RESEARCH GUIDE

Federal Procedure L Ed:

22 Fed Proc L Ed, Labor and Labor Relations §§ 52:878, 903, 904, 911, 934, 938.

Am Jur:

48 Am Jur 2d, Labor and Labor Relations §§ 13, 15, 16, 20, 164, 183, 271, 359, 432, 546, 628, 629, 631, 639, 649, 685, 970, 1190.
48A Am Jur 2d, Labor and Labor Relations §§ 1729, 1730, 1797, 2004, 2014.

Am Jur Proof of Facts:

Union's Breach of Duty of Fair Representation, 15 POF2d 65.

Forms:

12 Fed Procedural Forms L Ed, Labor and Labor Relations § 46:677.

WGL Coordinators:

10 Employment Coord, Coverage ¶ ¶ LR-10,702; 11,901.1; 11,904; 11,907.
11 Employment Coord, Prohibited Labor Practices ¶ ¶ LR-21,402; 22,505; 26,055; 26,677.
12 Employment Coord, Prohibited Labor Practices ¶ LR-35,005.

EXHIBIT 13.4   *(continued)*

29 USCS § 164, n 94   LABOR

outside state and also purchased materials in excess of that amount, despite employer's denial of substantially identical commerce allegations in complaint without asserted reason, where, having stipulated to jurisdiction, employer is estopped from denying it in absence of valid ground. Capitan Drilling Co. (1967) 167 NLRB 144, 66 BNA LRRM 1015, 1967 CCH NLRB ¶ 21706, enforced (1969, CA5) 408 F2d 676, 70 BNA LRRM 3258, 59 CCH LC ¶ 13360.

95. Orchestras

NLRB's retail jurisdictional standard applies to orchestras performing "club dates," defined as single engagements, such as at wedding, commencement, bar mitzvah, debutante party, fashion show, or other social event; however, bands selling music to commercial enterprises are governed by the prevailing nonretail standard. Levitt (1968) 171 NLRB 739, 68 BNA LRRM 1161, 1968-1 CCH NLRB ¶ 22512.

NLRB will assert jurisdiction over symphony orchestras having gross annual revenue from all sources of not less than $1 million, excluding only contributions unavailable for use for operating expenses because of limitation by grantor. 29 CFR § 103. 2.

96. Pharmacies

Pharmacy is retail enterprise governed by monetary requirements of NLRB's retail standard. Booker Family Medical Care Center (1975) 219 NLRB 220, 89 BNA LRRM 1702, 1974-75 CCH NLRB ¶ 16041.

97. Private clubs

NLRB has jurisdiction over nonprofit corporation operating private athletic club of 2,300 members, which, in addition to health and recreation facilities, also operates restaurant and furnishes hotel-type accommodations, where during prior fiscal year club derived over $500,000 from sale of food and beverages and made direct and indirect purchases of goods in interstate commerce exceeding $50,000. Denver Athletic Club (1967) 164 NLRB 677, 65 BNA LRRM 1136, 1967 CCH NLRB ¶ 21356.

NLRB will not assert jurisdiction over employer-membership corporation, operating nonprofit singing and eating club, where employer is basically retail enterprise with annual gross income of business, not including membership dues, of less than NLRB's discretionary standard of $500,000 for assertion of jurisdiction over retail enterprise. Syracuse Liederkranz, Inc. (1967) 166 NLRB 782, 65 BNA LRRM 1645, 1967 CCH NLRB ¶ 21651.

In determining NLRB's discretionary standard for retail businesses, membership dues will not be included in calculating volume of business of mem-

bership corporation, operating nonprofit singing and eating club. Syracuse Liederkranz, Inc. (1967) 166 NLRB 782, 65 BNA LRRM 1645, 1967 CCH NLRB ¶ 21651.

98. Public transportation systems

Where interstate commerce is unquestionably involved to extent not inconsequential, question of whether NLRB will require showing by bus company of dollar-amount of interstate traffic as predicate to jurisdiction is matter of Board's policy with which court will not interfere in absence of abuse of Board's discretion. NLRB v Parran (1956, CA4) 237 F2d 373, 38 BNA LRRM 2774, 31 CCH LC ¶ 70266.

Jurisdiction will be asserted over bus company, licensed by state and federal authorities, which supplies exclusive chartered and scheduled passenger transportation to nearby United States Air Force base and serves as interstate link with large bus company and numerous commercial airlines to and from such base, where bus company is not only required to maintain adequate transportation service but also to maintain employment conditions in accordance with Air Force regulations, and where labor dispute disrupting bus service would have serious and adverse impact on national defense, in that base served by bus company is vital link in air service between North American continent and Far East, and bus service is only public mass transportation available. Simmons (1968) 171 NLRB 1469, 69 BNA LRRM 1064, 1968-1 CCH NLRB ¶ 22588, supp op (1969) 179 NLRB 641, 72 BNA LRRM 1425, 1969 CCH NLRB ¶ 21362.

NLRB would assert jurisdiction over surface transportation company having tour business and operating buses in Honolulu, where company met standard for public utility or transit system, and for nonretail enterprises. Transportation Associates of Hawaii, Ltd. (1975) 216 NLRB 357, 88 BNA LRRM 1216, 1974-75 CCH NLRB ¶ 15452.

. Privately-owned toll bridge connecting mainland to island met Board's discretionary standards for jurisdiction as transit system. Margate Bridge Co. (1980) 247 NLRB 1437, 103 BNA LRRM 1335, 1980 CCH NLRB ¶ 16787.

Privately-owned toll bridge connecting mainland to island met Board's discretionary standards for jurisdiction as transit system. Margate Bridge Co. (1980) 247 NLRB 1437, 103 BNA LRRM 1335, 1980 cch NLRB ¶ 16787.

99. Public utilities

NLRB does not abuse its discretion in asserting jurisdiction over public utility by retroactively applying $250,000 "volume of business" jurisdictional standard, where, at time alleged unfair labor practice occurred, jurisdictional standard was $3,000,000 annual gross volume of business, which

☐   You may use the Parallel Table of Authorities and Rules in *CFR Index and Finding Aids*. If you look up the enabling statute, you will find a reference to the corresponding regulation.

One of these methods may be more effective than the others, so you should be flexible. In general, you will be able to identify a pertinent title and part, but probably not a specific section, through these methods.

Once you have identified and obtained a potentially pertinent section or part, you should, of course, examine the material carefully. Examine the table of contents for the chapter containing the pertinent material, and identify all pertinent parts. Be sure to look for definition sections, which may appear at the beginning of and apply throughout a chapter. Read through all sections within the pertinent part, because they are likely to be interconnected. Then, take note of the administrative history material in small print at the end of a section or the outline for a part. You may find there a reference to the enabling statutes as well as the regulation's date of final promulgation and citation to the *Federal Register*, discussed later.

Timing is important in regulations research. The regulation you find in the current C.F.R. probably is the correct one to use, but there are two situations in which you would not rely on the current C.F.R. regulation. First, if the key events in your client's situation occurred some time ago and the regulation was promulgated more recently, you will need to research historic regulations. There are several official sources of out-of-date regulations: GPO Access archives the C.F.R. from 1996 to date; you may be able to find an outdated paper C.F.R. set in a library; or you may use the *Federal Register*, discussed later.

Second, if your client's events are very recent or have yet to happen, you will need to check for very recent regulatory activity. To ascertain how current your C.F.R. research is, look at the first page of the C.F.R. paper volume you are using or consult the list of available titles on GPO Access. To bring your research up to date, you will use the *Federal Register*.

Researching regulations through government websites

▶ Select an appropriate agency-specific or broader regulation database.

▶ Run one or more searches.

▶ Read the pertinent regulation and related regulations.

▶ Check the website's currency.

Most if not all agencies have websites through which they provide a range of information to the public, and many include a regulations database with search tools. See Exhibit 13.5 (at page 333). While these databases are easily and inexpensively accessed, some caution is in order because these databases usually provide only regulations adopted or enforced by the agency hosting the website. If you know that your research involves only one particular agency, its database may be considerably easier to work with than broader C.F.R. databases. But if you are researching a broader legal issue, an agency-specific database is unlikely to lead you to pertinent regulations of other agencies.

In contrast to narrowly focused agency databases, the GPO provides access to the entire C.F.R. through GPO Access, its website located at gpoaccess.gov. The content of the website version is the same as the content of the paper C.F.R. (except that it does not include the C.F.R. index). To obtain a pertinent regulation through the website version, you may:

☐ search for the regulation by its citation, if you already have a reference from your other research;

☐ browse the Parallel Table of Authorities and Rules;

☐ select a title, then browse the chapters, parts, and sections within that title;

☐ run a key-word search in the entire database, using Boolean commands, truncation, and phrases, such as the agency's name; or

☐ use the search-and-browse function, in which you limit your keyword search to one or several titles or parts of titles. For an example of the results of a search, see Exhibit 13.6 (at page 336).

Exhibit 13.7 (at page 337) is the regulations template filled in to reflect our research in the Canoga case.

EXHIBIT 13.5	Regulations, from National Labor Relations Board Website (online source)

Site Map | **Search:** All of NLRB.Gov   Search Key Word

Advanced Search

Office Finder | Speakers | Careers | Contact Us | Text

HOME	**WORKPLACE RIGHTS**	**RESEARCH**	**PUBLICATIONS**	**E-GOV**	**ABOUT US**

Home > Publications > Rules & Regulations   **Saturday, March 29**

Manuals

Rules and Regulations

Guides

History

Reports

Spanish Publications

Other

*Adobe Reader is required to view PDF documents.

Click to download Adobe Reader 7.0.

Rules & Regulations

The online version of the Rules and Regulations is kept updated as changes are approved by the Board. Revised sections have been inserted to replace old sections. The printed version of this publication, available for sale through the Government Printing Office, was last reprinted in April 2002.

- Preliminary Pages (PDF*)
- Part 101--Statements of Procedure (PDF*)
- Part 102--Rules and Regulations (PDF*)
- Part 103--Other Rules (PDF*)
- Topical Index (PDF*)
- NLRB Organization and Functions (PDF*)
- The National Labor Relations Act

Site Tools

Add to favorite

Print friendly v

Email this pag

Questions

Related Links

Read the Natic
Labor Relation

Find the neare
NLRB office

Law Students:
Looking for a g
job?

back to top

Español | Inspector General | FOIA | No Fear

Privacy Policy | Disclaimer | Accessi

EXHIBIT **13.5**　　　　　　　*(continued)*

103.1–103.2　　　　　　　　　　　　　　　　　　　　　　　　　　　　　**OR**

considering all the various alternatives, the Board concludes that a gross revenue test is preferable, for it has the advantages of simplicity and ease of application. Board experience has demonstrated that such figures are readily available and relatively easy to produce, thereby reducing the amount of time, energy, and funds expended by the Board and staff as well as imposing less of a burden on the parties involved.

In light of the foregoing considerations, the Board is satisfied that the $1 million annual gross revenue standard announced today will bring uniform and effective regulation of labor relations to labor disputants at private, nonprofit colleges and universities, and at the same time enable the Board to function as a responsive forum for the resolution of those disputes.

Sec. 103.2 *Symphony orchestras.*—The Board will assert its jurisdiction in any proceeding arising under sections 8, 9, and 10 of the Act involving any symphony orchestra which has a gross annual revenue from all sources (excluding only contributions which are because of limitation by the grantor not available for use for operating expenses) of not less than $1 million.*

JURISDICTIONAL STANDARDS APPLICABLE TO SYMPHONY ORCHESTRAS

NOTICE OF ISSUANCE OF RULE

On August 19, 1972, the Board published in the Federal Register, a Notice of Proposed Rule Making which invited interested parties to submit to it (1) data relevant to defining the extent to which symphony orchestras are in commerce, as defined in section 2(6) of the National Labor Relations Act, and to assessing the effect upon commerce of a labor dispute in those enterprises, (2) statements of views or arguments as to the desirability of the Board exercising jurisdiction, and (3) data and views concerning the appropriate jurisdictional standards which should be established in the event the Board decides to promulgate a rule exercising jurisdiction over those enterprises. The Board received 26 responses to the notice. After careful consideration of all the responses, the Board has concluded that it will best effectuate the purposes of the Act to assert jurisdiction over symphony orchestras and apply a $1 million gross revenue standard, in addition to statutory jurisdiction. A rule establishing that standard has been issued concurrently with the publication of this notice.

It is well settled that the National Labor Relations Act gives to the Board a jurisdiction authority coextensive with the full reach of the commerce clause.[1] It is equally well settled that the Board in its discretion may set boundaries on the exercise of that authority.[2] In exercising that discretion, the Board has consistently taken the position that it would better effectuate the purposes of the Act, and promote the prompt handling of major cases, not to exercise its jurisdiction to the fullest extent possible under the authority delegated to it by Congress, but to limit that exercise to enterprises whose operations have, or at which labor disputes would have, a pronounced impact upon the flow of interstate commerce.[3] The standard announced above, in our opinion, accommodates this position.

---

* The following statement was published by the Board in the Federal Register on March 19, 1973, 38 F.R. 7289.

[1] See *N.L.R.B. v. Fainblatt,* 306 U.S. 601.

[2] *Office Employees International Union Local No. 11 (Oregon Teamsters) v. N.L.R.B.,* 353 U.S. 313; Sec. 14(c)(1) of the Act.

[3] *Siemons Mailing Service,* 122 NLRB 81; *Hollow Tree Lumber Company,* 91 NLRB 635, 635. See also, e.g., *Floridan Hotel of Tampa Inc.,* 124 NLRB 261, 264; *Butte Medical Properties, d/b/a Medical Center Hospital,* 168 NLRB 266, 268.

EXHIBIT 13.5   *(continued)*

OR   103.2–103.3

The Board, in arriving at a $1 million gross figure,[4] has considered, *inter alia*, the impact of symphony orchestras on commerce and the aspects of orchestra operations as criteria for the exercise of jurisdiction. Symphony orchestras in the United States are classified in four categories: college, community, **metropolitan, and major**.[5] Community orchestras constitute the largest group with over 1,000 in number and, for the most part, are composed of amateur players. The metropolitan orchestras are almost exclusively professional and it is estimated that there are between 75 and 80 orchestras classified as metropolitan. The annual budget for this category ranges approximately from $250,000 to $1,000,000. The major orchestras are the largest and usually the oldest established musical organizations. All of them are completely professional, and a substantial number operates on a year-round basis. For this category the minimum annual budget is approximately $1 million. Presently, there are approximately 28 major symphony orchestras in the United States. Thus, statistical projections based on data submitted by responding parties, as well as data compiled by the Board, disclose that adoption of such a standard would bring approximately 2 percent of all symphony orchestras, except college, or approximately 28 percent of the professional metropolitan and major orchestras, within reach of the Act. The Board is satisfied that symphony orchestras with gross revenues of $1 million have a substantial impact on commerce and that the figure selected will not result in an unmanageable increase on the Board's workload. The adoption of a $1 million standard, however, does not foreclose the Board from reevaluating and revising that standard should future circumstances deem it appropriate.

In view of the foregoing, the Board is satisfied that the $1 million annual gross revenue standard announced today will result in attaining uniform and effective regulation of labor disputes involving employees in the symphony orchestra industry whose operations have a substantial impact on interstate commerce.

Sec. 103.3 *Horseracing and dogracing industries.*—The Board will not assert its jurisdiction in any proceeding under sections 8, 9, and 10 of the Act involving the horseracing and dogracing industries.*

DECLINATION OF ASSERTION OF JURISDICTION

On July 18, 1972, the Board published in the Federal Register a notice of proposed rulemaking which invited interested parties to submit to it (1) data relevant to defining the extent to which the horseracing and dogracing industries are in commerce as defined in section 2(6) of the National Labor Relations Act, and to assessing the effect upon commerce of a labor dispute in those industries, (2) statements of views or arguments as to the desirability of the Board exercising jurisdiction, and (3) data and views concerning the appropriate jurisdictional standards which should be established in the event the Board decides to promulgate a rule exercising jurisdiction over those industries. The Board received 96 responses to the notice. After careful consideration of all the responses, the Board has concluded that it will not assert

---

[4] As reflected in the rule, this figure includes revenues from all sources, excepting only contributions which, because of limitations placed thereon by the grantor, are not available for operating expenses. These contributions encompassing, for example, contributions to an endowment fund or building fund, are excluded because of their generally nonrecurring nature. (Cf. *Magic Mountain, Inc.*, 123 NLRB 1170.) Income derived from investment of such funds will, however, be counted in determining whether the standard has been satisfied.

[5] The latter three categories are defined by the American Symphony Orchestra League principally on the basis of their annual budgets.

* The following statement was published by the Board concurrently with the issuance of this rule, 38 F.R. 9537.

| EXHIBIT 13.6 | Code of Federal Regulations Search Result, from GPO Access (online source) |

http://frwebgate.access.gpo.gov/cgi-bin/multidb.cgi

code of federal regulations

CFR Search Results

Search Database:

Title 29 All Volumes (2007)

For: "ORCHESTRA"

Total Hits: 5

[1]
((LIST OF AVAILABLE CFRs ONLINE))
  Size: 69603 , Score: 1000

[2]
[2007] 29CFR103.2-- Sec. 103.2 Symphony orchestras.
  Size: 785 , Score: 1000

[3]
[2007] 29CFR103-- Subpart A_Jurisdictional Standards
  Size: 1440 , Score: 880

[4]
[2007] 29CFR103-- PART 103_OTHER RULES
  Size: 8203 , Score: 652

[5]
Query Report for this Search
  Size: 640 , Score: 1

This document is sponsored by the Office of the Federal Register, National Archives and Records Administration on the United States Government Printing Office web site.

Questions or comments regarding this service? Contact the GPO Access User Support Team by Internet e-mail at gpoaccess@gpo.gov; by telephone at (202) 512-1530 or toll free at (888) 293-6498; by fax at (202) 512-1262.

2/12/2008 9:57 PM

EXHIBIT 13.7	First Regulations Template for Canoga Case

Issue:	Citation Information:
Does the National Labor Relations Board regulate orchestras?	• *Code of Federal Regulations* • *Title 29, part 103.2* • *2007*

Date of events: *Sept. 7, 2007*

Date of research: *Jan. 17 & Mar. 5, 2008*

Search and Find:

located regulation by . . . *29 U.S.C.S. § 164 Annotation 95 → orchestras. Second entry refers to 29 C.F.R. part 103.2.*	statutory authority: *29 U.S.C. § 164.*
	updated by . . . *See the second template, Exhibit 13.11.*

Information and Implications:

The Board regulates orchestras with gross annual revenues (excluding certain grants) of at least $1 million.

I need more info about the orchestra's finances to determine if it meets the gross annual revenue threshold.

Next Steps:

questions to consider: *Investigate orchestra revenues; available from public source?*	leads to follow:

> **Regulations in an administrative register (*Federal Register*)**
>
> ▶ Use List of C.F.R. Sections Affected (L.S.A.) to identify pertinent pages in fairly recent issues of the *Federal Register*.
> ▶ Use the tools updating L.S.A. to identify pertinent pages in very recent issues of the *Federal Register*.
> ▶ Read the material in the *Federal Register*, including the regulation itself and the explanatory material.

The *Federal Register* is a virtually daily publication covering the activities of federal agencies. It serves four research purposes:

- ☐ As noted previously, the C.F.R. is generally within a few months to a year of being current. New regulations (including amendments to existing regulations) are proposed and promulgated daily, so you must update your research beyond C.F.R. in the *Federal Register*, especially if your client is seeking advice about future conduct.
- ☐ If the pertinent regulation is not clear as applied to your client's situation, you may want to learn the agency's thinking behind the regulation. This information appears in the *Federal Register* when a regulation is finally promulgated. See Exhibit 13.8 (at pages 339–340). You may find pertinent information as well in the agency's notice proposing the regulation, which also appears in the *Federal Register*.
- ☐ A regulation that has been removed will no longer appear in C.F.R. You can find it in the *Federal Register* for its date of promulgation.
- ☐ You can learn about proposed regulations of interest to a client. Recall that interested parties generally may comment on proposed regulations.

The following discussion focuses on the first purpose: updating your regulations research.

The *Federal Register* is voluminous; a daily issue in paper may contain more than 100 pages. Although the material within each issue is arranged alphabetically by agency and there are indexes and tables, it would be burdensome to look through all of the daily issues published since the cutoff date for C.F.R. Several tools assist you in identifying pertinent material within the *Federal Register*.

The main tool is List of C.F.R. Sections Affected, or L.S.A. L.S.A. is available in paper in a set of softcover books typically shelved at the end of C.F.R. L.S.A. is published monthly, with later issues cumulating material from earlier issues. Because C.F.R. is republished on a rolling basis, L.S.A.'s coverage varies by C.F.R. title; you can find coverage information on the first page of the paper version.

Entries in L.S.A. are organized by title, subtitle, etc., so the standard means of access is to look up the title, subtitle, and chapter pertinent to your research situation. In each entry, L.S.A. identifies the nature of the recent regulatory activity, for example, addition of a new regulation, revision or removal of an existing regulation, and the page numbers in the *Federal Register* reporting that activity. Proposed rules appear at the end of a chapter's listing. See Exhibit 13.9 (at page 341).

EXHIBIT 13.8

Final Rule,
from Federal Register (paper source)

6176   **RULES AND REGULATIONS**

written statements of exceptions and allegations as to applicable fact and law. Upon request of any party made within such 20-day period, a reasonable extension of time for filing such briefs or statements may be granted and upon a showing of good cause such period may be extended, as appropriate.

(b) *By a court.* Where a case has been remanded by a court, the Board may proceed in accordance with the court's mandate to issue a decision or it may in turn remand the case to a deputy commissioner or judge with instructions to take such action as is ordered by the court and any additional necessary action and upon completion thereof to return the case with a recommended decision to the Board for its action.

§ 802.406 Finality of Board decisions.

A decision rendered by the Board pursuant to this subpart shall become final 60 days after the issuance of such decision unless an appeal pursuant to section 21(c) of the LHWCA is filed prior to the expiration of the 60-day period herein described, or unless a timely request for reconsideration by the Board has been filed as provided in § 802.407.

RECONSIDERATION

§ 802.407 Reconsideration of Board decisions—generally.

(a) Any party in interest may, within no more than 10 days from the filing of a decision pursuant to § 802.403(b) request a reconsideration of such decision.

(b) Failure to file a request for reconsideration shall not be deemed a failure to exhaust administrative remedies.

§ 802.408 Notice of request for reconsideration.

(a) In the event that a party in interest requests reconsideration of a final decision and order, he shall do so in writing, stating the supporting rationale for the request and include any material pertinent to the request.

(b) The request shall be sent or delivered in person to the Clerk of the Board, and copies shall be served upon the parties.

§ 802.409 Grant or denial of request.

All requests for reconsideration shall be reviewed by the Board and shall be granted or denied in the discretion of the Board.

JUDICIAL REVIEW

§ 802.410 Judicial review of Board decisions.

Within 60 days after a decision by the Board has been filed pursuant to § 802.403(b), any party adversely affected or aggrieved by such decision may take an appeal to the U.S. Court of Appeals pursuant to section 21(c) of the LHWCA.

§ 802.411 Certification of record for judicial review.

The record of a case including the record of proceedings before the Board shall be transmitted to the appropriate

court pursuant to the rules of such court.

Signed at Washington, D.C., this 1st day of March 1973.

PETER J. BRENNAN,
Secretary of Labor.

[FR Doc.73-4262 Filed 3-6-73; 8:45 am]

Title 29—Labor
CHAPTER I—NATIONAL LABOR RELATIONS BOARD
PART 103—OTHER RULES
Jurisdictional Standards Applicable to Symphony Orchestras

By virtue of the authority vested in it by the National Labor Relations Act, approved July 5, 1935,[1] the National Labor Relations Board hereby issues the following rule which it finds necessary to carry out the provisions of said Act.

This rule is issued following proceedings conforming to the requirements of 5 U.S.C. 553 in which notice was given that any rule adopted would be immediately applicable. On August 19, 1972, the Board published notice of proposed rule making requesting responses from interested parties with respect to the assertion of jurisdiction over symphony orchestras and the establishment of jurisdictional standards therefor. The Board having considered the responses and its discretion under sections 9 and 10 of the Act has decided to adopt a rule asserting jurisdiction over any symphony orchestra having a gross annual revenue of not less than $1 million. The National Labor Relations Board finds for good cause that this rule shall be effective on March 7, 1973, and shall apply to all proceedings affected thereby which are pending at the time of such publication or which may arise thereafter.

Dated at Washington, D.C., March 2, 1973.

By direction of the Board.

[SEAL]   JOHN C. TRUESDALE,
Executive Secretary.

On August 19, 1972, the Board published in the FEDERAL REGISTER, a notice of proposed rule making which invited interested parties to submit to it (1) data relevant to defining the extent to which symphony orchestras are in commerce, as defined in section 2(6) of the National Labor Relations Act, and to assessing the effect upon commerce of a labor dispute in those enterprises, (2) statements of views or arguments as to the desirability of the Board exercising jurisdiction, and (3) data and views concerning the appropriate jurisdictional standards which should be established in the event the Board decides to promulgate a rule exercising jurisdiction over those enterprises. The Board received 26 responses to the notice. After careful

consideration of all the responses, the Board has concluded that it will best effectuate the purposes of the Act to assert jurisdiction over symphony orchestras and apply a $1 million annual gross revenue standard, in addition to statutory jurisdiction. A rule establishing that standard has been issued concurrently with the publication of this notice.

It is well settled that the National Labor Relations Act gives to the Board a jurisdictional authority coextensive with the full reach of the commerce clause.[1] It is equally well settled that the Board in its discretion may set boundaries on the exercise of that authority.[2] In exercising that discretion, the Board has consistently taken the position that it would better effectuate the purposes of the Act, and promote the prompt handling of major cases, not to exercise its jurisdiction to the fullest extent possible under the authority delegated to it by Congress, but to limit that exercise to enterprises whose operations have, or at which labor disputes would have, a pronounced impact upon the flow of interstate commerce.[3] The standard announced above, in our opinion, accommodates this position.

The Board, in arriving at a $1 million gross figure,[4] has considered, inter alia, the impact of symphony orchestras on commerce and the aspects of orchestra operations as criteria for the exercise of jurisdiction. Symphony orchestras in the United States are classified in four categories: college, community, metropolitan, and major.[5] Community orchestras constitute the largest group with over 1,000 in number and, for the most part, are composed of amateur players. The metropolitan orchestras are almost exclusively professional and it is estimated that there are between 75 and 80 orchestras classified as metropolitan. The annual budget for this category ranges approximately from $250,000 to $1 million. The major orchestras are the largest and usually the oldest established musical organizations. All of them are completely professional, and a substantial number

[1] See N.L.R.B. v. Fainblatt, 306 U.S. 601.

[2] Office Employees International Union, Local No. 11 [Oregon Teamsters] v. N.L.R.B., 353 U.S. 313; sec. 14(c)(1) of the Act.

[3] Siemons Mailing Service, 122 NLRB 81; Hollow Tree Lumber Company, 91 NLRB 635, 635. See also, e.g., Floridan Hotel of Tampa, Inc., 124 NLRB 261, 264; Butte Medical Properties, d.b.a. Medical Center Hospital, 168 NLRB 266, 266.

[4] As reflected in the rule, this figure includes revenues from all sources, excepting only contributions which, because of limitations placed thereon by the grantor, are not available for operating expenses. These contributions encompassing, for example, contributions to an endowment fund or building fund, are excluded because of their generally nonrecurring nature. (Cf. Magic Mountain, Inc., 123 NLRB 1170.) Income derived from investment of such funds will, however, be counted in determining whether the standard has been satisfied.

[5] The latter three categories are defined by the American Symphony Orchestra League principally on the basis of their annual budgets.

[1] 49 Stat. 449; 29 U.S.C. 151-166, as amended by act of June 23, 1947 (61 Stat. 136; 29 U.S.C. Supp. 151-167), act of Oct. 22, 1951 (65 Stat. 601; 29 U.S.C. 158, 159, 168), and act of Sept. 14, 1959 (73 Stat. 519; 29 U.S.C. 141-166).

EXHIBIT 13.8   *(continued)*

operates on a year-round basis. For this category the minimum annual budget is approximately $1 million. Presently, there are approximately 28 major symphony orchestras in the United States. Thus, statistical projections based on data submitted by responding parties, as well as data compiled by the Board, disclose that adoption of such a standard would bring approximately 2 percent of all symphony orchestras, except college, or approximately 28 percent of the professional metropolitan and major orchestras, within reach of the Act. The Board is satisfied that symphony orchestras with gross revenues of $1 million have a substantial impact on commerce and that the figure selected will not result in an unmanageable increase on the Board's workload. The adoption of a $1 million standard, however, does not foreclose the Board from reevaluating and revising that standard should future circumstances deem it appropriate.

In view of the foregoing, the Board is satisfied that the $1 million annual gross revenue standard announced today will result in attaining uniform and effective regulation of labor disputes involving employees in the symphony orchestra industry whose operations have a substantial impact on interstate commerce.

§ 103.2   Symphony Orchestras.

The Board will assert its jurisdiction in any proceeding arising under sections 8, 9, and 10 of the Act involving any symphony orchestra which has a gross annual revenue from all sources (excluding only contributions which are because of limitation by the grantor not available for use for operating expenses) of not less than $1 million.

[FR Doc.73-4374 Filed 3-6-73; 8:45 am]

CHAPTER XVII—OCCUPATIONAL SAFETY AND HEALTH ADMINISTRATION, DEPARTMENT OF LABOR

PART 1952—APPROVED STATE PLANS FOR ENFORCEMENT OF STATE STANDARDS

New Jersey Plan; Plan Description; Amendment

In a document issued by this office on January 22, 1973, and published in the FEDERAL REGISTER on January 26, 1973 (37 FR 2426), the New Jersey developmental plan to assume responsibility for the development and enforcement of State occupational safety and health standards in accordance with Part 1902 of Title 29 of the Code of Federal Regulations and section 18 of the Occupational Safety and Health Act of 1970 (29 U.S.C. 667) was approved.

Provisions of that plan require that owners of any structures to be erected and used as places of employment submit plans for approval and comply with specific provisions of special State building codes. However, the decision did not indicate that the pertinent safety and health codes (N.J.A.C. 12:115—Building Code and N.J.A.C. 12:116—Plan Filing) have as their stated and clear purpose

the protection of employees even though the codes may afford some incidental protection to others. Codes that more directly concern other matters such as the protection of the environment and the public at large are properly not incorporated in the plan, and are dealt with elsewhere by the State of New Jersey and its political subdivisions.

The description of the plan in § 1952.140(b) is accordingly amended to indicate these features of the codes involved by adding a new subparagraph (3) to read as follows:

§ 1952.140   Description of the plan.

*   *   *   *   *

(b) * * *
(3) Safety and health codes which are established by the State of New Jersey to protect employees and which incidentally protect others are considered occupational safety and health standards for the purposes of this subpart.

*   *   *   *   *

(Sec. 18, Pub. L. 91-596, 84 Stat. 1608 (29 U.S.C. 667))

Signed at Washington, D.C., this 1st day of March 1973.

CHAIN ROBBINS,
Acting Assistant Secretary of Labor.
[FR Doc.73-4355 Filed 3-6-73; 8:45 am]

Title 32—National Defense

CHAPTER XVII—OFFICE OF EMERGENCY PREPAREDNESS

PART 1709—REIMBURSEMENT OF OTHER FEDERAL AGENCIES UNDER PUBLIC LAW 91-606.

Eligibility of Certain Expenditures for Reimbursement

1. Section 1709.2 is amended by deleting paragraphs (d), (e), and (f).
Effective date. This amendment shall be effective as of March 1, 1973.

Dated: March 1, 1973.

DARRELL M. TRENT,
Acting Director,
Office of Emergency Preparedness.
[FR Doc.73-4380 Filed 3-6-73; 8:45 am]

Title 41—Public Contracts and Property Management

CHAPTER 3—DEPARTMENT OF HEALTH, EDUCATION, AND WELFARE

PART 3-16—PROCUREMENT FORMS

Subpart 3-16.8—Miscellaneous Forms

Chapter 3, Title 41, Code of Federal Regulations is amended as set forth below. The purpose of this amendment is to inform the public of HEW's use of miscellaneous procurement forms.

It is the general policy of the Department of Health, Education, and Welfare to allow time for interested parties to take part in the rule making process. However, since the amendment herein involves minor technical matters, the public rule making process is deemed unnecessary in this instance.

1. The table of contents of Part 3-16 is amended to add Subpart 3-16.8 as follows:

Subpart 3-16.8—Miscellaneous Forms

3-16.804	Report on procurement.
3-16.804-2	Agencies required to report.
3-16.804-3	Standard Form 37, Report on Procurement by Civilian Executive Agencies.
3-16.852	Equal Opportunity Clause (HEW-386).
3-16.853	Request for Equal Opportunity Clearance of Contract Award (HEW-511).
3-16.854	Notice to Prospective Bidders (HEW-512).
3-16.855	Transmittal Letter (HEW-513).
3-16.856	Procurement Activity Report.

AUTHORITY: 5 U.S.C. 301; 40 U.S.C. 486(c).

Subpart 3-16.8—Miscellaneous Forms

2. Subpart 3-16.8 is added to read as follows:

§ 3-16.804   Report on procurement.

§ 3-16.804-2   Agencies required to report.

Each operating agency, the Office of Regional and Community Development, and the Office of Administrative Services, OS-OASAM, shall report its procurement to the Office of Procurement and Materiel Management, OS-OASAM, for the organisation as a whole.

§ 3-16.804-3   Standard Form 37, Report on Procurement by Civilian Agencies.

(a)-(e) [Reserved]
(f) *Frequency and due date for submission of Standard Form 37.* Each report shall be submitted in the original and three copies to arrive at OPMM not later than 30 calendar days after the close of each reporting period.

§ 3-16.852   Equal Opportunity Clause (HEW-386).

Use Form HEW-386, Equal Opportunity Clause, if it is prescribed.

§ 3-16.853   Request for Equal Opportunity Clearance of Contract Award.

Form HEW-511, Request for Equal Opportunity Clearance of Contract Award, is prescribed for use in communicating and transmitting information between the contracting officer and the Office of Civil Rights.

§ 3-16.854   Notice to Prospective Bidders (HEW-512).

Form HEW-512, Notice to Prospective Bidders, is prescribed for use with invitation for bids when bids are estimated to exceed $10,000.

§ 3-16.855   Transmittal Letter (HEW-513).

Form HEW-513, Transmittal Letter, is prescribed for transmitting awards which are subject to the Equal Opportunity clause.

§ 3-16.856   Procurement Activity Report.

(a) *General.* The Procurement Activity Report is designed to provide the Department with essential procurement records and statistics necessary for procurement management purposes and to

EXHIBIT 13.9   List of Sections Affected (paper source)

CHANGES JULY 1, 2007 THROUGH JULY 31, 2007

TITLE 28—JUDICIAL ADMINISTRATION

Chapter I—Department of Justice (Parts 0—199)

0.15 (h) removed..............................41624
0.19 (d) removed..............................41624

Chapter V—Bureau of Prisons, Department of Justice (Parts 500—599)

552.11 (a) through (c) redesignated as (b) through (d); new (a) added; heading and new (b) revised................................37631

Proposed Rules:

75...38033

TITLE 29—LABOR

Subtitle A—Office of the Secretary of Labor (Parts 0—99)

2.6 (a) and (b) amended.................37098
11.2 Amended................................37098
11.10 (c)(1) amended.......................37098
14.3 (a) revised; (b)(2) amended
.... 37098
14.4 (a) and (i) amended.................37098
14.20 (d) amended...........................37098
14.21 Amended................................37098
16.104 (a)(4) heading and (5)(i) amended..................................37098
16.107 (c) amended...........................37098
20.75 (c) amended...........................37098
20.76 (g) amended...........................37098
22.2 (l) and (q)(3) revised...............37098
70 Appendix A amended.................37098
71.51 (a)(5) and (34) amended..........37099
71 Appendix A revised.....................37099
75.1 (a), (b) and (c) amended..........37103
75.11 (a), (1), introductory text, (ii), (iii), (2), (3), (4), (b)(1) introductory text, (ii), (iii), (iv), (2), (4), (5) and (6) amended..................................37103
90.2 Amended 37103, 37104
90.11 (c) amended..................37103, 37104
90.12 Amended................................37104
90.13 (a)(2) and (d) amended............37104
90.14 (a), (b) and (d) amended..........37104
90.17 (a) amended...........................37104
90.18 (a) amended 37103, 37104

90.19 (c) amended...........................37104
90.21 (a) amended...........................37104
90.31 (a) amended...........................37103
    (a) and (b) amended................37104
90.32 (a) amended...........................37104
90.33 (c) amended...........................37104
90.34 Amended................................37104
90.35 Removed................................37104
95 Authority citation revised........37104
95.2 (ii) amended...........................37104
95.25 (c)(6) amended.......................37104
95.27 Amended................................37104
95.28 Revised................................37104
95.44 (b)(5) and (e)(2) through (5) amended................................37104
95.46 Amended 37104
95.48 (a), (b), (d) and (e) amended
.... 37104
95.71 (b) amended...........................37104
95 Appendix A amended.................37104
96 Authority citation revised........37104
96.54 Introductory text amended
.... 37104
96.63 (b)(4) and (5) amended 37104
97.4 (a)(3)(i) and (10) amended........37104
97.22 (b) revised...........................37104
97.26 (b) introductory text, (1) and (2) amended.....................37105
97.36 (d)(1) amended.......................37105
97.42 (f) amended...........................37105
98.530 (a) and (b) amended 37105
99 Authority citation revised........37105
99.200 (a) and (b) amended 37105
99.230 (b)(2) amended.....................37105
99.305 (a) revised 37105
99.400 (d)(4) amended.....................37105
99.520 (b)(1)(i) and (d)(2)(ii) amended..................................37105

Subtitle B—Regulations Relating to Labor (Parts 100—4999)

Chapter I—National Labor Relations Board (Parts 100—199)

100 Authority citation revised........40070
100.601—100.625 (Subpart F) Revised..40070
102 Authority citation revised........38778
102.117 Heading revised; (f) through (q) removed.................38778
102.119 Redesignated as 102.120; new 102.119 added...................38778
102.120 Redesignated from 102.119
.... 38778

Most of the time, you will need to update your research in L.S.A. Each issue of the *Federal Register* contains a Reader Aids Table of Parts Affected, organized by C.F.R. titles and parts, with entries guiding you to pages in that issue pertaining to the title and part you have selected. This table is cumulative by month, so you should check the last issue for every month since the current L.S.A. and then the most recent issue for the current month.

The GPO provides access to L.S.A. through its GPO Access website. Researching L.S.A. online may be more convenient than using paper volumes. You can find coverage information on the introductory screen and search for your regulation by keyword or citation.

In addition, GPO Access provides Last Month's List of CFR Parts Affected; and Current List of CFR Parts Affected, covering changes since the date of the most recent Last Month's List; and List of CFR Parts Affected Today. The information from Parts Affected Today is incorporated into the Current List, so Parts Affected Today is most useful when you are closely tracking a proposed regulation. See Exhibit 13.10 (at page 343) for print outs of the first page of search results from these online sources.

The final step is, of course, to read the material you have identified in the *Federal Register*. You may read it in paper, of course, or retrieve it from the GPO Access *Federal Register* database. Either way, you will find not only the language of the regulation, but also explanatory material, for example, a summary of the regulation, its legal background, information considered by the agency, and the evolution of the regulation. In addition, you generally will find the regulation's effective date and an agency contact.

As noted previously, you may use the *Federal Register* for purposes other than updating your C.F.R. research. You will use the same sources, albeit in different ways. For example, if you need to read an old *Federal Register* for background information on a current regulation, you could use GPO Access for 1994 to date, turn to a paper copy (which may be in microfiche), or use a commercial online resource described later. If you are checking for recent regulatory activity on a topic of interest to a client, you have several options. You could conduct a key-word search in the GPO Access database or look in the *Federal Register* subject index, which is organized by agency and topic.

Exhibit 13.11 (at page 344) is our completed regulations template, reflecting both our initial research locating the regulation and our updating using L.S.A. in paper and the GPO Access Current List of CFR Parts Affected and Last Month's List of CFR Parts Affected.

| EXHIBIT 13.10 | Last Month's List of CFR Parts Affected, from GPO Access (online source) |

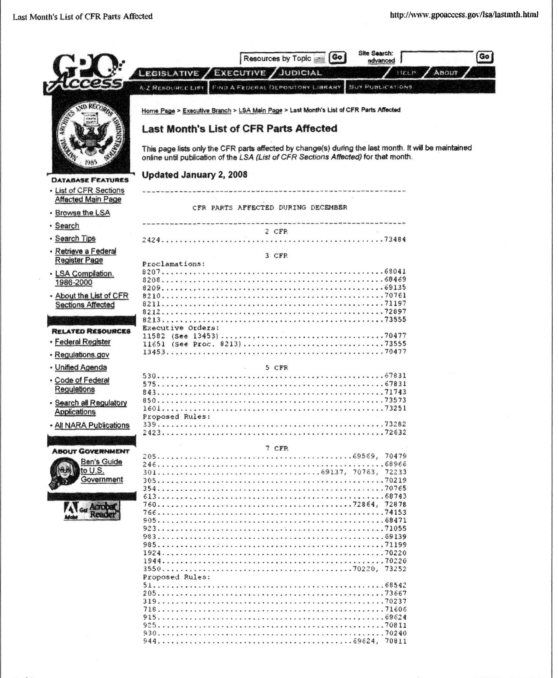

Last Month's List of CFR Parts Affected   http://www.gpoaccess.gov/lsa/lastmth.html

Home Page > Executive Branch > LSA Main Page > Last Month's List of CFR Parts Affected

Last Month's List of CFR Parts Affected

This page lists only the CFR parts affected by change(s) during the last month. It will be maintained online until publication of the *LSA (List of CFR Sections Affected)* for that month.

Updated January 2, 2008

```
-------------------------------------------------------------------
         CFR PARTS AFFECTED DURING DECEMBER
-------------------------------------------------------------------
                        2 CFR
2424................................................73484
                        3 CFR
Proclamations:
8207................................................68041
8208................................................68469
8209................................................69135
8210................................................70761
8211................................................71197
8212................................................72897
8213................................................73555
Executive Orders:
11582  (See 13453)..................................70477
11651  (See Proc. 8213).............................73555
13453...............................................70477
                        5 CFR
530.................................................67831
575.................................................67831
843.................................................71743
850.................................................73573
1601................................................73251
Proposed Rules:
339.................................................73282
2423................................................72632

                        7 CFR
205.........................................69569, 70479
246.................................................68966
301.................................69137, 70763, 72233
305.................................................70219
354.................................................70765
613.................................................68743
760........................................72864, 72878
766.................................................74153
905.................................................68471
923.................................................71055
983.................................................69139
985.................................................71199
1924................................................70220
1944................................................70220
3550.......................................70220, 73252
Proposed Rules:
51..................................................68542
205.................................................73667
319.................................................70237
718.................................................71606
915.................................................69624
925.................................................70811
930.................................................70240
944........................................69624, 70811
```

1 of 9   1/17/2008 4:53 PM

EXHIBIT 13.11	Second Regulations Template for Canoga Case

Issue:	**Citation Information:**
Does the National Labor Relations Board regulate orchestras?	• *Code of Federal Regulations* • *Title 29, part 103.2* • *2007*

Date of Events: *Sept. 7, 2007*

Date of Research: *Jan. 17 & Mar. 5, 2008*

Search and Find:

located regulation by . . .	statutory authority:
29 U.S.C.S. § 164 Annotation 95 → orchestras. Second entry refers to 29 C.F.R. part 103.2.	*29 U.S.C. § 164.*
	updated by . . . *LSA (paper): no changes.* *GPO website, Last Month's List: no changes.* *GPO website, Current List: no changes.*

Information and Implications:

The Board regulates orchestras with gross annual revenues (excluding certain grants) of at least $1 million.

I need more info about the orchestra's finances to determine if it meets the gross annual revenue threshold.

Next Steps:

questions to consider:	leads to follow:
Investigate orchestra revenues; available from public source?	

> **Regulations research in case law**
>
> • Judicial cases
> • Agency decisions

Courts evaluate, interpret, and apply regulations, much as they do with statutes. To research these judicial cases, you can use the sources discussed in Chapters 9 and 10, for example, digests, reporters, commercial databases. An efficient way to locate cases interpreting a regulation is by KeyCiting or Shepardizing the regulation. See Exhibit 13.12 (at page 346).

In addition, if the agency has adjudicatory powers, you should seek agency decisions interpreting and applying the regulation. Chapter 14 covers researching agency adjudicatory decisions.

Judicial cases and agency decisions also may be researched through looseleaf services, as discussed in Chapter 15.

2.   Citing Regulations

Regulations generally are cited to the regulatory code. Provide the regulation's name, if it is commonly known by a name; the code's abbreviation; the numbers needed to identify the regulation; and the date of the code. The format is the same under *Bluebook* Rule 14.2(a) and *ALWD* Rule 19.1:

☐   29 C.F.R. § 103.2 (2007).

Regulations not appearing in a regulatory code are cited to the register. Provide the register's name, the volume and the page number on which the discussion of the regulation or the regulation itself begins, the page number where the portion you are citing appears, and the date and the regulation's eventual codification. Here are two examples:

☐   *Bluebook* Rule 14.2(b): 38 Fed. Reg. 6176, 6177 (Mar. 7, 1973) (to be codified at 29 C.F.R. § 103.2).
☐   *ALWD* Rule 19.3: 38 Fed. Reg. 6176, 6177 (Mar. 7, 1973) (to be codified at 29 C.F.R. § 103.2).

EXHIBIT 13.12	KeyCite Report for Federal Regulation, from Westlaw (online source)

KEYCITE

C29 CFR § 103.2

Citing References

Citing Cases (U.S.A.)

▷ 1 N.L.R.B. v. Rochester Musicians Ass'n Local 66, 514 F.2d 988, 990, 89 L.R.R.M. (BNA) 2193, 2193, 76 Lab.Cas. P 10,850, 10850 (2nd Cir. Apr 28, 1975) (NO. 471, 74-1940)

Administrative Decisions (U.S.A.)

NLRB Decisions

C 2 Spring Library and Museums Ass'n, 221 NLRB 1209, 1210, 221 NLRB No. 194, 1975 WL 6564, *3, 91 L.R.R.M. (BNA) 1043 (N.L.R.B. Dec 18, 1975) (NO. AO-173) ★

▶ 3 Rochester Musicians Assn. Local 66, 207 NLRB 647, 648, 207 NLRB No. 110, 1973 WL 4660, *4, 85 L.R.R.M. (BNA) 1345 (N.L.R.B. Nov 29, 1973) (NO. 3-CB-1939) ★ ★

Secondary Sources (U.S.A.)

4 Employment Coordinator Labor Relations s 9:26, s 9:26. Nonprofit institutions (2008)

5 Federal Procedure, Lawyers Edition s 52:342, s 52:342. Monetary thresholds and other jurisdictional standards (2007)

6 Nonprofit Enterprises: Corps., Trusts, and Assoc. s 14:31, s 14:31. Labor Laws (2007)

7 Am. Jur. 2d Labor and Labor Relations s 632, s 632. Nonprofit institutions (2007)

8 THE BIRTH OF A RULE: THE NATIONAL LABOR RELATIONS BOARD'S USE OF INFORMAL RULEMAKING TO PROMULGATE A RULE FOR HEALTH CARE BARGAINING UNIT DETERMINATIONS, 1989 Det. C.L. Rev. 1105,   1132+ (1989)

C 9 AGENCY RULES WITH THE FORCE OF LAW: THE ORIGINAL CONVENTION, 116 Harv. L. Rev. 467,   592 (2002)

10 NLRB RULEMAKING ON HEALTH CARE COLLECTIVE BARGAINING UNITS: PREDICTABILITY, BUT AT WHAT COST, 9 Hofstra Lab. L.J. 483,   513 (1992)

C 11 RULEMAKING: THE NATIONAL LABOR RELATIONS BOARD'S PRESCRIPTION FOR THE RECURRING PAINS OF THE HEALTH CARE INDUSTRY, 9 J. Contemp. Health L. & Pol'y 377,   418 (1993)

C 12 QUESTIONING THE PREEMPTION DOCTRINE: OPPORTUNITIES FOR STATE-LEVEL LABOR LAW INITIATIVES, 5 Widener J. Pub. L. 35,   86 (1995)

C. What Else?

Regulations.gov. This federal government website includes a range of both simple and advanced search capabilities for researching federal regulations. Options include searching by key word, agency, type of action (e.g., legislative rulemaking, non-rulemaking), and type of document (notices, proposed rules, adopted rules, etc.). It is most useful for tracking the development of new regulations.

Commercial Online Resources. Westlaw, LexisNexis, Loislaw, and HeinOnline all provide databases with the *Code of Federal Regulations* and the *Federal Register.* Westlaw's C.F.R. provides a link to Notes of Decision for sections that have been interpreted in judicial cases; previous versions of the regulation; and references to agency decisions interpreting the regulation, commentary, and more through Regulations Plus. Westlaw also provides an index to the *Federal Register. LexisNexis Congressional* provides the text of federal regulations and the *Federal Register.*

Policy and Guidance Statements. Some agencies issue not only regulations but also less authoritative statements of the agency's approach to common situations. For example, an agency may issue a memo to employees who conduct inspections or prosecute cases. These statements can be very valuable and may be available from the agency or in a looseleaf service, described in Chapter 15.

Guides to Federal Agencies. To learn what federal agencies do, how to contact them, and what resources they provide, consult a source such as *The United States Government Manual* (available on GPO Access) and *The Federal Regulatory Directory.*

Presidential Documents. Two major types of presidential documents are executive orders (typically directed to government officials) and proclamations (general announcements and policy statements). These appear in various publications, including the *Federal Register*, title 3 of C.F.R., and *U.S. Code Congressional and Administrative News*; some also appear in the federal statutory codes. The National Archives website has links to Executive Orders, organized by the issuing president. LexisNexis and Westlaw provide some presidential documents. The *Weekly Compilation of Presidential Documents* and the annual *Public Papers of the President* compile not only executive orders and proclamations, but also other documents, such as announcements and nominations.

State Regulations. Many state agencies issue regulations. You may find them in an official paper code or public website, or in a LexisNexis, Westlaw, or Loislaw database. Many states have manuals similar to *The United States Government Manual.* BNA's *Directory of State Administrative Codes and Registers* provides background on the publications of administrative material at the state level.

AGENCY DECISIONS

CHAPTER 14

A. WHAT IS AN AGENCY DECISION, AND WHY WOULD YOU RESEARCH AGENCY DECISIONS?

Federal and state agencies make many decisions. Agency officials decide how to conduct an investigation, what technical or policy questions to study, whether to bring an enforcement action against an alleged offender, etc. This chapter focuses on decisions that are the output of administrative case adjudication; that is, the application of law — including regulations — to claims and disputes involving specific facts and parties before an administrative agency. These decisions fall into two main categories: formal adjudication and informal adjudication.

Formal administrative adjudication is broadly analogous to judicial litigation in several ways. Agency enabling statutes and administrative procedure acts set forth procedural rules that the agency must follow to adjudicate cases. A case generally begins with some form of notice, typically in pleadings, which may be construed fairly broadly. There may be discovery (or development of the facts by the lawyers) before the hearing, and preliminary issues may be handled by motion, i.e., by written and oral argument rather than presentation of evidence. The typical hearing resembles a trial with counsel, direct testimony and cross-examination, and exhibits; some evidence may be submitted in writing. The presiding official, often known as an "administrative law judge" (ALJ) or "hearing officer," then renders a recommended decision.

At this stage, however, formal agency adjudication and judicial adjudication differ in one important respect. Unlike a district court judge's order, an ALJ's recommendation is just that — a recommendation that is not always accepted by the administrative agency as the last word on a case. The agency's commissioners or other high-ranking members review the recommendation as well as the factual record and arguments of counsel. They may then choose to adopt the ALJ's recommendation as their own, or they may decide to develop their own decision.

Once finalized, a formal agency decision more or less resembles the opinion of a judicial court. It includes a statement of the facts as found by the agency, the agency's decision based on those facts, and the reasoning behind the decision. That reasoning typically includes discussion of the statute, any pertinent regulations, and previous decisions of the agency. Exhibit 14.1 (at pages 350–55) is an example of a decision by the National Labor Relations Board on whether nonunion employees are protected from discipline or discharge based on concerted activities.

Agencies are not always required to use these kinds of formal, court-like procedures. In fact, most agency adjudications are informal. Informal adjudications lack the procedural trappings of a formal administrative hearing, although they are still governed by some procedural requirements to ensure that parties receive due process of law. For example, an agency may have the authority to decide a dispute based only on written submissions from the parties, without providing the opportunity for a hearing before an ALJ. Even though these kinds of decisions do not use court-like procedures, they can still result in decisions that have the force of law.

Formal and informal agency decisions, like agency regulations, are subject to judicial review. The statute governing judicial review of an agency's decisions will usually specify whether such challenges are brought in a lower court or an appellate court. In either case, the agency's decision is generally reviewed as if it were an appeal from a trial court, because the agency's hearing served as the initial "trial" to determine the facts of the case. Thus, the issues before a reviewing court typically are limited to whether there is substantial evidence in the record to support the agency's decision, whether the agency has exceeded its statutory jurisdiction or failed to follow required procedures, and whether the agency has abused its discretion.

EXHIBIT 14.1	Agency Decision, from Decisions and Orders of the National Labor Relations Board (paper source)

Morton International, Inc. and Martin D. Howell.
Case 9–CA–30898

November 10, 1994

DECISION AND ORDER

BY MEMBERS DEVANEY, BROWNING, AND COHEN

On July 20, 1994, Administrative Law Judge Claude R. Wolfe issued the attached decision. The Respondent filed exceptions and a supporting brief.

The National Labor Relations Board has delegated its authority in this proceeding to a three-member panel.

The Board has considered the record in light of the exceptions and brief and has decided to affirm the judge's rulings, findings,[1] and conclusions and to adopt the recommended Order.

ORDER

The National Labor Relations Board adopts the recommended Order of the administrative law judge and orders that the Respondent, Morton International, Inc., West Alexandria, Ohio, its officers, agents, successors, and assigns, shall take the action set forth in the Order.

---

[1] The Respondent has excepted to some of the judge's credibility findings. The Board's established policy is not to overrule an administrative law judge's credibility resolutions unless the clear preponderance of all the relevant evidence convinces us that they are incorrect. *Standard Dry Wall Products*, 91 NLRB 544 (1950), enfd. 188 F.2d 362 (3d Cir. 1951). We have carefully examined the record and find no basis for reversing the findings.

Joseph C. Devine, Esq., for the General Counsel.
David J. Millstone and *William A. Nolan, Esqs.*, for the Respondent.

DECISION

STATEMENT OF THE CASE

CLAUDE R. WOLFE, Administrative Law Judge. This proceeding was litigated before me at Dayton, Ohio, on May 17, 1994, pursuant to charges filed on July 15, 1993, and amended on August 24 and October 22, 1993,[1] and complaint issued October 25 alleging Martin D. Howell and Robert Boerner were unlawfully suspended and discharged for engaging in protected concerted activity. Morton International, Inc. (the Respondent) contends the suspensions and discharges were for cause and did not violate Section 8(a)(1) of the National Labor Relations Act (the Act) as alleged.

Upon the entire record, and after considering the demeanor of the witnesses and the posttrial briefs of the parties, I make the following

---

[1] All dates are 1993 unless otherwise stated.

FINDINGS AND CONCLUSIONS

I. THE RESPONDENT'S BUSINESS

The Respondent is a corporation engaged in the manufacture and nonretail sale of adhesives at West Alexandria, Ohio, and during the 12 months preceding the issuance of the complaint, sold and shipped its products valued in excess of $50,000 from its West Alexandria facility to points located outside the State of Ohio. The Respondent is an employer engaged in commerce within the meaning of Section 2(2), (6), and (7) of the Act.

II. SUPERVISORS AND AGENT

At all times material to this proceeding, the individuals named below held the positions set forth opposite their names and have been supervisors and agents of the Respondent within the meaning of Section 2(11) and (13) of the Act.

Randall Bittner—Plant Manager
Jane Paxton—Manager for Human Resources
Leigh Walling—Polyester Supervisor
Bob Napier—Maintenance Supervisor

III. THE ALLEGED UNFAIR LABOR PRACTICES

A. *Chronology*

The facts are not in dispute with respect to the conduct of Boerner and Howell which led to their discharge, and all these facts were known to the Respondent at the time the two were discharged.

On the morning of June 14, at about 2 or 2:30 a.m., Boerner was lunching with a custodian named Snider "Butch" Neusock, and another employee. All were smokers. Snider had placed a memo on the table.[2] The memo was addressed to the Respondent's safety committee and signed, "Morton employee." The memo, in substance complained that the Respondent was not rigidly enforcing its no-smoking policy. The last sentence in the lengthy memo reading, "Also, what about the employees who do not use tobacco products—when will we be able to have a 'non-smoke' break of ten minutes or more every hour?" was composed by Brenda Holfinger, an assistant to the health and safety administrator. Holfinger is a regular hourly paid employee.

Indignant at the content of this memo, Boerner wrote comments on it in bold letters reading in one instance, "Chicken Shit" after the anonymous "Morton employee" appearing as the originator of the memo, and at another point made the observation, without an aquerbian mark "could this be racist" in reference to a sentence reading, "I hate to see them [the Respondent] back down because of pressure from a minority of the employee [i.e., smokers]" warning to his task, Boerner enlarged his commentary by noting at the bottom of the purloined memo. Again in very large letters, "I think the non-smokers should quit their damm [sic] crying and put their thoughts to a more useful purpose for the company!" In the course of his composition of this broadside, Boerner sought assistance in the spelling of a word from Neusock

---

[2] The custodian was later discharged on the ground he had removed the document from company records in a locked office.

EXHIBIT 14.1   *(continued)*

MORTON INTERNATIONAL, INC.   565

who obliged. What word he assisted with is not specified, but I seriously doubt it was, "Damm."

Apart from the minuscule assistance included by Neusock, who made no other contribution to Boerner's effort, none of the three men lunching with Boerner, whom he states shared his views, were in any way party to the writing on or posting of the memo by Boerner, nor is there any evidence they designated him as their representative for any purpose. Boerner left the area after posting the memo with his comments on it.

Enter Howell. At about 4 a.m. he entered the empty lunchroom. Noticing the posted memo with Boerner's amendations, he took it to a table and read it. A smoker himself, Howell was then inspired to add further commentary on the memo. At the very top of the memo he wrote, "Gee, Brenda this isn't you is it? Get a real job you glorified secretary." In response to a statement in the memo referring to "the old days" he penned, "What do you know about the 'old days.'" Directing his attention to the memo claim the company was retreating from a policy, he noted, "what policy? be specific Brenda." Concerning a statement in the memo to the effect that forcing smokers to do so outside in all weather would deter smoking, Howell wrote, "then more of us would miss work for being sick." To this point none of the memo was composed by Brenda Holfinger who typed the memo. Now, however, her sentence quoted above closed the memo and moved Howell to expound, "has production suffered, no, so shut up and stay the hell out of the trailer."[3] Finally, at the bottom of the page, Howell commented on Boerner's adjuration to nonsmokers that they should put their thoughts to a more useful purpose, stating this would be quite difficult for this nonsmoker cause *she* has no "useful thoughts!" Finished with his commentary, Howell made copies and posted them in the breakroom, the smoke trailer, and on a bulletin board by the health and safety office.

Discovering the altered and posted memo, Respondent launched an investigation. As a result the custodian who admitted taking the document from company files as a joke was fired. Boerner and Howell each candidly advised the Respondent of their conduct with reference to the memo. They were suspended pending the results of the Respondent's investigation. Each received a letter from Jane Paxton dated June 15 and reading as follows:

Subject: Suspension Notification Without Pay

As we discussed, the Company is investigating concerns that you may have violated our policies. In particular, we are reviewing policies including but not limited to:

    a. Harassment or intimidating language or conduct, . . .

    b. Conduct that reflects unfavorably upon the Corporation.

    c. Making malicious, false or derogatory statements that may damage the integrity or reputation of the Corporation, its products and performance, or its employees.

    d. Destruction, damage, improper disposition, or unauthorized possession or removal from Company

premises of property that does not belong to the employee.

    e. Posting, distributing, or circulating any written materials in work areas deemed inappropriate or disruptive.

Pending the outcome of this investigation, you have been suspended. I will be the person investigating these concerns.

What you can expect was discussed as the investigation is conducted. I will review the information and documentation you provided. As appropriate, I will consult with other employees and managers to assist in addressing and resolving the issues, and I will strive to keep you informed of the progress of this investigation.

I want to emphasize some of our expectations of you during this investigation. If you have any questions or concerns about any of these expectations, or about any part of this investigation, please contact me immediately. The expectations for you include the following:

You are expected to cooperate fully throughout the investigation, and be completely honest in answering questions and providing information to the Company.

You are expected to provide us with all of the information and documentation that you believe may help us in conducting this investigation. If you have any information or documentation that may be relevant to this matter and which you have not already provided, please provide immediately.

While this investigation is being conducted, you will be suspended without pay. During this time you must devote your full efforts to help bring this matter to closure. You must remain available during normal working hours to meet and/or provide information to Company representatives.

This is a confidential investigation. You must not discuss this investigation with any person who does not have a legitimate business need to know this information. If you have any questions or concerns about this requirement at any time, please feel free to discuss it further with me.

If you have any questions or concerns about any of these expectations, or about any part of this investigation, you will contact me immediately. I will contact you within the next three days to let you know of the progress of the investigation.

Please let me know if you have any questions, additional information, or want to discuss any of this. As you know, you can reach me at 839–4612.

Completing its investigation, the Respondent gave Boerner and Howell identical dismissal letters dated June 18 and reading as follows:

Subject: Investigation—Termination

We have completed the investigation of the alleged violation of policy listed in your suspension letter of June 15, 1993.

Our conclusions, based on interview with employees and your statement are:

---

[3] Respondent has a trailer to which employees may repair to smoke on their breaks.

EXHIBIT 14.1   *(continued)*

While working third shift on Sunday night, June 13th, an employee removed a confidential memo from the locked office of Health & Safety, made a copy and gave it to the Polyester third shift employees. You and one other Polyester employee co-authored derogatory, inflammatory and false comments on the memo, made additional copies and distributed it.

WAL cannot tolerate such actions and multiple violations of company policy. Therefore, your termination is effective immediately due to misconduct. Your final paycheck will include 32 hours of vacation payoff.

B. *Discussion and Conclusions*

The facts are clear and undisputed, but do they show the discharges were unlawful or legitimate? As I have previously stated in *Gatliff Coal*,[4] the answer to such questions depend on whether concerted action is present, whether that action is protected if it is in fact concerted, whether the General Counsel has set forth a prima facie case, the terminations were precipitated by protected concerted activity, and, if General Counsel has such a prima facie case, would Respondent have taken the same action in the absence of the protected activity? The first step in the process of determining these issues is measuring the facts found against the guide set forth in *Meyers Industries*, 268 NLRB 493, 497 (1984) *(Meyers I)*, in the following terms:

> In general, to find an employee's activity to be "concerted," we shall require that it be engaged in with or on the authority of other employees, and not solely by and on behalf of the employee himself. Once the activity is found to be concerted, an 8(a)(1) violation will be found if, in addition, the employer knew of the concerted nature of the employee's activity, the concerted activity was protected by the Act, and the adverse employment action at issue (e.g., discharge) was motivated by the he employee's protected concerted activity. [Footnotes deleted.]

and as recited in *Meyers Industries*, 281 NLRB 882, 887 (1986) *(Meyers II)*:

> We reiterate, our definition of concerted activity in *Meyers I* encompasses those circumstances where individual employees seek to initiate or to induce or to prepare for group action, as well as individual employees bringing truly group complaints tot he attention of management.

General Counsel, relying on *Meyers I*; *Amelio's*, 301 NLRB 182 fn. 4 (1991); and *Dayton Typographical Service*, 273 NLRB 1205 (1984), contends Boerner's conduct was concerted because other employees were opposed to the suggestions in the memo, Neusock assisted Boerner in the drafting of his comments on the memo, and Boerner's posting of the memo was a solicitation of employee actions and a logical outgrowth of the employees' joint complaint about the memo's stance on smoking.

I do not believe Boerner's conduct was concerted merely because others were opposed to the memo's suggestions inasmuch as there is no persuasive evidence the other three

memo readers, or any one else, authorized him to act on their behalf, or, with respect to the reference to the footnote in *Amelio's*, that Boerner's writings on the memo were necessarily a logical outgrowth of the concerns expressed by the group at the lunchroom table. Moreover, I do not agree that mere assistance in the spelling of a word threw Neusock into concert with Boerner. I do, however, conclude in accord with *Meyers II*, supra, that Boerner was engaged in concerted activity because his uncontroverted and credible testimony that he posted the memo, with his comments thereon. "To let the other people in the plant know—the other smokers know that this had been written and to see if—maybe if they had any comments or any hard feelings, maybe they would express their feelings" warrants a fair conclusion that he was seeking "to initiate or to induce or to prepare for group action" by fellow smokers in opposition to the sentiments expressed in the memo which were contrary to the interest of employees who smoked and in support of his writings on the memo.[5]

When Howell added his words to the memo, he endorsed and joined Boerner's effort in protest of the memo's attack on the existing smoking policy. That he did not then know Howell was the one who added the commentary to the memo is of no consequence. Here two employees reacted adversely to the memo and took complementary action to oppose it because they were smokers concerned in a common goal of preserving the status quo as it related to the policy on smoking. Howell's conduct in copying the notice, with his comments added thereon and posting it in several additional areas was an enlistment in and enlargement of Boerner's effort to inform other smokers of the threat the memo posed to existing smoking policy which was acceptable to employees who smoked.

The Respondent's smoking policy is a term or condition of employment, *Allied Signal*, 307 NLRB 752, 754 (1992), and the concerted activity of Boerner and Howell directed at protesting any change in policy thus concerns a term or condition of employment and is protected. The dismissal letters given to Howell and Boerner flatly stated the reason for their discharge to be "You and one other Polyester employee co-authored derogatory, inflammatory and false comments on the memo, made additional copies and distributed it." This evidences that the Respondent believed they were acting concertedly in writing on and posting the altered memo, and terminated them for engaging in such activity. It is well settled that discharges based on suspected concerted activities violate Section 8(a)(1) of the Act even if the suspected concert did not exist. See, e.g., *American Poly Therm Co.*, 298 NLRB 1057, 1065 (1990); *Gulf-Wandes Corp.*, 233 NLRB 772, 778 (1977).

I conclude the evidence warrants an inference the known or suspected participation of Boerner and Howell in protected concerted activities was a motivating factor in the Respondent's decision to discharge them. The burden rests on the Respondent to show the discharges would have taken place in the absence of protected concerted activity. *Wright Line*, 251 NLRB 1083 (1980); *NLRB v. Transportation Management Corp.*, 462 U.S. 393 (1983).

---

[4] *Gatliff Coal Co.*, 301 NLRB 793 (1991).

[5] The testimony of Jane Paxton that her investigation received a report that the comments at issue were designed to start up trouble evidences that the Respondent recognized the comments were of interest to other employees and would tend to inspire debate.

EXHIBIT 14.1   *(continued)*

MORTON INTERNATIONAL, INC.   567

The Respondent asserts Boerner and Howell were terminated for misconduct because each had violated company policies prohibiting conduct described in the Respondent's handbook as follows:

1. Harassment or intimidating language or conduct.

2. Destruction, damage, improper disposition, or unauthorized possession or removal from Company premises of property that does not belong to the employee.

3. Posting, distributing, or circulating, any written materials in work areas deemed inappropriate or disruptive.

4. Making malicious, false or derogatory statements that may damage the integrity or reputation of the corporation, its products and performance, or its employees.

Items 1 and 4

Respondent argues that the comments added to the memo by Boerner and Howell were merely personal attacks against the memo's author and therefore are not protected. It is the content of the memo, not the identity of the author, which caused Boerner and Howell to react to what they perceived to be a threat to the existing policy and practice concerning smoking. Howell credibly states his comments were directed at the memo and its author. Boerner credibly states he wrote what he did because he was upset at the content of the memo. Respondent's contention that the conduct of the two men was solely personal anger unrelated to terms and conditions of employment and therefore not protected concerted activity is simply without merit. The two were angry it is true, but that anger was raised by what they reasonably perceived as an effort to change the smoking policy, a term or condition of employment, in a manner detrimental to the interest of those employees who smoked. They were angry at the content of the memo. That this anger was also directed at its author is not surprising. I do not believe that employees protesting a change in a condition of employment are required to surgically express their protest in a prescribed manner leaving out any spirited or even profane aspersions directed at the memo or its author. Here the Respondent is exercised at the language used by Boerner, i.e., the term "chicken shit," and Howell's direction of his attack at Brenda Holfinger whom he thought was the author but was merely a coauthor. The Respondent characterized the language of Boerner as profanity and that of Howell as "malicious defamatory . . . obnoxious, and wholly unjustified" and therefore not protected. With respect to the references to the memo author as "chicken shit," I do not believe the Respondent is as terribly upset about the use of this term as it claims to be, given the uncontroverted and credible testimony of Boerner that "shit" is a common expression in Respondent's facility. Be that as it may, I have found Boerner was engaged in protected concerted activity directed at rousing smokers to unite in opposition to changes to existing policy. The Board, with court approval, has found that an employee who characterized an acting supervisor in writing as an "a– hole," an obvious contraction of "asshole," was engaged in protected activity when he resorted to this sort of rhetorical hyperbole to emphasize disapproval of the acting supervisors, and the use of the term did not make his conduct unprotected *Postal Service*, 241 NLRB 389 (1979), enfd. 615 F.2d 1366 (8th Cir. 1979), citing *Linn v. Plant Guards Local 114*, 383

U.S. 53, 63 (1966), and *Letter Carriers Local 469 v. Austin*, 418 U.S. 264, 283 (1974). The use of "chicken shit" as a descriptive term of disapproval does not strike me as more offensive than "a–hole." In so concluding I am well aware that such matters of degree of offensiveness can be argued ad infinitum by determined opponents without any agreement ever reached. Suffice it to say that in my view the distinction is not worth the argument.

With respect to Howell's comments directed to Holfinger, I doubt very much that their publication had or will have "an inevitable negative effect on [her] status in the eyes of the employees" as Respondent contends, or may damage the integrity or reputation of the Respondent, its product and performance, or its employees. Holfinger is allied with the employees who oppose the smoking policy, presumably the nonsmokers. Howell and Boerner belong to the smoking group. There is no showing Holfinger ever had a favorable status in the eyes of employees who smoke, and the fact she was vilified by a smoker is not likely to lower her status in the eyes of the nonsmokers. Respondent has not shown there has ever been any disciplinary action against any employee other than Boerner and Howell for "harassment or intimidating language or conduct." I do not believe it likely that no other employee ever violated the rule against such conduct, or that no other employee was ever known by supervision or management to have done so. The absence of any proffer by Respondent of evidence this rule has ever before been applied or been cause of discipline or discharge leads me to believe it has not been so applied until the situation before me arose, and, further, that Respondent probably does not regularly police such conduct. It is somewhat ingenuous to claim that Holfinger was falsely accused inasmuch as she did type the memo and took the opportunity to add her own opinion which is clearly not a measured and unbiased view.

Item 2 and 3

There is no evidence whatsoever that Boerner or Howell was aware they were dealing with a purloined document, the memo does not on its face show its possession by employees was unauthorized or in any way contrary to Respondent's policy, nor is there any evidence they should have known that was the case. I therefore conclude item 2 is an excuse for the discharges rather than a tenable reason. The conclusions of item 2 are unsupported by probative evidence and their proffer is, I find, part of a shotgun approach to see what might hit the targets, Boerner and Howell.

Turning to Respondent's posttrial brief contention that both men violated the policy against posting disruptive materials, I first note that the policy which appears in the employee handbook exactly as set down above as item 3 makes specific reference to posting, distributing, or circulating written matters in work areas. Boerner only posted the memo in the employee breakroom, which is patently not a work area. The rule therefore cannot apply to hidden conduct. Howell credibly testified he posted copies by the timeclock, in the breakroom, in the smoking trailer, and on the bulletin board by the health and safety office. Respondent proffers no persuasive evidence that any of these postings were in a work area, and Howell's description of the posting areas would seem to indicate they were not work areas. Respondent has

EXHIBIT 14.1   *(continued)*

therefore not shown the rule was violated,[6] and I find it was not because no postings were made in work areas. The use of the rule by Respondent as a defense therefore can not prevail. Here again, I conclude Respondent has consciously manufactured a reason that does not exist in order to disguise its true motivation.

The evidence shows Howell and Boerner were engaged in protected concerted activity when they placed their comments on and posted the memo, those activities were a motivating factor in Respondent's decision to discharge them, and General Counsel has made out a prima facie case the Act has been violated. The burden on the Respondent to prove the discharges would have taken place in the absence of any protected activity has not been met. Accordingly, I find General Counsel has proved by a preponderance of the credible evidence that Howell and Boerner were discharged in violation of Section 8(a)(1) of the Act.

To the extent the complaint alleges their suspension during investigation violated the Act, I do not so find. It was not unreasonable for the Respondent to suspend the employees involved in the handling of a document wrongfully extracted from its files while it conducted an appropriate investigation. It is its conduct after it ascertained the facts which runs afoul of the Act.

CONCLUSIONS OF LAW

1. Respondent is an employer within the meaning of Section 2(2), (6), and (7) of the Act.

2. Respondent violated Section 8(a)(1) of the Act by discharging Martin Howell and Robert Boerner on June 18, 1993, because they engaged in protected concerted activity.

3. The unfair labor practices found affect commerce within the meaning of Section 2(6) and (7) of the Act.

THE REMEDY

In addition to the usual notice posting and cease-and-desist requirements, my recommended Order will require Respondent to offer Howell and Boerner immediate and full reinstatement to their former jobs or, if those jobs no longer exist, to substantially equivalent positions without prejudice to their seniority, or other rights and privileges previously enjoyed, and make them whole for any loss of earnings suffered as a result of the discrimination against them. Backpay shall be calculated and interest thereon computed in the manner prescribed in *F. W. Woolworth Co.*, 90 NLRB 289 (1950), and *New Horizons for the Retarded*, 283 NLRB 1173 (1987). I shall further recommend that Respondent be required to remove from its files any reference to their discharges and notify them in writing that this has been done and that the discharges will not be used against them in any way.

On these findings of fact and conclusions of law and on the entire record, I issue the following recommended[7]

---

[6] Whether the posting rule is valid or not is not before me.

[7] If no exceptions are filed as provided by Sec. 102.46 of the Board's Rules and Regulations, the findings, conclusions, and recommended Order shall, as provided in Sec. 102.48 of the Rules, be adopted by the Board and all objections to them shall be deemed waived for all purposes.

ORDER

The Respondent, Morton International, Inc., West Alexandria, Ohio, its officers, agents, successors, and assigns, shall

1. Cease and desist from

(a) Discharging or otherwise discriminating against employees because they engage in protected concerted activity.

(b) In any like or related manner interfering with, restraining, or coercing employees in the exercise of the rights guaranteed them by Section 7 of the Act.

2. Take the following affirmative action necessary to effectuate the policies of the Act.

(a) Offer Martin D. Howell and Robert Boerner immediate and full reinstatement to their former jobs or, if those jobs no longer exist, to substantially equivalent positions, without prejudice to their seniority or any other rights or privileges previously enjoyed, and make them whole for any loss of earnings or benefits suffered as a result of the discrimination against them, in the manner set forth in the remedy section of this decision.

(b) Remove from its files any reference to the discharges of Howell and Boerner on June 18, 1993, and notify them in writing that this has been done and that the discharges will not be used against them in any way.

(c) Preserve and, on request, make available to the Board or its agents for examination and copying, all payroll records, social security payment records, timecards, personnel records and reports, and all other records necessary to analyze the amount of backpay due under the terms of this Order.

(d) Post at its place of business in West Alexandria, Ohio, copies of the attached notice marked "Appendix."[8] Copies of the notice, on forms provided by the Regional Director for Region 9, after being signed by the Respondent's authorized representative, shall be posted by the Respondent immediately upon receipt and maintained for 60 consecutive days in conspicuous places including all places where notices to employees are customarily posted. Reasonable steps shall be taken by the Respondent to ensure that the notices are not altered, defaced, or covered by any other material.

(e) Notify the Regional Director in writing within 20 days from the date of this Order what steps the Respondent has taken to comply.

---

[8] If this Order is enforced by a judgment of a United States court of appeals, the words in the notice reading "Posted by Order of the National Labor Relations Board" shall read "Posted Pursuant to a Judgment of the United States Court of Appeals Enforcing an Order of the National Labor Relations Board."

APPENDIX

NOTICE TO EMPLOYEES
POSTED BY ORDER OF THE
NATIONAL LABOR RELATIONS BOARD
An Agency of the United States Government

The National Labor Relations Board has found that we violated the National Labor Relations Act and has ordered us to post and abide by this notice.

Section 7 of the Act gives employees these rights.

To organize
To form, join, or assist any union

EXHIBIT 14.1   *(continued)*

MORTON INTERNATIONAL, INC.   569

To bargain collectively through representatives of their own choice

To act together for other mutual aid or protection

To choose not to engage in any of these protected concerted activities.

WE WILL NOT discharge or otherwise discriminate against any employees because they engage in protected concerted activity.

WE WILL NOT in any like or related manner interfere with, restrain, or coerce you in the exercise of the rights guaranteed you by Section 7 of the Act.

WE WILL offer Martin D. Howell and Robert Boerner immediate and full reinstatement to their former jobs or, if those jobs no longer exist, to substantially equivalent positions, without prejudice to their seniority or any other rights or privileges previously enjoyed and WE WILL make them whole for any loss of earnings and other benefits resulting from their discharge, less any net interim earnings, plus interest.

WE WILL remove from our files any reference to the discharge of Howell and Boerner on June 18, 1993, and notify them in writing that this has been done and that the discharge will not be used against them in any way.

MORTON INTERNATIONAL, INC.

As with agency regulations, the reason for researching agency decisions is that they constitute the law. The agency is subordinate to the legislature and courts: The decision must comport with the constitution, applicable statutes, and the judicial standards described previously. It must also comport with agency regulations, which are also law. A decision meeting these requirements is itself law and functions as a kind of precedent for other similar situations coming within the agency's jurisdiction. Although stare decisis does not operate as forcefully with agencies as with courts, an agency must generally explain deviations from earlier decisions.

B.   HOW DO YOU RESEARCH AND CITE AGENCY DECISIONS?

1.   Researching Agency Decisions

Research in administrative decisions is similar to research in judicial cases, as suggested by a comparison of our agency decisions template, Exhibit 14.2 (at page 356) and our case law template, Exhibit 9.3 (at page 160). The main steps are to develop a well-honed issue statement, identify one or more pertinent decisions, read those decisions carefully, verify that the decisions are still good law, connect that law to your client's situation, and plan your next steps.

As with judicial cases, the agency issues a decision in slip form, typically without editorial enhancements. Decisions traditionally are compiled periodically into paper reporters, and many decisions are posted quite promptly in the agency's website. Each such reporter and database contains the decisions of a particular agency. Some of these sources are commercial, while others are official government sources. This chapter focuses on official sources; Chapter 15 discusses commercial resources.

EXHIBIT 14.2	Agency Decisions Template

Issue:	Citation Information:
	• decision name
	• reporter, database, or other source
	• volume and page number
Date of events:	• date
	• GOOD LAW?
Date of research:	

Search and Find:

located decision by . . .

Information and Implications:

- facts
- procedure
- outcome and holding
- rule
- reasoning
- dissent/concurrence
- connection to client's situation: application of rule and case comparison

Next Steps:

questions to consider:	leads to follow:

Only rarely will you research only agency decisions. Most of the time, you also will research the enabling statute and judicial cases reviewing the agency's decisions; in some situations, you also will research the agency's regulations. Thus this part starts with a few words about research in statutes and regulations and concludes with a few words about research in judicial cases. See Exhibit 14.3 (below) for an overview of agency decisions research.

This part focuses on the National Labor Relations Board, whose decisional law is extensive and easily researched. For other federal agencies and for state agencies, the official sources may be fewer and more difficult to use. One good first step is to contact the agency directly; if you represent a party that is currently in a dispute with the agency and the agency is represented by counsel, the rules of professional conduct may require you to contact the agency's counsel instead. Other good options include visiting the agency's website and consulting with reference librarians in an academic law library.

> **Agency decisions research in statutes and regulations**
>
> ▶   Read the enabling statute for the legal standard and the agency's adjudicative authority; seek references to agency decisions.
> ▶   As needed, research applicable regulations.

Agency decisions may involve legal issues governed by statutes or by regulations adopted under statutory authority. Chapter 11 covers statutory research generally, and Chapter 13 covers regulations research. As you read the pertinent agency's enabling statute, look for a description of the agency's authority to adjudicate cases, the process the agency must follow, and the standard governing the case. Once you learn that the agency in your situation can indeed adjudicate cases, you should look in the annotation for references to pertinent agency decisions (as well as judicial cases). You should also look for indications of the agency's authority to promulgate regulations on your research topic as well as references to those regulations in the *Code of Federal Regulations*; citing the regulation may lead to pertinent agency decisions.

Exhibit 14.4 (at page 358), from the United States Code Service, lists several agency decisions.

| EXHIBIT 14.3 | Overview of Agency Decisions Research |

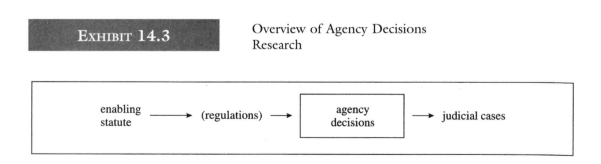

EXHIBIT 14.4	Descriptions of Agency Decisions in Annotated Code, from United States Code Service (paper source)

29 USCS § 157, n 45　　　　　　　　　　　　　　　　　　LABOR

A conversation may constitute a concerted activity although it involves only a speaker and listener, but to qualify as such it must appear at the very least that it was engaged in with the object of initiating or introducing or preparing for group action or that it had some relation to group action in the interest of the employees. Mushroom Transp. Co. v NLRB (1964, CA3) 330 F2d 683, 56 BNA LRRM 2034, 49 CCH LC ¶ 18921.

In order to protect concerted activities in full bloom, protection must be extended to "intended, contemplated or even referred to" group action lest employer retaliation destroy incipient employee initiative aimed at bettering terms of employment and working conditions. Hugh H. Wilson Corp. v NLRB (1969, CA3) 414 F2d 1345, 71 BNA LRRM 2827, 60 CCH LC ¶ 10205, cert den (1970) 397 US 935, 25 L Ed 2d 115, 90 S Ct 943, 73 BNA LRRM 2600, 62 CCH LC ¶ 10724.

Activities of employees engaged in, with, or on behalf of, other employees, and not solely by or on behalf of particular employees themselves, are concerted activities for purpose of mutual aid or protection within meaning of 29 USCS § 157. Top of Waikiki, Inc. v NLRB (1970, CA9) 429 F2d 419, 74 BNA LRRM 2678, 63 CCH LC ¶ 10999.

"Concerted activity" means the employee must be acting with or on behalf of other employees, and not solely by and on behalf of the discharged employee himself. NLRB v C &I Air Conditioning, Inc. (1973, CA9) 486 F2d 977, 84 BNA LRRM 2625, 72 CCH LC ¶ 14048.

For individual claim or complaint to amount to concerted action, it must not be made solely on behalf of individual employee, but must be made on behalf of other employees or at least be made with object of inducing or preparing for group action and have some arguable basis in collective bargaining agreement. ARO, Inc. v NLRB (1979, CA6) 596 F2d 713, 101 BNA LRRM 2153, 86 CCH LC ¶ 11250, 56 ALR Fed 728.

Concerted activity includes activity of individual employee when that employee is acting on behalf of only one other employee. Wilson Trophy Co. v NLRB (1993, CA8) 989 F2d 1502, 143 BNA LRRM 2008, 124 CCH LC ¶ 10622, reh, en banc, den (1993, CA8) 125 CCH LC ¶ 10740.

Two employees as well as a dozen or a thousand can act in concert for their mutual aid and protection. Tex-Togs, Inc. (1955) 112 NLRB 968, 36 BNA LRRM 1129, enforced (1956, CA5) 231 F2d 310, 37 BNA LRRM 2768, 30 CCH LC ¶ 69849.

It is not necessary for employees to band together and overtly manifest by physical action discontent before NLRB will find that concerted activity, for even individual protests which resound to groups' benefit are protected concerted activity. Aro, Inc. (1976) 227 NLRB 243, 94 BNA LRRM 1010, 1976-77 CCH NLRB ¶ 17662, enforcement

den (1979, CA6) 596 F2d 713, 101 BNA LRRM 2153, 86 CCH LC ¶ 11250, 56 ALR Fed 728.

Contrary to prior decision in Alleluia Cushion Co. (1975) 221 NLRB 999, Board will not find protected concerted activity unless employee engages in or with or own authority of other employees, and not solely on behalf of employee himself. Meyers Industries, Inc. (1984) 268 NLRB 493, 115 BNA LRRM 1025, 1983-84 CCH NLRB ¶ 16019, remanded (1985) 244 US App DC 42, 755 F2d 941, 118 BNA LRRM 2649, 102 CCH LC ¶ 11346, cert den (1985) 474 US 948, 88 L Ed 2d 294, 106 S Ct 313, 120 BNA LRRM 3392 and cert den (1985) 474 US 971, 88 L Ed 2d 320, 106 S Ct 352, 120 BNA LRRM 3392, 103 CCH LC ¶ 11585, on remand (1986) 281 NLRB 882, 123 BNA LRRM 1137, 1986-87 CCH NLRB ¶ 18184, affd (1987) 266 US App DC 385, 835 F2d 1481, 127 BNA LRRM 2415, 107 CCH LC ¶ 10226, cert den (1988) 487 US 1205, 101 L Ed 2d 884, 108 S Ct 2847, 128 BNA LRRM 2664, 129 BNA LRRM 3016, 109 CCH LC ¶ 10534.

46. Activity of single employee, generally

Employee who was discharged after acting alone in complaining to employer about violation would have been protected from discharge under 29 USCS § 157 by simply getting together with co-workers to complain. Prill v NLRB (1987) 266 US App DC 385, 835 F2d 1481, 127 BNA LRRM 2415, 107 CCH LC ¶ 10226, cert den (1988) 487 US 1205, 101 L Ed 2d 884, 108 S Ct 2847, 128 BNA LRRM 2664, 129 BNA LRRM 3016, 109 CCH LC ¶ 10534.

Activity of single employee in enlisting support of fellow employees for their mutual aid and protection is as much concerted activity as is ordinary group activity. Owens-Corning Fiberglas Corp. v NLRB (1969, CA4) 407 F2d 1357, 70 BNA LRRM 3065, 59 CCH LC ¶ 13356.

Truckdriver engaged in concerted activity by refusing to drive truck which he felt unsafe where he obtained instructions to do so from union official, sought to involve other union members and have them present during dispute with employer, and employer was aware of union involvement. McLean Trucking Co. v NLRB (1982, CA6) 689 F2d 605, 111 BNA LRRM 3185, 97 CCH LC ¶ 10166.

Single employee's filing of worker's compensation claim is not protected concerted activity, notwithstanding employee is member of collective bargaining group. Flick v General Host Corp. (1983, ND Ill) 573 F Supp 1086, 114 BNA LRRM 3576.

Employee who, in good faith, refuses to drive tractor-trailer truck on ground that condition of truck constitutes abnormally dangerous working condition is engaged in concerted activity under 29

> **Agency decisions in the agency's own reporter or database**
>
> ▶ Discern the scope, coverage, and means of access of the compilation.
> ▶ Locate potentially pertinent decisions.
> ▶ Carefully read the pertinent decisions.

Some agencies publish decisions in paper reporters, others in databases made available through public websites, and others in a combination of the two. *Bluebook* Table 1 and *ALWD* Appendix 8 (available through the website alwd.org) list official reporters of federal agency decisions. Each such compilation has its own particular features. The following discussion focuses on the National Labor Relations Board's compilations; you probably will find other compilations similar in general design if not identical in detail.

For many decades, the Board has published its decisions in paper reporters, called *Decisions and Orders of the National Labor Relations Board.* As with reporters of judicial cases, decisions are published in the order issued. Thus a digest is needed to identify pertinent decisions within the various volumes. The Board employs a highly structured and detailed outline of the issues it considers, called the "classification outline." See Exhibit 14.5 (at page 360). Board staff members write brief descriptions of each decision and categorize them using the topics within the classification outline. The classification outline and the decision descriptions function like the West key-number system and headnotes, discussed in Chapter 9.

For most recent Board decisions, dating from 1992 to the present, you may use the Board's classification system through NLRB CITENET. A standard approach is to scan the list of chapters and select a potentially pertinent one, then scan the topics within that chapter and select a potentially pertinent topic, then run a key-word search of the descriptions assigned to that chapter and topic. You will thereby obtain the descriptions of pertinent decisions, but not the decisions themselves. See Exhibit 14.6 (at page 361).

For older cases, you will use the *Classified Index of National Labor Relations Board Decisions and Related Court Decisions,* a set of hardcover volumes, each covering several years of Board decisions. Despite its title, this publication is really a digest, in which the decision descriptions are presented within the classification outline.

When you use the classification outline to identify potentially pertinent decisions, you learn about the range of issues addressed by the Board and how the various issues relate to each other. But if you do not need this information, and you believe that you can state your research topic well in a Boolean search, you could run a search using the Board website's "quick search" feature. Exhibit 14.7 (at page 362) is the first page of a citation list obtained using the search terms `smok*` and `''concerted activity''` in case text contained in bound volumes.

| EXHIBIT 14.5 | Classification Outline, from Classification Outline with Topical Index for Decisions of the National Labor Relations Board and Related Court Decisions (paper source) |

---

506 EMPLOYEE RIGHTS PROTECTED BY SECTION 7

0100	GENERALLY
0114	RIGHT OF SELF-ORGANIZATION
0128	RIGHT TO FORM, JOIN, OR ASSIST LABOR ORGANIZATIONS
0142	RIGHT TO BARGAIN COLLECTIVELY THROUGH REPRESENTATIVE OF OWN CHOOSING
0156	RIGHT TO ENGAGE IN OTHER CONCERTED ACTIVITIES FOR PURPOSE OF COLLECTIVE BARGAINING
0170	RIGHT TO ENGAGE IN OTHER CONCERTED ACTIVITIES FOR MUTUAL AID OR PROTECTION
0180	ATTITUDE TOWARD MANAGEMENT REFLECTING DISSATISFACTION WITH WORKING CONDITIONS AND/ OR LACK OF SUCCESS OF UNION CAMPAIGN, ETC.
0184	RIGHT TO REFRAIN FROM EXERCISE OF SECTION 7 RIGHTS
0184-0100	Generally
0184-5000	Subject to membership requirement of valid agreement
0188	RIGHT TO BE FREE FROM UNFAIR, IRRELEVANT, OR INVIDIOUS TREATMENT BY REPRESENTATIVE
0188-5000	Differentiation on basis of sex
0192	RIGHTS DERIVED FROM OTHER FEDERAL LABOR STATUTES
2000	NATURE OF ACTIVITIES PROTECTED
2001	GENERALLY
2001-5000	Concerted activity defined
2017	NOT ALL CONCERTED ACTIVITIES PROTECTED
2017-0800	Activity of such character as to render employee unfit for further service
2017-1700	Activities tending to disrupt employer's or union's operations
2017-2500	Activities relating to intra-union affairs
2017-3300	Cessation of work for personal reasons
2017-4000	No impact upon terms and conditions of employment
2017-5000	Resort to prohibited means
2017-6700	Activities prohibited by statute
2017-8300	Conduct violating valid provisions of contract
2017-9100	Conduct in derogation of bargaining representation
2033	BOARD HAS FUNCTION OF BALANCING CONFLICTING EMPLOYEE AND EMPLOYER INTERESTS
2033-5000	Exercise of economic pressure not unlawful per se
2050	EMPLOYER'S MISTAKEN BELIEF AS TO ACTIVITY'S PROTECTED STATUS IMMATERIAL
2060	EMPLOYEES' MISTAKEN BELIEF AS TO VALIDITY OF GRIEVANCE IMMATERIAL
2067	UNION MEMBERSHIP IMMATERIAL
2083	UNION ACTIVITY NEED NOT BE INVOLVED OR COLLECTIVE BARGAINING CONTEMPLATED
3000	REFUSAL TO CROSS PICKET LINE
3001	GENERALLY
3001-5000	Employer may replace non-striking employee refusing to cross line if business reasons so require
3033	AT PREMISES OF ANOTHER EMPLOYER
3033-0100	Generally
3033-2500	Right protected by 8(b)(4) proviso
3033-5000	Primary picket line
3033-7500	Secondary picket line
3033-8700	Picket line at state subdivision
3067	AT OWN EMPLOYER'S PREMISES
3067-0100	Generally
3067-1700	Primary line of another union at employee's place of work
3067-3300	Primary line of union representing unit of which employee is not member
3067-5000	As result of sympathy strike
3067-6700	Secondary picket line which is primary line of another union
4000	OBJECTIVE AS DETERMINANT OF PROTECTED STATUS OF ACTIVITY
4001	GENERALLY
4001-5000	Racial discrimination
4033	OBJECTIVES WARRANTING PROTECTION OF ACTIVITY
4033-0100	Generally

82

| EXHIBIT 14.6 | Agency Decisions Search Result, from NLRB CITENET (online source) |

NLRB

National Labor Relations Board
Classified Index - The Electronic Network
Skip Navigation   Comments

| NLRB Home | ▆▆▆▆▆ | Search Heading | Search Digest | Search Case Name | User Guide |

Classification Digest Search Results
Total Found: 2   Criteria:: 506-2001-5000: smoke

Do Search Within Search   **View CiteNet Abbreviations**

List All Results in new window (this will allow you to view and/or print the entire list)

Next Last

506-2001-5000-0000 Concerted or protected activity defined

Digest: [E's suspension and discharge of 2 Ees for writing on and posting memo dealing with enforcement of E's no-smoking policy, unlawful, since Ees were engaged in protected concerted activity; Ees' action of altering memo was taken to initiate or induce other fellow **smokers** in opposition to sentiments of memo; Ees took action to oppose memo in attempt to preserve status quo as it related to smoking policy; E's smoking policy is term and condition of employment and Ees' concerted action directed at protesting change in policy thus concerns a term and condition of employment and is protected activity; E's dismissal letters, stating "You and one other ... Ee," indicates E believed Ees were acting concertedly in writing on and posting altered memo]

Case Name: Morton International, Inc.

Case Number:9-CA-30898 **Decision Date:**November 10, 1994

Type: Board   **Citation Number:**315 NLRB No. 71

Members:DBC   **Tracking ID:**1994-784

Next Last

| NLRB Home | CiteNet | Search Heading | Search Digest | Search Case Name | User Guide | CiteNet Abbr. | Comments |

Today's date: February 13, 2008

Once you have identified potentially pertinent decisions, you would obtain the decisions in the paper *Decisions and Orders* or through the NLRB Decisions database available through the Board's website.

Of course, you should read with care the decisions you have obtained. As with judicial cases, you should learn the outcome of the case, discern the rule used by the agency to decide the case, understand the facts of the case and the agency's reasoning about those facts, identify the leading authorities cited in the reasoning, and examine any dissenting and concurring opinions. Be sure you fully understand how the decision is structured. Many agency commissioners incorporate the recommended findings and conclusions of the ALJ.

| EXHIBIT 14.7 | Key-Word Search Results, from NLRB Website Quick Search (online source) |

Site Map | **Search:** All of NLRB.Gov | Search Key Word

Advanced Search

Office Finder | Speakers | Careers | Contact Us | Text

| HOME | WORKPLACE RIGHTS | RESEARCH | PUBLICATIONS | E-GOV | ABOUT U! |

Home > Research > Decisions > Board Decisions   Thursday, March 6

Board Decisions

Site Tools

Add to favorite

Online NLRB decisions are offered in PDF and HTML format. Slip opinions are subject to revision before publication in bound volumes. Use the Quick Search on the left to search within these documents. You also might try doing E-Research using CiteNet.

Print friendly v

Email this pag

Questions

Frequently Requested Documents

Decisions

Board Decisions

Bound Volumes

ALJ Decisions

Regional Directors

Memos

Appellate Court Branch Briefs and Motions

Weekly Summary

Classified Index the Electronic Network (CiteNet)

Quick Search
Find what ?

smok* and "concerted

Search

Search within:
○ Case Name
○ Case Number
○ Case Text
◉ All

*Adobe Reader is required to view PDF documents.

Click to download Adobe Reader 7.0.

Slip Decisions   Bound Volumes

Volume : 352   Go   Documents Found: ‹

Slip Opinion # ▾	Case Name (HTML or PDF* version)	Issuance Date	Case Number
351-094	**Valerie Manor, Inc.** View: HTML | PDF (266kb)	Dec 28 2007	34-CA-11162
351-092	**Alstyle Apparel** View: HTML | PDF (233kb)	Dec 28 2007	21-CA-37029
351-043	**Metropolitan Transportation Services** View: HTML | PDF (658kb)	Sep 29 2007	17-CA-20061
347-016	**Smoke House Restaurant** View: PDF (195kb)	May 31 2006	31-CA-26240

back

Español | Inspector General | FOIA | No Fear

Privacy Policy | Disclaimer | Accessi!

Updating and validating agency decisions

- Judicial cases
- Shepard's through LexisNexis or KeyCite through Westlaw

As with judicial cases, the law made through agency decisions evolves over time. Later agency decisions may affect the validity of an earlier agency decision in various ways, for example, overruling, modifying, distinguishing, or citing with approval. By researching agency decisions thoroughly, you should obtain more recent agency decisions on your research topic and should thereby learn of any changes in the law at the agency level.

In addition, you should research judicial cases, with several purposes in mind:

☐ You should learn whether the agency decision on which you plan to rely has been reviewed by a court and what the outcome was.

☐ You should learn whether the agency decision has been cited in other judicial cases involving different parties but addressing your research topic.

☐ You should discern whether judicial cases addressing your research topic but not citing the agency decision use the rule articulated in the agency decision or some other rule.

To research judicial cases, you can use the sources described in Chapters 9 and 10, such as digests, reporters, and commercial databases. Because the agency decision and related judicial cases involve a statute and possibly also a regulation, you can use the sources described in Chapter 11 to locate cases involving a statute, such as the case descriptions in an annotated code, and the sources used in Chapter 13 to locate cases involving a regulation, such as citing the regulation.

Citing agency decisions is a key step, just as it is with judicial decisions. You may Shepardize agency decisions through LexisNexis and KeyCite them through Westlaw. Both services provide the history of the agency decision and a list of authorities citing the agency decision, including other agency decisions, judicial cases, and commentary. Both services also supplement the list in various ways, for example, through the use of symbols indicating the status of the cited agency decision and words or symbols indicating how the citing authority treated the agency decisions. See Exhibit 14.8 (at page 364).

Also keep in mind that the legislature may amend the statute or the agency may amend the regulation on which an agency decision relies and thereby change the law. You should discover this through your research in statutes and regulations, as discussed in Chapter 11 and Chapter 13.

Our agency decisions template for the Canoga case appears as Exhibit 14.9 (at page 366).

EXHIBIT 14.8

Shepard's Report for Agency Decision,
from LexisNexis (online source)

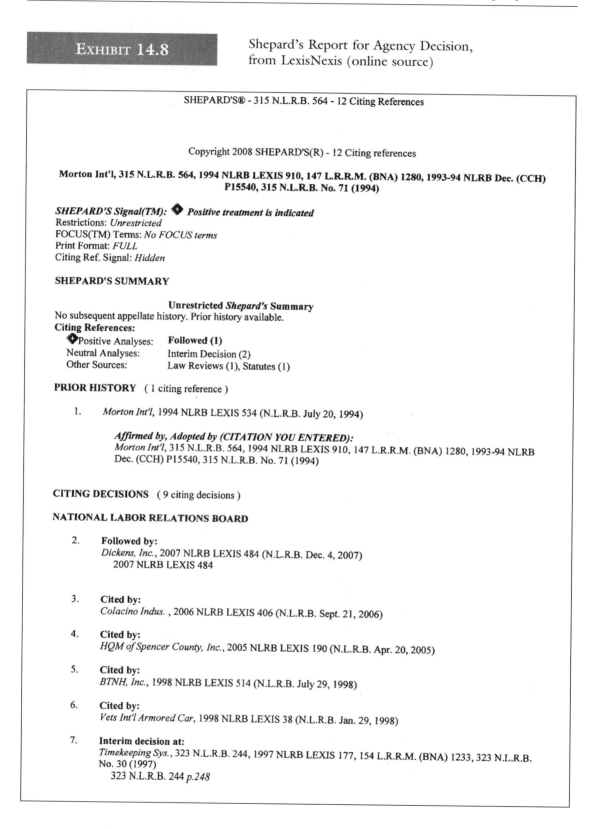

SHEPARD'S® - 315 N.L.R.B. 564 - 12 Citing References

Copyright 2008 SHEPARD'S(R) - 12 Citing references

Morton Int'l, 315 N.L.R.B. 564, 1994 NLRB LEXIS 910, 147 L.R.R.M. (BNA) 1280, 1993-94 NLRB Dec. (CCH) P15540, 315 N.L.R.B. No. 71 (1994)

SHEPARD'S Signal(TM): ◆ *Positive treatment is indicated*
Restrictions: *Unrestricted*
FOCUS(TM) Terms: *No FOCUS terms*
Print Format: *FULL*
Citing Ref. Signal: *Hidden*

SHEPARD'S SUMMARY

Unrestricted *Shepard's* Summary
No subsequent appellate history. Prior history available.
Citing References:
   ◆Positive Analyses: **Followed (1)**
   Neutral Analyses: Interim Decision (2)
   Other Sources: Law Reviews (1), Statutes (1)

PRIOR HISTORY (1 citing reference)

   1.   *Morton Int'l*, 1994 NLRB LEXIS 534 (N.L.R.B. July 20, 1994)

         Affirmed by, Adopted by (CITATION YOU ENTERED):
         Morton Int'l, 315 N.L.R.B. 564, 1994 NLRB LEXIS 910, 147 L.R.R.M. (BNA) 1280, 1993-94 NLRB
         Dec. (CCH) P15540, 315 N.L.R.B. No. 71 (1994)

CITING DECISIONS   (9 citing decisions)

NATIONAL LABOR RELATIONS BOARD

   2.   **Followed by:**
         Dickens, Inc., 2007 NLRB LEXIS 484 (N.L.R.B. Dec. 4, 2007)
            2007 NLRB LEXIS 484

   3.   **Cited by:**
         Colacino Indus. , 2006 NLRB LEXIS 406 (N.L.R.B. Sept. 21, 2006)

   4.   **Cited by:**
         HQM of Spencer County, Inc., 2005 NLRB LEXIS 190 (N.L.R.B. Apr. 20, 2005)

   5.   **Cited by:**
         BTNH, Inc., 1998 NLRB LEXIS 514 (N.L.R.B. July 29, 1998)

   6.   **Cited by:**
         Vets Int'l Armored Car, 1998 NLRB LEXIS 38 (N.L.R.B. Jan. 29, 1998)

   7.   **Interim decision at:**
         Timekeeping Sys., 323 N.L.R.B. 244, 1997 NLRB LEXIS 177, 154 L.R.R.M. (BNA) 1233, 323 N.L.R.B.
         No. 30 (1997)
            323 N.L.R.B. 244 *p.248*

EXHIBIT 14.9	Agency Decisions Template for Canoga Case

Issue:	Citation Information:
Is a protest against a new smoking policy protected "concerted activity" under 29 U.S.C. § 157?	• *Morton International, Inc. and Martin D. Howell* • *315 NLRB No. 71* • *November 10, 1994* • *Updating: followed in 2007 NLRB decision*
Date of events: *Sept. 7, 2007*	
Date of research: *Jan. 21, 2008*	

Search and Find:

located decision by . . .

Used NLRB Classification Outline to identify chapter 506 topic 2001-5000, Employee Rights Protected by Section 7, Concerted Activity Defined. In NLRB CITENET: Chose "search heading" option. Chose chapter 506 from dropdown list and entered "2001" in "classification detail number" box. Initial search lead to 191 results under topic 506-2001-5000-0000. Returned to previous screen and entered "smoke" in digest search string box to narrow results; lead to Morton.

Information and Implications:

An employer issued a new smoking policy. Two employees wrote critical comments on a copy of the policy in the lunchroom. The employees were suspended/discharged. The Board held that the employees engaged in protected concerted activity because they acted together to protest the employer's change in terms and conditions of employment. The employer therefore engaged in an unfair labor practice.
The key factual issue is whether other employees acted with Canoga.

Next Steps:

questions to consider:	leads to follow:
Was anyone else also protesting the policy?	*Dickens, Inc., 2007 Board decision, 2007 NLRB LEXIS 484.*

2.   Citing Agency Decisions

To properly cite an agency decision, provide the decision's name, official reporter citation, and date. The *ALWD* rule also requires the agency's abbreviation in the parenthetical.

☐   *Bluebook* Rule 14.3: *Morton Int'l, Inc.*, 315 N.L.R.B. 564 (1994).
☐   *ALWD* Rule 19.5: *Morton Intl., Inc.*, 315 N.L.R.B. 564 (N.L.R.B. 1994).

C.   WHAT ELSE?

LexisNexis and Westlaw. Both services provide databases of agency decisions, which are kept current, generally extend back in time farther than agency website databases, and provide additional search options. For example, Westlaw's database of NRLB decisions dates to 1935, the date the Board was established.

State Agency Decisions. It may not be easy to locate decisions of a state agency. Good first steps are contacting the agency or its legal counsel or visiting its website.

Informal Opinions. Some agencies issue opinion letters about specific situations on which advice is sought, so as to avoid litigation. An example is the private-letter ruling of the Internal Revenue Service. To learn how to research such informal decisions, contact the agency or the agency's legal counsel, check its website, or check a library catalog.

LOOSELEAF SERVICES

A. WHAT ARE LOOSELEAF SERVICES?

For some areas of the law, commercial publishers compile comprehensive and current collections of the law and commentary in a single resource. The traditional term for these subject-specific mini-libraries is "looseleaf service" or simply "looseleaf," because these resources do indeed appear in multi-volume paper looseleaf volumes. An increasingly common alternative is a subscription online service that does the same thing. We discuss these sources in this unit because they are particularly useful for locating administrative materials. Although they vary considerably, looseleafs do share three important characteristics.

First, they bring together, into one source, a wide range of legal authorities. Comprehensive looseleafs include judicial case law, statutes, administrative regulations, and agency decisions, at the federal and state levels. Many looseleafs also contain commentary. Some also include practice materials, such as forms; reports of pending cases or bills; and summaries of interesting conferences or studies.

Second, looseleafs are updated frequently and thereby provide fairly current material. They are published in formats that facilitate updating.

Third, the best looseleafs provide significant assistance to the researcher through refined finding tools, such as indexes, topic outlines, and case digests.

Because a looseleaf covers only one area of law, these tools can be very detailed, and one set of tools covers various types of legal authority.

B.   How Do You Research in and Cite Looseleaf Services?

1.   Researching in Looseleaf Services

Because each looseleaf is unique, research practices vary from source to source. The following discussion sets out the steps you might take in a paper looseleaf service, then describes options available online. The discussion features *Labor Relations Reporter*, a looseleaf service published by the Bureau of National Affairs, and its online counterpart. The federal concerted activity issue featured in this unit serves as the example.

Administrative materials in paper looseleaf services

▶   Locate an appropriate looseleaf service.

▶   Examine it and its instructional material.

▶   Consult the general index.

▶   Read the commentary for background and references.

▶   Locate and read the statutes and administrative regulations.

▶   Use the case digest to locate pertinent cases.

▶   Read judicial case law and agency decisions.

▶   Citate the primary authority.

Locate and examine the looseleaf. To determine whether an appropriate looseleaf service exists, for your research topic consult a library catalog, examine *Legal Looseleafs in Print* or check Table 15 in *The Bluebook* (abbreviations for services).

A paper looseleaf service uses binders that can be easily opened for insertion and deletion of pages; as new material arrives, it is slipped into the binder, adding to or replacing older material. The set of materials usually includes several binders, each with one or more sections set off by tabs. Extensive looseleaf services also include separate volumes for older material, such as cases or agency decisions. Once you have identified a pertinent looseleaf, look over the entire set:

☐   Examine the binders, and gain some understanding of the materials each contains.

☐   Look for a section describing how to use the looseleaf, typically located in the first binder, and read it.

☐   Look for a statement indicating the currency and updating of the various components. See Exhibit 15.1 (at page 370). Pages are reissued as needed, and most pages bear a date of issuance.

☐   Locate the general index and any updates, as well as tables of authorities, such as statutes or regulations.

☐   Figure out where the commentary material, statutes, regulations, and cases appear.

☐   Locate the most recent information, typically in a separate binder or section of a binder; also locate any hardbound or other volumes containing more dated information, such as judicial cases or agency decisions.

Consult the index(es). Many looseleafs are divided into several parts by types of authority, e.g., commentary, statutes, as well as by jurisdiction, i.e., federal, individual states. Thus there may be more than one index: a general index for the entire looseleaf and subsidiary indexes for the various parts. Furthermore, these indexes may have one or more updates, so you should be sure to note the currency of each index. As a general rule, consult the general index first and then any pertinent subsidiary indexes. See Exhibit 15.2 (at page 371).

As you move from the index to the text, take special care to discern the looseleaf's numbering scheme. The looseleaf may be organized and numbered by chapter, section, paragraph, or page, or, most likely, a combination of these.

Read the commentary. Ordinarily you will move from the index to the commentary portion of the looseleaf. The commentary is likely to be fairly current, present a detailed discussion, and contain references to primary authority. See Exhibit 15.3 (at page 372).

Research statutes and regulations. If you are using a looseleaf service to research an area of law governed by an administrative agency, you will want to read the pertinent statute and any regulations the agency has promulgated on your research topic. Most looseleafs afford several means of locating statutes and regulations: through the general index, through references in the commentary section, through a subsidiary index to the statutes and regulations sections, through a table of contents at the beginning of a set of statutes or regulations, and through tables of statutes or regulations.

Research cases and decisions. A looseleaf service covering an area of law governed by an administrative agency may also contain agency decisions and judicial case law. Indeed, a looseleaf service may well include judicial cases not reported in general case reporters, informal agency decisions that are difficult to locate in government sources, and very new decisions.

Looseleafs also typically contain detailed, topically arranged digests of decisions and cases. The general index, commentary, or subsidiary index for the case sections may point you to pertinent topics within the digest; you also may find it useful to skim the digest outline. The digest may appear in multiple volumes, for example, the newest digest material in the looseleaf binders, the

| EXHIBIT 15.1 | Looseleaf Service Updating Material, from BNA's Labor Relations Reporter (paper source)* |

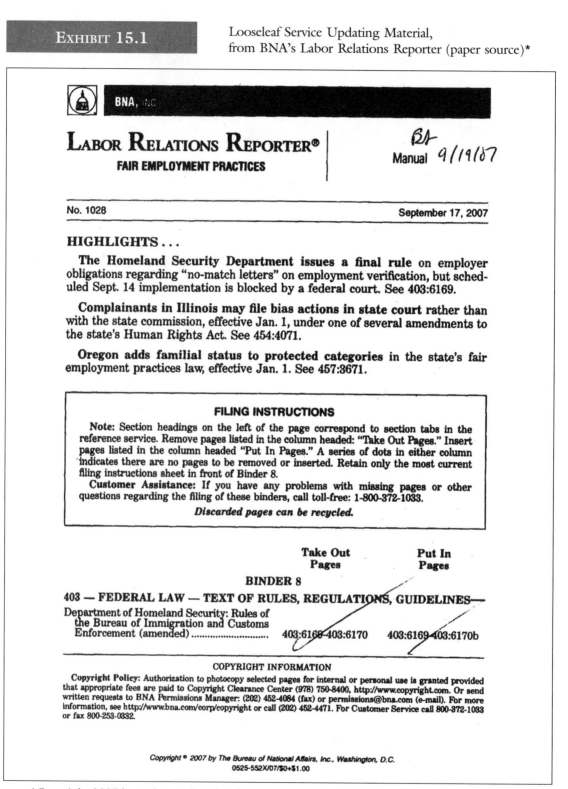

BNA, INC

LABOR RELATIONS REPORTER®
FAIR EMPLOYMENT PRACTICES

BA
Manual 9/19/07

No. 1028   September 17, 2007

HIGHLIGHTS . . .

The Homeland Security Department issues a final rule on employer obligations regarding "no-match letters" on employment verification, but scheduled Sept. 14 implementation is blocked by a federal court. See 403:6169.

Complainants in Illinois may file bias actions in state court rather than with the state commission, effective Jan. 1, under one of several amendments to the state's Human Rights Act. See 454:4071.

Oregon adds familial status to protected categories in the state's fair employment practices law, effective Jan. 1. See 457:3671.

FILING INSTRUCTIONS

Note: Section headings on the left of the page correspond to section tabs in the reference service. Remove pages listed in the column headed: "Take Out Pages." Insert pages listed in the column headed "Put In Pages." A series of dots in either column indicates there are no pages to be removed or inserted. Retain only the most current filing instructions sheet in front of Binder 8.

Customer Assistance: If you have any problems with missing pages or other questions regarding the filing of these binders, call toll-free: 1-800-372-1033.

Discarded pages can be recycled.

	Take Out Pages	Put In Pages
BINDER 8		
403 — FEDERAL LAW — TEXT OF RULES, REGULATIONS, GUIDELINES—		
Department of Homeland Security: Rules of the Bureau of Immigration and Customs Enforcement (amended)	403:6168–403:6170	403:6169–403:6170b

---

COPYRIGHT INFORMATION

Copyright Policy: Authorization to photocopy selected pages for internal or personal use is granted provided that appropriate fees are paid to Copyright Clearance Center (978) 750-8400, http://www.copyright.com. Or send written requests to BNA Permissions Manager: (202) 452-4084 (fax) or permissions@bna.com (e-mail). For more information, see http://www.bna.com/corp/copyright or call (202) 452-4471. For Customer Service call 800-372-1033 or fax 800-253-0332.

Copyright © 2007 by The Bureau of National Affairs, Inc., Washington, D.C.
0525-552X/07/$0+$1.00

*Copyright 2007 by and reproduced with permission from The Bureau of National Affairs.

EXHIBIT 15.2   Looseleaf Service General Index,
                 from BNA's Labor Relations Reporter (paper source)*

TER

GENERAL INDEX   **A 835**

TERMINATION OF EMPLOYMENT—Contd.
Modifications or reductions of penalties, LA
  ▸ 118.03, ▸ 118.806
—Public employees, LA ▸ 100.559565
Moonlighting, LA ▸ 118.6482
—Public employees, LA ▸ 100.552560
Motives
—Employer, LRX 510:202
—Mixed, LRX 510:201
—Union animus, LRX 510:202
—Union in seeking discharges, union-security con-
  tracts, LRX 730:305
Name calling
        LR ▸ 118.640
        LA ▸ 118.640
National origin discrimination, FEP ▸ 108.1215
—Federal employees, FEP ▸ 110.6515
Negligence
        LR ▸ 118.651
        LA ▸ 118.651
—Public employees, LA ▸ 100.552535
No reason given, evidence of discrimination,
  LMRA, LR ▸ 52.2780
Notice, LA ▸ 118.305
—Public employees, LA ▸ 100.5520
Obscenity
        LR ▸ 118.640
        LA ▸ 118.640
—Discrimination, LMRA, LR ▸ 52.2728
—Management, employee use toward, LA
  ▸ 118.6523
—Public employees, LA ▸ 100.552510
Off-duty or off-premises misconduct, LA
  ▸ 118.634
—Public employees, LA ▸ 100.552505
Overtime, refusal to work
        LR ▸ 118.658
        LA ▸ 118.658
—Discrimination, LMRA, LR ▸ 52.2731
—Public employees, LA ▸ 100.552570
Past practice, LA ▸ 24.355
Performance. See Incompetence and inefficiency,
  this heading
Personal appearance, LA ▸ 118.639
—Public employees, LA ▸ 100.552529
Personnel files, remedies for discrimination
        FEP ▸ 228.251
        AD ▸ 228.251
Physical disabilities. See Disabled employees, this
  heading
Physical tests, failure to submit, LA ▸ 118.655
—Public employees, LA ▸ 100.552565
Picketing
        LR ▸ 118.660
        LA ▸ 118.6601
—Discrimination, LMRA, LR ▸ 52.341
Political affiliation. See POLITICAL ACTIVITIES,
  subheading: Affiliation
Polygraph tests. See Lie detectors, this heading
Post leaving, LA ▸ 118.654
—Public employees, LA ▸ 100.552555
Pregnancy, FEPM 421:506
—Excessive weight, fired for being "too fat,"
  FEPM 421:502

—Federal employees, FEP ▸ 110.4018
Procedure
        LR ▸ 118.301 et seq.
        LA ▸ 118.301 et seq.
—Public employees, LA ▸ 100.5523
Productivity. See Incompetence and inefficiency,
  this heading; Loafing, this heading
Promotion before, LRX 650:107
Protected activities, discrimination, LMRA
        LR ▸ 52.2532 et seq.
        LRX 510:204
Protest against, picketing objects, LR ▸ 81.257
Psychological evaluations, LA ▸ 118.655
—Public employees, LA ▸ 100.552565
Public employees
        LR ▸ 100.641, ▸ 100.647
        LA ▸ 100.5501 et seq.
—Mitigation of damages, LA ▸ 100.559525
Public policy violations, emotional distress claims,
  IERM 533:104
Quitting jobs distinguished
        LR ▸ 118.07
        LA ▸ 118.07
—Discrimination, LMRA, LR ▸ 52.257
Racial discrimination, FEP ▸ 108.30251
—Abolition of job, FEP ▸ 108.30263
—Absenteeism, FEP ▸ 108.30257
—Availability of work, FEP ▸ 108.30263
—Dishonesty of employees, FEP ▸ 108.30259
—Falsification of job applications, FEP
  ▸ 108.30259
—Federal employees, FEP ▸ 110.3515
—Incompetence, FEP ▸ 108.30255
—Insubordination, FEP ▸ 108.30253
—Job qualifications, FEP ▸ 108.30255
—Misconduct of employees, FEP ▸ 108.30253
—Performance on job, FEP ▸ 108.30255
—Tardiness, FEP ▸ 108.30257
—Theft, FEP ▸ 108.30259
Reasons
        LR ▸ 118.632 et seq.
        LA ▸ 118.632 et seq.
See also specific reasons for discharge
—Discrimination, LMRA, LR ▸ 52.2672
—Public employees, LA ▸ 100.552501 et seq.
Refusal to give doctor's certificate, LA ▸ 118.655
—Public employees, LA ▸ 100.552565
Reinstatement. See REINSTATEMENT
Religious discrimination, FEP ▸ 108.1118
—Federal employees, FEP ▸ 110.5015
Remedies
        LR ▸ 118.801 et seq.
        LA ▸ 118.801 et seq.
—Discrimination, LMRA, LRX 510:209
—Public employees, LA ▸ 100.559501 et seq.
Resignation, FMLA benefits. See FMLA, this
  heading
Restitution by public employees, LA ▸ 100.5512
Retaliatory discharge. See RETALIATION
Safety, LA ▸ 118.659
—Public employees, LA ▸ 100.552575
Severance pay. See SEVERANCE PAY
Sex discrimination, FEP ▸ 108.4112
—Federal employees, FEP ▸ 110.4016

Consult individual Manual indexes for more recent information.
LA▸ = Labor Arbitration Outline; LR▸ = Labor Relations Outline;
*LRX = Labor Relations Expediter; *SLL = State Labor Laws;
WH▸ = Wages and Hours Outline; *WHM = Wages and Hours Manual

| EXHIBIT 15.3 | Looseleaf Service Commentary, from BNA's Labor Relations Reporter (paper source)* |

LRX 510:204   LABOR RELATIONS EXPEDITER   No. 860

Threatening to impose difficult or unpleasant conditions alone is not sufficient to establish a constructive discharge.[35] Those conditions must actually exist.

A second theory of constructive discharge is referred to as Hobson's Choice.

Under this theory, an employee quits rather than comply with an employer's requirement that the employee abandon the LMRA's § 7 right to engage in concerted activity.[36]

Discharge or Discipline in Violation of § 8(a)(1)

Section 8(a)(1) of the LMRA makes it an unfair labor practice for an employer "to interfere with, restrain, or coerce employees in the exercise of the rights guaranteed in § 7."[37] Section 7 guarantees employees the "right to self-organization, to form, join, or assist labor organizations, to bargain collectively through representatives of their own choosing, and to engage in other concerted activities for the purpose of collective bargaining or other mutual aid or protection . . . ."[38]

Protected Concerted Activity

For activity to be protected under § 7, and thereby § 8(a)(1), it must either be a union-related activity or some other concerted activity that is for the employees' mutual aid and protection.

Concerted Activity

"Concerted activity for their mutual aid or protection" has been broadly interpreted to include activities beyond mere collective bargaining or grievance settlement. It also includes efforts by employees "to improve their terms and conditions of employment or otherwise improve their lot as employees through channels outside the immediate employee-employer relationship."[39] The courts and the NLRB have given a broad interpretation to the meaning of "concerted" for the purposes of the LMRA.[40] The actions of an individual employee may be considered "concerted" as long as

that individual is acting under the authority of and on behalf of at least one other employee.[41] Additionally, concerted activity includes an individual employee acting with the intent of initiating group action.[42]

"An individual employee's reasonable and honest invocation of a right provided for in his collective bargaining agreement" has been considered concerted activity because the "invocation of such rights affects all the employees that are covered by the collective bargaining agreement."[43]

Protected Activity

The activity in question also must be protected by § 7 of the LMRA.[44] Employees engage in protected activities by participating in work stoppages over unfair labor practices and in economic strikes and sympathy strikes as permitted by the collective bargaining agreement. Employees who stop work because of a good faith belief that abnormally dangerous working conditions exist at their place of employment are engaged in activity protected by § 502 of the LMRA.[45] See the chapter, *Strikes and Lockouts*, for more information on work stoppages.

Filing or processing a grievance according to the collective bargaining agreement is protected activity. See the

---

[35] *Adson Inc.*, 290 N.L.R.B. 501, 131 LRRM 1145 (1988).
[36] *Intercon I*, 333 N.L.R.B. No. 30, 168 LRRM 1145 (2001).
[37] 29 U.S.C. § 158(a)(1).
[38] 29 U.S.C. § 157.
[39] *Eastex Inc. v. NLRB*, 437 U.S. 556, 98 LRRM 2717 (1978).
[40] *NLRB v. Wash. Aluminum Co.*, 370 U.S. 9, 50

LRRM 2235 (1962).
[41] *Wilson Trophy Co. v. NLRB*, 989 F2d 1502, 143 LRRM 2008 (8th Cir. 1993); *JCR Hotel Inc.*, 338 N.L.R.B. No. 27, 173 LRRM 1109 (2002).
[42] *NLRB v. Caval Tool Div.*, 262 F.3d 184, 184 LRRM 2180 (2d Cir. 2001).
[43] *NLRB v. City Disposal Sys. Inc.*, 465 U.S. 822, 115 LRRM 3193 (1984).
[44] 29 U.S.C. § 157.
[45] 29 U.S.C. § 143.

---

older materials in softcover or hardbound books. Thus you typically must work through recent material and then back in time.

Once you have identified potentially pertinent cases, you would, of course, read them in the looseleaf service. The looseleaf may or may not give the official citation to material published in official reporters.

Citate primary authority. To update and expand your research, use the looseleaf's citator, if one exists. If there is none, use Shepard's or KeyCite, especially for agency decisions and judicial cases.

Options for administrative material research in online looseleafs

- Search the table of contents or indexes.
- Run a Boolean search in one or more components.
- Peruse the case digest.
- Use the embedded links.
- Use the citator.

Increasingly, commercial publishers are offering looseleafs through subscription online services. Like paper looseleaf services, online looseleafs offer a wide range of frequently updated material, including the law and commentary, organized into components and accessible through finding tools such as indexes and digests. An online service also offers options not available in a paper looseleaf service:

☐ You can perform a Boolean search, typically by use of truncated words, phrases, and proximity connectors.

☐ You can elect to search one or several of the components simultaneously.

☐ You may be able to move quickly from one component to another through embedded links.

☐ The online materials may be completely cumulated so you need not look in several places for current materials.

However, the retrospective coverage of the online service may vary from the paper service, especially as to cases and decisions, so it is important to determine its beginning date of coverage.

Before you use an online service, you should explore a bit; a good strategy is to read the orienting materials, which may be found in the opening screens, a tutorial, or descriptions of the various components. In particular, seek to discern the following:

☐ what types of authorities are included in which components;

☐ what the coverage of each component is, e.g., how far back the case collection goes, how up-to-date the statutory materials are;

□ whether you can browse or search a table of contents or index;

□ what the key-word search protocols are; and

□ how readily you can link from one component to another.

Exhibit 15.4 (at page 375) reflects the range of content and search options available through the BNA Labor & Employment Library, an online looseleaf service.

2. Citing Looseleaf Services

Most authorities located in a looseleaf appear elsewhere in preferred sources, such as a code of regulations or official reporter of agency decisions. Nonetheless, you may cite to a looseleaf on occasion. The most common situation is when you are citing to a very recent agency decision not yet available in the agency's official reporter. When citing to a looseleaf, you must provide information about the authority as well as its location in the looseleaf. Here are two examples, on the assumption the decision is not yet published:

□ *Bluebook* Rules 14.3 and 19: *Morton Int'l, Inc.*, 315 N.L.R.B. No. 71, 147 L.R.R.M. (BNA) 1280 (Nov. 10, 1994).

□ *ALWD* Rules 19.5 and 28.1: *Morton Intl, Inc.*, 147 L.R.R.M. (BNA) 1280 (N.L.R.B. Nov. 10, 1994).

C.   WHAT ELSE?

Mixed Media. Although this chapter presents two distinct versions of a looseleaf, one in paper and the other an online service, you may well use a combination of the two. A publisher may offer, or a library may have, some parts in paper and others online.

Current Awareness Publications. Comprehensive looseleafs have current awareness publications, which are frequently published pamphlets that permit a regular reader to keep abreast of recent developments. The pamphlet may synopsize recent legal authorities, analyze significant new laws, recount the results of recent studies, report on important conferences, and list upcoming events. In addition, some legal authorities, especially new statutes and regulations, often are first available in paper media in pamphlets issued by looseleaf publishers.

Westlaw and LexisNexis. Westlaw and LexisNexis offer databases containing some looseleaf materials. The offering may be selective, that is, only portions of a paper looseleaf service may be available.

EXHIBIT 15.4	Online Service Overview, from BNA's Labor and Employment Library (online source)*

HOME   ABOUT   CONTACT US   SITE MAP   PREFERENCES   HELP

Labor and Employment Law Library

SEARCH   * Favorites

• Saved Searches   • Search History

Welcome. Log in to your preferences.

INDEXES

Topical Indexes provide access to all content in this Library.
Search Indexes »

SITE LINKS

▸ **Analysis**
Editorial explanations, with complete citations, of labor and employment law categorized by subject area.
Search Analysis »

▸ **Laws, Regulations, and Agency Documents**
Text and summaries of federal and state material grouped by subject area.
Search Laws, Regulations, and Agency Documents »

▸ **Practice Tools**
Practical aids for the labor or employment attorney, such as checklists, forms, and a model HR Handbook.
Search Practice Tools »

▸ **News**
Regularly updated reports on developments in labor and employment law, disabilities law, collective bargaining, and wage settlements.
Search News »

▸ **Library Update**
See what content has been added most recently to the Library.
Search Library Update »

GETTING STARTED

Phone support is available at 1-800-372-1033

▸ First-Time User Setup
▸ Take a Quick Tour
▸ Frequently Asked Questions
▸ Instructor-Led Training Options
▸ Quick Reference Card
▸ Training and Support

▸ Sign up for E-mail Highlights

FIND CASES

Find a Case by Citation
Use this search to find a specific case.

Search all Cases and Decisions
Find court, NLRB, and arbitration decisions by searching the Library's entire collection of decisions by word, phrase, tribunal, date, and other parameters.

See Most Recent Cases
Review the decisions most recently added to the Library.

Headnote Finder
Find decisions by first viewing the Headnotes sorted by classification number and, optionally, by court and date.

Find Classification Numbers by Searching the Outlines
Find the best Classification Numbers for viewing the Headnotes, by searching the Classification Outlines.

Find Classification Numbers by Browsing the Outlines
Find the best Classification Numbers for viewing the Headnotes, by browsing the Classification Outlines.

SEARCH OPTIONS

Choose the Specific Collections you wish to search
Search the Library — or limit your search to specific collections — by word, phrase, tribunal, date, and other parameters.

Choose a Guided Search
Use the Guided Search option to search specific collections by specific parameters.

TODAY'S HIGHLIGHTS

Login to the Daily Labor Report to see all highlights.

▸Firestone Fibers Reasonably Accommodated Worker's Religious Needs

▸Bias Claim Involving Anti-Muslim E-Mails at NYPD to Move Ahead

▸House Panel Hears Witnesses Divide on Workplace Legislation

EDITORS PICKS

▸ 2nd Circuit Rules Hospital Staff Doctor Raised Jury Issue of Employee Status

▸ 7th Circuit Allows Deckhand Who Reported Crew's Drug Use to Pursue Retaliation Claim

▸ Amendments to FMLA Allow Military Family Members to Take Leave

FAVORITE COLLECTIONS

Customize this area with your choice of links to the Labor and Employment Law Library's collections.

Go to preferences »

See all collections »

FAVORITE DOCUMENTS

No favorite documents have been selected to display. For help with this feature, view the Help file.

Edit Favorite Documents

↟ Top

Home | About | Contact Us | Site Map | Help

*Copyright 2008 by and reproduced with permission from The Bureau of National Affairs.

Interlude No. 5: Research in Administrative Materials

Researching the Canoga case, we learned that § 7 of the federal labor statute protects not only union activity but also other "concerted activities for the purpose of . . . mutual aid or protection." So, we were interested in administrative materials relating to the National Labor Relations Board because that administrative agency regulates unfair labor practices under federal law.

Our research led us first to an administrative regulation with jurisdictional implications. We learned that a federal statute, 29 U.S.C. § 164, gives the Board the authority to decline to assert jurisdiction over categories of employers where the impact on commerce is not sufficient to warrant federal involvement. Using the United States Code Service version of the statute, we followed the annotations to a pertinent administrative regulation, 29 C.F.R. § 103.2. See Exhibit 13.1 (at page 324). Section 103.2 provides that for the Board to take jurisdiction of Ms. Canoga's case, the orchestra must have revenues (excluding certain grants) of at least $1 million.

We next checked this regulation's effective date and currency. C.F.R. indicated that the regulation was promulgated on March 7, 1973. Researching in the spring of 2008, we found that C.F.R. was current through July 1, 2007. So we perused the necessary L.S.A. and the website supplements. This research confirmed that the regulation is still in force and has not been changed.

To learn more about § 103.2, we read the material accompanying it in the 1973 Federal Register, as provided after the regulation on the Board's website. Not surprisingly, the Board's regulation attempts to draw a line between major orchestras whose activities have a pronounced impact on interstate commerce and other orchestras. The Board noted that the $1 million standard could be revised in the future.

We did not locate a regulation on the topic of concerted activity. However, in the extensive annotations in United States Code Service, we did find references to various agency decisions, as well as many judicial cases. To try to uncover a Board decision with factual similarities to the Canoga case, we turned to the Board's publications. We used the classification index to identify chapter 506 topic 2001-5000, Employee Rights Protected by Section 7, Concerted Activity Defined. A search for that topic and the term smoke in NLRB CITENET yielded the *Morton International* decision. In that case, when two employees handwrote comments on a memo posted by the employer addressing the employer's no-smoking policy, they engaged in protected concerted activity, because they acted together to protest a change in the terms and conditions of their employment. See Exhibit 14.1 (at pages 350–55)

We updated this research by Shepardizing *Morton International*. We learned that it was followed by the Board as recently as December of 2007 but has not been cited by any courts.

RULES OF PROCEDURE AND LEGAL ETHICS

INTRODUCTION

This unit explores the methods and materials used to research rules that govern litigation and the practice of law. Because they are created by various government bodies acting in their official capacities, both types of rules are law — indeed, laws that a lawyer must know because they govern his or her day-to-day conduct. This unit has two chapters.

Chapter 16 discusses rules governing the procedural aspects of litigation in the courts. Each jurisdiction has its own rules of procedure, and most have several sets for different phases and types of litigation. These overarching rules for a jurisdiction may be supplemented by rules developed by a single court or district.

Chapter 17 discusses the law governing the ethical conduct of lawyers, known as rules of professional responsibility. The chapter focuses on state rules of professional responsibility and the model rules and codes prepared by the American Bar Association, on which many state rules are based.

For examples, this unit turns again to the Canoga case, stated on pages 3–4. Assume that, as Ms. Canoga's lawyer, you have identified viable claims and unsuccessfully sought a settlement from the orchestra. With reluctance, Ms. Canoga has decided to pursue litigation, and you have agreed to represent her. The two specific issues to be researched are stated within the two chapters.

RULES OF PROCEDURE

16

A. What Are Rules of Procedure, and Why Would You Research Them?
B. How Do You Research and Cite Rules of Procedure?
C. What Else?
D. Interlude: The Canoga Case

A. WHAT ARE RULES OF PROCEDURE, AND WHY WOULD YOU RESEARCH THEM?

Although the distinction is not always clear, lawyers distinguish substantive law from procedural law. Substantive law governs the rights, duties, and powers of people and entities as they carry out their personal and business affairs. By contrast, procedural law regulates how a case is brought before a particular tribunal and how the case proceeds from its inception until a final outcome is reached. Lawyers and litigants must observe procedural law throughout litigation, and procedural law assists the court and lawyers in administering justice fairly and efficiently.

	Civil Cases	*Criminal Cases*
Pre-trial pleadings discovery motions	civil procedure	criminal procedure
Trial	evidence civil procedure	evidence criminal procedure
Post-trial	civil procedure	criminal procedure
Appeals	appellate procedure	appellate or criminal appellate procedure

EXHIBIT 16.1   Rules of Procedure

In most jurisdictions, some procedural law appears not in the rules of procedure, as this chapter uses that term, but in the statutes of the jurisdiction. For example, statutes typically govern how quickly you must bring a claim (statutes of limitation) and which court has the power to adjudicate a claim (jurisdiction). Chapter 11 covers statutory research; this chapter focuses on rules of procedure.

Reflecting our federalist system, rules of procedure exist at both the federal and state levels. To ascertain which set of rules applies, determine whether your claim will be pursued in federal or state court and which district. A federal court applies federal rules, and a state court applies its state's rules. Federal procedural rules apply even when a federal court is adjudicating a claim based on the substantive law of a state, as occurs in diversity jurisdiction cases.

Most jurisdictions have several sets of rules of procedure, each addressing certain phases and types of litigation. Exhibit 16.1 (above) sets out the typical arrangement.[1] Furthermore, a particular court such as family or small claims court, or a district may have additional rules outlining the details of its practice; these are generally called "local rules" or "court rules." In essence, rules of procedure cover major topics, local or court rules minor points.

Rules of procedure are created by the legislature, by the judiciary, or through interaction of the two. At the federal level, it is not clear in the United States Constitution whether primary authority for creating procedural rules belongs to Congress or the federal courts. Most commentators believe that Congress has the right to prescribe rules of procedure for the federal courts, while the individual federal courts may issue local rules on matters not covered by Congress' rules. As a practical matter, Congress has delegated a great deal of authority to the United States Supreme Court.

---

1. Non-judicial forums, such as arbitration, generally have their own rules or strong customs, which are beyond the scope of this book.

The enactment of the Federal Rules of Civil Procedure (FRCP) is an example of this delegation. In the Rules Enabling Act of 1934, Congress gave the Supreme Court the power to prescribe rules of procedure for the federal district courts and the District of Columbia, as well as the obligation to report to Congress. In 1935, the Supreme Court appointed an Advisory Committee on Civil Rules to prepare a draft. After making some changes, the Supreme Court adopted the rules in 1937 and submitted them to Congress via the Attorney General. Although these rules were never formally adopted by both houses of Congress, the rules became effective in 1938. The FRCP have been amended by the Supreme Court from time to time since then.

Most states have delegated authority to make procedural rules to the highest state court or a special governmental body; some state legislatures then review and adopt the rules. In other states, the legislature or other advisory body drafts a bill containing the needed procedural rules, and the legislature enacts the bill according to its usual process of statutory enactment. Many states' procedural rules are modeled after the federal rules.

Each set of rules is organized topically, generally chronologically. The FRCP, for example, are arranged roughly in the sequence in which litigation usually proceeds in the trial court:

- introductory rules;
- commencement of a lawsuit, including service of process, filing of pleadings, the forms of pleadings and motions, and designation of parties to the suit;
- discovery, such as depositions and interrogatories;
- the trial itself;
- judgments and remedies; and
- specialized and miscellaneous matters.

Each rule describes the litigation practice it covers, stating what is permissible or required. Each rule is separately numbered, often with subdivisions. Accompanying the rule may be notes or comments prepared by the advisory committee, which typically discuss the purpose of the rule, previous rules that have been superseded or amended, and perhaps proposed but rejected amendments. Although the notes of the advisory committee do not carry mandatory authority, they are highly persuasive (as is the legislative history of a statute).

Rules of procedure are law. If your client's case is being or likely will be litigated, you would research procedural rules to learn the proper steps for carrying out the litigation. Procedural rules are binding, of course, on the litigants and their lawyers. Failure to follow the applicable procedural rules impedes the efficient resolution of the case and may be grounds for dismissal of the suit or for sanctions against the party or the lawyer.

The illustrations in this chapter pertain to the following variation on the Canoga case: Assume, as Ms. Canoga's lawyer, that you decided to file suit on her behalf. The complaint concludes with a signature block: a blank for your signature, your name typed below the blank, and information about your firm typed below that. Somehow the complaint was filed with the clerk of court without your signature. Instead, it carries the signature of Ms. Canoga, who came into your office the day the complaint was filed to review it and sign some other papers. So, you need to learn whether the complaint is valid as filed, and, if it is not valid, how to correct it, if possible.

Federal Rule of Civil Procedure 11(a) governs the signing of documents submitted to the courts in a civil case and the significance of the signature. See Exhibit 16.2 (at pages 383–85). Local Civil Rule 10 of the U.S. District Court for the District of New Mexico addresses various details of papers filed with that court, including defects in the signature. See Exhibit 16.3 (at page 386). The New Mexico state rule of procedure on the same topic is Rule 1-011, Exhibit 16.4 (at pages 387–88).

B.   How Do You Research and Cite Rules of Procedure?

1.   Introduction

As Exhibit 16.5 (at page 389) indicates, procedural research entails framing a procedural issue; locating the pertinent rule or rules, based on which court is handling the lawsuit; reading the rule and its comments carefully; reading a treatise discussion, as needed; connecting the law to your client's case; and planning your next steps, which very often entails locating and reading cases applying the rule. The focus of research in procedural rules is, of course, the text of the rule, but the rule is not often the endpoint of your research. Often you will look to the following authorities as well, listed from most to least weighty:

- ☐   cases interpreting and applying the rule,
- ☐   advisory notes or comments, and
- ☐   commentary.

You may look at these sources in a different order, such as looking for cases last.

As with any type of research, jurisdiction matters. For example, if you are researching a state rule of procedure, you would focus on cases from that state's courts, read the advisory committee notes from that state, and seek commentary regarding that state's rules. However, if you find no pertinent case from your state's courts and the state and federal rules are identical or very nearly so, you may want to look at federal cases and commentary. Similarly, federal courts fairly often, look to decisions from other districts or circuits.

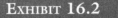

EXHIBIT 16.2   Federal Rule,
from Federal Civil Judicial Procedure and Rules (paper
source)

PLEADINGS AND MOTIONS   **Rule 11**

Each claim founded upon a separate transaction or occurrence and each defense other than denials shall be stated in a separate count or defense whenever a separation facilitates the clear presentation of the matters set forth.

(c) Adoption by Reference; Exhibits. Statements in a pleading may be adopted by reference in a different part of the same pleading or in another pleading or in any motion. A copy of any written instrument which is an exhibit to a pleading is a part thereof for all purposes.

Proposed Amendment of Rule

Effective December 1, 2007, absent contrary Congressional action, this rule is amended to read as follows:

Rule 10.   *Form of Pleadings*

(a) Caption; Names of Parties. Every pleading must have a caption with the court's name, a title, a file number, and a Rule 7(a) designation. The title of the complaint must name all the parties; the title of other pleadings, after naming the first party on each side, may refer generally to other parties.

(b) Paragraphs; Separate Statements. A party must state its claims or defenses in numbered paragraphs, each limited as far as practicable to a single set of circumstances. A later pleading may refer by number to a paragraph in an earlier pleading. If doing so would promote clarity, each claim founded on a separate transaction or occurrence—and each defense other than a denial—must be stated in a separate count or defense.

(c) Adoption by Reference; Exhibits. A statement in a pleading may be adopted by reference elsewhere in the same pleading or in any other pleading or motion. A copy of a written instrument that is an exhibit to a pleading is a part of the pleading for all purposes.

ADVISORY COMMITTEE NOTES

1937 Adoption

The first sentence is derived in part from the opening statement of former Equity Rule 25 (Bill of Complaint—Contents). The remainder of the rule is an expansion in conformity with usual state provisions. For numbered paragraphs and separate statements, see Conn.Gen.Stat., 1930, § 5513; Smith-Hurd Ill.Stats. ch. 110, § 157(2); N.Y.R.C.P., (1937) Rule 90. For incorporation by reference, see N.Y.R.C.P., (1937) Rule 90. For written instruments as exhibits, see Smith-Hurd Ill.Stats. ch. 110, § 160.

2007 Amendment

[Effective December 1, 2007,
absent contrary Congressional action.]

The language of Rule 10 has been amended as part of the general restyling of the Civil Rules to make them more easily understood and to make style and terminology consistent throughout the rules. These changes are intended to be stylistic only.

Rule 11.   Signing of Pleadings, Motions, and Other Papers; Representations to Court; Sanctions

(a) Signature. Every pleading, written motion, and other paper shall be signed by at least one attorney of record in the attorney's individual name, or, if the party is not represented by an attorney, shall be signed by the party. Each paper shall state the signer's address and telephone number, if any. Except when otherwise specifically provided by rule or statute, pleadings need not be verified or accompanied by affidavit. An unsigned paper shall be stricken unless omission of the signature is corrected promptly after being called to the attention of the attorney or party.

(b) Representations to Court. By presenting to the court (whether by signing, filing, submitting, or later advocating) a pleading, written motion, or other paper, an attorney or unrepresented party is certifying that to the best of the person's knowledge, information, and belief, formed after an inquiry reasonable under the circumstances,—

(1) it is not being presented for any improper purpose, such as to harass or to cause unnecessary delay or needless increase in the cost of litigation;

(2) the claims, defenses, and other legal contentions therein are warranted by existing law or by a nonfrivolous argument for the extension, modification, or reversal of existing law or the establishment of new law;

(3) the allegations and other factual contentions have evidentiary support or, if specifically so identified, are likely to have evidentiary support after a reasonable opportunity for further investigation or discovery; and

(4) the denials of factual contentions are warranted on the evidence or, if specifically so identified, are reasonably based on a lack of information or belief.

(c) Sanctions. If, after notice and a reasonable opportunity to respond, the court determines that subdivision (b) has been violated, the court may, subject to the conditions stated below, impose an appropriate sanction upon the attorneys, law firms, or parties that have violated subdivision (b) or are responsible for the violation.

(1) How Initiated.

(A) By Motion. A motion for sanctions under this rule shall be made separately from other motions or requests and shall describe the specific conduct alleged to violate subdivision (b). It shall be served as provided in Rule 5, but shall

Complete Annotation Materials, see Title 28 U.S.C.A.

EXHIBIT 16.2   *(continued)*

Rule 11   RULES OF CIVIL PROCEDURE

not be filed with or presented to the court unless, within 21 days after service of the motion (or such other period as the court may prescribe), the challenged paper, claim, defense, contention, allegation, or denial is not withdrawn or appropriately corrected. If warranted, the court may award to the party prevailing on the motion the reasonable expenses and attorney's fees incurred in presenting or opposing the motion. Absent exceptional circumstances, a law firm shall be held jointly responsible for violations committed by its partners, associates, and employees.

(B) On Court's Initiative. On its own initiative, the court may enter an order describing the specific conduct that appears to violate subdivision (b) and directing an attorney, law firm, or party to show cause why it has not violated subdivision (b) with respect thereto.

(2) Nature of Sanction; Limitations. A sanction imposed for violation of this rule shall be limited to what is sufficient to deter repetition of such conduct or comparable conduct by others similarly situated. Subject to the limitations in subparagraphs (A) and (B), the sanction may consist of, or include, directives of a nonmonetary nature, an order to pay a penalty into court, or, if imposed on motion and warranted for effective deterrence, an order directing payment to the movant of some or all of the reasonable attorneys' fees and other expenses incurred as a direct result of the violation.

(A) Monetary sanctions may not be awarded against a represented party for a violation of subdivision (b)(2).

(B) Monetary sanctions may not be awarded on the court's initiative unless the court issues its order to show cause before a voluntary dismissal or settlement of the claims made by or against the party which is, or whose attorneys are, to be sanctioned.

(3) Order. When imposing sanctions, the court shall describe the conduct determined to constitute a violation of this rule and explain the basis for the sanction imposed.

(d) Inapplicability to Discovery. Subdivisions (a) through (c) of this rule do not apply to disclosures and discovery requests, responses, objections, and motions that are subject to the provisions of Rules 26 through 37.

(As amended Apr. 28, 1983, eff. Aug. 1, 1983; Mar. 2, 1987, eff. Aug. 1, 1987; Apr. 22, 1993, eff. Dec. 1, 1993.)

Proposed Amendment of Rule

Effective December 1, 2007, absent contrary Congressional action, this rule is amended to read as follows:

Rule 11. *Signing Pleadings, Motions, and Other Papers; Representations to the Court; Sanctions*

*(a) **Signature.** Every pleading, written motion, and other paper must be signed by at least one attorney of record in the attorney's name—or by a party personally if the party is unrepresented. The paper must state the signer's address, e-mail address, and telephone number. Unless a rule or statute specifically states otherwise, a pleading need not be verified or accompanied by an affidavit. The court must strike an unsigned paper unless the omission is promptly corrected after being called to the attorney's or party's attention.*

*(b) **Representations to the Court.** By presenting to the court a pleading, written motion, or other paper—whether by signing, filing, submitting, or later advocating it—an attorney or unrepresented party certifies that to the best of the person's knowledge, information, and belief, formed after an inquiry reasonable under the circumstances:*

(1) it is not being presented for any improper purpose, such as to harass, cause unnecessary delay, or needlessly increase the cost of litigation;

(2) the claims, defenses, and other legal contentions are warranted by existing law or by a nonfrivolous argument for extending, modifying, or reversing existing law or for establishing new law;

(3) the factual contentions have evidentiary support or, if specifically so identified, will likely have evidentiary support after a reasonable opportunity for further investigation or discovery; and

(4) the denials of factual contentions are warranted on the evidence or, if specifically so identified, are reasonably based on belief or a lack of information.

*(c) **Sanctions.***

*(1) **In General.** If, after notice and a reasonable opportunity to respond, the court determines that Rule 11(b) has been violated, the court may impose an appropriate sanction on any attorney, law firm, or party that violated the rule or is responsible for the violation. Absent exceptional circumstances, a law firm must be held jointly responsible for a violation committed by its partner, associate, or employee.*

*(2) **Motion for Sanctions.** A motion for sanctions must be made separately from any other motion and must describe the specific conduct that allegedly violates Rule 11(b). The motion must be served under Rule 5, but it must not be filed or be presented to the court if the challenged*

| EXHIBIT 16.2 | *(continued)* |

PLEADINGS AND MOTIONS   **Rule 11**

new Rule 26(g). Discovery motions, however, fall within the ambit of Rule 11.

1987 Amendment

The amendments are technical. No substantive change is intended.

1993 Amendments

Purpose of revision. This revision is intended to remedy problems that have arisen in the interpretation and application of the 1983 revision of the rule. For empirical examination of experience under the 1983 rule, see, *e.g.*, New York State Bar Committee on Federal Courts, *Sanctions and Attorneys' Fees* (1987); T. Willging, *The Rule 11 Sanctioning Process* (1989); American Judicature Society, *Report of the Third Circuit Task Force on Federal Rule of Civil Procedure 11* (S. Burbank ed., 1989); E. Wiggins, T. Willging, and D. Stienstra, *Report on Rule 11* (Federal Judicial Center 1991). For book-length analyses of the case law, see G. Joseph, *Sanctions: The Federal Law of Litigation Abuse* (1989); J. Solovy, *The Federal Law of Sanctions* (1991); G. Vairo, *Rule 11 Sanctions: Case Law Perspectives and Preventive Measures* (1991).

The rule retains the principle that attorneys and pro se litigants have an obligation to the court to refrain from conduct that frustrates the aims of Rule 1. The revision broadens the scope of this obligation, but places greater constraints on the imposition of sanctions and should reduce the number of motions for sanctions presented to the court. New subdivision (d) removes from the ambit of this rule all discovery requests, responses, objections, and motions subject to the provisions of Rule 26 through 37.

Subdivision (a). Retained in this subdivision are the provisions requiring signatures on pleadings, written motions, and other papers. Unsigned papers are to be received by the Clerk, but then are to be stricken if the omission of the signature is not corrected promptly after being called to the attention of the attorney or pro se litigant. Correction can be made by signing the paper on file or by submitting a duplicate that contains the signature. A court may require by local rule that papers contain additional identifying information regarding the parties or attorneys, such as telephone numbers to facilitate facsimile transmissions, though, as for omission of a signature, the paper should not be rejected for failure to provide such information.

The sentence in the former rule relating to the effect of answers under oath is no longer needed and has been eliminated. The provision in the former rule that signing a paper constitutes a certificate that it has been read by the signer also has been eliminated as unnecessary. The obligations imposed under subdivision (b) obviously require that a pleading, written motion, or other paper be read before it is filed or submitted to the court.

Subdivisions (b) and (c). These subdivisions restate the provisions requiring attorneys and pro se litigants to conduct a reasonable inquiry into the law and facts before signing pleadings, written motions, and other documents, and prescribing sanctions for violation of these obligations. The revision in part expands the responsibilities of litigants to the court, while providing greater constraints and flexibility in dealing with infractions of the rule. The rule continues to require litigants to "stop-and-think" before initially making

legal or factual contentions. It also, however, emphasizes the duty of candor by subjecting litigants to potential sanctions for insisting upon a position after it is no longer tenable and by generally providing protection against sanctions if they withdraw or correct contentions after a potential violation is called to their attention.

The rule applies only to assertions contained in papers filed with or submitted to the court. It does not cover matters arising for the first time during oral presentations to the court, when counsel may make statements that would not have been made if there had been more time for study and reflection. However, a litigant's obligations with respect to the contents of these papers are not measured solely as of the time they are filed with or submitted to the court, but include reaffirming to the court and advocating positions contained in those pleadings and motions after learning that they cease to have any merit. For example, an attorney who during a pretrial conference insists on a claim or defense should be viewed as "presenting to the court" that contention and would be subject to the obligations of subdivision (b) measured as of that time. Similarly, if after a notice of removal is filed, a party urges in federal court the allegations of a pleading filed in state court (whether as claims, defenses, or in disputes regarding removal or remand), it would be viewed as "presenting"—and hence certifying to the district court under Rule 11—those allegations.

The certification with respect to allegations and other factual contentions is revised in recognition that sometimes a litigant may have good reason to believe that a fact is true or false but may need discovery, formal or informal, from opposing parties or third persons to gather and confirm the evidentiary basis for the allegation. Tolerance of factual contentions in initial pleadings by plaintiffs or defendants when specifically identified as made on information and belief does not relieve litigants from the obligation to conduct an appropriate investigation into the facts that is reasonable under the circumstances; it is not a license to join parties, make claims, or present defenses without any factual basis or justification. Moreover, if evidentiary support is not obtained after a reasonable opportunity for further investigation or discovery, the party has a duty under the rule not to persist with that contention. Subdivision (b) does not require a formal amendment to pleadings for which evidentiary support is not obtained, but rather calls upon a litigant not thereafter to advocate such claims or defenses.

The certification is that there is (or likely will be) "evidentiary support" for the allegation, not that the party will prevail with respect to its contention regarding the fact. That summary judgment is rendered against a party does not necessarily mean, for purposes of this certification, that it had no evidentiary support for its position. On the other hand, if a party has evidence with respect to a contention that would suffice to defeat a motion for summary judgment based thereon, it would have sufficient "evidentiary support" for purposes of Rule 11.

Denials of factual contentions involve somewhat different considerations. Often, of course, a denial is premised upon the existence of evidence contradicting the alleged fact. At other times a denial is permissible because, after an appropriate investigation, a party has no information concerning the matter or, indeed, has a reasonable basis for doubting the credibility of the only evidence relevant to the matter. A party should not deny an allegation it knows to be true; but

Complete Annotation Materials, see Title 28 U.S.C.A.

EXHIBIT 16.3	Local Court Rule, from United States District Court for the District of New Mexico Website (online source)

10.2 Titles of Papers.

    (a) **Identification of Substance.** The title of a paper must clearly identify its substance.

    (b) **Responses or Replies.** The title of a response or a reply must identify by title and approximate date of filing the paper to which it responds.

    (c) **Affidavit.** The title of an affidavit must identify by title and approximate date of filing the paper it supports.

10.3 Filing of Non-Conforming Papers.

    (a) **Acceptance of Papers.** The Clerk will not refuse to file any paper because it is not in proper form.

    (b) **Signature.** Any paper filed without signature will be stricken unless it is signed within fourteen (14) calendar days after the omission is called to the party's attention.

    (c) **Non-Conforming Papers.** The Clerk will give to the submitting party written notice of a deficiency and deadline for correcting the deficiency. The Clerk will also provide any applicable forms and instruction sheets. Failure to remedy a deficiency or to show good cause for non-compliance within forty-five (45) calendar days from the date of notice may result in dismissal of the action without prejudice in accordance with D.N.M.LR-Civ. 41.2.

10.4 Attachments to Pleadings. Exhibits are not attached to a pleading unless the documents attached form the basis for the action or defense.

10.5 Page Limit for Exhibits. Exhibits to a motion, response or reply, including excerpts from a deposition, must not exceed fifty (50) pages unless all parties agree otherwise. If agreement cannot be reached, then the party seeking to exceed the page limit must file a motion in accordance with D.N.M.LR-Civ. 7. A party may file only those pages of an exhibit which are to be brought to the Court's attention.

10.6 Highlighting of Exhibits. The portions of an exhibit the party wishes to bring to the Court's attention must be highlighted in the original, the copy for the Court and the copy for each party. Highlighting must be apparent on exhibits that are scanned and filed and/or served electronically.

10.7 Non-duplication of Exhibits. An exhibit should be submitted only once and may later be referred to by document title and filing date. An exhibit may be submitted more than once, however, if the submitting party wishes to bring to the Court's attention portions of the exhibit different from those previously highlighted under D.N.M.LR-Civ. 10.6.

RULE 11. Signing of Documents.

    11.1 Signatures. The Court will treat a duplicate signature as an original signature, and a document filed or served by electronic transmission is considered signed in accordance with FED. R. CIV. P. ll(a).

EXHIBIT 16.4	State Rule, from New Mexico Statutes Annotated (paper source)

Rule 1-011   **RULES OF CIVIL PROCEDURE—DISTRICT COURTS**

RULE 1-011. SIGNING OF PLEADINGS, MOTIONS AND OTHER PAPERS; SANCTIONS

Every pleading, motion and other paper of a party represented by an attorney, shall be signed by at least one attorney of record in the attorney's individual name, whose address and telephone number shall be stated. A party who is not represented by an attorney shall sign the party's pleading, motion or other paper and state the party's address and telephone number. Except when otherwise specifically provided by rule or statute, pleadings need not be verified or accompanied by affidavit. The rule in equity that the averments of an answer under oath must be overcome by the testimony of two witnesses or of one witness sustained by corroborating circumstances is abolished. The signature of an attorney or party constitutes a certificate by the signer that the signer has read the pleading, motion or other paper; that to the best of the signer's knowledge, information and belief there is good ground to support it; and that it is not interposed for delay. If a pleading, motion or other paper is signed with intent to defeat the purpose of this rule, it may be stricken as sham and false and the action may proceed as though the pleading or other paper had not been served. If a pleading, motion or other paper is not signed, it shall be stricken unless it is signed promptly after the omission is called to the attention of the pleader or movant. For a willful violation of this rule an attorney or party may be subjected to appropriate disciplinary or other action. Similar action may be taken if scandalous or indecent matter is inserted. A "signature" means an original signature, a copy of an original signature, a computer generated signature or any other signature otherwise authorized by law.

[Amended effective January 1, 1997.]

Committee Commentary

New Mexico has enacted an Electronic Authentication Documentation Act which provides for the Secretary of State to register electronic signatures using the public key technology. See Section 14-15-4 NMSA 1978.

Library References

Attorney and Client ⊂⇒24.
Costs ⊂⇒2.
Pleading ⊂⇒287, 288, 351.
Westlaw Key Number Searches: 45k24; 102k2; 302k287; 302k288; 302k351.

C.J.S. Attorney and Client § 138.
C.J.S. Costs §§ 2 to 3, 8 to 9.
C.J.S. Pleading §§ 478 to 485, 624 to 625.

United States Supreme Court

Frivolous actions,
In general,
   Jurisdiction, frivolous actions and proceedings, lack of subject matter jurisdiction, see Willy v. Coastal Corp., U.S.Tex.1992, 112 S.Ct. 1076, 503 U.S. 131, 117 L.Ed.2d 280, rehearing denied 112 S.Ct. 2001, 504 U.S. 935, 118 L.Ed.2d 596.
   Reasonable inquiry, frivolous pleadings, signer of documents, see Business Guides, Inc. v. Chromatic Communications Enterprises, Inc., U.S.Cal.1991, 111 S.Ct. 922, 498 U.S. 533, 112 L.Ed.2d 1140.

Withdrawal of assigned public defender not action "under color of state law", frivolous claims, civil rights suit brought by indigent defendant, see Polk County v. Dodson, U.S.Iowa1981, 102 S.Ct. 445, 454 U.S. 312, 70 L.Ed.2d 509.

Sanctions,
   Sanctions, attorney's law firm, see Pavelic & LeFlore v. Marvel Entertainment Group, U.S.N.Y.1989, 110 S.Ct. 456, 493 U.S. 120, 107 L.Ed.2d 438, on remand 907 F.2d 145.

Notes of Decisions

Admissions 5
Appropriate and reasonable, sanctions 12
Appropriate procedure, violations of rule 8

Attorney sanctions 14
Construction and application 1
Discretion of court, sanctions 11

82

EXHIBIT 16.4   *(continued)*

PLEADINGS AND MOTIONS

Rule 1–011
Note 6

1.   Construction and application

Where sanction awarded is based on what attorney failed to disclose to court, as opposed to defect in his or her pleading, Rule 11 is not implicated. SCRA 1986, Rule 1–011. Cherryhomes v. Vogel, 1990, 111 N.M. 229, 804 P.2d 420. Attorney And Client ⬅ 24

2.   Purpose of rule

Primary goal of Rule 11 is to deter baseless filings in district court by testing conduct of counsel; although rule should be read in light of concerns that it will spawn satellite litigation and chill vigorous advocacy, any interpretation must give effect to rule's central purpose of deterrence. SCRA 1986, Rule 1–011. Rivera v. Brazos Lodge Corp., 1991, 111 N.M. 670, 808 P.2d 955. Costs ⬅ 2

3.   Disqualification of judge

Trial judge who has previously held defendant, an attorney, in contempt was not required to recuse himself in subsequent criminal contempt hearing, where trial judge stated that he had no personal animosity toward defendant due to his past dealings with him, and defendant had appeared many times before same judge without incident. SCRA 1986, Rule 1–011; SCRA 1986, Canons 21–300, subd. A(3), 21–400. Purpura v. Purpura, 1993, 115 N.M. 80, 847 P.2d 314, certiorari denied 115 N.M. 79, 847 P.2d 313. Judges ⬅ 39

If judge becomes so embroiled in controversy that he or she is unable to make fair and objective decision, judge must recuse himself or herself. SCRA 1986, Rule 1–011; SCRA 1986, Canons 21–300, subd. A(3), 21–400. Purpura v. Purpura, 1993, 115 N.M. 80, 847 P.2d 314, certiorari denied 115 N.M. 79, 847 P.2d 313. Judges ⬅ 49(1)

Bias requiring recusal must arise from personal, extrajudicial source, not judicial source. SCRA 1986, Rule 1–011; SCRA 1986, Canons 21–300, subd. A(3), 21–400. Purpura v. Purpura, 1993, 115 N.M. 80, 847 P.2d 314, certiorari denied 115 N.M. 79, 847 P.2d 313. Judges ⬅ 49(1)

4.   Verification of pleadings

Attorney's failure to prosecute appeal of sanction imposed by trial court in his own name did not deprive court of jurisdiction where pleadings from first day of case bore caption that did not include attorney

and where Court of Appeals knew it was attorney and not client prosecuting appeal; attorney was obviously present before court and vigorously pursuing his case even though he had erroneously designated someone else as appellant. SCRA 1986, Rule 1–011. Mitchell v. Dona Ana Sav. and Loan Ass'n, F.A., 1991, 111 N.M. 257, 804 P.2d 1076, on remand 113 N.M. 576, 829 P.2d 655. Appeal And Error ⬅ 422

Every pleading must be, under our practice, subscribed by the party making the same, or his attorney, and, when any pleading is verified, every subsequent pleading, except a demurrer, must be verified. Hyde v. Bryan, 1918, 24 N.M. 457, 174 P. 419. Pleading ⬅ 294

Where a verification is required, as is the case under our statute, and is omitted, the pleading may be stricken out or judgment may be had on the pleadings. Hyde v. Bryan, 1918, 24 N.M. 457, 174 P. 419. Pleading ⬅ 355

5.   Admissions

Where defendant, in subsequent suit on admittedly unpaid balance owing on a note, admitted that her since deceased husband signed answer in prior suit on the note as attorney for defendant and her husband and where defendant raised no question as to deceased husband's authority to sign answer as defendant's attorney or make admission of the debt on defendant's behalf in the answer, husband's signature on the answer in prior suit had same effect as if defendant had personally signed, and defendant was bound by the admission in the subsequent suit. Rules of Civil Procedure, rule 11; 1953 Comp. § 18–1–10; Supreme Court Rules, rule 3–5, subd. A. Smith v. Walcott, 1973, 85 N.M. 351, 512 P.2d 679. Evidence ⬅ 248(1)

6.   Good ground requirement

The "good ground" provision of Rule 11 is measured by a subjective standard and is appropriate only in those rare cases in which an attorney deliberately presses an unfounded claim or defense. Rangel v. Save Mart, Inc., 2006, 140 N.M. 395, 142 P.3d 983. Attorney And Client ⬅ 24

In deciding whether good grounds exist for pleading or other paper, or whether sanctions may be imposed against attorney for party who signed pleading, court employs subjective standard, which depends on what attorney or litigant knew and believed at relevant time, and which involves question of whether litigant or attorney was aware that particular pleading or paper should not have been filed. SCRA 1986, Rule 1–011. Air Ruidoso, Ltd., Inc. v. Executive Aviation Center, Inc., 1996, 122 N.M. 71, 920 P.2d 1025, rehearing denied. Attorney And Client ⬅ 24

Good ground provision of Rule 11 is to be measured by subjective standards at time of filing of pleading; any violation depends on what attorney or litigant knew or believed at relevant time and involves question of whether litigant or attorney was aware that particular pleading should not have been brought. SCRA 1986, Rule 1–011. Rivera v. Brazos Lodge Corp., 1991, 111 N.M. 670, 808 P.2d 955. Costs ⬅ 2

Good ground requirement of Rule 11 cannot be satisfied with respect to any alleged proposition known to be false at time of filing. SCRA 1986, Rule

EXHIBIT 16.5	Rules of Procedure Template

Issue:	Citation Information:
	• set of rules
	• rule number
Date of events:	
Date of research:	

Search and Find:

located rule and comments by . . .	treatise information, as needed:

Information and Implications:

- rule language
- comments or notes
- connection to client's situation

Next Steps:

questions to consider:	leads to follow — especially cases:

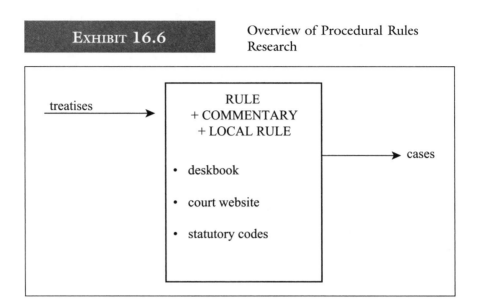

EXHIBIT 16.6   Overview of Procedural Rules
                                 Research

To obtain this range of authorities, you may use paper and online sources also used in researching substantive law; indeed, researching rules of procedure is much like researching statutes. You very likely will also use a deskbook, a source that is unique to rules of procedure (as well as rules of professional responsibility, discussed in Chapter 17). See Exhibit 16.6 (above). The following discussion suggests a standard sequence and focuses primarily on research in federal rules; you will use comparable sources and methods when you research state rules.

Rules of procedure

- Commentary, especially treatises
- Deskbooks
- Court websites
- Case law sources
- Statutory codes

2.   Commentary

Especially if your research topic is new to you, you should consider beginning your research in commentary. The standard choice is a well regarded treatise, many of which provide the rules and committee notes as well as the author's analysis. On the federal side, many lawyers turn to *Federal Practice and Procedure* by Charles Alan Wright, Arthur R. Miller, and others, or *Moore's Federal Practice*. Both are multivolume treatises covering civil, criminal, and appellate procedure; Wright and Miller also covers evidence. LexisNexis carries the Moore treatise; Westlaw carries Wright and Miller. In many states, there is a comparable treatise on state law. Exhibit 16.7 (at page 392) is from the Wright and Miller treatise.

Once you become fairly well versed in procedural law, you probably will begin your research in the rules themselves and consult commentary at a later point, to obtain an expert's discussion of the law or find citations to leading cases.

3.   The Rule and Comments

Treatises on procedural topics typically include the rules and advisory committee notes. Two often used resources for this information are deskbooks and court websites.

Deskbooks. Procedural rules are published in their most compact form in deskbooks. A deskbook is a one- or two-volume publication that usually contains the text of a jurisdiction's various sets of rules of procedure, notes or comments of the advisory committee on those rules, and some model forms. Exhibit 16.2 (at pages 383–385) is from a deskbook. However, deskbooks do not contain case annotations or extensive commentary. Because most deskbooks are published annually and are not updated until the next edition is published, they are fairly current but not necessarily completely up to date.

To locate a pertinent rule within a deskbook, use a lead from commentary or other source, the index to the pertinent set of rules, or the table of contents at the beginning of a set of rules. Read the rule much as you would read a statute. The rule describes what should or may occur. The consequence of failing to follow a procedural rule often is not stated but implied; for example, failing to respond to a proper discovery request may lead to a motion to compel discovery by the other side and a court order to provide the discovery.

You should read the entire rule, not just a subdivision that seems to be on point; skim nearby rules; and closely read any other rules to which your rule refers. Look as well at the first part of the set of rules; those provisions generally cover matters arising at various stages of litigation, such as calculation of time and modes of serving other parties and filing documents with the court.

In addition, read the advisory committee notes to learn about the drafters' intent and any amendments to the rule. The language in effect at the time of litigation governs, so you will want to focus on the current language. You need to know about amendments so that you work with cases arising under the current language and avoid relying on cases arising under the old language.

Exhibit 16.7	Treatise Discussion of Rule of Procedure, from Federal Practice and Procedure (paper source)

---

§ 1333   **SIGNING OF PLEADINGS**   **Ch. 4**
Rule 11

pro se litigant's pleadings a more liberal construction than those drafted by an attorney. Moreover, the failure to sign a pleading shields an attorney from responsibility and accountability for his actions. Consequently, we have determined the failure of an attorney to acknowledge the giving of advice by signing his name constitutes a misrepresentation to this court by both the litigant and attorney. For these reasons, we have held "any ghostwriting of an otherwise *pro se* brief must be acknowledged by the signature of the attorney involved."[34]

Furthermore, the practice of "ghostwriting" has been "condemned as a deliberate evasion of the responsibilities imposed on counsel by" Rule 11 by another federal court because the attorney responsible for drafting the paper has not certified the document's legal and factual merit by including his or her signature.[35]

The 1993 amendment to Rule 11 requires that "[a]n unsigned paper shall be stricken unless omission of the signature is corrected promptly after being called to the attention of the attorney or party." Accordingly, the Advisory Committee Note to the 1993 amendments to the rule explains that "[u]nsigned papers are to be received by the Clerk, but then are to be stricken if the omission of the signature is not corrected promptly after being called to the attention of the attorney or the pro se litigant."[36] This language is virtually the same as it was under the 1983 amendment to Rule 11.[37] Thus, in the absence of prejudice, the district court can treat the defect as technical and should grant leave to correct a failure to

---

34. Tenth Circuit explained

Id. at 778 (Brorby, J.), quoting Duran v. Carris, C.A.10th, 2001, 238 F.3d 1268.

35. Deliberate evasion

Johnson v. Board of County Comm'rs for County of Fremont, D.C.Colo.1994, 868 F.Supp. 1226, 1231–1232 ("What we fear is that in some cases actual members of the bar represent petitioners, informally or otherwise, and prepare briefs for them which the assisting lawyers do not sign, and thus escape the obligation imposed on members of the bar, typified by F.R.Civ.P. 11, but which exists in all cases, criminal as well as civil, of representing to the court that there is good ground to support the assertions made. We cannot approve of such a practice. If a brief is prepared in any substantial part by a member of the

bar, it must be signed by him.") (Kane, J.).

See also

Wesley v. Don Stein Buick, Inc., D.C.Kan.1997, 987 F.Supp. 884.

36. Advisory Committee

Advisory Committee Note to the 1993 amendment to Rule 11, reprinted in 1993, 146 F.R.D. 577, 584, and in vol. 12A, App. C.

37. 1983 amendment

The 1983 amendment to Rule 11 stated that "[i]f a pleading, motion, or other paper is not signed, it shall be stricken unless it is signed promptly after the omission is called to the attention of the pleader or movant."

EXHIBIT 16.7   *(continued)*

Ch. 4   SIGNATURE BY ATTORNEY OR PARTY   § 1333
Rule 11

sign;[38] if that is not done, an unsigned complaint may be dismissed or an unsigned paper stricken, as the district court deems appropriate. Although the rule requires that only the original of any paper submitted to the court must be signed,[39] as a matter of courtesy all copies should identify the person who signed the original document.

For a number of years, prior to the 1993 amendment of Rule 11, federal courts were divided on the question of who became sanctionable under Rule 11 when an attorney working for a law firm signed a pleading, motion, or other paper submitted to the district court. Some judges expressed an understanding that when a team of attorneys is conducting the litigation, the person who sign the paper may not necessarily be the one responsible for either the decision to file it or its preparation; for example, an associate or junior partner in a law firm may prepare, sign, and file a paper at the direction of a senior partner who made the relevant substantive decisions regarding the paper.[40] The rule's emphasis on the respon-

38. Defect technical

Becker v. Montgomery, 2001, 121 S.Ct. 1801, 532 U.S. 757, 149 L.Ed.2d 983.

Kovilic Constr. Co. v. Missbrenner, C.A.7th, 1997, 106 F.3d 768, 772, appeal after remand D.C.Ill.1997, 1997 WL 269630 (district court should not strike paper for failure to sign absent severe prejudice).

U.S. v. Kasuboski, C.A.7th, 1987, 834 F.2d 1345, **citing Wright & Miller.**

Operating Engineers Local 139 Health Benefit Fund v. Rawson Plumbing, Inc., D.C.Wis.2001, 130 F.Supp.2d 1022.

Stroud v. Senese, D.C.Ill.1993, 832 F.Supp. 1206.

Williams v. Frame, D.C.Pa.1992, 145 F.R.D. 65.

Duke v. Crowell, D.C.Tenn.1988, 120 F.R.D. 511.

See also

A legal malpractice complaint signed by the malpractice lawyer's wife was similar to one filed inadvertently without any signature, and therefore it was not necessary to strike the complaint as being in violation of Rule 11 when counsel's omission was a simple mistake, and a technically correct plead-

ing was filed shortly thereafter. Edwards v. Groner, D.C.Virgin Islands 1987, 116 F.R.D. 578.

Grant v. Morgan Guar. Trust Co. of New York, D.C.N.Y.1986, 638 F.Supp. 1528, 1531–1532 n. 6, **citing Wright & Miller** (irregularities treated as technical defects).

39. Original

Porto Transp., Inc. v. Consolidated Diesel Elec. Corp., D.C.N.Y.1956, 20 F.R.D. 1.

Pallant v. Sinatra, D.C.N.Y.1945, 7 F.R.D. 293.

Anderson v. Brady, D.C.Ky.1945, 5 F.R.D. 85.

40. Signing for another

Judge Schwarzer has remarked that "in such a situation, sanctions are more appropriately imposed on the principal rather than the agent carrying out his orders, and nothing in the rule bars its application in that manner." Schwarzer, Sanctions Under the New Rule 11—A Closer Look, 1985, 104 F.R.D. 181, 185.

521

Finally, check for forms that accompany your rule. These forms in a deskbook are intended only to illustrate an appropriate format of pleadings. Forms generally appear in an appendix to the set of rules. See Exhibit 16.8 (at page 395), a federal form for various types of jurisdictional allegations.

Court websites. In recent years, to improve accessibility and efficiency, many courts have developed websites that offer a wide array of information. Federal court sites are easily located through uscourts.gov. In particular, the court's local rules and standard forms used by that court should appear on the court's website. Exhibit 16.3 (at page 386) is from a court website.

4.   Cases Interpreting the Rule

Sometimes the rule and supporting material suffice. Much of the time, this is not true. Although rules of procedure read as straightforward directions, there can be considerable ambiguity when they are applied to specific cases. Judicial decisions discussing rules of procedure abound; indeed, nearly every case has at least a brief mention of the point in the litigation at which the court has been asked to rule, which lawyers call the case's "procedural posture." Some cases discuss the procedural rule only briefly, others extensively. Thus, over time, the courts have created a significant body of case law for most rules, stating the principles underlying the rule and establishing patterns of outcomes based on the type of claims involved in the cases.

As you look for cases, you should focus on cases that are binding precedent for the court handling your case. Look as well for cases that state important principles; favor your client, for example, set a low standard for granting a motion if your client is the movant; and arose in a factual context similar to your client's situation. To find cases interpreting rules of procedure, you may use commentary, discussed previously, as well as paper or online annotated rules and case law sources.

Annotated Rules. Although rules of procedure are not enacted in the same way as statutes are, they generally appear somewhere in or along with the jurisdiction's statutory code. See Chapter 11. For example, *United States Code Annotated* presents the FRCP after Title 28, the judiciary title; *United States Code Service* presents rules of procedure in rules volumes at the end of the set. Or you may find procedural rules with the state's administrative code rather than the statutory code.

Just as with statutory research, you should use an annotated rules source when available. Annotated rules sources provide the rules and advisory committee notes, as do deskbooks. Annotated rules sources also permit you to expand your research beyond the material provided in a deskbook:

☐ You will find descriptions of cases interpreting the rule.
☐ You will find citations to commentary.
☐ Annotated rules sources are updated more frequently than deskbooks, so you may find recent amendments to the rule that do not yet appear in the deskbook.

See Exhibit 16.4 (at pages 387–388), drawn from an annotated New Mexico rules source.

EXHIBIT 16.8	Form, from Federal Civil Judicial Procedure and Rules (paper source)

PROPOSED APPENDIX OF FORMS

Amendment of Forms

Forms 1 to 82 effective December 1, 2007, absent contrary Congressional action.

For forms effective until December 1, 2007, see Forms 1 to 35 preceding this Appendix of Forms.

Form 1.   Caption

Form effective December 1, 2007, absent contrary Congressional action.

<pre>
A B, Plaintiff   )
)
v.   )
)
C D, Defendant   )
)
v.   )
)
E F, Third–Party Defendant)
(Use if needed.)   )
</pre>

(Name of Document)

(Added Apr. 30, 2007, eff. Dec. 1, 2007.)

Amendment of Forms

Form effective December 1, 2007, absent contrary Congressional action. For forms effective until December 1, 2007, see Forms 1 to 35 preceding this Appendix of Forms.

Form 2.   Date, Signature, Address, E–Mail Address, and Telephone Number

Form effective December 1, 2007, absent contrary Congressional action.

(Use at the conclusion of pleadings and other papers that require a signature.)

Date _____

_____

(Signature of the attorney or unrepresented party)

_____

(Printed name)

_____

(Address)

_____

(E-mail address)

_____

(Telephone number)

(Added Apr. 30, 2007, eff. Dec. 1, 2007.)

(Use on every summons, complaint, answer, motion, or other document.)

United States District Court
for the
_____ District of _____

Civil Action No. _____

Amendment of Forms

Form effective December 1, 2007, absent contrary Congressional action. For forms effective until December 1, 2007, see Forms 1 to 35 preceding this Appendix of Forms.

Form 3.   Summons

Form effective December 1, 2007, absent contrary Congressional action.

(Caption—See Form 1.)

To *name the defendant*:

A lawsuit has been filed against you.

Within 20 days after service of this summons on you (not counting the day you received it), you must serve on the plaintiff an answer to the attached complaint or a motion under Rule 12 of the Federal Rules of Civil Procedure. The answer or motion must be served on the plaintiff's attorney, _____, whose address is _____. If you fail to do so, judgment by default will be entered against you for the relief demanded in the complaint. You also must file your answer or motion with the court.

Date _____

_____

Clerk of Court

(Court Seal)

(Use 60 days if the defendant is the United States or a United States agency, or is an officer or employee of the United States allowed 60 days by Rule 12(a)(3).)

(Added Apr. 30, 2007, eff. Dec. 1, 2007.)

Complete Annotation Materials, see Title 28 U.S.C.A.

378

As with statutory codes, LexisNexis, Westlaw, and other commercial sources provide rules of procedure in various configurations, within a full statutory code database or in a rules database, with or without annotations. For the most part, you will want to search an annotated rules database; it is narrower than a full statutory code database but also includes case descriptions that may contain your research terms.

Case Law Sources: In addition to commentary and statutory codes, good options for locating pertinent cases are the West digest and reporter system; commercial online services; and rules citators, such as Shepard's and KeyCite. See Chapters 9 and 10. If you are researching federal law, you may use, in addition to the other West reporters, *Federal Rules Decisions*, which contains federal district court cases discussing the Federal Rules of Civil Procedure and the Federal Rules of Criminal Procedure (as well as proposals for rule changes and articles on procedural topics by judges, lawyers, and professors).

Exhibit 16-6 (at page 390) is our template filled in to reflect our research of the Canoga case.

5.   Citing Rules of Procedure

A citation to a rule of procedure is very spare, consisting of the abbreviation for the set of rules and the rule number. The format is the same under *Bluebook* Rule 12.8.3 and *ALWD Citation Manual* Rule 17.1:

☐   Fed. R. Civ. P. 11.

You may, on occasion, cite the notes of an advisory committee. Here are two examples:

☐   *Bluebook* Rule 3.4: Fed. R. Civ. P. 11 advisory committee's note.
☐   *ALWD Citation Manual* Rule 17.1: Fed. R. Civ. P. 11 advisory comm nn.

If there is more than one set of advisory committee notes, you may want to add a date for clarification.

C.   WHAT ELSE?

Notice of Rules Amendments. Various publications provide prompt notice of amendments to rules of procedure. For example, advance sheets of West's federal reporters do so for federal rules. State legal newspapers and bar publications typically do so for state rules, and some states have advance rules services similar to advance legislative services. Other good options are court or bar association websites. Some courts send e-mail alerts to lawyers admitted to practice there.

EXHIBIT **16.9**	Rules of Procedure Template for Canoga Case

Issue:	Citation Information:
What are the consequences of filing a complaint with Canoga's (the client's) signature and without mine?	• *Federal Rules of Civil Procedure* • *11(a)*

Date of events: *Sept. 7, 2007*	
Date of filing: *Feb. 1, 2008*	
Date of research: *Feb. 10, 2008*	

Search and Find:	
located rule and comments by . . .	treatise information, as needed:
Wright and Miller discussion. FRCP table of contents.	*Wright & Miller: The court should treat a defect as technical and grant leave to correct the lack of signature "in the absence of prejudice." § 1333 p. 520 vol. 5A, 2004.*

Information and Implications:

- *Every pleading must be signed by an attorney. An unsigned paper shall be stricken unless the omission is corrected promptly after being called to the attorney's attention. FRCP 11(a).*
- *Correct the omission by signing a filed pleading or submitting a signed duplicate. 1993 Amendment Advisory Committee Notes.*
- *This must be done within 14 days. Local Rule 10.3(b).*
- *However, an electronic submission is considered signed. Local Rule 11.1. The court's Case Management/Electronic Case Files protocols also say that submission with use of a login and password is "signed"; the document is sent as a PDF.*

Next Steps:	
questions to consider:	leads to follow—especially cases:
How do these paper and electronic rules go together? *Re-file with my signature.*	*Operating Engineers Local 139 Health Benefit Fund v. Rawson Plumbing, Inc., E.D. Wis. 2001, 130 F. Supp. 2d 1022. [from Wright & Miller].* *No N.M. or 10th Cir. cases retrieved in Westlaw search.*

Form Books. Many practitioners rely on form books, which contain sample forms and pleadings. These sample forms can be useful, but they must be used with care. Major difficulties can result from selecting the wrong form, an outdated form, or a standard form that does not precisely fit the needs of a particular case. Sources of forms for use in federal courts include *Bender's Federal Practice Forms; West's Federal Forms; Federal Local Court Forms;* and *Federal Procedural Forms;* some are available online. State forms may be available in state practice treatises and continuing legal education materials.

Specialized Courts. Some specialized courts, such as the federal bankruptcy courts, have their own rules of procedure. You can research these rules through the sources described in this chapter.

D.   INTERLUDE: THE CANOGA CASE

If the Canoga case included a federal claim, the rules of interest for the signature issue would be the FRCP and any local rules of the U.S. District Court for the District of New Mexico. In Thomson West's *Federal Civil Judicial Procedure and Rules*, in the table of contents for the FRCP, we quickly found Rule 11 in part III. Pleadings and Motions. Subdivision (a) requires a pleading to be signed by the attorney (or the party, but only where the party is not represented by an attorney); an unsigned pleading is stricken unless promptly corrected after being called to the attorney's attention. See Exhibit 16.2 (at pages 383–85). The Advisory Committee Notes to the 1993 Amendments explain how to correct the omission: by signing the filed pleading or submitting a signed duplicate.

We next sought a local rule on the topic and found Exhibit 16.3 (at page 386) through nmcourt.fed.us, the website of the U.S. District Court for the District of New Mexico. Local Rule 10.3(b) adds some detail to Rule 11 by indicating that a pleading filed without a signature will be stricken unless signed within fourteen days following the notice to the party of the omitted signature.

Although the rules themselves are clear, for the purpose of illustration, we did a quick search for cases, first by reading the Wright and Miller excerpt in Exhibit 16.7 (at pages 391–92). A Westlaw search focusing on the rule number and the lack of a signature yielded sixty-nine cases — none from the New Mexico district court or the Tenth Circuit. In *Operating Engineers Local 139 Health Benefit Fund v. Rawson Plumbing, Inc,* 130 F. Supp. 2d 1022 (E.D. Wis. 2001), the case cited in the treatise, a company's officer who was not an attorney signed the company's answer; the court declined to treat this as a default but rather ordered the company to file an answer signed by an attorney within twenty days.

The notion of "signing" is interesting, indeed almost quaint, in this era of electronic communication and in light of courts' conversion to electronic filing. The New Mexico federal court's local civil rules describe the type of paper on which a paper must be printed (Rule 10.1) and yet also define "signature" to include not only a duplicate signature but also "electronic transmission." On the court's website is a description of the court's required electronic filing system. The protocol calls for documents to be submitted as a PDF (portable document format); a PDF resembles a snapshot of each page, so one could see whether a specific person wrote his or her name by pen on the document. Yet the protocol also states that using the lawyer's login and password is considered a signature. The court's website sends a mixed signal. Electronic transmission may suffice, but the client's, instead of the lawyer's, signature on a PDF pleading still seems problematic. In these situations — and they arise often in the practice of law — the best choice is to play it safe. In the Canoga situation, electronically sending in a properly signed PDF would be a good idea.

For the future, figuring out the electronic filing system would also be a good idea; a good place to start would be the protocols memo on the court's website.

RULES OF PROFESSIONAL RESPONSIBILITY

CHAPTER 17

A. What Are Rules of Professional Responsibility, and Why Would You Research Them?
B. How Do You Research and Cite Rules of Professional Responsibility?
C. What Else?
D. Interlude: The Canoga Case

A. WHAT ARE RULES OF PROFESSIONAL RESPONSIBILITY, AND WHY WOULD YOU RESEARCH THEM?

Lawyers have a unique role in our society. Lawyers affect the decisions of their clients and the outcomes of matters that often are confidential and difficult. Because of their expertise and training, lawyers often serve as judges, legislators, executive officers, or administrators. Lawyers also are major participants in law reform efforts. Thus, lawyers often are in positions to exercise considerable influence over the conduct of their clients and the public welfare.

With this power comes the obligation to assure that lawyers act responsibly and are held accountable for irresponsible actions. Early on, the legal profession policed itself. Over time, that approach has given way to modified self-regulation. Regulation of the legal profession now is a matter primarily of state law. Either the state supreme court or the state legislature promulgates rules of professional responsibility. Typically, an advisory committee recommends and drafts new rules and changes to existing rules, which are then published for review and comment by the legal community and the public before adoption.

The rules thus adopted govern the conduct of lawyers in that state. Professional responsibility rules are enforced through various mechanisms. In a typical model, a state disciplinary committee or board hears complaints regarding allegations of professional misconduct, issues decisions, and disciplines non-compliant lawyers. Disciplinary cases are then reviewed in state court. Professional sanctions include private or public censure, suspension of one's license to practice law, and disbarment. In addition to the state regulatory entity, some local bar associations have ethics committees that hear complaints about attorney misconduct and make findings and recommendations to the state authorities.

The American Bar Association (ABA) has played a major role in the development of rules of professional responsibility. The ABA adopted its first rules in the 1908 Canons of Professional Ethics. These canons were not mandatory, but bar associations and courts did look to them for guidance in establishing standards of conduct and in disciplining lawyers. The ABA later adopted a more comprehensive set of rules, the 1969 Model Code of Professional Responsibility (Model Code), which was widely adopted. It had a three-part structure: the Canons serving as broad principles; Ethical Considerations (ECs) providing aspirational and explanatory provisions; and Disciplinary Rules (DRs) setting minimum, mandatory standards.

In response to criticism of the 1969 Model Code, the ABA appointed a special Commission on Evaluation of Professional Standards (the Kutak Commission) to study and revise the Model Code. After wide debate, the ABA adopted the Model Rules of Professional Conduct (Model Rules) in 1983. The Model Rules, which have a simpler structure than the Model Code, have been adopted by many states, often with some modifications. The Model Rules have been revised from time to time, including a major revision known as Ethics 2000, completed in 2002.

The overall organization of a set of professional responsibility rules is, of course, topical. See Exhibit 17.1 (at page 402), which lists the topics of the current ABA Model Rules. The format of an individual rule varies from state to state, depending on whether the state follows the three-part structure of the Model Code, the unitary rule structure of the Model Rules, or a variation on these models. Most publications of state rules include some type of commentary, whether the ABA commentary, commentary from the state's drafting committee, or both.

As important as rules of professional responsibility are, they are not the only laws governing lawyers. Egregious professional misconduct can result in criminal penalties. Failure to provide competent representation to a client may constitute legal malpractice, for which the client may recover monetary damages from the lawyer.

EXHIBIT 17.1	List of ABA Model Rules of Professional Conduct

The illustrations in this chapter pertain to the following variation on the Canoga case: After researching the legal claims Ms. Canoga could pursue, you have tentatively decided to represent her in New Mexico state court as to her breach of contract and Employee Privacy Act claims but not to pursue a claim under the federal Americans with Disabilities Act (ADA). You have various reasons for this decision, including doubts about the validity of that claim, concerns about the time and expense needed to litigate that claim, an already heavy caseload, and significant family obligations in the coming months.

Limiting the scope of representation is a topic governed by rules of professional responsibility, in New Mexico by Rule 16-102 C, which follows the ABA Model Rules. See Exhibit 17.2 (at pages 404–06).

B. How Do You Research and Cite Rules of Professional Responsibility?

1. Introduction

As indicated in Exhibit 17.3 (at page 407), research in legal ethics entails framing the issue; locating the pertinent rule for your jurisdiction; reading that rule and its comments carefully; researching in your state's case law; and, as needed, expanding your research to include your state's ethics opinions, if available, and persuasive materials, including ABA materials. As this statement suggests, researching an issue of legal ethics centers on the state's rules of professional responsibility but rarely stops there. A rule is rarely so specific that its application is self-evident; many situations involve complex facts and competing interests. Thus, you very often will consider the following authorities, in addition to the rule, listed from most to least weighty:

- ☐ your state's cases interpreting and applying the rule;
- ☐ your state agency's or bar association's ethics opinions;
- ☐ comments to the rule;
- ☐ cases from other states;
- ☐ ABA materials, including ethics opinions from the ABA Standing Committee on Ethics and Professional Responsibility; and
- ☐ commentary.

You may well look at these sources in a different order, for example, comments before cases.

EXHIBIT 17.2   Professional Responsibility Rule,
                      from New Mexico Statutes Annotated (paper source)

Rule 16–102   RULES OF PROFESSIONAL CONDUCT

RULE 16–102. SCOPE OF REPRESENTATION

A. Client's Decisions. A lawyer shall abide by a client's decisions concerning the objectives of representation, subject to Paragraphs C, D and E, and shall consult with the client as to the means by which they are to be pursued. A lawyer shall abide by a client's decision whether to accept an offer of settlement of a matter. In a criminal case, the lawyer shall abide by the client's decision, after consultation with the lawyer, as to a plea to be entered, whether to waive jury trial and whether the client will testify.

B. Representation Not Endorsement of Client's Views. A lawyer's representation of a client, including representation by appointment, does not constitute an endorsement of the client's political, economic, social, or moral views or activities.

C. Limitation of Representation. A lawyer may limit the scope of the representation if the limitation is reasonable under the circumstances and the client gives informed consent.

D. Course of Conduct. A lawyer shall not engage, or counsel a client to engage, or assist a client, in conduct that the lawyer knows is criminal or fraudulent or which misleads the court, but a lawyer may discuss the legal consequences of any proposed course of conduct with a client and may counsel or assist a client to make a good faith effort to determine the validity, scope, meaning or application of the law.

E. Consultation on Limitations of Assistance. When a lawyer knows that a client expects assistance not permitted by the Rules of Professional Conduct or other law, the lawyer shall consult with the client regarding the relevant limitations on the lawyer's conduct.

[Amended effective March 15, 2001.]

CODE OF PROFESSIONAL CONDUCT COMMITTEE COMMENT

Paragraph D

The New Mexico rule differs from the ABA model rule in that the New Mexico version inserts "engage, or" and "or which misleads the court" in Paragraph D.

Paragraph E

Limitations on the scope of representation may include drafting specific, discrete pleadings or other documents to be used in the course of representation without taking on the responsibility for drafting all documents needed to carry the representation to completion. For example, a lawyer may be retained by a client during the course of an appeal for the sole purpose of drafting a specific document, such as a docketing statement, memorandum in opposition, or brief. A lawyer who agrees to prepare a discrete document under a limited representation agreement must competently prepare such a document and fully advise the client with respect to that document, which includes informing the client of any significant problems that may be associated with the limited representation arrangement. However, by agreeing to prepare a specific, discrete document the lawyer does not also assume the responsibility for taking later actions or preparing subsequent documents that may be necessary to continue to pursue the representation. While limitations on the scope of representation are permitted under this rule, the lawyer must explain the benefits and risks of such an arrangement and obtain the client's informed consent to the limited representation. Upon expiration of the limited representation arrangement, the lawyer should advise the client of any impending deadlines, pending tasks, or other consequences flowing from the termination of the limited representation.

[Revised, effective January 20, 2005.]

ABA COMMENT TO MODEL RULES AS PROPOSED TO BE MODIFIED

Scope of Representation

Both lawyer and client have authority and responsibility in the objectives and means of representation. The client has ultimate authority to determine the purposes to be served by

42

EXHIBIT **17.2**   *(continued)*

CLIENT–LAWYER RELATIONSHIP   **Rule 16–102**

legal representation, within the limits imposed by law and the lawyer's professional obligations. Within those limits, a client also has a right to consult with the lawyer about the means to be used in pursuing those objectives. At the same time, a lawyer is not required to pursue objectives or employ means simply because a client may wish that the lawyer do so. A clear distinction between objectives and means sometimes cannot be drawn, and in many cases the client-lawyer relationship partakes of a joint undertaking. In questions of means, the lawyer should assume responsibility for technical and legal tactical issues, but should defer to the client regarding such questions as the expense to be incurred and concern for third persons who might be adversely affected. Law defining the lawyer's scope of authority in litigation varies among jurisdictions.

In a case in which the client appears to be suffering mental disability, the lawyer's duty to abide by the client's decisions is to be guided by reference to Rule 1.14 [Rule 16–114 NMRA].

Independence from Client's Views or Activities

Legal representation should not be denied to people who are unable to afford legal services, or whose cause is controversial or the subject of popular disapproval. By the same token, representing a client does not constitute approval of the client's views or activities.

Services Limited in Objectives or Means

The scope of services to be provided by a lawyer may be limited by agreement with the client or by the terms under which the lawyer's services are made available to the client. When a lawyer has been retained by an insurer to represent an insured, for example, the representation may be limited to matters related to the insurance coverage. A limited representation may be appropriate because the client has limited objectives for the representation. In addition, the terms upon which representation is undertaken may exclude specific means that might otherwise be used to accomplish the client's objectives. Such limitations may exclude actions that the client thinks are too costly or that the lawyer regards as repugnant or imprudent.

Although this rule affords the lawyer and client substantial latitude to limit the representation, the limitation must be reasonable under the circumstances. If for example, a client's objective is limited to securing general informa-

tion about the law the client needs in order to handle a common and typically uncomplicated legal problem, the lawyer and client may agree that the lawyer's services will be limited to a brief telephone consultation. Such a limitation, however, would not be reasonable if the time allotted was not sufficient to yield advice upon which the client could rely. Although an agreement for a limited representation does not exempt a lawyer from the duty to provide competent representation, the limitation is a factor to be considered when determining the legal knowledge, skill, thoroughness and preparation reasonably necessary for the representation. See Rule 16–101 NMRA.

Although Paragraph C does not require that the client's informed consent to a limited representation be in writing, a specification of the scope of representation will normally be a necessary part of the lawyer's written communication of the rate or basis of the lawyer's fee as required by Rule 16–105(B) NMRA.

All agreements concerning the scope of representation must accord with the Rules of Professional Conduct and other law. *See e.g.*, Rules 16–101, 16–108 and 16–506 NMRA.

Criminal, Fraudulent and Prohibited Transactions

A lawyer is required to give an honest opinion about the actual consequences that appear likely to result from a client's conduct. The fact that a client uses advice in a course of action that is criminal or fraudulent does not, of itself, make a lawyer a party to the course of action. However, a lawyer may not knowingly assist a client in criminal or fraudulent conduct. There is a critical distinction between presenting an analysis of legal aspects of questionable conduct and recommending the means by which a crime or fraud might be committed with impunity.

When the client's course of action has already begun and is continuing, the lawyer's responsibility is especially delicate. The lawyer is not permitted to reveal the client's wrongdoing, except where permitted by Rule 1.6 Rule [16–106 NMRA]. However, the lawyer is required to avoid furthering the purpose, for example, by suggesting how it might be concealed. A lawyer may not continue assisting a client in conduct that the lawyer originally supposes is legally proper but then discovers is criminal or fraudulent. Withdrawal from the representation, therefore, may be required.

EXHIBIT 17.2   *(continued)*

Rule 16–102

RULES OF PROFESSIONAL CONDUCT

Where the client is a fiduciary, the lawyer may be charged with special obligations in dealings with a beneficiary.

Paragraph (d) [D] applies whether or not the defrauded party is a party to the transaction. Hence, a lawyer should not participate in a sham transaction; for example, a transaction to effectuate criminal or fraudulent escape of tax liability. Paragraph (d) [D] does not preclude

undertaking a criminal defense incident to a general retainer for legal services to a lawful enterprise. The last clause of paragraph (d) [D] recognizes that determining the validity or interpretation of a statute or regulation may require a course of action involving disobedience of the statute or regulation or of the interpretation placed upon it by governmental authorities.

Historical Notes

The Comment to Model Rule 1.2 published after Rule 16–102 includes proposed revisions to the ABA

Comment that were included in the ABA Ethics 2000 Committee report.

Library References

Attorney and Client ⬦32(4), 108.
Westlaw Key Number Searches: 45k32(4); 45k108.
C.J.S. Attorney and Client §§ 45 to 46, 236.

Notes of Decisions

Appeals 9
Client funds 3
Duties and obligations of attorneys 5
Grounds for discipline 6
Guardian ad litem 2
Jurisdiction 7
Officer of court 1
Right to effective assistance of counsel 4
Suspension from practice 8

1. Officer of court

Lawyers are officers of court and are always under obligation to be truthful to court. Code of Prof.Resp., DR1–102(A)(3); DR7–102(A)(5). Woodson v. Phillips Petroleum Co., 1985, 102 N.M. 333, 695 P.2d 483. Attorney And Client ⬦ 14; Attorney And Client ⬦ 32(4)

2. Guardian ad litem

Conflict between appellate guardian ad litem's perception of best interests of child in child abuse and neglect proceeding involving allegations of sexual abuse and child's expressed position that abuse never took place did require that guardian withdraw as counsel or that guardian's appellate answer brief be stricken, where guardian's brief advanced what she thought was in child's best interests and also indicated that child disagreed with guardian's position. NMSA 1978, § 32A–1–7, subds. A, D(2); SCRA 1986, Rules 16–102, subd. A, 16–114, subd. A. State ex rel. Children, Youth, Families Dept. In Matter of Esperanza M., 1998, 124 N.M. 735, 955 P.2d 204. Infants ⬦ 205; Infants ⬦ 241

Guardian ad litem is required to advocate child's expressed position only to extent that child's desires are, in guardian ad litem's professional opinion, in child's best interest. NMSA 1978, § 32A–1–7, subds. A, D(2); SCRA 1986, Rules 16–102, subd. A, 16–114, subd. A. State ex rel. Children, Youth, Families Dept. In Matter of Esperanza M., 1998, 124 N.M. 735, 955 P.2d 204. Infants ⬦ 85

3. Client funds

Attorney's expectation that he would be able to replenish the law firm trust account with a settlement from another case, and the fact that the funds eventually were replenished and delivered to their rightful owner, several months later, did not change the conclusion that attorney had violated disciplinary rules by misappropriating client funds. NMRA, Rules 16–102, subd. D, 16–115, subds. A, B, 16–804, subds. C, D, H. In re Chavez, 2000, 129 N.M. 35, 1 P.3d 417. Attorney And Client ⬦ 44(2)

Attorney's acceptance of money from client for purpose of investing it, informing client that money had been invested in real estate contract assigned to client, and informing client that his money was lost and failing to repay client despite promise violates subsections of disciplinary rule proscribing misconduct, disciplinary rule proscribing attorney's intentionally prejudicing or damaging client and subsections of disciplinary rule providing for preserving identity of funds and property of client, where client's money is placed directly into attorney's office checking account and there is no evidence that the money was ever invested in real estate contract. Code of Prof.Resp., DR1–102(A)(3, 4, 6), DR7–101(A)(3), DR9–102(A), (B)(3, 4). Matter of Gallegos, 1986, 104 N.M. 496, 723 P.2d 967. Attorney And Client ⬦ 44(2)

Attorney's failure to submit appropriate forms for transfer of liquor license to Department of Alcoholic Beverage Control and depositing in his own account and converting to his own use money client gave him for purpose of having license transferred, and attorney's failure to advise client of offer to purchase her property or of his receipt of $625 tendered to him as payment by purchaser's attorney, and his failure to refund money when transaction for purchase of real property was not consummated violates subsections of disciplinary rule proscribing misconduct, disciplinary rule proscribing attorney's neglecting legal matter entrusted to him, disciplinary rule proscribing attorney's intentionally prejudicing or damaging client, and vio-

EXHIBIT 17.3	Professional Responsibility Rules Template

Issue:	Citation Information:
	• set of rules
	• rule number
Date of events:	
Date of research:	

Search and Find:	
located rule and comments by:	treatise, Restatement, or other commentary information, as needed:
located ABA information by:	information from ABA sources:

Information and Implications:

- rule
- explanatory material
- connection to client's case

Next Steps:	
questions to consider:	leads to follow — especially cases:

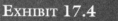 EXHIBIT 17.4   Overview of Professional
                                                Responsibility Research

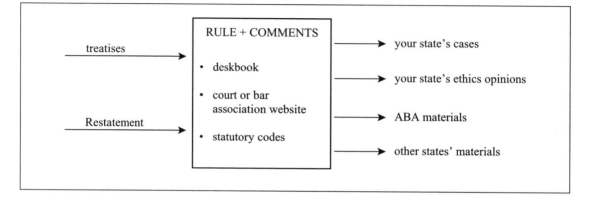

As with any other type of research, jurisdiction matters. That is, a mandatory precedent is weightier than a persuasive precedent, and an ethics opinion from your state is weightier than one from a sister state. Before you rely on authority from a sister state or the ABA, you should ascertain whether your state's rule is identical or very similar to that of the sister state or the ABA model; there are variations from state to state.

To obtain this range of authorities, you will use a variety of sources, both paper and online. While some sources are not unique to ethics research, for example, treatises and annotated codes, others are. The following discussion suggests a standard sequence, from sources one nearly always turns to to sources used mostly for difficult or unusual topics. For an overview, see Exhibit 17.4 (above).

Rules of professional responsibility

- Commentary
- Your state's rule and comments
- Your state's judicial decisions
- Your state's ethics opinions
- Persuasive authorities, especially ABA materials

2. Commentary

Especially if your research topic is new to you, you should consider beginning your research in commentary, especially treatises. Two good options are *The Law of Lawyering* by Geoffrey C. Hazard, Jr. and W. William Hodes, which includes analysis of illustrative scenarios, and *ABA/BNA Lawyers' Manual on Professional Conduct*. See Exhibit 17.5 (at pages 410–11).

A fairly new type of commentary in the area of legal ethics is the Restatement (Third) of the Law Governing Lawyers, promulgated in 2000. The Restatement draws not only on rules of professional responsibility but also on case law, including legal malpractice cases. In some areas, the Restatement position departs from the Model Rules as they read before Ethics 2000. The format of this new Restatement parallels that of other Restatements (see Chapter 7).

Once you become fairly well versed in legal ethics, you probably will begin your research in the rules themselves and consult commentary at a later point in your research.

3. The Law of Your State

Your state's rules and comments. For most states, the text of professional responsibility rules is published in the same deskbook that contains the state's rules of procedure. A state deskbook typically contains the rules of professional responsibility and some explanatory material as well, such as the comments of the advisory committee or adopting authority, but not references to cases or other authorities. Deskbooks are issued annually; thus, very recent amendments and new rules will not be included. See Chapter 16.

Most state codes include professional responsibility rules. In an annotated code, the rules are annotated as statutes, typically including any comments of the state advisory committee, historical notes regarding previous rules, case descriptions, and citations to commentary. Exhibit 17.2 (at pages 404–06) is from an annotated code. See Chapter 11.

Professional responsibility rules are available online as well. You may find the rules through a public website, such as one belonging to the state supreme court or a bar association. Westlaw and LexisNexis both provide professional responsibility rules in their state rules databases.

Reading a professional responsibility rule is in many ways similar to reading statutes and procedural rules. Most rules delineate permissible and prohibited conduct; implicit in the rules is that conduct contrary to a rule may lead to discipline. You should attend carefully to the nuances in the language. Many rules address situations in which there is some tension between two of the three concurrent roles of a lawyer: a "representative of clients" and "an officer of the legal system" (as stated in the preamble to the ABA Model Rules). The language is finely honed to strike the right balance between these roles. The third role is a "public citizen having special responsibility for the quality of justice." This role is less squarely and forcefully addressed; the ABA and some state rules call on — but do not require — lawyers to provide legal assistance to people who cannot afford it and to perform public service in other ways.

EXHIBIT 17.5	Treatise Discussion, from ABA/BNA Lawyer's Manual on Professional Conduct (paper source)*

No. 240   SCOPE OF THE RELATIONSHIP   31:309

Tactics

On the other hand, decisions that involve tactics and trial strategy are reserved for the professional judgment of the criminal defense lawyer after consultation with the client. See, e.g., *People v. McKenzie*, 668 P.2d 769 (Cal. 1983) (lawyer makes tactical and strategic decisions such as what witnesses to call, how to conduct cross-examination, choice of jurors, and motions); *State v. Davis*, 506 A.2d 86 (Conn. 1986) (general rule is still that witness selection is tactical decision for lawyer, notwithstanding state constitutional provision that gives defendant right "to be heard by himself and by counsel . . . and to have compulsory process to obtain witnesses in his behalf"); see also *Strickland v. Washington*, 466 U.S. 668 (1984) (judicial scrutiny of counsel must be deferential and indulge strong presumption that counsel's conduct involved reasonable professional assistance and was sound trial strategy); see generally ABA Standards for Criminal Justice, ch. 4, Defense Function 4-3.1(b), 4-5.2(b) (3d ed. 1993).

Although the line between substantive and tactical issues may at times be difficult to draw, courts have deferred to the lawyer's judgment in a wide variety of matters. See, e.g., *New York v. Hill*, 528 U.S. 110 (2000) (lawyer may make scheduling decisions; lawyer agreed to trial delay outside time limits of Interstate Agreement on Detainers); *Darden v. Wainwright*, 477 U.S. 168 (1986) (defense lawyers in capital murder case did not render ineffective assistance by not introducing mitigating evidence at sentencing, as such approach would have opened door to evidence in rebuttal); *Sexton v. French*, 163 F.3d 874 (4th Cir. 1998) (whether to file pretrial motion to suppress confession is tactical decision for lawyer to make); *Poole v. United States*, 832 F.2d 561 (11th Cir. 1987) (defense lawyer's decision to stipulate to easily provable matter—that institutions defendant allegedly robbed were federally insured—was tactical; therefore, client consent was not needed); *United States v.*

Clayborne, 509 F.2d 473 (D.C. Cir. 1974) (lawyer may decide to decline cross-examination); *State v. Gibbs*, 758 A.2d 327 (Conn. 2000) (lawyer may decide whether to file motion to dismiss for lack of speedy trial); *People v. Segoviano*, 725 N.E.2d 1275 (Ill. 2000) ("The only trial-related decisions over which a defendant ultimately must have control are: whether to plead guilty; whether to waive a jury trial; whether to testify in his own behalf; whether to appeal; and whether to submit a lesser-included offense instruction"); *State v. Mecham*, 9 P.3d 777 (Utah 2000) (lawyer retains responsibility for making tactical decisions, including whether to pursue motion to suppress evidence); *State v. Oswald*, 606 N.W.2d 207 (Wis. Ct. App. 1999) (change of venue request is tactical decision for lawyer to make); *State v. Burnette*, 583 N.W.2d 174 (Wis. Ct. App. 1998) (lawyer may decide whether to strike potential juror for cause).

Limiting Scope of Representation

A lawyer may limit the scope of the representation provided that "the limitation is reasonable under the circumstances and the client gives informed consent." Rule 1.2(c). Such limitations have long been recognized. For example, a lawyer and a client can agree that:

- the lawyer will handle only certain types of claims and not others, see, e.g., *Delta Equipment & Construction Co. v. Royal Indemnity Co.*, 186 So. 2d 454 (La. Ct. App. 1966);
- the lawyer will represent the client on a specific transaction without assuming any general duties to the client beyond the sufficiency of the relevant documents, see, e.g., *Grand Isle Campsites v. Cheek*, 249 So. 2d 268 (La. Ct. App. 1971), modified, 262 So. 2d 350 (La. 1972); or
- litigation will be conducted only at the trial level, see, e.g., *Young v. Bridwell*, 437 P.2d 686 (Utah 1968).

The requirement of reasonableness generally means that the limitation may not impair a client's rights or the lawyer's legal or ethical obligations. *Hartford Ac-*

EXHIBIT 17.5   *(continued)*

31:310   LAWYER-CLIENT RELATIONSHIP   No. 240

cident & Indemnity Co. v. Foster, 528 So. 2d 255 (Miss. 1988) (insurance policy may not contain provisions limiting ethical duties owed by insurance company lawyers to insured clients); *Greenwich v. Markhoff*, 650 N.Y.S.2d 704 (App. Div. 1996) (law firm may be liable for malpractice for failure to file personal injury action on behalf of client even though retainer agreement purported to limit scope of representation to workers' compensation claim; agreement did not obviate firm's duty to apprise client that personal injury action might lie); *Parents Against Drunk Drivers v. Graystone Pines Homeowners' Ass'n*, 789 P.2d 52 (Utah Ct. App. 1990) (retainer agreement may not grant lawyer control over settlement of case, in contravention of ethics rules).

The lawyer must clearly explain any limitations. See, e.g., *Johnson v. Freemont County Board of Comm'rs*, 85 F.3d 489 (10th Cir. 1996) (although separate representation is permissible for government official sued in both official and individual capacity, for lawyer to limit representation to official capacity, lawyer must consult with client about exposure in individual capacity and client must consent to limitation); *In re Bancroft*, 204 B.R. 548 (Bankr. C.D. Ill. 1997) (in context of bankruptcy proceedings, Rule 1.2(c) requires lawyer to explain to debtor "the nature of the bankruptcy process, what problems could or will be encountered, how those problems should be addressed, and the risks or hazards, if any, associated with those problems. Consent involves a clear understanding on the part of the debtor as to these factors and the possible results of a debtor proceeding without an attorney being present"); *Indianapolis Podiatry PC v. Efroymson*, 720 N.E.2d 376 (Ind. Ct. App. 1999) (when limiting scope of representation, extent of required disclosure to client is "similar, if not identical, to that required in the context of a conflict of interest"); Colorado Ethics Op. 101 (1998) (lawyer providing unbundled legal services must explain limitations of representation, including types of services not being pro-

vided, risks associated with limitations, and warning that client may face legal issues he may not understand); New York City Ethics Op. 2001-3 (2001) (lawyer may limit scope of representation to avoid conflict with current or former client, provided that client whose representation is limited consents after full disclosure and limitation does not so restrict representation as to render it inadequate); see also ABA Formal Ethics Op. 96-403 (1996) (lawyer hired by insurer to represent insured must advise insured that lawyer plans to proceed at direction of insurer in accordance with insurance contract).

'Unbundling'

Representation that is limited in scope, often referred to as "unbundled" legal services, is a means of giving clients a choice of something between obtaining full representation with respect to an entire legal matter and no representation at all. These types of services may be particularly useful for those who cannot afford to hire a lawyer to represent them but who may desire limited legal advice or may want assistance in drafting a document. See Colorado Ethics Op. 101 (1998) (approving provision by lawyers of unbundled legal services in litigation and nonlitigation contexts); see generally Hyman & Silver, *And Such Small Portions: Limited Performance Agreements and Cost/Quality/Access Trade-Off*, 11 Geo. J. Legal Ethics 959 (1998); McNeal, *Redefining Attorney-Client Roles: Unbundling and Moderate-Income Elderly Clients*, 32 Wake Forest L. Rev. 295 (1997); Zacharias, *Limited Performance Agreements: Should Clients Get What They Pay For?*, 11 Geo. J. Legal Ethics 915 (1998).

Ghostwriting

Lawyers who are asked to provide limited, behind-the-scenes legal services to pro se litigants should be cautious, particularly if asked to "ghostwrite" documents to be filed with a court. Some courts have found such conduct to be improper because it misleads the court and may violate civil procedure rules (e.g.,

Your state's judicial decisions. Once you have explored these sources, you will be ready to read cases interpreting and applying the pertinent rule. In addition to the case descriptions in an annotated code, you can use case digests, searches in a case law database (probably a commercial service, possibly a public website), and citators covering the applicable rule to identify pertinent cases, which you can read in a reporter or cases database. As with all case law research, be sure to cite each case. See Chapters 9 and 10.

Your state's ethics opinions. If your state ethics agency or bar association issues ethics opinions, you should research these next. See Exhibit 17.6 (at pages 413–14).[1] You may find them or descriptions of them in one or more of the following sources:

- ☐ the website for your state's ethics agency or bar association;
- ☐ the office of the ethics agency or bar association;
- ☐ a Westlaw or LexisNexis ethics opinions database covering your state;
- ☐ a specialized reporter, such as *ABA/BNA Lawyers' Manual on Professional Conduct*, and
- ☐ a state bar association publication.

Be sure that you know whether any opinion you find is binding or merely advisory. Keep in mind that it is, in any event, less authoritative than a judicial decision.

4. Persuasive Authorities

If, after exploring the sources listed previously, you still need further guidance, you should turn to persuasive materials. If you have not already done so, a good first step is to consult a treatise, the Restatement, a periodical article (several journals focus on legal ethics), or other commentary.

Very likely, your research at this stage will come to focus on the ABA rules because of their influence on state rules around the country. Not surprisingly, several ABA publications provide a wide range of useful information:

- ☐ *ABA Compendium of Professional Responsibility Rules and Standards* is a deskbook containing the current Model Rules; its predecessors; other ABA standards, such as the Standards for Imposing Lawyer Sanctions; and selected ethics opinions from the ABA Standing Committee on Ethics and Professional Responsibility.
- ☐ *Annotated Model Rules of Professional Conduct* provides a concise discussion of and citations to leading judicial decisions and ethics opinions along with the rules.
- ☐ At the ABA Center for Professional Responsibility website, abanet .org/cpr, you will find the Model Rules and a database of the ABA's formal ethics opinions, along with many other useful resources (including an e-mail address for a research service staffed by experts in legal ethics research).

1. We selected a Pennysylvania opinion on the Canoga topic, for lack of an available pertinent New Mexico opinion.

Exhibit 17.6	State Bar Association Ethics Opinion, from Westlaw State Ethics Opinions Database (online source)

Westlaw.

PA Eth. Op. 94-172, 1994 WL 928104 (Pa.Bar.Assn.Comm.Leg.Eth.Prof.Resp.)   Page 1

PA Eth. Op. 94-172, 1994 WL 928104 (Pa.Bar.Assn.Comm.Leg.Eth.Prof.Resp.)

Pennsylvania Bar Association Committee on Legal Ethics and Professional Responsibility

Informal Opinion Number 94-172

November 9, 1994

You were retained by Client to represent her in a criminal matter. As part of your initial negotiations, you agreed to represent Client up through and including a jury trial, for a certain fee. After the jury trial, you agreed with Client to represent her at the sentencing for an additional fee. You explicitly discussed with Client that this fee did not include representing her at any appeal. On October 14, 1994, following the sentencing, you sent Client a letter advising her of the November 14, 1994 deadline for filing an appeal, summarizing the possible issue on which she might want to appeal, indicating that your "representation of [Client] has terminated with the sentencing hearing", setting forth your rates for handling the appeal, and advising her that she most likely would be eligible for the Public Defender and should make an application as soon as possible.

Yesterday you received a telephone call from Client's sister. She related that Client had made an application to the public defender's office, which said that it would not process the application, that you were obligated to file the appeal, and that if you did not, you would be brought before the Ethics Committee [Disciplinary Board.] You telephoned the Public Defender's office to determine whether sister had accurately communicated its position. A lawyer at the PD's office confirmed that the PD's office will not process Client's application for assistance until after you have filed the Notice of Appeal and the Docketing Statement (which includes a Statement of Matters Complained of, and will list you as attorney of record.) The Public Defender representative did not assert that Client believed she had retained you for the appeal. Rather, this representative said that it was the office practice to require the private attorney to file these items.

You inquired whether you are ethically obligated to represent Client in the appeal. In particular, you asked whether you are ethically able to limit the scope of your representation to the trial representation only.

It is my opinion that ethically, a lawyer may limit the scope of the lawyer's representation of a client. I know of no ethics rule which would require a lawyer who has handled a criminal trial to always handle the criminal appeal. (And, indeed, I can think of strong reasons against a rule that **required** the criminal trial lawyer to always handle the appeal. This kind of obligation might serve to discourage lawyers from handling certain criminal trial.)

EXHIBIT 17.6   *(continued)*

PA Eth. Op. 94-172, 1994 WL 928104 (Pa.Bar.Assn.Comm.Leg.Eth.Prof.Resp.)   Page 2

The basis for my opinion is Rule 1.2(c) of the Rules of Professional Conduct. This provision, entitled "Scope of Representation", says: "A lawyer may limit the objectives of the representation if the client consents after a full disclosure of the circumstances and consultation." I believe that my interpretation is supported by the leading commentators and treatises in the area. See, e.g., G. Hazard & W. Hodes, The Law of Lawyering §1.2:401 (2d ed. 1994) ("Rule 1.2 recognizes that the client-lawyer relationship is based on contract. In the normal course of events, lawyers and clients should be able to agree that for larger or smaller sums of money, the lawyer will commit more or less time and energy, and assume more or less responsibility."); **ABA/BNA Lawyers' Manual on Professional Conduct, Main Volume,** 31:306-07 ("the client-lawyer relationship is contractual and rests upon mutual assent both as to its existence and its scope. Thus a lawyer and a client can agree …that litigation will be conducted only at the trial level"). I have seen no reference to the fact that the ordinary scope of representation rule does not apply in a criminal case.

*2 Thus, assuming that you consulted with Client and that Client consented to the limited nature of your representation, (i.e. your agreement to represent at trial only for a certain fee), then I think you ethically may refuse to represent her on appeal. Based on the facts you have told me, and your October 14, 1994 letter, it certainly appears that you limited your representation of Client to the trial stage and that she consented to this limitation. (This conclusion is supported by the fact that you both negotiated for your further representation of her at the sentencing stage for an additional fee.) Thus, I conclude that you need not represent Client on appeal. I would note that you have not indicated any statement by the Public Defender's office which suggests a belief that you did not comply with the provisions of Rule 1.2(c).

I would add two caveats at this point. **First**, my opinion is confined to the issue of what the Pennsylvania Rules of Conduct require. Committee members are not permitted to opine on substantive law. Thus, it may be that there is substantive Pennsylvania case, of which I am unaware, that overrides the ethics rules and requires a lawyer who accepts a criminal trial to handle a criminal appeal. I am unaware of such a case, however.

Second, one might argue that the normal scope of representation rules should be suspended at least with respect to filing a notice of appeal, if the lawyer's inaction would materially prejudice a client by causing her to lose her right of appeal. Thus, on the one hand, if the PD's office refuses to process Client's application, you might want to prepare a pro se Notice of Appeal for Client's signature, together with a Motion for Appointment of Counsel if she is indigent.

I would point out that in quickly researching this point, I have not found any material exactly on point. The closest example I found is an illustrative case in Professor Hazard's treatise. In the hypo, a Lawyer has previously represented a couple with respect to their small business. He is now consulted concerning an auto accident in which their son was involved. Professor Hazard concludes that the

As a first critical step, be sure to compare the language of your state's rule to that of the ABA's rule. The commentary to your state's rule in the deskbook or annotated code may provide this information; if not, you will need to do the comparison yourself. If your state's rule is identical to the ABA rule, you can adopt what you learn about the ABA rule; if your state's rule differs from the ABA rule, you will need to adapt what you learn about the ABA rule.

In addition, you may find it helpful to read judicial decisions and ethics opinions from other states. You will find references to these in many of the sources discussed previously. A good paper option is the *ABA/BNA Lawyers' Manual*. Strong online options are Westlaw's METH-CS and METH-EO, multistate judicial decisions and ethics opinions databases, respectively (the latter is the source of Exhibit 17.6 at pages 413–14), and LexisNexis' ETH-CAS (covering cases and ethics opinions).

Exhibit 17.7 (at page 416) is our professional responsibility rules template filled in to reflect our research of the Canoga case.

5. Citation

A citation to a state rule of professional responsibility consists of the abbreviation for the set of rules and the rule number. Here are two examples:

☐ *Bluebook* Rule 12.8.3 (by analogy): N.M. R. Prof'l Conduct 16-102.
☐ *ALWD Citation Manual* Rule 17.1: N.M. R. Prof. Conduct 16-102.

Citation to a state ethics opinion includes the issuing organization; type of opinion; number; and date, if the date is not part of the number. Here are two examples:

☐ *Bluebook* Rule 12.8.6: Pa. Bar Ass'n Comm. on Legal Ethics and Prof'l Responsibility, Informal Op. 94-172.
☐ *ALWD Citation Manual Rule* 17.4: Pa. B. Assn. Informal Ethics Op. 94-72.

Citation to ABA ethics materials is fairly similar to the forms described previously.

C. WHAT ELSE?

Proposed State Rules. Proposed amendments to a state's rules generally appear in a state bar journal or legal newspaper, as do newly adopted rules.

Proposed ABA Rules. Drafts of new rules and the reports of studies that the ABA undertakes concerning new rules often are published as separate publications to permit the ABA membership to make comments. Furthermore, proposed amendments as well as recently adopted rules and comments are published in the *ABA Journal* and on the ABA website.

EXHIBIT 17.7	Professional Responsibility Rules Template for Canoga Case

Issue: *Is litigating some but not all claims ethically permissible?*	Citation Information: • *New Mexico Rule of Professional Conduct* • *16-102C*
Date of events: *Sept. 7, 2007*	
Date of research: *Jan. 14, 2008*	
Searching and Finding:	
located rule and comments by: *Rule only at nmlaws.org.* *Rules and comments in West's New Mexico Rules Annotated.*	treatise, Restatement, or other commentary information, as needed: *Limitations have long been recognized, including handling some claims but not others — cite to Louisiana case. Limitation may not impair client's rights or lawyer's obligations. Lawyer must clearly explain limitations. ABA/BNA Lawyer's Manual on Professional Conduct § 30:301 (2002).*
located ABA information by: *Comment appears in N.M. Rules Annotated. Search in abanet.org yielded an ABA journal article and website re unbundled legal services.*	information from ABA sources: *Comment stresses agreement between lawyer and client and desirability of written communication.*

Information and Implications:

Rule 16-102C permits limiting the scope of representation if the limitation is reasonable and the client gives informed consent.
Other sources provide examples, e.g., New Mexico comment raises preparing a specific discrete document.

The claims to be asserted are the strongest; the claims we will not pursue are weaker. Be sure Ms. Canoga is fully informed and consents.

Next Steps:

questions to consider: *The legal weakness of the omitted claims supports the limited representation — but does my personal situation count?*	leads to follow — especially cases: *Delta Equipment & Construction Co. v. Royal Indemnity Co., 186 So. 2d 454 (La. Ct. App. 1966) [from BNA treatise].*

Specialized Rules of Professional Conduct. In addition to the Model Rules, the ABA has promulgated several specialized sets of standards, such as the Model Code of Judicial Conduct and the Model Rule for Temporary Practice by Foreign Lawyers.

Citing Ethics Materials. You may Shepardize ABA materials on LexisNexis.

D. INTERLUDE: THE CANOGA CASE

Researching the issue of limiting the scope of representation to some claims, we found the rule, but only the rule, at nmlaws.org. West's New Mexico Rules Annotated provided not only the language of the New Mexico rule, but also the comments of both the New Mexico and ABA committees and case descriptions. We learned that limiting the scope of representation is permissible if the limitation is reasonable and the client gives informed consent. The New Mexico comment provides the example of preparing a specific discrete document — so long as the lawyer advises the client of pending matters and the consequences of terminating the representation. The ABA comment stresses written communication between lawyer and client.

Lacking a pertinent case, we went to the New Mexico Bar Association website. We found ethics opinions from 1983 to date, synopses, a simple index, an ethics hotline. We found no pertinent opinions.

Turning to persuasive materials, we looked for ethics opinions from other states in Westlaw's METH-EO database, which contains opinions from twenty states. We found a recent Pennsylvania discussion of limited representation in the provision of basic legal services to the poor. Although Ms. Canoga's situation is different, some of the analysis could carry over.

Turning to ABA materials, we read the discussion in the ABA's *Annotated Model Rules of Professional Conduct* and then the *ABA/BNA Lawyers' Manual on Professional Conduct*. This treatise provided a thorough discussion of permissible limitations and precautions to be taken; it also refers to a handful of cases, ethics opinions, and periodical articles on point. Our next step would be reading these sources. If we wanted to pursue the topic even more, we could look at the wide range of materials collected at the ABA's Pro Se/Unbundling Resource Center, which we learned about from a 2004 article in the ABA Journal that we found via a search in the abanet.org/cpr website. Our research in ABA materials is a good example of how one thing often leads to another in legal research.

An aside: On the ABA website, we found a link to a compilation of professionalism creeds adopted by various state and local bar associations. These creeds recognize that professional responsibility rules cover some matters well but do not set sufficiently high standards for the area of civility. See Exhibit 17.8 (at pages 418–21), the New Mexico Creed of Professionalism. Most lawyers also look to their own moral standards as well.

EXHIBIT 17.8	Professionalism Creed, from Compilation Linked to ABA Website (online source)

A Lawyer's Creed of Professionalism of the State Bar of New Mexico

Preamble

As a lawyer I must strive to make our system of justice work fairly and efficiently. In order to carry out that responsibility, not only will I comply with the letter and spirit of the disciplinary standards applicable to all lawyers, but I will also conduct myself in accordance with the following Creed of Professionalism when dealing with my client, opposing parties, their counsel, the courts and the general public.

A. In all matters:

"My Word is My Bond."

B. With respect to my client:

1. I will be loyal and committed to my client's cause, but I will not permit that loyalty and commitment to interfere with my ability to provide my client with objective and independent advice;

2. I will endeavor to achieve my client's lawful objectives in business transactions, in litigation and in all other matters, as expeditiously and economically as possible;

3. In appropriate cases, I will counsel my client with respect to mediation, arbitration and other alternative methods of resolving disputes;

4. I will advise my client against pursuing any course of action that is without merit and against insisting on tactics which are intended to delay resolution of the matter or to harass or drain the financial resources of the opposing party;

5. I will advise my client that civility and courtesy are not to be equated with weakness;

6. While I must abide by my client's decision concerning the objectives of the

EXHIBIT 17.8   *(continued)*

representation, I nevertheless will counsel my client that a willingness to initiate or engage in settlement discussions is consistent with zealous and effective representation.

7. I will keep my client informed about the progress of the case and the costs and fees being incurred;

8. I will charge only a reasonable attorney's fee for services rendered;

9. I will be courteous to and considerate of my client at all times.

C. With respect to opposing parties and their counsel:

1. I will endeavor to be courteous and civil, both in oral and in written communications;

2. I will not knowingly make statements of fact or of law that are untrue;

3. In litigation proceedings I will agree to reasonable requests for extensions of time or for waiver of procedural formalities when the legitimate interests of my client will not be adversely affected;

4. I will endeavor to consult with opposing counsel before scheduling depositions and meeting and before rescheduling hearings, and I will cooperate with opposing counsel when scheduling changes are requested;

5. I will refrain from utilizing litigation, delaying tactics, or any other course of conduct to harass the opposing party;

6. I will refrain from engaging in excessive and abusive discovery, and I will comply with all reasonable discovery requests;

7. In depositions and other proceedings, and in negotiations, I will conduct myself with dignity, avoid making groundless objections and refrain from disrespect;

8. I will not serve motions and pleadings on the other party, or his counsel, at such a time or in such a manner as will unfairly limit the other party's opportunity to respond;

9. In the preparation of documents and in negotiations, I will concentrate on matters of substance and content;

EXHIBIT 17.8   *(continued)*

10. I will clearly identify, for other counsel or parties, all changes that I have made in documents submitted to me for review.

D. With respect to the courts and other tribunals:

1. I will be a vigorous and zealous advocate on behalf of my client, while recognizing, as an officer of the court, that excessive zeal may be detrimental to my client's interests as well as to the proper functioning of our system of justice;

2. Where consistent with my client's interests, I will communicate with opposing counsel in an effort to avoid litigation and to resolve litigation that has actually commenced;

3. I will voluntarily withdraw claims or defenses when it becomes apparent that they do not have merit or are superfluous;

4. I will refrain from filing frivolous motions;

5. I will make every effort to agree with other counsel, as early as possible, on a voluntary exchange of information and on a plan for discovery;

6. I will attempt to resolve, by agreement, my objections to matters contained in my opponent's pleadings and discovery requests;

7. When scheduled hearings or depositions have to be canceled, I will notify opposing counsel, and, if appropriate, the court (or other tribunal) as early as possible;

8. Before dates for hearings or trials are set — or, if that is not feasible, immediately after such dates have been set — I will attempt to verify the availability of key participants and witnesses so that I can promptly notify the court (or other tribunal) and opposing counsel of any likely problem in that regard;

9. In civil matters, I will stipulate to facts as to which there is no genuine dispute;

10. I will be punctual in attending court hearings, conferences and depositions;

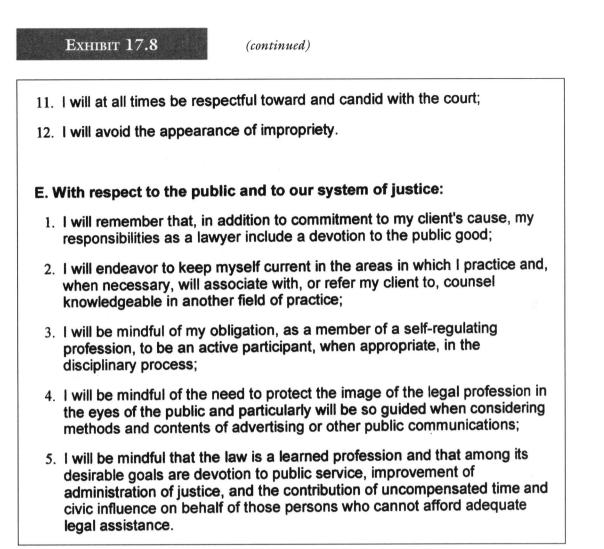

EXHIBIT 17.8 *(continued)*

11. I will at all times be respectful toward and candid with the court;

12. I will avoid the appearance of impropriety.

E. With respect to the public and to our system of justice:

1. I will remember that, in addition to commitment to my client's cause, my responsibilities as a lawyer include a devotion to the public good;

2. I will endeavor to keep myself current in the areas in which I practice and, when necessary, will associate with, or refer my client to, counsel knowledgeable in another field of practice;

3. I will be mindful of my obligation, as a member of a self-regulating profession, to be an active participant, when appropriate, in the disciplinary process;

4. I will be mindful of the need to protect the image of the legal profession in the eyes of the public and particularly will be so guided when considering methods and contents of advertising or other public communications;

5. I will be mindful that the law is a learned profession and that among its desirable goals are devotion to public service, improvement of administration of justice, and the contribution of uncompensated time and civic influence on behalf of those persons who cannot afford adequate legal assistance.

CONCLUSION

UNIT VII

DEVELOPING AN INTEGRATED RESEARCH STRATEGY

A. Introduction: The Older Persons' Housing Dilemma
B. Four Research Journals
C. Our Observations

Exhibit 18.1   Overview of Four Research Logs

A.   INTRODUCTION: THE OLDER PERSONS' HOUSING DILEMMA

Now that you have worked with a range of legal research sources, you should realize there is no one "right" or "best" way to research any particular situation. You have options as to which commentary to explore and which sources to use for various types of law. Fundamentally, your task is to locate and understand the governing law.

To help you see how varied legal research can be, we asked four law students to research the following situation, which we invented for this purpose. We asked each to record the steps they took while completing the research. Rather than focusing on the sources of law discovered, we want you to note the varied research strategies undertaken, each leading ultimately to similar results.

> Charles and Beca Swee bought a two-bedroom condominium in Costa Brava Towers, a large "older persons only" building, located in Delray Beach, Florida, shortly after they both retired from full-time work. They now live full-time in the unit. The building has more than 250 units, and there are many condominium association rules restricting who may live in this building, principally focusing on the age of the residents. Children and younger adults may visit only for short stays on holidays, vacations, or weekends; otherwise, permanent residents must be at least age fifty-five. Indeed, about ninety percent of the residents are over fifty-five. Charles is sixty-two, and Beca is fifty-three.

Costa Brava Towers is a new condominium building. Although they pay a hefty monthly association fee, Charles and Beca greatly appreciate the large number of amenities provided to the older adults who live in the building. Because of Charles' medical needs and limited mobility, they have particularly appreciated the fact that all parts of the building, including the swimming pool, are accessible for persons with disabilities. Additionally, they have often used the social and recreational programs earmarked for seniors (e.g., fitness programs, organized outings, and group educational programs) and appreciate the emergency healthcare programs maintained by the Costa Brava Condo Association. Charles and Beca dine regularly in the Costa Brava community dining hall.

A few weeks ago, their son and daughter-in-law died in a tragic traffic accident. Charles and Beca became permanent guardians for their grandsons, Vincent, age eleven, and Lek, age thirteen. Charles and Beca bought bunk beds and moved the two boys into the second bedroom in their condominium.

Although the boys are good kids, they act their age. At times, they make loud noises when playing in the unit, run in the hallways, and talk loudly when waiting for the elevators. The building manager recently advised Charles and Beca that residents in the building had complained about the noise. Although sympathetic because of the circumstances under which the boys came to live with Charles and Beca, the manager advised Charles and Beca that he was obliged to enforce the rules regarding residency and that they were obliged to remove the boys or vacate their condominium unit.

They were aware of the age restriction when they first moved into Costa Brava Towers, but are unwilling to relinquish custody of their grandsons or move out. Specifically, Charles and Beca now seek to learn whether the restrictive covenant regarding the age of permanent residents in Costa Brava Towers unlawfully discriminates based on age and whether the property restrictions are enforceable under these circumstances.

B.   Four Research Journals*

1.   Adine Momoh, Representing Charles and Beca Swee

The hypothetical presents three issues: (1) whether the restrictive covenant regarding the age of permanent residents in Costa Brava Towers unlawfully discriminates based on age; (2) whether the restrictive covenant is enforceable under these circumstances; and (3) if the restrictive covenant is enforceable and the Swees refuse to comply, what remedies are available to Costa Brava Towers.

* For ease of reading, we have not provided complete and proper citations.

I started by brainstorming terms for the following categories:

- ☐ Who: grandparents, grandchildren, homeowners' association, guardian;
- ☐ What: condominium, property, building, discrimination, covenant, restrictive covenant, age, exceptions;
- ☐ Where: Delray Beach, Florida; condominium;
- ☐ Why: invalidate restrictive covenant, enforce restrictive covenant, avoid liability, remain owners of unit, retain custody of grand-children;
- ☐ Legal: restrictive covenant, homeowners' association, Fair Housing Act, breach of contract; and
- ☐ Remedy: damages, equitable relief, injunctive relief.

Based on my first-year contract and property law classes and given that restrictive covenants are essentially contracts, I know that restrictive covenants generally present state law issues. However, a restrictive covenant can also present a federal issue depending on the sort of activity that the restrictive covenant is trying to restrict or the facts of the particular case. To gain more insight on this preliminary issue, I consulted the encyclopedia Am. Jur. 2d. I started with the index, looked up "restrictive covenant," and found pertinent sections to read in the *Covenants, Conditions, and Restrictions* topic. I also checked to see whether the sections I had selected were updated in the encyclopedia's pocket part; they were not.

Generally, equitable principles govern the enforcement of building restrictions. Building restrictions will not be enforced if, under the facts of the particular case, it would be inequitable and unjust. Whether injunctive relief will be granted to restrain the violation of such restrictions is a matter within the sound discretion of the trial court, to be determined in the light of all the facts and circumstances, and the appellate court will not interfere unless such discretion is manifestly abused. Given this general rule, I looked to see if there were rules regarding restrictive covenants dealing with age. Age-restrictive covenants have been upheld against constitutional challenges where such restrictions fulfill a legitimate public need. *Hurd v. Hodge*, 334 U.S. 24 (1948). Nevertheless, these restrictions can be struck down pursuant to state statutory requirements.

Given this information, I decided to look at the Florida Statutes Annotated because the condominium is in Florida. I wanted to know what general rules were applicable to condominiums in Florida. Accordingly, I looked for relevant statutory provisions under "homeowners' associations" in the index. However, most of these statutes were unrelated to the restrictive covenant issue. I then looked up another search term in the annotated code, "Fair Housing," to see what Florida's terms were regarding the Fair Housing Act. The index referred me to Florida Statutes section 760.20, which provides the general fair housing provisions.

Under section 760.23, it is unlawful to discriminate against any person in terms, conditions, or privileges of sale or rental of a dwelling, or in the provision of services or facilities in connection therewith, because of, among other things, familial status. I looked through the act, and found section 760.29, which provides exemptions to the act. Specially, subsection 4(b) says that housing for older persons, where at least eighty percent of the occupied units are occupied by at least one person fifty-five years of age or older, are exempted. Costa Brava qualifies in this instance because about ninety percent of residents are over fifty-five.

I then focused on the provisions within the "condominiums" section of the annotated code. I looked at Florida Statutes section 718.104(5), which says, "[t]he declaration as originally recorded or as amended under the procedures provided therein may include covenants and restrictions concerning the use, occupancy, and transfer of units permitted by law with reference to real property." Subsection (6) states, "A person who joins in, or consents to the execution of a declaration subjects his or her interest in the condominium property to the provisions of the declaration."

Looking at the annotations interpreting these provisions, I found cases that are relevant to the first issue. I KeyCited these cases and found that they are still good law. I also checked the annotated code's pocket part, but no additional cases pertaining to age restrictions were listed.

Hidden Harbour Estates, Inc. v. Basso, a Florida District Court of Appeals case from 1981, states the general principle that restrictions found in a condominium's declaration are clothed in a very strong presumption of validity, which arises from the fact that each individual unit owner purchases his or her unit knowing of and accepting the restrictions to be imposed. Regarding restrictive covenants on age specifically, *White Egret Condominium, Inc. v. Franklin*, a Florida Supreme Court case from 1979, discusses the significance of restrictive covenants in condominiums, relying on section 718.112(3)(b). The court reasoned that age limitations or restrictions are reasonable means to accomplish the lawful purpose of providing appropriate facilities for the differing housing needs and desires of the condominium residents' varying age groups.

Applying the standard articulated in *White Egret*, the court in *Roth v. Normandy Shores Yacht & Country Club, Inc.*, a 1987 Florida District Court of Appeals case, upheld a declaration provision prohibiting children under the age of twelve from residing in an adult condominium. However, *Roth* can be distinguished on its facts from the present case. In *Roth*, a unit owner argued the declaration restriction was invalid given a county ordinance that prohibited discrimination in sale, purchase, or lease of housing on the basis of age. In the Swees' case, there is no ordinance involved.

In brief, the first issue can be answered: the restrictive covenant regarding the age of permanent residents in Costa Brava Towers does not on its face impermissibly discriminate based on age. The purpose of the restrictive covenant is to provide a quiet, safe atmosphere that most senior citizens desire. In addition to making the condominium accessible for persons with disabilities, the condominium offers emergency health-care programs and social and recreational programs earmarked for senior citizens.

However, the inquiry does not end there. The restrictive covenant could be deemed unconstitutional as applied if it is used to unreasonably or arbitrarily restrict certain classes of individuals from obtaining desirable housing.

Restrictions on individual rights based on age need not pass a "strict scrutiny" test, because age is not a suspect classification. *White Egret* provides that whenever an age restriction is attacked on due process or equal protection grounds, the test is: (1) whether the restriction under the particular circumstances of the case is reasonable, and (2) whether it is discriminatory, arbitrary, or oppressive in its application. In *White Egret*, the condominium association was estopped from selectively enforcing the restrictive covenant on age because the record revealed that at least six children under the age of twelve were living in the condominium. In the present case, an estoppel argument may be unsuccessful, since the building manager recently advised the Swees that residents had complained about the children and that he was obliged to enforce the age restriction rules.

To find additional cases that might support the argument that the restrictive covenant in the present case is unenforceable given the circumstances, I turned to online resources and did a Westlaw search using the key number assigned to the *White Egret* rule above. I later restricted the key-number search by adding `age & restrict!`. I found one new case that was relevant; I had already found references to the other relevant cases in the annotated code and within cases I had already found. I KeyCited the following case and found out that it is still good law. The court in *Constellation Condominium Ass'n, Inc. v. Harrington*, a Florida District Court of Appeals decision from 1985, reasoned that when unit owners moved into a condominium with knowledge of a ban against small children, a showing that the birth of the owner's child was unexpected was insufficient to justify the denial of the enforcement of the rule. The Swees could distinguish *Constellation* on its facts and argue that as a matter of public policy, the unexpected death of one's children and need to raise their grandchildren are substantially different from the unexpected birth of a child, such that the restrictive covenant can be deemed unreasonable and arbitrary in its application.

If the restrictive covenant is enforceable under these circumstances, the next issue is: what remedies are available to Costa Brava Towers if the Swees refuse to comply and breach the restrictive covenant? Looking at the annotations following section 718.104 under "injunctive relief," I found a pertinent case from the Florida District Court of Appeals in 1982, *Del Valle v. Biltmore II Condominium Ass'n, Inc. Del Valle* holds that injunctive relief in enforcement of regulations contained in a declaration of condominium is appropriate. The KeyCite search indicated the case is still good law.

Conclusion. I conclude that Costa Brava Tower's restrictive covenant regarding the age of permanent residents does not on its face unlawfully discriminate based on age. Nevertheless, if the Swees decide to stay in the condominium unit and want to maintain custody of their grandchildren, I would counsel them to challenge the restriction by arguing that it is unconstitutional as applied. They will have to establish that the restriction is unreasonable under the particular circumstances of the case, and that it is discriminatory, arbitrary, or oppressive in its application. The Swees should make a public policy argument that the unexpected death of their children and the need to raise their grandchildren suffice to justify non-enforcement of the restrictive covenant.

2.   Marcus Ploeger, Representing Charles and Beca Swee

After a thorough reading of the facts, I identified the two primary issues faced by my clients, the Swees. The first is whether the age restriction is unlawful discrimination, and the second is whether Costa Brava Towers may lawfully enforce the restriction.

I began my research with periodicals, starting in Westlaw's Journals and Law Reviews database (JLR). After creating a list of possible search terms derived from the facts and issues of the case, I performed a terms-and-connectors search in the JLR database: ''age restriction'' & discriminat! & resident! & apartment condo! Using these terms I sought to identify articles that discussed the discriminatory effects of age restrictions for residents of apartments or condominiums.

Reading the titles and related paragraphs, I selected a 2004 Iowa Law Review article by Robert G. Schwemm and Michael Allen, *For the Rest of Their Lives: Seniors and The Fair Housing Act.* I skimmed the table of contents for relevant section headings and identified "Fair Housing Act" (FHA) and "The 'Housing for Older Persons' Exemption" (HFOP). I scrolled down to the HFOP section and learned that certain housing designated for older persons is exempt from the FHA's prohibition against discrimination based on familial status (children in the home). The citation directed me to a particular section of the Fair Housing Act, 42 U.S.C.A. § 3607(b)(1). I clicked on the link to "Chapter 45" at the top of the screen to quickly skim the Act for its general rule and other relevant sections, including §§ 3602(k), 3604(a), and 3607(b)(1), (2), (5).

Having identified a federal statute with which the Costa Brava Towers must comply, and relying on the common knowledge that Florida is a relatively popular place for retirees, I searched for relevant state legislation. Returning to the JLR database, I performed a terms-and-connectors search, seeking to narrow the topic down to Florida law: Florida & ''housing act'' & ''age restriction'' & discriminat! Again skimming the titles and accompanying paragraphs, I identified a 1999 St. John's Law Review article that seemed to be right on point—Nicole Napolitano, *The Fair Housing Act Amendments and Restrictive Covenants in Condominiums and Cooperatives.* This article states that Florida has its own Fair Housing Act but does not cite the Florida statutes.

Then I went to Florida's Annotated Statutes' table of contents. I clicked on Civil Rights, then Discrimination in the Treatment of Persons, and found the Fair Housing Act and its relevant sections, Florida Statutes Annotated sections 760.22, .23, and .29. After comparing the state and federal sections, I determined that they were identical in all material aspects. I reviewed the annotations of each statute, but I did not find any cases on point.

Once I had the statutory language, I decided to conduct a more specific search of Florida state and federal cases. I performed a terms-and-connectors search using the phrase: ''fair housing act'' & ''age restriction'' & ''housing for older persons.'' That search generated several cases, the most relevant of which seemed to be *Massaro v.*

Mainlands Section 1 & 2 Civic Association, Inc., decided by the Eleventh Circuit in 1993 (Florida is in the Eleventh Circuit). That case holds that exemptions are to be narrowly construed and identifies regulations from the Secretary of Housing and Urban Development, which I remembered being addressed in the federal act. While the court provided an analysis of an organization's qualifications as an HFOP, the court declined to rule on the enforceability of the age restrictions at issue. After reading the case, I followed the link to the regulations, 24 C.F.R. §§ 100.304–.307.

In search of more relevant case law, I performed numerous terms-and-connectors searches and found several cases that addressed the modification of association bylaws to comply with the Fair Housing Act when enacted by Congress as well as the application of the Fair Housing Act and Housing and Urban Development regulations to determine whether a particular association qualified as an HFOP. Because most of those cases focused on facts not disclosed in the Costa Brava Towers case, such as age verification procedures and publication and notice requirements, they were not particularly helpful. In light of the statutory language and its application in the cases reviewed, it seemed clear that Costa Brava Towers qualified as an HFOP.

Now focusing on the issue of enforceability, I returned to periodicals. I performed another terms-and-connectors search in the JLR database, and I found a 1998 University of Miami Law Review article that seemed right on point — Jonathan I. Edelstein, *Family Values: Prevention of Discrimination and the Housing for Older Persons Act of 1995*. It began with the true story of a nine-year-old girl who had to live with her grandparents because her mother died of cancer. The grandparents' condominium complex, however, was an adults-only complex, and it attempted to evict Jamie and her grandparents. Shortly thereafter, Congress amended the Fair Housing Act to prevent discrimination against families with children, and because the complex did not qualify for the HFOP exemption, the girl was allowed to stay. Although the story had a happy ending, it also ended up rendering a seemingly perfect precedent nearly irrelevant. However, it provided the argument that "Congress enacted the [amendments] to prevent discriminatory treatment similar to that faced by the [girl and her grandparents]."

Needing to find some legitimate argument for my clients, I decided to broaden the scope of my research by searching the general contract principle of estoppel in the JLR database. I found a 1993 Stetson Law Review article with a great title — Lewis A. Schiller, *Limitations on the Enforceability of Condominium Rules*. The article indicates that contract theories generally apply to restrictive covenants in homeowners' association agreements and are presumed valid. The article identifies a Florida Supreme Court case from 1979, *White Egret Condominium, Inc. v. Franklin*, that holds that age restrictions are generally reasonable, unless they are selectively enforced. Additionally, covenants may not be enforced where there is a failure to adhere to required procedures, such as those identified in the cases mentioned previously. The principle of estoppel may apply and bar the enforcement of a seemingly dormant restriction.

The article also briefly mentioned hardship, so I decided to perform another search in the JLR database focusing on hardship, which generated an encyclopedia in the Westlaw WebPlus Results column. In Am. Jur. 2d *Specific Performance*, I learned that courts will not enforce a contract if it will result in undue hardship on one party, with consequences unforeseen at the time it was made. The article cited many cases from various jurisdictions supporting this proposition.

In conclusion, periodicals provided an excellent starting point for researching the various topics and issues in this case. The statutes and regulations identified by the law review articles and courts in the controlling jurisdiction lead to the conclusion that Costa Brava Towers likely qualifies as an HFOP. Therefore, the age restriction is likely enforceable. However, because exemptions are to be construed narrowly in favor of curbing discrimination against families, the Swees may seek to avoid enforcement of the restriction on the basis of selective enforcement, estoppel, or undue hardship.

3.   Karen Hazel, Representing Costa Brava Towers

When compiling my list of search terms, I rely on the five "Ws" — who, what, when, where, and why. This gives structure to the initial phase of my research and strikes an efficient balance between thoroughness and remaining targeted and focused. I started with the following concepts:

- ☐ Who: condominiums, associations, unit owners, senior citizens, grandparents, disabled adults;
- ☐ What: restrictive covenants, restrictive housing covenants, unlawful discrimination, age-related housing restrictions, enforceability of private property restrictions, Florida housing statutes, federal housing statutes, Fair Housing Act, property owners' rights, condominium association rights, waiver of age restriction requirements, civil rights;
- ☐ When: early 2008;
- ☐ Where: Delray Beach, Florida; olderpersons' condominium complex; and
- ☐ Why: breach of restrictive covenant, enforceability of such a covenant.

Encyclopedias are a sound starting point because of their broad scope and extensive indexes. I consulted Am. Jur. 2d, starting with the update supplement to access the most updated information first. I chose to research entirely in paper until I had uncovered a list of binding, primary sources, reserving online research for checking the history of individual cases and for any follow-up tasks.

I began with Am. Jur. 2d's New Topic Service to check recent updates to my areas of focus and found none. I moved on to the General Index which helped me refine my search terms to "covenants: conditions and restrictions," "condominiums and cooperative apartments," "housing laws and breach of promise," and "civil rights and Fair Housing Act."

In the individual volumes, I narrowed my research nicely. In the *Covenants* topic, I found that age-restrictive covenants have been generally upheld against constitutional challenges where such restrictions fulfill a legitimate public need. In addition, in seeking to enforce this age-related provision, my client must show that it has followed its procedures, that those procedures are fair and reasonable, and that they are not levied arbitrarily or capriciously. I also found the West's key number listings for this topic as well as two relevant leads: *Enforceability of bylaw or other rule of condominium or co-operative association restricting occupancy by children*, 100 A.L.R. 3d 241, and *Validity and construction of covenant restricting occupancy of premises to person over or under specified age*, 68 A.L.R.3d 1239.

In the *Condominiums* topic in Am. Jur., I found some good general descriptions of the rights and obligations of condominium ownership: in choosing to purchase units, owners must give up certain rights and privileges that traditionally attend fee ownership of real property and agree to subordinate their interests to the group's interests. In each section of a specific volume, I scanned all footnotes to capture any Florida cases.

Because the sources up to this point frequently referred to A.L.R. annotations, this was my next step. I began with the A.L.R. Index, and under "Age Discrimination → Condominiums," I found sources referring to "Enforceability of bylaw or other rule of condominium/co-op association restricting occupancy by children." I also found a wealth of sources under "Civil Rights → housing → children → condominium/co-op association restricting occupancy by children."

This step directed me to the A.L.R. digests, as these contain concise references under broad headings. In addition, the A.L.R. digests offer summaries of actual cases, so I can scan the gist of each decision and quickly see if it applies. As usual, I checked the supplements first for updates. Nothing related to "condominiums" had been updated, so I relied on the bound volume's content. I discovered several Florida cases, mindful that I would need to consult a Florida-specific case law source later. I discovered *Roth v. Normandy Shores Yacht & Country Club, Inc.*, a 1987 Florida District Court of Appeals decision, holding that a provision in a condo's bylaws restricting occupancy based on age was valid and enforceable under certain conditions.

In *White Egret Condominium, Inc. v. Franklin*, a 1979 Florida Supreme Court case, the court held that a condo restriction does not inherently violate fundamental rights and may be enforced if it serves a legitimate purpose and is reasonably applied. Age restrictions are reasonable means to accomplish the lawful purpose of providing appropriate facilities for the differing housing needs and desires of various age groups. Checking the history of this case online, I discovered it had only been distinguished by a Michigan court in 1999 and thus remained good law. This case also referred to Florida Statute section 718, as well as the Fourteenth Amendment of the U.S. Constitution. In the KeyCite report for this case, I found related Florida cases, including many I had discovered in paper. Finally, this path led me to a Harvard Law Review article on the subject of association rulemaking, reinforcing the concept that age-related restrictions in condominiums will more likely be deemed enforceable if the restriction is enforced evenly, reasonably, and for a legitimate public purpose.

Back in A.L.R., two Florida District Court of Appeals decisions in particular aligned with my client's situation from a factual standpoint: *Constellation*

Condominium Association, Inc. v. Harrington, from 1985, and *Everglades Plaza Condominium Association, Inc. v. Buckner,* from 1984. In both cases, the court upheld age-related restrictions in condominium bylaws when children were introduced as occupants after purchase of the units and where there was adequate notice of the restriction prior to purchase.

In 68 A.L.R.3d 1239, I found *Riley v. Stoves,* a 1979 Arizona case. Although a persuasive precedent, its major issue was whether the age discrimination embodied by a particular restrictive covenant violated the equal protection clause of the Fourteenth Amendment of the United States Constitution. The court upheld the constitutionality of the covenant, declaring that fulfillment of the legitimate need of older buyers who seek to retire in an area undisturbed by children was a proper objective, particularly in the absence of testimony as to any shortage of housing in the area.

After doing an online check to ensure these cases were still valid, I felt ready to move on to my focused search for Florida cases and statutes, so I consulted West's Florida digest and reporters (in paper). There, I found several relevant cases, happy to see cases I had already pegged as relevant reappear. However, one case in particular jumped out: *Massaro v. Mainlands Section 1 & 2 Civic Association, Inc.,* decided by the Eleventh Circuit in 1993. This federal case holds that a residential subdivision that passes a bylaw limiting occupancy of housing units so that at least eighty percent of the units would be required to contain at least one person over fifty-five years of age satisfied the "policies and procedures" requirement for the "55 and older" exemption to the Fair Housing Amendments Act of 1988 ("the Act").

From the guidance offered by this case, I concluded that Costa Brava will need to show it has a credible process developed for enforcing bylaws. The fact that the Towers offers a full range of services bodes well for my client in light of *Massaro,* in which the court held that a residential community did not qualify for the "housing for older persons" exception under the Act due to its lack of these offerings. Finally, the restriction must have been clear to the Swees upon sale.

Although *Massaro* seemed right on point, I continued, mindful that after this stage I would need to identify any Florida statutes either nullifying or permitting such a restrictive covenant in the context of a condo association. I wondered if I had missed a nuance by not more fully expanding on my search terms, which remained somewhat general. While researching in A.L.R., I had found a subcategory "written/express covenants." This led me to *Rocek v. Markowitz,* decided by the Florida District Court of Appeals in 1986, which holds that an age-restrictive covenant was valid and enforceable under certain circumstances. As with all cases, I did an online check to ensure it still represented good law, and it did.

While I obtained leads for statutes from my cases, I conducted paper research for statutes directly. I consulted West's Florida Statutes Annotated, beginning with the General Index. Here I found subcategories under "condominiums," with the appropriate statute section number cited after each.

My best success came from section 760.29, "Exemptions of prohibited discrimination in land use decisions and in permitting development." Section 760.29 (4)(a) spells out the exceptions for housing/residential property that qualifies under this statute as "housing for older persons," thereby exempting such facilities from the federal Fair Housing Act of 1988 regarding age discrimination. Although section 760.29 was addressed in *Massaro*, it was reassuring to find this statute directly in paper.

In addition to checking the pocket part in the back of the annotated volume, I also checked the most recent cumulative supplement that shows updates to the entire Florida statutes. This did contain a short update on section 760.20, but none of it was relevant. To finalize my paper research, I found Florida's advance legislative service pamphlets, West's Florida Session Law Service 2007 Laws. No updates had been made that related to section 760.29, so keeping my client's needs and costs in mind, I believed I had at this point sufficient law to advise my client.

Conclusion. Based on both federal and Florida case law, the age-related residency restriction is likely enforceable. The provision would not likely be viewed by the courts as a violation of the Swees' constitutional rights because my client's condominium likely qualifies for an exemption under federal anti-discrimination law, provided that it continues to enforce the restriction even-handedly and consistently; at least eighty percent of occupied units are held by at least one person age fifty-five and over; a full range of social, medical, recreational and other services are offered (including accommodations for the disabled); and procedures for enforcing this restriction are fair, reasonable, and not levied arbitrarily. Also working in my client's favor is the fact that the Swees were aware of and understood the restriction when they agreed to uphold it, as well as the fact that federal courts have long recognized that providing housing tailored to older occupants is considered a legitimate public need.

From a nonlegal perspective, however, Costa Brava faces a more precarious position. Notwithstanding the law in its favor, forcing an older couple to move under such unfortunate circumstances could injure my client's reputation and, possibly, future sales. In addition, I would need to inquire as to whether the Towers has allowed children to live in units before this event, because from the facts, we know that at least some occupants are *not* over age fifty-five, including Beca. I suggest that the Towers offer to buy back the Swees' unit, subsidize their moving/closing costs, encourage the association to approve giving the Swees adequate time to relocate, or a combination of these gestures. Mindful of the fact that Costa Brava must enforce the provision in light of the needs of its other owners, it still faces a dilemma in light of the Swees' unfortunate bind; thus I recommend that we negotiate a mutually acceptable plan so both parties eventually achieve results at or near their goals.

4. Jesse J. Klick, Representing Costa Brava Towers

Once I felt that I had a sufficient understanding of the fact scenario, and the relevant research terms, I began my research by using legal treatises. I found this to be a great place to begin, because I had a limited understanding of the law in this area. To locate a relevant treatise, I first searched the law school's library catalog. I used various terms in my key-word searches, including "condominium association," "restrictive covenant," and "property law." Because I was not happy with the results, I decided to peruse the library shelves where relevant treatises might be found. To find this area, I located the Library of Congress call number for real property, KF 560–698.

I located two relevant treatises. First, I searched the index of the treatise *Powell on Real Property*, under the heading "covenants," then "restrictive covenants," and then "age restrictions." Second, I researched in a more narrowly focused treatise, *The Law of Condominium and Cooperatives* by Vincent Di Lorenzo. For each treatise, I checked the relevant supplements to ensure the information was up to date. From my treatise research, I learned that the controlling law would likely be found in a federal statute, the Fair Housing Act.

Taking what I learned from my treatise research, I moved on to statutes. I began by entering the citation I found in the treatises for the Fair Housing Act. I learned that discrimination on the basis of familial status was prohibited by 42 U.S.C.A. § 3604(a). However, I found that under 42 U.S.C.A. § 3607(b)(2) certain facilities are exempted under the "older persons exemption." Having found the relevant federal statute, my next step was to look through the cases listed in the annotations to determine if any would be useful. One relevant case was *Massaro v. Mainlands Section 1 & 2 Civic Association*, an Eleventh Circuit decision from 1993.

Next, I decided to see if Florida had a state statute covering this issue. I used Westlaw's Florida Statutes Annotated database (FL-ST-ANN). I prefer to use the table of contents when researching statutes online, as this is more useful than doing a terms-and-connectors or natural-language search. Using the table of contents, I clicked on Title XLIV Civil Rights, then on Chapter 760 Discrimination in the Treatment of Persons. Here, I found Florida's version of the Fair Housing Act, Florida Statutes sections 760.20–760.37. Like the federal version, the Florida statute contains an "older persons exemption" under section 760.29.

Now, having located a state and federal statute that seemed controlling, I moved into case law research. I again chose to use Westlaw for this stage. I used Westlaw's Florida State and Federal Cases database (FL-CS-ALL). In this database, I tried a number of terms-and-connectors and natural-language searches. I likewise used relevant terms from the two statutes I found that, I believed, would produce cases on point. Examples of the various searches I used are: ``older persons exemption,'' ``55 years of age'' /p ``older persons,'' and ``reasonable'' /p ``age restriction.'' I then used the citing-reference feature to find additional cases. I find the citing-reference feature to be helpful in locating more current cases. One of these cases, *Rogers v. Windmill Pointe Village Club Association*, an Eleventh Circuit case from 1992, directed me to 24 C.F.R. § 100.304. This section of the federal regulatory code contains the federal regulations for complying with the "older persons exemption" under the Fair Housing Act. Surprisingly, I did not find a reference to this citation in the annotations for the Fair Housing Act. Lastly, I made sure to KeyCite the cases I planned to use to ensure they are still good law.

Conclusion. I believe that Costa Brava Towers ("the Towers") would prevail if the Swees bring a lawsuit challenging the restrictive covenants regarding the age of permanent residents. Under both the federal and Florida Fair Housing Acts, the Towers would likely qualify for the "older persons" exemption. The Towers appears to meet the requirement that eighty percent of the occupied units are occupied by at least one person over the age of fifty-five; it provides amenities, services, and special programs designed for older persons; it appears to have published policies and procedures relating to the age restriction that have been followed; and the Swees had knowledge of the restrictive covenant when they moved into the Towers.

Moreover, I believe that the Swees would be unsuccessful if they sought to challenge the restrictive covenant, as applied to their circumstances, on the basis of equity. Two Florida District Court of Appeals cases, *Constellation Condominium Association v. Harrington* from 1985 and *Star Lake North Commodore Association v. Parker* from 1982 provide helpful case law for the Towers. In both of these pre-Fair Housing Act cases, the courts upheld the application of similar restrictive covenants regarding the age of permanent residents. In both cases, couples who were aware of the restrictive covenants prohibiting permanent residents under the age of sixteen unexpectedly had a child. In both cases, the courts upheld the condominium associations' attempts to prohibit the unit owners from living with their underage child in their condominiums. I would argue that these unexpected births are analogous to the situation here, where the grandparents have unexpectedly become permanent guardians of their grandchildren. Thus, not only is the restrictive covenant not illegal discrimination based on age, but it is likewise enforceable under the circumstances presented.

C. OUR OBSERVATIONS

Exhibit 18.1 (at page 438) shows the commentary sources, codified law, and cases the four students found and used to analyze the case of the Swees and Costa Brava Towers. Although they proceeded in various ways, some overall patterns are discernible:

- ☐ They all used commentary first.
- ☐ They all found federal and state law.
- ☐ They all found a mix of codified and case law.
- ☐ Three of the four used a mix of paper and online sources.
- ☐ Their analyses are nearly identical, regardless of client.

The four students were in their second year of law school and were chosen because they excelled in the first-year legal writing course. With hard work, you too can become skilled in legal research.

| Exhibit 18.1 | | | | Overview of Four Research Logs |

	Representing the Swees		Representing Costa Brava Towers	
	Adine Momoh	Marcus Ploeger	Karen Hazel	Jesse Klick
Commentary Type	Am. Jur. 2d	periodicals Am. Jr. 2d	Am. Jr. 2d A.L.R.	treatises
Federal Law				
U.S. Constitution	✔		✔	
Fair Housing Act (FHA)		✔	✔	✔
FHA Regulations		✔		✔
Massaro		✔	✔	✔
Rogers				✔
State Law				
Florida Fair Housing Act	✔	✔	✔	✔
Florida Condominium Statute	✔		✔	
White Egret Condominium	✔	✔	✔	
Constellation Condominium	✔		✔	✔
Roth	✔		✔	
Hidden Harbor Estates	✔			
Del Valle	✔			
Everglades Plaza Condominium Association			✔	
Rocek			✔	
Star Lake North Commodore Association				✔

Index

Italic page numbers denote illustrations.